To All My Addictive Patients

and

To My Daughters
Julie and Jane

so that

we may all live in a world freed of addictions

CONTENTS

FOREWORD

This important new book reflects the growing awareness that addiction is a central human experience. Addiction is a process that transcends specific "substances" upon which the addict becomes dependent. The power of *The Pleasure Addicts* rests less with Dr. Hatterer's brilliant review of the theoretical issues than it does with his intimate and absolutely compelling evidence of first person accounts of addiction to alcohol, drugs, food, sex, and even work.

Surely no nation in history has experienced a soul-searching about its drug dependence more intensely than has the United States during the last decade. What began as a national outcry by adults about youthful marijuana use in the late 1960s has by the early 1980s developed into an embarrassing—and perhaps even a frightening—awareness of the widespread existence of "substance abuse" in our society. We have for the first time, now defined alcohol and tobacco as drugs, despite the two industries' attempts to turn aside this thrust. We have put labels in our medical diagnostic manuals—the ultimate evidence of our definition of the disease— for alcohol and tobacco dependence. The addictive process far transcends these by now traditional "substances." We are now aware that dependence on marijuana and heroin not only have much in common with dependence on alcohol and tobacco, but that these processes can also extend to obesity and gambling and even to the use of such medicines as sleeping pills, stimulants, and tranquilizers. Dr. Hatterer goes even beyond this to show that sex and work can also deteriorate into self-destructive addictions.

When putting this broadened concept of addiction into perspective, we must keep in mind that it is not a new process. As soon as human beings had choices about what they ate, drank, smoked, snorted, and, most recently, shot, we have had problems with addiction. In fact this problem is deeply rooted in the choices themselves—addiction is nothing so much as it is a disease of choices. Our feelings of pleasure trigger for each of the addictive "substances"—in some but not all people exposed to them—a dependence which, when severe, can dominate, distort, and even destroy life. This vulnerability to pleasure is not uniquely American and it is not limited to this decade. Addiction is global and all but timeless despite the contemporary concern. The choices of "substances" people have all over the world are increasing and as they do the vulnerability to addiction rises. One of the most important functions of traditional cultures and religions has always been to curb the excesses to which individual behavior is subject. These forces are globally on the wane today. A rise in addiction is one result.

There can be little doubt that in the next decade there will be an enormous global increase in the awareness of the importance of the addictive process. Today we appear on the threshold of a new understanding of the biological basis of addiction as we begin to understand the role of the body's own morphine-like neuro-transmitters, the endorphins. These normal brain chemicals help us understand the power of morphine—the prototypical dependence-producing substance. These endorphins appear to control our pleasure and our pain at a chemical level in our brains. Addiction, however, has dimensions beyond biology.

Beyond even this new frontier, however, is the sober realization that the greatest potential for health gains in the last two decades of this century is not to be found in improvements in our already terribly expensive health care system. What gains there are to be made will come from changes in individual choices of pleasure-producing "substances." Cigarette smoking looms largest but the effects of alcohol and other drugs are also now profound drags on our nation's health. Think about it. The best way to cut our death rate from cancer, heart disease and auto accidents—as well as many other killers—is to curb our appetites for addictive "substances." The fact that addictions are widespread and growing need not lead to passivity about dealing with them. During the last decade there has been a twenty-five percent reduction in the heart attack and stroke death rate in the United States. This unprecedented good news appears to be the result of curbing the pleasures that we are discussing: the dramatic decrease in smoking by those over 40; the increase in physical activity; and the reduction in the use of cholesterol and saturated fats.

When the health planners and the tough-minded scientists begin looking for ways to achieve the goals of reducing our appetites for addictive substances, they could do no better than to turn to *The Pleasure Addicts* to understand the process in both theoretical and human terms.

Dr. Hatterer brings to each page a generosity and an openness to the human experience of his patient. His respect for his often tortured patients is contagious. The reader who might be tempted to wall himself off from the addictive experience is pushed more deeply into these lives, and ultimately, into his own addictive experiences with a new fascination and appreciation. *The Pleasure Addicts* will help shape the response of psychiatry and of the public to addictions in the 1980s.

Robert L. DuPont, M.D.
President
Institute for Behavior and Health,
Former Director of the National Institute
on Drug Abuse

ACKNOWLEDGMENTS

Acknowledgments and thanks to everyone who contributed to the production of this book are impossible. They would entail the story of my own and several hundred other lives. However, there are some people without whom this book could not have become a reality.

I am indebted to all of my addictive patients, from my very first, an alcoholic schizophrenic whom I treated during my psychiatric residency and then in private practice (1950-1955), up to my recent two-year intensive care (1977-1979) of a former anorexia nervosa patient with acute and chronic alcoholism and multiple drug addictions. Between these were the many others who revealed their sufferings to me at the Payne Whitney Psychiatric Clinic, in my practice, and in private life. Working with them, I was privileged to hear, to help, and to live with the essence of addictive thought and behavior which is the fabric of this book. The intense experiences with these people who needed me, and whom I sometimes needed, were responsible for my drive to communicate what I learned about addictions.

There were also special people in my life whose belief, dedication, talent, patient listening, and work with my verbal and written outpourings was immeasurably helpful. The major contributor at the top of my list is Elizabeth Strong Williams, who digested, sorted out, and edited down, line by line, many cartons full of my free associative writing to bring to life the first nine-hundred-page draft of the book. She devoted two years and more of her time, heart, profound insights, literary skills, and knowledge of specific milieus and addictive people to augment and sharpen the portraits and clarify the text.

A long list of creative mentors helped make the seed of an idea flower over a ten year period. In 1969 Audrey Wood, a vice president of International Creative Management, called me from Florida to say she liked a TV script of mine entitled

Hooked People: Food, Sex, and Drug Addicts. Her enthusiasm spurred me on to do it as a book, which I submitted six years later to Bob Mills, an agent, who believed in what I'd written. In the interim, Nathaniel LeMar and Arno Karlen skillfully edited the first and second drafts. My close friend Andrew Anspach shepherded the manuscript, orphaned for three years, to publisher Tom Yoseloff, who had the courage to publish this book.

I use the word courage with intense emotion because the saga of the reactions to the manuscript could have become a book in itself. I never received a neutral response. The heated feedback from publishers and editors was incredibly subjective and polarized. It ran from instant enthusiasm after overnight, non-stop readings to returning the manuscript many months later with hostile, moralistic criticism. These polarized excesses of emotion emerged from unconscious biases provoked by reading about addiction. Another common, predictable reaction was either total acceptance or a powerful objection to one or several of the addictions being in the book. ''Just do a drug and alcohol addiction book. . .we've all got a little junkie in us.'' ''That fat girl and workaholic were total bores.'' ''The sex addict disgusted me, it's really just porno.'' ''My god, it should sell like hotcakes, everyone has one of these.''

No one bought the book until the brave Mr. Yoseloff, who after several non-stop readings told me at our first meeting, ''I know this book better than you do.'' How was that for an excessive statement for a book on excess? It was these powerfully polarized and paradoxical reactions that kept refueling my belief in the validity of what I had written.

Over the years of producing this book, a number of other people contributed. Dr. Myra S. Hatterer, my wife, helped clarify the manuscript at different stages with her many readings and incisive critiques. My children, Julie and Jane, read and critiqued the story of Ellen and provided insights into current adolescent behavior and language. Research was done by Gary Frohlich, Steve Gullo, Ph.D., and Patricia Hilton. The many drafts were typed by Beverly Friedman and Susan Agrest with skill, devotion, and patience. Finally, I am indebted to Charles Buckwald, PHD and Bruce Parker, MA's permission to reprint portions of their extraordinary compilation of resources contained in their *Handbook of Drug Abuse and Alcoholism* that they have prepared as part of the *Career Teacher Resource Handbook* which can be requested from the Career Teachers Center, 450 Clarkson Avenue, Box 32, Brooklyn, New York 11203.

THE PLEASURE ADDICTS

PART I
THE ADDICTIVE PROCESS

Addictive behavior has invaded every aspect of American life today. We all feel the cloud of concern about becoming addictive—preoccupation with weight, smoking, drinking too much, or being caught in an excess of spending, acquiring, gambling, sex, or work.

No one escapes the media's power to promote or curb excess. Billion-dollar businesses sell both gluttony and dieting, smoking and cancer precautions, eroticism and the idea that work conquers all. Ours is a society of polarized excesses that is the essence of addictive life.

Much has been written about the "addictive personality" and specific addictions. I do not believe that any one addictive personality type exists, but that people become addicted because they are vulnerable to the *addictive process,* * which is rampant in our culture. I want to describe that process, its common causes, and its symptoms as I have seen them in my practice as a psychiatrist and in society. Then I will present some examples of addiction from my practice and describe the psychodynamics that I believe explain addictive behavior. Finally I will show some ways to prevent and reverse it.

The vast majority of writings on addiction are about its chemical and behavioral aspects. Far less has been written about what this book deals with—the psychological diagnosis, dynamics, and therapy of the addictive process. Such factors as the genetic, constitutional, chemical, physiological, socioeconomic, political, and epidemiological

* Robert A. Savitt, M.D., also used the concept of the Addiction Process as it relates to narcotics, hypersexuality, and food (see bibliography).

15

are beyond the scope of this book.* However, these *always* play roles in addiction and must be taken into account in understanding any addict.

The phrase "I am addicted to" is now used to describe a state beyond the definition of the World Health Organization—a state of "periodic or chronic intoxication produced by the repeated consumption of a natural or synthetic drug for which one has an overpowering desire or need (i.e. compulsion) to continue to take. . ." Today we extend the concept of addiction to almost any substance or activity. People say that they or others are addicted not only to drugs or alcohol, but to food, smoking, gambling, buying, or some form of work, play, or sex. I believe that all these addictions have a common denominator, which is a process that depends on constitutional, family, peer, environmental, and sometimes genetic physiologic chemical and ethnic factors, and which serve one or several functions in a person's adaptation to life.

In this book the term addictive must be distinguished from obsessional thoughts and compulsive acts and the obsessive-compulsive neurosis. Neurotic *obsessions* are repetitive, meaningless, unwelcomed, afford *no pleasure*, and always produce loss of energy, ambivalence, and doubt that destroy mental functioning. Neurotic *compulsions* are repetitive, unwelcomed, alien, meaningless, trivial, or ritualistic behavior performed against one's will. The behavior can be silly or terrifying, and the individual usually consciously attempts either to free himself of it or to ensure its continuance. It gives *no pleasure* and is not necessarily dangerous to the psyche or body. In both neurotic obsessions and compulsions, there is always *awareness of pain, dysfunction,* and sometimes a conscious need to hide the thoughts and behavior because of shame or embarrassment. The individual often seeks help because of his admitted pain and awareness of the crippling nature of the disease. Compulsive acts and obsessive thoughts are not easily hidden, denied, suppressed, repressed, dissociated, or split off, but are consciously painful and are admittedly destructive to the self and others. There is no evidence of tolerance, withdrawal, or abstinence phenomenon, toxicity, or destruction to bodily functions.

The following characteristics are common at every stage of the *addictive process.* The person has an overpowering desire or need for a substance, object, action, inter-action, fantasy, or milieu that produces a psychophysiologic reaction—a "high." This reaction is sought repetitively, impulsively, and compulsively. At first it is felt as a pleasurable way to cope with a psychic conflict or stress that has caused conscious or unconscious pain that seems intolerable. In the early stages of the process, one feels partial or total relief. There is a false sense of resolving conflict or stress because it is masked or extinguished by psychic and/or physical pleasure. This pleasure diminishes as the process continues; one feels less relief, less sense of coping

---

* Recent research has uncovered and documented the importance of physiological, chemical, and genetic factors in the predisposition, vulnerability, and perpetuation of obesity, heroin addiction, and alcoholism.

or resolution. One can no longer rationalize or deny the pain because of symptoms that I call ''hangover phenomena''—tension, depression, rage, guilt, and physical distress. These result from an inevitable deterioration of intimate and social relationships. Dependence exists because of disturbed ego (self-esteem) and superego* (conscience) functioning in early life. The addictive process can be continuous, cyclic, sporadic, or periodic, but it always involves tolerance, abstinence, and withdrawal.** Sometimes a person shifts from one form of addiction to another, but the process remains the same.

A person should be considered addicted when an overpowering, repetitive, excessive need exists for some substance, object, feeling, act, milieu, or personal interaction at any cost, along with a denial of the destructive consequences to one's physical, emotional, and social well-being and, in some instances, to economic survival. In true addiction there is almost always excessive use of pleasurable activities to cope with unmanageable internal conflict, pressure, stress, and confrontation. The person has little tolerance for frustration and cannot balance pleasure and pain, work and play. There is also impaired self-esteem, and conflicts about dependence, control, discipline, passivity, and aggressiveness. An unfailing diagnostic sign is that his free associations are saturated with references to addictive needs, milieus, and life styles. The person's life history reveals a period of maladaptation in the work-play axis of his life and the presence of addictive milieus, agents, and practices in his immediate family and peers.

It is the very fact that pleasure is being used dysfunctionally as a coping mechanism that makes it difficult for both a diagnostician and an addict to recognize and treat addiction. The addict cannot admit or identify his pain, let alone see that his

---

* The *ego* is that part of the person that relates to perception, self-perception, self-awareness, adaptation *to reality*, and self-preservation. It mediates between demand of primitive drives (i.e., the id) and internalized parental and social prohibitions (i.e., the superego) and of reality. It is the capacity for rational thought and action.

The *superego* is that part of the personality structure associated with ethics, standards, self-criticism formed by the infant's identification with important and esteemed persons in early life—particularly parents. The real and supposed wishes of these significant persons are taken on as part of the child's own personal standards to help form the conscience. It is the representative of society within the psyche, morality, judgment that an act is ''right'' or ''wrong,'' self-critical observation, self-punishment, self-love or self-esteem as the ego reward for having done right.

** *Tolerance* is increasing resistance to the effects of a drug. The need for increasing dosage to maintain or recapture the desired drug effect; in general, the more saturated body cells become with any substance, the longer the period required to rid them of all traces of a drug. Related to physical dependence—the need to have some quantities of drug presence within the body, or at least within some of its cellular elements. With other than drugs, the term refers to a need for increasing amounts of addictive agent, interaction, or activity with less and less satisfaction taking place. The ability to endure without ill effect increasing amounts of addictive agents with decreasing effects to continued use of the same dose of the drug.

Abstinence is voluntarily refraining from the use of an addictive agent, interaction, or activity. It is the denial of gratification that comes from physiological and/or psychological dependence.

Withdrawal is abstaining from an addictive agent interaction, or activity on which the patient has become dependent. It produces physiological and/or psychological symptoms.

addictive behavior is excessive and a way of coping.

It is almost impossible to pinpoint exactly when, how, and why a given person becomes involved in the addictive process. There may be shifting combinations of causes at different times in his life; these become increasingly complex and elusive as vulnerability evolves into full-fledged addiction. Then the process becomes autonomous and self-perpetuating; it has a life of its own, often unrelated to the initial causes.

Constitutional and genetic factors may be involved. The qualities and capacities someone is born with and how people react to them can strongly affect proneness to addiction. These are the causative factors one can least control, and are often the last to be recognized. We do not know how much one's genes or constitution contributes to addiction, but vulnerability to addiction does seem to run in families. Often a real or imagined constitutional factor makes someone see himself as inferior or superior to family members or peers; as a result, he cannot identify with them, and the tensions rising from this isolation and sense of alienation can help provoke early addictive behavior.

Family factors are always present. Every addictive adult I have treated has told either of excesses of inconsistencies or of deprivation or overindulgence in early life. There were shifts from too much to too little love, protection, or discipline. In many families one parent was too strict, and the other asked for too little discipline. Such situations impair the development of the child's superego and create a feeling of lack of support from either parent. The child cannot develop an adequate superego because it has identified with a parent who has a confused or absent superego. One or both parents may also have little ability to delay gratification and a low tolerance of frustration; the child sees that the parent has little control of his own behavior. There is no parental model to teach that reward emerges from consistent, orderly efforts. Unrealistic expectations of success result in the development of a low tolerance for psychic pain, so pain must be immediately relieved.

Too much permissiveness or indulgence also allows the child either too many or too few options in coping with boredom, conflict, or stress. This interferes with the development of self-monitoring and the ability to make constructive, conscious choices in dealing with psychic pain. One solution for such discomfort is an addictive practice.

The child learns of addiction directly from family models—the sights, sounds, and smells of parental excess. From the very beginning of life he is cared for by a parent who smokes, drinks, eats, or works too much or who is drugged or overeroticized. The constant smell of tobacco, the touch of a tense and overworked body, being left hungry and neglected by a parent addicted to alcohol or a drug, all leave deep marks that may be passed from generation to generation.

Later in life the person may adopt a different addiction, consciously rejecting the behavior of his family but not addictiveness itself. For instance, an addiction-prone child avoids the addiction of parents who gamble, drink, or overuse drugs or sex, but turns to addictive eating or work.

Also common in the parents of the addictive are chaotic, unstable lives—frequent separations, divorces, or experimental living arrangements. The most malignant forms of addictiveness develop where the family was literally or psychologically absent (gross neglect by one or both parents). This lack of support impairs ego development and self-esteem and fails to give the child ways to deal with frustration and failure.

Frequently found in the family backgrounds of those prone to addictiveness are marked swings from unrealistic praise to destructive hypercritical behavior. This is another form of polarized behavior that thwarts the growth of a child's realistic self-esteem and keeps him from establishing realistic goals and self-control. Addictiveness is provoked by continuous frustration and lack of self-realization.

Where there are gross sex-role and gender-role* distortions in one or both parents, especially in a family of a weak, nondisciplinary, passive, or absent father and a detached, unnurturing mother, the potential for addiction can reach malignant proportions.

Previously the study of addiction has focussed largely on the addictive agent, not on the people and situations that fuel addiction. I am convinced from my clinical experience that we must also concentrate on the *addictive complement*, a term I have coined for any person, group, or environment that keeps the addictive process alive. For example, a work-addicted, nagging parent with an excessive superego becomes the complement of a drug-addicted or play-addicted child, who is subject to no control or consciously ignores and denies the parent's practices and controls. Another is the spending-addicted wife who keeps her husband's work addiction alive. Many an addict finds a person whose addiction feeds into and seems to justify his own.

The addict also needs people who can provide what he feels is lacking in himself or with whom to make exchanges of what each lacks. He becomes bound to such people—relatives, spouses, lovers, peers—with his addictive substance or practice as the catalyst.

Often the parents of an addiction-prone child prematurely and inappropriately depend on the child. One or both can make him their alter superego, impose their roles on him, or reverse their roles and especially during adolescence they can manipulate him into a position of controlling their addiction or of being responsible for its destructive consequences. He becomes their everyday addictive complement, an integral part of the parents' addictive processes. He can eventually become a complement to someone else's addiction or develop his own addiction. If the latter

---

* The word gender refers to social behavior (masculine or feminine) considered appropriate to one's sex within the culture. The word sex refers to such physical matters (male or female) as the genes, hormones, genitals, erotic appetite, and genital behavior.

occurs, he searches for and finds his own addictive complement.

A preaddictive child usually shows signs of family and interpersonal maladaptation early in life. Among the most common are inability to cope with authority inside or outside the home and trouble getting along with other children. Because he feels removed from his family and peers, he has concentration and school-performance problems. He is likely to become isolated and bored. This isolation, whether externally caused or self-imposed, increases tension, provokes depression, inappropriate agressivity or dysfunctional passivity, unexpressed hostility, and periods of emotional withdrawal. Finding an addictive activity, peer, complement and/or agent not only combats his conflict, boredom, and negative emotions but can give him a false sense of being effective and active. For the first time he feels secure and less isolated, because he has found peer models and a milieu that enables him to gain a sense of belonging along with relief of his psychic pain.

Even if low self-esteem is not apparent in the early life of the addiction-prone person, it will be clear once his addiction-prone pattern emerges. Addictiveness becomes his primary way of dealing with feelings of physical, social, emotional, or interpersonal inadequacy; it anesthetizes tension and psychic pain. Furthermore, excessive early social isolation from his family and peers causes a paucity of intimate, nurturing relationships or, at the opposite pole, overidentification with an addictive family member. These leave the child poorly equipped to relate to individuals or groups. His interpersonal inadequacies become progressively more painful and result in many actual or provoked rejections by family, peers, and authorities. He grows unable to tolerate the tensions of intimate relationships or extended social inter-actions, and withdraws into addictive behavior as a solution. Others begin to react negatively to him; he then sees most relationships as potentially dangerous and hostile. Ultimately his isolation from family and peers forces him to retreat to a life with addictive peers and to become excessively dependent on them and the addictive activity or agent. As a result, he withdraws further from his everyday familiar contacts and experiences. His withdrawal can be a reflection of rebellious over-reaction and a pseudo-independence from his family, nonaddictive peers, and society.

The addictive process can continue to be rooted in an inability to deal with authority or to rebel satisfactorily and establish status and self-respect among family and peers during adolescence. Later there are difficulties in larger social arenas such as advanced education, jobs, and the law; because of increasing alienation, these become amplified as the process progresses. The inability to accept control or to exercise sufficient controls leads to dysfunction and attempts at psychic repair by destructive domination or excessive submission. Inability to tolerate any imbalances in control, dominance, and submission continually fuels addictiveness.

The addict has a history of disturbed perceptions of pleasure and pain in relation-ships and an inability to balance work and play. What others clearly see as pain, he experiences as pleasure. These distortions emerge from having been cruelly overcontrolled or neglectfully undercontrolled in these spheres of life; one or both parents were too punitive or not punitive at all about the child's pleasures and work requirements. As a result, the child continues throughout his life to wish others to punish him or learns to punish himself for any pleasure or neglect of his work. This behavior is reinforced by having identified with one or both parents' inability to nonpunitively balance their own or each other's pleasures and pain (play and work lives). Interpersonal and value system distortions within the family and in the addict's own psyche can ultimately make him mistake giving or receiving pain as pleasurable. The pleasure-pain, work-play distortions later become reinforced by addictive peers and complements. The addictive person has thus developed a need to repeat the interfamilial sado-masochistic relationships by punishing those who interfere with, deny, or thwart his addictive practices—practices he must use to cope with or to balance pain and pleasure, work and play. He lives in a vicious cycle; one cannot easily determine which came first, the current destructive interactions or the addiction. A person can continue addictive behavior to ensure his role as the submissive, dependent, overindulged child or as the overcontrolling, omnipotent, punitive parent.

Lack of self-esteem is crucial in addictiveness. The addictive process occurs because the development of the ego and superego are disrupted in childhood. In adulthood there remains a high degree of narcissism* and unrealistically high self-evaluation as defenses against deep-seated low self-esteem. The addictive person has excessive expectations of himself but little ability and willingness to discipline himself to perform in ways that enable one to realize them. The frustration that inevitably occurs provokes addictive behavior. The process is inflamed by self-contempt over lack of control of the addictive practice and continued poor performance in many aspects of life.

Inability to be accepted by peers and have high status among them can also set off addictive behavior. A youngster who shows excessive passivity is particularly vulnerable to peer pressures that can provoke addictive practices and entry into an addictive subculture. However, addictive behavior can have a quite contrary role in adolescence. Many youngsters need to disguise or deny any fear of passivity and dependence with a show of aggression through exhibitionistic addictive behavior. The addictive practice can bring peer leadership that cannot be gained in more con-

---

* *Narcissism:* the term was first used to indicate a form of nonsexual self-love. Now it includes sexual self-love. It refers to a state in which the individual has a heightened, exaggerated awareness and estimation of the self, negates the existence and value of others, and perceives only people who focus solely on their needs and will act as a source of pleasure, to be used and discarded with ease. The state is often accompanied by omnipotence, grandiosity, exhibitionism, superficial relatedness, immaturity, and sometimes, a wish to return to infantile or childhood periods of dependence and to be the center of attention.

Negative narcissism is a state of exaggerated underestimation and negation of the self with unrealistic ideas of inadequacy and self-accusation accompanied by unrealistic overevaluation of others.

ventional ways. If a youngster once had social, academic, physical, or creative leadership but lost it by having moved into a more competitive peer group, addiction may offer pseudoleadership.

An adolescent's lack of or a sense of masculine or feminine security, of sexual confidence, or of a sense of acceptability can also provoke addictive behavior. So can failure to meet peers' social, competitive, academic, erotic, or other standards. Not uncommonly the youngster is introduced into the addictive practice by a ''closet'' addictive peer, to deal with the guilt or anxiety adult or public pressure might provoke.

Once the adolescent addict moves into early adulthood his failure to achieve socioeconomic status or to be upwardly mobile can cause a great deal of psychic pain and make him seek continued addictive anesthesia. Rapid, frequent, and frustrating shifts upward or downward at crucial developmental periods in life can provoke addiction. The psychic pain is even greater when a person becomes aware of the luxuries and opportunities that members of other classes have.

Extreme economic pressures, the loss of wealth or security, or having much money but few limits or values to guide its use, can also be significant factors in addiction. In fact, the addictive life style can become a way to establish economic security or support an addictive practice. Winning economic status by selling an addictive agent or practice can lead a vulnerable person into addiction. Finally, addiction can be a way to deal with failure to achieve materialistic goals set by oneself, one's family, or by society.

Once many of the above factors are at work, their interplay with society can start or perpetuate addiction. A society that makes addictive agents and behavior highly accessible and fosters them through the mass media is fostering addiction in every vulnerable member of that society. The media, like many parents, sends out contradictory messages about both the pleasure and the danger of an addictive agent or life style.

Society also contributes to addictiveness by swinging from prohibition to permissiveness. This leads to confusion about what is benign and destructive, relatively legal and illegal (i.e., as in the case of marijuana). These polarized positions depend on the emotional blind spots of the addictive elite in media or those who have an economic interest in selling addictive agents or sufficiently warning or educating those most vulnerable to becoming addicted. The continued commercial support of addictive milieus, regardless of their danger for many, is furthered by the ambivalent attitudes of society's leaders. Addiction must increase in our society because our media, mores, and social rituals promote excesses in pleasure (food, sex, drugs) while they equally value and promote the ability to endure excessive work, physical violence, and pain. Billion-dollar businesses will continue to sell excess and the curbing of excess, exploiting addiction-prone people by saturation. Our society has a decreasing number of social and religious rituals to help monitor man's inevitable vulnerability to excess; in fact, we have an increasing number of rituals that promote addiction. We need public education and increased efforts to promote moderation and the monitoring by self and by society of our growing populations who are vulnerable to addiction.

It is difficult to be aware of the social forces that provoke addiction, and even more difficult to recognize the roots of the addictive process, because people find pleasure and relief in their addictive practices. The obsessive and compulsive elements are in concert with the ego, and the destructive ones are denied. Symptoms begin to appear only when the pleasure is outweighed by the pain (*hangover* phenomena). A person's life is then disrupted by his addictive behavior and in turn affects other lives. After a while, the addictive agent no longer serves its original purpose; paranoid reactions can appear, such as suspiciousness, insecurity, and blaming others for one's failures. In the later phases of addiction, there are commonly excesses in dependency and passivity, poorly handled aggression, and hypersensitivity to slight feelings of failure or rejection. As the addictive act is constantly called on for instant relief of psychic pain, emotional control declines, and there are impulsive behavior and mood swings of which the person is often unaware.

Because the addict always denies the nature, depth, duration, and impact of his addictiveness, distortions of time sense occur during addictive behavior. The addict is invariably not able to account for time spent in addictive fantasies and acts.

Characterologic defects are always present; when addictive practices often become a life-style, they further impair the superego and ego. At various stages of the addictive process, a person may well show dishonesty, unreliability, and irresponsibility, lack of control, overcontrol, manipulative or immature behavior, mild or hardcore criminality, demandingness, grandiosity, exhibitionism, insatiability, impulsiveness, and inability to delay gratification.

The greater a person's characterologic defects before the process begins, the more destructive is the addiction., The addictive process can plateau and become merely automatic. It may die out if it ceases to serve its original functions, but it will persist as long as it offers even the least relief from inner discomfort.

It is important to realize that the addictive process does not always have its inception in the childhood or adolescent years, when vulnerabilities to becoming addicted are most often established. Many people become addicted later in life because of a variety of circumstances that are unendurable. Obviously those whose childhood patterns cultivate addictiveness remain the most vulnerable throughout their lives. They can develop a more malignant process, depending on the vicissitudes they experience. They are less easily treated than those who develop later-life situational addictiveness. Regardless of the phase of life in which the addictive process surfaces, a person develops along with an addiction, a set of trigger mechanisms that make it self-perpetuating. These are stimuli, conflicts, or pressures that provoke a fantasy, feeling, or thought that leads to an addictive act. They may be psychological, physical, environmental, or interpersonal.

Trigger mechanisms are an integral part of the addictive process. Each trigger leads to an addictive act, and each addictive act makes the addict more acutely sensitive to future triggers. This circular process becomes more powerful because the addictive act produces physical or psychological euphoria without resolving the problems that cause the addiction.

Trigger mechanisms occur in clusters and vary from person to person. Their number and nature may change over an addict's life, but most are repetitive and predictable. They have their roots in the addict's early family history and the circumstances and pressures he has to deal with at the present.

The addict is unaware of his many trigger mechanisms. The pleasure of anticipating and experiencing the addictive gratification wipes out any awareness of what triggered it. Even if someone tells him—or, more likely, complains to him—about his addiction, he will quickly deny or repress the unwanted insight.

The diagram opposite describes the cyclic aspects of the addictive process.

To understand addiction and help an addict help himself, one must discover and help him identify (i.e., become conscious of) the specific triggers that spark and perpetuate his addictiveness. They may be depression, isolation, loneliness, boredom, situational life crises (divorce, death of parent, etc.), severe failures (at work, in love, over money), sex and gender dysfunctions, unbearable pressures, stressful competition, fatigue, overwork, excessive exposure to other addicts (i.e., addictive agents/milieus), psychosis (i.e., the addictive agent is used as self-medication), and so forth. This list could go on and on if one were to carefully examine the literature of addiction (see bibliography). I and others who have studied the addictions in depth tend to single out the triggers most common in each author's own skewed population, and based on their own emotional bias. But if one asks the addict what he believes to be the reason for his addiction, his first and perhaps only answer is, "I do it because I like it" or "It makes me feel good," or "I get high on it and wipe out bad feelings." He reduces the reason for his addiction to pleasure alone. This awareness of pleasure is for him the paramount emotional trigger. Not only does the addict identify an emotion as *the* most important trigger of his addictiveness but so do the clinicians and researchers who have observed him.

There is a large body of research literature on the connections between the addict's specific emotional developmental disturbances, his past and current emotional life, and his addictiveness. The majority of authors single out the emotions as causative in their analysis of the addictive process (emphasizing either the chemical or psychological factors, depending on their disciplines and biases). Because addictions emerge from the pain/pleasure axis of life, emotional damage or dysfunction is a key to understanding addiction. Developmental disruptions, traumas, imbalances, inhibitions, loss of contact with one's emotions, or becoming overwhelmed by them are the essence of high vulnerability to becoming addictive.

THE ADDICTION PROCESS

Cycles

EXCESSIVE PAINFUL STIMULI (Triggers)

1. Psychological (Emotional/Blockage-Denial)
2. Physiological – Chemcial
3. Environmental
4. Familial (Absent, Polarized Discipline)
   (Addictive Model/Complement)
   (Peer Model/Complement)
5. Interpersonal (Situational)
6. Constitutional/Genetic

Stimulates →

Conflict
Pressure
Crises
Anxiety/Depression
Loss (Death/Divorce)
Imbalances (Work/Play)

Stimulates →

EXCESSIVE PLEASURABLE STIMULI (Triggers)

Impulsion   to →   **Instant**   to →   **Fantasy**
Drive   Chemical   Thought
Craving   Synthetic   Feeling
Need   Natural   Imagery

                           Addictive
                           Paraphernalia
                           Milieu   to →
                           Model/Complement

(Escalates)
Tolerance

Addictive Act   to →   **Impulse**
Pleasurable   Feeling
(total/partial)   Thought
(masks pain)

Denial

Dissociation
Depersonalization
Derealization
Splitting Off
Guilt
Fear
Suppression
Repression

Hangover
(Somatic symptoms)

Evokes →

High
Psychic
Chemical/Rush
Physiological
Euphoric
Altered Effect

No Resolution
No Relief
Escalates

Therapies

Psychological Therapy

Confrontations
Psychotherapy
Psychoanalysis
Hypnotherapy
Family Therapy
Psychodrama

Therapeutic Community
Milieu Therapy

De-addicting Activities & Environments

Behavioral Therapy

De-addicting Peers
Alcoholics
Gamblers
Overeaters   ANONYMOUS
Pot Smokers
Pills
Weightwatchers
T.O.P.S.
Smokenders

Chemotherapy

Antagonists
Methadone/heroin

Aversive
Disulfiram/alcohol

Substitutive
Lobeline/nicotine

Withdrawal/Abstinence Therapy

Detoxification Center
Medical/Psychiatric
Hospitalization
Therpeutic Community
Closed Unit
Research Unit
Medical
Community

Replacement Therapy

Non-addictive
Pleasures/Peers
Athletics
Hobbies
Health Club
Yoga
Transcendental Meditation
Religion
Balanced Work/Play/Sex

Detoxification Activities & Environments

Because our internal chemistries control our emotional lives, and external chemicals that affect them are so available, these chemicals easily become a prime way of adapting to emotional malfunction. This is particularly prevalent in our society, because powerful advertising media and the medical establishment promote the instant availability and use of chemical relief for every human discomfort and as a major source of pleasure. When emotional illness or disturbance occurs, a person is encouraged to turn at once to natural or synthetic chemicals to alter, control, or expand his emotional life. Every day, chemicals are prescribed, promises are given that one can go from depression to euphoria, anxiety to relaxation, inhibition to erotic abandonment, boredom to excitement, shyness to gregariousness, loneliness to intimacy, if only the right chemical is taken. Chemicals have long given mankind instant relief of pain and instant gratification. Modern technology has refined chemicals and made them more available than ever. But when the excessive use of chemicals is denied as being the sole source of relief for unidentified or unresolved emotional conflicts, they become dangerous coping mechanisms.

What emotions do the majority of these authors believe to be at the heart of the addictions? Some are negative emotions—anxiety, depression, agression, hostility, rage, panic, terror, shame, guilt, loss, feelings of inferiority or inadequacy, dis-illusionment, disappointment, hurt, injured pride, boredom, lonliness. Some are regressed emotional states—infantile dependency, orality, greedy incorporation, primitive rage, undifferentiated paneroticism, or the absence of emotion that is variously called depersonalization, dissociation, detachment, derealization, and emptiness. These are all referred to without fail in most literature on addiction.

The reasons for attributing addiction to these emotional states is that they are poorly tolerated, produce pain and frustration, and are at the heart of man's major problems within himself and others. The literature on addictions is replete with extensive histories of people whose past and current emotional lives have been distorted and disrupted by their families, lovers, peers, legal authorities, and the social milieus with which they come into daily contact. These backgrounds cause severe damage to the development and stabilization of a person's emotional life, making him highly vulnerable to addictive coping mechanisms. He inevitably experiences excesses in suppression and repression, blockage, denial, imbalance, confusion, dissociation, splitting off, poor recognition of emotion, and misidentifying emotional pain as pleasure and pleasure as pain.

Authors less often explain addictiveness as emerging from a disturbed capacity to cope with positive emotions—warmth, affability, happiness, lust, love, joy, abandonment, tenderness, intimacy, and playfulness. I have observed in my own patients that the absence, suppression, repression, denial, misunderstanding, and misidentification of positive emotions are just as important in understanding addictive behavior as are negative emotions. We invariably identify addiction in its middle and latter phases, when the addict (and sometimes those around him) experience more negative than positive emotions. Because of his denial, dissociation, regression to infantile negative emotions, etc., we ignore his use of addictive agents to cope with positive emotions. Even in the advanced stages of addiction, the addict usually continues to cover his impoverishment of genuine pleasure, living a pseudo-pleasurable life. Scratch the surface of any addict's life and you will find a long gamut of dysfunctions in his capacity for satisfying experience or for coping with positive emotions. In treatment it is vitally important to identify and pinpoint these dysfunctions and their origins.

What must helper and addict do? They must enable the addict to identify his emotions accurately and understand their dysfunctions. Does he deny, misinterpret, confuse, dissociate, or split them off from reality? Unless the addict can answer these vital questions, he cannot see the function his addictive agent or practice serves in dealing with emotional dysfunctions. Does his addictive agent displace, replace, ward off, defend, deny, suppress, or repress his positive and/or negative emotions? Is he partly or entirely incapable of developing a balanced, functional emotional life without his addictive practice? Is his addictive act his only emotional language? Perhaps instead of expressing anger and being in touch with other emotions, he eats, takes heroin, drinks, gambles, smokes. Does he do this to hurt someone close to him, his society, or himself?

There is much in recent research literature about the difficulties of distinguishing addictive states from the various depressive illnesses. The degree and kind must vary in each case. It isn't easy to determine whether a depression is caused by cessation of addictive practice or induced by the addictive act. Obviously the end of any pleasure, whether it's crashing from cocaine or feeling blue because there's no junk food available in the house will bring some degree of mood change. The inevitable down must follow every up. If depression reaches pathological dimensions (interfering with work, sleep, social interaction, and sex) and has physical effects (such as sleep and weight loss), a professional should be called upon to make a differential diagnosis.

Effective diagnosis and treatment depend on singling out which emotions relate to a person's addiction and why his specific addictive agent/practice has come into play. This knowledge leads to accurate diagnosis, the best choice of therapeutic inter-action, and ultimately to insight, relearning processes, and constructively replacing the addictive practice. There is now a growing body of literature that has attributed the choice and nature of certain addictions to specific emotional dysfunctions.

1. *Alcohol, barbiturates and mild tranquilizers:* to reduce anxiety, relieve depression, release inhibitions and repressed emotions, relieve shyness and erotic weakness, and to cope with loss, loneliness, and feelings of inferiority.

2. *Narcotics:* to reduce rage and aggression, relieve psychic and physical pain, deny isolation, achieve an identity, cope with loss, rejection, overwhelming emotions, weakness, shame, boredom, loneliness, and absence of emotions.

3. *Amphetamines:* to remove fatigue, increase speed and energy, enhance action,

   eroticism, and ability to perform, and to extend perceived time span.
   4. *Hallucinogens:* for escape and fantasy, to resolve identity and body-image
      disturbances and inability to feel emotion, and to permit oceanic feelings.
   5. *Food:* to reduce tension, relieve depression and anxiety, resolve inaction, and
      promote erotic withdrawal.
   6. *Nicotine:* to reduce tension, to take or replace needed action and control,
      replace, express or repress emotions indirectly.
   7. *Work:* to increase self-esteem, deny isolation, avoid intimacy, gain acceptance,
      reduce anxiety, exercise emotional control, and avoid competitive pleasure.
   8. *Sex:* to reduce isolation, absence of emotion, loneliness, and tension, to
      resolve conflict, and to gain power.

These specificities probably relate to what each chemical or activity can provide.
Some have been used in controlled ways by physicians to treat illness. But physicians
must discover the individual's unique chemical and psychological responses to the
potentially addictive agent—the dosage—how much is required to produce the
reaction, the margin of safety in their use—which are all barometers forecasting
potentials for addiction. As we gain more through sophisticated chemical and
psychological research and in-depth psychoanalysis of the connections between the
emotions and addictions, we will achieve more skill and accuracy in predicting the
choice of addictive agent and practices. Because so many other variables are involved
—family background and identifications, legal sanctions, social acceptability, availability, cultural rituals, economic forces, group response, social attitudes, vogues,
chemical, genetic and other constitutional predispositions—it will never be easy to
closely define the relative importance of emotional factors in provoking a given
addiction. We do know that failures to cope with or stabilize one's emotional life
make one highly vulnerable to the addictive process.

   Despite the many other emotions that play a role in addiction, every addictive
practice at first seems to give more pleasure than pain, and seems to resolve
pressures and conflicts. Eventually the act becomes more important but less pleasurable. The addict must then find ways to deny the pain the addiction itself is beginning
to cause, and to reinforce the illusion that he is experiencing greater highs. Usually
he is helped by the people around him. It is as important to fellow addicts as it is to
him to deny the addiction. His family may also need to deny the guilt, pain, and fear
that his addiction causes them. Allowing him to remain addicted may satisfy their
own psychological needs—selfishness, denying their own addictions, controlling or
indirectly punishing the addict, or avoiding guilt about his disgrace.

   At first an addict can deny his addiction by shifting to another activity immediately
after an addictive act. Often he completely blocks or represses any memory of his
addictive fantasies or acts. He also resorts to rationalization; if someone tries to make
him face his addiction, he produces a host of explanations for his actions, denies that

the practice is addictive, says he only acted as he did because someone upset him, and claims he is doing what everyone else is doing. He may go as far as to admitting that the other people he knows may be addicts, but he says that he can always stop.

Even when his addiction has begun to interrupt his work and social life, he continues to deny what has happened. If asked to describe his day, he cannot account for much of his time, unaware that it was spent in addictive reveries or acts. In the final stages, he still cannot connect his near paralysis and the addiction that has brought his life to a halt.

By the time he becomes addicted he has built up an environment of stimuli—fantasies, other people, the paraphernalia of his addiction. Ads, movies, reading matter, bars, and various social milieus all continue to act as powerful environmental triggers.

Naturally, he is most vulnerable when subjected to unusually intense pressure or to many pressures at once. His mounting failure to cope increases his tension, which he tries to resolve with addictive behavior. Early in the addictive process, the addictive act is pleasureful and effective. The drink, candy bar, cigarette, or masturbatory act dissolves tension, relieves depression, resolves conflict, provides the energy to meet a challenging life situation or to take action that seemed impossible before. But unlike normal coping practices, it becomes excessive, repetitive, and serves many functions other than dealing directly with life. In advanced stages, the practice becomes the addict's sole coping mechanism and only source of pleasure. Then it no longer helps him cope and is causing symptoms that produce new problems that must be coped with. In this vicious cycle, the cure becomes the disease.

The word addict comes from the Latin *addicere*, which means to assign or surrender. An addict, or *addictur*, was someone bound over to another person as a captured enemy, slave, or serf. Every addict has an excessive need for dependence, either overt or hidden. The emotional excesses, deprivations, and swings to which he was subjected as a child, his imbalanced ego and superego, and a variety of resulting problems, leave him with dependency problems others cannot tolerate. Usually he is unaware of how dependent he is, how paralyzing his dependency needs are, and how insatiable his needs seem to others. He is aware of only painful rejections and failures when these needs are not met by society and those closest to him.

If someone tries to exert excessive controls over an addict, either openly or covertly, the addict consciously or unconsciously perceives it as unjust. The things most likely to trigger an addict further into addictive behavior are exerting over-control or unrealistically denying the need for any control.

The addict invariably seeks and finds another addict or an addictive complement who will resolve his guilts, anxieties, hostilities and vulnerabilities or balance his excess or lack of ego and superego. The fellow addict's addiction need not be of the same kind or degree. The addictive complement can have a severe superego which serves the addict's need to keep his addictive behavior alive. In many such cases an addicted parent had reversed the child-parent roles, creating in the child an adult superego; when the child grew up, he gravitated to an addicted person with whom he could play the role of addictive complement.

There are usually many people in an addict's environment who find him a convenient scapegoat. They can consciously or unconsciously collude with him to fill their own excessive needs. They can be addicted parents, peers, and anyone in close daily contact who needs an addictive complement—someone they can depend on to support or provoke their own addiction. Obviously, if the addictive model or addictive complement is in the family, the impact is more powerful and damaging and will increase the depth and duration of the addiction. Addictiveness is then passed on from generation to generation.

Sometimes an addict can make people close to him his addictive complements, manipulating them into providing the triggers he needs to justify his addictive acts. He may force them to reduce his self-esteem, make him feel guilty, overprotect him, or reject him; he may seduce them into exploiting or abusing him. Then, instead of expressing his anger directly to the person who aroused it, he feels justified in acting out his addiction.

Because addictiveness is always highly stimulated by media, environment, social attitudes, and addictive subcultures, the addict always finds collusive partners and a steady source of complements. His addiction is continuously fueled by the abundance of milieus that supply what he needs—a drug-saturated disco, bar-filled streets, a porno district, thirty-flavor ice cream parlors, and the off-track betting places. Our society richly provides these pleasure emporiums as needed outlets, since they serve everyone with vital relief from pressured lives. They are high-profit-baring pleasure domes. For the addict they can become danger zones. An addict may not realize how persistently he seeks out his fellow addicts and addicting environments. He knows that they make him feel alive, more adequate, and relieved of the pressures that triggered him to turn to them.

Usually an addict who is just entering his subculture finds as a complement either a fellow addict in a more advanced stage of addiction or one who is older and more experienced. They seem to him to function adequately or even well, so they serve him as models and provide the rationale that addiction can be a viable coping mechanism. Once fully at home in the subculture, he spends more and more time with peer addicts; they trigger further addictive behavior by making it seem more valid. In their company, it seems easy to deal with all sorts of social interactions and tensions. He sees his fellow addicts as adjusted to their problems; they convince him that he, like them, has found the best way to deal with the injustices and difficulties that seem to beset them. Soon the addict feels comfortable only with those to whom he can relate in a state of excess. He considers moderate people dull; their real shortcoming is being incapable of the level of excess that can turn an addict on. He has acquired an addictive identity, which he can use to rationalize all his addictive acts. Eventually he begins to serve as a complement to other neophyte addicts. By bringing them "out" he feels justification of his own practices and enlarges his circle.

If an addict is absorbed by an addictive subculture, he finds his complement in one other addict, with whom he forms a closed, symbiotic relationship. But since he finds it almost impossible to feel alive and intimate except during addictive acts, he is in great danger when he invests his entire emotional life in one other addict. No matter how intense addictive relationships seem during a high, they are by their nature transient. An addict is not really interested in the other person, only in the pleasure the other person can provide. When two addicts become locked in a relationship, they may fuel each other's addictions, easily become isolated and suspicious, and even find it difficult to integrate into society. No one else seems able to fill their addictive needs as well as each other.

When an addict becomes acutely aware of the danger of society's harsh disapproval, he may withdraw from it completely. He may for the first time realize that people around him are aware of his addiction and are hostile, rejecting, or intimidating to him. He then often feels guilty and unjustly set upon; this can drive him into isolation that only deepens his problems and aggravates his addiction. He finds that he is no longer able to use his addiction as a means of emotional contact. He may then begin to practice his addiction alone, feeling unreal and detached from the world. His withdrawal, injustice-collecting, and paranoia can become even greater if he persists in believing that no one is aware of his addiction or if he himself continues to deny its existence.

A major trigger mechanism is that of *polarized narcissism*. Authors who have researched and written about the addictions inevitably focus on the importance of narcissistic imbalance as a common cause and perpetuation of the addictive process. Because the addict has suffered from early disruption, damage, or trauma to the development and establishment of his ego and superego and to his nurturance and dependency needs, he must incur narcissistic disturbances. These disturbances are reflected in his relationships with others and attitudes toward himself. Imbalances occur in his ability to perceive himself accurately or to deal equitably with others. Narcissistic dysfunctions continually trigger addictive coping mechanisms. What do these authors describe as narcissistic that has also appeared in my own addictive population? When someone is addictive, he is described as having to have what he wants, when, where, and how he wants it and often immediately. He needs instant and excessive rewards for inappropriately small exertions in work or relationships. He shows little or no appropriate awareness or appreciation of other's contribution to his life or their sacrifice on behalf of his addictive behavior. He is more often than not unable to delay gratifications, is easily frustrated, and overreacts to failure. Rarely does he concern himself with his excessive negative emotions, which are provoked by any level of discomfort, nor does he care about their unpleasant consequences to anyone around him. He can shift from arrogance to indifference, from the pain of total self-negation to the pleasure of complete self-absorption, from aggressive self-preoccupation to pseudo-compliance, solicitude, and a passivity that camouflages his excessive needs. He believes that his addictive act will magically repair any injury to his ego regardless of its excessive nature and damaging byproducts to himself or others. He lives through a series or narcissistic crises that are outgrowths of his polarized, unrealistic, and at times unrecognized fluctuations of his self-esteem. These distortions in self-assessment and needs and his inappropriate, inequitable, detached and selfish behavior finally trigger hostility and retaliation when others refuse to tolerate his behavior and meet his excessive needs. Their retaliation makes him feel devalued. He suffers narcissistic wounds that perpetuate his addiction. He uses addictive behavior either to repair his ego, reinforce his negative narcissism, or cope with his rage, shame, or guilt provoked by these retaliations.

Sexual problems can be a common trigger to addictive behavior. The literature on addictions is full of accounts that connect the first signs of addiction to problems caused by faulty or impaired gender and erotic identity in childhood, adolescence, and early adulthood. Many an adult's sexual insecurity and dysfunction either provoked addictive behavior or emerged as a byproduct of the destruction caused by post-addictive symptoms and hangovers. The addictive act can become a coping mechanism, form of substitution, sublimation, way to deny, excuse, or withdraw from sexual confrontations, frustrations, and dysfunctions. For some, the very nature of an addictive high is equated or unfavorably competes with orgasm as life's ultimate pleasure. Physical and emotional deteriorations caused by addictions result in a high incidence of sexual failure and rejection, which the addict may deny or refuse to identify as a source of his feelings of sexual inferiority. The addict is then caught in the circular web of turning back to addictive practice to cope with sexual failure and not knowing he has failed because of his addiction. Sexual prowess is so strongly equated with nonsexual prowess in our culture that any sexual insecurity makes one highly vulnerable to addictive coping in order to repair the loss of this highly valued pleasure. Meeting exaggerated, unchallenged sexual norms and variations can also trigger the individual who believes himself to be inferior or incapable of meeting these distorted norms.

The triggers an addict is most likely to identify on his own are failure, rejection, and criticism. His impaired ego and superego make it difficult for him to deal with any of these, so they are indeed frequent triggers. He is most vulnerable if his childhood was marked by unrealistic or excessive praise or criticism from those closest to him. Being devalued and minimized are especially destructive and can be the most severe triggers. He keeps searching for the totally accepting relationship he had or wanted as a child, and begins to distort the real nature of the rejection he receives. He may not be able to see that people reject his demands because they are excessive or made in ways that make them difficult to fulfill.

Our highly competitive society urges us to live up to many ideals, not all of them attainable by any one person; therefore many people's competitiveness is heavily covered by denial. We are supposed to be ''nice guys,'' but we all know that ''nice guys finish last.'' An addict may be especially vulnerable to competitive standards and comparisons. Although unaware of constantly comparing himself to others, he is often triggered into addictiveness by the wounds his comparisons deal to his ego. Money can bring comforts, education, and security and is equated with success, power, control, and even sexual power. It is no wonder that financial comparisons can also be addictive triggers. Furthermore, most of us today must cope with increasingly rapid changes in jobs, environments, attitudes, and relationships. This produces strain and, in those most vulnerable to strain, a need for some kind of anesthesia. For the addict, this means turning to his addiction. Such strain often triggers the addict to go on a binge and may cause a relapse in an arrested addict.

Most of us feel that ours is essentially a democratic, middle-class society that puts a high value on moderate living. Actually, our values are often contradictory and provoke polarized behavior and attitudes. We value youth, power, status, aggression, and wealth, but we praise the intellectual, intimate, peaceful, nonmaterialistic life. We condemn violence, yet our children have grown up watching dehumanizing and pointless wars on television. We are perpetually dieting, perpetually glutting ourselves. We smoke and put cancer and heart-disease warnings on the packages. We drink and even devise sweet wines that will be palatable to younger and younger adolescents, yet we post notices of Alanon meetings on school bulletin boards. We talk about sexual freedom and defend the production of addictive pornography, yet we restrain the sexual education of the young. Addictive value systems emerge from and reflect these contradictions. When an addictive person discovers that some of our professed values do not really give him the opportunities they promise, he may value his deviance as a form of rebellion and thus justify his needs.

We can be so excited by and involved in excess that we are blinded to the beginnings of addiction. We think of addicts in extremes—skid row derelicts as typical alcoholics, ghetto heroin addicts and hallucinating acid trippers as typical drug addicts. We separate them from ourselves physically and psychologically because of their extreme deterioration or dramatic behavior. That makes it easier for us to ignore the man who can tolerate the work demands of his success only by heavy social drinking; the woman who anesthetizes herself to the irritations of her life by just the right combination of liquor and tranquilizers; the teenager who takes hallucinogenic drugs on special occasions, but armors himself against the stresses of school with daily marijuana or barbiturates; the adolescent whose parents are relieved that she is getting drunk on weekends instead of taking other drugs.

We promise young people more options during their unrealistically prolonged adolescence than they will really have when they enter the adult world. The rights that seemed to be held out—new life-styles, sexual freedom, minority opportunities, meaningful but nonconformist and nonmaterialistic careers—are in fact not easily available. A young person and his friends may try to live in these ways, but they find themselves faced with a society far more rigid and conformist than they expected. When doing one's own thing collides with keeping up with the Joneses, many young addictive people find a rationale for continuing to do their own thing—to the point of irrational deviance, not only in spite of the Joneses but in spite of themselves. They equate this with individuality and make it a reason for insisting on whatever they feel they deserve. They have been led to expect great rewards for little effort, and they continue to insist on greater rewards for still less effort, and in the end find that nothing is enough. If they enter a subculture where hard drugs are the norm, they find that addiction is called not "having a monkey on your back" but "having a Jones."

The speed of change in our work and lives can also contribute to addictiveness. Most of us cannot keep pace with the rapid advances of technology, and we are often asked to make swift changes in our jobs and living arrangements—recurrent uprootings in the service of corporate structures. The faster we move or are moved, the more vulnerable we are to seeking something to help create the illusion that we are still on top of things. As we place more and more value on speed and action, we must devalue the contemplation that might allow us to face our frailities. We extend these attitudes to our opinions on addiction. Addictions that slow people down, such as food, alcohol, and opiates, incur far more disapproval than those which speed people up and give the appearance of greater activity, such as work, amphetamines, and sex. Many young people are torn between the high value placed on action and excess and their own reaction against it. They use drugs to slow themselves down or speed themselves up, trying to deal with or react against the culture.

Passive and dependent people are most vulnerable to these pressures—just as we are least tolerant of their qualities. A passive, dependent person may turn to excessive work, sex, or speedup drugs in reaction to his fears about having these characteristics, which threaten his self-love and sense of autonomy. But these addictions have crash periods when the addict is overwhelmed by depression, fatigue, and sleeplessness. He is then devalued by himself and society, because he is reduced to the same passivity as the addict who chooses a slowdown addiction.

Each person's addictive pattern has its own special sequence related to his needs, circumstances, and stresses. No pattern occurs in every addictive person, but eventually all addictions disrupt one's ability for daily living. Addictive patterns lower his level of consciousness and remove him from life's mainstream. He must spend a lot of time thinking about and carrying out his addiction; at the same time, he must deny it to avoid the pain of recognizing how much of his life it has invaded. Eventually it takes priority over everything else, and his ability to work, be on time, or even spend much time with nonaddicts suffers accordingly.

An addict has probably grown up feeling alienated from his family and peers. Even if he does try to live within the social mainstream, he still feels alienated; he devalues and denigrates it regardless of its real strengths and failures, and more openly values deviance. He may ally himself with people pushing for social change, but his interest is less in constructive change than in promoting an anarchic, excessive life style in which he can pursue his addiction freely. The addict feels that the counterculture offers him change for the sake of change and a certain amount of protective coloration. At first he is attracted by the promise of humane tolerance of sex, drugs, play, and a sensual life, but his real interest is in protecting hedonistic excess and addictive peers who depend and promote his use of addiction to cope with life. He often ends up denying central values of counter-culture groups and championing the most radical and militant elements of their life-style.

To better understand the addictive process, you must now listen to the addict's inner voice and know his environment, family, peers, and way of life. Having had the privilege of entering the heart and head of the addictive patient in my office and having lived and studied in depth my own and other addicts' lives outside my office have been the ways I learned about addictive disorders and how to treat them. I believe the best way to deepen your understanding of addictions is to see their essences and complexities through transcriptions of addicts' monologues and histories. What you are about to read are accounts of four people of different ages and backgrounds, each in a life crisis and at a different stage of the addictive process. These portraits and therapeutic vignettes are based on actual clinical data. Because of professional confidentiality, details that would make anyone identifiable have been changed, but this does not basically alter the accounts. Any resemblance to anyone I have ever treated or known is purely coincidental.

PART II
PORTRAITS OF ADDICTS:
THE CRISES, HISTORY, ANALYSIS

INTRODUCTION

Throughout fifteen years of studying the addictive process I have diagnosed, treated, and researched addictive people with the aid of audiotaped records of their sessions. The tapes enabled me to listen to the addict's inner voice and life, to hear his denials and evidence of his unrevealed levels of consciousness, and to analyze the mechanisms of his interactions with people. The tapes were valuable not only as a therapeutic tool but as documents of my failures and successes.

In the initial research with audiotapes, my assistants and I spent hundreds of hours condensing therapeutic sessions into what we considered their most meaningful and helpful elements. This condensation was called a *Taped Capsule*. The capsule was given to the patient to listen to at home between sessions. Over the years since these early experiments, I have tried to use the taped record of a session in other therapeutic ways. I recommended that the patient take the record of the entire session home to listen to and review, and then discuss its validity in following sessions. In later years, I suggested certain portions of the hour or self-chosen segments. I asked more ambitious patients to make their own tape capsules for us to review. Finally I researched the entire three year depth analysis of a sexual addict, all on tape and then transcribed. This gave me the rare opportunity to microscopically study the addictive patient and process.

Watching and listening to thousands of hours of addicts' free associations made me acutely aware of the nuances of their behavior and moods, their language, inflections, pauses, and shades of meanings. Replaying the taped records away from the emotionally charged context of a psychiatric encounter allowed both the addict and me to better objectify what we learned.

I also learned one very important fact over those years of listening: the most valuable time for any therapist to find out about and to treat an addict, the decisive moment to zero in on him, is when he is in a state of crises. He suffers pain and, more than at any other time, feels compelled to seek help. His mechanisms of denial are most feeble. His addiction—for the first and, in some cases, the only time—lies bare and raw for him and his helper. He is acutely vulnerable, undefended, and he can be reached as at no other time. His free associations reveal facts and give insights that are unobtainable when he is not in pain but relatively in harmony with his addiction. It is for these reasons that I have chosen to present the internal monologues of four addicts in states of addictive crises.

Catherine is forty-two years old, married, from an upper-middle class background. She returned to see me in a state of panic ten years after a period of therapy with me. Her entire life was falling apart, her marriage, family and career in chaos. She had deteriorated physically because of addiction to alcohol and other drugs. A number of incidents in her immediate life had brought her to total desperation; she needed to return to see me in order to stop what seemed to her the final wave of destruction sweeping over her and swallowing her up.

Tom is a nineteen-year-old who was sent to me from a crisis clinic. He was desperate over his sexually addictive life, which had played havoc with his entire life and reduced him to self-contempt, rage, and complete inability to trust anyone in the many worlds he turned to for love. He felt the pain of total isolation after a brutal rejection by his family, once poor and now utterly involved in making money. In the past, he had received debasing and sadistic treatment by others, culminating in the total devastation of his identity. Now, for the first time, he poured out his nineteen years of reactions to this cruel and ignorant treatment. Falteringly he reached out for help, full of angry defenses and suspicion yet craving answers that might help rid him of his demon.

Chris, a Wall Street lawyer of fifty-two, was referred to me by a doctor whom he saw at an emergency clinic where he was inaccurately diagnosed as being addicted to drugs. His addiction, it turned out, was work. He developed a mild paranoid reaction to having been trapped in a situation that tore away all his defenses and forced him for a moment to face the work-addicted shell he had become. His bloodless, detached, and driven character had a serious impact on every sphere of his life. He came to see me with distorted motives, still in a state of paranoia, defending the rigid structure that protected his work addiction. The cracks in his armor were wide and revealing.

Ellen is a fat fifteen-year-old adolescent whose obesity finally invaded and destroyed the rest of her life. She was brought to see me by her mother after having run away from home for a weekend that left her in a panic. She had been faced with more addictive stimuli at once than she could manage. But this was only the culmination of a disastrous year of failures, isolation, loneliness, hostility, fear, and inability to face her peers, schoolwork, or family. This made it imperative that she get help for her pain-filled addictive food odyssey. She desperately needed someone to help her untangle the destructive web spun by all the people, places, and things in her life that triggered her food addiction. She was in a state of angry hysteria, lashing out at everyone, but most of all hating herself and her body.

I present their internal monologues so you can hear the voices of addicts in crises. No labels or clinical summaries can tell you as much as their own words, their hesitations, their silences. Once you know each of them, we can look at their histories to see what brought them to their crises. There is also a brief analysis underlining the moments in their monologues and their histories that reveal the sources and mechanisms of their addictions.

CATHERINE

THE CRISES

Ten years had passed since I'd last seen Catherine Muller. They clearly had not been the good ones we both had hoped for when she'd ended her therapy.

When I left here, ready to marry Bill, everything in my life was going to go better. But I feel as if I've been suspended in some sort of half-life—or half-hell—since I don't know when. I've just been letting myself go along with it all. . .the way I always have, I guess. Whatever I do always seems forced on me by circumstances. I need to find the center of things. The only choice I can think of is that I'd like to feel better in an instant. Otherwise, everything seems too much to cope with. I simply don't have anything left inside.

Catherine looked emotionally burned out and physically ravaged. Her arms and legs, which had been long and slim when she was in her twenties, were now almost emaciated, the rest of her body seemed bloated. There were fine, premature age lines on her face from years of polite, forced smiles. Her grey-blue eyes were blood-shot and watery from held-back tears. The fine, unevenly streaked blond hair, that always used to be combed straight, was slightly disheveled and revealed the dark roots of neglect. Her skin was shiny, pale, and tightly drawn over her high cheek-bones and the sharp features of her aristocratic face. She spoke either in a soft, polite, seductive voice or in a hoarse rasp that revealed the toll of too much smoking and alcohol. Only her tense bearing and taut, cool facade were familiar to me. I thought back to the childhood she had described to me long ago, and I remembered that she had built that facade before she even knew why she needed it.

There never seems to be a middle of anything for me. I've always been either too good or. . .too bad. Everything that happened today. . .just happened to me. I didn't make any choice. Except, I suppose, what I did to Mother. . .but that was really inevitable.

God, no wonder Mother's so sick from. . .so many empty bottles hidden in her apartment. I couldn't believe it. My superaristocratic, superhypochondriac mother. She turns out to be the worst old closet wino in Manhattan. I won't know what to say when I see her. . .and. . .I can't believe she fooled all those doctors all these years. And me, too! And even Dad! I bet he died fooled. She'll die for having fooled everyone. Coffee, I need coffee, or something in me to get going. . .maybe something sweet or something else in my stomach, anything. I've got to be able to think clearly. But when I leave here, how am I going to manage it? I mean, face her? I'll never get to the hospital today. . .or ever, maybe. Maybe she'll die tomorrow. Lying there helpless with her broken hip and all her lies.

I'd like to feel better right away. I wish I could have Johnny right now. . .he's young, he can give me what I need. . .that's crazy, I'm a grown. . .getting older. . . woman. . .Bill, the kids. . .I'm out of my head. . .I'm going insane. Bill will know. He'll know, but he won't care. He'll just go on being whatever. . .it is he is. . . can't be. . .or do. . .for me. . .what I just had done all over me. He's never had all of him all over me. So little of us touches. I loathe him. And Mother, too. I didn't want to say that. . .shouldn't feel it, even to myself. . .it's too much. . .I have to keep it away. . .by talking. . .oh, the times I've needed to talk, to call somebody because I knew I couldn't handle it all alone. It's so good to talk to you, after all these years. I used to call Rob, rely on him. I had to call him. . .too often, yes, to cry and have breakdowns over the phone. He always used to be there. . .to. . .save my mind. I. . .Rob was someone for my soul, too.

I guess calling Rob to always come and rescue me was as much a reflex as. . .gulping down a pill with that dreadful coffee while I was waiting for him to answer the phone. . .or vomiting it all up, sometimes. And when he got there finally, Rob would always put his arms around me. . .I. . .I don't know why. . .probably just to distract me, keep me from what he called turning to all my chemical escapes. . .because of the mess I am. . . .

Mother. . .that's how all this mess started today. I was in her apartment and found this monumental collection of wine bottles. . .full, half-full, empty. . .the stink! My mother, sitting in the hospital, acting as if she's at death's door, lying, demanding that I gather up all her ridiculous papers, bring them to her. . .put everything in order. Order! Her whole damn lying life has no order!

Shelf after shelf of cheap wine. . .I thought I was going to faint. I felt so guilty, as if I'd exposed Mother naked. Now I'll. . .tell them at the hospital, and they'll. . .do something. I mean, now the doctors will have to cope. . .they'll be able to deal with her. But my God, if she starts again. . .I mean, when she gets out! That's probably how she fell and broke her hip in the first place. Well, the doctors will have to handle it. . .say something, make her stop. And all Mother's belongings, her stuff. . .that's all it is, stuff. I don't know what half of it is. Useless, probably. . .part of her props. . . just symbols of all the care that hasn't been given, the responsibility that hasn't been accepted. . .stuff. Worthless stuff I left with her before Bill and I married, stuff she gave back to me. . .more to resent, more for nobody to care about. And now I've got to cart it all around again. All the evidence of money wasted, time wasted, things passed by. . .God it's sad. . .evidence of nothing to show for a whole life. She wants me to keep it safe for her. . .oh, God, it's laughable except for being so crazy, so pitiful. And I'm still doing my numbers, too. But I'm learning. . .maybe I can learn to start getting straightened out. I know it has to have something to do with not drinking.

It isn't as if I didn't know it, from all the times Rob and I. . .in restaurants and our favorite little secret bars. . .always having too much, ending lunch smashed on too many bloody marys. The last time, we ate lunch at our favorite place. . .the Folly. . . aptly named! Rob suddenly made a thing of not having a drink with lunch. He made me feel guilty. . .unclean. I knew I shouldn't want one as badly as I did. . .so I. . .I ordered one, of course, a ramos fizz, and sat there sipping it, wanting a very, very dry martini in that cool, dark niche at the Folly. . .listening to Rob tell me that he'd gone off the booze because he'd finally met someone he felt he could. . .have a good relationship with. The man had told Rob he needed to give up drinking. Rob admitted to me how much of a closet drinker he really was. . .how good this new lover. . .friend. . .was going to be for him. . .telling me all that. . .suddenly I felt like crying. For me, too, it can't be just nothing either. I mean. . .oh, the things we've messed up, Rob and I. . . .Somehow I always seem to bounce back. I *have* to. Trying to help people, the way Rob does. We tried, at least, with the kids. Trying to do something real and honest for them. I know that wanting to is the only way to make what you do have any meaning.

And I can honestly say I'm happy for Rob and his trying to quit drinking. He thought I didn't notice how good he looked, how much bloat he's lost. I did notice. . .I'm just so preoccupied with me. . .I know if I don't keep trying to remember that I'm a person. . .that I'm someone. . .I. . .wouldn't be able to handle anything. I have to keep remembering I'm someone, or at least capable of becoming someone, something. I've never really believed I could be. . .maybe a writer or a teacher. Some day I'll know. . .I can't believe I've had to live through all this shit for nothing.

Right now I feel as if I can even put the business about the doctor in perspective. It's funny, just talking about it here, for the moment at least, makes me think I can. . .the doctor who makes. . .made. . .me forget all the crappy drudgery of Bill and the kids and keeping the apartment clean and cooking and giving Bill's damn "little dinners" so he can go on being successful and well thought of at the agency. The doctor. . .I should have known he was pumping false life into me. And it did feel good. . .it took. . .it only takes a few seconds after one of his shots to feel good. He promises the moon, and right away you feel as if you're on it! I should have known that Linda, with all her pills and Demerol, couldn't send me to anyone who could really help me.

But it did help me get a few pitiful hours of energy. . .a little high, a little sunshine before Mother's phone calls. . .and Bill asking where I'd been, and the kids always wanting to know when dinner is ready, and "Mummy, can we get the bicycles out?" And "Mummy, can we go to the movies Saturday?" And "Mummy, when are you going to take us to the museum?" Oh, God. . .anything to get rid of all the. . .details. . .I couldn't cope with. I thought at least the shots weren't the same as. . .alcohol. I really thought it was a way of getting off the drinks. But it was just a way of having both! Because the minute I'd come down from the shots, I'd be so depressed I needed a drink. . .more than one drink, lots more than one.

The thing that keeps coming back is, how can I know all this and still. . .I know that I've spent. . .wasted. . .whatever. . .more than ten precious years drinking at lunch, drinking after work, sneaking drinks when I knew nobody was going to find out. And when I think about that, everything adds up to one big fat zero! Zero! No guts, no purpose, no accomplishments. And dirty little things. . .all done with. . .the help of alcohol. Oh. . .how can I be sure that I'll ever, ever learn, and think, and stand on my own two feet and not on somebody else's. . .no shots, no Bill, no Warren, no David.

I have to know there's no policeman in my head to stop me from drinking, no. . . image. . .to. . .uh. . .prevent me. . .from. . .uh. . .destroying myself. I knew that when I was seeing you so many years back, while I still was working at the agency. Some of the things I. . .used to write down, my. . .most awful secret thoughts. . .that I never showed even to you because I was scared underneath. . .you didn't know how scared! I was writing to get around to telling you what the problems were! I. . .I knew even then that I. . .that there are the talkers and the doers, and that I was. . .I am. . .afraid of being. . .uh. . .just a talker. I wrote all this kind of stuff constantly when I was seeing you. On paper I could admit what I couldn't say sitting here in front of you, with you trying so hard to get the truth out of me. How could I have seen what I was so clearly then? Maybe I didn't really believe it. Was it all just thinking and writing, and never doing or wanting to face the facts? Oh, to speak it. . . scream it out to you, or maybe to anybody, would have made it real. But I did write it. . .admitted then, long ago, that I was sick in a way. I've gradually. . .uh. . . stopped admitting.

The solutions. . .not solutions, there's only one. . .to stop drinking. Simple enough. To stop drinking. . .kaput. Then why don't I stop? The. . .uh. . .answer is because somehow I want to destroy myself. It seems so easy for me to have all sorts of incredible insights talking like this. . .or writing out everything the way I did. So why don't these insights stay with me?

I know why. . .because I. . .ah. . .want to punish myself, for all the unkind, thoughtless, meaningless things I've done. For all the faceless men I've slept with while. . .ah. . .I was drunk. I have a good body. . .a pleasant face, and I. . .I know all these things have physically attracted men. But I. . .grew up with too much wrong discipline. . .sometimes none. ''I'm just a girl who can't say no,'' the song goes. It was all right at first, without all the drinking, when the numbers weren't high. Now it's not all right. No, it's not all right at all. Too many men! Too many nights I can't even remember. And too many I can! I've used booze and love for unlovely things. I know I drink partly to forget it. I still don't even know my own mother. I did learn to face the reality of my father. . .but not my genteelly poor, complaining, standard-bearing mother. Oh, it seems so hard to think. . .but it's all here.

Ah, I don't feel like being an interesting conversation piece any more. . .or being the dream-smasher I can be. . .was, sometimes. I just feel like being me. Now I've smashed so many dreams, for me and Bill and the kids. I've reduced myself to something that should be smashed first. My life is so tied up with mistakes. . .and reform, and judgment, and other people's ambitions, and being paid attention to for the wrong reasons. . .which I encourage. . .and I drift and drift until I. . .ah. . .who am I? You did try to find out ten years ago, but it got very complicated. . .thinking a session would be about one subject, something I'd just done, and I'd talk, and you'd ask a question, and. . .the question would seem strange, interrupt my thoughts. . .I wouldn't be able to think. Everything would end up. . .different. And while I waited to find out why, I twisted my fingers and smoked too many cigarettes. And drank. Oh, God, how I drank—and forgot about the whole thing two minutes later. And to amuse myself along the way, I listened to other people's stories. . .people who'd actually done something, good or bad. I hid out in their midst. . .and in my drunken evenings. If I stand alone now, with my own answer. . .can I do it? Just me, without any philosophizing? All by myself? I really don't believe I can. . .alone? I've been younger, stronger.

The thing is, I know that by not drinking I learn to care more about myself. I told you that the best thing you'd done for me in terms of drinking was saying I had to quit or you wouldn't treat me. You didn't really put it quite that strongly, but that was the message, and believe me, it worked. . .for a while. I've slipped back, but not into thinking it isn't important. My slip is thinking *I'm* not important. What depresses me, because I can't understand it, is. . .why weren't you able to keep me. . .keep it. . .from slipping away? I mean, the feeling that I wouldn't drink again? Maybe just because so many other problems piled up. They took so much of the strength and control I thought I had. . .leached them out of me.

I used to think I was strong by being all tied up in good, hard work. Now I know that isn't really true. I guess there was more pressure in work than strength. It was exciting, I'm not denying that, but it took a toll. Some of its crises became my crises, and I. . .I couldn't weather them without. . .well, what I seem to have done. Oh God, the same nights, after days of hard work! Oh, I know what my pattern was. The physically attractive man with a problem in his life, lonely, attracted to me. It drew me like honey draws a bee. Find out what he's like. . .make him like me because I can't like myself! Was it because I think I can find the answers to life's problems through osmosis? By going to bed with someone I thought I respected? I'd lie down, take off my clothes, and say, 'I want someone to love me.' What I meant was, I want someone who has the answers. So here I am, same old me. . .lots of experience, but no problems solved. . .it makes me feel old. Old, with my old hanging-on mother and her old hanging-on shreds of financial solvency. . .her bonds, handled for free by poor senile Mr. Jenkins because he always handled our family's affairs. He and Mother dwelling on pathetic scraps. . .disorganized, losing things. And I know this is ridiculous, poring over Mother's screwed-up past when so many things are screwed up. . .threatened me.

You said I chose drinking in imitation of my father. This makes its own kind of horrible sense. I feel very confused and sad about Daddy. I know he loved me. When he was still alive, there was a joy in our house. . .I've never felt that kind of love since. When he died, I missed him so. I. . .I hated him for leaving me, but I also. . . hated myself for hating him. And now, if only he. . .if I knew how to tell him the rest. . .how unfortunate a choice I'd. . .what a way I've found to dishonor your memory, Daddy. . .your poor, wasted life. . .I've found ways to outdo even you. And what I can't face now is whether I still have a choice after so long. . .and so much of the deck stacked against me. Are there choices any more for someone like me? I really don't want to think about it today. . .yet I. . .I'm obviously very preoccupied with it.

I read somewhere that we're overcivilized. It shouldn't and doesn't have to happen. But then, everybody has come such a long way from honesty that. . .we can't even face our own lives. We can't honestly face one another in business, or in sex. . .or love. . .or. . .oh, I'm exhausted, depressed by it. I'm exhausted even thinking how far I've come. And still not enough, obviously. You tried so hard to get the message across sometimes, but it was never enough. It vanished. God knows, none of it helped that strange night. . .a long time ago now, when I was still going to you. . .when I'd come home from the agency and drink and then half passed out. And at one-thirty the telephone rang. It was someone who said he was a friend of

David's. Obviously he'd had a good evening with lots of drinks. And because I didn't want David to forget me, I was listening to this man. He was saying that once David gave him the names of three women he could call, and he's calling me because he wants a woman. He said David told him that he'd had the perfect relationship with me, that I. . .I was just a call girl. . .that. . .that he'd made sure to keep things that way so I couldn't hurt him the way I'd hurt other men. I was so sick I hung up and burst out crying, hysterical crying.

I know in retrospect that David was a bastard. Sadistic. He did have passion, maybe that's what I loved in him. . .not the bastard, the passion. And that's missing in Bill, my life with him. . .passion. The lack of it has created all. . .or most. . .of this mess. I want somebody to love me that way. . .but. . .so many times. . .you used to point out what a Goody Two Shoes I'd been, Mother's and Daddy's and everyone's good little girl through all those ups and downs. . .God, how many more do I have left in me?

I did stop drinking. And everybody did react. That was when I first met Bill. I guess people who drink. . .or have to. . .do react. Others don't, and people who drink always seem to be with others who drink. So everyone is always reacting. It was good for my ego then, but it didn't last. . .only during that one fresh start, until my ego got its usual "indigestion."

It was all working at first. I could feel it in my words, "I *will* know what I want." That qualifying *will*. That's what I do now, too. . .qualify, and leave the back door open so I can fly out if I don't find what I want. Or slip off the right course or shut it out completely. . .which is what I had to do. Why, when I sounded so good? I did sound so sure.

When I was pregnant. . .oh my God, that was a time. I did want to never remember again. . .to ever go through that. . .but it's true, I wrote it all down. . .I had to talk to someone, even if it was only myself. I was glad to be rid of my roommates. What I needed was to be alone, without. . .the illusion of leaning on any-one. And as usual, lots of work, lots of details to block out the big things. . .lots of new resolutions. . .they all went their way, like everything else. I detested it! I needed it! And underneath I kept repeating, hysterically, all I want is someone to help me find a doctor so I can kill the child before he's born.

Since one of the men in question was my boss, I had to find a new job. You can't work for someone who thinks you're trying to frame him. I kept telling myself, he won't give me a recommendation because he hates me for this mess. To leave in a hurry, in a bad light, in trouble, after three years of service. . .no good! David was gone, but I'd found someone. And I was so tired from the tension that was building up day after day at the agency, tired because I'd been hurt by David again without seeming to be able to stop. I'll never forget how it felt knowing that three mornings from then I was going to wake up, take a bus to New Jersey, and have an abortion. It was the most awful, frightening thing I'll ever know. I wrote a note that said, "In the event of my death, please transfer all property to my mother."

I kept waking up that morning before the alarm. When it finally went off at seven-thirty, I got up. It was a cloudy, heavy day. Inside I was frightened to the core. I knew it had to be done, and I knew it would hurt, but I didn't know what the doctor would be like, how long would it take, what he would do. . .I was sure he'd ask me questions, and I'd get my story mixed up. I was scared I'd lose the money, and that it would be done with unsterilized instruments. My worst fear was that I'd never be able to have other children. There was no one I could call except my old practical roommate, Dorian. She said it wasn't so painful, the worst part was fear. That I had plenty of! Dorian told me, "Destroy all your personal references to this so that if your mother can't reach you, she won't know the real reason. Say you're so broken up over David you have to have a change. Don't eat, because you don't want to vomit there. Wear low shoes and a cotton dress and your raincoat."

I called the agency to say I wasn't coming in. I got Ken on the phone, and he didn't even give me a chance to say how sick I felt. Just said, "Keep cool." I passed by the building at ten minutes after nine and saw Jerry Burgess. I thought how different our days will be. I stopped at Forty-Second Street to go to the bank and see why my interest was so much on a loan of only four-hundred dollars. It was too complicated for me to understand. The interest was eighty-one dollars and sixty cents, I guess because I was borrowing the five-hundred dollar balance all over again. I cashed the check, got three-hundred and sixty-three dollars, and took a taxi to the Port Authority Terminal. I kept repeating, "I can't be late."

The bus for new Jersey went through the Lincoln Tunnel, turned off the highway around Union City, and went through streets of small towns I didn't know even existed. It stopped at every corner. Finally at the right stop I handed the driver my ticket and got off. I walked a couple of blocks until I came to the house with the doctor's sign out front. At least it said M.D. The nurse in the waiting room wasn't in uniform. She didn't ask my name or what I wanted, just told me to have a seat.

There were three other women ahead of me. One was plump and looked like a housewife and was very nervous. Another was about thirty-five, with a small boy, chewing gum and looking fairly relaxed. The third was slim, black-haired, intelligent-looking. The room was furnished with plastic and metal furniture, and there was a table stacked with magazines. . .magazines, at a time like that! There was no talk. Nothing but silence. All the others were wearing high heels. I felt like a schoolgirl. I was thinking, "And I am next." And exactly ten minutes after eleven the nurse came back and said, "Who's next?" and I said, "I am." I followed her through a windowed door.

"Who told you to come?"

"Mrs. Corbino."

"What do you want?"

"An abortion."

"Do you have the money with you?"

"Yes, three-hundred and fifty dollars. That's what I was told was right."

"You're very lucky. The doctor is going to Europe for six weeks on Wednesday."

I'd wet my pants a little in the waiting room, and I was worried about it. At a time like that! The nurse showed me the bathroom and told me to take off everything except my slip and underwear. I did it, and then I washed my hands and went with her into the doctor's office. He was small and unwashed and tired-looking. He had on rubber gloves. I kept thinking, "He's a doctor, it's all right." I told them my name was Ingrid, which of course they knew was made up.

"How long since you've had your last period, Ingrid?"

"The middle of March."

"Now, I want you to help me. You must relax. You're so frightened. Do you think I'm going to kill you?"

"Don't be so frightened," the nurse said. "You're very lucky. You'll be relieved when it's over. It'll hurt less if you aren't so afraid."

Then they started. My legs were up in stirrups, braced so I could open more. They kept telling me to lie flat and keep my hips down. It was supposed to make it hurt less. He put. . .a long tube up. . .into. . .my vagina. I don't know what other instruments. . .many, though. Cold, thin, sharp, blunt. The nurse had to take my hand. She kept telling me to keep my hips down and relax. She did hold my hand through all that pain and pressure. . .around and around inside my uterus. One of them kept saying, "Almost over now. . .just a little more. . .a little more. . .everything's going to be much easier now."

Finally I thought, "If you don't stop, I'll do something very bad. I'll jump, just get up. . .and then you'll really hurt me." I can stand pain, but not indefinitely. . .I. . . have to know it's going to be over soon. I'm. . .I'm so conscious of everything. When it was finally over, the long tube came out of my vagina, which was bleeding. My legs were shaking so much I could see them move, and I was wet with perspiration. I couldn't believe it was all over, and that it only took twenty minutes. As I walked out of there, I was sick to my stomach, even though I'd already thrown up some, and I kept thinking, some day I'll have many children. That was all mixed up with their directions of when to take my first postabortion douche and when I could have my first. . .postabortion intercourse. I thought, I *have* to have a Scotch. . .more than *a* Scotch. . .two. . .six! All the way back on the bus to New York, Dorian was working her curiosity on me, asking, "How much did it hurt?"

Facing work and the office even days after, and running into Bill. . .all of it. . .I felt total emptiness. The cold, frightening emptiness I felt this morning, in Mother's apartment full of bottles. . .with all its secrets uncovered. You know, I think that in some horrible way I am still a little girl in a starched pinafore. . .which is the way I felt. . .feel. . .when I'm with her. . .at the hospital, when she screams and lies and complains and finds fault. As if I'm the childish, guilty one. Am I? That's exactly how Bill and even my children are starting to react to me. It's the way they make me feel, too.

I can even believe that I may be getting more like Mother. . .sick. . .sicker, sickest. And what good in hell does it do me to know that? I can't go through any more confrontations with her on that so-called deathbed. This morning I screamed the truth at her. She preserved her dignity, naturally. That's her natural pose. Lies, denies it, does it again and again. . .all these hidden, hideous years. And when I tried to say how sad, how sorry. . .she. . .she turned her head and said in that hoarse, cracked voice. . .now I know it comes from all her boozing. . ."Catherine," she said, "I don't know what you're talking about. You're the one who is sick. Oh, far sicker than I am or ever will be. My only problems are on my hospital chart. My broken hip, my migraines, my colitis, those are my problems."

Yet I really do feel sorry, at this moment. Really terrible for having attacked her. All I could do afterward was reach out and sort of pat the bed. . .I couldn't look at her or touch her. I wanted her to. . .somehow. . .forgive me. . .as if that would make me the good little girl I've left so far behind. I know I wasn't attacking only her, but every other damn destructive person I've. . .I've ever managed to seek out all my life. . .everyone who's ever hidden their self-destruction from me and from themselves. I must have a talent for that!

Mother! She and I. . .there are some ways that we. . .I need her! And I know she needs me. . .to be honest, help each other. . .face each other. . .we haven't faced the truth at all yet. This morning when I looked at her rotting in that hospital bed, I saw her face dissolve for one second into a terrified, terrifying, old mass of pouches and lines. Then she saw me watching her and pulled herself right back together into that rigid, pathetic. . .oh, God! She yanked the sheets up around her and sat there like a ramrod, staring straight at me.

"Catherine!" she said. "You've spoken the last words I ever want to hear from you. You leave this room at once and don't ever come here again!"

I got up and walked out of that room. And as I closed the door, I looked back at her, her face all collapsed. And her eyes! She was dead to me, out of my life completely. . .unreachable. Ah. . .I'm numb over it. Completely. I have to be, because I can't believe it happened. I can't think how I could have done what I did to her. . .don't want to. I have to have. . .to go. . .somewhere. . .where am I going to go now? I'm shaking again. . .shaking all over. I'm not pulled together enough yet. If I only had somewhere to go. . .or could just pull everything over my head. . .my own place. . .without Bill and the children. . .hide and make it all go away.

I need. . .Johnny. . .no. . .just a shot or a sniff of something. . .even a vitamin! I can't, it would kill. . .killed her? She's dead? Rob. . .I couldn't call him. . .no, nothing from him. . .oh, my God, I had an appointment this afternoon with the doctor for my shot. I've been so many times and I still can never remember the address. No, not again. . .not after sitting in his waiting room with all the patients, all waiting to get. . .especially Jeff, an attractive guy, a successful young artist I see there every time I need a shot. The last time really turned me off because Jeff was so. . . nervous. He couldn't wait for his turn. He paced the floor and smoked cigarette after cigarette until suddenly he went running down that pale-green corridor screaming his head off. Completely out of control. Totally. The nurse and doctor had to come out and take care of him. . .take him in. . .like a child.

Well, I don't expect that to ever happen to me. . .but, God, I did need something today. . .to go somewhere. Ruth told me I need to go. . .to a hospital. . .but, no. . .yes, I really wanted to go to one then. . .to get help. . .that's why you came to my mind after all these years. Ruth said I'm. . .no, she's right. . .I felt as if I was going crazy. That's why I told you I needed an appointment immediately. . .I was in despair and fuzzy in my head. . .thought this must be what it's like to go insane. I can't remember. . .don't want to remember. . .how her eyes were. . .tears, and not just her telephone tears. How can I ever. . .face. . .their faces. . .they must know. . .hate me. I need something to get me through it all with Bill and the children. My heart was going so fast. . .I saw every face from my day. . .my whole life. . .Bill, the kids, Mother. . .oh, God! Mother's head was bobbing around on some ridiculous nurse's body. . .David, Johnny. . .and here I am groveling around in my bag for. . .a cigarette. . .so wrapped up. . .and I do need. . .something. . .now. . . I've come back to see you because I don't have anywhere else to go in my life. This is my last stop.

HISTORY

Catherine Muller's mother sent her to the same convent school she herself had attended. Although Dorothy Forster had left the Church when she married, she held on to whatever proprieties she could with a certain defiant flair. At school, seven-year-old Catherine made friends, but many of her invitations to birthday parties and afternoons of swimming at the club were prompted by her young friends' mothers; they were charmed by Cathy's neatness and prettiness and the long, shiny hair held back from her solemn face by taffeta ribbons. A lot of Cathy's friends thought she was a Goody Two Shoes, but they went along with their mothers when prodded: "Why don't you invite Cathy? She never gets too wild, and you two can have a nice afternoon." Cathy was never too anything, except perhaps too nice. Some adults thought she hardly even acted like a child and seemed to have no idea how to have real fun.

Catherine's parents had married against the wishes of her mother's family. Mr. Forster was not Catholic; neither was he ambitious or "social." But he was very handsome, and Dorothy felt that the strong sexual attraction between them was the most important thing that had ever happened to her. This was during the Depression, and the trust fund Dorothy had inherited from her grandmother was already not bringing in as much income as they had expected. But prices were still low, and Dorothy and Jack easily found a spacious apartment with charm. It was easy to find good servants, and everyone seemed sure that the Depression would soon end, so the Forsters told Dorothy's bankers they wanted to draw full income from her trust every year, even if they did occasionally have to dip into the capital.

By the time Catherine was born and the Depression had ended, the trust was depleted, and Cathy's father faced the reality of having to seek a job if they were to continue living as they had. During the early years of their marriage, her parents had pursued a life of intense sexuality, pleasure-seeking, and drinking, all well out of sight of Dorothy's family.

Now they had to turn to Dorothy's family for help. Because they had a child, Jack was given a position in one of the family's businesses. Dorothy was advised by her father and brothers to be sensible, and she began cutting expenses in order to rebuild her capital. Dorothy and Jack were very pleased over his new job, and Dorothy was sure he would be as good at supporting her as he was at having fun and satisfying her sexually. Therefore they paid little or no attention to financial advice, and since they had to "keep everything going" while Jack got established, they continued their extravagances. There was always the unspoken but reassuring thought that some day, when Dorothy's father died. . . .

But Jack, intimidated by the conservative, hard-working atmosphere of his office, began to drink at lunch. After only seven months he was dismissed after a violent argument with Dorothy's father and brothers. The reasons were "inefficiency and overindulgence." He turned to friends and found another job. But again, out of insecurity, he drank at lunch, after work, and finally in the office on bad days when everyone was keyed up and irritable about little mistakes. Jack was politely eased out of his second job by the friend who had given it to him. Friends were still sure it was just a matter of Jack "finding something really suitable"—maybe in sales, where he could use his outgoing personality and the contacts he still had.

When they moved to a smaller apartment, little Catherine first paid little attention to the changes on their lives. She didn't even care about her nurse leaving; she thought that now her mother would spend more time with her. But she did mind very much when her father came home trying to be cheerful and affectionate, her mother got angry and yelled at him, and he became sad. One evening, when he'd had to tell them he'd lost another job, her mother called him stupid and said he was no good at anything any more. He wept at the dinner table.

Catherine became terribly frightened, wanted to make it all stop. She felt she had to do something so that she would never again feel that frightening lurch inside her chest, as if the world was going to slip away. She loved her father very much. She always sat on his lap after breakfast before he went to work and she to school, and they read the comic strips together while her mother was still in bed. He always found time to be with her, telling her long stories about his childhood in the country or, better still, wonderful nonsense stories. She wanted to make him feel happier and stronger, to help him as he helped her, but she didn't know what she could do.

She did think of things she could do for her mother, perhaps because Dorothy expected, even exacted, a great deal from her. Catherine began to believe that if she did everything right for Mother, maybe Mother wouldn't get angry at Daddy, and then everything would be better. She tried to be superlatively neat, pretty, and appealing, so as to be popular at dancing school and the parties and dances she was sent to. She tried to do more and more around the house to help Mary, their only remaining maid, because Mother now yelled at Mary until she cried and talked about quitting—and if Mary quit, Mother would get even angrier at Daddy. At school Catherine tried to be best friends with all the girls Mother said came from the nicest families; she had to make sure she was invited to all the birthday parties. She was starting to worry, because Mother said she couldn't give any more parties for her because they had only Mary to help.

No matter how hard Catherine tried to do everything right, things kept getting worse. Her father now had a minor sales job based on commissions, which meant he never knew how much he would make. Her mother was constantly angry at him, and angry at the bankers, who couldn't seem to understand that she had to have more money because Jack was doing so badly. Cathy usually heard of such things in angry, tearful fragments after she'd gone to bed. She became so nervous that when her mother took her shopping for the velvet and taffeta dresses she needed for dancing school, she couldn't concentrate on which one she liked best. And she would forget to stand up straight until her mother sharply reminded her that she was getting too tall, and that slouching would make her look like a witch. When her father hugged her and told her how pretty she looked, ready for dancing class, she would smile to try to make him happy. She couldn't look into his eyes when he took her chin, tenderly kissed her, and told her he knew that all the boys would line up to dance with her.

There were more and more arguments late at night in her parents' bedroom. She lay half awake, hearing the angry voices and tears; they entered her dreams and nightmares. And there were grim, silent struggles in the living room in the evening while she tried to concentrate on homework in her bedroom. When she went in to say goodnight, her father would be shaky and befuddled, her mother tense and shrill. She'd first kiss her mother, then go to her father. He would grab her and try to pull her onto his lap. "You love your dad, don't you baby?" Catherine would stand there stiffly, wanting to hug him but watching her mother sitting taut in her chair, making Catherine realize it would be best to leave the room as quickly as possible.

The one part of herself that Catherine kept protected from the anxiety and tension of her dissolving family was the development of her mind. She liked schoolwork because it was the only thing that presented no complications if she did it well. The choices were clear. If you did your work badly, you stood pilloried at your desk or the blackboard in sullen resignation or desperate embarrassment. If you did your work well, you raised your hand, stood up, answered the question, and quickly sank back into your seat, satisfied with yourself, feeling that others were satisfied with you and relieved of wondering how you would do that day.

Catherine's greatest pleasure was the private use of her mind. She could not be without a book. She spent hours thinking and writing about what her life could become—fantasies usually based on the hero of whatever romantic book she was then reading, and never involving a pair of loving parents. Even on the rare occasions when she invited a friend home, she chose a quiet girl who would be content to spend the afternoon in her room, reading and making up stories with her. Often Dorothy embarrassed Cathy by swooping in on them and saying, "Why don't you two do something that's fun? Cathy, how can you have a good time sitting around all day? What will Laura's mother think if you don't do something to entertain your guest?" Later there would be a lecture about Cathy becoming too smart for her own good and probably scaring off the boys at dancing school with her vast vocabulary.

Gradually Cathy had to protect her private world more and more; it was becoming her only refuge from her parents' sadness and their increasingly shrill, downward course. Her father had become ill and no longer worked. Sometimes this made Dorothy and Jack seem more peaceful as they sat in the living room, mixing each other milk punches before lunch, sours and daiquiris before dinner, happily using the remaining shakers and stirrers of cut glass and silver. These times seemed the last vestiges of happiness in the home.

But even this situation degenerated. Cathy's mother began bringing the problems to her for sympathy and solutions. Cathy tried, inadequately, to bridge the gap between her adverse circumstance and her mother's increasing demands. Her father sat oblivious and numb. As it became clear that he would not be going back to work, Cathy's mind fled to the stormy moors of the Brontës. When her mother complained to her that the laundry was ruining the fine percale sheets which the maid had grown too arthritic to iron, Cathy suggested, with knowledge gained from a womans' magazine, that she get plain muslin sheets. Her mother called her "Miss Priss," and said she must have inherited her tacky ideas from her father's family. Cathy comforted herself with Thackeray and Jane Austen's acerbic heroines.

One afternoon, after a two-day fight between her parents, her father went out in the car and crashed into a toy store; the newspaper revealed that he had barely missed hitting a child and killed a man instead. Cathy spent the evening reading *Jane Eyre* and Dickens. She cried over them, forgot forever that the newspaper said there was a liquor bottle in the car. Later she forgot that when her fasther died three weeks after the accident, it was not from internal injuries but cirrhosis of the liver.

Cathy's mother adopted an attitude of pathetic, helpless, and demanding widow-hood. When the lawyers took Cathy aside and explained how little money there was, and how she must help her mother, she began to use her mind to create new objectives and defenses. She was now a sophomore in high school. The lawyers said there was not enough left for her to continue in private school or go on to a good college without forcing her mother to make terrible sacrifices.

Cathy immediately investigated scholarships. With hard work and quiet but relentless charm, she managed to stay on at her school, graduate, and enter Radcliffe on a full scholarship. Just before leaving for Radcliffe, she had to find a place for her mother in a small hotel that sheltered the shabbily genteel. Most of the older women there maintained dignified fragments of their past lives—silver-framed photographs, a favorite wing chair, a small Oriental rug. Cathy didn't know that sometimes they shuddered in their rooms at night when the halls filled with the screams of some old lady whose well-bred mask had disguised terror, loneliness, or a cruel thirst for sweet sherry. In arranging this new stage of her mother's life, Cathy felt guilt, fear, and relief. This was the end of the only home she had, insecure as it was.

Catherine approached college quietly and very seriously. She was immaculate in her grooming and dress, and a bit prim. She kept to herself; it did not occur to her that there was a place for her among any of the groups in her dormitory or her classes. She did not see much of the girls from her old school, because she did not want to go on pretending that her life was like theirs. But the college did become her home; she threw herself deeply into her courses and her scholarship job in the library. She stayed away from the college's social life—the "jolly-ups," the "mixers," the Harvard football games. She felt very alone, but could not imagine how not to.

Only once, in her junior year, did someone breach her privacy. Mason, a tall and handsome senior at Harvard, would not be discouraged by her determined reserve. It took Catherine a while to admit to herself that she was more stirred, and sensually so, by his pursuit than by anything she could remember. He was locally well known, and many classmates, male and female, admired him. Catherine was thrilled to receive telephone calls from him instead of her mother's long and maddening regular laments. She loved the nights when he ran with her to her dormitory, both of them laughing with the excitement of just making it before the watchman locked the door—Cathy, the grind, almost getting a late mark instead of studying for a high mark.

Most of all, Catherine loved the long, delicious weekend afternoons in his room, where he showed her the joys their bodies could find. Her only previous experiences with sex had been a few beery struggles on couches in fraternity houses. Her body offered itself to him, and they both reached greater pleasures than they had ever known.

One Sunday afternoon, Mason drove Cathy to the suburbs to have dinner with his family. Their rambling, shingled house was filled with polishesd old furniture, silver, books, and plants in every sunny window. His family, cultured and obviously very fond of him, awakened in her a hunger as surprising and deep as that stirred by Mason's lovemaking. Catherine carefully maintained her cool, intelligent charm and avoided his mother's discreet questions about her family. As the family talked of the week's events, she chilled inside, feeling that at any moment one of them would sense that she didn't "belong" didn't deserve to be present amid such happiness— she, who felt she had let her family fall apart.

When Cathy and Mason left, she felt she could never live through another such day. Once back in his room, she broke into tears. Not noticing how stiffly the boy was sitting, she sobbed out her loneliness, her fear, her lack of family. He finally took her in his arms and began their usual lovemaking, but Cathy was so shaken that she begged him to take her back to her dormitory.

Mason never asked her out again. But almost immediately one of his roommates called her. When she refused to go out with him, he said in an ugly tone that it was too bad, because from what he'd heard from Mason they could have had a really good time. She ended her years at Radcliffe a Phi Beta Kappa, with a B.A. in English, *magna cum laude*, a lonely mind, and bruised fantasies.

In spite of her intellectual skills, Cathy decided not to continue her education. Her experience with Mason had made her feel that she had no place in the university world. She did not realize how startling her emotional outburst had been to him, and whatever anger she had allowed herself to feel about the episode of his turning her over to another man in such a brutal fashion was transformed into the feeling that he had rejected her because of her disintegrated family. She never saw that she always used too many defenses too soon, before she had insight into a situation or people. She reacted very quickly and took people at face value, as she had always taken her parents. As her life rapidly became more complex, it was more difficult for her to live it than to change it or move on.

Cathy was ambitious and knew she would have to make a good living for herself, which meant typing school. She decided to stay in Boston because it seemed a home of sorts, and because it was less expensive than New York. She did not admit to herself that New York meant more involvement with her mother and her mother's endless complaints.

After answering a newspaper ad, Cathy found herself sharing a small apartment with a nurse and an airline stewardess, attending typing school, and trying to fit into still another world. Her roommates seemed strange to her, unlike the people in her previous spheres of genteel poverty and academia. Her college clothes, so carefully chosen, now looked somehow worn and wrong, so she imitated her roommates' way of dressing and allowed herself to be drawn into their social life. Through Linda, the nurse, she met Jim, a good-looking medical student who, as an undergraduate, had been a football hero. He was good-natured, but now his smiling face sometimes seemed a bit apologetic about a once muscular body going full and slack.

Cathy began to see Jim every night. He was spending the summer in Cambridge, trying to improve his marks enough to get through his last year of medical school and hiding from his problems and his ambitious, demanding family. Jim was also drowning his troubles in a great deal of beer. Catherine met him every day after school to go out to dinner and a movie or to help him study. But soon she began to spend the evenings drinking with him or sitting in a drive-in cafeteria, listening to the maudlin tales of his unsympathetic family and his resolutions to hit the books the next day. She felt tired, but told herself it was because she felt sorry for him, because the summer was so hot, because typing school was so dull. Finally she admitted that it was because she had to drive Jim home almost every night because he was so drunk; because he was weak and dependent like her father, and she resented it; because she had a slight hangover so many of those hot, dull mornings.

At the end of the summer, Cathy decided to stay in Boston to help Jim continue on his shaky course through med school. The only reasonable job she could find was in a publishing house. She felt a little depressed—because it was a dead end, she said, not because she was wasting her time on Jim, who was as unable to provide her with a future as her father had been. And during the winter of that year, she began to feel chafed and imposed on by her roommates. On many Saturday and Sunday mornings she would find one or the other of them asleep with a man on the living room sofa bed, and she began to feel that their life was cheap and sordid.

One night when the three of them were at home alone, washing their hair, drinking, and gossiping, Billie Sue, the stewardess, whose partners changed with startling frequency, confessed that she'd had an abortion in Mexico early in the fall. Catherine was shocked. When the girl went on to describe the dirty little doctor who'd forced her to have intercourse with him before he would perform the operation, she flared up and said she thought it was disgusting. Billie Sue collapsed in tears, and Linda turned on Catherine in anger.

"Who do you think you are to talk like that? I don't see what's wrong with doing it if you really enjoy it. It's better than wasting all your time on that impotent lush you're running around with! I know, I tried him! He's no good for anything, and the booze you're pouring into yourself is dissolving all that fancy Radcliffe veneer of yours pretty fast." Billie Sue, recovered from her tears, leaped in. "Those dexies I've been getting for you aren't helping any, either."

Catherine retreated to her room, shaken and confused. Well, she did drink with Jim, but she never got drunk. And he only got drunk because he was so worried about school. She only took dexies because feeling sorry for him made her feel so tired. How was she supposed to put up with her dull job without them? But wrong not to sleep around a lot? That really stung. Maybe most people did it with lots of people. She didn't know.

Catherine kept thinking about it all week. By Saturday she had decided to sleep with Jim. She blocked out Billie Sue's gruesome abortion; she did not ask Linda for the help with contraception she could have easily given. Catherine just got herself drunk for the first time, kept Jim fairly sober, and let him take her while she was in an anesthetic haze. Afterward she told her roommates; she soon stopped feeling so uncomfortable in the presence of their aggressive sexuality. But she still did not really think of herself as a woman. Neither did she let herself think much about sex. And she did not keep track of her periods, so it was only after she had missed two that she began to worry.

Finally her fears overcame her need to deny what might be happening. She made a terrified visit to a doctor, giving a false name, and then received the news on the phone. "Yes, Mrs. James, you are pregnant." Panicked, trying to calm herself with alcohol, she turned to Billie Sue for help. She sobbed drunkenly, never thinking that Jim should or could have helped her. Later that night Billie Sue told Linda, and together they persuaded her to tell Jim and said that Linda would try to arrange something at the hospital.

Cathy and Jim met the next night at their favorite bar, The Recovery Room, across the street from the hospital. When Jim heard the news, he panicked and drank. But he did extract some money from his parents and promised to get in touch with someone he'd heard about. Catherine was to meet him three days later, on Friday afternoon; it would be set for that night. She arrived fighting terror and guilt. Jim arrived drunk, and Catherine had three drinks before she could summon up the courage to ask about the arrangements. Jim looked at her, blank-eyed.

"I called the guy three times today, but the phone was always busy or out of order or something. I don't know. We'll have to try again next week."

Feeling desperate and abandoned, she said she had to go to the ladies room, rushed to the phone, called Linda, and hysterically sobbed out her story.

"Look, try to calm down," said Linda. "I've been asking around. There's an obstetrics-gynecology resident here right now, and there's an empty room in emergency. We can do it, so let's meet there. Just hurry."

When Catherine returned to the table, Jim had ordered fresh drinks for them. He finished his and passed out, head on the table. She looked at him, drained her glass, went outside, and found a taxi. She sat back in the cab; her body began to feel punished by the cramps she'd been trying to ignore all day. The relentlessly good little girl who was part of her deepest self pushed into her mind the realization that she was about to do something illegal and dangerous. There was now a dampness between her legs that she could not bring herself to investigate. She didn't want to think about that part of her body, of what it had done or what was about to be done to it.

She walked into the impersonal, cruelly lit emergency room, feeling exposed and humiliated. Linda appeared after what seemed an endless wait.

"Listen, Cathy, we can't do it now. Stan's got two emergencies stacked up. One is a fifteen-year-old kid who was bleeding like nobody's business.

She launched into the details. With unacknowledged anger and a swell of anxiety, Catherine clutched Linda's arm and interrupted:

"I can't just wait here. I'm having cramps. I think something's wrong."

"Well, if you're lucky there is," Linda told her. "Go home and wait for me to call, all right? Maybe it'll happen by itself."

Catherine fled back to the apartment and sat sipping Scotch, rocking against the pain that culminated in a miscarriage early the next morning.

The following week was nightmarish for Cathy. While she recuperated, she remained completely withdrawn throughout Linda's frantic apologies and both girls' fussing over her. She silently planned her flight from this life at which she had failed so badly. The scraps of strength and survival instinct that had pulled her through Radcliffe were severely weakened. She knew she could get no help from her mother, yet she did feel a need to see her at least briefly, for whatever emotional relief she might find.

As soon as she was able, she went back to New York. When she got there, her mother inundated her with her hypochondria, complaints, and demands. Once again Catherine had reached out in a time of fear, failure, and frustration to someone who was not really there and never had been.

She was determined to find a place in the city. First she installed herself in a large hotel for young women, safely at telephone distance from her mother. Then she began a feverish search for the good job she felt would restore her shaken ego. Every day she made the rounds of impersonal, sometimes insulting employment agencies and personnel departments. Late every afternoon she collapsed in the room of a large midtown Schrafft's and bent her head over a gibson amid a sea of grey- and ash- and blue-rinsed heads, all bent over their own frivolously named but high-proof cocktails.

The gibson reduced her anxiety and confusion and prepared her for the inevitable evening call from her mother, with its burden of overbearing and anachronistic advice. Catherine sensed the dangers of her mother's attempts to enmesh her in her own anxieties and demands. The thought that her mother's selfish, unproductive life had caused such emotional and physical deterioration hardened her own determination to succeed. But Mrs. Forster's calls still left Catherine tense, depressed, and sleepless.

The variety of girls and women in Catherine's hotel seemed to offer neither friends nor models, only disastrous alternatives. Abby, who had the room on one side of Catherine's, was mousy, in her early thirties, and had little contact with anyone except an occasional hesitant pleasantry murmured when she passed Cathy in the hall. More often, Abby scuttled down the hall with her head lowered, concealing a frightened smile.

On the other side lived Gail, from whose room Catherine heard incessant chattering phone calls. When Gail wasn't on the phone, she was knocking on Catherine's door or that of any new attractive resident on the floor. Abby's door she ignored completely. One night Catherine offered Gail a drink from the bottle of sherry she kept to help herself relax and sleep, and Gail began the first of a series of persuasions to loosen up and enjoy herself and the city. She told Catherine she could fix her up any time she wanted a date, and promised a really good time. She said loosening up a little might even help Catherine with her other problems, make it easier for her to find a really good job.

She progressed to telling Catherine that the way to live was to love, and confessed that she herself lived on loving and on supplying companionship for a long list of out-of-town businessmen. She reassured Catherine that it was all strictly first class, that she lived in the hotel because of the straight image it gave her, and that the dates did not necessarily involve ''what you think, Cathy, with that fancy society-school background of yours.''

After discouraging further intimacy with Gail, Catherine spent many evenings alone in her room, slightly high on gibsons and sherry, absentmindedly stroking herself between her legs and fantasizing about what Gail would be doing when she finished her phone calls and departed for the evening. One night, when she was feeling high enough on the surface and depressed enough underneath to be vulnerable to her fantasies, she heard Gail engaged in unusually frantic efforts to organize her evening. She was trying to line up two girls to go out with two oil men from Texas, ''real Glen McCarthy types, really loaded, looking for a good time.''

When Catherine, feeling no pain but loneliness, knocked on her door to offer her a glass of sherry, Gail seized her advantage and said, ''I don't mind having a sherry with you, but why have an old maid's tea party when we can go out and really have a party?'' Catherine anaesthetized her better judgment with another quick sherry and ventured out with Gail.

As the evening went on, it became clear that Gail was a fully professional hooker. The more anxious Catherine became about finding herself in a fully sexual situation, the more she drank—so much that she allowed herself to be taken to the men's hotel suite, where she passed out. She awakened to find herself lying half dressed under two hundred pounds of a drunk nude Texan, who was clumsily trying to plunge into her. As she tried to push him away, he moaned feebly and violently vomited all over her. Catherine's hysterical sobs brought Gail and her partner running into the room, both clutching towels that failed to cover the semen on Gail's leg or the man's half-erect penis. Gail grabbed Catherine, shook her angrily, and slapped her face.

"Do you want to have the house fuzz in here? Shut up and pull yourself together. You know I run a classy setup! You can't even handle a little plain fucking!"

Catherine never fully remembered how she got cleaned up, dressed, out of the hotel, and into a cab. She dimly remembered slurring the address of a building she'd lived in as a child, then staring at it without recognition as the driver said, "Wake up, lady, you're home now. What's the matter with you, anyway? Jeez, if there's anything makes me sick it's seein' a broad so drunk she don't know where she is." Finally she managed to direct him to her hotel.

She had several interviews lined up for the next day; she managed to get up and drag herself perfunctorily through the morning's two unpromising prospects. Her interview for the afternoon was a prize. It was for a spot on the training program of one of New York's largest advertising agencies. It had the reputation of being a "killer" agency, brutally competitive in handling its employees and manipulating the public, but it also had an aura of great glamor.

Catherine presented to the personnel man at the agency a charmingly frightened manner and impressive academic credits. The impersonal routine was broken by the appearance of a tweedy and extremely agreeable young man. He introduced himself as Warren Haight and said he was looking for a copywriting trainee, "someone really top-drawer intellectually." He wanted, he said, to throw some ideas at her and see how she handled them. She spent the rest of the afternoon roughing out plans for a beer account and a sanitary napkin account. Her ego was fed by this man's steady supply of admiration and approval. She fired out ideas with increasing confidence, and at the end of the day produced a slogan that was to help lift feminine hygiene advertising out of genteel ambiguity and into its present openness.

She felt no indignation at the personnel man's impersonal "Leave your resume, and we'll call you." Warren Haight had given her a warm handshake and said, "I know you're right for here, and you'll move up as fast as possible. We're going to make a great team."

Exhausted from the previous night and slightly let down from her afternoon's ego trip, she went back to her room, ordered a sandwich from the coffee shop, had more sherry than usual to celebrate, and crashed into deep sleep that lasted three hours. Sirens and an acrid smell stirred her. She opened her door to find firemen wielding axes and hoses and carrying a blanket-shrouded stretcher out of Abby's room. Catherine stood dazed in the hall, listening to the frightened sniffles and excited whispers, ". . .said they never saw so many bottles. . .fell asleep with a lighted cigarette. . .probably loaded. . .seemed sort of strange to me. . .I guess no one really knew her. . .did she kill herself?"

Catherine dreamed and woke through the night. In the morning she called the desk and asked where Abby was, and how she was. She heard:

"Oh, honey, she died on the way to the hospital. She wasn't burned that badly, you know, and of course they won't know for sure till the autopsy, but she had a lot of empty bottles and pills in her room. The druggist said this morning she had so many prescriptions, and they found even more from other drugstores, so. . . ."

Abby's death stimulated a temporary burst of intimacy among the girls on the floor, some of whom were trying to forget that they had never spoken to her. Cathy, believing Warren Haight's assurance of a job, started searching hard for a new place to live, away from the sad and sordid place the hotel had become.

She felt very lucky when she heard that Dorian, the younger sister of a girl she'd known at school, was looking for a roommate, and went right over to see her. She found three girls, two just out of junior college, and Dorian, recently expelled from junior college, living in a two-bedroom, rent-controlled apartment in the east Fifties. Dorian was now studying jazz dance with a young black choreographer whose integrated troupe was beginning to be well known in the city. She was a breezy, attractive girl. She laughed when Catherine mentioned her sister, laughed about her own role as the family rebel, laughed about having been expelled from two boarding schools and a college.

Catherine wanted to be part of this open, friendly group. When a message came to her that Warren Haight's agency wanted to hire her, she called Dorian and arranged to move in immediately. She did so as easily as she seemed to make all the other rapid changes during this period of her life. No one saw yet how quickly she became insecure and anxious about handling new, unprotected situations.

Dorian could show the girls anything they needed to know. She showed Catherine how to search out the best stores, how to make up her face and eyes; she found her a good hairdresser. Catherine looked better than she ever had. But she usually needed a last pat from Dorian before she felt she looked all right, and her carefully wrought appearance became rather disheveled by the end of most of her evenings.

To the young men in the agency training program, Catherine seemed smart, beautiful, and sexy. She was asked out a lot. Dorian's easy ménage, with its constant cocktail parties, informal Saturday dinners, and Sunday brunches helped Catherine through her frantic first year of socializing in New York. People from all sorts of milieus mixed with Dorian's marijuana-smoking Village friends—the old schoolmates, the once unpopular but now bitchily witty, the instantly friendly.

To Catherine, Dorian was like a blissfully permissive mother. Dorian taught her to use herself physically to attract and manipulate men; she had turned her old-maidish sherry sipping into a comforting social ritual that brought the relaxation she always felt she needed. Catherine could not see that Dorian wanted more than anything else the pleasure of exposing innocents to some new thrill, no matter what it was. Then Dorian could sit back and observe until, most exciting of all, she could move in and control things when someone went under.

Catherine was becoming more aware of Warren Haight's growing interest in her. She was hardly surprised when, groomed and socialized by Dorian, trained by the agency, she was told she was to work as a copywriter on one of his accounts. But since she knew that her sanitary napkin slogan was being used in a new campaign, she was surprised when she was placed on the agency's beer account. Warren said nothing about this, and Catherine, grateful to be working for this extraordinary bright, sympathetic, and complimentary man, remained silent.

Warren helped her to blossom socially. He took her out for the after-work drinks that were part of life at the agency. With Warren skillfully drawing her out, she found that for the first time in her life she felt secure enough to talk easily and freely. She gained a reputation for being witty and amusing. Men were attracted to her, but Warren was so possessive that people assumed she was his mistress. She did not deny the assumption, even colluded with Warren in fostering it, because it spared her from dealing with her uncertain sexuality.

Now that Catherine was safely launched, Warren sent her off alone more and more often, telling her she should enjoy herself and that he had too much work to go out much. He was extremely hard-working, had a wife and children in Greenwich—and, Catherine had heard, was dominated by a rich and unpleasant mother-in-law. She took Warren at his word, not seeing that his real but only genius was using others. She had not heard the common opinion that Warren milked ideas from those he came in contact with in order to advance himself.

Warren had two major accounts with high television budgets and some smaller ones with less exciting and less prestigious print-advertising budgets. The ambitious, the hustlers, the hangers-on and, most important, the weak and the drinkers he deployed throughout the agency to socialize with the people on other accounts, to hear the gossip, secrets, and weaknesses there. Once his mind had been fueled with this information, his real work began. He was an artful and pathological liar. Without dropping an inch of his almost unctuously agreeable facade, he moved swiftly upward, slicing each Achilles' heel exposed on the rung of the ladder above him. The rung he now coveted was occuped by David Lindner, his creative chief, who was less cerebral but equally unscrupulous. Warren was pleased to have Catherine, with her brilliance, beauty, and hidden weakness for drink, as a pawn in his game.

So Catherine moved, unknowingly, according to Warren's plans. She had his permission for her after-work social life, but he always cheerfully chose her companions. She sat with them in the frantically fashionable bars on Third Avenue, enjoying the easy intimacy, thriving on the crowds and martinis. The conversations always began seriously with business, degenerated into gossip, and finally drifted with alcoholic emotionality into the deep, vulnerable confidences that substituted for real intimacy.

Catherine was unable to sort out all the varieties of attention that came her way. She could not tell the real from the romanticized, the power-oriented from the narcissistically gratifying, so she allowed herself to live more and more loosely. After many drinks and a light dinner, she often had to be piled limp into a taxi by one of her admirers; and just as often she had to face the anger of Dorian, who was furious to see Catherine—inhibitions relaxing, weaknesses surfacing—slipping out of her grasp. But Catherine no longer needed to depend on Dorian; she moved the focus of her life away from the apartment to the office and to the bars that were extensions of it.

One morning as Warren deftly extracted the previous night's gossip from Catherine, he heard the facts he needed about a major new account that was coming into the agency. He fitted them together with what he already knew about the account's dealings with other agencies and with what he had ferreted out about the vulnerabilities of the others who would vie for the account. The competition would be complex and Machiavellian enough to match his talents. Warren quickly decided that this would be the struggle in which he would trap and defeat David Lindner. Before he set Catherine to work as his instrument of espionage, he tried to strengthen his control over her by taking her out to dinner and then trying to seduce her. His sensuality did not equal his lust for power, and finally he had to confess to her that he was impotent. He blamed his childish, willful wife and his castrating mother-in-law, and hoped that Catherine was too drunk to remember much anyway.

Everyone at the agency became aware that Warren was challenging David for the new account. When he invited his work group out for cocktails to celebrate Catherine's birthday, he deftly instigated the second phase of his plan; he invited David to join the party. Catherine was still unaware of the extent of her intellectual and physical impact on the men around her, but she and everyone else could see David's immediate interest in her. David's multiple seductions had long been an agency legend, fostered by his own boasting. Catherine was beautiful and intelligent enough to be indispensable to his reputation. She felt that her contributions to Warren's account had earned her the party, and her anticipation of being the star of the evening overshadowed her confusion about Warren's invitation to David. She sat sparkling amid the plentiful drinks and the attention of her confreres.

Warren greeted David as if in a gesture of truce in the agency tension; then, once David had been settled next to Catherine, he quietly withdrew. Suddenly, angrily, Catherine realized exactly what was to be won, and that she was the final pawn. She felt conflicting waves of disgust and of excitement at being the center of so much attention and intrigue and for Warren for attempting to use her so whorishly in order to indirectly control David. Finally she did let David make clear to their audience that they would eventually move the celebration elsewhere. The two of them had dinner alone and then went to David's apartment, where Catherine allowed herself the pleasure of being seduced by a master at making women feel wanted.

Warren sealed his usually eager ears with self-righteousness and allayed his anxieties with work. From that point on, the agency watched as Catherine continued to work and sympathize with Warren by day, in his lust to get ahead. By night and on weekends, she became more deeply involved with helping David maintain his vision of himself, which was almost a caricature of a man's man. She loved his world of hard drinking in all the spots where the social and the successful preened themselves. She loved the feeling that David had the central secret of selling almost any product. And above all, she loved the weekends in Westhampton with David's fast-talking, fast-moving, erotically predatory friends.

David moved through life swiftly, relentlessly. He began to demand every possible minute of Catherine's time. Warren could no longer ignore her morning fatigue, her too-long lunches, the gossip that followed her through the halls as her work life became more tense and demanding. But her mind and body were so constantly bombarded by David's addictive patterns that she forgot the office the minute she was with him, drinking, moving into a still-expanding social life, being made love to so much with a combination of abandonment and expertise she couldn't equal but could never forget.

Her attention was sharply called back to her job when David won the new account away from all his competitors. Catherine knew Warren would realize that David's decisive, persuasive campaign was based on an idea Catherine had given him. On the evening after the climactic announcement, Warren demanded that Catherine break that evening's date with David, who had promised her protection from whatever revenge Warren had in store. But Warren took Catherine for dinner and gave her such a verbal whipping that she fled from the restuarant in tears. He had threatened to have her fired and to see that she never worked in advertising again.

Catherine stayed home the next day, after her first sleepless night since the start of her affair with David. She called him at the office and at home, unable to reach him, becoming more and more frantic, finally crying and drinking. At midnight David's phone was answered by a woman's voice. When Catherine finally spoke to him, hysterically begging for help, wanting to know who was with him, he said in a slurred and brutal voice, "For God's sake, you sound like you need a psychiatrist more than a job. You'd better get yourself pulled together, and get over the idea that fucking a dry hole like you is any big deal for me."

The next four days ran together in a sleepless blur of alcohol and tears. Catherine didn't know which caused her more pain and fear, the prospect of losing her exciting, ego-feeding job world or David's betrayal and the discovery that the feigned orgasms she'd felt she owed him had been pitifully inadequate. She was rescued by Ken, one of David's art directors, a handsome, hedonistic bisexual. He enjoyed the security of his job too much to jeopardize it by overt intrigue, but he did relish an occasional opportunity for stirring up a little trouble. Ken had pieced together what had happened and went to see Catherine at home. He found her utterly vulnerable and ready for a long confessional lunch over numerous drinks. This was followed by seduction at his apartment. Then he gave her the information she needed for survival.

Ken and Warren had gone to New Orleans to see the president of one of Warren's accounts. Ken had been looking forward to enjoying New Orleans' more tempting debaucheries. Annoyed by Warren's prissy and power-driven insistence on work, Ken had amused himself by getting Warren drunk each night and maneuvering him into spending the evening alone with the client Ken knew was ambisexual. When he saw Warren the next morning, he found what he expected and spent the next few hours reassuring him:

"All you did was let it get sucked because you're too chicken to go out and stick it where you want. That doesn't make you a fag, just a guy who let his balls get too busted. . .let yourself get overworked and underlaid. Just forget it. One swallow doesn't make a summer. . .anyway it wasn't even your swallow."

Catherine went to the office late the next morning and found Warren ready to use her absence as an excuse to fire her. She knew she had to use the weapon she had been given, alien as it was to her. She stared at Warren and said:

"Sorry I'm late, but I've been working on something with Ken, and I've learned a lot. I know he's a talented guy, but he's just taught me that it's who you know, and what you know about them, that wins the game around here. What do you think about that, Warren?"

Warren never spoke to her again. He issued a typed memo that transferred her to work for Bill Muller, an earnest workhorse whose accounts demanded a grey sea of print advertising unrelieved by the glamor of television or the glossy magazines. But Catherine was determined to use all her creative ability and painfully won knowledge of power-playing to rescue herself from this limbo. In her passion to strike back at Warren and David, she worked harder than she ever had before. At first she was almost oblivious to Bill Muller, an unsophisticated mid-westerner with an uneasy awe of New York. His goodness, quietness, and steadiness went unnoticed until he began complimenting her on her work. Her ego had been so drained that she drank in Bill's praise thirstily.

When he invited her to lunch the first time, she was surprised when he took her to a quiet, romantic French restaurant quite removed from the part-fun, part-business, all power-play of the usual agency haunts. Catherine was even more surprised when the waiter's assumption that they'd start with a cocktail was dismissed with a request for the menu, and he suggested that she try their cold vichyssoise. It wasn't until Bill turned down the wine list and remarked that he couldn't handle drinks at lunch if he wanted to think clearly during the afternoon that Catherine realized that this was the first time she'd ever nonverbally turned down a drink.

Their lunches became increasingly frequent, and Catherine began to genuinely enjoy them. As her tension and fear diminished, her work grew stronger, steadier, and uninterrupted by hangovers. She and Bill found themselves responding so well to each other at work that he began to rise above the dull print accounts to which the agency had relegated him and she felt emotionally turned on by him.

Bill was dazzled by Catherine's flair and pleased by the steadying effect he had on her. She began to admire his goodness and strength; she wanted to reward him for them and possess them for herself. She knew that with Bill she could control the part of herself that with others could quickly run amok. He seemed eager to fill her needs, and she found herself involved in a genuine courtship, complete with flowers, dinners, nights at the theater, Sundays at concerts, and finally, without either of them quite knowing how or why, a proposal of marriage.

They both worked hard for Bill's success, but Catherine knew that hard work alone would never make a real coup in the agency. So while Bill labored late over his fledgling television spots, Catherine slipped easily back into the stream of agency politics. Once more she sat in the bars with all the young talents, with their loans and drinking money and precariously juggled bills, and their taxis to office because they felt a little hung over. And as thirstily as she drank the drinks, she took in the laughter, the admiration of her wit and the excitement. She began to think of the possibility of David and of nights that had become so imprinted in her mind that Bill's respectful lovemaking couldn't erase their revived impact.

Catherine, her ego restored by Bill, did not allow herself to think that he was too good, that the very traits she needed in him were too much for her to contend with. When she began to go out for lunches as well as for drinks, Bill didn't let himself think that she was playing office politics for him. And when she had a long lunch with Ken, and then another with a difficult young art director, each time losing her control and finding excitement and relief from Bill's gentility, Bill still said nothing. Finally, after another few weeks, there was David again—informed by Ken that Catherine was still available and vulnerable. He moved in rapidly, carrying her back into his world.

She loved being back at the good tables in the ''in'' places where rising celebrities, fringe glitter people, ''creative'' businessmen, and upper-class hustlers allowed the gawkers and tourists to stare while they enhanced each other's luster, drinking steadily. She listened again to David's promises of winter weekends in Jamaica and Christmas in Stowe, drifting into a comfortable cloud of alcohol and, later, reassuringly powerful and expert sex, never letting herself think what she'd tell Bill.

Through her ability and astuteness, Warren's beer account became Bills. And as Bill plunged harder into this new work, she could barely summon up conscious guilt. Suddenly a memo came down from David—now Bill's creative head—saying that he needed her for a special project. Catherine emptily promised Bill that once this campaign was over, they'd have more time to consolidate their work and their relationship. She ran quickly to David's discreetly lit corner tables, removed from the tackier elements in the bar and far more exciting than any other part of life. She was shocked when David did go away to Stowe for Christmas, but with someone else. She quickly turned back to Bill, working, spending all her time with him, reassuring him that it was only the killer pressures at the agency that had temporarily driven her away from their private and protected world.

When David returned from vacation, there was a startling shift in the agency structure. During his absence, the comptroller had been looking into David's accounts. Suddenly, in the restaurants and bars, everyone joined in fitting together bits of information; they led to the unavoidable conclusion that David had so blatantly mishandled his expense account and budget that it was only a matter of time until the administrative axe fell. Everyone anxiously curtailed his own expense accounts, but there was still money for drinks and, for Catherine, the sexual episodes that followed.

David called Catherine, and they had a last bout together, drinking as much as they could on David's remaining charge accounts and then working equally long and hard at sex, which always ended with Catherine's faked orgasm, essential to the gratifying David's ego. Exhausted, hung over, and working erratically, Catherine would stare sadly at Bill when she was no longer able to avoid him. He, reluctant to admit what was happening, could not look back enough to see her desperate wish to be stopped in this headlong rush to destroy herself.

After six weeks Catherine was waiting, half-consciously but desperately, for some sign of menstrual flow. She visited a gynecologist, who examined her coldly and impersonally, avoided her frightened eyes, and told her she could call the office Friday for the results of her test. But she did not wait for Friday to send a panicky note to David. She went to his apartment the following evening and found him drunk and ugly. She sat numbly before his storm of abuse. He told her she'd better not try to pin this on him, because she'd been fucking Ken and just about anyone else who'd get her drunk enough. He'd ruin her if she tried anything. No woman could do this to him. She should have stuck to tight-assed Bill. But now Bill wouldn't have her around to help him grab any more beer accounts; she was being transferred to another, far less creative head. She just couldn't handle anything—screwing, booze, or herself.

David left New York the next day without letting his landlord, creditors, or friends know where he was going. Catherine waited out the weekend, making incessant trips to the bathroom in the vain hope that she would find her pregnancy had suddenly disappeared. But it hung on. Beneath her consciousness she felt it was all she had. Her ''bad'' man had run from her, and she had chased her ''good'' man away; her mother, who had never really given, now could only take and complain that it was not enough; her job was in jeopardy; and she had reduced everyone in her life to a cardboard figure.

She appeared at the office Monday feeling shaky and ill, and collapsed in tears when Bill confirmed that she was being transferred.

"Listen Catherine," he said, "you're really sick. You don't seem to need me any more, but you certainly don't need the other people you've been seeing. Your mother can't help you, and no job can help you either, in the state you're in. I don't know too much about these things, but I really think you need to see someone. . .I mean, a psychiatrist, and I have the name of one for you." Despite the wave of indignation she felt, she smiled weakly at Bill, wanting him back, wanting to heal the wounds she'd caused so that she could have his help again. He continued, "Why don't we stop seeing each other for a while, until you've gotten things straightened out with the doctor. Then I'd really like to try again, Catherine, and I hope you will too."

Dorian, who had noticed Catherine's trips to the bathroom and guessed the reason, arranged a clandestine abortion for the next week in return for the pleasure of going along and hearing all the details of Catherine's love life and this humiliation.

The same week Bill had suggested that she go to someone for help, Catherine made an appointment with me. Although filled with fears of exposure and rejection, she felt stirred by the act of deciding to get help, and she began to write down some of the feelings deeply clenched within her. On her first visit, when I asked her why she had come, she let out a dry and strangled cry, the most she could squeeze through her tight defenses, and told me one of her truths. It was one that had rankled for years, but painful as it was, it wasn't as bad as facing the major truth of her life. She told me that although she'd been as loved as she felt she could be, she had never had an orgasm and feared she never could.

Her feelings of fear, desperation, guilt, and rigid morality would not let her lie completely to me, so she returned to this problem again and again in her cool, staccato speech. When my attempts to probe her past, her daily life, and her erotic conscious and unconscious became too much for her to bear, she lied and disguised her responses, letting out a burst of grief or anger at David or saying that only two men who'd made love to her had ever asked what she really wanted. But the pressure of my probings stayed with her, and from dozens of scattered references to drinking that slipped through in her free associations, I learned that she had much more than a sexual problem.

Unfortunately, I was too young to have the skill and experience needed for dealing with the subtleties and disguises of her addictive personality. I pounced on my discovery of her alcoholism with naive and self-congratulatory enthusiasm. Some of my inconsistent and blundering diagnostic thrusts did succeed in stripping away Catherine's denial that her alcoholism was the true focus of her problems. She allowed my interpretation and directive maneuvers to reach a few levels of her consciousness, and she cooperated nonverbally, but she would never say, "Yes, I'm an alcoholic." A gap remained between the feelings boiling inside her and the cool, low-key emotions she allowed to emerge, and this made her feel distracted and separated from her world. She could not bear to tell me all her truths.

She learned that I could be intrigued by the intricacies of her sex life and convinced that they were indeed a basic problem. And without my knowledge, she began to use another powerful resistance: She sublimated any confrontations with her drinking and the other hidden, guilt-ridden parts of her life by writing out her analysis instead of living it. In these sporadic confessional outbursts an almost fiendish voice emerged, a self she did not usually dare to like—a conscience less brutal and more willing to tolerate the usually intolerable. Catherine did, however, allow two of my interpretations to penetrate her screen of denial and emotionally edited truths, and to stay with her. I told her:

"You seem to want to give to a lot of people who don't give much to anyone, least of all you—like your mother. And it seems to me that you've been attracted to unavailable men who live with some kind of excess that destroys them and you—like your father. You seem to shy away from men who really do want to give you something, such as Bill."

These words remained in Catherine's mind as she gradually drifted away from me. She never told me then how much she felt for me or how much my acceptance had meant to her. Armed with my words, she fled back to Bill, feeling one terrible moment of fear about his kindness and his willingness to take her back despite her obvious lack of judgment.

Bill never knew that she hadn't stayed with me long enough or that she'd hidden away her most painful truths in a box of writings kept as "unfinished business." He never even realized that he didn't really want to know the full extent of Catherine's truths, didn't want to be frightened by her lacks and weaknesses.

Dorian tried to reassert her control over Catherine, but Catherine resented this, for she felt she needed a fresh start in every part of her life. She found an apartment she could afford alone. Bill was always there and supportive. Catherine felt somewhat crowded by his unrelenting good attentions, but she also felt safe. The pressures of Bill's job and Catherine's frustrating struggle to make something of her new assignment brought tensions. There were evenings when Bill had to work or was inattentive because he was tired, and there were days when she felt humiliated and depressed under her uncongenial new creative head.

Catherine turned again to her usual safety valve. Bill tried to ignore the change in her appearance, the excuses for her late hours and broken dates. But one night when she'd promised to be home, he waited alone in her apartment until after midnight. He stared at the sink full of dishes, the stale and overflowing ashtrays, the unmade bed, the disordered heaps of clothing waiting to be taken to the cleaners. He poked under the bed and found two highball glasses. He looked on the rickety telephone table and saw a week's unopened mail. He looked further and found a pile of overdue department store bills and a jumble of unattended tax and health insurance forms. He saw in it all the deterioration he had been trying to deny when he looked at Catherine. When she finally came home, she was so drunk that he couldn't have denied it anyway.

She dropped into a chair and began talking a contrite story about work pressures and late meetings. As he sat staring at her rumpled dress and smudged makeup, she began to spit out an angry tirade and jerked herself awake to relate each tale of incompetence, injustice, misunderstanding, and duplicity. Bill sat quietly, repressing his disappointment, his anger, and his new fear of her angry, aggressive behavior. Desperately he tried to think of a way they could save their relationship from destruction. When her outbursts finally ended, he proposed that they marry right away, saying that this was what she needed to steady her and that he needed and wanted her.

Gratitude for his acceptance washed over Catherine, healing all her raw guilt. It also buried in a dark recess of her mind the knowledge that just an hour ago she'd had her first orgasm, and that with Bill she could never have this experience. She woke early the next morning, determined in spite of a sickening hangover to cope with the indignities of her job. She would cancel all lunch and after-work dates; she would give herself completely to Bill. He, in turn, would help her collect the pieces of herself, which had become so badly scattered.

Bill moved in with her the next weekend, imposing his meticulous and slightly obsessive orderliness and helping her fix up the apartment to fit their new life together. Catherine could hardly believe that things were finally going so well for her. She bought new clothes, kept the bills paid up, and let herself enjoy playing house, nesting in, and bedding down with her future husband. Their wedding, which both had been secretly dreading, went well. It had been kept small and quiet. Catherine's mother carried it off with great style, as if the money she'd once had still existed and was being used with proper understatement. Catherine never asked her mother where the money came from for the small but elegant prewedding luncheon, the flowers and the bottles of excellent Champagne. Like her mother, she tried to remain unconscious of the increasingly frequent contributions from her most indulgent uncle. And she felt grateful to her mother for getting through the day without a single mention of her own maladies and problems.

Bill's inhibited father could sense Catherine's hidden smolder and appreciated his son's reasons for marrying her. His depressingly virtuous mother filled every awkward silence with declarations of how much Bill had told them about her, how happy she had made him, and how happy they all were to see him marry such a fine girl. Catherine smiled and hid her sadness and guilt about all the times she'd made their son unhappy and not been a fine girl at all.

The first year of their marriage was full of resolves and repressions. They both worked hard, and on many nights flopped into bed too exhausted for mental or physical intimacy. She stayed away from the excessive use of any drug for the longest period in her life, but she did look forward to the blissful two dry martinis before dinner, the only period of real relaxation in her day. She enjoyed the carefully chosen bottle of wine Bill sometimes brought home and usually finished most of it. Wine made Bill sleepy, and he dropped off after one glass. This left Catherine more lonely than after their brief, tired lovemaking and her faked orgasms.

This moderate, industrious life was rewarded with a new, time-consuming account for Bill. It brought Catherine further isolation in the dry world of a conservative financial account that advertised only in the *Wall Street Journal*. Bill began to spend several nights a week out on business and made a number of trips to the West Coast, where his new clients had their main office. Catherine tried to stifle her resentment at his abandoning her to further the success he probably wouldn't have reached without her. On lonely evenings she again found comfort in their after-work bars with co-workers, particularly with Shelley, an ex-henchman of David's who had survived the head-chopping following David's departure. Shelley well knew that Catherine's attempt to follow the solid, virtuous life her square husband was programming for her would not last long. During one of Bill's business trips, Catherine had two days of the kind of drinking and excitement she had thought she had banished from her life, and they ended in Shelley's bed. Her affair with Shelley was to continue for several years, but always as an underground part of her life. Catherine knew that Bill would not tolerate an openly adulterous wife.

With Shelley as her clandestine safety valve, Catherine did not drink a great deal on business evenings with her husband or at the dinner parties they occasionally gave. Still, the strain of her minimal marriage, her alcoholic affair, and her unfulfilling job led to outbursts of tears and resentment. Bill persuaded her that rather than juggling marriage and a job she should settle down and devote herself to starting a family. Rather wearily she agreed. Numbly she moved into a larger, better apartment and engaged in a more active sex life with her husband until her pregnancy was confirmed.

Bill was delighted with the daughter who arrived, but Catherine, after a brief flare of gratification, found herself trapped, shaky, and resentful. She felt unable to cope with her baby and got little help with her anxieties from her overworked pediatrician. Any plea for advice to her mother brought only a barrage of criticism. Her nights became desperate and sleepless. Bill went to bed earlier and earlier; then her mother would call, and Catherine sat for what seemed hours on the uncomfortable chair by the phone table in the hall, listening to confused complaints until she had to excuse herself and pour a quick Scotch to try to stop her hands from shaking. After another Scotch or two she went to bed, only to be awakened by the baby's crying. Then she walked back and forth with the child, too nervous to rock her or croon to her. The baby's cries escalated until Catherine had still another drink and sat with the baby until they were both calm enough to sleep.

After a few months of this, Catherine seemed so ill and irritable that both Bill and her mother suggested she see a doctor. She went to both Bills' doctor and her mother's and collected from each a prescription for tranquilizers and another for sleeping pills. Feeling more rested, she was able to look around at the pram-pushing women in the park and discover kindred spirits, each with a complaint, a new doctor, a few extra pills to give Catherine so that she could see if they helped. She listened to all the complaints and, with a list of symptoms, went to one doctor after another, collecting her own array of stimulants, sedatives, tranquilizers, and energizers to cope with her nausea, fatigue, dizziness, headaches—actually a nonstop hangover that grew more complicated with every remedy.

Before the birth of her child, Catherine's only release had been her decreasingly frequent meetintgs with Shelley. Motherhood without help, her waning physical attractiveness, and the unending fatigue that made arranging the meetings and dressing attractively for them a chore, gradually brought the affair to an end. Bill's work had overwhelmed his sexuality, and Catherine retreated further in fatigued withdrawal until their sex life almost vanished. One night, after a party that ended in a visit to a bar, Catherine shone with brief vitality, and Bill responded. When, to their surprise, they found themselves in bed and aroused, she had enough energy for sex but not for using her diaphragm. Thus their second child was conceived.

Dr. Bryan, her obstetrician, was shocked by her physical deterioration and had strong suspicions that she was drug-dependent. With a proper balance of kindness and firmness, he stressed the dangers of taking any drugs or allowing herself to be given shots by any of her array of specialists. For the first time, she enumerated to herself and then confessed to Dr. Bryan how many doctors she had been seeing for as many sketchily diagnosed maladies.

Filled with resolve, Catherine tried to organize her household. She redecorated her daughter's room and a room for the new baby; and one spring-cleaning morning she ceremoniously emptied all her caches in her medicine cabinet, the back of the disordered linen closet, and her cluttered drawers. The impact of a wastebasket entirely filled with this quasi-legitimate pharmacopoeia made the first break in the wall of denial that had sealed off her mind from her body for such a long time. It even made her remember my shots in the dark about her being an alcoholic.

With the birth of her son, Catherine's dependence on Dr. Bryan's firm guidance ended. Again she was fatigued and trapped at home. Postpartum blues combined with complete withdrawal from drugs produced a serious depression. At her six-week checkup, Dr. Bryan suggested she see a psychiatrist, and she finally decided that she had to return to me.

This time I was more experienced. I ordered her to stay away from the impersonal doctors who had given her drugs in such quantity and variety that her mind became fragmented. I also reminded her that alcohol itself was a drug and could only deepen her depression. I then replaced her crutch-drugs with an antidepressant, one drug she could take without wanting to increase the dosage. She began waking up in the mornings without headache or heartache, and I began to bring Bill into some of our sessions. Catherine had told me about faked orgasms and now a near absence of sexual activity. Now I saw Bill's deep passivity and lack of interest in improving the situation. Although I still missed some of the shattered pieces of their lives, I could put together enough for them to sustain Catherine and the marriage for a few more years.

Catherine now had the strength to strip away more of her shield of denial and to try for the health and happiness which I made her realize were possible. She believed she had hit bottom and now had both a doctor to care for her and a reformed husband who realized that she was starved for his consideration and interest. She learned that she needed not only help and support from others but from herself—from Catherine, the person, not Catherine, the failure. Bill was made to realize that she needed intellectual as well as emotional nurturing, and he gave her money to hire a part-time housekeeper. This released her from the continual child care and household routines that had been laced with nips of Scotch and either pepped or dulled with shots and pills. Once Catherine was free of having to do everything for her family, she was able to find things she wanted to do for them. She began to move about more comfortably in the outside world and look for things she wanted to do for herself. Sustained by antidepressants, and with vital activities beginning to replace her addictions, Catherine left me once more. Unfortunately, it was again too soon. She had learned and grown, but grave vulnerabilities still lay within her.

While in therapy, Catherine had made a friend, a woman struggling with her own problems. Catherine watched and shared in her successful struggle with herself. Ruth was a fellow member of the park's unhappy ''Librium brigade,'' quite beautiful when her body was not too fat and her face not pulled by tension and fatigue. She had struggled through a disturbed childhood; she and Catherine were drawn together by their resentments as well as their intelligence. Each tried to help the other, and each had insights into the other's problems, but Ruth was more insightful and more successful in extricating herself from her problems. Her food-focused life had never been as devastating to her as Catherine's devotion to drugs. She became a surrogate mother to Catherine, a constructive one, encouraging her to stick to her anti-depressant and nothing else, to see only me, complimenting her on her improved appearance, and gently teasing her about it being caused by Bill's increased attention. Ruth supported Catherine's forays into volunteer work while she herself applied to and was accepted in a graduate studies program.

Ruth's academic program, and her husband's insistence that she devote most of her remaining time to him and their child, slowly eroded her friendship with Catherine. There were phone calls and occasional lunches. Ruth usually stuck to the salads, pleased to be freeing herself of compulsive cravings for food and of her hated fat. Catherine avoided martinis, not aware that she was doing it for Ruth. When Catherine's life began to slip again, and martinis became harder to resist, she began finding reasons to cancel the lunches, unaware that she did so to spare Ruth the sight of her resumed deterioration.

Bill's job brought him increasing success and demanded more of his time. He began asking Catherine to create a better organized and more complex home life, yet he was spending less time with her. Without a doctor, no friend to support her, and her efforts to find an outside interest still unfulfilled, Catherine again sank passively into the increased demands of her family. As she sank, she reached once more for familiar numbing comforts.

The next few years brought boredom, stifled resentment, and further decay of mind and body. The more time she spent at home, the more chaotic and disordered the apartment became. The more time she spent with her children, the more alien and emotionally attached to their father they seemed. When Bill asked Catherine to use her connections to see that the children got into the proper schools, she had to ask her mother to round up some of her old friends to write references; her mother deluged her with criticisms about her failure to enroll them in dancing school to pave the way for junior dance lists. Finally both children were accepted at a coeducational school; her mother frowned on it, but Bill and Catherine's friends favored its unthreatening, progressive approach to education.

Bill began to insist that Catherine involve herself in some of the school activities. Her other forays into outside interests had been so incomplete and unsatisfying that she agreed only because she feared that her usual tactic of passive refusal would provoke an outburst of the unspoken hostility that lay between them. As she reluctantly dug out her best suit, she did not let herself remember how much her chronic fatigue and lateness, her inability to remember details and, above all, her anxiety in groups had contributed to her past failures. She remembered only her boredom and inability to find someone with whom she could feel relaxed. But she did go to the meeting on scholarships for disadvantaged children. It was being run by Rob Powers, head of the middle school, a young and apparently gentle bachelor who was much admired by the mothers. When he asked for volunteers to work on the scholarship fund brochure, perhaps someone with an advertising background, Catherine raised her hand.

The intimacy between them was immediate, and again Catherine did not pause to search for the flaw that had appeared in all her relationships with men. Their meetings soon moved from his harshly lit, chalk-dusty office to a cool, dim bar nearby. Catherine felt that Rob would be able to hold her, keep her from her tumbling into an existence she dreaded without really daring to imagine it. She loved him for his complete and unselfish appreciation of her mind, and they were both elated when the scholarship project was finished successfully and on time.

Catherine wrote other things and was nourished by Rob's appreciation of her creativity and of her need to be someone in her own right. They poured out their feelings, wishes, and ambitions to each other. Rob talked about his dissatisfaction at being removed from teaching to administration, which at that school meant catering to the hostilities of unsatisfied, overgiving mothers and overindulged, aggressive pupils who dominated their parents and teachers. He did not discuss his problem with alcohol because he knew it was sporadic, breaking only fitfully into his attempts to resolve other difficulties in his life. He was afraid to tell Catherine that he could see she was caught in a deeper, darker current of that same problem.

She talked to Rob about her emotionally impoverished marriage without betraying her restless curiosity at his failure to try to make their relationship sexual. She knew that he had been married and could tell from his brief, tense mention of it that he did not want to discuss it. One Saturday she found herself miraculously free of her family. Her mother had made one of her rare offers to take the children to a matinee, and Bill was not due back from his trip to the Coast until the evening. When Rob called her, sounding a little drunk and a little disturbed, she eagerly accepted his invitation to come to his apartment.

That afternoon far more drinks were poured down than feelings poured out, yet even in Rob's apartment she felt unable to break down his reserve about his private life. Suddenly they moved toward each other and were in his bed. Catherine, impassioned, worked frantically to produce an erection in Rob. He entered her with some effort and, moving in her mechanically, brought her to more orgasms than she could count; then he withdrew without reaching release himself. Exhausted and grateful, she lay on his chest and asked what she could do for him. In a voice as remote and passionless as his performance, he told her that this would never happen with them again; he was homosexual and had not had an erotic relationship with a woman since the marriage broke up.

Rob said that he had married only because he'd despaired of finding the monogamous, marriage-like homosexual relationship he had always sought. His wife had been beautiful, hard-working, and talented, had loved him for ''all the wrong reasons,'' and ended up castrating him. They ravaged each other in a screaming, sadomasochistic fight after she saw him emerging from one of the midtown homosexual haunts he had never been able to give up. Free of his wife and of the depression and guilt he'd felt every time he betrayed her, he'd resumed his search for the right man. And now he had lost another lover just the night before, a handsome and rich young man who had seemed to want the love relationship Rob was offering him. When Rob asked him to move in, the man was surprised and answered matter-of-factly that it was out of the question for him to let his family down by openly living with someone.

Catherine was shattered by Rob's statement that he still loved this man and couldn't imagine ever loving anyone else. She was further shattered when she got home drunk and late to find her children fed and put to bed by her furious husband. Bill caught her off guard by accusing her of having an affair with Rob and saying she'd have to pull herself together or they'd be divorced. He stopped short of telling her to stop drinking, get sober, and stay sober. Catherine fought away the sudden, desperate realization of how lost she'd be without Bill and the rigidities of their life, and battled to protect her fragile sexual high. She screamed at him that Rob was homosexual, but that if she were to have an affair with him, he could offer something a hundred times more satisfying than this sexless, loveless, deadening marriage.

They both backed away from this sudden laceration in their relationship. Bill removed himself completely from Catherine's life, driving himself deeper into his work, maintaining only the appearances that he felt necessary to his new status as a vice-president. Not sexually threatened by Rob, he let him take Catherine off his hands emotionally and left his wife, overripe and underused, to decay in whatever way she chose.

Catherine's friendship with Rob ripened as no other had. They sat in their corner of their bar and shared their frustrations of mind, heart, and ambition. Catherine gave Rob the courage to leave the safety and status of the school and look for the teaching challenge he sought in a public high school, and eventually in some innovative work. She helped him through many conflicts over relationships with men and gave support through the days and nights of depression that followed his compulsion. She saw and tried to show him the dead-end nature of the depersonalized homosexuality he turned to when one of his more stable relationships failed.

In return, Rob showed empathy for all the corners of Catherine's life that she revealed to him, and tried to be more than a barroom father confessor. He saw how badly she had let slip her appearance and her awareness of herself as a woman, and tried to make up for the loss of her husband's concern and her own self-esteem. He gently pointed out the rundown shoes, the low hems that concealed her still beautiful legs. He gave her the name of a hairdresser who could improve the hair she had such trouble keeping in shape, and generally tried to make her put some value on her feminity.

They gained insight into each other's blind spots and explored all but one—their unevenly shared struggle with alcohol. Catherine could always tell when Rob was having a little too much; he became overanimated, a little grandiose, and began making streams of promises to her and to himself which they both knew he'd never keep. But Catherine said nothing, glad he was matching her pace, and they grew maudlin, sometimes weepy, over their relationship. The only thing Catherine disliked was Rob's occasional gesture of physical affection. She would sit feeling sad and alone, knowing it could go no further than this tender stroke of her arm or impassioned squeeze of her hand. Rob was also quick to recognize the signs of Catherine's binges and hangovers. Although he could detect the puffy tiredness of her face, her more than usually unruly hair, her slip straggling below her skirt, he could not bear to face the sadness in her eyes—the desperate gaze of someone who's been there and back and fears she won't make it back the next time.

Catherine persuaded Rob that finding satisfying work would indirectly help him deal with many of his personal dissatisfactions. When he and two other teachers in his ghetto high school started an evening storefront school, he found it a source of great self-esteem. He began sending Catherine some of his more interesting students to be tutored in English; when she achieved some measure of success and satisfaction with them, he brought her to the storefront school.

One student there, Johnny, had spent most of his life in foster homes and had just returned to the streets from a detention facility. He had been supporting himself for several years as a drug pusher. His shrewdness and savage instinct for survival had taken him from schoolyard and barrio hallway dealings in marijuana and heroin to a Park Avenue trade in cocaine. The narcs had watched him deliver drugs along with groceries from the expensive market that employed him in the afternoons. They followed him in his dealings at school to the apartments on Park and Fifth in the afternoon, hoping to cath the bigger fish who supplied him. They did not know that at fifteen, he had been dealing profitably for three years and was holding enough not to need frequent contacts with suppliers. Frustrated, the narcs settled for Johnny alone. After copping a plea with unusual ingenuity, he was back on the streets in short order.

Rob and Catherine soon became more fascinated with Johnny than with the school itself. To them, he became a symbol of all those they hoped to save from the destructive elements of the world. Their struggles to control and develop this boy, whose values were so deeply rooted in basic survival and exploitations as to be alien to them, set off destructive shifts in their own personalities and relationship. Rob was struggling not only to channel Johnny's talents constructively but against what he saw as Catherine's competition for the boy's affection. Johnny had survived by a series of homosexual and heterosexual seductions; he was sensually attractive and knew how to make himself emotionally appealing to men and women. People wanted to help him, and he had quickly learned to control them by promising to become a projection of what they wished to become. Johnny felt Rob's and Catherine's excitement over him and understood how deep were their voyeuristic and messianic needs to capture him and transform him into something he knew he could not be.

Rob lacked the strength and aggressiveness to deal with both Johnny and Catherine. She seemed newly powerful in her satisfaction with her small successes in this world, so comfortably far from the realities of her own life. Rob dropped out of the struggle, consoling himself with Johnny's occasional smile. Catherine became deeply involved in trying to expand Johnny's skill at telling stories of his street life into the ability to write them. She felt that a collection of such stories, in his vivid Spanish-English, would be not only an important human document but a teaching tool; it would stimulate minds untouched by the insipid and condescending children's stories that she was ashamed to offer to her ghetto students. She did not realize that his web of stories, which exploited every phase of his drug life and touched all her emotional stops, also titillated her curiosity about drugs. She was impressed at how he was able to avoid addiction during his initiation with smack, which he despised, and excited by his descriptions of the highs produced by hash, cocaine, and combinations of other things she'd never heard of.

One night they stayed late together in the storefront. Johnny was skillfully detailing his victimization by society and his joy in sharing coke with the wealthy, powerful people he dealt it to. It did not take much urging to turn Catherine on, nor long for it to become her fix. After a few weeks, Johnny came less and less frequently to the storefront. One day Catherine found herself missing him and, suddenly and frighteningly, craving coke. She fled to Rob's apartment for consolation and reassurance and saw Johnny walking swiftly away from his building. When she went upstairs, she found Rob coming down from a cocaine high in tears and uncontrollable tremors of anxiety.

They sat through the night together while Rob poured out his guilt, anguish, and despair. The storefront project, which had brought him so much hope, finally brought him the greatest degradation and humiliation of his life. He had to admit to himself and to Catherine that he had wanted not only to bring out Johnny's creativity, and up to that moment had successfully struggled to restrain himself. Johnny had come to him that afternoon, offering once more the seductive possibility of shaping his savage mind, and had persuaded Rob to snort coke with him. Then he had forced Rob to his knees, and Rob, who had never before touched any of his students sexually—in his drugged state submitted to being orally raped by this boy.

Catherine confessed to her own cocaine addiction which she knew had come from her association with Johnny. She too was no longer able to deny the realities of her being destroyed by the association with Johnny. She and Rob clung together, feeling they needed each other more than ever. They abandoned the storefront project. Rob confined himself to teaching, and Catherine cut back to occasional tutoring. Bill remained locked apart in his deep, frozen hostility at the relentless deterioration of his home and his wife. Her children seemed nerve-shattering projectiles dashing through the dingy apartment, demanding peanut-butter sandwiches and soft drinks, school-play costumes and new clothes, already knowing not to demand love that did not exist for them.

Catherine could endure her desperate guilt and fear only by sealing her internal world from her outer self with powerful denial. Once again she shut away all her insights and transient confessions about her drug dependencies. Her only emotional contact was with Rob, to whom she clung in a static bond of survival. Even to Rob she could not confess how deeply she wished that Johnny had chosen her instead of him.

Catherine has periodically contacted me over the years, when she had to cope with major crises. Her insight into and control of her addictiveness is always short-lived. She has felt relief from her daily drive to drink only when she attended Alcoholics Anonymous groups. Even then she could never admit to her destructive identity, give up her powerful denial that she was and always will be an alcoholic. The last time she visited my office, I said to her once again, "Well of all the things you've done to help yourself, AA seems to be the only one that's helped for short periods." She replied, "So how come I'm back here and in the pits again? And I've told you ever since the first time I saw you, they're really all different from me. I know I won't spend the rest of my life like them."

ANALYSIS

Catherine's addiction to drugs—alcohol, tranquilizers, sleeping pills, cocaine, amphetamine—escalated over twenty years. For a while her controlled, polished facade and her skill at denial enabled her to live with it. She used one drug or another in her struggle to cope with conflict, pressure, stress, and disturbed relationships with her family, peers, lovers, husband, and children. She used drugs in her struggle to balance her erotic, emotional, marital, and career life. Her denial that she and those close to her were addicts or addictive complements made detecting her problem difficult and treating it impossible.

Only after she had had many crises and seen many doctors who incorrectly diagnosed her hangovers did I finally detect her illness. I, too, was first thrown off by her vast capacity for denial. Catherine faced her addiction too late, at an advanced stage of the process. Her mind was utterly dominated by thoughts of when, where, how, and with whom she could obtain a drug to relieve all other conscious concerns. Her facade had deteriorated, and she was suffering episodes of depression. Her cool denial was replaced with pain, guilt, self-loathing, poorly veiled anger, and insecurity. A puffy face, bloated body, and signs of neglect revealed that her addiction had taken control of her entirely. She had hit bottom. The shock of learning about her mother's alcoholism triggered her insight into her own addictive life. But she had become emotionally blunted; mere vestiges of emotion surfaced, and those only when talking or fantasizing about addictive substances, people, and milieus. Her physical and psychic hangovers, mood swings, and anxiety attacks left her chronically fatigued and unable to function.

Catherine's inability to sustain a stable work pattern at job or home lacerated her self-esteem. She also felt deep inferiorities about her periodic frigidity through most of her guilt-ridden, promiscuous sexual life. In fact, she eventually developed inter-locking addictions to both drugs and sex; one triggered the other, and both served many functions beyond affection, recreational joy, and relief. As a result, she developed a rigid body armor that isolated her from those who might have been close. She no longer achieved even transient relief from her addictive pattern.

The seeds of Catherine's addictive process were sown early in her life. Her father's and mother's narcissism and hedonistic lives, their neglect of her, and their respective overt and covert alcohol addiction, left her emotionally starved and disturbed her development. She was ignored, overprotected, seduced, and exploited by turns. Her parents' constant bickering over money and their manipulations to survive without working produced an insecure environment full of hostility. The fragile family bonds soon disintegrated.

Catherine's childhood was one of continual tension and overreactions to this unstable environment. She withdrew into fantasy and became an overcontrolled and compulsive student. She scavenged what self-esteem she could outside her home by total compliance with everyone who would feed her starved ego. She found it easiest to be nourished by a demanding authority and became a child work addict.

What little intimacy Catherine felt from her father's abortive attempts at affection when he was drunk ended traumatically with his death. Then she felt apart from everyone. Only her workaholic activity could control her anxiety. Her insecurities and vulnerability to depression deepened as her mother's dependencies emerged because of closet alcoholism, widowhood, loss of family support, and money problems. Their roles were soon reversed.

Catherine did not escape the oppression of this symbiotic relationship until she left home. She was ill-equipped to live securely as an independent young adult and falteringly attempted a relationship with Glenn. He was to fill the void in her by loving her. He did temporarily open her mind and body to sensual joy, but this soon ended. Once again her fragile security was destroyed by rejection. This paved the way for a shift from work addiction to other addictive behavior. She began using alcohol as anesthesia for the pain for loneliness and a catalyst for intimacy and sex. Her early alcohol addiction was reinforced by a rebound love affair with Jim, the passive, dependent, alcoholic medical student. Jim was her unconscious substitute for her mother. Catherine was both an addictive complement and collusive partner in this relationship. She also was vaguely aware of her recurrent sexual frigidity and tried to dissolve it with alcohol; she soon developed a conditioned pattern of needing alcohol to engage in even superficial social contacts. Eventually she used alcohol to deal with all pressures, conflicts, feelings of inadequacy, failures, rejections, and her inability to establish an identity. By doing so, she was able to go on denying that these problems existed.

Catherine's entry into the advertising world accelerated the middle stages of her addictive process. It was a provocative milieu in which addictive people and practice flourished. She was immediately singled out by and attracted to Warren, her workaholic first boss. From the beginning Catherine could cope with the pace, politics, and mutual exploitations by using alcohol. Soon she became an easy mark—the sexual, status, and work pawn of men whose own insecurities and addictive behavior required her collusion. Warren, David, Ken, and finally her husband Bill served as addictive models or as interlocking and collusive addictive complements. Her days and nights of addictive living culminated in the traumatic abortion that led to the end stages of addiction. She entered a futile round of guilt, resolutions, and relapse into drug use.

Her attempts to make Bill a family were her last ditch efforts to straighten out her life and led to still another failure. At first it seemed that her marriage was therapeutic; she had a brief period without addiction, because Bill became an undestructive addictive complement. His work addiction had abated to a mild level and did not trigger Catherine's addiction. But with the growing pressures of family life, boredom at home, frustrations in her relationship with Bill, and finally the reemergence of his work addiction, Catherine's old addictive rush returned. Then after she had suffered a post partum depression, her doctors aggravated her condition by giving her further addictive substances. The most malignant addictive contact was with the one who gave her amphetamines. At last her addiction reached autonomy.

Perhaps the most important source of Catherine's addiction was a lifetime of dependence on people who were unreliable and who could not rely on her. First there was the tortured, hostile relationship with a dependent alcoholic mother who first rejected and then clung to Catherine with cruel narcissism. Then, when Catherine entered the competitive adult world without the support of family, peers, or self-esteem, she turned to men to survive and fill her gaping dependency needs. Her father was the first man on whom she had depended; through his alcoholism and death, he had abandoned her. Glenn, her first love, Jim, her rebound lover, her mentor-lovers, Warren, David, and Ken, and finally Bill, her superego and addictive complement—and, of course, the many faceless men with whom she had spent blurred nights—all turned out to be unrewarding dependencies. Her most crippling dependencies were with Rob, Johnny, and David, full-blown addictive models who brought about her adoption of an addictive life style. These devitalizing mutual dependencies often provoked sadomasochistic interactions and exploitations that led her still deeper into her addictions. Catherine also had a series of dead-end dependencies on doctors who misdiagnosed her illness and created further dependencies on drugs. Her addictions sapped her mind and body and defeated her.

Throughout her adult life she continued to feel deep-seated needs to achieve, compete, and gain power and control over the men in her life. Her addictions were triggered by her failures to do so. She felt like and was seen by others as a used, devalued object rather than a person. The only exceptions were periods in her relationships with Bill, Ruth and Rob who transiently served as constructive, life-balancing helpers. Her frigidity and taking of drugs had become her way of expressing anger and retaliating against her exploiters and those she exploited. Drugs became a substitute for emotions, and talk about problems masqueraded as feelings. Catherine ended up with little or nothing to give. She was continually triggered to take drugs to combat everpresent painful realities; in her endless addictive cycles, she made empty resolutions that only triggered further addiction. She could not use the glimmers of insight that came occasionally from those who loved her—Ruth, Bill, myself—because of her pattern of denial. Acute physical and emotional symptoms kept triggering further addiction and finally eroded that denial. Only when she felt more pain than pleasure did she begin to acknowledge her addiction. Eventually she was forced to face her mother's long-standing addiction and then her own denial. Finally, she could not avoid facing that she was burned out.

TOM

THE CRISES

At our first meeting, Tom presented an artful array of shifting masks—man and boy, arrogance and innocence, cruelty and helplessness. His extraordinary good looks met a movie ideal; he had ruddy skin, a strong jaw, sandy-blond hair. He was thin-waisted, broad-shouldered, and had a taut, muscular body. An elaborately patterned nylon shirt clung to his torso, and skintight jeans to his small, firm buttocks. Even in his spaced-out state, he managed to convey the seductive coolness that turns most women's heads, and more than a few men's. His blue-grey eyes darted quickly and stealthily, cruising everything in sight. Sometimes his nostrils flared and his lips pursed as he controlled signs of smoldering anger and sensuality.

The taped record of his first session gives a clear picture of his feelings, fantasies, motivations, and life. At first Tom blocked much of his history; only later in therapy, after he had opened up with considerable anger about his relationship with his brother, did he discuss his sexual life. Then he said, "It's taken me a long time to look you in the eye and say I'm a fag. I guess I wanted you to say, 'Listen, stop pissing around and let it all out.' I've got to start getting it out if I'm gonna get out of this shit." It was after that crucial session that we could start piecing together the crucial facts of his story.

Tom's history led me to some of my earliest understanding of the common denominators of addictions. His connections with other addictive people made me see how they manage to find one another and sometimes stay connected through their addictions. Tom's sexual addiction solidified my thinking on the subject. Of all addictive behaviors, his sort is especially secret, rapid, and ephemeral, and it cuts through all levels of society. Frequent, instant contacts are made, often in tandem with other addictions, particularly alcohol and drugs.

80

I have to tell you from the start that I'm a little stoned. . .actually I feel great. I never could look at any guy. . .even a doctor. . .I never talked about it until this guy said I should see a shrink. In a way, I really believed that fucker. That's why I'm here, same place Neil goes. Why should he get all that help and not me, just because I don't have any bread? And I can't tell those fuckers at home, because they're the ones. . .or at least my brother sure fucked me up. . .and. . .I'm scared. . .I won't. . . go. . .here I end up bawling my head off. . .I never do that. . .I don't know what happened. . .I want to be a. . .I know I'm not a faggot! Well, I'll tell you every fucking thing that happened. I can sit here and let it all hang out for you just like that little rich prick, Neil, because he's one of the ones who blew my fucking mind. So I'm sitting here, in a real psychiatrist's office just like in a movie, with me the superstar who's all fucked up.

The big trouble started Friday night, after. . .I had. . .uh. . .no, I could never tell you that. I mean, well, you're a doctor, you can't fuck me up. You're supposed to straighten me out if I want it. So I'll tell you, every move, how I felt. . .coming out of the subway going home Friday night. It had stopped raining. Christ, what time was it? Shit. Late. And my mother had bugged me about getting home early. I didn't give a shit. I knew they'd all be sitting around the fucking table. But Jesus, what was I going to say about the shirt I had on? It was expensive. It felt good on me. He felt good. . .his leg, he left it there. . .left his hand around my arm. . .gave me money. . .and he gave me his phone number. He does want to see me again. I want to see him, too. I was thinking, maybe I'd call him Tuesday. . .Christ, that's tomorrow. I don't want it to come. I don't want to go through that door at the school again, either. Shit, I'm busted. But I can't let myself go under. Friday night I really hit bottom. . .my ass was sore. . .burned, ugh. . .it twitches like that now if I think. . .I don't want to think about it. . .afterward all I could think was, I needed a her, and just some other body to go out with, to cover everything up, forget it completely.

Another thing I keep thinking about is Mrs. Powers, my teacher. She said I have to do special tutoring, remedial crap. Shit, I'll never do it. Nothing's worked out in my whole life. Maybe I've had it. I hate to think. . .she said she'd put me in a special class. . .for weirdos. Fucking cunt, I know she's got the hots for me, that's why she'd called me up to see her alone. I saw her staring at my body like a piece of trade. Well, I don't give a shit. And she looked right at me. . .God, I had my cock shoved right up against her desk, and she looked! You better believe it! Looked like she'd go right. . .down. . .she got red. . .I caught her and she knew it. I looked back and smiled at her like, you fucker, I got your number. She jumped up so fast and ran to her closet like she had to find something. I knew she had to hide her hots. She bent down to pick something up, and I could have rammed her one right in the. . .

But the other thing, what happened to me in the bar. . .Jesus, it was like a dream or something, not real. It's the last. . .gotta be the last time. He said, "You'll get to like it." Does that always happen? No, it could never happen to me. Scared the shit out of me. It hurt. He'll never get me back there. It felt cold inside me. . .I hated that prick! That'll be the last time, ever. And Neil, what if I do call him? No, I won't, because it'll be like I'm back to my old tricking. But I've gotta return his shirt, and he's not that way. And I like him. I've got to get over this, back to something. I really can't take this any more, it's killing me.

And that lady helped me. I really feel like I miss her. I'll start dating again, really make out a little. . .maybe Lisa. She's beautiful, and I turn her on. Dresses great. I looked good with her. She turned me on. . .a little. . .everyone who went out with her made it with her. I had to say I did. . .God, I wonder if she'd expect me to ball her! I just don't feel like I could make it with anything right now. It won't be easy, but I will some day. I can't stay like this. What'll happen if I really try to make it with her? I really used to feel some stuff about Miss. . .Christ, she's gotta be as old as my mom. It would look awful. That's crazy, queer stuff. . .I'd like to call my old teacher. . .she'd help again. It'd be nice to see her again. I could tell how I needed someone. . .a girl. . .to wipe out what happened.

Well, when I got home Friday, sure as shit they were all in the dining room. No lights in the living room. . .I can never face them all together in there. One day I'm just gonna flip out with them. But they're getting suspicious, I know it. My brother's gonna know it. . .that prick, he's gonna be there just waiting to blow things wide open. I know. He's been wanting to do it all along. I don't look at him. . .after something like. . .what happened. . .I get to feeling he can tell. But he's so fucking busy with his bike and his broads he doesn't even see me when I'm sitting right across the table. . .looks right through me. I guess I can do it to him. . .he's outta my mind. . .not really, though. Outta me, though. Some day I'll get back at him, maybe tell them how he got me started in all this shit. . .it's over with all of them. . .they'll know. . .or I'll tell them. . .I feel like crying! But I can't even cry, can't feel anything, just dead inside.

Anyway, I opened the door and walked down that goddamn hall like I was going to the electric chair. The whole way I knew they could hear, but they sat there so fucking quiet, not saying a word. Finally my sister sticks her head out, looking really spooked. I could tell something was up, but I kept telling myself they couldn't know anything. I tried to get it together so whatever they were going to lay on me, I could hack it. But my sister started whispering at me like she's really shook up. "Mom and Dad have been waiting. We just finished dinner and we. . ."

I didn't want to listen any more. I just wanted to get it over with, so I just pushed her away. I couldn't even see her, I felt so freaked. I walked in, completely out of my head, thinking the shit would hit the fan. But for the first time in my life, my fucking spaced-out father was trying to act like he had some balls, like he was halfway like a man.

"Tom, your mother and I want to talk to you. The rest of you go in the living room, Mother and I want to talk to Tom alone."

Mom was sitting there like she was completely zonked, couldn't even open her mouth, just twisting her napkin around and staring at him while he was dragging this big liquor carton out of the closet. I hate to tell you what was going through my mind. They found my porno, the whole fucking box of it. I thought, oh Christ, help me. . .my face feels stiff, hollow, it must be red. . .no, white, all drained. I'm shaking so hard I'll fall down, please just let me keep standing. . .stand up to them. God, I knew this would happen. How did there get to be so much? What made them look? My brother, that prick? That fag at school, did he call? The money I took from his coat pocket! Did they finally miss it? Got to think, stop shaking. What else in my life? Will I have to tell everything? They're looking at me, they can always see what I do when they look at me. They must have looked at everything all afternoon while I was out. . .the pictures, the leather. . .where's the leather? Did they see my belt? And this damn shirt.

"Tom where did you get all of this? What is it for?"

I was still shaking, but when I heard his dumb voice, the dumb shit, asking me that fucking stupid way, I was shaking from being so fucking mad. . .not scared any more,

I just wanted to get it over with, like if they don't know it now, they'd fucking well better find out. I wanted to bust them up, kill them, kill all of them, and I screamed as hard as I ever did in my whole fucking life.

"I'm a fag! What do you think it's for!" And then I could like feel myself slipping right out of sight, like I was out of the room, out of my whole head, completely spaced, like I fainted, lost all of them, like I was in another world, wanted to let go. But then my mother, she's too much, too dumb to believe. She says, like a simple shit in her dumb soft voice. . .an idiot. . .like she never knew anything in her life. . . .

"What's a fag, Tom? You can't be that. They're like *women*. You're not one of those. You're a real boy!"

And then my father, just as dumb, I couldn't believe it, "Tom your mother's right, you don't know what you said. You don't even know what a real fag is. Kids just use that on each other when they are angry and they want to put someone down."

Well, that pulled me back into my head, and I really let them have it. I started yelling so loud it was filling my head, the whole room. I started pulling all that shit out of the box and throwing it around and yelling what did they think all this fucking stuff was all about? Do all the kids save up a pile of this kinda shit? It was all sliding around the floor, with my brother running in like he's the fucking fuzz, and my sisters and their husbands. There was so much I was stumbling around in it. I just kept throwing it and getting madder and madder, still looking for my leather, wanting to know where it was, and my brother was grabbing me, probably wanted to shut me up. So I let him have it, screaming in his dumb face.

"You bastard, you knew, and you threw out my leather. You bastard, you threw me out! My leather! Me!"

I almost knocked him right on the floor. I thought he'd knock the shit outta me or bust me in the mouth, so I split like crazy. If I didn't, I knew I might tell about him and how he was the one who started me, so I ran yelling down the hall.

"You fucker! You took me, and now you took my leather! You fucked me!"

I ran into my room completely freaked and started ripping into my closet, looking for my leather. It wasn't there, I couldn't find it anywhere, so I busted my fist through that goddam cheap cardboard wall they put up when my fucking brother thought he oughta have his own room. Then I ran down the stairs like a fucking animal, and I could hear my sister screaming. I was thinking, my God, I told them. I feel like I'm free at last. No, I really feel like shit. I can't take it. . .got to get out. . .I'm a queer and they all know. I'll get out of the city, go somewhere. I can't ever go back to them. . .I feel so spaced-out. . .I can't believe it's all out. . .it's okay now! No, it's not okay. I hate. . .myself. . .him. . .that prick, my brother. He knew and he's glad they know. He's fucking 'em all. This can't be happening to me. . .I'm nowhere. . .What'll I do?

I got out of the house. Walking the streets again. I turned into the subway. . . again! Smelling the warm, funky, sooty smell. The piss smell. There was a men's room. . .as usual. . .and I thought I'd go in for just a minute, to piss. . .and just to see. Thinking someone's in there. . .waiting. . .wanting. . .I want. . .need to be wanted. . .no, it'll kill me. . .shit I won't even get a hard-on. . .I'm dead down there. I should feel safe, warm, but I'm shaky. Everything's so flat, empty, I'm all alone. . .with no hard-on. . .nothing left of me. A guy at the end of the station looked at me. I thought, he's gay. . .but if I take a step, there's nothing under me. . .shit,

I've flipped. Someone was coming down the stairs. He was behind me, looking at my ass. God, what's happening? I was really out of it, my head hurt, and I thought I'd like to kill myself and just be dead, but I couldn't.

God, it was so bright in the subway car. There weren't too many people, though. I sat at the end, to be alone. I felt like I couldn't go anywhere, do anything. I was so shot! I thought I'd go back to that bar. . .but that was crazy. . ."Come back, you'll get to like it," he said. Did I like it? Yes. . .ah, my prick, felt something. . .I'm not sure what train I was on or how many stations I passed. Suddenly I just wanted someone to take me. And at the same time I felt like killing myself. But Neil was. . .I had his shirt. . .I thought, I'll call him tomorrow. . . .

My head hurts just going over all this stuff again. But I feel a little more like I know what I'm doing. I didn't even know where I got off that fucking train. I do know I paced up and down the station, going in and out of the phone booth, holding a dime in my hand. Finally I got it together and went over to get the Forty-Second Street train. My head was hurting bad. I was so tired, and I thought I might want to go and sit in a movie. But shit, I was out in the street now, in the cool air again, walking. Then in a window display I saw a cock! I thought, I'm outta my mind, but I decided to look just once. There were books and magazines, on one side all with chicks. . .the other. . .it was guys. . .I thought, I'll look at both kinds. . .just this once. Christ, it was a bunch of spooks in there, and quiet. No wonder, they had really kinky stuff there. . .rubber, chains. . .leather. . .Jesus, priests and nuns. There were signs, DO NOT READ HERE THIS IS NOT A LIBRARY. . .you better believe it. . .MOVIES. . .ADULT MATERIAL. . .NO ONE ADMITTED UNDER 21. There was a row of peep-show booths in the back. Suddenly I noticed an old creep staring at me. He was a fucking old fag. He looked right at my basket, had his eyes on it and wouldn't let go. It was unreal.

I strolled past the peep-shows back in the darkest room. I told myself it'd be the last. It was warm. . .stinking and smoky. It cost a quarter for each part and there were eight parts. There were movies of two girls, two guys, one girl, one guy, two guys. I needed a quarter. I hated to ask the guy up front because he was fat and ugly and needed a shave, but I wanted to so much I didn't care. So I picked a film of a guy and a girl because it looked like she was gonna give him a blow job. I decided that was a good one for me to see. I also wanted to see the two guys doing it, and I said to myself, who gives a shit! It's dark! I had four dollars and sixty-five cents and another five dollars I'd taken from his pants that morning. Shit, I felt like a thief, too. Were they looking for the money in my room? That's how they found my leather! Goddam!

Would you believe, as soon as I got into that dark peep booth, some fucker pushed in with me and had his prick stuck right up against my ass. I wanted to yell, but I couldn't. He said, "Calm down, kid, just thought you'd like a little fun like in the movies." I told him, "Get the fuck outa here, you fag." He scared the shit outta me. . .but that prick. . .well, fuck it, I felt. . .something. Those booths. . .they do blow jobs right in those booths! It's true. . .goddam place smelled full of it. Can you dig it, right in the next booth somebody was doing someone, going right down on him! The guy doing it looked like he was ninety! I could've vomited! I thought, I gotta get outta here! It was crazy, and the place was a bummer, but suddenly I started feeling horny. I started thinking about another movie place where I saw the ads. The movie was Rawhides. I felt like I wanted to rest in a real movie house. It was for adults, over twenty-one. Could I get in? It was late at night. . .I wanted to sit down, I felt weak. My head hurt, and I was having trouble thinking of the name of the movie house. But I figured I could flake out there for five bucks, so I found it and bought my ticket.

The place was loaded with people who looked so old! It felt good to get off my feet. I felt like I could've slept for a week. I never saw anything. . .so big. . .as the guys on the screen. A guy in leather, oh God, fucking another guy in the ass! The way he was doing it! And it was all there. . .so big. . .it was outta sight! Dynamite! And I had a hard-on. I was thinking, I've got to get outta here. I've gotta get my rocks off right here, now! Then, oh Christ, some ninety-year-old queen moved in next to me, with his eyes right on my cock. Like he wanted to eat it. "Want me to suck it, Sonny?" "Fuck off, grandpa," I told him. he said, "Listen, you little prick, who are you kidding?"

I wanted to get out of there. . .really I did. The old fags were all over the place. I looked back at the screen just once more, and then I was going to cut out. But Christ, the leather guy was exploding all over him! It happened. . .just like the guy in the bar did to me. I gotta get the hell outta here I said to myself. I decided to go to the john. There was someone young going in. Must've been the only other young guy in there. Good build, bright blond hair. . .small ass. . .so I went in. I just wanted to look. I bet myself he'd be trade. I started to piss, and then, God, he took it out and got to working on it. And it was big. . .the biggest. So I thought, I'll do him. I'll go down on him. And then, oh Jesus, I saw his face! Old, and mean, with hair like a wig! Curls, and blond. . .and tan crap on his face. A shit-eating grin. . .like the one who. . .the one who said, "You'll get to like it!"

Suddenly my prick went completely dead. And I started feeling panicky, and my head hurt again. I felt so sick to my stomach. . .I wanted to vomit, but I couldn't. Still, I felt. . .hot. . .like I had to go somewhere and get it. It was ten after eleven. I couldn't believe it got so late. I thought of taking the subway to the village. A leather bar? No, I wouldn't go there. . .I thought, maybe I want it in the ass again! God, never! No! I just wanted. . .I don't know. . .I had to have a place to sleep. . .I didn't want to ever let it happen, ever again. I wanted a place to crash. Not back home, with them all sitting around, waiting and worrying. I don't give a shit about any of them, because they don't really care about me. . .the whole fucking lot of them. And now I don't care! Maybe I do. But who else is there? No one. Yeah, I'd find someone down in the Village to crash with, and try to get a job to get enough bread to make it on my own. My stomach was hurting, burning, because shit, I hadn't eaten all day. In the subway some old number was coming out of the john, then some kid. I was almost sick to my stomach. I could smell that piss inside the subway john. I knew it would be dead inside there. It was worrying me not being able to get it up. . .and I had to wait and wait for the E train to come.

I was wondering, will I make it with someone tonight? I still felt horny. . .it was that. . .prick. I kept remembering, "You'll get to like it." I knew I'd never go there again. But I could almost feel it in my ass. . .thank God, the train finally got to Eighth Street, and I got out fast. I thought I'd go into one of the all-night places for something to eat. And that was the beginning of a real bummer.

I came up out of the subway, and right away I spotted this dude across the street. One quick shot and I could tell he was built. . .a beautiful body, great basket in his jeans, real blond hair. I thought, like I really stopped him dead with my cruise. I mean, he looked like he had a hard-on just looking at me. . .looking right at my prick. He looked about my age, with a face sort of like from a fancy school. His eyes were so blue, and his body. . .it was almost like we were twins! Then I began to think maybe he was a hustler. I was already wondering where we'd go, what would happen. . .who'd give in first.

Then he started looking the other way. That made me wonder what his scene could be. Then shit, he began walking away fast. I started to tag him because I thought maybe he was taking me to his place. . .or maybe he was a front for a gang-bang! Or just doing some cat-and-mouse number on me? I knew I was too tired to last long. My stomach hurt. I wanted it, and even more looking at the ass on him. I was hoping he was going to be "it" for the night. But he was walking so fast, practically running, not even turning his head to look at me. And he seemed like he was shaking. I just couldn't figure out what his scene could be. So when I caught up to him, at a red light, even though I was out of breath, I went right in.

"It's a warm night, man," I said. He turned around and looked at me. "Yes, it's very warm." The light changed, and we started walking along together.

"Hey, but you act like you're cold," I said. "You're shivering, even with a jacket on. All I've got is this shirt. Wanna get inside somewhere? Get a bite someplace?"

"Well, I'm on my way to. . .well. . ." His voice was trembling. I could tell he was freaked, so I figured he was new to the scene. But I also figured I better do my little game, because I still wasn't sure I was reading his scene, and I was so shot from the whole day. So I said, "I'm starved. Gotta eat somewhere and. . .'have' something."

That seemed to cool it a little, and we went into the all-night place, but he still seemed so spaced. He walked ahead of me down the cafeteria line, not looking around or saying anything. And I was so busy looking at his gorgeous ass that I kept grabbing one dish after another off the counter without even knowing what I was taking. So when we got to the cashier, there I was with this huge load of crap. . .desserts, salads, sandwiches. . .and all he had was a cup of black coffee.

I asked him, "Aren't you going to eat anything?"

"I ate earlier this evening." His voice wasn't shaking any more, and it had this real snotty, rich-kid sound. I was figuring I'd have to move in and take over quick before he started to do any numbers, when that fat-ass bitch cashier starts ringing up all my stuff. I could see I wasn't going to have enough bread, and he was already heading for the tables, so I called out to him as nice as I could.

"Listen, my name's Tom. What's yours? We might as well know each other's names. . .it's always nice."

When he turned around, he was coming on like he's some fucking prince or something. "My name is Neil, and we do know each other. We just met—outside."

I could feel my face getting redder and redder while that fucking bitch kept yelling out how much I owed. "Shit, I've only got. . .hey, Neil, am I glad we know each other, because I'm short about. . .I mean, I forgot to bring enough bread with me. Can you lay something on me?"

"Already? We've just met, and it's already 'lay something on me'?"

Then the little fucker pulls out a ten, drops it on the counter, and walks away without even waiting for the change. It was like he had all the money in the world, and ten meant shit to him. He was just too much! Points for him. Trying to put me down! Well, he might have the bread, but I had the balls. I could just tell looking at him that I'd been around more than him. But I still couldn't dig his number, whatever it was. So I said:

"Neil, don't forget your change. I'm not one of those lend-a-friend types. Listen, man, if you want, you can always take the interest out in trade later." Well, I thought, now you've said it. That's not cool at all.

Then he said, "You don't seem like any kind of friend, and I'm no John. For openers let's get the record straight. You seem nice enough, and I'm not out tricking tonight. In fact, the meal's on me. Let's just talk. I really just wanted to talk to someone tonight, and when I saw you come out of the subway, it was funny, I said to myself, that guy could be my double, and I stared because it was freaky to see someone like myself. I've never picked up anyone so young. I mean, I've got a problem about this kind of thing."

"Whatta you mean so young? How old are you?"

"Older than I look. I'm in college. I go to N.Y.U. And living in the Village, with it all around me, I mean, there's just too much for me to handle. I have a few hangups about this. . .like, what's my scene, and what I've done. . .I don't! And I didn't want to do anything tonight except talk to someone. I mean it."

After he said that, he looked kind of cold and alone. I still couldn't figure him out, but I started to feel sorry for him, in a way. You know, sometimes you can meet a guy and get the hots for him, not just to ball him, but for him as a person. I mean, you still want to ball him, maybe even more, but because you get interested in what he's like. I was thinking this was crazy. I'm not the love-at-first-sight type, but I was really turned on. It never hit me so hard before. I said:

"God, you sure look younger. Do you have your own place? Does anyone live with you? I'm flat broke, and I told my family I'd be at a friend's place for the weekend."

After I said that, I'd really have felt like he busted my balls if he told me to get lost. But then he really got to me. He said, really nice and soft, "Maybe we can talk somewhere else."

I guess I moved in pretty fast after that. I was almost afraid I was pushing too hard, but I didn't want to give him a chance to start thinking or get scared off. I just couldn't take one more down that day. I have to have him, or it, or something to get it off.

"I have two roommates, but they went home for the weekend. I've never really taken anyone back there. . .to just. . .talk. I really feel lonely tonight, and I don't want to do anything. All night I've been trying to stay out of trouble. It's funny, just as you came out of the subway I had it licked. . . .I was about to go back. It's really strange how we connected."

"Yeah," I said. "Let's get out of here."

By this time I was really feeling good. . .food, someone like this who could talk. . .I didn't have to try, and he seemed pretty smart. It made me think if I was like him I'd never have to get into all my shit. I wondered how it was to be like him. Then I was getting hot all over again, thinking maybe he'd let me get into him. I still wanted to have him. If I could get it up. Shit, why did I ever let that other creep get into me? I wanted so bad to forget that, get moving. . .I asked him if he lived far, and he said no, it was only five blocks. "We live in one of those new buildings near the school, myself and two guys I went to school with at home. They go back to their families almost every weekend."

"Where's home?"

"Uh. . .Scarsdale."

It was just like I thought. He was a rich kid, fancy school, apartment. But I wondered what he was doing in that butch-looking drag. Not even new stuff, kind of beat-up. He could probably buy good stuff, leather jeans. Even I had better-looking clothes than his!

He started up the conversation again. "I can tell from your face you must be wondering how someone like me is into this kind of thing. I keep wondering, am I really gay? You may not believe it, but you're the first young guy I've ever met I just felt like talking to. Anyway, my scene hasn't been people my age, not since years ago. I've never done anything with anyone young. In fact, what I do isn't all that much.''

''Tell me about your scene, man,'' I said.

''I've been telling someone my story, and next week I'm going to tell it to a whole group of people. It scares the bejesus out of me, but Tuesday it's going to be all out in the open.

I wondered what the fuck he meant. I started thinking it was going to be a bummer, because I couldn't figure out what kind of trick this was going to be. He lived in one of those fancy buildings near the school. He had to ring a bell to get in, and some old fart took a year to get his ass over to the door and then stared at me ten times before he opened it. I felt like shit. I was really ready to split, and even Neil started getting shaky again. We rode up in the elevator staring at each other like a couple of jerks. I still felt horny, and I thought I'd better turn him on again. I smiled at him, and right away he smiled back, and I thought he did seem turned on, but I knew I had to play him cool. He was smart, and he wasn't going to be anybody's pushover. But he was nice and gave off good vibes. I really liked him.

So when we got off the elevator—it was on a high floor—and I'm waiting for him to get his door open, I got the superhots for him and moved in right behind him, so close he could feel my cock on his ass. He started fumbling around with his key, and when he got the door open he ran in so fast I almost fell over. The minute we got inside he ran in the kitchen and asked if I wanted coffee, but that wasn't what I came for. I headed right for this big low sofa he had, and I could see him watching me over the counter. I lay down and spread my legs open so he could get a good look at my basket. Just like I thought he would, he copped a quickie cruise, and I started feeling a little hard.

''Got any booze?'' I said. I could really use a drink. It's been a long day and night.''

He looked away real fast and started fooling around getting out ice and glasses, like he was scared and stalling for time. I wanted him to turn around while I still had it up, but he wasn't even looking at me. I'd never wanted to get it on with someone so much before. He made me feel more than horny. . .something more. . .I was thinking maybe I'd even go down on him, and he'd have to let me do something. He was pouring the booze light, not enough, and I needed a real belt or I'd blow the whole scene. So I said:

''Hey, Neil, don't be so stingy with the booze. Why aren't you pouring some for yourself? Come on, man, join the party. Listen, don't be such a tight-ass.''

''Listen, Tom, there isn't going to be a party tonight. Let's get this whole thing straight. I said I wanted to talk, and that's all I want to do. If you don't, maybe you'd like to have your drink and split and find yourself a nice john for the night.''

He made me so mad I suddenly screamed, ''What the fuck do you mean find a john? I've never gone with anyone for money! You can't insult me like that! Whatta you think I am, some fucking whore?''

Well, I thought he was gonna pass out. He flopped down on the chair white as a sheet, shaking, grabbing the edge of the counter like he was holding himself together that way. At first I thought it was some new freaky come-on, but then I saw his eyes and I knew he was really flipping. I really felt bad. I didn't know what to do, but I tried to cool it as quick as I could.

"What'd I say? I didn't mean anything. Listen, man, please tell me, are you okay? Let me fix you a drink or something."

He still didn't say anything, so I poured him a stiff drink. His hands were shaking, but he belted the whole thing down. I sat down by him and patted his knee, trying to calm him down, and I just left my hand there while he sat there staring, completely spaced.

Then suddenly he turned around and looked right at me and smiled like I'm his best friend. . .like I just saved his life. . .smiled really beautiful, but like he was almost crying too. I could feel that smile right in my cock, like I could get a hard-on, so I just left my hand on his knee. I knew, in a way, that I'd scored, but I didn't. . . well, I just wanted to hold him, get close to him. Why the fuck didn't I close in for the kill, I was wondering. But no, I felt good toward him. And I felt sorry for him. . . something about the way he was letting me see how shook up he was. It made me feel horny for him, but without a hard-on. I know some guys really go all the way, kiss, call other guys their lovers, but I always hated that shit. . .too faggy. I really wanted to do something. . .stop him from crying or let him spill his gut and then see what happened. I said:

"Jesus, man, I didn't mean to fuck over your head like that. I mean, I'm sorry, whatever I did."

"It wasn't just you, Tom. I asked you up. I mean, what could you expect, just talk? I came on with you just as much as you did with me, and it blew me out because I really wanted it to be different."

"Different how? What do you want?"

Then he started to lay his whole scene on me, and that's when he told me about your group. He told me he comes here to see some shrink, and that he's in a group where they help gay guys who don't want to be gay.

I still remember everything he told me. Even after all the other things that happened to me over the past few days. I don't usually remember a lot of stuff, don't even like to, but what he said must've really got to me. There's a lot of difference between him and me. . .he's rich, and smart, but he had some of the same feelings I always had. Especially the first things he told me, like being an outsider and feeling lonely even when other kids wanted to get friendly or when girls would come on with him. He said his father was a doctor and wasn't home much, always out operating and teaching at a hospital, doing some kind of research. Then he'd come home and try to be a father, but he never made it because he was too tired and wasn't really interested. He said his mother was better, spent more time with him, but she was a teacher, even wrote books, and she always bugged him about his grades all through school. Half way through what he was telling me he stopped and asked if I wanted to hear the whole thing.

I said, "I've got nowhere to go. In fact, I was hoping I could crash here."

"Sure. I really need someone around tonight."

Then he told me how he always had arguments with his parents being so tight-assed about money. . .I mean, to a point where he'd take the train into New York with no bread, and on the train or in the city he'd find some old john to buy him dinner. Then he'd stay in the city overnight without his parents knowing where he was. That was even before he started going to college in the city. It was unreal, the way he got money. . .always from guys, and some of them were married.

He said the more he hustled and had all the extra money, the freakier he felt. . .like getting the shakes when he was putting the make on some old number, until it got so bad he was scared shitless about maybe freaking out. . .over being gay, or semigay, or whatever. That was why he went to some counselor at the college, and they sent him to you. And he told me you have groups where gay guys who don't want to be gay talk about what they do. He kept saying how many guys got help that way, got away from gaying around. . .even got married and had kids, really got to, like, making it with broads! He kept saying, "Tom, I'm really getting somewhere now," and I knew he really meant it. He said to me:

"The reason I was out when I met you was a telephone fight with my parents about not going home this weekend for my mother's birthday. It really got to me. I was out standing around when you came out of the subway, and you looked so much like me from across the street, and you kept staring at me. I wanted someone to talk to, and I figured I was better off with you than ending up with some john. I've never felt anything for anyone my age. I didn't want to! I really don't feel that way about you. . .I like you a lot, but not that way. I'm getting too together to start some new thing."

I didn't know what to say to him, he seemed so honest. I said, "Neil, just forget it. Don't get bugged." He looked beat, so I wasn't going to begin telling him my whole scene. I said why didn't we sack out, and I poured us two more big belts, figuring he'd get my message. But all of a sudden he had that tight-ass voice again.

"I don't want another drink. Booze really gets to me. I let go completely. So let's just each sack out. You can sleep in there."

I looked in the room he showed me and saw just this one small bed. Then he headed for the other room; it had two beds, and one of them was a double. I figured he was trying to let me know he was going to play it straight. But Christ, I wanted to touch him, hold him. I was trying to picture what he'd look like with his clothes off. But my head hurt, and I was dead tired, so I didn't argue with him. Can you believe, he shook my hand and offered me a pair of pajamas?

"No way," I said. "I go bareass." Then I said, "It's going to be cold alone in that room. I mean, aren't you going to be lonely? Two beds in one room, and you all alone. . .especially tonight?"

"Come off it, Tom, I think we'll both feel better. I won't feel so alone if I know I have a friend here. . .someone to talk to. Tom, you're my friend, aren't you? You said you were only five minutes after we met, but are you? Can you be?"

I could tell he was trying to be a friend and not come on to me, but damn, I was still horny. It was fucking up my head, because I kept thinking I might not be able to get it up, but I was really getting off on him.

"Neil," I said, "I really want to have a friend. I've never had a real friend. I promise you I'll stay on my side. . .I mean, in my room. I'll leave you alone."

He said goodnight. It was almost too much. I was wondering if I could just get one look at him undressed, maybe while he was getting out of his underwear. I could just ask him where the john was. When I got to his door and looked in, he was just about to drop his jeans, but the minute he heard me he yanked them up like he thought I was going to rape him.

He said, "What's the problem?"

"Nothing, Neil, I don't want anything. Where's the bathroom?"

"Right down that hall on the left."

He really had his mind made up that he was going to go straight. But his body! Even though I felt so dead inside, I wasn't feeling all that dead down there! It was crazy! I had some sort of heavy hots for him, but I kept thinking. . .or trying to think what it would be like. . .if I tried to go completely straight, too. Get a girl. . .screw nothing but broads all the time. . .go to some head-shrinker and have to spill my guts out. . .shit, not me. . .tell every fucking soul.

I just had to go in his room again. Now I wanted him to see all of my body. Maybe it would turn him on after all. I couldn't get it out of my mind how great it would be if I could just be close to him. So I went in the room again, and there he was, flaked out with his back to me. Not moving a muscle. It was like a fucking cop-out. So I eased into the bed and curled up against him, against his ass all turned to me. I didn't even care any more if he woke up and threw me out of the bed. I had to be near him. So I pressed up close to him. He didn't move, but I could tell he was awake. Finally he said, ''Tom, let's just be friends. It's okay, you can stay, but let's just be friends.''

I said, ''Yeah, no party tonight. I just want to be friends. You're right, and anyway, I gotta do a lot of things tomorrow to get my head straight. I'm beat anyway. I couldn't get it on tonight, so just relax and let's be friends. Can I hold on to you? Can I just stay this way? Is that okay with you?''

He said, ''Tom, let's just get some sleep.''

So I said good-night and rolled over, and we stayed curled up with our backs against each other.

When I woke up, I was alone, and it took me a while to get it together. you know, the only other person I ever spent a whole night in bed with was my brother. I felt like shit, but I guess I was glad I didn't do anything the night before. Neil was really a nice kid, something. . .different. I went into the kitchen, still feeling half out of it, and there he is, wearing straight-looking jeans and a shirt, fixing breakfast. He was like a different guy, and if that's what doctors think is a good job. . .I'm so fucking mad thinking about it I could tear this whole place to pieces. He was still being nice in a way, fixing me breakfast and still rapping about going straight an the shrink and the group. That bastard, he might not even have to get laid to go straight, like I. . . .

Well, I sat up the night before listening to his sad stories. Now when I started to tell him my scene, he freaked. But I wanted to tell him. I felt so nervous, I thought it would help me settle down. I didn't tell him everything, and I guess I made up some stuff. Sometimes I do that now without really knowing it. . .it just creeps up on me before I know what I'm doing. Mainly I told him how I can turn on any dude I want, and left out about the chicken-hawking. I don't know, maybe I told him too much. I was still trying to turn him on to me, and he might have known it. He was a spook about picking up on things. Anyway, he got cool and started acting like he was some kind of shrink himself. So I lied again and told him I'd made it with chicks, and his eyes almost fell out of his head. He started rapping away again, but he wouldn't let me get near him.

He started to get high on himself and getting shrunk. I think it might have set him a little crazy. He said you told him tricking like we do is like. . .an addiction. . .it starts different, but when it gets to be too much of a habit it makes you spaced-out and stuff, and you're like a sex head. That's sort of right. . .it's a little like that. . .I can't keep away from it. . .get uptight but keep wanting to go back to the same bad scenes.

Well, Neil wanted me to call home. Of course I couldn't, because they'd just think I'd been fucking around with fags all night. . .that's what they'll always think now, every time I go out. I couldn't take that shit. And I still don't know what to do.

I told him I couldn't call them. I was feeling so alone. . .really lousy. . .I asked him, I really begged that shit to let me stay there till I could get my head together, just for the day. And all of a sudden he looks really scared, like it's all too much. like *I'm* too much, and he says his roommates will be coming back and how can he explain it to them.

How do you like that fucker! Thought they'd know he tricked, find out he was a fag! A hustler, a cheap hustler. At least *I* never hustled anyone, and here he is hustling me with this going-straight number. . .how he wants to help me. And then he's putting me down, putting me out. Well, I really let him have it. I told the little bastard he could take his fucking help and shove it up his ass. If him and all his fancy group fuckers can make it, so can I. And I ran out of there before that shit could say another word.

I must've really flipped. I couldn't even wait for the fucking elevator. I ran down the stairs, all the way down. All I could think of was getting out of there, away from him, so my parents wouldn't send the cops after me. The same old fart was in the lobby, and he's still got the front door locked. I'm screaming at him like a nut, and he mumbles he's going for the key and goes in some little room. I thought he was going to call the cops. I was so freaked out I ran in after him and ripped the whole phone out and started swinging it at him. I guess he thought I was gonna kill him, and I guess I felt I was too. I was ready to bust anything in my way. I just hurt so much. . .I don't know why. . .shit!. . .I'm crying again! I was out of my fucking skull. I don't know how he got that door open, but finally I busted out of there and ran down the street. There was some damn police siren, so I ran for the subway.

I was completely freaked, and wouldn't you know, the minute I got out in the street I headed right for a fucking subway john, for another tearoom scene. The sign on the door said CLOSED FOR REPAIRS. Shit! I didn't know what was happening to me. I felt like killing myself. I was thinking about Miss Lyons. . .she did help me once. . . I could call her. . .if I could find a phone. . .it was only seven-thirty, so I went to the end of the platform and flaked out on a bench for I don't know how long. Suddenly I jerked awake and saw some old fart coming up to me. A fat old faggot. I guess he could see from the way I was glaring at him that I was ready to let him have it. . .him or anybody who wanted to touch me. . .or my ass! So he turned around and went farting off. I sat there kinda spaced, just letting the trains go by till I felt like I could get it together. I began thinking about Neil. . .that maybe he was right. . .not to go on gaying it. And thinking I could make it too, if I tried. . .if I could try. I was feeling so goddam down.

I remembered the two phone numbers I still had in my pocket, so I went into the phone booth. I said, "Hello, is this Mrs. Elizabeth Wilson? This is Tom Coder. Mrs. Powers from school called you about me. Or did she forget to tell you I was going to call? I'm the one that needs all the help. . .with tutoring. . .are you there?"

She says, "Oh, Tom, Mrs. Powers did call, last night."

"Well, I'm the one that needs help," I said again, "with tutoring."

The she apologized and said she wasn't expecting me to call so early, and morning wasn't her best time. "I don't really begin to function," she said, "without at least one cup of coffee, Tom."

My God, she sounded good. . .sounded warm. She called me Tom, and said she'd help me. She was a very fancy talker. She said:

"Mrs. Powers said we should get started very soon. She explained that you do need quite a lot of help. Tell me what you want to arrange, when we can meet, and what you need to do. My, you've certainly been good about getting in touch quickly."

I started feeling together. I wanted to turn her on to me, and I felt like I could. . .like I had to, because I needed something. . .someone. I suggested right away. . .that morning, after she had her cup of coffee. "Because I want to dig in," I told her, "and Mrs. Powers told me how great you've been with the others. You've helped them a lot, haven't you? And I really need help, too."

I came down really heavy with her. She was so convinced that she said we could meet as soon as the library opened. She said it was the most important tool I could use! That was a real screech, but I said it sounded great, I'd meet her anywhere that morning, just name the time and place. So we set it for ten-thirty at the Seventy-Ninth Street library, near her house. She said that would be a good time because her husband would be taking their children to the park for bike riding and to the zoo. After we hung up, I felt a lot better because she sounded nice. . .like she liked me. I could tell that because she called me Tom a lot. Then I started wondering what she'd look like. Maybe fat? And with a fat ass? Ugh! To fuck? No! I decided I'd just think about the tutoring bit.

I needed something to eat and a shower before I met her, so I took the shuttle to Grand Central and went in the wash-up department in the men's room, got a razor and towel and stuff, and got myself together. I came out feeling like, "O.K., here I come, Tom Coder, young body beautiful, superstar of "Going Straight." And wouldn't you know, when I pushed those doors open, feeling great, looking great, there was one of those tall, fancy, advertising type dudes with the suit and briefcase and the whole number, looking right at me. Jesus, he laid a fast, strong cruise on me. And the funny part was he. . .he looked so straight.

I could see he was starting to follow me, and I don't know what happened to my mind. I just freaked and started running through the place. And do you know, no one even noticed. I just kept running and pushing through doors until I got out on the street. Thank God, I lost him. He had to be some kinda freak. . .probably wanted to fuck me. . .no thank you! I felt psyched up and told myself I had to stay out of johns and stations and stuff like that. I decided to walk all the way to Seventy-Ninth and not look at anyone. Goddam eyeballs can be like a pair of balls. . .they turn on if you even look. But I felt. . .like. . .totally there. . .like maybe I could change. . .a little. . .so that none of those fuckers could get into me. . .ever. I swore I wouldn't let them. I'd get into someone, a her, a she.

I was wondering if that Mrs. Wilson would get to the library early. It felt good out in the fresh air, so I took my time getting up to Seventy-Ninth. I would have gone to sit in the park; but I knew it would be loaded with faggots, cruising, so I kept on walking and trying to think about school. How the hell did I know how to use a library? Maybe she really would help me. I felt like at least trying to do the work, the papers. . .pass the courses. I walked into one of the playgrounds and sat on a bench, digging the kids and stuff. I liked watching them play because, Jesus, they looked happy, and I thought it'd be nice to feel like that again. . .to be free to slide and swing and get kisses if you fell down. I was even thinking it'd be nice to have a kid someday. . .if I could ever get it up and in. Have a kid? Support a kid? Shit! Why not!

The time went by fast, and I headed for the library. I must have been a little early, so I leaned against the side of the steps to wait for her. I kept eyeing up all the chicks I saw, trying to guess which one would be her, feeling kind of turned on by the whole deal. Shit, I was thinking, look at that! That's gotta be her. Dynamite! But she's gonna be too much for me. I didn't think she'd be that young. Nice. Looking right at me. It had to be her, right? So I took a chance and said, "Mrs. Wilson? I'm Tom Coder." "Well, I'm not Mrs. Wilson!" The snotty bitch! Just my luck it wasn't her. By that time somebody else was walking by. So I said again, "Could you be Mrs. Wilson? I'm Tom." "No, sonny, I'm not," she snapped.

After that one, I thought I better let her figure out who I was. The waiting was getting to me, so I started thinking about the scenes I'd heard went on in the johns at colleges, in the libraries and everything. Everbody said the college dorm and library tearooms were like unreal. . .great. By that time I was feeling that was what I needed. . .some guy's mouth wrapped around my dick, sucking it to make me feel good. And maybe I'd mouth-fuck him, too. Then I told myself, shit, no more of that. But I could feel myself slowly getting a hard-on. What was I going to do? Stick it in her! Ha! Or maybe a quick fuck in her ass! Then maybe she'd enjoy it so much she'd get up and do me. . .or do my work for me because I fucked her. . . .

Suddenly I saw her and knew it had to be her, she was walking so fast. She started to walk up to the steps, and I lost my hard-on, thank Jesus! I said, "You must be Mrs. Wilson. I'm Tom Coder."

"Oh! How did you know who I was? I guess because you've been waiting so long. I'm glad to meet you, Tom, and very sorry about being late. I did need a cup of coffee, but here we are, so let's go inside and get going. I'm sure Mrs. Powers has told you, using the library is the absolute foundation of writing any paper. Do you know which areas you need to work on most? You haven't brought any notebooks or index cards. I. . .we won't be able. . .uh. . . ." She seemed very nervous all of a sudden.

"Well, you see," I said, "I was at a friend's house last night, and I ended up sleeping over. I didn't have anything with me, but I thought maybe I could talk to you first. I mean, I know it's really important, and then maybe we'd be able to spend the rest of the time, you know, going over my other problems in English. . .alone, somewhere. I mean. . .I could tell you about my hangups when it comes to work. How's that sound to you? Then when we meet next time, I can show you all the notes I made last year, on stuff I started and couldn't finish. Does that sound good to you? Anyway, I'm really lousy in libraries. I'm lost in them. About the only place I can find in them is the john."

I thought saying that would really get to her, coming on like that college-boy fucker Neil, and I had to laugh at my own private joke. And she got sort of shook up. But there was no way I could keep her out of the library. She marched right up and headed for those little drawers, you know, the card files. And she started in again about the library as a "basic tool". Ha! Very uptight and a little out of it, almost like I wasn't even there. So I got turned off and felt like I wasn't there, too. Next thing I knew I was cruising again, like an old sex head. . .turning to look at this one and that one right there in the library. While she was talking about primary sources. Shit. I knew I had to fake her out so I could get us out of there, because I couldn't keep my mind on the stuff. . .words just running in and out. Maybe she could help me get going on the papers, but not in there! I'd just end up flipping for some kid while she was rapping on and on.

She wasn't bad looking at all. The arms and legs were a little skinny, but nice. And sort of bags under her eyes, when she wasn't smiling. But good boobs, and as long as those look young, that's what counts, boobs. And her ass! Nice and small. . .almost like a boy's. The place was creepy quiet and making me nervous. I thought I could put her uptight, too, so I stood right behind her and said real loud, "Mrs. Wilson, do you mind if I call you Elizabeth?"

Well, she about jumped a mile in the air and got red, and her hands shook and she started fumbling with the cards. Suddenly I could feel that she wanted to split, too. She looked really classy, a real lady. But lady or not, anyone that gets that uptight isn't ready for any library number any more than I am. So I came on to her about how I had some problems, personal things that were hanging me up and keeping me from concentrating. She kept getting more and more jumpy, like she knew I was coming on to her. Then a couple of dumb bitches sitting near us started shushing away, and suddenly she said, ''All right, Tom, let's go,'' and we both split for the door like it was going out of style.

But when we got outside on the steps, she looked a little spaced out, and I couldn't quite figure what her scene was. I knew she had one, that's just something I can always tell. And I knew she was one of those people I could go ahead with, without knowing exactly how it would turn out, you know? I was getting her attention more and more with my ''I need help'' number, but letting my voice get a little hornier so she'd know there was something there for her even if she wasn't sure what it was. She fidgeted around, real nervous, but then she said we should go up to her place because we'd be alone there.

It wasn't far from the library, and while we were walking there in the hot sun my sex head started to work again, and I started wondering what it'd be like eating a girl. That would be a new scene for me. I started feeling hot about it, too. And I thought I could feel her digging me, looking my body over, getting turned on by me. I know when that happens. You can feel somebody doing it. . .right down to your balls. But I thought maybe I shouldn't allow myself to get that turned on. Maybe just try to concentrate on doing some work. . .letting her help me. Shit.

Her place was one of those old fancy buildings, fancy but kind of dead. She looked a little shaky and spaced out. Her apartment was nice but cluttered up, and the ash trays were all full and there were some dirty cups and glasses lying around. I said:

''Listen, Mrs. . .uh. . .Elizabeth. . .I'll bet you could use another cup of coffee. Can I. . .have something. . .with you?''

''Yes, do you drink. . .coffee, Tom?''

''Never touch it. Just milk or juice, please. Or maybe. . .something stronger? Nothing in between for me. I like it all the way. . .either way, I mean.''

''You do? You know, Tom sometimes you seem a lot older than you must be. How old are you?''

She was slowly dropping that superpolite teacher number, and I knew it was okay to laugh and say, ''Old enough to know better, and young enough to want to,'' even though that sounded kind of tacky. I kept watching her to see how she'd handle that. She looked a little spooked, but she started the ladylike number again while she went into the kitchen to make coffee. I don't care how much she tried, I knew I was getting to her. She was getting nervous. . .shaking. And when I saw how red her face and neck were getting, I was sure she had to have the hots for me. Shit, maybe I couldn't handle it, I thought. But I wanted to try. So fuck off, Neil, you smart-ass!

I was imagining going down on her, sucking her pussy. I'd never done that. . .of course I'd fingered some. . .that. . .it felt all soft around my finger. . .and slippery. . . but. . .I'd always been afraid. . .but I really didn't feel afraid with her. My ass felt. . .I was getting horny. . .I didn't want to think about getting fucked, either. I swear that really wasn't what was making me hard down there. . .hard, half-hard, on again off again. But I knew one thing for sure, nobody was going to get into me again. No way! Not with any gold dust or grass or. . .anything. I'd completely had it with that scene, the whole bit. . .the tired old fags, the queens who just want to fuck and can't even feel anything. . .some of them always trying to impress their tricks with who they are, and what they can do, and who they did it with last night. Crazy freaked-up old guys, and some younger ones, too! Anyway, I was thinking I had to get all that shit out of my head and get my cock up into Mrs. . .I mean Elizabeth.

I had the feeling it was getting to be high time to blow her mind. At the same time I was still thinking about Neil. What the fuck did he know about life? I made up my mind I was going to be the best Goddam fucker going! So I said, "Elizabeth, you seem a little. . .uptight. I mean, are you tired? It's all right with me if we just sit here and talk. Just get to know each other. . .forget about the work stuff for today. I like to relax. . .with someone nice. . .like you. You're really easy to talk to."

Well, maybe I did that a little too fast. She jumped up and ran over to that damn kitchen again. "How about a little more juice, Tom? Maybe you'd like something to eat before we get down to work. Did you have breakfast this morning? I'm sure I can find you some cookies."

"Hey, Elizabeth," I said, "I got something better than cookies for you and me. It'd make the cookies even better if you do find them. And it'd really relax you—and me, too."

Jeez, I took a chance saying that. I was afraid I'd lost her completely. She kept fiddling in front of those cabinets, and I thought what the fuck is she trying to hide? I got up and stood as close behind her as I could. I wanted to press myself into her ass, but she was spaced, just staring straight ahead. Then I saw what was inside the cabinet. Shit! I never saw so many empty wine bottles in my life! Half-gallons, gallons! She had to be the biggest wino of the world. I moved back a little, not sure if she was freaked because she could feel my prick or if it was because I saw the wine bottles.

"Well, someone around here really likes wine, unless they just collect them," I said.

Then it got kinda scary, maybe because I said too much again. She turned around real fast, dead white, staring at me so hard I couldn't figure out what was going on. She started shaking so hard I thought she was gonna faint. I grabbed her, and she felt outta sight. I really wanted to keep on holding her, and helping her.

"Elizabeth, come on, sit down," I said. "You look like you're about to pass out. Come on, let me help you."

"Oh, thank you Tom, it's nothing, really, just that I haven't been feeling too well lately. And frankly I feel pretty awful right now."

She wasn't putting me on. She looked flaked and shaky. She looked sad. . .and helpless. Jesus. . .that turned me on even more. Because I knew she needed me. And I knew if I could be strong, she'd feel better. Maybe feeling my prick behind her. . .maybe that made her upset. . .no. . .I knew I didn't get that close. What she needed was some sympathy. Yeah, and why not give it to her. I could see it might help her to have a little. . .loving. I said:

"Listen, you really look like you could use a shot of something." I didn't know whether to push the booze or the joint, but she looked so lost that I felt sorry for her. I said, "I'm really sorry. I was joking, Elizabeth."

She still didn't say anything, but she pointed at this little kinda hutch that had some old glasses in it, like antiques. I figured she meant for us to use them, so I got two and filled them up with red wine. I handed her one and made like a little toast with mine, to get her going again.

"Come on, Elizabeth, cheer up," I kept telling her. "Here's to you. Drink up and you'll really feel better! And these glasses are really fantastic."

Shit, I could feel the stuff hit me, on an empty stomach. I was really so turned on by her, and I was wishing she'd get out of her funky mood. I wondered if she just needed a drink or if it was me knowing that got her on such a downer. I didn't care. The place had class, and so did she. She must be rich. . .not that she was such a fancy dresser, but cool in a way, like those society babes that do things for poor kids. Anyhow, she finally took a sip of the wine, and it seemed like she got it together a little, but it was still like being with a sleepwalker. Then she said:

"These are lovely glasses, Tom. My family always had them. I remember how beautiful I thought they were when I was a little girl." She kept staring at me while she took long, slow sips. You'd have thought that cheap wine was, like, great hash the way she was taking it in, and I could tell she was starting to feel the hots for me. She was looking right into me, like she really wanted me. She was like another person, inside her eyes. And her lips were really beautiful, the slow soft way they moved. So maybe she'd be willing to wrap them around my cock. . .shit. I couldn't see how she could look so horny and so sad at the same time. Ah, I wanted to turn her on so much! To warm her up and bring her out of her downer.

"Come on, Elizabeth, here's some more," I said soft, very soft. "Drink up, you've gotta cheer up. Smile a little. . .for me." And put out for me, I was thinking. Oh, she was getting it on, slow but sure.

She said, "I guess I do need another drink, Tom. You're really being so sweet and kind. I feel so bad not doing something right now to help you. You must have problems of your own without having to put up with me." Then she started again about my getting a good start in school. Jesus! No matter what, she just couldn't seem to let go of that teacher crap. But it didn't last this time.

"Listen Elizabeth," I said, "school hasn't been my only problem lately. I've really been uptight, and rapping with you would do me more good than anything. You look like you're feeling better." I didn't want to rush anything. "I think this wine is doing you good, and another glass will do us both even better." I poured her some more, and she began to smile, still a little spaced out, but in her own way she was beginning to come on to me. So I did my little toasting thing again. She said:

"This is making me feel great, Tom, how about you? I guess we've both got our problems, but we won't think about them today. To tell the truth, I've just about had it with problems, and with a lot of things in my life. Right now, wine seems a lot better than worrying, for both of us." She had to do another little teacher number, but I could tell she really didn't mean it. "Do you think it's all right for you to be drinking this, Tom? I know it's just wine, but it's a little early in the day, and. . .well. . .how do your parents feel about. . ."

"Elizabeth, I'm really not so young, if that's what you're worrying about. Believe me, I'm a lot older. . .in a lot of ways. . .than you think. I've really lived, if you know what I mean."

"No, Tom. What do you mean?"

But shit, I knew she was getting my message. She said that so sexy, left herself wide open for me. I said to myself, no more library talk today! That wine was really loosening her up. And me, too. I was feeling great. And she was great, real understanding. . .and great boobs, too.

I told her, "I've done a lot of things that most kids just haven't done. . .ever. I'm sort of. . .advanced, in a lot of ways. I've gotten into and outta places no kid my age should've been."

She didn't say a word. She just smiled, and this time she filled the glasses. Now she was really getting with it. I knew we could both forget the kid shit and start to relax.

She was one of the coolest people I've met in a long time. I picked up my wine again and reached for her hand.

"Come on, drink up, and here's to being friends."

She swallowed the whole glass, and I felt her squeeze my hand. She told me I was a sweet person and that she felt better just having me there. She said I was nice, like a comfort she hadn't had in a long time. I was getting a little scared, but I figured there was something else she hadn't had in a long time either. So I poured down the rest of my wine too, and moved down the couch toward her until I slipped my leg right between hers, right up until my knee was just brushing her pussy. She looked a little scared, but she let me do it. I poured some more wine till I could think of what to do next. I was getting a hard-on just sitting there. God! It was great, but it was getting real hard and big. She was so warm. . .her whole body was warm, and my leg was right into her crotch and she wasn't stopping me. She just let me press it closer, like a big prick. And she liked it! I could imagine her cunt, warm and wet, just ready for me. I wanted to let her know then, but I wanted her to be looking at my hard-on. And then I'd feel her up and kiss her, yeah. . .or kiss her first, then feel her up so she'd let go completely. . .and then she'd open her legs more for me and let me go down on her and tongue-fuck her. Oh, shit, I was busting outta my pants and she was getting red and ready, turned on all the way up her crotch.

I leaned toward her and put my whole mouth against hers. Then I pressed my knee against her harder, and pressed my tongue against her lips. I could hardly believe the way it all felt. Her soft face, her mouth opening to let my tongue in, and I could feel her moving her pussy all around against my knee. We kept our eyes closed and kissed. I kissed her all over her face and blew in her ear, and then whispered like I heard once in a movie, "Elizabeth, don't do a thing. Let's just go inside and lie down."

Sure enough, she lay way back, and her legs were wide apart. She kept her eyes squeezed shut, and I moved my hand along her leg and pushed my finger inside her crotch. She let out this kind of cry just when I touched the tip of her cunt, and she was so hot and wet and all open for me, I kept going in and out of there with my finger and in and out of her mouth with my tongue. I really felt like she liked it, and I felt so great. . .like I've never felt before in my life. . .all together, on a whole new kind of trip. I loved being able to give it to a chick so she thinks it's the greatest, and me feeling like it was the greatest too. Then finally she put her hand on my hard-on, really started loving it, and I felt so out of sight! I was afraid I was going to come in my pants right there.

We kept on kissing, and the next thing she opened my pants and took my cock out. I was still afraid I'd come, so I took my hand away from her crotch and we stopped a minute. But then we started again. We had to! I put my fingers back into her and wet them and put that all over my cock. She touched the tip very softly, and I thought I'd go out of my head. I was afraid I'd come right then, all over her, so I grabbed both her hands and pulled her up from the couch. We stood there with our wet hands together, just staring at each other, and I began to lead her toward the bedroom. She started to say no, but I asked her please just to lie down with me. I wanted to be with her. . .wanted her.

Then suddenly she leaned against me so hard I practically had to carry her to bed. She flopped there with her eyes shut and her head turned away, but I could tell she wanted it. I pushed her legs open again and pulled up her skirt and got her panties off. I could feel my hard-on big and pushing against the bed. I closed my eyes and moved my head down between her legs to tongue-fuck her. God, it felt great. . .it was so warm, and. . .my tongue. . .was stiff like my prick. I kept moving it in and over her. . .tasting. Then my tongue was stiff in her. And when I ran it over her tip, it made her whine. She was squirming, but not hard.

She was getting wetter and wetter and moving all over my tongue and lips. She loved it! And her ass. . .I held her ass and pushed her closer to my tongue until my head was practically in her. Then she went wild. . .she must have been coming. She practically exploded, shaking all over me, and I kept tonguing her while I was getting my shirt off. I sucked her tits and then put my tongue back in her again and again until I knew my cock was ready to go in her. But then she was coming again. She took my prick in her hands and put it in. Into her, for me! Right up. . .way up! It felt so big sliding in and out of her. She had me feeling absolutely out of sight, and she was coming again, I think. Around my hard cock, and tight on it. I wanted to hold her ass. She was holding my ass, tight, and her nails scratching my back. She was keeping me in her. . .loving me in her. Until I couldn't hold back any more. I came into her, and she felt it. . .like it was. . .dynamite!

Then she started begging me to stay in. And all I could think was. . .I've had her, and she's under me, and I'm hot and sweating. I couldn't believe. . .me. . .in a woman! I made it! All the way! I came! And it got hard again, and she came, too. . .a woman came with me. She kept hanging on to me, wrapped her fucking arms and legs so tight around me, and pushed against me like she wanted it again. But I was really busted, so I rolled off her onto my stomach and closed my eyes so she could see I was shot. But then I thought maybe I'd want it again because I felt so great about making it, so I rolled over on my back, but I kept my eyes shut. All of a sudden I felt her mouth all over me, sticking her tongue in my mouth like it was a cock or something. It really blew my mind, so I jerked myself away and turned my back on her, trying to stop her clutching and get her out of me. She was begging me for more, saying how she needed me, and I did it so great for her, and the next thing, I couldn't believe it, she was all over me like some fucking nympho.

All I could think of was how I had to get out of there, right away, because she was between my legs, sucking, and around my balls. It hurt, but I was hard again, and I knew she was going to wrap her mouth around it. And keep it there! I was ready to come again! She was busting me! Like all of them! She was going wild, up and down me, eating me all up! Shit, I came again, and she still kept her face on my belly. I thought I couldn't stand it any more. All I wanted then was to call. . .Neil. . .tell him I made it! Ah! Shit! I made it, as a man! Wasn't that too much! But she was still lying on top of me, saying, "You'll stay, Tom, won't you? We can work together. I feel so sad." And she began to clutch at me and cry. Jesus! She was hanging on to me like she was drowning in her own tears. "Don't let me go, Tom, you've been the only one who's cared. . .to bring me out. . .of my sadness. . . ."

It really got to me. I felt like I was hurting as much as she was, and that never happened to me before with anyone, chick or trick or friend or anyone. I felt like I was the only man in the world, like I could save her, really had the balls for it. I rocked her back and forth, but all of a sudden she starts grinding her cunt on me, and clutching on me when I'm trying to get away.

"Don't leave me, Tom. I can't be alone, lonely, any more. It's too much for me. Please, come back."

"Listen, Elizabeth, you've got to cool it. Here, just let me give you something that'll make you feel great. You're really gonna love it. You'll forget everything."

"Anything, Tom, anything! Anything you want to do!" She kept holding our her arms toward me. "I'll do anything with you, Tom, for you, to you, please Tom."

Jesus! She completely flipped over me. She was high, hooked on me. I had to get something into her so she'd get off my back. Suddenly I couldn't wait to get out of there. I got my jeans on and left my shirt on the doorknob. I guess I didn't want to let her think I'd never want to make it with her again, but it had to be my scene. So I got out one of the joints and dragged her up on the pilow and started talking her into it.

"Here now, sit up. This will really relax you. You'll feel just great if you just let yourself go with it. Just float, baby, and let it take you along."

Well, I didn't need to bother. She grabbed it right away and busted it like she'd been at it for years. I couldn't believe it! She must be a real head! I was thinking, she is gonna be outta her skull, because that stuff is dynamite. And then she comes in with, "Tom, where'd you get this? Oh, I mean what kind of cigarette is this? Turkish or something? It's very different." And she starts laughing like she's ripped already. Can you believe!

"Come on, Elizabeth, come off it. You know goddamm well what that is. And you've been stoned before. No one who isn't cool busts a joint like you just did. You know dynamite shit when you try it! Come on, admit it." But she just kept dragging on it till she was coughing her lungs out, tears running down her face, the whole number. . .really wrecked. She just went right out of her skull, babbling and all. "Tom, where did you get this stuff? It's really something, sending me right out of my mind. Tom, you're too young for all this. . .Tom, bring me some wine, something to drink, and then promise you'll tell me how old you are, I mean really how old. . ."

Then she passed out cold, and I bent over her and whispered, "I'm seventeen, Elizabeth." I tried to get her hair out of her eyes, because they were wet with tears, and then I kissed them. I took the roach out of her hand and kissed her eyes again, and then her mouth. Then I said to her, and I really meant it like from the bottom of my heart, even if she was out cold, "Thank you, Elizabeth. Thanks for my first time from a seventeen-year-old fag who is never going to be a fag again, because you did something so great for me."

Then I split right out, and I was running down the street. I couldn't believe I got in, and she wanted me again! I just couldn't take any more of it. And I was beginning to feel dizzy and stoned, but sick, too. Everything was like. . .all stretched out, and that's when I began to think it would never happen again. It was like I was in a dream. I felt like I was going crazy, like those freaky, spaced-out feelings I'd been starting to get. So I thought I gotta go somewhere and flake out for a while or I'd end up in some booby hatch for good. I couldn't take one more hassle, one more person. My head was pounding, and I was sweating all over. Things were getting fuzzy from the angel dust and booze and all that fucking and sucking and cunts and cocks all mixed up like crazy in my head. My stomach was in a knot, my legs were shaking, and all of a sudden I thought I should get to a hospital, get a shot of something that'd maybe fix me up. I thought I could say I ate something or I was almost run over. . . like with that bastard yesterday. . .except he really was okay, he probably would have sucked me off if I'd. . .but he covered up his fagginess with that work shit, and that "you have a problem" number. . .God, it was only yesterday. It's been so much I can hardly keep track.

Anyway, next thing you know I'm standing in front of this place, and there's a red sign, CRISIS CLINIC. I felt like my head's in one place and my body's somewhere else. . .shaking all over. . .but going like it had a life of its own, right through the doors. I couldn't even see what it was like until I heard some chick asking me am I all right and would I like to sit down or lie down. Then she starts in like some machine with all these questions, my name, how old am I, where do I live, ever been there before, do I have a phone number, what happened to me.

I turned off and wanted to get the fuck out of there, but I couldn't even get up. So I sat there and lied about everything. It's so easy for me now, I can lie like a madman without half thinking, or sometimes I don't even realize I'm doing it. Then I heard her say she'd have to call the doctor. The next thing you know I'm being walked down some hall, with some big black dude on one side and some little jerk in doctor drag and big glasses on the other, yapping so many questions I couldn't get my head straight. I couldn't say a fucking thing anyway, because just when I thought I'd answer one thing so I could get the hell out, he'd ask me something else. They took me to this room and said I should lie down, I'd feel better. I kept thinking these guys are gonna fuck me up, and I wanted to fight them and get away, but I couldn't.

I can't remember it too well, but it seemed like I was there for hours. I must of passed out, and when I came to again that weird doctor was standing over me and looking like he wanted to put me away with the nuts. He asked me how I was feeling, and I said much better, I really had to split and go home right away. He said to lie back down, I'd been coming down from a rough trip. . .that fucker thought I'd been tripping.

So I did my best Neil-type number. I said I just ate something funny and maybe had too much booze, because something happened to me that never happened before, which was my real reason for coming there. Well, he grabbed a chair and sat down practically on top of me and zeroed in through those specs like he couldn't wait to hear all about it. So I told him I'd been meaning to come to a place like this for help, and I'd like to come back when I'm more together and could really talk. . .I'd come back if I could just split now. I really had to get home to my family, they were probably freaking out because I'd stayed out all night.

He gave me some bullshit about how this is a place for people like me, who got wrecked and need to talk. Since he probably thought I'd tripped or popped some smack, he might call the fuzz, so I jumped up to go. But the black guy came back with this other doctor, and he looked like the first dude there I could dig at all. He told the others to split so he could get me to cool it. He said he wanted me to answer his questions, but I could go home if I wanted. If it wasn't for him, I'd of never ended up here laying all this stuff on you.''

Anyway, I told him how I got laid for the first time and how I was worried it might never happen again. . .not about any gay stuff. . .and how I'd like to talk with someone but I needed something to get my head. . .my shit together. Then he tells me that this doctor who's doing some kind of research. . .runs a special group to help all kinds of junkies. . .even sex junkies. Can you beat it? Sex heads, fat heads, pot heads. He lays on me that this doc treats you in his own private office and it won't cost. I couldn't believe it all. . .thought I'm really too stoned and not getting it right. . .research my ass. He said I'd have to agree to listen to some tape shit. . .I got lost. . .but said okay, okay, at least let me outta here. I was pretty scared they'd lock me up, and I thought I'd go to anyone instead of that. . .shit, I really was busted and needed anything I could get. Then I agreed and said yes, yes, he gives me this name, and I said I'll go. He wrote out your name and address. I really grabbed the paper and he seemed to turn off all at once. Then that other fuckhead with the glasses came back in, and right away I felt like I was just a piece of meat again. . .like, he couldn't wait to get rid of me. He said, "You're okay now, kid. Why don't you go on back home to your mom and dad, where you should have been."

And I thought, you fucker, I ain't been home since I was born and I ain't never going back again! You're so blind behind those glasses, you wouldn't know what kinda freak you ran into if you fell over him! So I got up and ran out of there, but when things got spacy again, I remembered I had somewhere I could go. So here I am talking to you. I end up spilling out all of this shit. . .trying to get my head screwed on. . .straight. . .or do something to get over what I got. . .or maybe I'm just stuck with a mind that sucks.

HISTORY

Tom is the youngest child of work-dominated parents struggling to move upward by devoting all their energy to the two liquor stores they own. He was unplanned and unwanted, and he grew away from them emotionally and physically. They left him with no experience of closeness to them. But Tom did receive contact and sensory stimulation from the brother and two sisters to whose care he was relegated. At first they enjoyed playing with him and wanted to keep him quiet and happy, so they quickly met his every need.

When Tom was three, his maternal grandmother moved in with the family—his grandfather had recenly died of chronic alcholism, ending a long and miserable marriage. Tom's mother had been nagged by guilt for neglecting him; in her eagerness to have her own mother look after him, she blocked out any considerations that her mother might no longer have any capacity for the sustained emotional giving Tom demanded. She also forgot how eagerly she herself had once fled from her role as buffer between her own parents to marry a man very different from her undisciplined father.

When Tom's grandmother first arrived in the household, she responded to his charm as strongly as everyone else; she gave him what was, for her, an inordinate amount of love and attention. And he seemed an ideal child in every way but one. Whenever he was left alone, he had uncontrollable temper tantrums that disturbed the entire family. His grandmother could not tolerate this sign of his demanding appetite for love and attention; she lashed out on Tom the rage she had kept dammed up during forty years of accommodating her husband's addiction. Also, she had become arthritic, and this heightened her intolerance of Tom's behavior. Both were demanding and produced pain, and she unconsciously associated them with her husband.

At the same time, Tom's brother and sisters were developing social lives outside the family. They began to resent having to stay home with their demanding baby brother and their hostile, semiinvalid grandmother. Tom's parents had now acquired a second liquor store and were too overworked, tired, and driven to make money to acknowledge the increasing anger and disruption in their family.

Tom, desperate over his suddenly unfulfilled needs, fought in vain to keep his place in the center of the home. First he turned to his sisters for attention, and they soon learned he would do anything to keep it. They began to press him into doing their household chores; he not only accepted their exploitation but clung to their skirts, flattered them, even imitated them, hoping that his gestures of submission would keep them interested in him. But they grew impatient with his demands anyway, and more fickle in their own emotional needs, and they began to use their baby brother only sporadically. Finally, in desperation, they would shake him loose by ridiculing the very behavior they had first encouraged.

In what seemed a disintegrating world, Tom then focused on holding his brother's attention. But his brother, Robert, was more brutally determined than anyone else to be free of Tom's dependence. He chose an arena for their struggle that introduced Tom to a world of guaranteed attention. One night, when Tom was ten and his brother fifteen, they were left at home with their grandmother, who was now as demanding in her invalidism as her husband had been in his alcoholism. Robert was furious at being deprived of an evening with his friends to dance attendance on the burdensome oldest and youngest members of his family. Tom was surprised when his brother snapped off the television early and angrily announced that everyone was going to bed early. Tom was shocked almost senseless when he and Robert got into bed. Robert pulled down Tom's undershorts, stretched out on his back, and hissed, "You and that old bitch ruined my night, and now you're going to make up for it. Here—take my cock in your mouth!"

Tom was shaking from head to foot, as if he'd just been shoved into an alien, freezing world; at the same time he was in a state of exquisite sensual excitement. He tried to collect himself and respond. Robert gazed at the ceiling in a trance of self-gratification while he unemotionally but authoritatively instructed Tom in performing his new duties. Tom was transfixed by his bother's large, throbbing erection and by this incredible new activity. Suddenly, as his brother's arched, reddened body strained in orgasm, Tom realized that he was now in total control.

In the nights that followed, Tom turned to this new way of being instantly wanted, with or without his brother's prompting. He felt his own identity begin to emerge from the muddle of his reactions to a family who had emotionally serviced him without ever providing sources of consistent identification. He could stop wondering if he was like one sister or another, like his mother, his father, or his grandmother. He concentrated his unformed identity on his brother's nude body and on the feelings of jealousy, admiration, attachment, and consciously forbidden erotic excitement it aroused in him. He now felt that lying next to his brother in bed for so many years had made him want to be most like him. He didn't know that these new nights were destroying that possibility.

Every night Tom's brother was forced to stay home with him, he initiated Tom into new tricks of gratification. He insisted on every form of service but one: he never forced Tom to be entered anally. Despite Tom's manual and oral control of his brother, the ultimate control of their pleasure-power game remained Robert's refusal to submit to Tom's own need to be serviced. Tom was permitted to be pleased only by passively pleasing. The one time he tried to reverse their roles, Robert raged at him. "What do you think I am? Some kind of a fag or something?"

Tom's twisted but growing love for his brother was reduced to an unholy bargain. Tom spent the day after each of their sweaty pain-and-pleasure nights trying to obliterate the memory of it. Each day he feared becoming more feminized, but each night he planned against the time his brother might never again find new ways to artfully arrange his hand or mouth. Tom also lived with the numbing fear of discovery. As the brothers became hooked to each other, Robert constantly protected his own masculinity by threatening Tom with exposure.

Tom, though, realized that his brother could live without what he could not. He became obsessed with possessing in his brother what he did not feel in himself. He wanted to be a man. But Robert sensed that Tom was beginning to devour him and began to viciously reject his overtures by insisting that Tom would "become a fag for life" if he let him "keep that stuff up."

In the face of these threats and rejections, Tom began to experience panic and feelings of unreality. He wanted to vanish from the world, as he felt people had always disappeared from his life. He began to internalize his erotic world, submitting to others in fantasies that consumed much of his days and nights. He totally sexualized his mind and body. For the first time, he was feelilng the excess that controlled him.

At school Tom felt rejected; actually, he was making himself a loner. His grades deteriorated. He became tense and began losing weight. His mind was consumed by memories of what he had done with Robert and by erotic daydreams about boys to whom he was now becoming attracted.

One day he was slowly wandering home from school, wishing he would never have to return. He had been the last one chosen for baseball that day; it had unsettled him so much that he'd missed three easy catches and lost the game for his team. He began to cut across an empty lot and glanced at a little shack in one corner of it, wishing it could disappear there to hide forever. Then he realized it was the place his brother and the other older boys used for turning on and other activities from which he was always excluded. As if in one of his dreams, he saw the door open. Suddenly a boy stuck his head out and called to him.

"Wanna drag?"

Tom felt so neglected and emotionally impoverished that his first instinct was to refuse, but he hesitantly said yes and slowly walked toward this longed-for invitation. When he was inside the shack, in the darkness, all he could hear was smothered laughter and a taunting voice saying, ''Your brother says you give the best blow job in town, so get to work, kid!''

The next hour of Tom's life powerfully imprinted on him the experience of mingled terror and pleasure in being primitively wanted and taken. He was quickly stripped and surrounded by flesh eagerly wanting to be wanted. He submitted to the excitement of a roomful of adolescent sexuality, and it multiplied tenfold the impact of his previous experiences.

The shack incident quickly got back to his brother, who was panicked at what he had unleashed in Tom. He was also afraid that the story might be bandied about the school and get back to the family. Tom stayed calm in the face of Robert's outrage, because he felt that his attackers had become involved with him in a way they had never before experienced or expected. He had artfully brought each of them to such excitement that they had wanted him again when it was over. This submission of theirs would keep them silent. They had not expected to find themselves seduced.

Robert began to be frightened about himself, and from that time on rejected Tom completely. He told Tom that if he ever touched any man again, he would tell the family, and they'd send him away to ''the booby hatch.''

Tom felt as if part of his life had been amputated. He withdrew even more and masturbated daily, reliving his activities with his brother and in the shack. He covertly watched handsome boys, hid himself in the showers at school, tried to avoid gym class, and felt more and more separated from his family.

His loss of weight, agitated look, and air of helplessness again aroused his sisters' protective interest, and the slight simmer of seductiveness beneath his depressed behavior made them start taking him around with them. They even encouraged their friends to make a fuss over him. This brief surge of attention revitalized Tom a bit; but his parents were becoming frightened by his withdrawn, sullen behavior. They hit on the idea of sending him to the Boy Scout camp his brother had attended several summers before. Tom had always managed to evade camp by offers of what turned out to be rather half-hearted work in his parents' stores. This time his brother, eager to have him out of the way, assured his parents that Tom would be sure to pull out of it if he went to camp and got in with the bunch of guys, nice but fairly tough, who went there. They would teach him how to stand up to things and really ''take it.''

Robert's descriptions of the rough kids seduced Tom into agreeing to go. They stimulated vague, repressed dreams of the shack incident and made him feel that the challenge of the summer would lie in his mouth and loins and not in his muscles and fists. This unconscious yearning to test himself again in the game of sexual power led him into another crippling experience.

From the moment Tom arrived at camp, he made the jocks and hoods the major figures in his elaborate erotic fantasy life. This was the first time Tom lived among the embodiments of maleness and muscularity on which he had centered his masturbatory rituals for months. In his fantasies, each served as a victim of his sexual power, and he of theirs. But in reality, Tom felt trapped in his own eroticism, with no way to release it. He spent frightened nights under his blanket, an arm's length away from the boy in the next bunk. The damming up of his compulsion for orgasm, and his realization that there was no one with whom he could safely make contact, made him withdraw deeper into constant erotic fantasies.

The four ringleaders in Tom's cabin epitomized the maleness he desired. His behavior toward them alternated between submissive seductiveness and further withdrawal. Eventually his look of constant sexual hunger became evident to even the most naive boys in the cabin.

Tom's fantasies focused increasingly on Josh, the young "stud" who led the group. Josh returned Tom's attention with constant baiting and teasing. He was a more tantalizingly dominant and better endowed version of Tom's brother, and he brought Tom's preoccupation with the size of his own penis to an obsessive pitch. He seized every opportunity to compare his own organ with everyone else's. In the shower, every furtive glance brought Tom a despairing moment of truth as he checked out the glistening bodies around him. Each one seemed more virile than he could ever hope to be, and after each look he turned his own body farther into a corner to hide his inadequacy.

He slowly began to feel he'd perfected his secret peeking enough to concentrate on the chief object of his desires, first taking in Josh's whole body, then focusing on the penis he wanted to have so much in one way or another. Tom's tormentor was well aware he was being had visually. One day Josh caught Tom staring in an unguarded daze. Then he and three friends silently motioned the smaller boys out of the shower room, and the four of them circled slowly around Tom as if they knew they were arranging themselves for their parts in his fantasy—but not knowing who would be victim and who victor.

They opened their attack with a rapid-fire stream of put-downs about Tom's penis in its cold, frightened state. They began to shout: "Tiny Tom." "Just a little Twiggy." "Teeny Tom's teeny peeny." "Ain't big enough for a knot hole."

Then the ringleader began to bring Tom's fantasy to life. He grabbed Tom's hand, forced it down around his own penis, and said he had two minutes to bring him off or he'd have to suck it until he came. His brutal wanting made Tom know how to satisfy him. He grabbed some soap and worked away at the boy's penis as though no other part of his tormentor's body existed. In this moment of detached reality, he suddenly found himself uncontrollably erect and came seconds before his victor. He smiled at Josh, filled with a surge of conquest, feeling they were brothers under the skin.

Sensing the switch, the boy suddenly threw Tom against the wall and screamed, "You cunt, you! You're nothing but a fag."

The next day, in and out of the showers, Tom was the object of snickers from the bunk's smaller members. Each one, protecting his own position in the pecking order and elated at having escaped his hidden fears, called softly after him, ''Twiggy.'' ''Tiny Tom.'' ''Teeny Tommy teeny peeny.''

The camp director had to call Tom's parents and ask them to come for him that night. They were never able to find out from their silent, red-eyed son what had happened. But his brother heard a garbled story about Tom having been teased in the shower and angrily complained that Tom was getting so soft and spoiled that even the kids at camp were too much for him.

As a result, Tom went into total retreat at home, closing the door of his room and sealing off his mind from his parents' concerned questions. He became so deeply depressed that he could find relief only in continued sexual fantasy and the daily masturbatory rituals that accompanied them. He slept all day, refused to come out for meals, and wandered through the house only late at night. After a week of this, his parents demanded that he start making deliveries for one of their stores. He agreed to these chores because he was starting to feel a craving for people and for the seductive conquest that had surfaced in his fantasy life.

Tom discovered that on his delivery rounds he could usually find a ''fix.'' There were certain eager customers with whom he felt a wordless but deep and instant bond. He sensed that their feverish grab for his deliveries rose from the same frantic pressure that made him grab the part of himself that now demanded relief two or three times a day. And those who needed his service most often and urgently could be counted on to transfuse his ego with the recognitin of his attractiveness he craved so badly. Once he was invited in by a disheveled but beautiful woman in her thirties, and once by an older man who had come to the door with his bathrobe untied to reveal genitals so huge that Tom could barely hand over his package. Their yearning eyes held him at the threshold of an unbearable decision; but each time he turned away, speechless and terrified by his excitement and fear of being destroyed. These two episodes were rich material for hours of erotic dreams.

These two episodes and the few other emotional scraps Tom scavenged during the rest of that summer could not sustain his ego, let alone repair the damage it had suffered at camp. He dreaded returning to school to face his peers, and he felt too drained to ferret out a new ''victim'' who could weave together the frayed fibers of his masculinity. Yet he found just such a person the first day of school. As he shouldered his way through the crowd going into English class, his eyes lit on the teacher, hiding her lumpy, awkward body behind her desk. Her pockmarked skin reddened. Tom's face remained impassive as his eyes stripped away the fragile mask of her authority. In that moment, each recognized that the other had an impoverished life, but they could supply each other with what they needed for their flourishing fantasies.

Miss McGhee was in charge of the drama club, and each year had to round up students for parts in the required Shakespeare productions. She found that Tom could not only fulfill her fantasies but was the ideally beautiful, narcissistic lead for her plays. She became so devoted to Tom that by the end of the year his ego was replenished and bitten by the bug of applause. He'd begun to do body-building exercises and was regaining lost weight. He turned in physically appealing but artistically dull performances and failed two courses. His protectress kept him out of trouble by groveling before his other teachers and admitting she had had him excused from too many classes.

For the next two years, Tom's energies at school were divided between going on the stage for every moment of attention he could find there and studying just enough to earn passing grades. Quickly he became adept at cheating; although he was caught twice, and his parents were called in to the school, his protectress again stepped in and rescued him from serious consequences.

Miss McGhee became Tom's substitute mother. She agreed to tutor him, and the late afternoons and evenings she devoted to coaching him out of his failures sealed the bond between them. As Tom's mind and body filled out, the attraction between them took on a new dimension and became deeply rooted in his fantasy life. Before, his fantasies contained shifting images of his brother, the shack, and the shower at camp; now these were being replaced by his teacher. Often he imagined stripping her and throwing her sprawling across his bed, a helpless yielding mound of flesh that he would caress until it moaned and pleaded to be mounted. At the moment of his orgasm he felt only the exquisite pleasure of his own flesh, unimpeded by any sense of the body in which he imagined plunging himself. He developed new masturbatory rituals to accompany it. Sometimes he stood in front of his full-length mirror wearing only his jock strap and became aroused by watching the swell of his own excitement. When he tore off this last restraint, he became even more excited by his fully revealed erection, which he would then lubricate and massage until semen spurted onto the image in the mirror.

On days when Tom felt ignored, had failed at something, or had successfully cheated, he began to think that people could sense the secret dramas he played out with his prized physique. His fantasies invaded more and more of his life, until his flights into masturbatory rituals became an anesthetic for the guilt and depression they caused. As this fantasy world expanded, much of his real world closed down. To enhance his mirror image, he cut an ad out of a comic magazine and sent away for a course that promised to strengthen his pectorals, biceps, and gluteus maximus. He also sent away for more and more male magazines, which gave him an increasingly exciting progression of photographic images of what he yearned to become. Finally he started acquiring magazines showing athletic young men in seductive postures. These jock-strapped, G-stringed, phallic men were intended to seduce rather than to shape a boy's emerging male identity. Tom kept this hoard of homoerotic images hidden in his room.

As junior high school came to an end, Tom's fantasies shifted from his teacher to images of being protected by or beind tied down and taken by these men with bulging phalluses. His interest in acting under Miss McGhee's direction was replaced by the isolation and relaxation of going to the movies. He avoided his peers by sneaking away to neighborhood movies at every possible opportunity; sometimes he maneuvered his parents into forcing Robert to let him go along to more exciting Broadway movie houses. It was on one of these expeditions that he found a chance to escape from the cage of his fantasies and touch the reality he had been craving.

The show was a double feature filled with erotic aggression. But Tom's brother, angry at having to spend the afternoon with him, got up abruptly at the end of the first film and said he'd meet him outside when the show was over. Tom realized, as his brother left, that he'd had an erection for quite a while. As the lights went up for intermission, he stumbled dazedly down the aisle, suddenly desperate to masturbate. When he walked into the shabby, wine-smelling men's room, the first thing he saw was a tall, thick-necked, broad-shouldered young man standing with his back to him, displaying tightly clad and tightly clenched buttocks that seemed to be straining toward the same pleasure Tom was seeking. Tom was drawn to this figure as relentlessly as he had been drawn into his masturbatory fantasies, until he was standing beside him.

As in a recreation of the past, Tom felt his hand being pulled over and placed on what seemed to be the biggest erection he'd ever seen or imagined. Tom felt a pulsation throughout his own body, as if it had become suffused with the young man's power and energy. He wanted more, and the young man knew it when he saw how hungrily Tom stared at his phallus. Tom felt another hand on the nape of his neck, slowly and inexorably pushing him downward to incorporate this loved image. Tom's mouth was trembling and numb, but as he slowly, greedily engulfed this detached maleness, a sense of mastery almost washed away his flashes of panic. Then suddenly a tremor of his body made him realize that the rest of a human being was standing over him, alive and ready, and he withdrew, overwhelmed with the need to flee from danger.

He fled back to his seat, dizzy, heart pounding, grateful that the lights were dimming for the next feature. He was determined to wipe this new, terrifying reality from his mind. He managed to immerse himself in the film and make his mind as flat as the images on the screen.

After this ''coming out,'' Tom's high-school years were divided between utterly different worlds. In one he constantly tried to compensate for his growing frustration over failure to find ego nourishment in the other. His search sent him on unreal trips to public toilets, to wrap himself around any maleness he could find. It sent him ferreting out pornography in candy stores, downtown sex shops, movie houses that admitted him because he looked older than his years, and the pickups who took him home and turned him on by telling him every detail of their sexual experiences. He kept becoming more deeply immersed in the city's homoerotic underbelly with a momentum that allowed him no introspection, no recognition that the other world was being swept almost out of his mind.

That other world was a facade thrown up simply for survival; it grew flimsier and glossier every day. Defensively he acted seductive with girls and older women, but never all the way. His homosexual life and images had crowded out the possibility of anything more, and he feared that he might never be able to return to women. He fell into a series of paranoid panics, terrified that he would be lost in a world whose conversations, conventions, and identities seemed to him, at his deepest levels, alien, perhaps life-destroying. The slightest encounter with an aggressive, sensual, and predatory woman would profoundly depress him. And he was terrified that he might choose the wrong victim for one of his pseudoseductions, someone who would call his bluff, see it was impossible for him to follow through, and watch him turn on himself and destroy himself.

When he was at home, he fought with his parents constantly. They wanted him to spend his weekends and most of his other free time making deliveries for them. When they did pressure him into working, he took longer and longer to return to the store after each delivery. His trips to and from the store had become compulsive forays; he got off the subway at each stop, seeking a ''john'' whose phallus he could take into his mouth in the men's room, as though by controlling each one he could wipe out his ultimate destination. And thus he blotted out his parents' work demands, even let the entire family slip from his consciousness—except for those moments when he still needed them to feed some neglected part of his consuming narcissism. Tom's underlying rage never abated and was never recognized; and he was never satisfied in his search for other men's orgasms and never thought of seeking his own with them.

His failures at school were inevitable because of the ravenous appetite for admiration that demanded so much of his time, making him work on everyone to feed his addictive ego. He found his greatest nourishment in slightly older homosexuals and much older women. He felt most sated after he had teased or excited one of them to the edge of his control and then suddenly signaled or said, ''Look at me, love me, but don't touch me.'' But after these indiscriminate and sadistically tantalizing seductions, the inner emptiness returned; it drove him deeper into fantasies that brought him dangerously close to the submissive feelings he thought of as being truly homosexual, so again he went seeking their homoerotic embodiments. He felt as if he were searching for some ultimate trial by fire that would release him from the need for his journey into homoeroticism. And unconsciously he knew that he did not have much further to go.

Some of his recent pickups had almost completely destroyed him by trying to enter the last clenched, unviolated part of his body. The most recent and most persuasive of these was a mirror image of Tom's own beauty, but endowed with even greater seductive skills. They had met in a steamy, anonymous cafeteria and sat talking for over an hour, connecting because this man's story was Tom's story. He was older and had traveled further, had struggled with his own enormous problems, and was emerging from them. He was capable of a tenderness that made Tom realize for the first time that one of the endless string of partners whom he had made fantasy ideals had become a person. This man made Tom feel that he wanted not to use, abuse, or control him, but only to be with him, touch him, love him, and above all, listen and talk to him. The man knew who he was and what he wanted, and in every way except one seemed completely male. He confessed to Tom that he could not enter a woman, but more than anything he wanted to some day and knew that he would.

Filled with the warmth of the late afternoon of talk, Tom agreed to go to the man's room. He never forgot their long, affectionate embraces and allowing himself to be kissed for the first time. The slow hours of sensuality relaxed his fears of utterly losing his masculinity. He had the illusory but exciting feeling that he'd finally discovered the love image that had always stood in his mirror, unsatisfied and icy and flat. He was in a sweat of unconscious surrender when the man suddenly turned him on his stomach. Tom felt the warm, strong pressure of another body on top of his own, lips on the nape of his neck, arms circling his waist, and then the pressure of a phallus trying to enter him. His mind and body leaped awake. He rolled over quickly, dressed in frantic haste, sped trembling home, and fell exhausted on his bed.

After this incident, Tom reacted to his strong but unconscious fear of becoming some man's mutual lover—or, worse still, feeling womanized—by swinging back and forth between sexual pain and pleasure. To compensate for his fear and to rid himself of his unrecognized rage, he had to reject the possibility of ever again submitting to love—the love he'd known the first few years of his life, lost, and never regained. Now he had to become the predator. He became a chicken hawk, watching the youngsters in his neighborhood with the swift intuition of a bird of prey and seducing the vulnerable. The preyed-on youth would often be frightened, but unfailingly was controlled by Tom's skillful mouth and artful hand. Each time Tom scored, his tension and anger were relieved and his ego sated. But whenever he failed in anything, he was too shaken by his impotence and unconscious rage to bring out a new victim; he would orally rape the most submissive of his chickens.

His new role rekindled some of his old guilts and fears of exposure. He had to compensate by a compulsive return to subway toilets, where he lurked until he was orally raped. This brought him lower still. To console himself for his humiliation and shore up his still shaky image as a predator, he returned to the porno world hidden in his room. He began to send away for the leather trappings of the sadomasochistic cult. He used each new studded, grommeted, chained leather outfit to enhance his mirror image in his masturbatory rituals. He brought himself to more and more frenetic peaks as he made himself erect with his new ersatz supermale image. This image became mixed with his chicken-hawking; he had fantasies of newly discovered boys being forced into submission by his erection and his devouring mouth.

Since his descent into these new and precariously juggled worlds, women had almost faded from his fantasies, yet he sensed that if he were ever to escape his growing, obsessive entrapment, he would have to get back to the days when he could imagine subduing and mounting a woman. Now the only heterosexual image he could summon up was of a powerful, faceless woman who would tie him down and take him over.

He was beginning to find that his facade of gregariousness and charm, his genius for attracting adulation, was becoming as tenuous as his old fantasies of women. Because of his strong physical impact and practiced, casual seductiveness, he had always found it easy to come on strong with girls at school and make up convincing stories of conquests for the boys. But now he seemed to lack the energy or concentration enough to focus on this part of his life. As the hungry challenge in his eyes was being replaced by detachment, classmates met his come-ons and stories with joking disbelief. His paranoia translated this into a serious threat to his masculine facade. What would normally be his real world—family, work, school—became so castrating, failure-ridden, and unreal that he launched himself on the darkest, strongest stream in his life.

For a month he had been dressing up in various combinations of his new leather ego, going to Greenwich Village, walking around, and letting anyone who looked butch cruise him. He refused to be picked up, but got his excitement by turning people on and then abruptly turning them off with a cool ''look but don't touch'' reaction. The tougher someone looked, the better Tom liked it. He felt almost orgasmic pleasure if someone made a direct pass so that he could counter with ''Get lost!'' or ''Fuck off!'' or, if he felt safe enough, ''Go find yourself a fag!'' He felt as if the rough voice he used was another person speaking, the sadist he thought might emerge from the castrated masochist he thought himself to be. It was the voice of the rage he denied and which had to emerge in some way.

He had sent away through one of his porno magazines for a copy of *The Gay Life Guide*, a directory of homosexual movie houses, baths, parks, cruising grounds and, most important to Tom, a rundown on the specialty bar scene. He'd heard tales about these from some of his pickups, but the thought of them had only driven him to his usual fearful distraction and elaborate masturbatory rituals. But from his guide he learned the locations of the leather places, and driven by his compulsive urge to transform his fantasies into reality, he gathered courage for this final, dangerous descent.

Tom would dress up in his tightest faded jeans, thinnest body shirt, thickest leather belt, and the heavy leather boots he'd saved so long to get. As he located and entered each bar, he felt that this might be the place that would put him in touch with his most exciting and dangerous fantasies, but his fear would make things seem dreamlike as he walked the length of the bar. Only his awareness of the excitement he created with his young body, the cool blond face that floated in so many people's fantasies, the perfect balance of cruelty and innocence ambiguous enough to excite both victor and victim—only the quest for this ego nourishment gave him the courage to walk in aloof and apparently calm, pass in and out untouched, and then, safely back on the street driven to flee blindly to the next place.

He soon became confident enough to enter, quickly assess any touch of fraudulent masculinity in the hungry eyes of those who cruised his well-packaged virility. He immediately sensed the local pecking order and was able to ferret out the most aggressive males. He found that every bar had its own character. He checked out each one not knowing if he looked simply for the one that held the most danger or which one seemed to hold the exact image of masculinity he had to have. After several days of teasing and torturing himself with his carefully chosen ego-ideals and his "look but don't touch" routine, he settled on one bar.

This bar seemed always crowded, had the largest number of "straights," and was filled with Greek and French sailors and merchant seamen. Tom knew that because of his youthful virility he was a prized kind of prey. He was also quite aware of one man who was always there, standing beneath an overhead light near the end of the bar. He had a square jaw, deep-set eyes, a football player's body, and a sinister overlay of the gangster. His powerful body was always in the same faded denim, and a bunch of keys dangled from his belt, signaling his membership in this dark cult. He had spotted Tom on his first visit, with a look that searched and impaled him, and Tom knew that this was what kept drawing him back. He watched this man, who always stood in the thickest part of the crowd, yet apart from it, seeming to direct the action that moved so swiftly and tensely around him. The area where he stood seemed impenetrably dark and densely packed, and he seemed to be testing, choosing who would be allowed to enter there rather than remain at the front bar.

The day Mrs. Powers, Tom's academic counselor, called him in to discuss his failing grades, Tom rushed straight from school to the bar. He caught and held the man's eye longer than usual and, as if mesmerized, began elbowing his way to the far end of the bar. Dimly he wondered why it was so crowded, since this was the middle of the afternoon, but there was a heavy rain outside, and it was the Friday before Labor Day. As he shoved through the crowd, someone groped him so hard that he winced with pain, but he never took his eyes from his goal—the rock-like man who stood in this river of humanity and guided it into streams and eddies toward the dark pool behind him. Tom was afraid that this man could provide him with the final test he sought. When he presented himself, would he put the man in his place, get his "fix" that way, and leave? Could he lure him out of the dangerous current he controlled and make him his prey?

Tom stepped up to deliver his ultimate tease, but the man gave him a hard stare and said:

"You've come in here asking for it three nights in a row, kid, and I've got it for you right here."

Tom was so confused and panicky that he hardly felt the blood rush to his crotch, the erection that was so revealing to this hawk for whom he had become a chicken. He was trying to figure out what the man meant, what he had for him, and where "right here" was.

Suddenly Tom was shoved forward. The crowd in the dark back room parted to admit him, and he was submerged in a sea of flesh, heat, and sweaty smells. His last clear image was of the man's face as Tom glanced around in panic, wanting to be assured, and saw a cruel smile that told him this was the hawk that would make him a chicken. The man's powerful arms gripped his waist, locked him in a totally defenseless, exposed position. As he struggled to escape, something wet and hard thrust painfully into his anus and worked relentlessly in and out, controlling him completely no matter how hard he tried to eject it. All his fantasies of being so brutally wanted fled as this force pumped away, ignoring anything but its own satisfaction, forcing his submission. He twisted loose with a last desperate movement, felt semen all over his backside as he was pushed to the floor, and heard:

"Now you got what you came looking for, kid. Come back tomorrow and you'll get to like it better."

Tom picked himself up in a daze, jerked his jeans up over his sticky body, fumbled his belt closed with shaking fingers, and elbowed his way to the door on reflex alone. He was shaken with sorrow and pain deeper than anything he had ever felt. All his sexual fantasy and experience seemed to have rushed together, pushing him to this rock bottom where the last shreds of his masculinity were ripped off. As he stumbled into the heavy rain, his mind desperately tried to spin free of the assault and his part in inviting it. As the rain poured over him, he hoped it would wash away this last stop on his long and greedy search to incorporate the ultimate in masculinity.

Dazed, he headed toward the brightest lights, hoping they would lead him to a subway for home. He remembered that his mother had wheedled his father into letting someone else tend the stores tonight so they could have a "nice dinner," and had begged Tom to give up his elusive comings and goings for once, so they could all sit together like real family. Tom had no idea what time it was; his hidden life was timeless. He realized he'd lost his sense of direction, because he'd headed away from Tenth Avenue and was standing right at the edge of the West Side Highway.

Exhausted and near tears, he leaned against the low concrete wall. The sudden squeal of brakes and crash of metal made him flatten against it in terror as a black Mercedes skidded up over the curb like some final engine of destruction. The headlight smashed against the concrete inches from his leg, and one hubcap rocketed off and rolled away into the darkness. A tall, well-dressed man rushed out of the car and over to Tom, who was pressed against the wall, drenched, pale, and near fainting from this final terror. The man asked him if he was all right, and Tom felt a strong warm hand on his shoulder. He looked up into a face so concerned that it seemed to defuse all his terror and bring him back to reality. The man had a handsome face, clear blue eyes, and high cheekbones, and he wore very expensive clothes. Tom smiled a little shakily and said:

"I'm okay. What about you?"

The man explained that he'd felt one of his tires going flat and, afraid of the slippery highway, had swerved toward the edge and lost control of the car.

"I'm glad you aren't hurt," he said. "I guess we're both lucky to be alive. I wonder if I can find a phone or some way to get help. All the garages around here are closed. Maybe if I went into one of those bars. . .they seem to be the only places open."

In a flash of paranoia, Tom said, "Oh, no, don't do that. I can help you with the tire."

"I'd really appreciate that, and then I'll be glad to give you a lift somewhere. You shouldn't be in this area at night. It really isn't safe."

They struggled together in the cold downpour to put on the new tire and finally climbed into the car. They were both soaked. They stared at each other from their different worlds, and the man said with concern:

"You're drenched. I changed clothes at my office, so I have a dry shirt in the back seat. You can have that to wear home, and some time you can send it back to me."

Tom completely misinterpreted the man's intentions as he watched him fish a shirt out from beneath a huge pile of papers and folders in the back seat. He felt a warning flash of contempt that launched him on a quest to repair his lacerated ego. This man, he thought, must be one of the married Wall Street closet queens he'd heard about, and calculated how to use him to shoot from the bottom to the top again.

When the man had retrieved the shirt and turned to Tom, he was surprised to see that the pale, pathetic, frightened boy now seemed to flush and expand with something. The clothing, which had been plastered to him by the rain, now seemed as it dried to be tailored curiously tight. And he had never seen such a wide, elaborate leather belt.

When Tom saw the man studying him curiously, he was sure he had more on his mind than shirts, and proceeded to take his off. Carefully watching his host's face, he caught a flicker of admiration for his physique. The man commented, "Looks like you really work at keeping in shape. Do you work out?" Tom spread his legs and pressed hard against the man's thigh. He was surprised when the expected grab was not on his crotch but on his arm.

"Look, son, I think you have a problem."

Tom didn't know what to do next. The man had not moved his leg away, but his voice had a convincing, fatherly tone. Tom assumed a sad expression and, making another try to smoke the man out, said, "I do have a problem. I know it. You're my problem." And he gave the man his most appealing grin.

The man seemed stunned, and Tom thought he had broken his facade. But there was no response, so finally he dropped his hand and moved his leg away. Tom realized that he would not find his sexual fix in this dark car. He said dully, "Just leave me at the nearest BMT station," and began to struggle into his tight, wet shirt.

The man pleaded with him to take his dry shirt. "Please, take it. You can keep it. Really, I'm sorry about what I said, but. . .it's just that that's not something I know about. . .maybe you could concentrate on some real work and keep your mind off things like that."

Tom's face turned stiff and red with fury. He had listened all his life to such talk from his hard-working, disorganized, demanding family. But he knew he had reached the man somehow, opened him up a little; he would prove it some time soon. He looked the man in the eyes with his most seductive, sincere, and yearning look and said:

"You know, you're right, and I will borrow your shirt. I'd like to talk to you. Maybe we could meet somewhere when I return it. I've never had anyone to talk to about my problem. You're the first person I've ever told. Would you meet me again?"

The man said, "Son, I'm no psychiatrist, and my work keeps me very busy, but I'll try to help you. Now let me give you some money for a cab home. Your family must be wondering where you are."

Tom stuffed the five dollars in his pocket and automatically headed for the subway. On the way home, in a fever of frustration, he got off at two stations and tried to get blown in the toilets. But for the first time in his life, he found himself homosexually impotent. He rode the rest of the way home fighting off fantasies of his old dominating teacher and of the man's voice saying, "You really have a problem." He went inside to the family dinner feeling emotionally bankrupt, flattened, and trapped, with a ravenous ego he couldn't satisfy as he had in the past seven years. All his sources had dried up. He had to find new ways to feed himself, to connect with new kinds of people, if he were not to wither and die inside. Through a strange set of coincidences, he ended up at the clinic, had my name on a piece of paper, and had been told by Neil about my homosexual group. Life might not be so bad for him if he, too, went for therapy.

Tom did go for treatment, and stayed in the group for six months. He was helped to understand his addictive sexual patterns and realized that he could not tolerate or survive addictive homosexual sex. He left the group with many ambivalences about whether he would live as a heterosexual, a bisexual, or a closet homosexual. He told the group that he didn't want to come back because he had a night job, and that becoming independent of his family was the most important thing in his life. He had also begun dating a girl with whom he had a number of satisfying sexual contacts. He admitted to the group that he was still attracted to strong men and might allow himself to "get a blow job when I need one." His last words to the group showed some insight, and indicated a good prognosis. "So long, losers. I'll be back if I get hooked again. I hope you're able to split too. . .and that you aren't here if I have to hit the Doc for another group fix."

ANALYSIS

Tom's taped monologues constantly revealed his addictiveness. His hours of memories and free associations were saturated with sexuality; in fact, almost every action, feeling, fantasy, and impulse was sexualized. He was compulsively driven to one form or another of sexual interaction with the world around him. Even his language had become highly eroticized. He had reached the point of coping with every pressure, conflict, failure, insecurity, anxiety, or depressive reaction, by turning to a sexual act or fantasy.

His excesses in sexual thought and behavior had begun impulsively, were escalated and elaborated in early adolescence, and through late adolescence consumed him. Although he could still maintain a variety of defensive facades, he finally failed in his attempts to deny the degree of his addiction.

When not involved in his addiction, Tom developed many withdrawal symptoms, such as depersonalization, depression, panic, acute anxiety, and somatic complaints. He often had hangover responses—guilt, fear, paranoia, a feeling that every sexual experience was empty and devitalizing, and therefore he had to pursue increasingly intense and kinky sexual highs. His appetite for sex became insatiable. At the end of his monologue, it was clear that he would soon become vulnerable to alcohol and drugs as attempts to cope addictively with the increasing pressures of his life.

Throughout his life, Tom had a high degree of anxiety and frequent periods of depression. These were always related to his feelings of alienation, isolation, and rejection by his family and peers. He even felt rejected by homosexuals because of his contemptuous behavior toward them. His loneliness, fear, guilt, and rebelliousness provoked paranoid thinking and episodes of panic and depersonalization until he worried that he might be losing his mind. He became incapable of coping with failure and continuously fought the profound social and erotic passivity that kept him from taking effective action or sustaining work. Excessively dependent, preoccupied with himself, and unable to deal well with his aggressiveness, Tom could not properly assess his own worth.

There were periods when Tom lost track of time because of his involvement in pursuing addictive sex. This resulted in truancies and failures at schoolwork. He had begun to live more at night and in his fantasies than in daytime reality. Tom often withdrew for long periods into movies, bars, and lavatories—the world of the sexually addicted. He disregarded psychological and even physical dangers in his search for relief from the pain of lacking a secure identity or life style. A sense of being no one is a threat to any person's sanity, and living in a no-man's land between heterosexual and homosexual society provoked Tom's severest symptoms of anomie.

Many sources of Tom's addictiveness are clear. He was born with extraordinary physical endowment. His family first reacted by oversaturating him with sensual and emotional stimuli. Then his parents suddenly withdrew into their work; he experienced similar engulfment and then withdrawal with his inconsistent and destructive brother, sisters, and grandmother.

Tom became sexually addicted as a way of coping with a series of deeply traumatic rejections and abandonments to anesthetize the pain of feeling isolated from every member of his family. The deepest roots of his pain were in the shift of his grandmother's (mother surrogate) initial devotion, love, and overprotection to neglect and anger. Her reversal occured because of her age, infirmities, and having spent too many years of her own life as the addictive complement to her alcoholic husband. Soon after this, Tom was exposed to his brother's exploitive and premature arousal of his eroticism, which was to fixate his use of sexual seduction as an addictive coping mechanism. His brother Robert also shifted from aggressively demanding that Tom service him erotically to a brutalizing rejection. Robert made a final assault on Tom's ego when, in order to protect his own masculinity, he exposed Tom and accused him of becoming a fag. These assaults were compounded by his sisters' going from solicitous love to exploitation and then to rejection, because Tom rebelled against serving them and being femminized by their demands that he do their chores. Not the least of all the rejections was Tom's loss of both parents to their own workaholic patterns at the liquor store.

Hence, the most damaging causes of his addiction occured because his grandmother, brother, and sisters first sated his hunger for acceptance and admiration and fostered his narcissism; then, just as suddenly, they rejected him and shifted to feminizing exploitations to fill their own selfish needs. Finally they abandoned him. Tom's feminization by his family was followed by similar treatment from his peers, who inflicted on him a series of physical and psychological rapes. These set in motion serious gender and erotic conflicts.

Tom could not resolve these conflicts. His sexual addiction had him shifting between homosexuality and heterosexuality. In both fantasy and real life he shifted between passive and active sexuality, trying to resolve his sexual identity. Soon he began using sex to resolve other problems, such as his low self-esteem, inability to cope with authority, isolation from peers, and any work demand. In violently reacting against work, he had become an addictive complement to his work-addicted parents. Tom's brother also turned to excesses in heterosexual sex and speed in reaction to the parents' work pattern.

Another major cause of Tom's addiction was the increasing immersion of his mind and body in sexual media, paraphernalia, milieus, and practices. He moved from soft-core to hard-core pornography, public urinals, bars, parks, restaurants, and truck docks and travel stations where sadomasochists cruised. His addictive life was fueled and then made autonomous by these centers of addictive homosexuality.

Tom's addictiveness became both chronic and acute. His alienation made him feel isolated, and his depersonalized feelings provoked his paranoia. When sex eventually gave him no pleasure but only pain, self-loathing, and failures, he hit bottom. He could not make meaningful emotional contact with others and felt driven to further sexual excesses to cope with his alienation from people and from any life he might have aspired to. The absence of a sense of worth and of any firm identity—familial, social, economic, gender, erotic, work, peer—became the deepest, most malignant roots of his addictive process.

From birth, Tom experienced polarized excesses of acceptance and rejection. He learned that through overt or covert seduction he could temporarily win counterfeit love or at least acceptance. His impulsive, insatiable need for acceptance involved a search for dependable parent figures—first within his family, then among teachers and anonymous males. But each conquest of one of these became a defeat and led him to pursue the next victim, who again would vanquish him.

Another major emotional dynamic in Tom's life was his inability to deal with his powerful aggression and the dependent and passive elements of his psyche. His anger at the world increased over the years and finally smoldered steadily just beneath the surface of his addictive sexual behavior. His inner voice constantly raged at others for every trauma to which he had been subjected as a child, and for every new trauma he unknowingly provoked.

Tom acted out his sexual conflict in sadomasochistic fashion. This began with his sexual submission to his brother, continued in his seductions of peers at camp and in his chicken-hawking—and of such defenseless older people and authorities as adult homosexuals, his obese teacher, and an alcoholic tutor. He moved on to tormenting and being tormented by anonymous males in urinals, bars, movies, streets, and their apartments. Finally there was the barroom homoerotic assault on what he felt to be the last vestiges of his male identity.

Tom's encounter with Neil also revealed many of the dynamics of his life. He had just experienced the most painful confrontation he had ever had with his family. They had discovered his homosexuality and addictive paraphernalia and pornography. His humiliation and rage triggered a paranoid flight. Trying to regain some ego strength and acceptance, he made a desperate search for a homosexual fix—and, as it turned out, a narcissistic one. He ran into his ego-ideal in Neil, who looked somewhat like Tom. He tried to seduce and manipulate Neil into a sexual encounter, but Neil was trying to go straight and had joined a Homosexuals Anonymous group. In this group, as in Alcoholics Anonymous, the participants supported each other in changing addictive practices and life styles.

Through the encounter with Neil, Tom got his first insight into the development of another person's addiction. Neil's sexual addiction, like Tom's, was provoked by his parents' obsession with work and money. He turned to homosexual prostitution to rationalize his inability to cope with their absorbing materialism and unattainable standards of performance. But Neil could not satisfy Tom's need for a fix and an addictive model; neither would he collude with him. Worst of all, he acted as an addictive complement—an astringent superego force—when Tom was already contending with more social and family rejections than he could handle.

To remove his anxiety, rage, and enormous loss of self-esteem, Tom fell into an even greater, more frenzied need for homosexual contact; in his desire to establish some sense of control over himself and another person, he chose a sadomasochistic "leather" bar. He was also unconsciously driven to a fantasized tormenting scene with the man who ran the bar, the epitome of his desired male image—to attain his ultimate homosexuasl high by recreating the rape scenes of his past, in which he was totally controlled and in turn attempted to control. But instead of resolving his conflicts with relief and pleasure, as in any addictive process, he crashed. Instead of finding relief, he had a brutalizing confrontation in which he again felt humiliated, rejected, and inferior. His anal rape by the group of men was the ultimate humiliation. The pain, emptiness, and defeat that resulted broke what fight was left in him to hold on to the fragments of ego and masculinity he had clung to so desperately.

The other significant encounter in his life was with Elizabeth. She was collusive and acted as an interlocking addictive agent; her alcoholism was mutually reinforced by his sexual addiction. However, her loving support of his masculinity and affirmation of his ability to engage in coitus was the first optimistic note in his addictive life. Tom knew of Neil's contact with a psychiatrist's self-help group for homosexuals. In a final mixture of defeat, punishment-seeking, and glimmers of hope, he went for help.

Tom's addictive homosexuality emerged in part from his conflict over his sexual orientation; he could not accept homosexuality as a way of life. But even if Tom had been struggling to achieve a homosexual adjustment, he still might have become involved in addictive sex. This does not mean that all homosexual behavior and life-styles are addictive. However, Tom's history does show that it is not easy to enter homosexual society and avoid addictive milieus. The first places homosexuals chance upon or are guided to that offer anonymity, comfort, and peer support are commercial (homosexual bars, baths, movies houses, and discos) or public (cruising neighborhoods, parks, auto rest stops, urinals, transportation stations). Society is often hostile to nonprofit organizations for homosexuals—political, religious, educational, and social homophile groups and homosexual counseling, medical and sex-education organizations—which are the nonaddictive places to "come out" (A term used to describe a non-homosexual's entrance onto the homosexual scene and into homosexual practices.). These more constructive settings receive little economic or social support from the homosexual community and less from public and government agencies. Therefore, the homosexual remains much more vulnerable to addictiveness and its byproducts.

Ignorance and bigotry about homosexuality continue to be rampant, and the public is still polarized on the subject. Because of so much confusion, ambivalence, and lack of information, it is vital to make a distinction between addictive sexuality, both homosexual and heterosexual, and healthy sexuality. I chose to describe a patient whose sex addiction was homosexual because of many homosexuals greater vulnerability to being driven into sexual addictiveness. We live in a homophobic society that inhibits and degrades those who decide to or must adapt to homosexualtiy. Their lives can easily become filled with fear, anxiety, panic, paranoid feelings about exposure, housing, job and social discrimination, and family rejection—all along with the difficulties inherent in establishing a secure homosexual life-style. These pressures produce heightened susceptibility not only to sexual but to alcohol and drug addiction. All too often, during the early stages of adaptation, hedonistic abandon becomes a typical reaction against the pain provoked by so many adversities. Gay pride becomes a protection against the self-devaluation and secretive lives of those trying to survive economically and socially in a culture hostile to anyone who admits they are homosexual.

There is now an effort within homophile organizations and enlightened educational religious, legal, medical, and psychological communities to differentiate viable homosexual life-styles from addictive and asocial homosexual practices. In Los Angeles, a self-help group called *Sexual Compulsives Anonymous,* has formed under the wing of the Metropolitan Community Church. Its program is directred particularly toward those addicted to seeking sex in public rest rooms despite the threat of arrest. In a press release reprinted in *The Advocate*, a national homosexual newspaper, SCA said, ''Sex can be suicide'', and *The Advocate* added, ''At least some sex is.'' The group says it is ''structured to provide a step-by-step program of behavior modification for this and other sexual compulsions. It is constructed to re-gear sex drives to healthier ways that will place emphasis on long term relationships, utilizing the basic tenets of Alcoholics Anonymous-type groups. The goal is to modify sexual behavior to a socially acceptable point.'' This is an example of the kind of help that is emerging for those trapped in the depersonalized excess of addictive homosexual acts which can result in having to face emotional and legal dangers to their love and work relationships and to their physical beings (venereal diseases, herpes, hepatitis).

Our society remains polarized in its attitudes about sex. It still has destructive prohibitions and hypercritical laws and practices that exploit guilt, shame, and fear. One segment of our repressed public stifles the growth of healthy erotica and the dissemination of sex-education, when we need both. This hypocritical censorship guarantees the perpetuation of debased erotica that the sexually addicted use to cope with the pain and emptiness of their sexual lives. Therefore, the billion-dollar pornography business increasingly fuels both the hetero, bisexually, and homosexually addicted. In effect, it clouds awareness of heterosexual sex addiction, which brings damage through divorce, venereal disease, and destructive narcissistic life-styles. In fact, we sometimes admire and reward heterosexual sex addicts and set up such figures as role models from James Bond to the sex playboy. Therefore hetero-sexual sex addiction is less likely to be identified, and the addict is less likely to obtain help.

Tom's history dramatically illustrates this social travesty. Until his therapeutic encounter his insatiable addiction was fed by pornography and public way stations for the sexually addicted. Healthy erotic information outlets and social places were so much less accessible. He received no help in becoming aware of what had been destroying him until his chance meeting with someone engaged in a similar struggle. How different might his life have been in a less paradoxical society.

CHRIS

THE CRISES

Christopher Marshall was tall and compact and moved as if he had a rod up his back. His features were perfectly proportioned and conventionally good-looking, even handsome, yet nondescript. He had deep-brown deadened eyes and fine brown hair that lay flat on his head. He was immaculately groomed, nothing was out of place. He wore a funeral-dark suit with thin stripes, perfectly tailored but outdated, a blue oxford button-down shirt, red necktie, and heavy cordovan shoes that gleamed from years of proper care—every symbol that could instantly identify him as belonging to his class and life style.

Christopher was referred to me by an emergency clinic where he had arrived extremely agitated and complaining of stomach pains and nausea. Questioned about his symptoms, he became still more agitated and said they were caused by an unknown drug he had been tricked into taking. When told he could be treated best by referral to a psychiatrist, he first expressed some resistance; then he said he had experienced psychiatric hospitalization when he was nineteen, after taking a hallucinogenic drug. Finally he agreed to seek help.

When he arrived at my office, lean and rigid and fastidious, he seemed physically remarkable only because his face looked too lined and fatigued for the forty-seven years he had given as his age. He repeatedly assured me that he had never knowingly taken drugs and had no drug history except for the recent episode and one twenty years ago. When I broached the taping of sessions, Christopher was indignant. But as I stressed its medical and social usefulness as a research technique, he suddenly announced that he had some vital information about drugs and corruption in society that he had assembled in the past few days that would be invaluable to the psychiatric

123

profession. He stressed that he needed no help and that I should consider having the tapes played at a "closed professional meeting." He refused the offer of a tranquilizer and launched into one of the most compulsively detailed psychiatric histories ever offered to me by a patient. This account enabled me to reconstruct his past more accurately than any of the other addicts.

Chris constantly justified his elaborate confessional as a contribution to the exposure of corruption in our society, but he sometimes became disorganized by moments of acute anxiety and paranoid anger. I sometimes felt that in his need to elaborate his account, he was going to lose himself in rapture over the depths of his life and talk himself into exhausted collapse. It was obviously difficult for Christopher to discuss his relationship with his wife, children, and friends, his sexual life, or anything that did not relate to his work. He hesitated for long moments before revealing any of his present or past emotional life; he said that even when hospitalized after his breakdown in college he had avoided discussing sex with his doctors.

Although he assured me that he had never revealed himself so completely, I detected no sign that he was gaining much insight into the disordered parts of his life. In describing his play-obsessed sister he allowed himself some hostility, and he did seem to realize that his wife was far more manipulative than he had previously suspected; yet he continually de-emotionalized every aspect of his life, and cut short what may have been his most painful memories by returning to discussions of his career. Only when he talked about business did his voice become emotional and warm. At times his account seemed to verge on paranoid delusion.

After the therapy I never saw or heard from him again.

This whole thing is like a nightmare for me. I went to the clinic yesterday because I wanted treatment for the. . .nausea and stomach pain. When they told me I should accept a psychiatric referral, I almost told them they were the ones who needed that kind of help. Not I! Except I remembered that if you say that kind of thing, it may mean you really are. Now, I can usually handle any sitution pretty rationally, think it out, then act, solve things. . .well, the problems I've uncovered. . .they're something no one could really handle. I say. . .I've seen such things. . .

I know a lot of people think I'm dull. A compulsive worker. . .a square. . .but I've seen things, especially in the last few days. . .I'm beginning to see what's attacking our society at every level. I honestly wonder if people know what's going on. We're crumbling, like ancient Rome. . .I mean, every kind of perversion. I'm here more through a sense of duty than. . .than anything else. I'm not here because I'm sick. The world is sick. People are being corrupted by drugs and pornography and crime. . .and. . .the kind of man I'm going to tell you about. These people have to be exposed! It's the duty of responsible people to help save them.

It's all very, very clear to me now that I shouldn't ever have been in a position to find out. I should have obeyed my instincts. But my colleagues in the office kept pressing and pressing. I didn't have a chance to think the whole thing out. I let myself be persuaded to take this Paul Winkler into the firm. And that's where it began.

Once he was in, he showed he did have the ability to work hard. I've always been the hardest working partner. I'm the one who has to ride the others. It's getting difficult to get people to come up with. . .I mean, to work hard. . .imaginatively. I think all this new so-called leisure thing really just stalls productivity. I always seem to find myself in the position of standing for what everyone else feels he should be doing in life but isn't. Maybe I'm even doing more and doing it better, but I've trained myself to. It may rub people the wrong way sometimes, but I can't throw away my education and twenty years of discipline and hard work just to be popular and keep people from being a little jealous of me. It's just the way I am.

When I think of this man Winkler. . .what he did to destroy everything I stand for in the firm. . .people like him are destroying this country. . .I. . .I. . .ah. . .I could explode! I've never felt anything so deeply. Just thinking about it is. . .making. . .my stomach hurt again. . .whatever drug he gave me, trying to tear down my work. He! He tried so cleverly. I've had to collect all the information thoroughly, run the closest kind of check on his activities to document things. I keep it with me in my briefcase. . .it's here, I brought it. . .which is why I don't want to take anything that would dull my perceptions. I can't afford to lose track of a single thing, not a single idea.

I kept an eye on Winkler from the beginning. He began pretty well, better than I'd expected from someone from his background. He did work hard, with great concentration. I admit it, I even enjoyed working with him. He seemed to have enough extra energy to specialize profitably at business lunches and after hours with other members of the firm and with clients. Now, our comptroller was hired personally by me. He runs a tight ship, lets me know when things are getting out of hand. I don't like this whole expense account thing, on principle. Oh, I know everyone does it, but it's just a shade unbusinesslike. . .unethical.

I should have realized what Winkler was up to right away, but I didn't, because he was getting a lot of work out of the men in the firm he was seeing socially. I'd had trouble in the past with some of them. The usual kind of thing. . .having their secretaries tell their wives they were working late when they were really having extramarital affairs. . .even becoming involved with secretaries. . .right in the office. I have the girls fired, but it keeps on happening.

I was pleased to see more work turned out, but something didn't seem quite right. I noticed it was the men I'd had problems with who were working so hard with Winkler. I was worried. . .about his encouraging members of the firm to get in the habit of just the sort of thing I've tried to stamp out. The ethics of this firm are very important to me. Every time I tried to get Winkler alone to discuss anything, he'd suggest we go somewhere for lunch or dinner, and I was never quite able to turn the conversation onto the subject. Then I began to realize that those rich lunches, dinners, and drinks were taking the edge off my drive. And I didn't like it or approve of it. I still couldn't see how he was getting that clique of men to work harder. . .by showing them how to play harder? Whatever it was, I felt it would be destructive to the firm, to everything I've worked for. That was when I finally began checking up. I hired a very discreet investigator, highly recommended, and I began to find out that Winkler was more depraved and destructive than I ever could have imagined.

It turned out that Winkler was actually a panderer. I'm. . .it. . .makes me sick to even have to. . .think about what he. . .uh. . .was doing. I. . .feel. . .ah. . .confused when I think of that. Well, I'm going to expose him. No matter how personally repellent I find it, I can meet anything head on.

I found out that Winkler was providing one of our older partners with a series of young, really young Puerto Rican girls, fourteen and fifteen years old. I could hardly face that particular individual after I found out. His own daughters are grown and married. With some of the others, it was just girls. . .ah. . .set up in an apartment. . .at least discreet. But then I found out about Mr. Slobin, the man who runs the mail room and supervises the office boys. This person was efficient, a bit old-maidish in a way, and dull. Just right for the job. And it turns out the man's actually a homosexual. It's something I never would have even thought about, but Winkler found out right away. Incredible how someone comes into a group and discovers the most hidden, weak part of everybody else. God knows what his own private life must be like. I've. . .uh. . .discovered some other. . .things. I. . .I can expose him before the board next week, and I'm going to.

Anyway, apparently Slobin hires only little fairies as office boys and then terrorizes them by threatening to tell. That's why they work hard and never ask for raises. Slobin always keeps the late-and-absent reports, so they can't qualify for unemployment if he fires them. Slobin gets good, big bonuses. I guess he. . .uh. . .just keeps those boys under a reign of terror. When Winkler caught on, he. . .it's unbelievable, he was also acting as a pimp for those. . .uh. . .one of our own men, another good family man has been having. . .uh. . .affairs with those. . .homosexuals. Winkler even arranged something for one of our clients! A Middle Eastern businessman. I guess in that part of the world men take young boys as lovers. But doing it in my firm. . . .

I have it all down here. I typed it myself, because I wouldn't trust my own mother to transcribe material like this. Winkler had discovered everybody's Achilles' heel but mine. When he began inviting me to have lunch and dinner so often, I accepted so I could find out everything he was up to. That was my one and only reason. I'm being gut-honest when I say this, believe me. I still had absolutely no complaints about his work. He kept right up with me, so in a way I really had to go along with him for those dinners. And I found him offensively personal, but that's due to. . . uh. . .background. He was constantly, incessantly, coming after me about my all-work-no-play approach to everything. It was depressing, and I was afraid it would. . .I mean, might have some kind of an effect on my work.

And I didn't like the way he could draw me out sometimes. He kept getting me to try all kinds of wines he's interested in, and I'm really not used. . .uh. . .not accustomed to that, and to talking about personal things. I keep my private life private. Well, also because my private life certainly isn't unusual. . .just the usual husband-and-wife things, like too many decorating bills and clothing bills and not enough weekends in the country. Besides, if I'm going to talk about myself, it has to be like this. I'm doing it on my own. . .working on myself for the good of. . .I'm going to tell everything that. . .uh. . .happened. . .to get rid of. . .clear my head so I can get back to concentrating on all the work. I've been working very hard all week, collecting the evidence on Winkler, all his pandering, and. . .something worse, much worse. . .I. . .honestly believe Winkler is deeply involved in international drug traffic! He travels abroad for the firm. . .definitely, and. . .I'm being absolutely honest when I tell you I'm sure he's been using these trips for his drug dealings.

Yesterday at lunch I ran into an old law-school friend. His father's well known downtown, George is under the old man's thumb. . .always was, never could hack it for himself. George tried to tell me there was something about Winkler, although he wouldn't say what, and George never sticks his neck out on anything. If he. . .I mean, since he was trying to warn me. . .not in so many words, but to let me know, it has to be true.

Winkler must be involved in international drug trafficking. . .just the kind of thing that's destroying the country. I was planning on facing Winkler privately today. I think I could force him to resign quietly and avoid scandal. But now I realize he was playing for time, and obviously he was trying to trap me, too, because he kept saying I looked tired, and asked me to meet him after office hours at his health club. Sometimes I go to the Princeton Club. It turned out he belongs to a private club in a big office building on Madison Avenue. I should have known. I've never thought much of that drink-your-lunch advertising crowd and the places they go to. That was where he tried to frame me. Obviously he realized that was the only way he could get me. I just don't fit into his kind of. . .uh. . .whatever, so he had to drug me and try to frame me.

All right. We meet there. I was completely wound up about facing Winkler once and for all. I had a couple of martinis to calm down. I. . .believe me, somehow I just lost track of how many after that. I'm usually a very moderate drinker. I never let myself get drunk that way. Just a couple, and then I let him show me around. The place had dark, shiny walls with chrome and mirrors, wall-to-wall carpeting, almost like a tacky expensive cocktail lounge. I was curious, but I was determined to keep on collecting my evidence, because Winkler kept telling me he was really going to show me how to live, and I knew he was ready to do almost anything to trap me.

We went through the gym and the steam room, and I guess we swam for a while, even though I was starting to feel high. I was still biding my time, because I *knew* he was trying to trap me, and I could trap *him* whenever I wanted to.

Then he took out a key to the door of what he called the private. . .the ''private'' club. That's when I. . .uh. . .began to be sucked. . .I. . .when he. . .tried to victimize me. And I began to know something strange. . .some wrong was. . .inside me. I mean, I was high, but it was more than that. My hands became four times their size, and everything was bleeding blazing colors as if I was inside a kaleidoscope and I was spinning around on the pieces of glass. My body and skin felt hot. . .so alive. . .it made me almost forget why I was really there, to follow him and trap him. I still didn't actually say to myself that he'd put something in my drink. It all became so confused. . .so fast. . .I. . .it still makes me sick to. . .I know I was practically out of my head. . .I feel confused again just thinking. . .it's still here. . .the previous information. . .all in order, the way I put it down. Some people may think I'm naive, too work-oriented to know the score, but my standards and instincts tell me who can be trusted and who can't. Anyone who doesn't believe that is barking up the wrong tree. . .I mean. . .anyway, I make up for any lack of experience by being able to really think things through. . .I can. . .uh. . .unpeel any complicated situation. That's why I had to make a record what goes on in that place. I. . .it s my word against his, and it's his sickness. . .not mine. Anyone who'd be involved with that place has to be a degenerate!

At first, I admit, it was relaxing, totally relaxing. I was leaning back in a huge, revolving ball-like chair. There was music piped in all around me. It was dark. . .black. . .just light from a projector throwing sex pictures on the walls. And this pretty girl, not what you'd expect at all, but really clean and nice looking. . .talking, bringing me some little things to eat, like Chinese food, I think. . .some sweet, some spicy, and another cold drink. . .I mean, I couldn't refuse. . .she was so nice. . .telling me to enjoy the pictures. . .touching me. . .she had long soft fingers. . .

When I think about it now I feel ill, but I admit I didn't then. . .all rotten underneath. . .that room was where. . .if it wasn't in the drinks, they drugged me there,

with those bits of food, in the dark. . .that girl. . .she led me into another room. . .I'd
heard they were all over New York now, but I thought it was all filthy, like Forty-
Second Street and Eighth Avenue, but here it was beautiful. . .set up to trap victims.
There were two other girls. . .a live sex show. . .I saw things. . .nobody could ever
believe unless he'd been there. Then she took me into another room. . .little
rooms. . .and I had less and less on. . .till I was down to nothing. I was
drugged. . .my skin was hot and slippery. . .like some animal's. . .I was
helpless. . .becoming the victim. . .I felt sick. . .and excited, I was excited. . .my
heart beating so hard. . .pounding from something she stuck under my nose for me
to sniff.

Finally I was alone in one room with just one girl. . .stripped bare, no clothes. . .
massaging me all over. . .and her tongue was everywhere on. . .and in my body!
Everything began whirling, and the colors were like stained glass. . .I can't get over
her tongue, up my. . .I. . .suddenly I vomited. . .so sick I couldn't stop. I knew I was
completely out of control, and she got scared. I don't know how long I stayed like
that, but finally somebody helped me clean up and get dressed, and I got my briefcase. . .got out of there. . .desperate just to get out. My evidence is right here in my
briefcase. . .and it's on this tape, now, too. I got a cab. . .holding my briefcase. . .I
felt so sick I thought I'd better go to a hospital.

I know I was momentarily. . .sick. . .to let it happen to me. . .weakened enough to
get taken in by people like that, when I knew what he was all the time. I lost my
grip. . .I. . .my intuition failed. I weakened! I let him suck me into it! But I've done
my duty. It's on your record now that I've told you all this, and I hope you'll regard
it as a contribution to. . .against the drugs and all the filth. . .that's around us. . .and
that's why so many people are getting sick these days from overindulgence of everything. Too much preoccupation with sex, drinking themselves to death, and not
keeping their noses to the grindstone is why our society's getting soft and rotten to
the core.

I think that as a doctor you'll realize that's why I live by my belief that work never
killed anyone. As a professional man you can see from my whole story how work has
always saved me, not destroyed me. You can see why I've made work the one most
important thing in my life.

HISTORY

From his birth at the exclusive maternity pavilion where his grandfather was
chairman of the board, Christopher Marshall's life was shaped—by parents and
grandparents, by peers and their parents, by exclusive private schools—to have the
intelligence, discipline, aggressiveness, good manners, and education for an
outstanding career in law or finance. This was all done according to the rigid ethic
that had governed his family for five generations.

Baby Chris was a model toddler. His mother liked to say it was because of his
innate moral fiber, but it was also because of his nurse, Hilda, an owlish spinster
who exercised severe discipline over the children in her charge. Hilda, it should be
added, was the opposite of Bertha, a well-meaning permissive woman who had been
nurse for Chris's sister Anne, his senior by three years. It was because of Bertha's

deficiencies, Mrs. Marshall believed, that Anne daydreamed, had tantrums, left-handedness, and the unspeakable habit of masturbating in front of whoever would watch.

When the time came for a nanny rather than a nurse, Chris' mother chose someone who seemed a replica of Hilda. Nanny Griggs, approaching seventy, handled Christopher and Anne with the same spartan severity as had Hilda. Nanny Griggs's ''you-must-not'' approach was very ''successful'' with young Chris; but she had trouble with Anne, who not only had sloppy habits and bursts of temper but constantly gravitated to the kitchen or servants' quarters of the town house. Secretly Anne laughed and cried with them and talked to them about their lives or their dead husbands or their boyfriends.

Under Nanny Griggs's supervision, Chris was making a much-praised transition from model toddler to model little boy. He ate and napped at the right times, never wet his bed, and was fastidious about arranging his expensive toys at the end of every play period. His consideration and politeness toward his playfellows made people think of little lord Fauntelroy or a Gainesborough formal portrait of a boy.

One summer evening, in the middle of an elegant ''seated'' dinner party, Chris's mother heard sobs from upstairs. She rushed into his room and discovered that Nanny Griggs had welted the boy's arms and buttocks with a leather belt she always carried coiled in the pocket of her housecoat. Her reason had been Chris's inexplicable refusal to put away a set of Lionel train tracks. Nanny Griggs was immediately replaced by a seemingly less rigid caretaker.

Mr. and Mrs. Norman Marshall were tall, healthy, and handsome. They observed social proprieties, followed the family traditions of hard work, an active social life, and devotion to civic, cultural, and philanthropic projects. They lived without ostentation on the interest from considerable wealth inherited from both sides of the family. The one thing they failed to give Chris and his sister was deep emotional contact.

Eleanor Marshall was well groomed, sensible, and unfrivolous. Her manner was always cool, except on those rare summer days in the Hamptons when she suddenly became exhilarated after an especially exciting game of tennis or an afternoon of sailing. Despite her apparent lack of any passionate involvement, or of any emotion at all, she harbored with almost sexual secretiveness a fierce ambition for her son. This cool, horsey matron had heard what detractors, obviously hangers-on and have-nots, had whispered. Her husband, they said, good as he was—a bank president, head of prestigious charities, board member of almost every important foundation in the city—was in some way inadequate, a phony. Not ethically, of course, nor physically, and certainly not financially; but they said he was merely a product of the money, pull, and power wielded in the past by his and his wife's families. ''A not-too-perfectly functioning bank president, my dear.'' ''Hell, it took buying Manhattan from the Indians to get him where he is.'' ''If it weren't for their combined capital, the whole thing would have been in receivership years ago, love.''

Although Eleanor was too strong and loyal to let the whisperings affect her, mightn't there be a flaw after all? And couldn't she sometimes, while watching Anne grow lovely with a face somewhat lax and languid, see that flaw? But there was another possibility. It was obvious that Norman Marshall's feelings and drives were rightly channeled—into his family, his work, a competitive passion for athletics. But Eleanor had just missed being valedictorian of her class at Smith; the reasons were not as important now as the "just missed." Was the flaw in her?

It never occurred to Eleanor to want her son to be a musician, a writer, or a doctor. What she did fiercely want was the true cloth-of-gold, unflawed. "I think Chris is going to be creative, I mean really creative, in business," she often said to close friends in a voice that sounded as if her jaws had been wired together with platinum thread. And the Marshalls went on competing almost frantically—Chris against his parents in tennis and sailing; Anne in her development as a young horsewoman.

Chris could not remember any significant communication with his father except praise when he excelled at work or in sports. As he grew older he observed his parents' communication with each other. His father left the apartment at eight each morning, opening and closing his briefcase to check its contents while his mother asked if he really would be home in time for them to get to the theater or to a dinner party. When he did arrive home on time, he always seemed to have left some preoccupying unfinished business at the bank. And on evenings when he worked especially late, Chris's mother seemed indifferent.

As a boy, Chris saw nothing unusual in his family's life style. It became increasingly predictable and was interrupted only by sister Anne's occasional bursts of rebellion. Even when Chris became aware that his father was rich enough not to have to work at all, he felt that his choice of a rigorous work life was what had kept the present generation of the family from drifting into the decline and excesses he saw in some of his friends' families and in his own sister, who was doing poorly at school.

Chris was sent to one of the best private boys' schools in New York. The students were encouraged to be very aggressive and competitive in scholarships and other activities, so that they would be accepted at equally good boarding schools and then the best colleges. At times Chris felt frustrated when his aggressive urges were stifled by city life and his family's rigid social regime, but he knew that all this was "good training" for the discipline of boarding school. He accepted that students could not raise their voices during recess periods on the wire-fenced roof because it might disturb people in nearby apartments. He learned not to be wild at birthday parties and not to run up and down the hallways at his friends' town houses or duplexes. He did not even talk at the Friday afternoon dancing classes, which required wearing white gloves and being polite to little girls from girls' schools. To the dancing-school teacher Chris showed the required bow and his impeccable manners.

Chris was accepted at the Episcopal boarding school where he had been registered at birth, the same one his father had attended. This very strict school was obviously far better than Anne's horsey Southern school, which had done nothing to improve her marks or her self-discipline. Chris felt that his school would give him an edge over boys from places that allowed more weekends, smoking privileges for seniors, and more frequent ''care packages'' from home.

The school was of a piece with the early shaping of Chris's fiercely ''virtuous'' nature; it began to short-circuit what little abandon, humor, or zest he had. He saw even leisure time as a series of projects and skills to be mastered. It became more important for him to excel at a sport through self-discipline than to throw himself into it for enjoyment or aggressive release.

There was a strong religious emphasis at school—compulsory chapel every morning, church attendance every Sunday, a lecture every Sunday evening by a guest minister from a well known New York, New England, or even English church. The student government held informal but compulsory prayer meetings. In his junior year, Chris became a member of the student government; most of his classmates had realized by the end of his freshman year that they would nominate and vote for him as their student representative to the faculty as soon as he became eligible.

If Chris had many rebellious or sensual urges, they were buried in his unconscious, safely hidden from himself and everyone around him. He rigorously pushed away any leanings toward self-indulgence and sexuality. He worked hard at perfecting his tennis game and strove to become captain of the swimming team. The only times any strain showed was when Chris's roommate complained of being kept awake by the dim glow of Chris's flashlight under his blanket. Chris would mumble apologetically that he wasn't tired and was trying to read himself to sleep. Later he lay awake, feeling the full weight of his anxiety about all the things he hadn't done quite to his satisfaction that day and all those he'd set for himself for tomorrow.

One assumption ran through the school's religious and academic training. Because all the boys came from privileged families and were fortunate enough to be there, and if they took full advantage of what it offered socially and scholastically, they would move on smoothly to the best colleges, where they would belong to the best clubs; then to the top graduate schools; and then to the best hospitals, legal firms, banks, and investment houses, where they would become editors of law reviews, senior partners, presidents, and chiefs of staff. Most of the boys thought that college would be an extension of boarding school, with some exciting new freedoms added. But they didn't grasp what life would be like when school was finally over, because they didn't know any people or life styles but their own. People from other worlds were merely vague images, acknowledged with the automatic good manners that took the place of genuine feelings or recognition.

Chris was accepted at Princeton, his first choice among colleges; here, too, he had been registered at birth, for the men in his family had gone there for generations. He and the other ''preppies'' knew that from the moment they arrived they must prepare themselves for the following February, the time to be chosen by the eating clubs. It was very important to be among the first chosen by the best clubs, so Chris maneuvered to make himself sought-after and respected for his muted excellence and "low profile."

However, Chris was soon bombarded by incidents and awakenings that made him realize college could be very different from his previous schools, and his life there far less sheltered. Clearly people like himself were a very small part of the college and of the world outside it; yet because he had been trained all his life to be courteous to everyone, he got along pretty well with students from very different social backgrounds. They tended to regard him as somewhat apart, but overlooked the occasional blunders he made out of his ignorance of their worlds.

Chris's first roommate came from Texas. The college had tried to assign freshmen roommates of roughly similar backgrounds, so Jeff was also the well educated son of a rich and respected family. To Chris, the difference between them seemed enormous; he felt awkward, frightened, and sometimes slightly repelled. But gradually he found himself very attracted to one trait that seemed to sum up all the differences, freedom—the freedom with which Jeff could accept an unsatisfactory grade; his freedom in talking about masturbation and exploring sex with girls, as little as either of them had; his freedom talking about and using his family's money to go out, and, as Jeff put it, "raunch around" and enjoy himself.

The more Chris felt shaken and aroused by these new impressions, the more he tried to tighten his self-discipline. He had walked onto the academic and athletic battlefields superbly armored, he had thought, but the competition here was confusingly disguised as non-competition. It really had little to do with grades, sports, and self-discipline, but with noblesse oblige and becoming powerful independent survivors.

Besides, for his parents' satisfaction and his own, Chris also felt burdened by having to make up for his sister, the family black sheep. He felt contempt to the point of nausea at her lying, cheating, and academic and disciplinary rebellion. He did not admit to himself that he felt burning jealousy when Anne made her blatant pronouncements, puffed out on the smoke of her cigarette with a hoarse, vulgar, but distinctly debutante laugh. "I just love fucking, brother dear, don't you? Or do you?" "Chris, really, your half-assed lectures on fucking. . .I mean, who gives a flying fuck about the socalled fucking family name!" "Chris, brother darling, you're just like Prince Valiant in the funnies, I mean, dear little brother, that's *absolument passé.*"

After barely scraping through a very "social" boarding school and a junior college for rich but not very bright girls, Anne had been caught having intercourse with the school's attractive, hard-drinking riding teacher in an empty jumping field. She was expelled, her lover was fired, and they eloped. The Marshalls swiftly gave Anne part of a trust fund from her grandfather to set up her and her husband in a small riding school—severance pay, Eleanor Marshall called it.

During the summer after his freshman year, Chris visited Anne and Doug. With a recurrent erection swelling embarrassingly through his madras slacks, he suffered through a long evening of their drinking, jokes, and allusions to their sex life. When Anne and her husband finally fell asleep in each other's arms on the living room floor, Chris went into the bathroom and, in darkness, masturbated twice in twenty minutes without any emotion.

In their sophomore year, Jeff and Chris chose to remain roommates. Jeff continued to chip away almost sadistically at Chris with his friendly aggressions and breezy style. In reaction, Chris kept studying harder, went out for prevarsity Lacrosse with a vengeance, and masturbated more and more frequently.

Both of them went up to New York for Thanksgiving weekend. Chris went to see his parents and attend the traditional ''little'' parties and dances that precede the big Christmas coming-out season. Unlike most of the East Coast college group, Jeff did not stay at the Biltmore; instead he held forth at the Plaza and ran with a pack of rich, raucous Texas friends who had descended on New York with the quiet delicacy of Huns. At Jeffs' urging, Chris slipped out of a Thanksgiving Friday dance early to join Jeff's group. They ran from bar to bar on Second and Third Avenues, bumping into other twos and threes of the young Texas rich who thronged there. At first, painfully self-conscious, marked by his white tie and his inability to yell and pound shoulders, Chris felt shy with the Texas girls; they seemed much more sexy, more made up and dressed up, than the girls he knew. But he smiled his usual pleasant, neutral smile, began matching drinks with the others, and ended up feeling warm camaraderie with the boys and febrile arousal over the girls.

That night Chris made his debut as a ''booze hound,'' with all the determination he had used in attacking every project in his life. As the drinking grew more competitive, Chris consumed an enormous amount without showing any signs of drunkenness. This made him the winner and something of a hero among his increasingly woozy, incoherent companions. He talked more and laughed louder than he ever had, and he kept feeling the warmth and slight throb of his semierection as he pressed his thigh against that of one of the girls. He loved that night. He felt as if it had released a spring that had been coiled inside him so tightly and for so long that he hadn't known it was there. For the first time in his life he felt some relief from the edge of anxiety that had always kept him tensed against others.

The next week, back at school, Chris was distracted from his usual sharp discipline, thinking of that evening, of how much he would like once again the abandonment of those dark, hot, noisy Third Avenue bars, swallowing the icy, sour, biting drinks, getting a great glow, then a buzz, wanting to come as thigh pressed against thigh. Another episode like that and he just might have the courage, as Jeff put it, to ''get a little.''

During this year, for the first time in his school career, Chris couldn't concentrate on his work. He began to fantasize about girls in extravagant detail and became obsessed with sexuality, planning his daily "spree" of masturbation. He wanted to go back to the city and spin out into pleasures he'd never known before—all of them, whatever they were.

During the three-week study period in January and during spring vacations, Chris went to New York with Jeff to party as much as he could. He was willing to try anything and go anywhere. He continued to drink the most, yell the most, and try to get the farthest into every girl's pants. Yet the minute he was back at Princeton, he felt guilty, depressed, and driven by an obsessive urge to masturbate. Furtively, like an animal trying to burrow, he tried to get back into his studies, but often he suddenly needed to get up from his desk and go into the bathroom and masturbate. Afterward he felt lonely, almost panicked, yet this ritual became necessary, even on grey Saturday afternoons when he forced himself to go to the library. Suddenly, in the middle of a paragraph of a book, he would get up, go to one of the bathrooms in the library, and masturbate behind the door of a stall. He hated it, he told himself, because it didn't pick him up and didn't even help him study. But he kept on doing it.

More and more Chris tended to leave some or all of his work unfinished to pursue even half-pleasures. For the first time he cut classes, because he felt unprepared to answer teachers' questions or discuss the material. He began going to a local townie bar for beers in the afternoon or evening. But now he had to drink until he was almost reeling to get the buzz that eased his tension. Usually there was only a brief hour or two of relief, and he'd wake up the next day with a beer hangover, feeling no closer to anyone, no more relaxed, hardly remembering the town girl he'd met and made out with.

By a few months after he first had intercourse, Chris had run through all the easily available local girls at his town hangout. The first was a thirty-year-old alcoholic who was always there and available. They were both drunk, and it happened so fast and made him so dizzy that he couldn't understand why everyone said fucking was so great. Then he tried again and again, often in such alcoholic confusion and frenzied anxiety that it ended with premature orgasm, Chris exhausted, the woman unsatisfied, and both filled with hostility.

By spring vacation in Chris's junior year, his marks had begun to slip. His parents questioned him, but not too severely, because they had no idea what his life or feelings were. Norman Marshall was going through a siege of intensely demanding work, and Eleanor was spending an increasing amount of time alone at the house on Long Island Sound. The Marshalls seemed most concerned with whether Chris was keeping up contacts with his old friends and doing the right things with the people they knew.

Chris, however, no longer cared about his former social life—carefully structured, active but antiseptic, well mannered, with an occasional beer, no smoking, and the carefully and almost properly scheduled light petting with nice girls at dormitory doorways. This had been replaced by compulsive drinking and frenetic but lackluster sex.

Word somehow spread through the parental grapevine about his drinking and running around in Princeton with fast girls and hoody boys. As Chris received fewer invitations to the ''right'' parties, he became more attractive to the people who had once found him impossibly square. As mothers crossed him off the top of their ''eligible'' list, others were waiting to accept him—people like Eleanor would have described as ''rich and gross.'' He had met them at a party given by friends of Jeff's parents one winter evening. They owned a ranch in Texas, a house in Mexico, and a large co-op in New York where they spent part of the theater season because they backed one or two Broadway musicals every year.

This apartment and everyone in it seemed worlds away from Marshalls' almost severe, wood-panelled duplex. The living room had crystal chandeliers dangling like diamond earrings, rugs so thick and soft they suggested walking on flesh, walls papered in deep-toned flocked velvet, enormous vases of exotic flowers that suggested a gorgeous and vaguely sinister tropical rain forest. Chris drifted through the rooms, a bit dazed and enjoying everything his eyes took in, tasting all the food, drinking the drinks, smelling the cigar smoke and perfume, looking at people who seemed more glamorous than any he had ever met. They were dressed in the height of quiet good fashion, modestly but richly jeweled, and had the not-too-shiny patina by which the rich immediately recognize each other.

Chris noticed a girl who seemed as different from those he knew as the women there were from his mother. And when she saw him looking at her, Wendy cut straight through the crowd and introduced herself. She was small and dark-haired and wore preppy clothes except for heavy beads and a Bulgarian peasant blouse. She had the boldest, most direct manner Chris had ever encountered. She instantly got under his skin as no girl had. She had a way of finishing all his sentences for him in her husky voice so that he felt somehow clever and relieved of his usual social anxieties. For an instant he felt like backing away, when her driving monologues tapped briefly at the defensive shell around his feelings. And she interspersed her outrageous stories about her family's unconventional behavior with direct questions about his taste, values, and fun life. He felt at moments she might strip away all his defenses and get right to his most hidden secrets. But he was overwhelmed by her, and more than ready to leave the party with her.

Wendy asked him to take her to her favorite place in Greenwich Village, a small restaurant near her apartment; she also made clear by the intentness with which she swirled them out of the party that she intended more than a quiet dinner. As their cab sped downtown from Park to Greenwich Avenue, Wendy told Chris in telegraphic sentences how she had been shipped out of Beverly Hills by her filmproducer father and social New York mother. Instead of attending the proper junior college they'd selected for her, Wendy, always rebellious, took an apartment in the Village and attended drama classes.

She began to reel off what she and her coterie of close friends were doing to themselves and each other in the world of drugs, drink, and sex. Chris could hardly believe what he heard, and listened so hungrily that she felt compelled to talk on and on. Most of all, he was concentrating on the sensuality her talk revealed and how he could have sex with her. Wendy solved this problem by abruptly stopping her monologue in the middle of dinner to say, "Chris, I'm very attracted to you," and sliding her hand up his thigh. He paid the bill quickly, and they walked in silence back to her apartment.

This was Chris's first all-night, unhurried sexual experience. He was so excited by Wendy's bold sensuality that for the first time he felt no awkwardness or anxiety, only a seemingly endless capacity for arousal that kept them going almost constantly until morning, and then again that afternoon until Chris had to make the last train back to Princeton. On the way, he kept falling into exhausted naps, then jerking dizzily awake, aroused just by the motion of the train, then falling asleep again amid memories and fantasies of exploring Wendy's flesh.

He saw Wendy in the city almost every weekend. They went to parties given by her drama-school friends and to bars in the Village, on Third Avenue, on the West Side. At all of them Wendy knew people, and Chris greedily tried everything that was offered—drinks, marijuana, benzedrine inhalers, dancing to bongos or rock-'n-roll. Most greedily he tried sex in all the varieties Wendy taught him, and then ways he had fantasized and began to teach her. Being with her became an obsession, and each new sexual twist led to another. Chris bought and studied pornography to find more. Wendy was thrilled to find herself a little frightened by him when he acted out some mildly sadomasochistic scenes taken from sex magazines.

Chris was now so excited by her that he began a stream of half-humorous obscene phone calls to persuade her to come to Princeton during the week or on the few weekends when he absolutely had to do some studying. Her fantasies of Chris and the excitement of their "telephone sex" soon had her on instant call. Wendy would have nothing to do with most of Chris's friends; she found them "too goddam straight." Instead she and Chris went to out-of-the-way hangouts, where she always managed to discover off-beat students or townies whom Chris would never have noticed. He was not interested in wasting their time together even on these people; he could never seem to get enough of being in bed with her. But Wendy loved to collect "types," and Chris, stimulated by her interest in them, ended his junior year with a new group of friends who were a close approximation of the people Wendy had hung out with in high school in California.

Chris returned to his parents with the lowest marks of his life, a warning from his faculty advisor, and rooming arrangements that involved two outsiders—a preppie with a bad case of Marlon Brando worship and a handsome black boy who had reached Princeton from Harlem on a scholarship. His parents were angrier than he had ever seen them. If he had not been determined to conceal and protect his new life, the three of them might have been more honest with each other than ever before. But Chris retreated behind a sullen, proper mask and suggested that he stop spending summers with them in Edgartown and take a summer job in a brokerage house.

This seeming sacrifice of summer pleasure had been planned to free him and Wendy. She was to spend the summer with an aunt and uncle in Southampton, where her parents hoped she would meet ''the right kind of people.'' The uncle and aunt entertained a great deal. At first they had done so to launch their daughters in society, but gradually their parties had become known locally as free-for-alls open to anyone with a presentable face and wardrobe. Wendy had been there the previous year and knew that as the summer passed, her aunt and uncle, in their own pursuit of amusement, would become oblivious to what their guests did—to the nude swimmers in their pool and the twosomes and groups half-naked and naked in the back of station wagons in the late hours. People also used a ramshackled old house that Wendy's uncle and aunt had rented across the road, with warrens of bedrooms for servants and for guests invited by their daughters.

Chris spent hot, gritty, lonely, fantasy-ridden weeks in the city, working as a runner in his father's friend's brokerage house. Then every weekend he exploded in the huge, damp house in the Hamptons. He and Wendy and their group tore up and down the Montauk Highway from large, elaborate cocktail parties to the discotheques just beginning to spring up. From there they went to the old roadhouses where their parents came late and drunk to foxtrot in red linen pants and flowered linen dresses. And last, on to the homosexual dance place back in the scrub woods to do the hully-gully in huge chorus lines of prancing, shrieking men.

And always, finally, Chris and Wendy went back to his guest bedroom for sex, dizzy and sometimes half unconscious from drinks, marijuana, and dancing. Even when he finally managed to sleep, usually on the beach during the afternoon, surrounded by Wendy's chattering, hopped-up friends, he had to be careful to stay on his stomach so that his erection wouldn't be visible. He lay pretending to sleep, hiding his rage at Wendy for her restless socializing when he wanted to be alone with her to act out the new fantasy that had caused his erection.

Chris began to feel that his life was a state of continual tumescence, relieved and renewed on weekends, and consuming his mind as he moved like a zombie through his Wall Street weekdays. During the week he masturbated two or three times a day in the men's room. And as the week wore on, he had to have enough beers at lunch to help him slide over his feelings of rage and entrapment.

His parents called him one Wednesday night in August, at the end of an especially frustrating, fantasy-ridden day, because a friend of his mother's had written from

Easthampton hinting that Chris was running with a wild crowd. They questioned him relentlessly about not having accepted invitations to sail with family friends at various yacht clubs, and about how many of his prep-school friends he was keeping up with. They received only bland, noncommittal replies.

Soon afterward Wendy called to tell Chris that a group of her California friends had shown up on their motorcycles with someting new and fantastic for them to try. It always excited her to introduce him to a new thrill, because he could get into it so much that it heightened the thrill for her. Only he, of all the pseudosophisticated preppie and social types she knew, had the nerve to do things as hard and as wildly as they were done in California.

She asked him to come early and to bring Jason, his black roommate. Her uncle and aunt were already so revved up about a party they were giving that they'd scarcely noticed the armada of Harley Davidsons across the road; Wendy had promised they'd confine their own party to the guest house.

Chris called in sick and took the Friday morning train to the Hamptons. He was excited about having Jason with him; he had been a good source of marijuana and a guide in Harlem when Chris and his friends sought music and bars there. Now he could show Jason something in return. Chris knew that bringing a black house guest would seem daring and shocking to Wendy's Southampton group, and that they might seem even more shocking to Jason, who was relatively innocent about this overprivileged world where kids ran after expensive thrills and dangerous, escalating excesses because they'd already had too much of everything and nothing was enough to relieve their boredom.

When Chris arrived at the house, the usual group, Wendy, and her five California friends looked as if they had stepped out of a motorcycle movie. For three days they had been drinking, smoking marijuana, and taking bennies. The something fantastic Wendy had promised was peyote, which her friends had picked up on their way through Arizona. Amid growing sexual tension and the bikers' studied crudity, they ate the peyote.

Chris would never be able to allow himself to remember that night completely, but flashes of it came back even twenty years later when he was tired and under great stress. Wendy with Jason, then Jason with a biker, one girl with all the bikers, the chains they wore being used, then himself, Wendy, and Jason together. And finally a screaming flight through the undulating basement tunnels of the house, onto the beach, and into the water—where Chris tried to drown himself?

Chris's parents had to be called down from Edgartown, and he spent the next four months at a sanitarium that provided the finest care for the nicest sort of patients, just as his schools had given the finest education and discipline to boys from good families. The therapy was didactic; the patients attended lectures about how to live a balanced life. Strenuous exercise, fresh air, farm foods, and attendance at the non-sectarian Christian church were mandatory. Too much introspection was discouraged. That an ordered vigorous, rigorous day would cure any disordered mind was the tenet of Dr. Wrightman, who had autocratically ruled several generations of patients and their heirs. Chris's parents, who visited on weekends, were reassured by his relatively quick return to "his old self" and by their pleasant chats with his doctor. The doctor was never specific about Chris's treatment, but he somehow relieved their unspoken fears that the breakdown or cure might teach a young person to hate his parents and be obsessed with sex.

Chris began his senior year at mid-semester, quieter than ever, working harder than he ever had, regulating his life minutely and rigorously. He made up his missing semester the following summer, graduated with excellent grades, and was accepted at Harvard Law School. His parents were pleased; Harvard Law would equip him for a distinguished career and eventually to succeed his father as the head and money manager of the family.

That fall Chris found two other Princeton alumni for roommates and determined to immerse himself in the grind of first-year courses and outdo the plodding, thorough types aiming at corporate law and the quick-thinking, fast-talking ones who would excel at litigation. The time Chris spent away from study was now so unimportant to him that at first he didn't notice that his roommate's sister, Sally Brower, was taking up more and more of his free hours.

Chris's roommate, George Brower, was very close to his younger and only sister. Their mother had died when they were quite young, and from George's vague references Chris gathered that some serious breach existed between George's father and his "artistic" daughter. George said, "Dad wanted her to go to Wellesley, but she didn't make it—didn't want to make it, really. If she really likes all this art stuff at the museum school maybe she'll be another Matisse or something." As he said this to Chris, even George Brower didn't believe it.

Chris's few dates with Sally didn't reveal to him her willful extravagance of exquisite little Chinese jade snuffbottles, and her obsessive acquiring of expensive art supplies. Tubes of acrylics, thin-handled mink and sable brushes, power tools for metal casting, all were strewn, unused, over the bare wood floors of her one-room "studio" on Beacon Hill.

What Chris did recognize in Sally was her hedonism and sensuality. She had intense brown eyes that could stir him in the groin. Her seductive smile came on quickly and at will. She often threw back her long, blond-tipped hair or slowly ran her hand through it. His sex drive had returned, and he began to masturbate to fantasize about sex with her; sometimes erotic memories of himself and Wendy merged with those of Sally. He recognized that this eroticizing seemed like that with Wendy but was somehow safer. Straight family. Better family. Right people.

Gradually Sally began luring Chris out of the library to drive to the Cape on sunny spring weekends and go to informal parties in the studios and lofts of her Beacon Hill friends. By fall of Chris's third year, she had firmly set her sights on him as husband material: good looks, good background, industrious to the point of obsession, which worried her a little, but definitely an excellent provider. Now Sally also drew Chris out of his rigorous schedule for more time at sex—not just straight sex but things she had learned from the Beacon Hill kinky types. It surprised her at first that Chris responded wildly and then went her one better. When they were lying in bed, too exhausted to do anything more, she wondered where he'd learned. Fabulous, if he just wouldn't study so fucking hard.

After these episodes Chris retreated into harder study to prove to himself that this time he wasn't out of control. Sometimes it meant not even telephoning Sally for days, a week, two weeks. During these silent periods, Sally felt chilled by Chris's neglect and started seeing other men and having sex with them, usually men from her set on the Hill. At least half her enjoyment was letting Chris know, through her brother, who was doing her this week. Then, as she expected, the phone would ring, and Chris's voice would be almost hoarse with needing sex.

"Yes, my darling, all right. I'll see you in about twenty minutes."

"On the Hill?"

"On the Hill."

In his junior year, Chris had made the *Law Review*. In his final year, his preoccupation with working as one of its editors, along with his determination to keep racking up A's, made it obvious to Sally that because of his determination to be first and best, she would have to give up many of her demands after they married. But, she thought, she couldn't exactly call that neglect.

In the last months of school, Chris became aware that he needed Sally not only sexually but socially. In fact, she was practically the only nonacademic friend he had. Evening after evening, even though she complained, she sat on the cot by the wall in his tight little law review office and read magazines until it was time to have brief but abandoned sex. Then he returned to more study, more work.

One night, a couple of weeks after an encounter on the office cot, Sally called to say she was afraid she was pregnant. While she drove from Boston to Cambridge, Chris was thinking that for all her complaints about being neglected for his work, she had stuck to him. Chris and Sally announced their engagement even before the rabbit-test results came back negative, and Chris found himself being moved properly, relentlessly, but not unwillingly toward becoming Sally's husband. Sally dashed to florists, caterers, Bergdorf's, Bendel's. She and her mother entered a whirl of silver, china patterns, and new clothes.

Meanwhile, Chris faced the exciting challenge of his first job interviews. He applied to only the very best firms in Boston and New York. He was pleasantly surprised that in those weeks Sally did nothing to "break his circuit," interrupt his final, crucial sprint. She was the right girl, she did understand his obsession—his "thing," she called it—about getting the best.

For the first time, Chris experienced a true work high, a dizzy euphoria after intense job concentration, a study session, or an oral honors exam. Yet these highs, like the ones brought long ago by sex, quickly faded and left him empty, weak, and trembling, as if from a coffee hangover.

Soon before the wedding, Chris was interviewed at one of the most prestigious law firms in New York. Being there, Chris knew, was what he wanted more than anything or anyone. He had been seen by one of the partners, who'd bowled him over by sharply warning that they expected long nights of work, weekends of labor at home, total devotion. Chris was deeply stirred by this man, knew him immediately for a kindred spirit. Yet at the many moments when aggressive answers were expected, he felt himself faltering and unable to counter quickly or brightly enough. He left certain that the one man he wanted to work for had already rejected him for being ineffectual. These thoughts consumed his attention during the week of pre-wedding parties. He walked through the marriage ceremony perspiring, cold, and clammy, panicked over failure.

The honeymoon was a disaster. For Sally it was ten days of stifled anger. For Chris it was depression over the absence of work and fear of failure. He pushed himself into the familiar exertions of tennis, golf, and snorkeling. He met other discreetly honey-mooning couples at cocktails before dinner and made love to Sally perfunctorily. He didn't eat well and couldn't sleep; and despite occasional rushes of sensual enjoy-ment, Sally knew he wasn't really with her even during sex.

When they returned to New York and walked into their new apartment, Sally immediately rushed around inspecting wedding presents that had been delivered there. She was too absorbed with her possessions to notice Chris standing, holding the letter that welcomed him to the law firm. She did not understand the rush of pleasure he was feeling through his whole body as he led her into the bedroom and made love to her urgently on the sheetless new bed.

For Chris, the first year was the happiest in his marriage. The disappointments of the honeymoon quickly gave way to weeks of enthusiastic lovemaking, and he was genuinely pleased by Sally's efforts to be a good wife. She dutifully filled her days with improving on the mix of parental donations and wedding presents that furnished their apartment. She also conscientiously set about meeting the wives of the other new men in the firm. Chris believed everything in their lives had finally fallen into place. They were not aware that both of them were asking little or nothing of each other, which erected a false facade of a balanced, equable life.

When the sharp competition of that first year ended, Chris emerged as by far the most energetic and hard-working new member. He was rewarded by being assigned to Mr. Elwood, one of their youngest, richest, most demanding, and most capricious clients. All the young men at the firm continued to stay late; Chris, whose special client might phone at any hour, stayed even later, worked even harder. Sally began to notice this with growing annoyance.

Chris could not remember ever discussing starting a family with Sally, yet suddenly there was an announcement that she was pregnant, and this time it was true. Throughout her pregnancy she complained bitterly of his lack of attention; he could not understand why she failed to realize how important it was that he spend every possible minute tending the demands of his prize client. When the delivery occurred, Chris was on the phone with the client rather than in the labor room helping her ''breathe.''

Mr. Elwood sent Sally lavish baskets of rare orchids when their son Josh was born, but Sally was implacable in her resentment of Chris's work and his special client. When Chris suggested making Mr. Elwood's name their son's middle name, Sally became angrier than he had ever seen her. For weeks she remained withdrawn, until he gave in to her demand that they buy a large co-op in the fashionable East Sixties. She had failed to draw him to her by having a baby; now she began trying another way. She plunged back into painting, entered the Art Students League, hired a housekeeper, bought thousands of dollars worth of art supplies and new clothes in which to paint and attend classes, and she joined and redecorated two rooms to create a studio.

Chris was aware of the influx of new artists and pseudo-artist friends. But his time now and over the following years was almost totally dominated by work. The firm gave him every demanding, hard-driving client. Knowing that he was the only man in the firm capable of both intense attention to detail and understated competence with clients gave Chris the strongest rushes of emotion he felt during this period.

He became increasingly aware of Sally's parties and the new people she seemed to be constantly phoning, running around with, and bringing in for cocktails and dinner—a husband-and-wife team of art critics who openly snorted cocaine; a lesbian (or so Chris suspected) high-fashion model who claimed she wanted to paint and was in Sally's class at the Art Students League; a bearded twenty-year-old actor-director from the Theater of the Spontaneous. Chris questioned Sally about these people only casually, in passing. He was, in fact, relieved that they kept her from making demands on his time, attention, and sexuality that he could not fulfill.

Now when he felt a rush of excitement it was always at some stressful, inconvenient moment in the office, where he spent most of his time. Almost without realizing it, he resumed the old habit of masturbating two or three times a day in the men's room—at ten in the morning, at five, when the office was emptying out, and at ten at night, after dashing out for a sandwich and coffee. On the increasingly rare occasions when Sally did complain of neglect, he countered by pointing out her bills for art supplies, clothes, hairdresser, exercise classes, and gifts to friends.

With astutely paced ambition Chris left the firm to join a newly formed, forward-looking investment house as a founding partner and chief legal counsel. His and Sally's life was now even more elaborate. They became involved in art collecting through Sally's ''turtleneck'' set. Chris wrote the checks and kept grimly at work while Sally went to gallery openings and parties with one of her friends.

Things got out of hand between them only on those rare occasions when Sally bought tickets or made reservations or when they took little Josh to the new house in the Hamptons for a vacation. Chris suffered depression, a painful reminder of their honeymoon, but now of increasing depth and duration. In the past year or so he had begun to feel that Sally and her group were relieved when he was rescued by the inevitable phone call summoning him back to work sooner than planned, and he left them to their art talk, sailing, and partying.

He did not attribute his rise from depression when he returned to a work crisis to escaping the family from which he'd become so detached, as his own parents had been detached from him. By now Chris had come to feel that life was work and that work was his life, his salvation from all the weaknesses to which everyone around him seemed helpless prey.

Chris's ability to defend himself from any emotional intrusion by people close to him might have remained unchallenged, but his elaborate defenses suddenly collapsed. The panic and indignity of having to go to an emergency clinic because of being drugged shocked him temporarily out of his closed world. For a brief time he faced the pain of isolation and emptiness that lay beneath his life of unceasing work. He leaped at the clinic psychiatrist's referral to me as an opportunity to prove to himself that he was not sick, that the architecture of his life was flawless. In fact, being told by the doctor that I was conducting a taped research project gave him a perfect rationalization. He would see me at once in order to provide me with the latest information on how new powerful emporiums of sex and drugs are destroying society. He could do this because he had just been victimized by one of them.

Christopher Marshall remained in therapy longer than I had expected. His narcissism and workaholism explained his vigorous use of the tapes—for long, obsessive, and painfully detailed reporting of every aspect of his past and current life. He recorded reel after reel of tape on his own, allegedly so that I would have a complete in-depth account of the corruption all around us. Often I barely kept myself from saying, "Enough already, I get the picture." He chastised me for not doing my homework when I reported to him that I had not listened to all his tapes that week. He gave my alleged delinquency as one of the many reasons that helping me was wasting his time.

The treatment failed. He stonewalled every insight offered. When I tried to have him use tapes to see that he was addicted to work, he continued to use them as merely another kind of compulsive work. Any innovative therapeutic efforts on my part fell on resistant ears; he perceived every interpretation as a destructive attack on his total being. He made it clear that to expose and rid himself of his work addiction would remove the vestiges of his frail and failing human contacts. The people he worked with were the only ones left for whom he could feel anything.

He finally terminated therapy after I firmly insisted that the only way he might recover would be by joining my addicts' group. This attempt to cut through the roots of his denial aroused a protective self-righteous anger that enabled him to rationalize ending therapy. How dare I cast him in with a "bunch of addicts." His final words were these:

"I have taken far too much from you, and given you too much of my precious time in order to contribute to your research on other people's addictions. And now your gratitude is to lump me in with all those sick people, when you know I got here by accident. Your theory that people can become addicted to work is foolish. At first it was relaxing to have someone to talk to each week. But let's face it, I don't need to go to a psychiatrist to relax, my work is my relaxation. . .my real pleasure in life. I was enjoying the work we did together until you recommended this last thing. I've done enough of your research, which has now begun to upset me. You'll come to realize one day that some of us are not what you call sick workaholics but healthy people at peace with themselves because they know that their work is the essence of the good life and a way of giving to everyone's welfare."

Many years later, I learned from a patient who knew Chris that he had had several minor heart attacks. He refused to slow down after any of them and was now a candidate for open-heart surgery. His wife had left him, and his children were living as ski and tennis bums in resort towns. He lived alone. He had been made the head of his firm, but recently had been kicked upstairs because of his illnesses. When last seen, he was chronically depressed and had withdrawn socially because of his enforced inactivity. He told my patient that he felt all he had to do to get over his long slump was to find another law firm that would appreciate the true value of an "old-fashioned nuts-and-bolts kind of worker."

ANALYSIS

Chris worked obsessively and compulsively, and most of his free associations were related to his work. His work excesses blocked out any social, family, marital, and erotic life. His perfectionistic, rigid, and slightly paranoid description of his present situation showed that he overworked himself to the point of exhaustion. Work had so dominated his life that it had become his only way of relating to others. It was the only subject of conversation or fantasy that aroused his emotions. He handled all his conflicts, pressures, and inability to confront disturbed relationships by turning to work. His narcissistic denial of people's needs was also dealt with by one form or another of work. Work superseded every other value in his entire life.

His need to work had escalated over the years; he had to do more and more of it to feel sufficient gratification. He finally became a "work freak" with no other identity, isolated from others in social or play situations. He developed withdrawal symptoms during vacations and social events, became depressed, tense, and alienated, and suffered physical symptoms such as stomach pains and tension headaches.

Chris had some physical symptoms and periods of paranoid behavior, but neither he nor those around him were aware of his problem, for the symptoms of work addiction are very subtle. His worst depressions occurred when he could not engage in some form of work. He had considerable underlying anxiety and was constantly fatigued and detached. His depressed, joyless nature and emotionally constricted, self-righteous manner inevitably separated him from people. He constantly over-controlled himself and others and could not sustain intimate contact or express anger. He was essentially fearful and distrustful, and he refused to face his failures or his insensitivity to people who did not live up to his merciless standards.

Chris's addiction flowered when he was well into adulthood. Work-addicted people are easier to identify then, because it is easier to withdraw into work when one is independent of one's family. It is not as easy to identify the work-addicted child; the young work grind who is a loner may be tolerated by peers and often is lauded by adults. Parents and teachers may hold up his work excess to others as a virtue or even as model behavior.

The seeds of Chris's addictions were sown early in life by a series of tyrannical, rigid, and compulsive nurses. Their severe regimentation was approved by his parents until they discovered that overt sadism had been used. Besides this cruel overcontrol by surrogate parents, he had emotionally detached parents, the father progressively obsessed with work and the mother fiercely ambitious. Both parents valued him only in terms of his work performance and adherence to standards of social behavior.

Chris also had to contend with a play-addicted sister, who developed patterns of asocial excess (delinquency, excessive drinking, addictive sex) to retaliate against her parents' and nurses' overcontrol and coldness. Chris's behavior was, in part, a reaction against her rebellious hedonism.

Chris's education contributed further to his developing an addictive life. He complied with the very strict, religious, conservative atmosphere, the stress on achievement, and competition, the work ethic that dominated all other values. There he showed social isolation and alienation; he could relate to others only on the most superficial social plane. He even worked at play, taking part in sports to compete rather than for enjoyment.

His work addiction mounted during his last year in prep school. In college he changed to other addictive practices. This brief but intense shift into the early phases of other addictions resulted in total collapse. He could not tolerate the radical changes, became completely disorganized, and had to be hospitalized. At the hospital he was prepared for even more pernicious forms of work addiction, fed by his fear of once again losing control and endangering his emotional life.

Chris had many contacts with addictive work, play, sex, and drugs from his college days on. They reinforced his addictive process either by acting as *models* and *complements* or in *collusive* or *interlocking ways.*

The most important fact of Chris's earliest years, we have seen, was the absence of any real emotional bond with his parents and parent substitutes. This created a need to compulsively and obsessively order his life and perform to perfection. Over the years, his emotional isolation triggered him into increasing work; the work allayed anxiety produced by detachment. At first this worked, for it brought some acceptance from others and the rewards of achievement; but it also began to strengthen an already overdeveloped superego (conscience) which had first been formed by his nurses, parents, schools, and as a reaction against his sister's weak superego. His own superego soon became tyrannical.

The first crack in his armor appeared in adolescence. He could not deal with all the emotional, erotic, physical, and interpersonal changes in his life. This inability and his work excess triggered him into compulsive masturbation. He continued to use this to relieve anxieties rising from nonsexual stresses he could not cope with.

The most significant trigger mechanism in his last year of prep school was exposure to Wendy, who was herself multiply addicted to sex, drugs, and speed. She provoked Chris's short foray from work addiction into excesses of play, sex, and drugs. It is important to recognize that Wendy's and Chris's behavior was not that of two normally lusty teenagers. There is a difference between healthy adolescent rebellion and the insatiable need for sexual and drug-taking excesses that led to Chris's hospitalization.

As a reaction to his breakdown, Chris returned increasingly to excessive work. He made few or no emotional contacts and remained isolated except from those who pursued him or arranged his life. Despite a surface appearance of independence, he was deeply dependent on others to arrange his emotional, social, and erotic life. Soon he was to be overcontrolled by another woman, Sally. She directed his social and erotic existence and ultimately maneuvered him into marrying her. This reveals the high degree of passivity in his personal life. Sally's manipulation of Chris's social life triggered further work excesses. He felt the first work high of his life, and then the first signs of withdrawal when he had to abstain from work on his honeymoon.

Chris managed to find a career with competitive demands that played into his addictive process. He was intuitively attracted to a work-addicted employer who could trigger further work excesses. After marriage, his wife's addictive spending and abandoned pleasure-seeking continued to trigger his work addiction. The breakdown of their erotic life pressured him still further into addiction, and he again practiced addictive masturbation to cope with the anxieties produced by his emotional detachment and isolation.

Chris's role in life soon became that of everyone's superego. His self-rightous behavior could only make others respond with hostility or withdrawal. This in turn made Chris even more isolated and caused further withdrawl into work-addictive behavior.

The crisis that brought Chris into therapy involved a temporary breakdown of his usual defenses—repression, denial and projection. This breakdown produced an acute paranoid reaction, but it did arise from his confrontation with someone—Winkler—who was himself addictive and understood Chris's problem. Winkler attacked Chris's facade and broke him down. In treatment, Chris became even more self-righteous and temporarily reconstituted his ego through hours of confessional—detailed reports of every aspect of his life. This acted as an emotional catharsis and allowed him to relax more than he had in recent years. But eventually he had to deny the value of his catharsis, and despite unearthing his repressed erotic history, he had no ability to gain insight from his therapy. He merely supplied detailed information for me to piece together for my research. He often defensively said to me, ''I hope this gives the complete picture of what I felt. . .did. . .saw. Mark my word, I never told anyone that such things went on in my mind, not even when I was hospitalized years ago. I have done this to let you understand how one gets corrupted, and about the cesspools of my past that I have rid myself of through good, hard, honest work.''

These hours of reportage became for him a work binge. They enabled him to temporarily cope with a traumatic situation that might again have resulted in hospitalization. For the time being, his paranoid mechanism had helped stabilize his life.

Because of Chris's extreme denial of his addictions, extended therapy was impossible; he left before follow-up could take place. This is typical of work-addicted people. Of all addictions, theirs is least assailable, and it is not accompanied by the many obvious character defects that appear in other addictions. These defects are submerged under a self-righteous surface. Only the people close to Chris experienced these defects—his detachment, tyrannical superego, selfishness, tightness, passivity, social dependencies, need to control everyone by work, and denial of the sensual and intimate aspects of everyday living. Others felt them as insensitivity and even cruelty.

Chris's addiction left him alone and without humor or joy. Without help for his problem, he will be vulnerable to profound withdrawal symptoms, depression, compulsive masturbation or loss of libido, psychosomatic illnesses, and a physical breakdown because of overwork.

ELLEN

THE CRISES

Ellen Smithers' plump cheeks and full red lips were set off by deep, clear, sparkling brown eyes and a luxurious mop of auburn ringlets. She had a big frame, and her arms and thighs had grown disproportionately large; they carried a great deal of weight that added to her bulky appearance. If you looked only at her pretty face, you might disregard the rest of her body.

All summer Ellen had been dreading the first day of her junior year of high school. I could see from the way she looked at me, however, that visiting a psychiatrist for the first time was not her idea of an ideal escape. She had been brought by her mother, Ceil, because she'd run away over the weekend and returned confused, disheveled, and apparently dazed from some drug. She angrily announced to her family that she'd done everything they could possibly imagine, then retreated to her room and refused to say anything more.

She didn't say much at that first session, when I saw her and her mother together. Ceil talked at great length about Ellen's problems, asking me why her daughter was so moody, so difficult to handle, and unable to control the constant eating that made her overweight. She answered her own questions so rapidly that I imagined few people could do much more with her than listen.

She had talked about Ellen's problems so constantly that Ellen had adopted her mother's version of her childhood as her own. As I looked at both of them—the slightly overweight, physically imposing, and emotionally aggressive mother and her pretty but very overweight daughter hunched defensively in her chair—I could see that each was causing the other a great deal of pain. From what Ceil said I gathered that the whole family was in trouble.

We arranged for Ellen to see me for individual therapy and see a nutritionist about a weight-reduction program, and for the whole family to come together for additional therapy sessions. Clearly she and I could accomplish little that would be lasting if she continued to feel that she was the focus of her family's problems. Finally Ceil left us alone together, and she described the crisis that had brought her here.

I feel alone, like I don't even have a life. Just. . .eating, and even that. . .I guess it doesn't make me feel much better. And now all the things I've. . .done since I left home that night. . .and now a real psychiatrist asking me please tell my story. . .I feel like I don't have anything worth telling. Even all the things I did since yesterday made me feel like I have absolutely nothing. Everyone has so much more happening to them, stuff they can look forward to. I just feel trapped. The same old Ellen. . . never changed in my whole life except to get fatter! I've always been fat, so what difference do a few pounds make? I'll never be thin. . .probably end up with even more problems after. . .the things I did since I left home.

I wanted so much to be like my friend Margie, but I get stuck in front of the damn TV. And the minute I switch it on, there has to be one of those dumb cake commercials where everybody loves everybody. I know that's probably why I watch it so much. . .constantly, my mother says, she's always nagging me about it. But watching food commercials isn't as bad as being surrounded by her cooking! I mean, really. All my mother ever does is fix, fix, fix, food, food, food! And she's always saying we all eat too much, we ought to cut down. But when we cut down at family dinner, it seems like we have that much more at company dinners.

God, how I hate those company nights! She invites all those assholes, fixes food for two days, gets horrible, and yells at me no matter what I do. She even wrecks her own meals by yelling at me right at the table. Sometimes I pretend I'm sick and stay in my room. . .then I don't have to see any of them. I never have anything to wear anyway. . .I just made it into my jeans this morning.

I hate looking in the mirror. I used to do it so much, just to check. . .see if. . .I wish I didn't have any mirrors in my room. Zach. . .my brother, he's such a creep. . .he just waits to catch me looking at myself and calls me "Big Ass." He'd like to have a sexy sister. . .that's the only thing in his dumb head. . .I'm glad Margie turned him off when he came on with her. He's so stupid he doesn't even realize she wouldn't go out with someone that dumb. He needs someone to put him down, anyway. He's always showing off in front of his mirror. . .flexing those muscles, lifting his weights. He thinks he's so cool. . .like parading in front of Margie with his shirt off, like he didn't know she was here. . .God's gift. . .sucking in his stomach, sticking out his chest. And he wouldn't look so hot if he did let his stomach stick out. He'll get his some day. Someone'll prick his big balloon for good.

Now I feel like something to eat. . .even while I'm here talking like this. . .about problems. . .like when I'm looking at TV. Seems like it's the only thing I do these days. But what else can I do? God, I can't even get away from supermothers on television. "She did it all without any grease. Country Crust is the lovin'est way to frah chicken for your family." My mother's always at me to do a hostess act for her, just like on TV. . .feed 'em and they'll love you.

"Ellen, would you watch the oven for me? The layers for my torte are in, and I don't have time to wait. I have to get the hors d'oeuvres from that new place everyone's using, and then I've got to stop by Mrs. Koster's for her caesar salad recipe and some of her garlic croutons for it.'' Ya. . .ya. . .ya! That's the way it goes. Or, ''Ellen, what are you going to wear tonight? You acted so terrible last night. I skipped my Thursday Gourmettes to take you to Alexander's. Then you carried on like a baby, saying all those things to the saleslady and everyone could hear you!'' Ya. . .ya. . .ya. Hysterical! I can't stand it!

I keep begging her, ''Mother, will you just leave me alone about what I'm going to wear?'' But she won't, and then she snoops around all the time and uncovers my nibbles. . .her nibbles that she says are for cocktails, like the banana flakes and the macadamia nuts! I hid them under the couch in the living room, I admit it, so I could sneak a handful when I was watching TV. . .because watching TV. . .I mean, the ads make you feel starved. But she doesn't fool anybody. The cans and little cellophane packs of nibbles are right there in her bedroom at night, right on her bedside table, because she's a closet eater. She sneaks it, just like I do!

Why does she say she'll tell Daddy? Fat chance he'd care. What could he do, anyway? She's got him snowed. . .he's just another one of the fats in this family! Doesn't care about me either. . .I hate her, and I hate him too. All he can think about is his Knicks and his Mets and his Jets. . .and his beer. The only thing he does is eat. He eats all night. I can't stand him lately. . .making terrible jokes about me with Zach. I hate them all except Margie. She was so nice to me yesterday. . .I will call her. . .we'll do something tomorrow. She'll still be my friend, even though she lost all. . .that weight. . .oh God, that word! I can't stand thinking about it any more. . .about me. . .my. . .size. . .that last dinner with all of them. . .Nana, Aunt Belle, Uncle Willie and Jeff. . .it was too much, all of them at once. Aunt Belle and Nana wanting to know if I'm dating. . .Jeff snickering with Zach. . .Aunt Belle raving about that diet doctor of theirs and how he got them to lose so much weight. Then they come to one of our dinners and put it right back on! And whenever they're feeling thin, they really let me have it. . .handing me ten pounds of clippings about every new diet they've heard of. I never go on any of them any more. . .they make me hate them so much the way they tell me about them. Anyway, if I did try, I'd be the one person who wouldn't lose a pound. Even if I did lose, it'd take me a year. . .and so what? Who'd want to take me out?

I'm so tired of crying alone in my room. Looking at myself sideways in the mirror, pushing my stomach out as far as it'll go. I know I look horrible this way. . .I'd like to cut it all away. Someone even said I look like I'm pregnant. I hate them, all of them. . .all the fooling around they do. . .but I do look awful. I could just die. No one would ever want to have a baby with me. The way I look. . .I really want. . .a. . .

Here I am, thinking. . .I'm thinking about food again. I mean. . .now, even while I'm talking like this. . .about my mother, and her cakes and tarts and desserts. How can I stop thinking about them? If only she wouldn't nag at me, make me help with those big fancy things like the cakes. . .frosting the cakes. And the screaming and picking on me. ''Ellen, you let it get scorched!'' I mean, she's hysterical about food herself. ''Help me do this! Help me do that!'' Nothing but food and cooking. My God, no wonder we all eat so much in our family! We think about food all the time. I bet even my so-called sexy brother's a closet eater, too. And he is a sex maniac, with all that porno stuff hidden in his closet under that smelly pile of gym clothes! That's no better than my buying chocolate chips and cream fills and hiding them! Just so I can take a handful now and then. . .when I absolutely can't stand it any more. So what if I do love the cookie jar? At least I know what I'm doing. . .I. . .uh. . .know I shouldn't. But it's better than hiding that porn and looking at it. . .and. . .oh, what's the use. I know I'm a mess.

A fat freak, that's what I am. Zach! I hate that bastard! He actually screams at us all for eating too much. Him, with his pimples! Oversexed bastard, making love to himself, looking in the mirror all the time. I can't stand it. And I can't even get into this summer's jeans, much less anything. . .good looking, new. . .sexy. I can't even face. . .uh. . .trying to squeeze my ass into tight French jeans. . .or a stretch sweater. Maybe if I grew my hair and fluffed it out, got that soft look. . .I. . .Christ, that's not going to help, and I know it. But maybe something to make my face. . .my cheeks. . . look a little smaller, narrower. But I know damn well that nothing's gonna make my other cheeks. . .God, I'd be so humiliated to even try to squeeze into something. . .things like Margie can wear now.

If only I could do it. . .she did it. . .lost so much. I. . .I've looked at all the diets. . .so many diets in all the magazines, even the newspapers Aunt Belle keeps sending me. She even bought me a happy-face scale that I'm afraid to get on. . .I just don't want to know how much fat. . .maybe an all fruit diet, just fruits and some water. . .no, I know I couldn't. . .I mean, I wouldn't stick it out. I know I couldn't.

Fat ass, that's what Zach calls me, the bastard! Sometimes Mother does try to understand how cruel. . .how he treats me. The other night after I'd gone through this huge crying jag, she came in my bedroom and sat down on the bed a little while to talk and said, "Ellen, really, you've got to get out of yourself. Staying in your room so much, watching TV all day, it just isn't healthy." She said I'd end up at a. . .a psychiatrist or something. She says I've got to stop moping around and feeling sorry for myself. God, I don't want to be this way! I don't want to keep on feeling sorry for myself and hopping from the candy store to the bakery to the ice cream stand on the way home from school. . .or from Margie's house. I just can't stop, but she's going to keep telling me to go out and be with someone. . .a friend. . .I don't have any friends. . .except Margie.

Oh, I know what Mother wants. . .a tall, thin, popular, beautiful daughter. She'd love to show me off at her parties and to her friends. Goddamn it, I hate them! Why do I put up with her? And with them? "Now remember, Ellen, the salad plates go on the left. . .be sure to leave some room for the scalloped potatoes. . .I'm using that new recipe with sour cream. . .make another place for the fried eggplant and zucchini sticks. . .we'll use the crescent salad plates for the corn, so people can get the melted butter on the corn instead of losing it in the rest of the food." Jesus Christ, it goes on forever!

God, and she wants me to be thin and gorgeous! She's absolutely impossible. I do this, that, everything. . .trying to please her. I set the table and let her boss me around like I'm an idiot or some kind of freak. I try to be nice, ask her if it's okay about the things I wear, and when I finally manage to think of something I'm happy to wear, all I get is, "Find something clean, find something cute." Me. . .cute! What in the world would look cute on me? Yeah, cute, as long as it isn't a cute tent. Something that makes me look adorable so everyone will think I'm sweet. Maybe I should just dip myself in marshmallow fluff and we'll see who gets a case of sticky fingers for me. If I don't eat it all off myself. . .before I waddle into the living room.

She's really like an absolute maniac before one of her precious family dinners, when we all gorge ourselves like animals. You should hear my father trying to calm her down. "Listen, Ceil, try to calm down. You're tearing around this kitchen like a steam engine. You'll be worn out by the time the family gets here. Where's Ellen? Why isn't she here helping you get things ready?" It just doesn't let up, ever. Then she says it's better if I don't help, because I'm so sullen and mope around in my room. . .just watching TV and eating, eating. Then she starts on how I screamed at

Zach. . .that shit. . .and our fights are going to drive her wild. It all. . .ah. . .ends up with me in tears again, running back into my room like. . .like a goddamn animal. Back in your cage, Fatso. In the end, all my father can do is try to calm everyone down. . .which means he usually ends up taking her side. Oh, God!

"Ellen, I won't have this disrespectful behavior from you. Ellen! Do you hear me? And I don't want to hear you slamming the door of your room again or I'm going to take it right off the hinges." Can you believe this is my father talking? Unbelievable! But he has to, partly because of her. . .she's standing right there, waiting to see what he'll do to me. I just can't stand the way they make him hassle me like that. It always ends up with me jumping on my bed and crying all over again. Fat, sick crybaby, that's what I'm turning out to be. And I don't want to!

You can't imagine how horrible it was on Saturday night. She said it was going to be extra special. The last family dinner of the summer. Well, it was the pits, really the worst. I felt like staying in my room. I just couldn't face them, that same bunch of stupid assholes, Aunt Belle and Uncle Willie, Nana, Jeff, all doing the same stupid things. Daddy always makes his great new drink of the week and keeps pouring it out for all of them, even Nana. She's getting deaf and sort of senile, and she gets completely out of it when Daddy gives her a drink. And Jeff and Zach snicker around in the kitchen, sneaking drinks and telling their slutty jokes. . .I can't stand hearing them or thinking about them any more. I stay up in my room as long as I can. I guess I must seem. . .more weird and screwed up to them than I really even am.

When I went in there last Saturday, they were all smashed, including Nana. My mother was pushing food at them, and they kept gobbling it up and laughing their stupid heads off. They didn't even notice me standing there at first. Then they started in with their usual asshole talk.

"Ellen, dear, let me bring you your plate from the oven."

"I'm so glad you came out to see us. Are you feeling better? Sit here next to your Aunt Belle and tell me all about it."

"Gee, you look tired, you musta flaked out in there. You still look like you're dreaming."

"Come here and give your old Uncle Willie a kiss, honey."

"Sit down, Ellen, and have something to eat. It'll pick you up, like that old Kickapoo Joy Juice I fixed for everybody."

I usually say, "I don't really want anything. Don't bother bringing it out. I'm still half asleep."

"What's that you said, dear? What did Ellen say? You want to go out? Have something first. Do you want to go back to sleep? You have to have something to eat first."

"Listen, Nana, she doesn't really need it. It'd be okay if she missed a meal or two."

"That'll be enough of that, Zach. Just stop it for now. I won't take any more of this."

My mother came marching out of the kitchen with a huge plate of food and plunks it down in front of me. I know she was saving it in the oven just to show them all how good she is to her darling daughter. I sat there staring at it. Then I shoved my arm straight out, with my palm out facing them, and pushed my plate away, and everything went tipping over all around. Mother jumped up again to grab everything. The rest of them were so smashed they just sat there like dummies. I just don't know why I did it. . .suddenly seeing their greasy faces and those piles of food. . .it's a kind of a blur. . .I don't really remember what they did or what I did. I know I suddenly began to feel starved, but I didn't want them all sitting and staring at me while I ate.

The whole thing was like a nightmare. For a second, they were absolutely stunned. Then everyone except my father just pounced on me. I could feel my face getting red, and then I felt red all over, with this scream building up inside me. My mother was grabbing napkins and mopping stuff up, grabbing my plate away and yelling about the mess. Aunt Belle was saying to everyone:

"Look how she treats her mother! All that work, and she ruins the whole dinner and gets everything in a mess. And she comes to the table looking like a mess herself. It's no wonder all they have is trouble with her."

Jeff and Zach were laughing like mad. I thought, well, if I just eat something. . .I reached for the cake, and I was just pulling the plate over to take a piece. . .I wasn't going to eat the whole thing. . .and Zach jumped up and hit my hand, mashed it right into the cake, and started yelling. . .I don't even want to say. . .he was horrible. I jumped up so fast my chair fell over, and then I really yelled at them all.

"I'll kill myself! You're all killing me!"

I ran out of the room screaming as loud as I could. I guess I really scared them. . .their faces really looked scared. I could hear my father calling out that it was okay, that I helped make the cake and I should come back and have a piece. I didn't know what I was doing. All I knew was that I couldn't stay one more minute at that table or in that house. . .or with any of them. . .because they're killing me, they really are!

I went in my room and rummaged through my bag. Thank God I found three dollars and sixty-cents in it and all my eye makeup and other stuff, just enough to last me through the night. I was thinking, where could I go? What could I do on three dollars and sixty-cents? I was wishing I'd told them all what I'd really like to do to them. Who could I go to? Who really cares about me? No one. . .no one!

I was out of the house, and I started crying again, stumbling down my own street as if it was some strange dream place, alone. . .lost. . .I wanted to go into a deli and buy something. . .I felt hungry. . .I hated them! I bought a cupcake, and. . .ugh, it was too thick, too sweet, but I finished it fast and called Margie with change I got in a candy store. . .I told myself I had to buy something to get change for the phone. Anyway, I called Margie, but no luck. Her line was busy. Typical! I can't ever reach her when I want to. At least I had my Milky Way. I. . .imagined Margie was telling someone right then about how she did it. . .so proud. . .of being thin. But she is nice, really good to me. . .the only one.

Still, I was really feeling mad. Dialing and dialing, getting a busy signal, and then a wrong number. Finally I slammed down the phone and decided to wait. Meanwhile I was getting more and more hooked on the idea of going into that new Flavor Heaven that just opened. It was only a few blocks. . .they had the windows covered with posters of the flavors of the week. . .Peachy Cream Shortcake and Black Forest Chocolate Mint.

Everyone at the Flavor Heaven was taking tickets and waiting. It took me a while to make up my mind. I had a chance to look at all the flavors. . .the Banana Boats, the Softee Swirl. "Try our Celestial Zodiac Spin-a-Flavor and see what the stars say." You pressed the button for your sign. . .Taurus. . .then you spin the gadget around and it tells you a choice of two flavors. I got, "For you, friendly and courageous Taurus, Apple-Cherry-Cheesecake or Berry Bubblegum. Take this double-ended spoon, show the counter boy your card, and he will be glad to give you a taste of each.'' Oh, wow! Just then he was calling my number. I said, ''Here I am!'' I asked him if I could try the Black Forest Chocolate Mint instead of the Berry Bubblegum. He sort of glared at me at first, but he loaded both ends of the spoon. I thought, oh, wow, now I can't decide between these two or the Peachy Cream, which is one of my real golden oldie favorites.

Suddenly I felt better, and he started being nicer. He told me if I were Pisces, maybe it'd be easier, because their choices this month were Peachy Cream and Funky Fudge. Then he said he'd just transform me into a Pisces! I told him I'd always had good vibes with Pisces.

He was real cute, and he was paying lots of attention to me. We started fooling around and went through most of the zodiac, when some nasty kids started making a fuss and the manager came out. He was really mean. . .uh. . .all the people waiting in those places get so horrible, because everyone is so impatient to get what they want. I felt as though they were all ganging up on me, just because I was having a good time. . .and that boy was being nice to me. It seems when someone treats me nice, someone else always louses it up.

Anyway, they were terrible. I don't even want to remember what they said. I ended up running out of there, crying again. . .for a change. Sometimes I feel as if I don't have any control over myself any more. I can be feeling just terrible, and then something will get me laughing when I don't even expect it. And then when I feel okay, the least little thing will make me cry and ruin it all.

I went to a phone booth and tried to finish up that messy ice cream while I called Margie again. Her mother answered, and when I told her it was really important, she said Margie was at a meeting. I felt kind of funny. I was afraid Margie had been lying to me or something, because she'd told me she had a date that night. But I couldn't think of anything else to do, so I got the address from her mother and went to meet her, fifteen blocks away. I started walking there, and suddenly I noticed I'd dripped ice cream all over my jeans. It looked awful, chocolate and tangerine spots! But I felt as if I had to go, because there wasn't anywhere else to go.

I wondered what kind of meeting she was at, and what she'd say when I told her what they all did to me tonight. I kept thinking and walking and hating them because I felt so bad. I started thinking maybe Margie and me would go out for something after the meeting, maybe just a hamburger, some place where they butter the bun. A rare hamburger, with the juice soaking into the bun, and maybe green relish, or mustard and onions. . .and a Coke. . .a fountain Coke, because they're better than the bottle kind.

When I finally got to the place, there was a sign, SECOND FLOOR—WEIGHT WATCHERS. I thought, my God, what's she doing? Why? How could her mother send me there? Maybe Margie had been sitting there the whole time and told her mother to send me! Maybe she'd been trying to push me into this. On top of everything else being so awful. . .how could she! She's supposed to be my friend! I started to go a little bit out of my head as I climbed up those damn stairs, feeling. . . just as mad as I'd be at home. I hated it! It almost made me start crying again.

At the top of the stairs they had all these big signs about dieting that would piss anyone off and they really hit me. It. . .was awful, disgusting! I just stood there with my head buzzing.

I thought it must really be a horror show. . .I can't. . .can't go in. . .but. . . where else? Maybe I'll just go in, get some booklets or some information. . .as long as I'm already here, and feel miserable. I really have to do something right now or I'll die. . .just get a few folders and then get right out and call Margie, tell her I found out how to join and everything. Then she'll invite me over. But I hate it here. . .now I'll have to hate everyone. . .never forget what she's done to me, and how she did it. Maybe it was meant to be, like fate, because if I stay for a minute I can phone Margie and ask her if I can sleep over tonight so we can talk about this. . .awful place. . .I'll call later, when she's back from her date, and it'll be a good excuse. She'll have to do something for me. I'll forgive her for this. . .and maybe for the first time in my life I'll do it, really get going on a. . .stay on. . .get so I can. . .be part of the human race. I feel brave. . .I'll be strong, go in.

I finally got up enough courage to open the door and peek in the room. It was filled with more fat people in more sizes and shapes than I'd ever seen. . .a lot of girls, but mostly women. It seemed like all of them had platinum blond hair in the same hairdo, all grinning away with bright teeth. They all looked like big old Barbie Dolls! Maybe that's supposed to be what Weight Watchers makes you into. There were lots of tables with pamphlets and books on them, and each table had one of those ladies behind it. One of them saw me. I think she knew I was upset, because she grinned at me even harder than all the others but in a sort of kind way.

"Come on in, honey. We won't bite."

I walked over to her table and saw those booklets, stuff like *How to Avoid Temptation. . .Schedule Your Eating. . .To Keep Track. . .Break the Chain. . .How to Tell When You're Angry. . .Manage Crises Eating. . .Boredom. . .Tension. . .The Blues. . .Eating Out. . .How to Get Help from Loved Ones, Friends. . .To Shop Prudently. . .To Meet Special Challenges. . .*My God, reading all these I felt kind of scared about that and didn't know what I should do, but the lady was really nice. She asked my name and told me not to worry about paying now, and said meetings were every Monday, Wednesday, and Friday. Then she gave me a membership card to fill out and lots of pamphlets. Well, I was still pretty upset, so I just took the stuff and went to a chair near the door so I could get out fast. The whole thing was making me feel horrible.

There was a tall lady at the end of the room talking like a machine. . .like. . .uh. . . my mother. . .asking and answering questions I didn't even want to know about. Her hair so yellow, and this big red mouth of hers just kept moving. . .it was unreal. All those crazy people began looking fuzzy to me. I. . .uh. . .began to feel a little sick to my stomach, wondering how Margie could stand it. Suddenly I wanted a hamburger. . .a big, soft, rare, juicy one. . .so much I could taste it.

Then this big tall woman rapped on the table and called for everyone to listen to her. She said, "Now, everybody, we're going to have weigh-in results to see whose weight's off. If anyone didn't weigh in tonight, just raise your hand and let me know. It isn't too late, you can still go back and weigh in. You may even find a happy surprise in what you see." Everyone actually laughed, like they thought she was funny. She said, "Tonight I'm proud to tell you that Mrs. Blah-Blah is our top Lady Loser, with five pounds off this week and fifteen for the month."

That lady, the winner, stood up, and they all started clapping and cheering. She still looked like a dump truck to me, but she was smiling and bowing. Then somebody else who'd lost three pounds, and a man who lost twenty since he'd joined. . .he was the biggest one yet. I couldn't imagine that he'd lost any weight at all. It was too much!

But suddenly I thought maybe I'd join. . .then it would be easier seeing Margie, talking to her. I leafed through some of the those booklets the lady had given me, something about vegetables, thinking it just wasn't possible. I'd never make it, never be able to remember all that shit. And I didn't like those vegetables or their salad recipes. . .no blue cheese or sour cream dressing, just lemon juice. I thought maybe I could stand the fish and chicken, but they said no fried chicken, and that's the way I really like it, or chicken pot pie with really thick crust. They even said no watermelon. . .can you imagine. . .there's nothing to it, it doesn't even fill you up, but they say it's full of calories. The more I read, the worse I felt. If you really want to know, I felt like I wanted to eat everything. I hated every word in those books.

That lady said, "And now, everybody, here's a first-time speaker who, I might add, is also one of our youngest and prettiest members. Let me introduce our Speaker of the Week, Miss Marjorie Sloan!"

They started their stupid clapping again, and I looked up and saw Margie. I'd been so out of it I hadn't seen her there, up near the front. She was heading for the platform, and she really looked great. Beautiful new pair of suede pants, platform shoes, great new clothes I hadn't seen before. She really looked thin, and calm, too. But when she started to talk, I could tell from her voice she was a little nervous. Her speech was good, though. I still remember some of it because it got to me. . .even if it hurt a lot to hear it. She said:

"You can all see what's happened to me. I've kept on my program really easily. I found I like it because, like, I can still eat lots of different things and stay this way—if I may say that word I used to hate to hear—thin! Now I love to hear it. Thin. When people said that word, it used to cut into me like a knife. . .just like that other word, which I'm not going to say tonight because I hope pretty soon it's not going to be true about any of us. I guess that's why I love to hear people say thin now, because it describes me and it seems like it's being said in a nice way."

I couldn't believe it, but I started feeling sort of happy. I was even laughing and clapping along with those stupid people. Then she went into a whole long thing about her eating habits and how she got fat, and sneaking around to get food and hiding herself in big sloppy clothes. . .everything I do. I know it'd be great to be able to stop all those things, but. . .I don't know. . .the whole thing started to make me feel guilty. I don't know if I could ever do it. . .or if I did, whether. . .I'd look pretty. . .or have friends. . .or if it would make any difference in my horrible life.

Then Margie went into this number about how Weight Watchers was the thing that helped her, and how they'd all helped her by all trying together, and she could face things now. . .all kinds of people, and especially boys. It was really corny. I listened to all that crap and looked at all those creeps, and I felt worse and worse. I mean, who'd want to be with those people or end up that ridiculous? I just couldn't take it. I was ready to get out of there when I heard them clapping and cheering really loud, and Margie was running down the aisle toward me. I found myself jumping up, and we grabbed each other and hugged each other, and I was crying again. But she was crying too. She said how great it was that I came there, and how great she felt, and how happy she knew I'd be. So I knew she really did care, but I still didn't want anything to do with the rest of those people. I just hung on to her like we were in our own little world together.

She kept saying how brave I was to come all by myself, that she didn't try to push me into it because she knows I get enough of that from everybody else. I felt terrible! Finally I had to tell her I'd only come because of the way my family bummed me out that night. I started crying again, and she promised we'd get out of there right away. But she did say something about me coming to the next meeting. And when I looked up, a whole bunch of those creepy people was standing around us like they were ready to pounce, saying things like, ''Ellen, you'll be able to talk to us, and you'll feel so much better.'' I ducked my head down against Margie's shoulder again, and she was really great. She told them I had a horrible day and I was sleeping over at her house, so we had to go right away. She said something about me calling home, but I was so relieved to be getting out of there I just ignored it.

''Margie,'' I said, ''let's go. You're really great to ask me to stay at your place tonight and everything. I don't know if I can face my family, I'm still so upset. Can't we just go somewhere and sit?''

I was hoping it would be a place where I could finally relax and get something to eat. That Wunder Burger. I could have a double, with. . .it'd be my last, forever. . . with mustard and relish. . .instead of a double, maybe two, a cheeseburger and a hamburger, one each way, and French fried onion rings. But she wasn't into that. Maybe I wouldn't be either, if I was asked out like she is now. She reminded me that she was meeting some people. She'd promised this guy Max she'd meet him in front of the Super Scoop at nine-thirty. . .I'd forgotten she was seeing a guy tonight. I told her not to worry. I'd just go on my way somewhere, I knew I'd been enough trouble for her already.

She said, ''Oh, Ellen, come off it. You'll stay over at my place, and no more hassling. We'll go into the Super Scoop and sit and talk until Max gets there. Then maybe you'll feel better. Go tell your family you're okay and where you'll be.''

There I was, with Margie being so nice, making that place seem almost like I might join and really do something, and all I could think about was food. I can hardly stand to think how it takes over all the time, like I can taste it and smell it and feel my mouth and my stomach getting ready for it. I felt miserable. . .angry. . .I wanted to be funny about it. . .but mostly I wanted to get out, because what I really felt was lousy.

I grabbed Margie and started coming on the way I used to at school last year. I started yelling, ''I pledge allegiance to the flag of the Weight Watchers of America, and to the diets for which they stand.'' And we started marching around on our way to the door while I made up words to the tune of *America the Beautiful*, singing it at all those creepy ladies until we finally ran out of there laughing. I felt as if I'd gotten out of prison! And I think Margie felt that way a little, too. Anyone in their right mind would have to! My mind was loaded with. . .thoughts. . .and I don't think Margie even realized we were both running until she noticed I was ahead. She called after me to slow down. I felt kind of embarrassed, because it made me realize why I was running and where. . .the Super Scoop. It hurt to know that, and I could tell Margie probably knew too. So we stopped and got on the bus, and I told Margie about the whole horrible evening. I felt as if I had to tell her every word, like I'd never have another soul in the world to tell it to, and it was the most important thing in the world for her to hear it all.

She was really nice, said I wasn't alone in all this, and if I'd only stop and remember, she'd been exactly like me. She kept me from crying all over the bus, but she turned me off, too, and made me mad with her martyr speech. That crap just makes everything worse. All I could really think of was the maple walnut ice cream at the Super Scoop, or the buttercrunch. I'd have even settled for vanilla then, with butterscotch sauce getting just a little hard from the ice cream, and whipped cream on top. . .I couldn't stop myself any more, and no one else would either. I hated them all, and I wanted to die. . .and get a hamburger!

Then. . .I couldn't believe it. . .Margie started after me again. It was crazy, like she was picking up all my vibes and saying something that would really hit me.

She said, "Come on, Ellen! You've just got to stop worrying about all this so much. You can really be above all this if you face it. Come to the next meeting Monday. They even have them on Labor Day because people really need them. Are you listening to me? I want you to promise me you won't miss a single meeting. I went to all three every week for months. At first people say they can't make it all the time, but believe me, if you really want to, like I did when I'd finally had it with myself, you manage to do it."

I could hardly stand all that preaching, especially when Margie started about her family all helping her lose weight. It made me mad to hear about her mother letting her get her way. . .I guess I know why. . .because that'll never happen to me! Anyway, I was getting so depressed I couldn't think of anything to say. Then I saw the Super Scoop sign up ahead. I never thought that stupid wild West saloon lettering would look so great. I could see kids pushing in and out of those batwing doors. I really wanted to get in there so much it even gave me strength to be nicer to Margie. I had to have a Coke. . .or something. . .I was so nervous I was ready to jump out of my skin. I really wanted some ice cream, but even a Coke would have helped.

"I didn't want to meet him here," Margie was saying, "but he'd already told Debbie and Josh we would. I'd have felt silly saying I didn't want to set foot in this place. For me it could be the Super Slip. You don't just stop drooling over everything that easily! I don't want to go someplace that's going to be torture. But I feel so great tonight. . ."

We went inside. I'd only been there by myself in the afternoons, when it's quiet, but I'd heard from everyone that it was the place to be at night, so I'd been hoping I'd get there. And it was great, like an old western saloon, with a real old mahogany bar and a mirror behind it, only now it's for serving fantastic sundaes and ice cream. There are old wagons fixed up for serving hamburgers and hot dogs and French fries, and one part fixed up like an old dance hall, with great music, sometimes a live group on weekends. I always wanted to see that part of it with a group of people or someone cute. But none of it was the way I expected. . .everything just turned out wrong. . .one more place where everyone fits but me.

You know, everybody has to turn around and stare when you come in, like they all think they're so cool, and I didn't even have on any dark-red nail polish, besides being in those dirty jeans and T-shirt. And everybody else had on a great-looking outfit. I. . .I guess I've lost track of what everyone's wearing, and some of the kids had new fall stuff already. There were kids looking tan and great in cut-offs and halters, and kids with terrific high-waisted pants. . .not baggies, the kind that really fit. . .I felt terrible.

I felt completely out of it. It was really crowded, and the music was so loud, and all the smells of food from the different sections. . .I didn't know what to do. . .their hot fudge sauce is the best. . .I thought I was going crazy. I knew I could only have a Coke with Margie there, and the smell of those hamburgers. . .I don't know why I couldn't stop thinking about having a hamburger! At least I had to get into a booth, away from everyone. It didn't look like we could get one, so I grabbed Margie's arm and dragged her through the crowd. When she saw the sign over the counter, with all the fantastic TREATS FOR THE WEEK, she said, "Ellen, do we have to sit and look at that? Well, I hope it won't be for too long." But I knew it was a hell of a lot easier for her. It's all so easy for her now!

I was thinking I couldn't sit there with just a Coke, I was practically drooling at all the things on the sign. I just didn't care. I was getting confused by everything in there, I had to get somewhere I wanted to be, so I got on the stool in front of all those fantastic toppings. . .Fantastic Fudge, Tangerine Ambrosia Thriller, Strawberry Banana Shortcake. I guess Margie could tell I was getting into them. When the waiter came, she ordered two lemon Tabs. . .can you believe that! He acted really horrible, like some of those people do. I guess she was feeling as nervous as I was, because she kept preaching and explaining why she'd gone in there.

"I guess it'll just never be easy. I should stay out of places like this. Still, you have to try and get used to it, because it's around you all the time, like, three times a day at the table and everything. I haven't been near this place in at least four—well, definitely three months."

She seemed relieved when she spotted Debbie and Josh. They were in the ice cream section, giggling over a huge Tropical Delight. When they saw Margie, they started toward us, laughing and waving that pineapple shell around. I felt terrible, thinking, oh God, here they come. . .I was hoping they'd get stuck on line and be late. . .and they look so. . .oh God, I feel so ugly. . .she's really tiny, looks so good in those pants. . .and I never saw anyone look so skinny in a Kurta. . .I always have to look for the big heavy cotton kind, but hers is see-through, it's adorable. . .and no bra. . .no wonder she has such a cute boyfriend. . .both so straight and blond. . .everyone's noticing them. . .why did I ever come in here? I wish I could crawl in a hole. . .wish I'd ordered something else. . .getting really hungry. . .hamburgers. . .somewhere alone. . .warm. . .in a big chair, with a lot of hamburgers. . .rare. . .with French fries and a chocolate frosted. . . .

Josh and Debbie kept laughing and talked about what to do for the rest of the evening. Josh said, "Listen, let's make it over to Ron's after the movie. He's had a bash going ever since his dad let him stay alone in the house. He's got some kids there now who just split from some Jesus commune in Vermont. No more getting high on Jesus, man. Ron copped some great stuff that gets you off a lot better."

They were fantastic. I mean, all the things they were talking about. I didn't know Margie knew anyone like that, and I never thought I'd get to be with them. It was exciting, but I was getting a little nervous, and I think Margie was too, because she talked like she was trying to get out of it. Even Debbie sounded like she didn't want to go to something that wild, and she was kind of wild herself, at least a lot more than Margie.

While they were talking, a really cute boy snuck up and grabbed Debbie and Josh and clunked their heads together. Then he put his arm around Margie and said, "Hey, you look really beautiful." That had to be Max. I felt completely out of it, because he looked like he really meant what he said about Margie. And there she was. . .with him. . .laughing at everything he said and getting all psyched up by him. They looked much more stoned than anyone ever got when I was with Melvin. . .they did have the munchies. . .they looked so cute. . .and they were Margie's friends now that she's. . .but they must've really been heads. They do more than grass, all those people they know. How could Margie go to Ron's? That guy did a lot of dope. I was wishing I could get out of there. . .or have a Tropical Delight. . .alone. . .Jesus freaks are supposed to be really weird. I was thinking, what if Margie goes there? Those people must've been into a lot of sex, too. How could Margie be doing that?

Finally Margie remembered I was still there and introduced me, kind of nervously. Max was sort of nice to me, and so were Josh and Debbie. Max said, "Is Ellen coming along? I've got plenty of room in the car.'' Josh and Debbie said, ''Yes, Ellen, come along,'' and so did Margie.

Suddenly I stopped feeling so bad. Margie wanted me to be with her new friends, and I was pretty excited about it. Max said to me, ''Hang in and you'll be up in no time. A couple of tokes in the car and you'll be mellow by the time we get Stanley.''

I wondered who Stanley was and if they were setting up a date for me. Their friends sounded scary and. . .I've really only gone out with Melvin. I wouldn't know what to do. I started to feel awful, wanted to crawl away and be in a hole somewhere. I guess I ended up staring at Margie with my dumb helpless look, because they were all looking at me, and then Debbie and Josh stopped paying any attention to me and said they'd wait outside while we made up our minds. I could tell they didn't think I belonged with them, and they didn't want me around. Max kept asking me to come, and that made me even more nervous. Finally Margie asked him to wait outside, too, because we had to talk about a problem.

I felt grateful to her for getting me out of it, because I was really scared underneath. I felt I'd get hurt somehow, like I always do when I'm not wanted. And I felt especially ugly. . .fatter than usual that day. The whole thing was making me feel terrible. . .you know, having a chance to do something you always wanted to do. . .the kind of thing everyone else does. . .and then being such a mess that all you want is to get away from it.

Margie and I went to the phone booth, and she called her mother and told her I'd be going there right away and sleeping over because I didn't feel too good. She also told her I was too tired to talk and not to bug me, just let me watch TV or go to bed or whatever I wanted. Then of course she had to say to me, ''You can call your family from my place and tell them you're sleeping over.'' I guess she saw the look on my face, because she went right on, ''I know you probably feel like you never want to see them again, but you have to start telling them you aren't going to let them hassle you any more. Just call, and then we'll talk tomorrow about what to do with them next. Listen, I have to go or they'll be looking for me. I'll tell them you're meeting someone else here, okay? I'll see you later.''

I gave Margie the biggest hug, because at that moment I loved everything she did for me. She went out those swinging doors, and I felt like I'd been set free. It was such a relief to be alone again and stop worrying about every little thing about myself, so I let my mind go off again. Then that same rude waiter caught me staring at some people sharing a delicious-looking sundae. He smiled, just like my shitty brother, and pointed to the sundae and then to me. That really finished me off. I turned around and started to run out of the place like someone was after me trying to hit me. I was so humiliated I just pushed my way through all those kids and the noise, and I went through the swinging doors so hard I almost fell down, and kept running on down the street.

The bus was pulling up to the stop ahead, and I didn't want to have to wait for the next one, so I started yelling and waving my arms for the driver to wait. I almost made it into the bus, but he didn't see me, and the door closed on the belt of my coat. The bus started to take off and practically tore my coat in half. I fell right in a horrible filthy puddle of water filled with. . .ah. . .I don't even want to think about it. It was the end! I was lying there in a complete daze until I felt the driver grab my arm and shake me, and there were voices floating around me. People were saying, ''He could have killed her. . .they never wait for anyone. . .should we call an ambulance?''

It was like another nightmare in that whole horrible day of nightmares. I just sat there on the curb, completely gone. I mean, it was almost like I'd tried to kill myself or something. Then I realized I was really all right, and I looked at all those faces staring down at me, half scared and half angry like it was my fault or something. I thought they were going to pounce on me like everyone else that day. . .I had to get away from there.

I must have started running again, because suddenly I realized I'd gone tearing up to another bus stop as if I was chasing another bus. But then I realized there wasn't even a bus there, just a bunch of people waiting and staring at me like I was a goon. When the bus did come, I got on and saw that it was full of English muffin ads. Not another ad in the bus, just pizza English muffins, hamburgers on English muffins, English muffins for breakfast! So of course I started to starve all over again, and I got into such a daze that I missed Margie's stop and had to jump up and beg the driver to stop. He stopped with a big angry jolt, so everyone on the bus had to start making remarks about how rude kids are these days and about what a mess I was, and I ran out of the bus with my head buzzing like mad.

When Mrs. Sloan answered the door, she probably didn't know whether she should put me in the garbage can or the booby hatch. I was so dirty and sweaty and upset that the second she asked what was wrong I threw myself all over her and started crying like a real hysteric. I know it was awful, but I couldn't control myself, and the more she patted me and tried to be nice, the harder I cried.

Finally she led me to a big armchair and got me to sit down while I tried to stop shaking and gasping. She asked what on earth happened, but I don't know her that well, so I didn't know what to say for a minute. But finally I began, still gulping and blubbering. When I finished telling her everything, I still couldn't stop crying. I started telling everything again, but she wouldn't let me. She told me to try and calm down, which I didn't mind. At least she didn't yell at me like it was my fault for being upset. . .the way my mother does. She even said she understood about my having problems with my family, and she'd help me straighten things out with them in the morning. And she said Margie always talks about me and I'm really her best friend. That made me start to feel great.

She said I should get my clothes off so she could run them through the washer, and wouldn't I like a nice hot bath, and then she started that Weight Watchers crap. God, I couldn't believe it! I'd been thinking how great she was, and then she had to start the same number I've been hearing all my life. . .the same old songs as my mother. I was so hungry I could hardly breathe. . .I still wanted a hamburger. . . really needed a doubleburger. . .with special sauce and French fries. . .a chocolate frosted. . . . Who needed a hot bath? Who cared how I looked or how I smelled? Or what happened to me, or what was going to happen? Didn't she realize. . .couldn't she feel? I was getting more and more into that horrible mood of having your whole mind and mouth and stomach just crawling and angry for something, when it seems like all you're getting is trouble.

I guess she must have recognized my expression from seeing the same one on Margie's face, because she finally speeded things up, got my bath ready, and said she was on her way to the kitchen to make me a Weight Watchers seafood salad if I'd give her my clothes and take an old robe of Margie's she'd dragged out of some closet. I jumped up and grabbed the robe, ran in the bathroom, but I didn't care. I just didn't want to cope with anyone for a while.

I filled up the tub with lots of Margie's bubble bath and collapsed in there, letting the warm water run in, twiddling the plug with my toes to let the old water out and then letting a little more warm water in until I began to feel better. . .or at least like moving. I picked up the washcloth and began to slosh some of the mess off me. Margie's bath stuff was great, a new kind of organic peach oil thing, and by the time I finished, I was beginning to feel better than I had all day. I even started thinking about myself being like her that night. . .one thin person in the middle of a whole room of fat people.

I got out of the tub and decided I could face the mirror in the bathroom. . .Margie had daisy decals stuck all over it. I turned in all directions, catching sights of my body in the surrounding mirrors. The worst was my profile. My fat as bulging and it looked like I was pregnant, and my arms and thighs were four times bigger than I thought they were. . .and I had no chin. . .just a lot of flesh that went into my neck. . .it was a nightmare! I squeezed my eyes shut. . .I could have burst out in tears from the pain of what I saw in the mirrors.

I didn't know if I was facing things or just trying to punish myself. But I finally had to do something, so I jumped on the scale and looked at the dial. It said a hundred and fifty-five. . .and a half. . .and I'm only five-foot three. I couldn't believe it! I gained so much since. . .when? The last time I weighed myself was. . .God, I guess I stopped when Aunt Belle gave me that happy-face scale for my last birthday. I went on thinking of myself as a permanent 147. But I decided that I was going to be part of my past. I'd weigh in every time I had to and tell them all how much less. . .get myself right in the middle of their Losers Winners Circle! I knew right then I could become one!

I wrapped myself up in that robe, even though it was probably some reject Margie used to slop around in, and marched out in the living room and asked fast and loud for that Weight Watchers dinner. But I sort of crashed when Mrs. Sloan put that dinner in front of me. . .a toasted muffin with water-packed tuna and stuffed olives. . .and a carrot curl, a cucumber slice, tomato with no dressing. I decided that since I was stuck with that, I might as well eat it the way they said in those booklets. . .you know, small bites, chew, chew, put your fork down between mouthfuls. It was awful. It probably showed on my face, because Mrs. Sloan got very fidgety. Thank God she went back in the living room.

I finished and went into the living room. Mrs. Sloan was into her needlepoint and didn't pay much attention to me or to the TV program she had on. I was feeling kind of down, so I just watched the TV. It was. . .would you believe it. . .a documentary about starvation all over the world. I couldn't believe it. I mean, I'd heard about Bangladesh and even some places here in this country, but I never saw. . .so much of it. . .babies with legs like sticks sitting in the dirt, dry and leathery like old people. . . old in three years from never, never having enough. I couldn't believe I was where I was. . .all comfortable. When the program was over, I wanted so much to do something, help somehow, so I got a pencil and paper to write down the address of the organization that's sending food there.

I saw that Mrs. Sloan was paying attention to it, too. I said how terrible it made me feel to see all those people. . .those children looking like they're dead, and people not doing anything about it. I said, "I wanted to do something for them right away. I wanted to write a letter and tell them how I feel, and that I was going to try and help." I was surprised when she really liked my idea.

"Why don't you write the letter and tell them how you feel? I'll get letter paper for you, and I'll send some money myself."

I couldn't believe it. No one in my family gets excited over things like that. In fact, if it came on our TV, they'd run and switch fast to a ball game, grab another beer, and forget it. They think it's all right to yell at me for every little thing I do, but they never think about anything unfair in the world, and they sure don't want me to get worked up about it. . .it might disturb their stupid heads.

I sat down and began the letter, but Mrs. Sloan kept talking about how wrapped up in herself she was, and how she worries about petty things like how good the TV reception is and whether the butcher gave her the best cut of meat. Well, at least she admits it. But then she started a whole long thing about how she used to worry about Margie, and how she was afraid that she'd been partly responsible for her gaining so much weight. She said Margie was so pretty until she was twelve, and then suddenly she got really tall and self-conscious and wouldn't stand up straight and all that stuff. Then two years ago she broke her leg in a skiing accident, and that's when she got fat. She got really depressed when she was stuck in bed at home, and her mother fed her all kinds of candy and desserts to keep her happy, and that's how she started getting fat.

God, no wonder it was so easy for her to lose it! I don't know why she even needed that stupid Weight Watchers. At least she knew what it's like to be thin. All I know is what it's like to be fat. . .your whole life, and have everyone picking on you. Mrs. Sloan said it was only when she made up her mind to keep her mouth shut that Margie made her own decision to lose and went to Weight Watchers. And even then she felt like nagging Margie to get thin. I couldn't stand any more inspirational crap, but she went on about how she told Margie she'd been fat herself when she was a teenager, and that that helped them understand each other. . .I didn't want to find out any more. I said I was dead tired and went to bed.

It felt great to escape under those covers. I had a dream, though. . .actually a lot of dreams, all confused, that I don't remember. . .yes, the one thing I do remember is that I kept waking up and thinking it was morning, but it wasn't. Every time I woke up, I looked at the little clock beside the bed and it seemed like hours had passed, but it would only be fifteen minutes or a half hour. I guess part of it was waiting for Margie to come in. And the funny thing is that when she did come in, I didn't hear her. I must have fallen asleep one last time, and then Margie was waking me up, laughing and asking how much longer was I going to sleep. She told me I'd been sleeping hard, but twitching around like I was having a nightmare.

I told her I'd had lots but I couldn't remember any, even though they were scary while I was having them. . .maybe that was lucky or something. I told Margie how great her mother had been, and how much her mother cared about her, and how we watched TV together and everything.

"Yes, she told me about that," Margie said. Then she said she hoped I hadn't told her mother anything about Max and Debbie and Josh. . .she'd gone with them to the movie and then the party at Ron's for a little while, and then right home. She said she was never going out with Max again.

"But he's really cute," I said.

"He's cute, but he wants to hang out with those people at Ron's. I thought it would be terrific there, but it was scary. You heard what they were saying about what goes on there. If Mom knew, she'd kill me. You know, she's always reading dumb magazine articles about drugs and sex and kids, and she talks to her friends about them and asks me all kinds of questions."

"Yeah," I said, "there really is some pretty heavy stuff going now." Then I came right out and asked what I was really curious about. "What was all that about

Charlene and Don and Mr. Donegan? I heard Charlene turned into a big head, and I knew she and Don were making it, but I couldn't believe it about Mr. Donegan. I mean, everyone says he's a fag, and he used to be a priest or something. Right?''

''Well, the way I heard it, Don put some DMT in Charlene's chocolate milk at lunch about two weeks ago, and she was really tripping. Don was mad because he thought she was making it with Mr. Donegan. What he didn't know was that she was pregnant, and she freaked out and told him. He got scared and told her to lay it on Mr. Donegan. Well, she cut classes to meet Mr. Donegan in one of the boiler rooms during his free period. She was going to tell him, but it ended up with them getting it on together. Well, Don had been sneaking after them, partly because he wanted to catch Mr. Donegan at something because he was afraid Donegan knew about him selling reds at school. Anyway, he caught them, and everyone else got in on the act—Mr. Ferris and the nurse and two of the janitors. You know, Mr. Donegan and Charlene never came back to school. Don told some of it to Josh, which is how I heard. Really, all that group are scary. They look so great when you see them at school, but what they're always laughing about is dope. I really found out that you can't fool around with them. You're in all the way or forget it. When Max took me to Ron's, Josh was terrible to me when I wouldn't take DMT, and then Ron started in about how everyone should be cool about sex.''

Suddenly I didn't want to hear about all the things Margie was into. It was exciting, I guess, but it was scary. I jumped out of the bed and said:

''I should get up. You've probably all finished breakfast.''

''Mom and the boys did, but I waited so we could eat together. After they go, we can have a great day.''

That meant a Weight Watchers breakfast. I wanted to eat alone. . .muffins with butter and. . .but I'd have to follow Margie and do what she does if I was ever going to make it. I put on my clothes that Mrs. Sloan had washed for me, but I still didn't want to face any of Margie's family. I could hear her brothers and her mother getting ready to leave, and it sounded kind of nice. . .everyone joking around, Brian and Roger kidding Mrs. Sloan when she started fussing too much, instead of everyone exploding in a fight. But I wanted to be alone, so I fiddled around in Margie's room, putting on some of her eye makeup till they left. Then Margie came back and said we had to go down and eat.

It was awful! Grapefruit. . .not even pink, like when Mom's on a diet kick. . .but when she did that I never got stuck, just got up early and had chocolate milk, and cream cheese on date-nut bread, and cocoa with marshmallow if it was cold. Then I'd heat up some frozen blueberry blintzes with sour cream. . .and then sit with them. . .and listen to Mom lecture about how she was starting our day right. But she never knew what I'd had earlier. I'd just let her talk, leave a little early for school, and stop at Mister Pancake on the way. . .it's so nice in there. . .they always gave me extra cups of whipped butter.

Anyway, as soon as I choked down that God-awful breakfast at Marge's, she said we were going to play tennis. I felt absolutely trapped. She got one of her brother's old rackets for me and said I could use an extra pair of her sneakers. She even said she had an outfit I could wear.

I knew why she wanted to go. It was José, one of the student-teachers at school. He was going to give free lessons over the summer and have some kind of tournament. It was supposed to give kids something to do in the summer and keep them from doing drugs. I wouldn't be caught dead at a stupid thing like that, but I think Margie had a crush on José last spring. Sure enough, she started gabbing away about how José told her Ron played there before he started doing drugs, and José had said Ron could have been good enough to play competitions. But one morning he showed up there after he'd dropped some acid and really freaked. He started running away from the ball instead of trying to hit it, and yelling that something was chasing him around the court. José didn't call Ron's parents, just got someone to help him talk Ron down. But he told Ron that if he ever caught him fooling with drugs again, that would be the end. Ron did show up stoned again, and José called his father, but Ron's father didn't do anything.

Margie kept dragging out tennis balls and sneakers and socks, telling me about the Ron business. Finally she got out some horrible Mexican blouse, really baggy, and old white pants for me to put on. I'd never seen her in them, but I could tell they were from her old fat wardrobe. Then I had to watch her put on a leotard and new jeans that really looked great. She's got so many mirrors in her room now it was practically impossible to find a place to stand where she couldn't see how big my breasts were while I was getting dressed. But she was busy going on about all the places she wanted to go—the museum, the park, some flea market they have weekends. She was trying to be nice, saying there were lots of old clothes I'd like at the flea market, so I might want to go with her.

Just as we were about to leave, Margie asked if I'd called my family last night. "You really ought to now if you didn't, because no matter how awful they were, they'll really be worried by now."

Well, I lied, of course, and told her I'd called them before I went to bed. Then I charged to the door ahead of her so she couldn't get after me about it any more. If I'd have to go through all that Weight Watchers crap, they ought to have some suffering of their own.

I imagined how they'd be that very moment. . .getting really worried. . .Zach not even able to concentrate on his sex magazine, and Mom screaming that I'd probably been. . .attacked. . .by some man. . .I'd be helpless, but then he'd realize I was nice. . .and I'd tell him how horrible they are and stay with him. . .big and strong. . .and Daddy would cry, realize how awful he'd been last night when it wasn't my fault at all. . .I could imagine Aunt Belle calling all morning, and Mom having to lie, or both of them crying. . .probably thinking I was dead. I wanted all of them to cry, especially shithead Zach, for having been so mean to me.

When Margie and I got to the courts, José was just finishing a lesson with three guys. Margie whispered, "Isn't he cute? When I'm on the court with him, I forget all my problems. Just wait till he puts his arms around you to show you how to hold the racket and follow through."

She went on and on. She'd really gone wild about him. I sure couldn't picture him putting his arms around me! I thought he'd be mad that Margie'd brought along a draggy, baggy mess like me. He'd probably want to be alone with her, and then she'd be sorry I came, and I'd have nowhere to go.

But I have to admit, at least that part of the day wasn't too awful. José was nice to me, even gave me a little lesson and put his arms around me, but he probably does for everyone. He acted like he was interested in giving me lessons. . .maybe even like he thought I was nice. And the lesson didn't make me as hungry as I thought, so when Margie dragged me into the museum for a salad lunch, it didn't seem too bad. I guess I wanted to get it over with so we could get to the flea market.

The flea market was great. I found just the kind of stall I like, with all kinds of great old stuff. I began putting together great outfits and even gave a costume lecture to Margie and some people who were hanging around. But when I said, "a woman's body, overexposed and underexplored throughout the years," the old bag who runs the stall said we should buy something or leave. Margie started dragging me away even though everyone else was laughing and enjoying it. Damn Margie! She's so crabby and inhibited. She doesn't realize how funny I am. . .get into the whole thing. . .can't let anyone have any fun!

I was feeling great. . .those old hats and shawls make your face look so good that no one notices the rest. So after that old biddy was so shitty to me, and Margie did her number, right away I began feeling slightly desperate over not having had one decent thing to eat. . .just that awful dry, crunchy breakfast and rabbity lunch. . .no dressing, just boring salad and cottage cheese.

Then we saw one of those crêpe carts. Margie started dragging me along faster, babbling about fixing a Weight Watchers frappé as soon as we got back to her house. . .called it our big treat. God, sometimes I just don't believe her! I began to wish I wasn't stuck with her, but I couldn't go home.

When we finally got to her house again, she took me into the kitchen and showed me the pantry closet her mother set aside for her. She had diet posters up, and pictures of skinny models, and one of some horrible fat old woman with an open refrigerator of food fallen over on top of her. And there were tons of diet books and receipe clippings. I mean, all of that might make you stop wanting to eat, but it wouldn't stop you from thinking about food.

Margie loved it all. She got out her own special blender and counted out four medium strawberries! Can you believe it, grading them by size for the rest of your life? She added some horrible powdered skim milk and lots of water, and lectured me about how I could make the same kind of goodies for myself at home. I couldn't take another minute of it.

"Margie," I said, "you're just as hung up on these dumb diet recipes as my mother is on her gourmet stuff. You sound like Mother and Aunt Belle and Mrs. Koster rolled up into one. You're still just thinking and talking food, and you're driving me absolutely bananas. I think those people are just making money by getting you to pretend to forget food, but they've got you so hung up you can't get off the subject. I mean, I really like food. If I'm not going to eat too much food, I've got to stop thinking about it all the time. So if you don't mind, I think I'd better get started home. I told my family I'd be there early. I'll be just in time for another table scene."

She stood there staring at me, looking really hurt. She said, "I'm really sorry, I didn't. . . ."

"I'm sorry too, Margie," I said. "I didn't really mean that. Maybe I really am ready to turn over a new leaf. And I didn't mean to hurt you."

I smiled and gagged down that awful plastic shake so she wouldn't be mad at me. And I guess she wasn't, because she went and got me a great embroidered Mexican dress to wear home and face my family in. It was the usual long, loose kind from her old days, but by the time I fixed myself up with some more of her eye makeup and got her to lend me a great scarf for a headwrap, I really looked good. She even admitted it looked better on me than it did on her. I really can put things together well when I want to.

She made me promise to go home and face my family, and go to the meeting Monday night. I. . .guess I. . .just kind of let her think I would. But secretly I couldn't wait to get out of there. As soon as I left, all I could think about was how much I wanted to sit down alone and have a nice, quiet, big meal. . .where it smells good. . .the Super Scoop, where they have big high booths. . .and a really fantastic dessert. You know, you can have a Triple Fudge Delight if you want one. Then I started thinking maybe I really should get home for supper. But I knew if I stayed out longer, they'd suffer more. . .but they might really go crazy. . .Mom might flip out. . .they all would.

As I walked along, I wondered if I should go to a movie. . .the one Margie. . .and Max. . .saw. . .the one everyone's talking about. Then I could talk about it, too. About what a trip it is. . .like they did. . .say things in school. . .to kids that belong. I could even let shitty old Zach know that I saw it. It looked like it might rain, so I finally got the bus and sat staring at the ads and the people, trying to figure out what to do. . .almost dreaming. . .when I noticed that the boy sitting across was looking right at me. And he was really cute, with the kind of real silky hair I like. I couldn't help wondering if I'd ever go out with someone like that. He was smiling at me, in my Mexican dress. I couldn't believe he was actually thinking about me. . .probably about his girl friend. Then he got off the bus, and that was that.

I never have any luck with boys. If he'd seen how fat I was, he would have been turned off anyway. I thought, what if I never get asked out? Why don't I ever meet anyone cute like that? Will I always be alone? Or end up with Melvin? I really want to have someone. . .not another. . .another freak like Melvin. . .and not just all that laughing and giggling. I'd like to have a boy to be alone with. . .to kiss. . .who'd think I was pretty. . .hold each other. . .feel so good. . .Melvin was such a movie freak. I know he never takes out anyone any more. . .probably just sits alone in the movies. And what if he was on line for this one and he saw me? I wouldn't want to wait on line with him. I want to change everything. . .get to look good. . .so someone like that boy. . .smiling and silky hair. . .would stop and talk to me. I'd smile back. . .no, I get too scared to even smile, feel like a big bag of. . .never know what to say or do. . . .

I felt down by the time the bus got to the movies. There was a huge line. It was awful being in that crowd. I could hardly stand it. That kind of thing always happens to me. I want to get away from home, away from my family, but when I do I feel even lonelier, more terrible. It seems like everyone else knows exactly what to do, what to wear. . .has someone to be with, so no one even notices me. Probably if anyone did, they'd just think I was a creep and make me feel worse.

I'm sure no one else in that movie line noticed how loud everything was, Muzak going, everybody laughing and talking, the usher marching up and down and yelling at people to move closer together. I was getting more and more nervous, and I kept asking him when he went by if I'd be able to get a good seat, but he stared right over my head and said, "Ticketholder's line. Five o'clock showing." Then when the line started moving, everyone was pushing and shoving and making me nervous. I knew I wouldn't be able to stop at the candy machine if I was going to get a good seat. Then just when I almost got through the door, that usher stuck out his arm in front of me and said: "All right, that's it! Line now for the next show!"

I couldn't believe it! It just wasn't fair. I was so mad I forgot all about being scared. I jumped in front of him and said, "What do you mean? I bought a ticket for the five o'clock show."

That bastard just stared right over my head again and said, to no one at all, "This is the line for the seven o'clock show. Five o'clock show sold out."

I was so mad I didn't know what to do. I couldn't stand the idea of waiting there, so I started running down that horrible crowded street. I decided to go to the Super Scoop for my last big fling. I guess it was my last big mistake, too. I know I shouldn't have gone, but the way I felt I couldn't get there fast enough.

It was just as crowded and noisy as the night before, almost worse than the movie line. I needed to get into a booth, so I was pushing back and forth with everyone else, looking for a place. Finally I saw a couple getting up near the back and made a mad dash for it.

I sat down and grabbed the menu, feeling so relieved to be alone in that booth. All I wanted to do was concentrate on what I was going to have. . .something I really wanted, my absolute last fling. A waitress came over and asked if I'd made up my mind. I hate having to decide like that, with someone standing over me. I guess I'm afraid they'll get mad. And if it takes a long time to get my order, I always think they're getting back at me for taking so long to make up my mind.

I asked about the banana split and what flavors they had, and she said, "They're all right on the menu. But the almond mocha fudge and strawberry cream cheese cake are sensational. I usually have them myself."

I said I'd take those, and Mountain Raspberry Ripple. And for topping I said to put marshmallow on top of the strawberry, fudge mint on the mocha fudge, and crushed pineapple on the raspberry.

She wrote it all down fast, like she'd get it right and bring it right away. I began to feel a little better, and I peeked around the edge of the booth to see what was going on. I saw Josh standing in the middle of a group of guys who all looked pretty wrecked. There was a girl right in the middle of them, laughing like crazy, and touching all of them like she knew they were all turned on to her. She was actually sort of grabbing at Josh, but he was the only one who wasn't paying much attention to her. In fact he was looking straight ahead, almost as if he was mad at her. Then I realized he was looking right at me! I felt really scared and ducked back into my booth. But he began to look like he was going to come over and talk to me. I thought he couldn't be. . .he was so fantastic looking. And no one had ever come on to me before, not even Melvin. Why me? I was sure it must be a mistake. He probably thought he saw someone else he knows.

But he was coming over. I felt like I was about to die right on the spot. And at the same time I was thinking, what if she comes with my banana split right now? Then I realized it was the booth. He could see it was empty except for me and he probably wanted it for himself, to sit in with that skinny girl they were all turned on by. But he was the best looking. I figured she probably wanted to be with him.

He said, "Hey, Ellen, what's happening? This place is such a hassle tonight, and you look so cool sitting here by yourself."

"Oh, I'm just doing the same thing as everyne else in the place."

"Oh? You look like you're waiting for someone."

I sat back and sort of laughed. "Oh, no, I always travel alone."

The waitress came back with my banana split. I didn't know what was going to happen. I sat there feeling like an idiot and clutched my fingers together under the table.

He laughed and said, "Don't tell me you thought you were going to have this all alone!"

"Well, I was, but be my guest. I'll order another spoon."

I was surprised at myself, but he made me feel good, and I began thinking he really wanted to stay. I was so excited by the idea of having him to share the banana split that I jumped up and waved at the waitress so she'd come right over. He gave her that smile of his and asked for the spoon and a napkin. Then he turned back to me and said, ''That's all I need—for now. But maybe later on we'll have fun my way.''

I felt a little scared when he said that, and he started smiling that way at the waitress again. It seemed like he was coming on with her, and she was digging him, and I started hating them both. I was getting into a really bad mood again. But then he turned around and scooped the cherry from the top of the dish along with a lot of whipped cream and pressed it gently against my mouth. It was so great the way he smiled at me and said in a soft voice:

''Come on, try it and see if you like it. Especially the cherry. That's special from me to you, or will it be from you to me?''

I was ready to flip. I just closed my eyes and opened my mouth and took it. I leaned back and smiled at him like I was floating. I felt shivery all over. . .my God, I was in a dream. . .and his lips, the way he smiled! And when he ate, he almost looked like he might want to kiss me right there. . .right in front of everyone. He was so beautiful I thought I'd like to kiss him. . .his lips, the way they moved. . .his whole face. . . eyes. . .shoulders and waist. And he acted like he was having fun and liked me. I was looking right into his eyes. . .just tingling and warm. . .and the ice cream was so good. . .but I didn't care.

''Come on, Ellen,'' he said. ''Let's figure out some way to eat this delicious mess. You start at one end, and I'll start at the the other. Then when we're both finished, we'll be together.''

I don't think I ever ate anything so fast in my life, and with such shaky good feelings inside me. It was like nothing ever before, and he actually wanted me to eat! I was so happy right then I could have screamed. I'd have done absolutely anything he wanted. . .even stop eating if he told me to. I wanted to just touch him, he looked so delicious. . .to sit there all night with him. I didn't even care about eating. . .I could hear and feel so much, it's all still in my head. I'll never forget it. I can still hear the Stones record. . .we were practically eating in time to it. It's been running through my head ever since.

> I went down to the Chelsea Drugstore
> To get your prescription filled.
> I was standing in line with Mr. Jimmy.
> A man said he looked pretty ill.
> We decided that we would have a soda,
> My favorite flavor-cherry red. . .

Something, something, something. . .then it goes:

> No, you can't always get
> What you want.
> But if you try sometimes
> You just might find. . . .

Finally we just sat there listening and staring at each other. When the high soprano part started at the end, it was like the ice cream was melting the way the music was melting and the way I was melting over him. When it ended, he sort of made a kiss at me and sat there staring until I began feeling nervous again. I was scared he was going to get up and leave. Maybe he'd only sat down with me because there wasn't any place else. I got up enough courage to say, "Well, Josh, eat and run time, huh?"

"No, no way. You just stay right here and. . . ."

"Sure, and I'll order another banana split."

Then he said, "Just wait, I've got a surprise for you."

"Listen, after the weekend I've been having, the last thing I need is any surprises. I'd go bananas." I couldn't believe what he said next.

"Come on, Ellen, you looked like one of the happiest chicks I've ever seen till just now. So just hang in and I'll be back."

I felt terrible, but I couldn't stop staring after him. I thought I'd never see him again, and I wanted to remember how he looked. Then he went and sat with his friends, and I could see them all laughing and shoving each other, and that girl wiggling all over him. I felt so horrible and sick I put my head down in my arms on the table. When I felt someone patting my shoulder. I looked up, trying to keep from crying. There was the waitress with the check. She said:

"Listen, you don't have to leave the booth right now. It's just that if I don't get my checks in, I get the cashier on my neck. Don't feel bad, honey. It happens to all of us. Some guys'll use you every time. Now you let me know if you want something else."

I couldn't see her because my eyes were blurred with tears. I put my head back down on the table. Then all of a sudden I felt another hand running over my shoulder, bigger and warmer, going through my hair and down my neck and squeezing my other shoulder. I looked up and it was him again, with his fantastic smile. He was swinging some keys back and forth on a chain with two red lucite balls, like he was trying to hypnotize me. He acted like nothing had happened, just laughed and said:

"Look what I've got for us. Wheels. Hurry up, Ellen, let's go."

He practically yanked me out of the booth and through the crowed till we were outside. He didn't say where we were going or what we were going to do, just rushed us around the parking lot, swearing because he couldn't find Ron's car. It was supposed to be red, with a special license plate with Ron's initials. I realized we'd already gone past it twice. I touched his elbow, a little scared because he seemed so mad.

"Isn't that it in the next row?"

He stopped dead for a second, then grabbed me again and started pulling me over to the car. He seemed to relax a little once we got in. He looked right at me for the first time since we left the booth, and smiled.

"It's a great car, just like he said. We're going to have a great time in it together, Ellen."

He started the car and we roared out of the parking lot so fast I was terrified. He drove like a wild man, swerving in and out of traffic, yelling at other drivers, practically sideswiped another car. I thought he'd go out of his mind when we got stuck in traffic on the Fifty-Ninth Street Bridge. Once we got to the other side and into the dark side streets, he began to kiss me every time we stopped for a red light. First it was on my cheek, then on my neck, and then on my lips. I felt myself turning red all over. Then he started asking what boys I'd been out with and everything. Oh, wow, the way he kept looking at me! And squeezing my hand! I was feeling good and warm all over again. I wanted to squeeze his hand. . .I wanted to do anything for him! But I couldn't understand why he kept asking about other boys I'd been out with.

I said, "Oh, not too many, I'm just a sophomore this year."

He began kissing me on my neck, laughed, and kissed me again. And the way he smiled at me after he kissed me! Maybe he could see from my face. . .maybe I looked shocked, like this never happened to me before. . .except with one other person. . .and he was. . .fat. . .so it wasn't because. . .it felt too great. But he asked me how far I went with other guys. I didn't know what to say. I wish I'd talked about all this stuff with Margie or someone instead of just overhearing kids at school. . .or reading those dumb dating columns. I began getting very nervous, so I said:

"Well, just like all the other kids, you know."

He kissed me again, so I guessed that must be okay. We went racing along. . .like out of this world! And between my legs. . .down there. . .I felt warm. Wet, too. . .and. . .kind of all swelled up. I couldn't even hold my legs together. . .didn't even want to. I feel funny talking about all this, but it really never did happen to me before. It was confusing, and I was. . .scared. . .I couldn't figure out why he was being nice one minute and then acting like I was hardly there the next. Right after he was kissing me and asking those questions, he started that horrible fast driving again.

I asked, "Do we have to get some place? I mean, are we going some place special?"

"Somewhere very special, babe. We're both going to get right where we want to get!"

He turned a corner so fast I almost fell in his lap, and then he started squeezing my hand harder and driving faster through all these dark, empty streets.

I guess he could tell I was scared, because he said, "We're going to the marina. It's a great place, a beautiful view of the city, and hardly anyone to bother you this time of night. So it's, you know, really a great place."

"For what? What kind of place is it, Josh?"

"Nothing to get worried about. Just McGuire's boat yard."

He was screeching the tires going around corners, and all of a sudden we were bumping down this unpaved road. He stopped so suddenly I almost hit my head on the dashboard, and he didn't even notice. I was in a daze. I didn't know what to do, and now I was too scared to say anything. He sat there absolutely quiet, looking at me. His eyes seemed sort of turned off and dead. The whole thing was spooky. I started looking around for my bag, just for something to do, because I was getting so upset. It had fallen on the floor when he stopped so fast.

I said to him, "This place is really a little weird. It's getting sort of late, too."

He said, "Oh, it's a great place. You must have been here with other guys. You said you liked out-of-the-way stuff, so come on, tell me, what kind of stuff? I mean, how do you really like to get it on?"

I said, "Oh, you know, like rapping and laughing, you know, really laughing a lot over things and. . . ."

"You mean, like, you like to get high?"

"Oh, no! Just planning different skits and stuff."

His questions were making me so nervous that I started saying all this stupid stuff about the view, if you can believe it. He didn't seem to mind, he just smiled and leaned back in his seat and sprawled his legs apart.

"Yeah, I like it here, too. You're just out of this world. Have you ever been alone with someone in a place like this, so beautiful, where you can just make your own world?"

"Do you like to make out?"

It was starting to get awful. . .I can hardly even stand telling you about it. . .I wanted to get out of that car, to stop him talking that way, and I had to let him know. I was so scared I didn't answer, and I think he took it the wrong way. He leaned forward with a cold look on his face.

He said, "So lets."

"Listen, I think you're getting the wrong idea. I mean, I just don't think it's such a good idea to get so involved right away."

"What kind of involvement do you mean?"

I didn't say anything again and he took it wrong, 'cause he said, "Don't you think it makes things dull? I mean, if you just do boring things all the time, it's a drag. I think you should at least try everything just once. . .like, you wouldn't want to eat just banana splits in life."

I felt I'd better say something or he'd start to go too far, so I tried to make a joke and said:

"Oh, I like sucking on a lemon."

"You mean you like kind of kinky things? Is that what you like, Ellen?"

"Well, I don't know what you think is kinky?"

"Oh, come on, Ellen, you know, don't put me on."

I was wishing I'd never gotten in his car. I didn't know what to do. . .right after he said "put me on," he said, "Let me turn you on." He ran his hand across my shoulder and right down near my. . .uh. . .breast and asked in this kind of sexy voice, "You like to start like this?" I said, "Please, no, not really," but he was reaching across me and opening the car door. "Let's get out for a minute." So I got out, feeling sort of shaky, and he pushed the seat forward and before I realized it he'd pulled me into the back with him.

I guess he could see that I was shaking all over. My teeth were even chattering, I was so scared. He even looked a little nervous himself. He reached in his pocket and pulled out a really big, fat joint. I never did anything but take some little pretend drags of grass at some parties, because everyone else was. I just don't smoke dope or take any drugs. . .lots of kids at school don't, and I don't, either.

But he lit it and took a deep drag and then practically shoved it in my mouth. He said it was something special, to really take it in. I was so scared that I did. It hurt my throat and made me feel dizzy, and I did it some more when he told me to. After smoking that dope. . .I know it had to be something more than grass. . .he got all sort of wild-looking, and I got so dizzy I thought I was going to faint. But I wouldn't let myself pass out. I was too afraid of what would happen to me. I did feel sort of. . .looser. . .suddenly I was warm all over. . .but I was still scared.

I expected him to try and do things to me that I didn't want. But also I sort of wanted him to. . .because if he didn't try, I'd feel terrible. I feel chilly and then warm just thinking about it now. I feel. . .some of the other things, too. . .I'm embarrassed. . .but I guess I better tell it, because I can't forget how I felt every second. Maybe telling will help me put it out of my mind. . .well, maybe I don't want to forget all of it. . .even if it was scary. . .because some of it was good. There isn't anyone else I could say these things to, not even Margie. I don't think parents and doctors or any older people really know how kids feel, how we really think. . .how horney our minds can get. But we do have these feelings. . .and I remember what he did. . .all the feelings I had.

When I was in that back seat with him, I was practically collapsed from dope. I just. . .let him go ahead and start doing all those things. . .first his hand on my leg. . .pushing up my dress. . .squeezing inside my leg fast. . .making it feel so good. I couldn't close my legs. . .all swelling up there so. . .I wanted to feel it. . .move. . . it was warm, and. . .my legs were warm, and shaky. . .I felt all wet again. Then he was moving closer. . .and. . .kissing. . .in my ear. . .I never knew I could feel so good. . .his hand kept moving further. . .I felt so wet in there, and then he got his finger inside me where I was so wet. . .he touched something, and it felt so. . .made me dizzy. . .his finger was going all over my insides, and then outside. I wanted him to kiss me more, be closer. My legs were so open. . .to let his hand be. . .inside, where I wanted it. . .no, I didn't want it. . .to be. . .it felt so. . .no I didn't want to go too far. . .I closed my legs on his hand so his finger couldn't go on. . .but I'd gotten so wet. . . .

He kept kissing me. . .my mouth. . .running his tongue in and out till I thought I couldn't stand it any more. Then his other hand was under me. . .on my. . .back and my bottom, and he was grabbing me so hard. . .I wondered why he was grabbing me there. I thought I'd die unless I could stop him. Then I remembered my bag was in the front seat, so suddenly I managed to sit up and grab it. And I started rummaging around in it like mad, looking for something, anything. He sat up and glared at me, but in a way it was the first time he seemed to realize I was there. He watched me for a minute and then he asked:

"Ellen, what are you looking for? Have you got something in case. . ."

"Nothing, really," I said.

"Come on. We're really getting into it. What've you got?"

"I haven't got anything on me, Josh, I'm just looking for. . . ."

"What? What do you usually use?"

"Nothing."

"We better do something or it could be bad."

"Bad to what?" I said.

He moved away from me. His face had that cold look, and he wasn't touching me any more. I'd found what I wanted in my bag, a big Baby Ruth, and I offered him some. I guess that was the last thing he wanted in the middle of what we were doing. . .but not me! Actually, I wasn't really getting hungry. I thought I could get him to stop. I felt like I was getting sicker from what he gave me and what he was doing to me. It was all too much, and it was like. . .if I got something in my stomach, I'd feel better. Then suddenly Josh started smiling at me, completely changed his mood again. He was back in a trance, making out with me again and saying:

"Ellen, I've got something much better for you."

But I was feeling worse than ever, and I was more and more sure it was from what I smoked. Then he was putting my hand on his. . .so hard. . .I. . .I dropped my Baby Ruth because he was kissing me. . .in my mouth with his tongue. I couldn't even think any more. Then he was pressing it against me. . .right where. . .I felt. . .dead. . .scared. . .but. . .all open. His hands were up my leg again. . .with his finger inside me again. And he kept on pressing on me. . .lying on top, squeezing me, rubbing me all over. . .feeling. . .kissing my neck like he wanted to smother me.

I thought I felt his hand. . .finger. . .in me again. . .except it wasn't his finger. . .it was his. . .thing. . .and it was big. . .hurting inside me so I thought I couldn't stand it. I kept saying, "Let's stop! Let's get out." But he just kept going on. I think what we'd smoked hit him even more than me, because he was really out of it. His eyes were just cold and dead, and I couldn't stand what he was doing to me. But I was too weak to stop him. . .still dizzy. But I was wide awake. My eyes were stretched wide open, not missing one second of what was happening. He kept pushing into me. . .spreading me too far. . .it hurt. He had his pants off, naked. . .and he was moving so fast. . .and his thing was big! I kept saying, "Stop, Josh! Please!" But he kept pushing into me until I was so scared he'd hurt me inside that I started yelling.

He did stop for a minute, but before I could get myself together he started again, going at me like I wasn't a person, just a. . .a body. . .spreading my legs. . .put his face down between my legs. . .with his tongue up and down. . .and into. . .like somebody in another world. . .I felt weak and sick but he just put his thing into me again and now I really begged him to stop hurting me, but he wouldn't. I kept yelling, "It hurts, please don't, it hurts!" But he kept on till finally, thank God, I don't know, he got out and it felt a little better. Then I realized he'd wet me. . .all over my stomach. So it must've been. . .ah. . .over. I. . .knew somehow by the way he was. . .uh. . .breathing. . .the way he. . .acted. I guess we were both upset by the whole thing, because we were stammering in this dumb way. I couldn't understand him, and I couldn't get him to understand what I needed. I mean, I think he would've started all over again or something, because he kept saying:

"Ellen, you were wonderful, great. . .I can't believe it, Ellen. . .it's so. . .did you ever. . .do. . . ."

"Do what? Josh? What. . .no. . .never." Then I said, "Do you have a handkerchief? I have to. . .get all this. . .off. . . ."

He finally found his pants and rummaged around and got a hanky and cleaned that stuff off me, but I still felt like a mess.

"Listen," I said, "I really think we've got to go."

He said, "Please, Ellen, let's stay just for a while."

But I had to get out of there because he was trying to start again, making me all nervous and disgusted. And almost before I knew it, he was down with his face between my legs again! That was when I suddenly went completely out of my mind. I don't know if it was what he gave me, or maybe I was sick, or scared he'd kill me right there if I didn't get him to stop. I pushed his head off me and started to scream. I felt like I was going wild, and I guess it must have scared him, too. I don't know if he thought it was the dope or what he did to me or what. All I know is that I kept screaming and screaming, feeling like I was going out of my mind. I don't think he even said anything, just asked me where I lived and drove me right home.

Well, when I got there, it was as bad as I thought it would be. . .all of them yelling, my mother accusing me of being a drug addict, my father asking if I wanted to turn myself into a whore, Zach looking so full of himself, laughing and asking who'd want me. It was the end of a nightmare. I mean, why should I remember my sleeping nightmares when I can find one at home any time I want?

I hated being dragged here by my mother. I thought it would be more of what I get at home. I don't even know why I decided to talk to you. Maybe things had just gotten so bad I felt like nothing mattered any more, or things just had to change. The talking has helped, though. I know I've got problems, but at least I know it isn't just me. I'm not. . .I don't want to be. . .the only sick one in the family. It helped me realize that all of us were making each other sick. I mean, we all sort of always knew it anyway, right? Never saying it, just living with it shut inside us, so it was making us madder and madder at each other.

HISTORY

Ellen's life has been created by her size for most of her fifteen years. Every feeling, thought, action, and reaction was related to food. Her family was food-focused. When her parents were newly married and poor, eating was their most available pleasure; eventually it also became entwined with pain and anger. Ellen eventually felt that the eating all centered around her—that she was both the cause and the victim of her family's food obsession. Partly this was because her mother, Ceil, talked about Ellen's current and past eating problems so constantly that Ellen adopted her mother's version of her childhood.

Ellen was born prematurely when her brother Zach was four years old. At first, her mother was delighted to have the baby girl she'd wanted for so long. And although she would not have admitted it, she was relieved to have a sickly, under-sized child who required so much attention. Ceil had never been able to handle her physically active son, and she seized on Ellen's birth as a way to punish Zach whenever he angered her. She set up a schedule of three-hour feedings for Ellen, then gradually shifted to unscheduled and frequent feedings on demand. Months later she was describing her struggle to "keep Ellen alive" so constantly and so dramatically that no one seemed to notice that the infant girl was becoming sturdy and plump, pulling herself up on the sides of her crib and screaming vigorously for her next unscheduled feeding. Already Ellen had found a way to control her environment and her family.

When Ellen began to crawl and then walk, Ceil started complaining that her baby daughter was "always getting into everything" and becoming as hard to handle as Zach had been. Ceil had thought that a girl would be quiet, dainty, and obedient. Over the years she did not hesitate to elaborate on her disappointment to her family, her friends, and to Ellen.

"Can you imagine, there was a time when we actually had to try to fatten you up? After a while you never seemed to get enough—especially late-night feedings. As soon as you were through, and I got back to sleep, you were up and screaming for more. You did your fair share of crying, even after you caught up in size."

Ellen could argue little; few people could do anything but listen to what Ceil wanted to say. She was a big-boned, slightly overweight woman, physically imposing and emotionally aggressive. She would not listen and felt compelled to outtalk every-one, rapidly answering her own stream of questions or offering a stream of unasked for advice and commentary.

Ellen usually got along better with Carl, her father, than with anyone else in the family. He worked in a bank at a low executive level. He was considered a ''good guy'' by the cronies with whom he went out for big lunches, beer, drinking, and baseball games. Carl, too, was heavy, but he managed to avoid real obesity.

Ellen received her father's sense of humor, and she was grateful for the unpleasant moments he sometimes spared her by cutting short her mother's often hysterical behavior. But Ellen thought he was afraid of Ceil; usually he sat quietly, letting his wife's constant flow of opinions and complaints wash over him. When Ceil became too loud or too insistent, he would simply rise, leave the room, and settle in front of the bedroom television with a beer to watch a sports program.

Ellen also feared that her parents had fallen out of love. As a teenager, she could not remember a time when there wasn't tension between them. She was often awakened by her mother's midnight expeditions to the kitchen and sometimes kept awake by the muffled fights that usually followed. Sometimes she overheard them. Eventually Ellen no longer ''heard'' her father complain that Ceil would rather stuff herself than make love, just as she no longer ''heard'' Ceil complain about Carl staring at other women.

Then Ceil developed a new complaint. She incessantly announced that she was a nobody, no better than the family maid. She loudly resolved to leave them all to cook and clean for themselves so that she could go back to school and learn to operate her own catering business, make mountains of money, and escape her boring family life. Ellen couldn't decide whether, beneath all the bombast, Ceil was the kind, generous, long-suffering mother she declared herself to be, or was really a selfish woman whose generosity with food hid her need to dominate her family.

Actually, Ceil could not tolerate anyone confronting her about her selfishness and wanted to deny that it existed, deny even that she had needs. Ceil's own mother had seen her only function in life being to cater to her children's and her husband's needs, to give of herself without limits. Food was love, and she offered more of it than any member of her family needed or wanted. She silently suffered with many sicknesses and over the years secretly went to many doctors, who never could pinpoint a diagnosis. Ceil finally came to realize that her mother was a martyr and hypochondriac. It made her feel guilty, angry, and determined to avoid that fate herself. Still she continued to battle her unconscious identification with her mother. Her father was an openly selfish man; he believed that a man was entitled to total control and made no bones about insisting on being catered to by everyone. Ceil fought him and vowed never to fall in love with any man who could dominate her.

The only person in the family about whom Ellen was not ambivalent was her brother Zach. Both had disappointed their mother, Zach by being a boy and Ellen by not being the ''right'' kind of girl. In fury and anguish at being rejected by their mother, Ellen and Zach turned against each other, each sure the other was getting the love that neither received.

Zach was relegated to second-class citizenship when Ellen was born. His earliest way of teasing her was to snatch away her bottle, cookies, and snacks, and later Ellen blamed him for most of the tension that surrounded mealtimes. It was true that Zach always interrupted the family food discussions with complaints about the family being overweight and descriptions of his latest social conquests. Zach was the only thin, athletic-looking member of the family. Though not afflicted with their food obsession, he was preoccupied with his lean, muscular body and the social success it brought him, particularly with girls.

Teenage Ellen blamed her brother for the "fat odyssey" that began when her mother took her to her first diet doctor when she was eleven. There followed a succession of specialists in obesity and glandular problems—to no avail. The only medical suggestion Ellen remembered was the she be allowed to eat alone instead of with her family. She remembered it because whenever Ceil was especially angry, she continued to threaten Ellen with leaving her to eat alone and go without dessert.

Ceil was often angry at mealtimes. Sometimes she was hungry and frustrated herself, because she had launched the family on a new diet fad. She constantly argued, and Ellen found herself goaded into trying to outtalk her mother. When her father and Zach managed to passively fade out of the fight, it left Ellen to carry on the battle alone. Finally she felt that she and her mother had been at war since the first day she opened her mouth. She didn't know why she couldn't resist the challenge, for she knew that Ceil would never stop her own talking long enough to find out what Ellen really wanted, let alone give it to her.

Things were even more painful for Ellen when her father and brother did not retreat from the fighting, for then they sided with Ceil. Ellen was used to fighting with Zach, but when her usually indulgent and affectionate father joined in sadistically teasing her about her appearance and demands for attention, she fled to her room in tears. At fifteen she could hardly bear to think about him; she loved him too much when he was kind to her, and hated him too much when he wouldn't defend her against her mother and brother.

Away from her family, Ellen seemed less moody and difficult. But she smiled too much and too easily, to ward off all the hurts she automatically expected. She found it difficult to fit in with her peers from her first day at school. Set apart by her size, she was the target of constant name-calling and teasing. At first she fought with her tongue, screaming and name-calling as her classmates did and as she did at home. But when the first boy-girl parties began, when she was twelve, she had almost given up. At fifteen she still remembered her first "real" party: the grim and humiliating struggle with her mother over what to wear; her late arrival with eyes reddened by tears; the nervousness that made it impossible for her to eat even the ice cream and cake; the boys' teasing; the frantic phone call to beg her mother to come and take her home right away.

Within a year she developed a new set of defenses. She began to experiment with ways to change her despised self-image. Impulsively she cropped her long, curly, red hair into an extravagant bush. She tried to wear at least one piece of clothing that was in fashion with her peers—a top with sleeves that made skinny wrists look appealingly frail, pants that would make narrow hips look sexy; but because she was too heavy, the tight clothes only emphasized her bulges.

No matter what she wore, Ellen looked fat to herself. And no matter how hard she tried, she could not walk into a room in a way that showed any pride. She was always conscious of her slightly lumbering gait, the insides of her knees brushing together, the signs of a body that has carried a little too much weight for too long. More often, Ellen gave up all efforts with her clothing; she lived in a battered raincoat even in warm early autumn and spring, when it was time for T-shirts or thin dresses.

She stopped having the shrill fights at school that had marred her earlier years there, but they continued at home. Acutely afraid of being attacked for being fat, she began using her keen sense of humor to defend herself. She could not see that her tongue was as much a weapon as ever, and that she had begun to defend herself before she could be attacked. Neither did she see the hurt and fear she sometimes caused with her quick put-downs and her barrage of jokes at other people's expense. When her classmates started to avoid her hostile, aggressive jokes, she retreated into sulking and eating—complaining that everyone was taking advantage of her good nature.

In spite of her damaged emotions, Ellen still liked people and wanted to be liked. She started high school determined to make new friends with whom she could feel relaxed and have fun. The friends she found were outsiders and loners like herself; she kept them amused with constant takeoffs on herself, her critical family, and the popular and square kids at school. These monologues brought her all-too-short periods of approval and respite from hurts.

Despite Zach's loud complaints that Ellen's presence, appearance, and friends threatened the all-important social success of his senior year, she brought them home. Ceil was as outraged as Zach. "The people she brings home are horrible. The boys look like hippies or whatever you call them, and the girls look so awful I can't understand how they have any boys around them at all. I don't even know why they bother to visit. I never hear them having any fun. They just mope around that messy room of hers."

Ceil's own needs were so great that she could not understand why Ellen retreated in angry tears from her constant family dinner parties. Still, she baked huge batches of goodies to entertain Ellen's small group of silent, scruffy friends. Ceil was not aware of how feeding and cooking for Ellen's friends turned Ellen on.

At the beginning of Ellen's sophomore year, her friends were still with her. She felt enough relief from her oppressive body image to admit and occasionally indulge an aspiration to act. She tried out for the school's drama club and was accepted. But she played only funny fat-girl parts, and the acceptance did not give her enough courage to stop defending herself and placating others.

Still, what attention she did attract brought her relative acceptance and happiness at school. Melvin, a clinically obese but keenly intelligent and sensitive sophomore, began taking her out. Although Melvin's mimicry and humor had earned him status as class comedian, he could not possibly measure up to Zach's standards of attractiveness and sexiness. Underlying feelings of shame and defensiveness kept Ellen from having any real pleasure in her first boyfriend.

Ellen and Melvin carefully hid from everyone else. When they did go out in a group, she felt they were lumped together as a "gruesome twosome." She would hunch miserably into her seat at the movies or into her corner of the booth at the pizza place, always acutely aware that their combined hulk made it impossible for them to avoid touching each other. But Ellen and Melvin went out quite a lot and had heady moments of being at the center of attention with their clowning. To Ellen, the best moments came at parties where everyone turned on; then she and Melvin became part of a whole group of giggling, greedy people instead of separate, insatiable hulks.

Alone together, Ellen and Melvin felt free only when discussing nonemotional, intellectual subjects. The rest of their conversation was restricted to sarcastic jokes about others and hesitant humor about being loners. They carefully avoided any mention of fat, sex, or physical attractiveness. Melvin was even more defensive about himself than Ellen, especially about relationships and sex. He lacked her ability to reach out to others or to give of himself except on the most superficial level. Ellen rarely knew what he really felt about anything.

One night shortly before spring vacation, Ellen's parents allowed Zach to give a party. They insisted that he allow Ellen to be there and invite some of her friends. She apprehensively invited Melvin, her good friend, Margie, and Doug, the boy Margie was going out with. They all felt ill at ease among Zach's friends, who seemed carefully selected for their popularity and physical appeal. One of Zach's friends turned off the lights, and Ellen felt more and more nervous as the giggling around them subsided into rustling and urgent breathing. Melvin's arm moved hesitantly around her shoulder, and she turned toward him. Just as their faces bumped clumsily together, the lights went on, and Ellen looked up to see her brother standing at the light switch, watching her and laughing. Zach disappeared into the hallway with his girlfriend, and Ellen jumped up and ran angrily after them. She stopped when she heard the girl giggling to her brother, "You better not let her make out, Zach, she looks pregnant already."

Melvin did not call Ellen during spring vacation; neither did he ask her out after school resumed. He continued to be the class comedian, making the only kind of contact with people he could. Now Ellen was more isolated than ever, and it drove her deeper into the secret patterns she had been building up. She no longer felt safe enough to eat much in front of other people and began to keep food hidden in her clothing, her locker, her book bag. She bought candy bars from subway vending machines and gobbled them secretly on the way to and from school. When Margie, her only remaining friend, went away to camp, Ellen spent an utterly isolated summer and organized her life around who and what to avoid so that she could have time to eat alone. She began to believe that if she was not seen eating, people would say, ''Why, she eats like a bird.''

Her family did not notice how withdrawn and chronically depressed she had become. They were annoyed by her zombie-like TV watching and by the days she spent eating nothing, only to start after dinner and eat steadily until bedtime and beyond. To her mother she seemed only a threat to the smooth operation of her dinner parties. Ceil would go into a frenzy of perfectionism that left her no time to relieve Ellen's social fears by giving support or encouragement. Instead, confronted by Ellen's bad moods and baggy jeans, she swooped down and attacked her in the futile hope of relieving her own anxieties about her daughter.

The only thing Ellen looked forward to all summer was Margie's return. She counted on her friend to rescue her from relentless family pressure and secret ''escape'' eating. But Margie returned looking as if she had never been fat—so normal, acceptable, even sexy in her new clothes, that Zach suddenly became interested and asked her to go to a party with him.

Suddenly Ellen couldn't remember when she'd last been to a party or had any fun. She reached under the sofa and filled her hands with the food she had hidden there. She sat dully in front of the television and watched it flicker meaninglessly, aroused only briefly by images of crisply snapping pizza chips, butter melting on ears of corn, mouths inviting peaks of frosting on cakes. As each image stirred her, she ate, numbing herself to the reality that eating could only make her less accessible to new friends, less loveable to herself, less confident, less anything but fat.

ANALYSIS

Throughout Ellen's life, her weight and appearance dominated her feelings, thoughts, actions, and reactions. She was obsessed with the subject and compelled to eat excessively because of her tensions, depressions, family conflicts, insecurities about her body and sexuality, and disturbed relationships with her peers.

Her nighttime ''closet'' eating, squirreling away food at home, furtive extra breakfasts, sweet-store hopping, and constant food-filled fantasy life were all diagnostic clues to her addictiveness. So was her daily emotional overreaction to the conflicting messages she absorbed from an environment saturated with them—television food commercials, magazine articles and ads about food and dieting, and a family preoccupied with food, weight, and appearance.

Diagnosing the addictive process depends not only on weight but on the psychological criteria stated in Part I. In Ellen's case, the surest clue was the role of food and eating in her psychic economy. She was only marginally overweight during infancy and childhood; only in her teens did she develop clinical obesity.* In fact, many people who do not show clinical obesity have all the signs of food addictiveness. But being overweight may reflect the early stages of addiction, as may having a history of large shifts in weight. Recently a growing number of people seem to have become food addicts in reverse—anorexics, who starve themselves to the point of illness or even death. Many of these people have shifted from overweight to underweight.

Ellen experienced tension and anxiety all her life, but they became acute in her adolescence. They were broken by periods of depression that led her to withdraw from others. She also began to experience inner rage that erupted in tantrums and outbursts of hysteria, disrupting her relationships with family and peers. She had increased depressions and severe mood swings and suffered rare sensitivity to their reactions to her eating and appearance. When under too many pressures and unable to cope with her crippling emotions, she became mildly confused and detached. Distortions developed in her body image; she either denied her actual size or thought herself more obese than she was. This finally produced borderline paranoid reactions.

Since Ellen's birth, her mother Ceil continued to further her addictiveness. Determined to be a martyred mother and wife, she found Ellen's birth a mixed blessing, even after her difficulties with an overactive son. At first she denied these feelings, but her unconscious anger about what she perceived as an oppressive domestic life showed in her overreactions to Ellen from birth. Ellen's premature arrival and early frailness seemed an added pressure. The foundation was laid for a destructive symbiotic relationship. Ceil's reaction to her infant daughter's excessive demands had been to submit and even be controlled by them. Her repressed anger over this produced anxiety, which was compounded by continued resentment of her son's uncontrollable aggression. She totally neglected him, causing the jealous rage that led to his sadistic abuse of his sister.

A period of chaotic demand feeding made a mark in Ellen's psyche. Ceil's hostile and contradictory double messages during feeding made Ellen's relationship with her more disturbed each year. She had wanted Ellen to grow up to be the beautiful thin girl she herself had always failed to be. Forever fighting her own weight problem, Ceil would swing from one extreme to another about eating, food, and its preparation. She was a bundle of polarized excess—a dieting gourmet cook who hosted elaborate dinner parties with lush desserts her daughter was forbidden to eat. Her disciplining of Ellen's confused reactions kept them in continual tension and anger. Bathed in mutual hostilities, they could only foster each other's food-addictive reactions. Ellen

---

* "Obesity is where there is a 15%—20% increase over the standardized weight-life expectancy charts and where the overweight endangers that person's emotional and/or physical health." (Morton Glenn, M.D.)

became a painful mirror image of those excesses in Ceil which Ceil most denied. This made it even more difficult for Ellen to accept herself or identify with her mother. They erupted in full warfare in Ellen's adolescence.

Ellen's addictiveness also had roots in her father's behavior. He was passive and inconsistent and shifted from seductive to sadistic, especially in reacting to her weight and eating habits. His conflicts with Ellen's mother and their inability to take a united stand on Ellen's discipline made Ellen even more troubled.

The selfishness, hostility, and rejection of Ellen's family, to her and to each other, left her feeling threatened and isolated. They became more food-focused and overvalued appearances instead of human relations. Ellen continued to retreat into eating as the family fragmented. Her parents' marriage was unhappy, and no family member could get along with the others. The only thing they shared, if only negatively, was preoccupation with food and diets. They had all become narcissistically very concerned about their appearance and about what and where they ate. Finally they all used Ellen's weight problem as a forum for their own anxieties, angers, and frustrations. She became the family scapegoat.

In turn, Ellen reacted to the traumatic family dinners with rage, withdrawal, and a growing compulsion to eat even more. This became a vicious cycle: the more the family baited her, the fatter she became and the more she was baited. Her brother's erotic, narcissistic, and sadistic behavior was especially damaging during her adolescence. His attacks of her most vulnerable areas, her body and her sexuality, badly shook her fragile ego. Ellen's father reacted to her defiance and depression with impotent unconscious hostility; unknowingly he joined in his son's cruel humor. His behavior produced profound conflicts in Ellen's relationships with boys. It is also significant that other members of Ellen's family, such as her aunt and grandmother, were preoccupied with food and used alcohol to excess. Their nagging presence supported the reactions of Ellen's immediate family to her weight problem.

The reactions of Ellen's peers to her being fat were the second most potent cause of her becoming addictive. Their cruel teasing, incessant rejections, discharge of hostilities and need to scapegoat Ellen left her with psychic scars. Even her addictive collusions with Melvin and Margie eventually failed. The damage done to her ego could not easily be undone, because her addictive process had become more deeply rooted. She retreated further into food fantasy and relieved her pain by eating.

In her adolescence, then, Ellen suffered with a weak ego, passivity, vulnerability, a lack of family support, and peer pressure—all of which made her take refuge in her addictiveness. Food and drug addictions are prevalent among adolescents, and subcultures can sway or intimidate a fat, unattractive, and rejected teenager into food addiction in order to cope with ideal standards of appearance. Facing the arenas of sexual, social, and athletic competition makes a teenager like Ellen more vulnerable to addictiveness as a solution to daily feelings of inadequacy or failure.

Many cumulative pressures, then, fell on Ellen. She could not keep friends. She could not cope with her mother's daily hostile nagging, and insensitivity, or with her conflicting messages and behavior about food. And men—her father, brother, friends, and finally Josh—teased her and traumatically exploited her vulnerabilities. Her food-obsessed environment presented a steady stream of subliminal temptations and prohibitions about eating. She also had addictive models in her mother, marginally in her father, in her hypersexual brother, and in addictive peers. Her diets, instant-fat-cure doctors, and exposure to food, also fostered her addictive process.

Even Ellen's wit and intellectual performance at school did not compensate for her feeling that she was a hopeless failure. She developed a thin facade of proud humor and sarcasm and also used emotional blackmail, withdrawal, projection (blaming others), and denial to cope with her overwhelming lack of self-esteem and inability to control her food addiction.

The more pressures and controls imposed on Ellen by her family, friends, doctors, Weight Watchers, and de-addictive media (diet charts, posters, and pamphlets), the more addictively she reacted. When she was totally uncontrolled, she would skillfully provoke people close to her (mother, friend) into curbing her eating excesses. Ellen did this by unconsciously leaving a trail of clues that induced them to overreact. But their responses only made her further justify her drive to eat. She engaged in power struggles with those she involved in these maneuvers, particularly her mother. These struggles went beyond eating and obesity, to clothing, spending money, and cleaning her room. She used guilt as a weapon and in turn was made to feel guilty. Her social life, lack of discipline, and dissatisfaction with her body image, led her into fantasy identifications as substitutes for constructive models,, and periods of mock exhibitionism to compensate for her self-loathing and denial of her own self-image.

Ellen finally became unable to cope with her everyday life, withdrew from people, and developed feelings of panic. The crisis that made her seek help can be explained by the cumulative effects of *trigger mechanisms, addictive complements, collusions,* and *interlocking addictions.*

Ellen's traumatic sexual encounter was her first important *interlocking addiction.* Josh's powerful assault on her body and ego tipped her precariously balanced emotional life. His sexual addictiveness turned her on to sex; she tried to turn him on to food. It is incredible how often one addicted person spots another and is attracted, even if they have different addictions. This was the case in Ellen's and Josh's instant attraction to each other.

Ellen's major trigger mechanism was her constant food-focused fantasy life. She responded to the endless environmental stimuli that augmented all the addictive people and complements in her life. Other trigger mechanisms were anger, need for tenderness and intimacy, humiliation, isolation, boredom, anxiety, fear, depression, and other emotions she could not express.

Because Ellen had deep-seated problems about self-esteem, body image, appearance, and sexual emergence, her addictiveness was also triggered by any assault on her ego that related to her appearance. Her oversensitivity verged on the paranoid; she was often triggered into eating by conversations about appearance, diet, food, or sex that were not about her.

Last, Ellen was triggered by her inability to deal with the painful competitive comparisons with peers that happened every day of her life. Others seemed to her to cope easily with adolescence, looked secure in their skinny clothes, were able to rebel, handle sex, alcohol, drugs—and most of all, could eat and not get fat. Comparing herself with successful peers became the most devastating thing she had to face.

Finally Ellen's adolescent crisis forced her into doing something about her addiction. The clinic recommended that she see me because I had treated young people with food addictions. Ellen was very responsive to therapy. In a short time she understood the many factors that had made her addicted to food. She immediately followed my recommendation that she religiously attend Weight Watchers meetings. Fortunately, she had been prepared to accept this valuable self-help group by how well Margie had done before. The de-addictive people there helped her recover. She found a path out of a process that had sealed her mind and body in fat. Eventually she found pride in her thinner self and body image—a self she could respect in a body she could accept and believe others accepted.

PART III

THERAPY OF THE ADDICTIVE PROCESS

It is not possible to include in this book the multidimensional and combined therapy programs that have been devised to meet the needs of the many addictive populations. And I have not included a discussion of psychopharmacologic and aversive agents, maintenance therapies, vocational and other social rehabilitations for chronic and untreatable addicts. A massive and growing literature deals with the sophisticated use of multidimensional approaches by clinics, professionals, and paraprofessionals. There is a strong movement toward collaboration by self-help groups, therapeutic communities, and physicians. (see bibliography) And there are attempts to utilize all social agencies, therapeutic communities, and volunteer services to help *de-addict* the addictive patient and his *addictive complements*.

The therapy of an addict and his addictive complements always depends on a *helper*, someone who chooses to be part of the therapeutic process. He may be a mental-health professional—psychiatrist, psychologist, social worker, nurse or counsellor—but may also be a family member, friend, lover, co-worker, peer addict, or staff member of a therapeutic community, self-help organization, mental hygiene clinic, or hospital. It is essential only that he or she is constructively involved with the addict.

A helper should be emotionally accessible to the addict, keep his confidences, and have a strong ego, and the capacity to tolerate other people's anxieties, depressions and emotional blackmail. He must be willing to give of himself without always expecting a proportional return—an above-average willingness, short of masochism,

185

to endure inequities in a relationship. He should be able to postpone immediate gratifications in order to achieve his goals and to cope with his failures.

It is, of course, essential that a helper understand the addictive process and how one becomes addictive. For that reason, a former addict can often do the job best.* Training in and experience with the many forms of behavioral and/or insight therapy is also a strong qualification. The very fact that a helper is motivated to engage in an addict's therapy, willing to be involved in his introspection and behavior modification, is a positive sign. Other good signs in a helper are having expressed a wish to learn about the addictive process and to attend self-help groups such as Weight Watchers, Smoke Enders, Pot Smokers and Pills Anonymous, Alcoholics Anonymous (Alanon/Alateen), and Gamblers Anonymous, or to be trained by a professional therapist. Above all, a helper must be a caring person; the least desirable traits are being moralistic, punitive, judgmental, or highly authoritarian. One should not be a helper if one cannot set limits for oneself or if one projects unattainable goals for the addict. A helper should be aware of his task before and during his commitment to the addict's therapy. He must learn about the limitations of any addict's therapy; modest goals are safe and most realistic. He must know which addicts will never be capable of overcoming the process and require life-long support or custodial care.

The therapeutic principles given here for identifying and treating addicts have emerged from hundreds of trials and errors over twenty-five years of clinical practice and research. My deep conviction of their validity comes from long self and group analysis of my own addictive process. My struggle to comprehend and arrest my work addiction has given me the best evidence of what is and is not therapeutic. I have lived through many battles and have tried to learn why and how I won or lost them—not only with myself but with my addictive patients. And I believe I gained something in each combat. Sometimes I won a battle but lost the war.

I have also learned from living in an addictive society, with its hundreds of alleged cures and home remedies offered through all the media. I have drawn from the professional and layman's literature and the popular media (see the selected bibliography). I have studied and been both therapist and participant in self-help and psycho-therapeutic group therapy. However, I learned most from doing thousands of diagnostic interviews as an admitting psychiatrist at the Payne Whitney Psychiatric Out-Patient Clinic and in my private office. I developed methods and skills for identifying and diagnosing addictiveness which is usually very obscure early in the process. I learned still more from careful listening with my third ear to thousands of hours of addicts' free associations and from meeting their addictive complements and other important people in addicts' lives.

---

* Paraprofessional and professional training might soon become a reality when sufficient funds, personnel and programs are made available to meet community needs to train people in the treatment of addictions.

Many medical and sociological studies, autobiographies and novels, and theater and film presentations show in detail the different facets of the disadvantaged addict, his family, and his subculture. The majority of these scientific studies and other literature (see bibliography) has been about chemical addictions, such as alcohol, nicotine, heroin, amphetamine, barbiturates, cocaine and multiple drug addictions. More recently gambling addiction and the food addictions, such as obesity, anorexia, and bulimia have received increasing attention. We still have little significant research but an increase of popular literature on the nonchemical or partly chemical addictions, such as sex, work, spending and television.

All of this literature dramatically shows that vulnerability to the addictive process is high in people who suffered gross or covert traumas and brutalization in childhood —constitutional defects, extreme physical, socio-economic and environmental deprivations, beatings, incest, rape, abandonment, emotional isolation, and families destroyed by neurosis, psychosis, or multiple addictions. This vulnerability seems directly proportional to the damage done to a person's developing identity, self-esteem, and capacity for emotional, economic, and physical survival.

A significant percentage of people with the most traumatizing backgrounds turn quickly to natural and synthetic chemical addictions, because the chemicals are so accessible, they offer immediate relief and there is a high incidence of peer and family role models with chemical addictions. These chemicals allow a brutalized person to dissociate and split off the unbearable realities of his painful present and past life. They help replace that pain with an escape into pleasure. Generally the greater and more protracted the damage, the stronger an addictive agent is demanded. The wide availability, to the advantaged and disadvantaged alike, of many legal and illegal pain-killing and euphorant chemicals explains their extensive use, medical and otherwise. Because of these facts, abuse of chemicals is bound to continue to be our society's major addictive coping mechanism. The sources of conflict and pain for too many people go totally neglected by society and families. Their suffering goes on relentlessly until the addiction finally surfaces in courts, hospitals and public places at the end stages of addiction. By then, social control and treatment are mandatory but usually the damage is already beyond repair. Now the addict can find relief only in addictive agents, addicted peers, and addictive subcultures.

From the beginning of my work with addicts, I experimented with therapeutic techniques, trying to suit each to the specific addiction and addict. I used some of them to deal with my own addiction and to cope with my relapses. The majority of my work has been with people from the white lower, middle, and upper classes who were alcoholics or were multiply addicted to various combinations of drugs, food, sex, and work. What I learned from them has been useful in my fewer therapeutic contacts with smoking, gambling, anorexic, and spending addicts. From all of them I obtained information that enabled me to see common denominators useful in treating the addictive process.

I have worked less with poor, inner-city addicts. Much of my information about them comes from scientific literature and from my patients who occasionally crossed into their worlds. These reports did suggest to me the enormous challenge in their therapy. The majority of my patients did not have to contend with the daily pressures of poverty, unemployment, discrimination, lack of education, and a struggle to merely survive. It is difficult enough to treat privileged and overprivileged addicts; with the poor and oppressed, a helper encounters social and practical obstacles that must be overcome or dealt with if the addict is to recover.

I learned that many addicts I treated had moved from one addiction to another or were at times multiply addicted. Because I, like others, often failed with the chronic and multiply addicted, I became involved in two therapeutic experiments that spanned four years. For two of these years I worked with a homogeneous group of sexually addictive men; for the other two years with a heterogeneous group of men and women addicts (food, drug, alcohol, work, and gambling). Both projects grew from a three-year audiotaped study of the therapy of a sex addict.

The most valuable research tool I used over eighteen years of investigation is the audiotaped record. These tapes not only documented my findings but became therapeutic aids. I spent thousands of hours listening to and editing these tapes, learning addicts' inner voices. The nuances of their language, pauses, inflections, denials, distortions, blocks, all became intimately familiar. They often resembled my own inner addictive voice. Some of the tapes captured decisive moments of addicts' fantasies, impulses, and acts. They were portraits of the addict in crisis. Facing them destroys the camouflage of denial and lies the addict relies on.

Treatment begins the moment any helper helps an addict face that he is indeed an addict. The diagnosis can be made only by someone who understands the addictive process. This knowledge may not be complete or even fully conscious in the helper's mind, but he must be aware of or sense these hallmarks of addiction: polarized excesses in the person's past; pleasurable excesses used to neutralize physical or psychological pain; tolerance and withdrawal phenomena; progressive excess until there is severe damage to any or all of the following—self-image, social life, erotic life, economic and work life, emotional function, and people who live and work with the addict.

Every person's unique history determines the kind and degree of such problems. Uncovering the things that spark and perpetuate addictive behavior is also essential to an accurate diagnosis, but ferreting them out is no easy or rapid task. It is particularly difficult in the early phases, when many signs and symptoms are still hidden, and the addict fights attempts to point out his addictiveness. Addiction is more difficult to diagnose than most ills because the addict and his collaborators have an incredible ability to hide, deny, repress, rationalize, and sustain the process. The guilt, shame, and social stigma attached to addiction push one to deny to self and others the facts that reveal addiction.

Often the people who know most help least. Family, loved ones and close friends may fail to tell the truth, for they fear emotional blackmail, rejection, and the hostility which they have learned follows blocking the addict's pleasure. Some, as we shall see, have an unconscious vested interest in the addict's illness. All these defenses must be chipped away by the addict and those who know him before diagnosis and therapy can begin. They are the major barriers to seeking help, changing, and sustaining change.

Aside from these subtle and often slippery defenses, the addict's most challenging protection is his capacity to tell open and indirect lies. At first these deceptions are about only his addiction; eventually they encompass his life and become the addiction's guardians. The addict becomes a polished actor—perhaps unaware of this talent, but rarely without it and unwilling to give it up. When addiction becomes malignant, the addict believes his own lies and manipulates others into believing them as well. Even when not successful in such maneuvers, he may continue in his convictions, quite unaware that more and more people are on to him. His truths have become delusions, the seeds of paranoia. In fact, the addict is invariably the last person to know or want to know that he is an addict.

One cannot, then, get an accurate history from the addict; his defense of his addiction negates the facts or misleads a listener. There is always some conscious and unconscious withholding of the whole story. Therefore one must not only seek the inadvertent revelations in his talk and daily behavior, but use other informants.

Still another difficulty in diagnosing addiction early is that every addict first experiences his addiction as more pleasurable than painful. Addiction is itself the excessive use of pleasure to remove pain. As long as the addict would rather live with his disease than without it, he submits to it without admitting it exists. First he denies, ignores, or represses his hasngovers; then he dismisses them as minimal discomforts. They still greatly outweigh his real and anticipated highs, which wipe out pain and camouflage the psychological and physical distress produced by previous addictive acts.

During the middle phase of addiction and after any crisis, the addict starts becoming aware of discomforts. He does not connect his slight, emerging pain with his addiction. Addictive pleasure still outweighs these hangover effects. Some people who are being hurt by his addiction will finally try to speak to him or get him to seek help. This can bring his addiction into blurred focus in his consciousness for the first time, but it rapidly vanishes in a blaze of denial. He may even pay some lip service to his glaringly visible excesses by intellectually admitting he is excessive. He then is quick to add, ''Aren't most of us addicts?'' Or, ''So what? It makes me feel good.'' He minimizes the impact of his addiction on his life and others, for it has become his security, his means of inner balance.

Destructive as this balance may be, the addict sees it as better than none, and better than fear of the unknown, which he faces should he change his life. Often at this stage his balance is strongly supported by addictive environmental complements, other addicts, the propaganda of his subculture, and the mass media. Surrounded by people like himself, he gains security from no longer feeling deviant; his addiction becomes a norm.

In the early and middle phases of the addictive process many medical, psychological, and community service professionals fail to diagnose addiction. They rarely get the whole truth from the patient, who may arrive with another problem or diagnosis or against his own wishes. These first contacts rise from physical and psychological symptoms which the addict doesn't connect with his addiction because he doesn't consider himself ill. Only a highly skilled clinician or other helper can spot his addiction and break through his denial and repressions to lay bare the facts. Other informants are too often ignored or dismissed as overreactive. Some are addictive complements, peer addicts, or relatives with an unconscious investment in maintaining the addict's illness. They are more of a hindrance than help in diagnosis and therapy.

Unfortunately, diagnosis is easiest in the end stages of the process, when it may be too late to help. The addictive pattern is now quite obvious, but social stigma and fear of confronting the addict still silences people aware of his problem. Only when hangovers and withdrawal begin to outweigh pleasure is the addict and those about him forced to face the truth; how his symptoms disrupt his life and others'. People begin to pressure him into recognizing his addictiveness and its destructive consequences. Some try to guide or browbeat him into changing or getting help.

The people who can best diagnose addiction before it becomes malignant are those who have lived close to an addict and felt the pain, helplessness, frustration, anger, and other destructive by-products of addiction. For the professional helper, a person who accurately observes the addict's daily failures in his emotional, social, sexual, and work life is an invaluable informant. This person, fully aware because of his own ravaged life with the addict, will nail down the diagnosis. If he has been drained by or made responsible for the addict's life, he is relieved by spilling out the truth. Sharing his long-withheld feelings is an overdue release; even if at first he is reluctant, evasive, guilt-ridden, or hostile, his information will soon pour out, charged with emotion.

His story and the addict's will differ, sometimes enormously or even shockingly. This revelation is born of the pain of inequity or of having masochistically lived with an addict beyond the call of duty. He has probably reached extreme exasperation, withdrawal, or an unconscious wish to retaliate for what he allowed to happen or felt he had to endure. In more cases than not, he has suppressed his emotions and behavior with the addict. He is rarely the addictive complement (someone with an interest in maintaining the addict's addiction) or another addict; he could be called a nonaddictive complement. He is one of the addict's healthy contacts and has lived through enormous frustration trying to raise the addict's awareness of his behavior, lies, denials, and regressions. Often he is the one who became most entangled in the addict's guilt traps. The addict has set him up as his everyday monitor—and as the person he blames most for provoking his addiction. The addict then punishes him and defiantly escalates his process.

When the very late stage of addiction arrives, healthy helpers give up in helpless exasperation and smothered retaliatory anger. They feel they have lost not only many battles but the war, and they withdraw to avoid being sucked into the addict's destructive life. They can no longer give of themselves without feeling totally exploited. If healthy and capable of separation (not easy in marriage and other close relationships), they remove themselves from what has become a web of sadomasochistic interactions. Dead ended power struggles between addict and helper(s) ensue with someone whose addiction has progressed unchecked, and who has totally refused to accept the diagnosis of addiction. Therapy then becomes impossible.

After a healthy helper, the best diagnostician is an addict in remission or a former addict. The saying, "It takes one to know one," is quite true of the addictive process. Addicts, however different their addictions, seem to have a sixth sense for recognizing and communicating with one another. Having recognized an addict, the former addict is fearless in confrontations and confident in his convictions. He leaves the addict no space to lie, repress, or deny. He himself has lived through all the addict's deceptions and manipulations, so he cannot be made to feel guilty or forced to withdraw. Having been there and back more than once, he is compassionate but relentless.

Every helper must continually keep in mind that the diagnosis is itself the kernel of therapy. The addict must face his identity and perhaps sustain that awareness all his life; otherise there is no change. Every therapeutic step must help raise his awareness. Addicts usually go from zero to one, and some up to almost a hundred as they learn the overt and subtle defense mechanisms that kept their addiction alive.

Certain facts are needed to determine the treatability and most suitable techniques for each addict. This book can give only guidelines for therapy; the bibliography points to many kinds of treatment. The earlier addiction began in a person's life, the greater are the frequency, intensity, and depth of the destructive by-products, and the more difficult is treatment. Those who have suffered going from one addiction to another, and come from multiply addicted families have a poor prognosis. So do people who have spent long periods with addictive peers and subcultures and have had many relapses. Goals for them must be minimal.

The nature and number of addictions also shape the outcome of therapy. Addictions that destroy body chemistries and tissues are more dangerous; they lead to secondary physical diseases and then are less treatable. Chemical dependencies are now thought to have lives of their own; they often go beyond psychological management once irreversible damage is done to some organ or chemical system.

The earlier addiction is identified, and the fewer spheres of life it affects, the easier treatment is. Recent studies show that when addictive behavior occurs only within the family and is diagnosed and treated early within groups, the results are best. Unfortunately, most statistics on treatment programs and individual therapy are based on incomplete histories and misinformation; many do not distinguish addictive phases and do not describe the depth, duration, frequency, and intensity of addictive behavior in each phase. Few or no reports exist on addictive complements other than close relatives and addictive peers. More often than not, professionals ignore the multiply addicted; only recently are they seeing the significance of an individual having more than one addiction at a time or moving from one addiction to another.

Many self-help groups get more information than most professionals, but use it primarily to get the addict to accept the existence of his illness. The addict's history is used to show him there can be no significant recovery without abstinence, and he is treated only with behavorial methods. Behavioral therapy alone does not teach an addict the roots and trigger mechanisms of his problem, the causes of relapses, or how to avoid moving on to another addiction.

The addictive process cannot be treated uniformly or predictably, because crises and surprises are so frequent. Each crisis feeds the addiction, which leads to still another crisis. In fact, addicts thrive on crises, for they prevent him from confronting his addictive identity and process. They detach him from the very people who could help him and to whom he should feel responsible. They remove his guilt and help him avoid other feelings about the process. In short, crisis can become the addict's excuse for protecting his addiction. Then he needs the addictive agent for relief from his provoked or self-induced crises, which continue to destroy his life and the lives of others.

There is more benefit from a combined psychoanalytic, psychodynamic, and behavioral approach. It can fortify the addict and those around him with insights and ways to prevent relapses. Here I divide treatment into stages; actually these stages overlap, as no therapy progresses by orderly steps.

From the start, a helper must expect surprises, not a smooth therapeutic road. He will feel the same frustrations, anger, and wish to retaliate as anyone else who deals with the addict. Therefore he must set limits and not be trapped in exploitive and draining dependencies, masochistic interactions, or acting in provocative, guilt-producing ways. The addict will try to set up the helper as the enemy, the person who wants to take candy from a baby, interfering with the pleasure that is the addict's survival defense.

Whatever therapeutic goals the helper and addict set, a good rule of thumb for both is to cut them in half, expecting modest change and frequent relapses. At their first meeting the helper must convince the addict that he needs people; he cannot make it completely alone, or solely in one-to-one therapy. In twenty-five years of one-to-one depth analytic and behavioral therapy, I have never cured an addict on my own! I warn anyone grandiose, narcissistic, or naive enough to believe he can do so to be prepared for failure. Therapy with an addict requires humility as well as knowledge and skill.

The addict needs help not from a subculture of addicts but from all who can join heads and hearts to shed or limit their addictions. Because so much addiction is rooted in the family, peer groups, and an addictive environment or culture, therapy is best accomplished by immersion in nonaddictive environments—with formerly addictive surrogate families and peers. The helper can be the catalyst shepherding the addict to people and places that counteract his addiction. They become antibodies that combat the addict's fantasies, impulses, and acts.

The addict, I have said, tries to make the helper his monitor—his conscience, his addictive parent, his executioner. Sometimes he reverses the roles and makes his helper a victim. The helper must beware of being manipulated or blackmailed into these roles. Effective treatment is helping the addict become capable of self-monitoring; otherwise he becomes resigned to relapses, moves to other addictions, or unconsciously seeks and finds other monitors (addictive complements), perpetuating the process. Thus he makes each new addictive complement fuel his addiction, and both suffer the erosion of addictive life. Eventually it wears people down and tears them apart.

After setting the ground rules for his relationship with an addict, a helper must assert that the addict needs many other helpers as well, and that the most important ones are former addicts. If he is a professional therapist, he must tell the addict that he cannot be treated by office visits alone.

An addict and his helpers put in therapeutic work proportional to the depth, duration, and intensity of his addiction. No crash treatment works; only sustained daily work does. A reasonable goal for those whose addictions first appeared in childhood and those with ten or more years of addiction is a lifetime of vigilance, periodic self-help, and occasional relapses under pressure. They can expect only extended periods of freedom from addiction, and periods of controlled addiction.

The addict must be told that sustaining change depends on both behavioral therapies and an understanding of his unique psychological and physical trigger mechanisms. Without knowing his particular motivations, the functions his addiction serves, and how his triggers are protected by his defense mechanisms, sustained change is unlikely. That is, behavioral techniques help reduce addictive behavior, and insights change addictive attitudes. Using both is vital to combat the inevitable relapses and to secure the longest possible periods of addictive-free living.

But neither therapeutic technique is effective if the helper does not immediately start to discover, reveal, and block the addict's denial of the process. The best way to begin is by questioning him about his daily addictive life in thought and fantasy as well as in action. How many hours does his addiction consume each day? What preparatory time and energy does it require? The helper soon learns that the more consuming the addiction, the greater the addict's evasion, lies, denials, and other defensive behavior. The number, quality, and intensity of these defenses is also a barometer of his resistance to being helped, and thus of prognosis.

Delusional denial is untreatable outside a hospital, where the addict is removed from his addictive agents, environments, peers, and complements. At the other end of the scale is the addict who admits some degree of excess. He will say such things as, ''I do drink more than I should.'' ''People do tell me my work seems to be the only thing in my life.'' ''I get fat on and off—just eat a little more than is good for me.'' ''They tell me I always turn a conversation to sex, so I guess it really is on my mind a lot every day.''

Another way to detect denial is observing the addict's verbal and nonverbal reactions to questions about the process. One may observe a blank, detached expression, a nervous smile, eyes glazed or focused in the distance, frequent hysterical laughter, a provoked look, or a hostile grimace. He may fill an ash tray with cigarettes, seductively thrust the pelvis or eye your genitals, have shaky hands, sweat profusely, or have to munch on something. How often does he change the subject, get annoyed, find an excuse to blame others, or engage in controversy on the subject? Does he always reply that everyone is addicted in some way? Does he engage in a power struggle when confronted about his addiction? For example: ''I drink like my friends, no more no less. Everyone drinks a lot these days. You have to get high on something just to survive.'' ''Are you trying to suggest that I'm some sort of pervert? You know, sex is here to stay; you have too many middle-class hangups. . .probably don't get laid enough.'' ''Do you expect me to start a day without a cigarette and cup of coffee? Who does?'' ''I'm just an average housewife trying to get through a day. Lots of people smoke three or four packs a day.''

Another step in assessing an addict's defensive maneuvers is taking a detailed history from someone close to the addict—relatives, friends, lovers, co-workers, or others who have seen how he acts under pressure. The person should be asked:

''Does anyone in the family smoke, drink, eat, spend, work, or do anything else to excess? How much? For how long?''

''Has any of them been physically or mentally sick or been hospitalized or jailed because of these excesses?''

''Who did the punishing in the family? Did one parent do too much, and the other too little?''

''Has the parent's excess interfered with his work, play, love life, economic survival, getting along with others? For how long? In what ways?''

''Does he lie, cheat, try to overcontrol or manipulate, or blame others too much?''

''Does he get very angry when you try to stop his addictive behavior or tell him he's an addict?''

''Does he do his addictive thing twice as much when you suggest he control himself?''

Obtaining a complete history from the addict himself prepares the helper to confront his resistances and to cut through his denials, lies, and other defenses. The addict may inadvertently confirm his illness: "My mother and grandmother were sort of heavy drinkers. So was my father; he ran away when I was twelve, but they threw him out of the house lots of times before that because he lost the food money gambling. I don't blame them for drinking so much after he left." "I got in with a gang that was into grass and other stuff, but with me it was mostly just grass. My brother was working day and night. He was the golden boy. Me, I guess I was the black sheep, the playboy. . .ass-man. . .my brother called me a suck and fuck head. I called him a work freak. My dad's brother was into booze and didn't work much when he lived with us. They said I looked like him."

Another way of gathering information is letting the addict free associate; his mind is saturated with addictive associations, and it is difficult or impossible for him to keep screening them out. If none appear, he will seem blocked, unable to speak freely, or make irrelevant conversation to cover his addictive thoughts. That is why he may seem "spacey," perhaps described by professionals as schizoid or alienated. Actually, his inner world has become so fixed on his addiction that he draws blanks when asked to free associate, and planning his next addictive act may so absorb him that he doesn't make contact with others. Listening carefully to his language and asking for a record of what he does hour by hour each day will uncover what he blocks in free associations—and what he denies he does. Blanked-out or hidden memories indicate times when he pushed from awareness his addictive preoccupation and practices. For example:

"You know, come to think of it, I don't really know what I did last Tuesday and Thursday afternoons. You're right, I must have been doing something. . .I guess my boss tells me I look like I'm out of it in the afternoons when I come back from lunch. But you know how in the advertising business you have to drink at lunch, and besides, it oils my mind and releases my creative juices." A lot of things I take a hit of turn me on. I feel a real warm rush, and then I'm able to talk about myself. Otherwise I'm pretty shy and stay by myself most of the time." "I have a bad memory for the details. . .of what I do each day. . .most of my day I really don't plan. . .it just happens. I live at the office a lot. . .I have a cot there. . .my wife tells me I only come alive when I talk about my business."

Major clues may also come from investigating how and with whom the addict spends most of his leisure time. Most people relieve tension by doing and using things that have addictive potentials, but addicts use them to excess for psychic survival. What activities spark his greatest feelings? How does he relieve anxiety and depression? How resolve conflicts? One should ask whether he has any friends who drink, work, or are sexual to excess. How much time does he spend with these people? What is his major form of relaxation? When he has a problem, feels tense or depressed, what is the first thing that comes to his mind, and what does he do for relief?

After getting as much historical knowledge as possible from the addict—usually it is sparse and inaccurate—the helper should try to interview healthy informants and the addict's complements. More often than not, their stories contradict the addict's:

"You have to be kidding. He's been on at least a quart a day for months, and sometimes he has the shakes. I can't believe he told you he's strictly a two-martinis-before-dinner drinker." "For years she keeps telling me she has to go to shops every day and spend money. I'm supposed to be a workaholic. She's sure a spendaholic." "I can't believe he didn't tell you about the three breakfasts he has in different coffee shops on his way to work. He said he eats like a bird? You just have to look at him to know it's not possible. I guess he just doesn't eat much in front of people. But all that fat has to come from somewhere." "He hasn't been able to pay a bill for a year. I hide the money. He's at OTB or the track or some kind of card game every night. That stuff about his making house calls at night to sell insurance—he handed you a crock. It's what he's told me for ten years. If he sells so much, how come we're broke and het gets calls from bookies saying they'll hang him out a window if he doesn't pay up?"

The discrepancies between the stories of informants and the addict show how badly the process has invaded and destroyed the addict's life. One should keep asking him about his life, for properly timed confrontations expose discrepancies, and these are prognostic of therapeutic collaboration. Discrepancies also show the depth, duration, and extent of his denial mechanisms, which are major blocks to effective therapy. The way he handles confrontations of his denials with truths from informants indicate the extent of his resistance to change.

The helper should be direct but cautious and nonjudgmental. Addicts need compassion but not sympathy, empathy but not patronization. One should never devalue or ignore the addict's struggle to gain self-esteem and recognition of valuable aspects of his personality that have been masked by his addiction.

Most addicts consciously or unconsciously harbor enormous guilt, shame, and fear of being nobody. Some claim that they do not know who they really are aside from their addictive identity. But any recognition or praise must be genuine. If one lies to the addict, the deceptions always boomerang. He will manipulate them to justify the lies he uses to protect his addiction, and to involve one in situations that allow him to engage in and rationalize addictive behavior.

It is difficult for a helper to maintain patience. The addict's demands for attention are usually insatiable, and no one should be expected to fill a bottomless pit. The helper has to set limits and plan what reasonable demands he can fill, particularly during times of crisis. He should make sure that there are other, temporary sources of help to get the addict through these difficult times when his addictiveness is inflamed. The helper must not monitor any aspect of his addictive life—the agent, the practice, or contact with fellow addicts. He should not volunteer to disentangle the addict no matter how the addict tries to get him to do so. Neither should he let the addict trap him into being critical of his addictive complement; he will seize any opportunity to use the criticism to justify his addictive reactions to his complements. Rather the helper should make him as aware as possible of the factors that perpetuate his addiction and those that can remove it. The helper must be a catalyst to an expansion of the addict's awareness of what he must learn to become an effective self-monitor of his addiction and how to prevent relapses.

A helper can tell an addict, ''When you want to stop, change, give it up, you're the one who can do it. No one can do it for you. Don't make it seem that others are responsible or to blame for your addictive activity. Don't get others involved in your control. If you have to depend on someone temporarily, make it someone who has been there and come back or at least has gained control over his addiction. He'll know that the only way to help is for you to learn to help yourself. He may lead the way, even temporarily pick up both you and the pieces when you're in trouble, encourage you to take the next step, or tell you that everyone slips sometimes. The best helpers never take control or let you control them.''

Timing is important in any confrontation. The further addiction is from a person's awareness, the greater the need for confrontation; however, the helper has to use an emotional style suited to the addict's unique nature and subculture. He should intuitively judge when, how often, at what pace, and in what tone to confront addictive denials. He cannot confront an inner-city drug addict as he would a closet-drinking suburban housewife. Of course if there are psychological or physically dangerous emergencies that demand immediate confrontation, it is best done in protected environments such as hospitals, detoxification centers, and on-going therapeutic groups and communities where strong support systems exist.

I have devised a number of techniques to help the addict face his addictive behavior. One of the most valuable ones is listening to audio tapes made during therapy. Heard outside the therapy session, they give the addict some idea of the extent of his addictive free associations, fantasies, dreams, and interactions with others. He has to face how deeply enmeshed he is in the process and how he defends it. And he can better see his faltering starts at ridding himself of his addiction.

Another device I use is what I call the daily blueprint (see chart) of an addict's life. I have the addict make a week-long chart of hour-by-hour activity from (AW) awaking to (SL) sleep, using the headings: (W) work, (CW) creative work, (S) social activities, (TM) trigger mechanisms, (AI) addictive impulses, (AF) addictive fantasies, (AP) addictive practices, (CC) creature comforts, and (P) physical exercise. Reviewing the chart each week and justaposing the four charts for a view of a month show how addictiveness has affected his daily functioning. This is like many behavioral techniques used by self-help groups such as Smoke Enders, Weight Watchers, Alcoholics Anonymous, and Gamblers Anonymous, all aimed at making the addict aware of what, when, where, how much, and with whom his addictive behavior occurs. The calorie counting, wrapping and unwrapping of cigarette packs, recording of thinking about betting, all are used to this end. The device must be acceptable, practical, and not too bizzare to be integrated in the addict's life style. Even doing an all-encompassing *Life X-ray* is merely a different way of expanding the addict's consciousness of when, what, where, how, and sometimes why he engages in his addictive practice, makes his addictive contact, or persists in living in addictive milieus. They are the most accurate barometers of moment-by-moment, day by day addiction. They are also a very sensitive index of the addict's capacity to use behavioral techniques—the degree of his discipline, motivations, and will, and every discrepancy between his spoken good intentions and his undone deeds.

Addict:	Oh, those ridiculous charts, you need a PH.D to understand them and have to be a Price Waterhouse bookkeeper to fill them out every day.
Therapist:	So just put down how many ounces of alcohol you consume each day.
Addict:	That's ridiculous, I don't need a chart for that. Except when I have blackouts, I pretty much know roughly what I drink from our liquor bills. . .at least when I'm home, 'cause no one else drinks every day in our house.
Addict:	I keep leaving those tapes in the country. I guess I do that because I'm afraid to have them at home or in my office.
Therapist:	But you also said your calorie counter broke and you never got it fixed, and that my idea of timing your eating was driving you crazy and that this X-ray chart took too much time even though we found that filling it out really only took sixty seconds. Then we decided you'd better just do three after you brushed your teeth, 'cause you said that was the most disciplined moment of your whole day.

The addict's resistances are as many and elaborate as the forms of denial that emerge in any therapeutic encounter with him. Ferreting them out, even when the addict himself is totally committed to using a behavioral device, is necessary in any treatment program. You must tailor the various designations of the *Life X-ray* chart (or any other behavioral technique) to each addict's specific needs and limitations. Asking him to fill in a twenty-item chart when he won't even bring in the chart is a ludicrous therapeutic request. A rule of thumb is to expect minimal follow-through and ask of him only what is proportional to his current addictive pathology. The less, the better! Often confronting his negative reactions and slippery contradictions is as helpful as any of the daily conscious-raising techniques.

The following is an actual chart of a polydrug user (amphetamine, gold dust, amyl nitrate, Quaalude and sometimes L.S.D.) who initially did report weekly and sometimes daily use of one or more of these drugs. We discussed his trigger mechanism in therapy and I suggested that he use self-monitoring audiotapes for the other items. The latter was not successful, and he stopped bringing his tapes to the sessions. At first, he also failed to fill out the hour-by-hour chart completely; there were many blank spaces on it. He did not wish to look at how "spaced out" he was each day. He could not face the fact that many hours of his life were totally unaccounted for. After three months every space was accounted for, even though he had continued to try to con me into believing he was working at his art for more hours each week than he actually was. This was a graphic reminder to me, even after twenty-five years of knowing that the tapes, charts, counted records are as deceptive as the patient's words and protests. But any effort whatever toward awareness and self-monitoring is always better than none!

He was an artist and had chosen to make large charts on an 11" X 14" drawing pad, which he now proudly spread before me during each session to exhibit his progress. This chart which he brought in after four months of therapy, reflected a radical change. As you can see, he chose to report on six items that were an index of his limitations and focused on his motivation which, in his case, was to give up his addiction to drugs in order to be able to return to his creative career (painting).

Directions For Filling Out Life X-Ray Chart

1.	Fill out this chart at the end of each day, before you retire or in an optimal time in your day. Do *not* wait a day, for you will block and deny addictive activity that occurred.
2.	Fill in each and every hour and make sure you identify your activity according to the code below, which covers the variety that any person's day includes.
A. W.	When you awaken in the morning to start the day.
C. C.	Any creature-comfort activity (eating, preparing meals, toiletry, shopping, chores, dressing, etc.).
W.	Activity that produces income, saves income, household cleaning, repairs, clothing preparation (ironing), home contracting, entertainment to generate income, meetings, conventions.
C. W.	Creative work, hobbies, etc., any activity that does not produce income and provides pleasure but is also a form of work (i.e. gardening, repair, gourmet cooking, house decoration, etc).
P.	Physical exercise; passive or active sports; spectator.
S. A.	All leisure activity that is exclusively for pleasure, with or without other people. Sexual activity (recreational-procreative).

T.V., movies, reacreational reading, theatre, music, museum, travel, dining, parties, dancing.

A. I.   Addictive impulses are sudden feelings that occur throughout the day, last more than a few seconds, and occur without conscious forethought.

A. F.   Addictive fantasies are internal verbal monologues and visual images that suddenly appear and are repetitive, last more than a few seconds, and relate to addictive (agent/interaction/milieu/previous addictive) experience.

A. P.   Addictive practice (see definition of an addictive act).

T. M.   A trigger mechanism is any factor that triggers an addictive impulse/fantasy/act (the addict should know definition and list of common trigger mechanisms. It is important to list these as clusters of T. M. They will forewarn the addict of situations, environments, agents, complements, clues, etc., to which he is most vulnerable.

It is important to line up four consecutive weeks of charts after you have done the following:

a)   Add up hours for each of the above for each day, week, and month.
b)   Look for consistent patterns of vulnerability.
c)   Look for specific trigger mechanisms.
d)   Look for any changes that relate to therapeutic practices and behavioral exercises (tapes, etc.) that are constructive/destructive and prove to be either positive or negative reinforcers.

The nature and degree of resistance to any behavioral device shows a helper how and why the addict resists change. It permits him to say, ''You think you're motivated to find out about your addiction and change, but it's only in words, not deeds. You forgot to bring the chart and listen to the tapes last week, and today you bring in the information on scraps of paper without any mention of how many ounces of alcohol you drank each day—just a note that you drank before, during, and after dinner. You do this after telling me three times at the last session what a terrific idea it is to fill in a life chart and listen to a tape. Two weeks ago you told me that your tape machine was broken, and that you misplaced the charts. I'm beginning to

TIME SCHEDULE

	Friday	Saturday	Sunday	Monday	Tuesday	Wednesday	Thursday	Friday	Saturday	Sunday	Monday	Tuesday	Wednesday	Thursday	Friday
9-10	Wake	Wake		Wake	Wake										
10-11					Wake	Wake									
11-12				Creative Work		Wake	Creature Comfort	Creative Work	Creative Work		Creative Work	Creative Work	Creative Work	Creature Comfort	Creative Work
12-1	Creative Work	Creative Work		Creative Work	Creature Comfort		Creature Comfort	Creative Work	Creative Work		Creative Work	Creative Work	Creative Work	Creature Comfort	Creative Work
1-2	Creative Work	Creative Work		Creative Work	Creature Comfort	Creative Work	Creature Comfort	Social	Creative Work		Creative Work	Creative Work	Creative Work	Creature Comfort	Creative Work
2-3	Creative Work	Creative Work		Creative Work	Creature Comfort	Creative Work	Creature Comfort	Social	Creative Work		Rest	Creative Work	Social	Creature Comfort	Creative Work
3-4	Creature Comfort	Creative Work		Creative Work	Creature Comfort		Creature Comfort	Creature Comfort	Social		Creative Work	Creative Work	Creative Work	Creature Comfort	Creative Work
4-5	Creature Comfort	Creative Work		Creative Work	Creature Comfort		Creature Comfort	Creature Comfort	Social		Social	Social	Creative Work	Social	Social
5-6	Creature Comfort	Rest			Creature Comfort		Creature Comfort	Creature Comfort	Creative Work		Social	Social	Social	Social	Creature Comfort
6-7	Creature Comfort	Rest		Social	Rest		Social	Creature Comfort	Creative Work		Social	Therapy	Creative Work	Social	Creature Comfort
7-8	Creature Comfort	Social		Social	Rest		Social	Creature Comfort	Social		Social	Social	Social	Creature Comfort	Creature Comfort
8-9	Social	Social		Social			Social	Social	Social		Social	Social	Creative Work	Creature Comfort	Creature Comfort
9-10	Social	Social		Social	Social		Social	Social	Social		Social	Social	Creative Work	Social	Social
10-11	Social	Social		Social	Social		Sleep	Social	Social		Sleep	Social	Social	Social	Social
11-12	Social	Social		Social	Social			Social	Social			Sleep	Social		Social
12-1									Social						Pot
Totals	3 Creative Work 4 Social 5 Creature Comfort	5 Creative Work 5 Social		5 Creative Work 6 Social	3 Social 6 Creature Comfort	2 Creative Work	4 Social 6 Creature Comfort	2 Creative Work 6 Social 5 Creature Comfort	6 Creative Work 8 Social		4 Creative Work 6 Social	5 Creative Work 7 Social	7 Creative Work 5 Social	6 Creature Comfort 5 Social	4 Creative Work 4 Social 4 Creature Comfort

wonder if you say one thing and do another when it comes to confronting how your addiction has affected your life.''

When the addict denies he is addictive, the helper might say, ''Then why is it so important for you to continue the activity? If I asked you to count how many strawberries you ate, you wouldn't react quite so emotionally, would you? You must have a greater investment in doing this than you're aware of—or why are you so angry every time the subject of how much you smoke comes up?''

Another sign of what phase the addiction has reached is how negative the addict's emotional responses are and how much he sabotages a helper's efforts to bring his addictiveness into focus or interfere with it. Behavioral as well as verbal power struggles appear. For instance:

Helper: ''You missed the past four sessions and angrily tell me that Weight Watchers is a bunch of dull, disgustingly fat housewives who turn you off.''

Addict: ''I told you I've gone a few times to all those groups. Weight Watchers, Weigh of Life, Fattys Anonymous—you name it, I've tried it. Mostly women without much on their minds except their bodies and spending their husbands' money. I'm a busy man. . .a high-powered executive doer in a roomful of losers. You've got to come up with something I can sink my teeth in and get this blubber off, but right away! Say something, do something, but don't just sit there and look at me. I'm spending my money for you to do your job, which is to get me thin.''

Or, in another case:

Addict: ''I think you're making a lot out of nothing. I just like to drink. You work from seven in the morning till ten at night, so look who's talking. . .everybody in my family loves to eat, and we're all a little big, but my doctors are more worried about my blood pressure than I am. You're no different than my husband, not having ashtrays or matches in this office, when you know people have smoked one thing or another for centuries to relax. . .and in religious ceremonies they drink, don't they?''

Such power struggles are subtler when the addict artfully engages the helper in intellectual discussions about his addiction being normal behavior, practiced by most or all people. It must be pointed out to him that his practices are excessive, his motivations never purely recreational and relaxant. He will invariably deny these facts or find ways to engage the helper in controversy. He wants to put the helper in either a defensive or overtly offensive position, even create a crisis. Then he can use the helper's reactions to justify escalating his practice or dismissing the helper as unrealistic and useless to him. He will accuse the helper of ignorance in assessing the addictive practice and its destructive impact, and argue its normality in the past and present.

The helper has to point out to the addict that he is using his practices destructively and dysfunctionally. Examples of this must be given in a neutral tone without devaluing the addict, making him feel guilty, inadequate, and inferior, and without comparing him to people who adapt to pressures and crises nonaddictively. If the addict is not ready to confront himself, the helper should use examples that are emotionally less charged and more acceptable. For instance, by giving histories of changing of former addicts whom the helper has known for years, he can more easily show how change, though slow, is possible. Accounts of the struggles of those who mastered their addictions despite relapses are powerfully therapeutic.

The helper can then focus on the value of addict self-help groups. He must emphasize that the addict can change only with the aid of people with whom he can establish rapport and share more than addiction. Too often the addict's social, economic, and intellectual values are alien to the self-help groups available to him. He finds communicating and identifying with the members difficult or impossible. He then tends to use his difficulty connecting with them as a rationalization for not attending the meetings. This happens when one recommends an upper-class, educated heroin addict to a self-help drug community of inner-city street addicts. Having nothing else in common with the group destines his treatment to failure. Similarly, one cannot put skid-row alcoholics, middle-class obese housewives, and uneducated sex-addicted male prostitutes into one therapy group. The differences between their worlds block communication and hinder mutual support.

I have formed two self-help psychotherapy groups from my own middle- and upper-middle class practice. No other such groups existed for them, or they had found none with which they could share much except their addictions. Typically one member said to me, "I was going to Gamblers Anonymous, but practically all of them live a way I don't know about. With me, it's backgammon. With them it's bookies, taking contracts out on people to collect, and going in and out of jail." Even in AA, each group in one community has its unique character. I have extensive clinical evidence that alcoholics need more than alcoholism in common if they are to integrate in a self-help group. In twenty-five years of recommending my alcoholic patients to AA, I have found that each had to find the particular group to which he could relate. If he felt dislocated and alien, he refused to continue.

Still, where only one group exists, it is imperative to get across to that addict that any group is better than none. Sharing addictive experiences and how they can be mastered sustains change more than any other therapeutic activity. It becomes the ultimate confrontation that cuts through the walls of denial and repression. The addict is forced to face his addiction for hours on end instead of using it to withdraw from people and life. He must feel, react, interact, or at least voyeuristically identify with professed addicts.

The intensity of the addict's anger and how strongly he rejects the group experience are also indices of addiction and the depth of denial. A rule of thumb is that the longer addiction has existed, the greater an addict's resistance to suggestions that he join peer self-help groups. Typical responses are: "I know I'm not a alcoholic because I met one of those crusading AA types, and he's only replacing one disease with another. . .all that goddam preaching." "Those people are really fat. I'm not that far gone." "I can't stand groups, any groups. I'm a loner and always have been." "What if someone in the group tells about my going to toilets and doing things with young boys."

Unfortunately, homogeneous self-help groups do not yet exist for addictions to work, sex, spending, T.V. or multiple addiction. There are now groups only for drug, alcohol, food, gambling, and smoking addicts.

The early sessions are crucial to diagnosis, which I have said is itself a major part of treatment. The addict tries to maintain the illusion that he is only engaging in pleasure as any normal person does. He reaffirms that he can drink, smoke, or eat in moderation. Each time he tells a helper and himself that he has learned to control his excess once and for all. In the early stages of addiction he can be convincing, but in most advanced addictions moderation is clearly impossible. Once an addict has had five, ten, or more years of addictiveness, and certainly if he has had several addictions since childhood, he cannot expect to become moderate or to live totally addiction-free, without relapses. He must develop constructive defenses to deal with his relapses, so as not to be engulfed by them.

After the addict has accepted the diagnosis, he needs ongoing reinforcements of his awareness of his addictiveness and what triggers and fuels daily activity. He has to learn thoroughly what has been occurring out of his awareness that triggers addiction—sometimes clusters of circumstances, reactions, and inhibitions. For example: "Every time I get angry at him, I think, what the hell, I'll have something to eat, that'll calm me down." "Yesterday the shit hit the fan. I lost my job, found out my daughter had an accident, and finally admitted to myself that I'm not in love with my wife. So I hit the bars to wipe it all out of my head." "I just can't face people without lighting up a joint. . .I don't feel connected with anything or anyone unless I'm stoned. So I have to be high most of the time." "I know the only way I can control the family is by letting them know I work seventy hours a week. They can't do a thing to me, because I have them all feeing guilty that they do nothing compared to me. And without my money, who would I be?"

Only when the addict can pinpoint his multiple trigger mechanisms, how they emerge from his relationships, and how they are compounded and amplified by environmental triggers will he be sufficiently protected from his unconscious addictive impulses. For instance: "I think I finally understand what you've been trying to get me to face. Every time my mother starts nagging about spending too much on clothes because I need bigger sizes, and I'm alone on Saturday nights with nobody and nothing but the tube and an ice box full of leftovers from her cooking class, I'm a goner. So I see it's loneliness, my mom, money, looking lousy in clothes, and all the damn extra food in the house."

So far, most studies have stressed the addict's Pavlovian response to the stimuli in his environment. Helper and addict must analyze that environment to discover whether it is addictive or not. Addicts become less addictive when removed from addictive environments. Sometimes controlled settings without pressures (detoxification centers, therapeutic communities, self-help peer groups, etc.) help bring rapid improvement. Certainly very addictive environments contribute to progressive addiction:

"Whenever I'm near Forty-Second Street, with a porno shop every twenty feet, it's like I'm in a fever. Or in those movie houses, where everyone's wandering around looking for a blow job or to get jerked off. But in our country house, with nothing but kids and families and the woods, there's not a chance unless I pull out my porno. . .and I usually don't." "It's all those food ads, the restaurants and talk about food during our vacation. We get so heavily into rich food. . .in fact, just going to a supermarket is enough to turn me on for the week." "All I know is potheads, and the disco's loaded. . .man, if you just stand there you get a contact high. . .at least I do."

The point must be made to the addict that there are hundreds of environmental stimuli to fuel his addiction. Some are more easily discovered and more potent than others. As many as possible should be detected and repeatedly identified. The addict must find ways to avoid contact with addictive people, situations, provocative addictive complements, and environmental stimuli; only thus can he change his behavior and release emotions for which his addiction can remain uncovered:

"You mean he buys that paper for you, knowing it has all those ads for porno movies you can't stay out of? You told him that every time you read an ad, you want to go to the movies and a whorehouse." "Every time you're in that house, you can smell the smoke in all the rooms, and you keep your mouth shut about her hacking cough. You get angry, but your father makes you feel like a child, so as soon as you get out of that place, you go right on a buying binge—last week a thousand dollars you didn't even have, so you're up to your elbows in debt." Daily vigilance about these connections will keep increasing the addict's awareness. He should make notes or reminders (mental notes, written lists, charts), compare experiences with other addicts, and make phone calls to helpers, peers, or friends. He needs to do these things when he feels threatened that he will lose consciousness or control of his addiction and needs role models and encouragement that he can self-monitor his own activity. It is also helpful if he listens to audio tapes or watches video tapes of crucial therapy sessions and reads books about addicts who have either destroyed themselves or survived their addictions. The more techniques of self and mutual help the addict learns, the better. They reinforce one another and help him toward the first experiences of briefly seeing and feeling the blue sky of recovery.

Consciously admitting addiction and discovering the rewards of breaking it lead to the next phase—intellectual and emotional awareness of the physical and psychological rewards of abandoning addiction. For the first time the addict will say that he feels better, ". . .as if a cloud has lifted. . .stronger and more confident. . .not so worried about what other people think. . .not blaming everyone for what goes wrong. . .clearer, more in touch with my feelings. . .I can get angry instead of drinking to hide my feelings. . .it's like being set free.''

Finding out which form of reinforcement (positive, negative, or both) best suits the addict can help avoid relapses.* Such suitability usually relates to early interractions with family members. Addicts themselves give clues: ''I was always taught by being criticized and made to feel like a failure, and it just never worked.'' ''My mother built up my confidence unrealistically, and my brother and father didn't pay any attention to me. I need someone to be honest with me about how far along I've come.'' ''When I don't get any attention at all, it wipes me out for the day.''

Mastering daily addictive responses is a continual learning process. All signs of greater self-respect and reduction of guilt and self-contempt must be underscored by helpers; this assures the addict that he will continue to experience emotional and practical rewards for having given up addictive practices. When people respond more positively to the addict and congratulate him on his change, he loses some of the psychic pain caused by addiction. He will feel closer to people from whom he has withdrawn, and who have withdrawn from him.

The next step is for the addict and helper to learn which techniques best break through daily resistances to awareness of his addiction. Besides group interaction, the addict needs one or more peer helpers and/or a therapist who are alert to when he reaches out for help or has set up situations that trigger addictive activity. These latter maneuvers usually are not conscious. Provoking disapproval is a common tactic to rationalize addictive activity.

The addict always tests his helper's limitations, probing a hundred ways for his Achilles' heel. He is particularly intuitive in finding any excess in his helper. How the helper balances pleasure and pain in his life concerns the addict greatly. How does he cope with the factors in his life that might lead him to addictive behavior? The addict also will put the helper's values on trial and try to seduce him into believing that everyone uses pleasure in excess to reduce pain.

The helper must remain empathic even during the most destructive phases of the process, and be compassionate when the addict expresses helplessness, even utter impotence. The exception is when the addict directly harms the helper and others. Then the helper should objectively and directly tell the addict how he and others are

---

* *Positive:* becoming aware of other forms of nondestructive pleasure; receiving attention, verbal and nonverbal praise and affection, acceptance and support from others; experiencing increased physical well-being and a balanced emotional state; increased self-esteem; achieving the rewards attained from reaching one's goals; finding people attracted to one.

Negative: experiencing one's own and other's aggressive, critical, punitive, devaluing, hostile, and rejecting attitudes and behavior; pointing up the loss of self-esteem, failure, and absence of any rewards; experiencing physical and emotional pain (i.e. hangover symptoms); stressing the inability to achieve one's goals.

being hurt, how negatively people react to him in these circumstances, and what this costs him in self-esteem.

If the helper himself has been addictive or has known addicts who have mastered their addiction, he is better able to understand the nature of the inevitable relapses, how they can be managed, and that they need not make the addict feel hopeless. When he has become aware of the chronic nature and limited treatability of some addicts, he must go on believing that he still contributes to the addict's welfare.

Caring is part of the core of help for an addict. Being able to honestly bolster his self-esteem in varied, inventive ways is essential. Singling out the addict's hard-won gains each day helps him become addiction-free. It is difficult but essential to find the right balance of accepting and rejecting the addict's self-destructive nature, hostility, and narcissism without rejecting him as a person. Being too rigid for some permissiveness at certain times disrupts the helper-addict relationship. And the helper must accept that he alone can never help an addict. The process is bigger than both of them, and that they both need as much help from others as they can get. As I said, I have not cured a single addict alone in twenty-five years, and I know of no one who has. A helper cannot afford grandiosity, omnipotence, or a messiah complex. The greater one's humility before the challenge of helping an addict, the better one's qualifications for the job.

When a helper tries to aid an addict in changing his daily life, he meets with sabotage. This can be an unconscious cry for help or a sign of resistance to change. The addict long ago discovered verbal and behavioral ways to manipulate others—especially by making them uncertain whether he is addicted—to frustrate their attempts at interfering with the process. His ambivalent reactions in therapy reflect a mixture of resistances and genuine desire, even resolution, to give up his addiction. Having admitted to addiction, the addict can make more conscious efforts to give it up. These efforts are never easy; even after pledging to change, he cannot make and carry out the decision to control his addiction without resorting to manipulative, defensive behavior. He finds himself automatically returning to such familiar defenses as denial, repression, and suppression. Awareness compels part of him to commitment to change, but often this commitment slides away.

After coming out of the addictive closet, the addict tells about untreatable addicts he has spent time with and addictive environments he has recently frequented. He sprinkles these almost offhand accounts liberally in his conversation and free associations, never relating them directly to his own addictive behavior. ''I saw a fantastic movie the other night with Will and Mary [two other known addicts] about some guys who deal coke [cocaine] and fight all these Southern rednecks all the way. They really let the limousine liberals have it. Nicholson played a middle-class Establishment guy who was stoned out of his mind for most of the trip. I think they're saying something like we're all stoned or have to be to take all the pressures and creeps in this society. They say the only way to really enjoy a flick like that is to be a little stoned yourself. Don't you think so?'' ''You know I'm just one of lots of kids on grass, uppers, or ludes (Quaaludes) to get into music at that stadium rock concert. Anyway, if you don't have anything of your own you can still get a contact high.''

The addict sends out many such double messages about his addiction: ''I went to those goddam AA meetings every night and took my Antabuse pills every day, but don't think I have to do all that much to stop boozing. Let me make it clear. I have no intention of giving up what you call my booze battalion of friends. Who'd I have left in my life to hang out with? Don't tell me they're my friends just because I see them at my favorite watering holes.'' He is denigrating the group, but he is also asking the helper for control or perhaps testing how controlling the helper will become when he sends out double messages. Will he set limits? Will he fall into the trap of being judgmental, moralistic, punitive, and authoritarian?

The addict will provoke, cajole, seduce, or enrage the helper—somehow involve him in talking about the pros and cons of his addiction. If he cannot snare the helper into acting controlling, he will try to control him, make him impotent before arguments about addiction. The helper who is an ex-addict can greatly aid a non-addictive helper; he is more able to aggressively pinpoint the addict's denial tactics and effectively confront him with them. He can also quickly identify the addict's manipulations through ambivalence, rationalizations, and projected hostility and guilt—all used to set up and justify further addictive behavior. The ex-addict helper, aided by a group, can more safely exert pressure, express dissatisfaction or anger, and even directly ask the addict to try to control his addiction, as other members of the group have in the past.

Addicts can use each other as role models as a way to learn to control their addictions. Sometimes an addict becomes competitive with his mentor and wants to match or supercede him or even sabotage his progress. These destructive interactions must be identified by helper, mentor, and addict. They can be a cry for help, resistance to change, or an attempt to prove change is utterly impossible:

''I know exactly how John feels when he says if Bill can get off the sauce and stay dry this long, why not me? I felt angry at first, because I didn't want to believe I was an alcoholic like both of them. I was convinced I could still drink socially and handle my liquor and if I went off booze I'd do it cold turkey, not take all the time they took, that's crazy. If you do it, do it all at once! I'm basically a lot more aggressive than those guys anyway. Do you think going to those AA meetings with them helps? I guess I should at least continue to let them pick me up in their car to get to the damn meetings. My wife says if they can do it, why not me.''

''I guess I stayed in the group to hear the grizzly stories and have them tell me I was like the rest, and now maybe to show them I could lick my hangup just as easily as any of them. Believe me, they're in no better shape than me. After I left the group the last few times, Mike and Ben stopped off to have one shot with me on the way home instead of going for coffee with the rest of our gang. I said one for the road never killed anyone. Mike told the group it's the first drink he had in months, which I know must be bullshit.''

The helper will have to face the addict's failure complex and his repeated provocative statements that he and other addicts are destined to fail at whatever they try. This attitude becomes a self-fulfilling prophecy. The addict has failed many things and people because addictiveness itself promotes failure. He is caught in a web of maladaptive feelings and responses that range from ineffective to destructive. Until he stops using his addiction as a way to function, he will anticipate failures and then use them in a circular fashion to perpetuate his addiction. ''Let's face it. Every time I put on that much weight, the guys stop calling and I just give up on myself and get depressed. So I eat more, can't shop for any clothes, and don't even meet my writing deadlines. Then it's money problems because the bills pile up, and I go on weekend binges and get superangry at everyone at the beach house. And of course everyone clears out to the beach because I'm such a bitch. You know, I won't go with them even if they did ask me. Who can put on a bathing suit looking like me? I've blown up like a balloon!''

The addict tries to trap the helper in his morass of failures by getting him to listen to endless, obsessive accounts of his addiction. This talk reflects how completely his thinking and feeling have become saturated with addictiveness. He comes alive only when talking about his or others' addictions, and tries to make his addictive free associations the sole catalyst of emotional exchange with helpers. This is also a pitfall in group interactions; counter-addictive talk and activity replace the addiction. Other ways of getting along with people are neglected. The helper may not be aware that the addict is ''getting off'' or ''high'' on obsessive talk against his addiction. Helper and group have to point out to the addict that he does this to thwart change.

At this point, the addict must consciously use behavior modification and psychological insights each day to continue mastering his addiction. He has to see that the time he must invest in changing is proportional to the depth and duration of his addiction and the frequency and number of relapses. Those who have had one or more addictions for many years must put in hundreds of hours of work and daily vigilance.

Each of the addictions requires its own combination of behavioral techniques and psychological insights. Addictions that are chemical or involve daily body functions require special treatment. I will give a variety of therapeutic examples to illustrate how a helper can shape his approach to the addict and his therapeutic requirements.

First, as I have said, the addict should be shown at every contact with him that he uses his excess pleasure to reduce pain, resolve conflict, hide or withdraw from situations that produce uncomfortable emotions—or to replace those emotions in order not to have to deal with them. In short, his addiction has become his major or only coping mechanism. One can say, for instance: ''Every time you start to think about getting out of the house and away from your kids and husband, say to decide on a career, you immediately think about taking some kind of upper or downer or actually take one." "You tell me that meeting new people gets you so tense that you have to light a cigarette. With your new selling job, you're smoking even more than the four packs you smoked when you worked with the same four people every day." "It isn't easy going to casting calls with hundreds of other actors and being rejected. You were on seven calls this week, and you went on an ice-cream binge every day. Being rejected for a job is like not being loved. It seems your only compensation is as much soft sweets as you can get in your mouth. Then you tell me it doesn't help because you're still hungry afterward. You're like a bottomless pit, never filled with enough love or acceptance. And your work means having to cope with a steady diet of rejections."

The addict may reply: "But couldn't it just be that I'm bored or plain hungry? I eat because I like eating more than anything else, certainly more than being rejected. Anyway, you have to eat to survive. . . and I'm not surviving too well in acting, so why not at least enjoy myself?" "Things are fine at work all day because there are people there who really care about me. When I got to my apartment at night, it's empty and lonely there. My only way to shake the day is to turn on. I told you I'm not too good at making the first contact. . .getting on the phone and saying, 'Are you free tonight?' So isn't it better for me to get stoned, take out my porno, jerk off, and hit the sack? Then I just pass out. I don't even know what time I fall asleep."

The next step is to help the addict identify and deal with his trigger mechanisms. Helper and addict must learn which ones are most powerful and where in the addict's life they cluster; thus they discover how the triggers relate to his history, relationships, values, and current struggles. This is best done through detailed accounts on audio tapes made in or out of the session and through written reports of the settings, thoughts, events, and addictive contacts before, during, and after each addictive fantasy and impulse.

Recording trigger mechanisms on a chart or audio tape is itself therapeutic. Identified trigger mechanisms become red flags the addict can watch for. Sometimes several trigger mechanisms occur together; the greater their number, frequency, and intensity, the more intense and frequent are the addictive impulses.

Many trigger mechanisms have been identified by researchers who have conducted in-depth studies of addictions, especially alcohol, tobacco, food heroin, amphetamine, gambling, and poly-drug addictions. But the populations in these studies were skewed in one or more ways—geographic, cultural, ethnic, religious, age, sex, socioeconomic, intellectual, psychopathology, physical pathology, and stage of addiction. Each researcher pinpointed triggers in his particular population, with its specific vulnerabilities. Those most often found were anxiety, depression, family conflict, interpersonal and socioeconomic stress, isolation, loneliness, boredom, gender-role and erotic conflict, low self-esteem, situational crises, life passages, deaths, and any frustration of needs. Also found were excessive dependencies (orality), distortions in dominance-submission, sado-masochism, aggressiveness, hostility along with emotional inhibitions, misidentifications, and an inability to cope with failure or to establish a social career and personal identity. In some reports, one or several triggers are said to be those most responsible for addictive behavior.

Because the addict is always faced with a variety of depressive phenomena once he has admitted his addiction, and is willing to embark on some degree of detoxification, the helper must be prepared to obtain an accurate (often professional) diagnosis of the depression. Unless its roots and meaning are defined, all forms of help are short-circuited. Trying to stabilize and detoxify the addict is futile as long as he remains depressed, for he does not have enough strength or movtivation to use the insight and behavioral techniques offered him. Addict and helper have to discover whether the depression is internal (chemically or genetically based), reflects his recent altered chemical state, or results from the removal of the life he has so long cherished and protected. This knowledge is necessary in order to coldly confront his addictive dependencies. It is seeing himself for the first time as others have seen him, or worse, still not being able to look at how he has devastated his mind and body through years of addictive living. His confrontation and changes are traumatic, because he is giving up the only relief he had in life for the unknown. So he is bound to be depressed.

Treating any of these depressions always requires the means (i.e. chemo-therapy, psychotherapy, hospitalization) suggested by a professional. He will keep in mind that treatment is effective only if it is in concert with the addict's total history. Having an alcoholic use an addictive tranquilizer is as inadvisable as giving pornography to soothe a suicidal sexual addict. Managing depression in an addict still remains one of the most difficult diagnostic and therapeutic challenges to meet because it often seems that the only cure available holds the potential for perpetuating the disease.

In short, research revealed that almost every known discomfort in human adaptation has been singled out as an addictive trigger. I believe various addictive populations reveal one cluster of triggers rather than others because the researcher projected his bias or the group was exposed to more or different triggers than others. *What remains vital is for the addict to discover and remain aware of his unique, prevalent, and predictable set of triggers.* He must vigilantly recognize them at every turn. He has to be warned that they vary in impact, time of occurance, and multiplicity at different periods of his life. He has to be alert that they can shift, depending on his life circumstances. He will find out that the most persistent triggers are those that emerged from his childhood. Here is a typical exchange between addict and helper that illustrates the multiplicity and impact of addictive triggers:

Addict: "I couldn't believe it until I thought of what you said about my day being loaded with triggers. I hadn't realized there were so many. My boss made me feel like an ass. . .put me down the same way my father used to. I wasn't able to handle the money thing with my wife. . .she says checks always bounce. The straw that broke my back was having this guy come on to me in my own office with the porno he was selling. I just flipped out at lunch. . .right into the baths again. Then I got loaded at the bar station and missed the seven-ten train. She blasted me on the phone when I called her. I called up one of the group and talked and talked. Otherwise I just would have gone on drinking and tub crawling [visiting homosexual baths] the rest of the night."

Helper: "Well, at least you stopped yourself this time, with a little help from our friends. Did you realize what the triggers were?"

Addict: "Yes. My father's put-downs. He's done that to me all my life. It was worse after my boss let me have it, and then my wife. . .about how badly I handle money. . .but she scares me because she says that kind of thing when she's on one of her spending binges. I get like a real up-tight ass. . .and then. . .well, I couldn't fight the last bit with this fantastic hunky-looking guy who walked into my office trying to sell me all the cock-sucking hetero porno. . .can you believe it, he had a hard-on right in front of me and cruised my crotch! That did it! I thought I'd kicked that problem forever. I guess I was too weak after everything that happened. What made me feel good is that I did pull myself out of that nose dive when I called Ron. He was a saint to listen so long and tell me he'd slipped too and went to the track again yesterday. He blamed it on those OTB signs all over town. He said that not even the caution on the sign. . .you know, GO TO THE NEAREST GAMBLERS ANONYMOUS. . . helped him. My call actually helped him. He said he'd been thinking about going to the trotters, but after we talked he said, 'You make the nine-ten train, and I'll take Sally out to a movie.' So I got the train and he took Sally to a movie."

If a consistent, reliable helper shows an addict rejection or inconsistency, the addict will experience it as a very severe setback. This is less likely if the primary helper keeps in touch with peer addict helpers, learning from them which behavioral techniques have best produced change. Addicts gain a great deal from self-help groups, both by talking in person and on the phone and by identifying with peers who are learning to monitor their addictions. The addict can imitate and identify their peers' insights and behavior to control his addiction. Ultimately, each addict and his helpers must determine why, where, when, and how often each resource and therapeutic technique works best for him. They cannot be limited by any one form of help. Using all possible resources—helpers, peer addicts, audio and video tapes, and charts—keeps the addict on the road to recovery and reduces the number of relapses. An addict who is effectively using a variety of therapeutic techniques would say:

"I can't stand any more analysis of all the drunks I've been on. . .but I did listen to that two-minute tape of what you said to me—you know, the one about why I think no one at the office knows I'm a lush? Then, how come my boss sent me to that doctor about my missing so many days? And how come the doctor laid it on the line and said that I'm not fooling anyone in the company, and that if I don't go to the company's AA program I shouldn't bother to pick up my next paycheck. That hit me right between the eyes. I had to realize the answers to those questions. I listened to that tape every morning while I brushed my teeth and finally it got to me. I want to do something right now! I've been asleep so long, and I don't want to and can't kid myself or any one else much longer. I just know I'll hate the jabbery confessions at the AA. I've heard all about what goes on. It's like going to church, but at least I'll be with drunks who aren't drinking—even if they talk a hell of a lot about how they kill themselves at it. And at least I'll get my next paycheck!

Helpers should point out what they observe to be the most dangerous trigger mechanisms for each particular addict. Experiments have shown that absence from the addictive agent, other addicts, and addictive environments is the most effective single way to stop the addictive process. This is not possible in most addictions; food, sex, drugs, tobacco, and alcohol are always present in our society, and some are essential to a normal life. But if the addict understands the power of environmental stimuli, he may eventually be better able to control his contacts with environmental triggers. Such control must be extreme in the malignant stage of addiction; the only therapy is full commitment to a detoxification program.

One person becoming aware of his triggers and beginning to change said: "I'm a bit of a TV addict, too, and when I filled in the chart on when, where, and why I think of food, I realized that while everyone else picks up a paper or goes to the bathroom during commercials, I watch them. . .I never realized how many there are during four hours. Well, it's during those commercials that I think of food. On top of that, my wife takes cooking courses and talks about food all the time. And at our office I'm working on a food advertising account, so I rationalize that I'm doing my homework by watching so much TV. But who am I kidding? It shocked me when I realized how much of my life is tied up with my mouth and stomach. . .TV, my wife, my job. . .it's a twenty-four-hour number on my head. Do you know what I dreamed of when I cut down this week on the TV and ice-box raids? Food. Goddam fudge pouring over coconut mounds like a volcano exploding. . .which is what I'm like if I can't get something to eat when I want it.''

Four trigger mechanisms are very commonly reported: rejection, loss of self-esteem, loneliness, and boredom. Any addiction flowers because it is deeply rooted in early-life rejection, excessive nurturing, or neglect. Early relationships have left the addict ill prepared to deal with normal rejection and acceptance. In his past and present, he has been triggered by too much or too little emotional and physical caring and by excessive control of his behavior.

The addict compensates with addictive behavior and seeks out people and situations that will meet, or can be manipulated to meet, his excessive needs. Sometimes he misinterprets their conduct so as to delude himself that they have met them when his needs have not been met. The people who nourished excessive dependencies or had unrealistic expectations in his early life cannot meet his bottomless needs later on, but he relentlessly clings to their apparent support. His nurturers regret having set the excesses in motion; they say they gave too much, asked for too much, or expected too much or too little. Subsequently they give less, give inconsistently, or withdraw completely. This triggers feelings of rejection, which fuel further addictive acting-out. The addict perceives requests that he be self-supporting, independent, and responsible as rejections.

The addict must become aware of these distorted reactions and gain the strength to make sound judgments that will help him control his addiction. He must understand and cope with his loneliness and boredom. He has either had to be constantly stimulated by pleasure or has been unable to balance pleasure and work. Addictive practices have further reduced his self-esteem and created restlessness and boredom. Perhaps more than ever, he expects too much or too little and gives or takes inappropriately. His inability to give of himself emotionally and materially makes him seek masochistic providers or others who are crippled in giving and taking. Inequities, rejections, boredom, and isolation escalate in his life because other addicts and addictive complements behave as he does. Also, frequent and intense contacts with addictive relatives constantly act as triggers without his realizing it.,

The addict is also unknowingly triggered by a sea of cultural contaminants. Our society promotes a need for continuous excitement to relieve tension and boredom. People are sold one new high after another—speed, violence, the biggest, the best. Less value is placed on a moderate, slower-paced, shared existence. There is also a narcissistic youth ethic of ''do your own thing,'' but too little attention to whether a person does his thing excessively or in ways to affect others. Packaged excesses are constantly and powerfully communicated by all the media—violence, sex, drugs, and drinking. Our culture triggers addicts with a bombardment of stimuli that spawns new addicts in each generation.

The addict can also be triggered by difficulty becoming integrated with normal society. He protected himself with an addictive subculture and then tries to rejoin society during recovery; he must then contend with prejudice against addicts. Life becomes more difficult and painful for him. In fact, if he has lived in an addictive subculture for long periods, he may never again feel accepted or acceptable among nonaddicts. He will always feel deviant and have to support his deviant identity—by addictive acts and by living among others with a similar identity. For instance:

"Since I was sixteen I've been getting it off with 'heads.' You know, it's been seven years of hanging out only with them. Straights bore the shit out of me. I just can't seem to connect with any of them, even though I've been clean for months. I get so uptight. . .don't know who I am with them. . .don't talk or feel at home. . .and for sure they can't get into my scene. Like last night at the disco I said to some straight guy, 'It's hard to get it on without poppers,' and he shot back, 'Man, are you gay?' He knew right away where I was coming from. He said, 'No thanks,' and walked away."

Therefore the addict must be aware each day, even each hour, how and why his addictive identity, practice, and life style provoke rejection. He has to see how his belief that he will be rejected, which verges on paranoia, has become a self-fulfilling prophecy. In the past he ignored and denied the real impact of his behavior and provoked rejection by those who loved, lived and worked with him. Even while improving, he forgets that he must sometimes expect to be rejected justifiably, and sometimes unjustifiably, for people will accuse him of addictive behavior even if it is no longer occurring.

As the addict starts to become aware of these problems, he will tell the helper about them. For instance: "Yesterday, for the first time I can remember, I tried to listen to what my brother said. . .even my folks. . .to give some thought to what they said. I stopped myself from running off at the mouth. I said to myself, shut up, you're so full of what you want. I realized that I always try to overwhelm them all so they'll just give up and let me have whatever I want. . .usually money to gamble. All those calls to them when the bookies are after me. . .I think they're on to me by now anyway. They lie or I get suspicious about why they're telling me they weren't home. . .I think they don't pick up the phone sometimes because they know it's me about to go down the drain again! I guess I bring a lot of this on by myself, but finally I can't take it any more, so I do what I do. . .put another bet on the nags to soothe my burned feelings."

Feeling rejected by those who matter or even those who no longer matter sets up another common trigger, loss of self-esteem. Every in-depth study of addiction speaks of the addict's low self-esteem. These studies are full of such terms as devaluation, self-hate, self-loathing, low opinion, and inferiority. In many addicts these feelings are acute but not at a high level of awareness. They can be rooted not only in early development but in how the addict is regarded and treated by those he has most damaged. He may develop feelings of guilt, shame, failure, low expectations of his ability to meet his own or others' expectations. In advanced or chronic addiction, he does not believe he can accomplish anything. When the addictive process has a life of its own, with destructive symptoms and by-products, low self-esteem is based on real failures. Because of these failures, people treat him in personal, social, and professional ways that confirm his self-devaluation.

He must therefore try to kill one of the most malignant sources of his low self-esteem—his addictive behavior. He soon learns that any mastery, however small, is a step in that direction. At first he may not see that his painful sacrifice will bring him such a reward; often it seems to do nothing. The addict feels he is giving up something too valuable to be balanced by a small gain in self-worth.

Every helper should recognize those early faltering sacrifices—the addict's first form of giving, and jump in with support and praise. He should assure the addict that he will gain self-esteem for what he has sacrificed. His helper seeds the pearls of those first compliments from others who begin to value him again or value him for the first time. The addict builds on this first praise, making it the foundation of a new, more secure identity.

Helper: "I realize how hard it was for you to give up your uppers and downers this past month. Your wife told me it was the biggest thing you'd given her in a long time. Do you realize that after that she and your family started treating you as if you had real value? That's a terrific beginning."

Addict: "I know I've been the shit heel of the family and down at our shop. I realized how much people's respect means to me. When my wife said I was like my old self again, and my partner said that I'm not as spacey, I managed to turn out my first good design in a year. I can't believe what giving up that stuff has done for me. You said all I had to do was to do it to see how good I'd feel about myself."

The consequences of giving up addictive practices—improved relationships and better psychological and perhaps physical health—contrast vividly with his past. This success is a wellspring of self-esteem. The impact of addiction on work, social, personal, erotic, and economic life gradually diminishes. Such changes in any facet of life are enhanced by the reactions of those close to the addict who see the change. It is important not only for helpers to emphasize and reinforce the changes but for the addict to do so himself—by talk, by playing audio tapes, and by comparing his behavior and moods in addictive and nonaddictive periods. He must still expect to feel moments of indiscriminate, sometimes gratuitous anger toward those close to him in nonaddictive periods. Such frustration and other residual withdrawal symptoms may appear, and he may exploit them to deny the value of giving up his addiction despite his gains in well-being. He should be reassured that once the withdrawal period passes, the improvement in his self-esteem will be more sustained. Here is an exchange I had with one addict as this was happening to him.

Addict: "Every time I turned on, I felt like the lowest, too weak to control this or anything in my life. Sure, a pot head is the pits to everyone. . .lower than a drunk. . .can't think things through. . .so a job, money, even my own pad, they're out for now. My family still wants to believe I've got talent, but it's hard for me to believe. The last thing I painted was a mess. . .it's two years since I picked up a brush. How can I even say I'm an artist? I'm a nobody. . .at least I was till this past month. The group made me feel like at least some kind of person. They asked to see my old paintings. Those four days I went cold turkey I was depressed, like a zombie, or else I was kicking everyone's ass. But on the first day, for the first time since I don't know when, I felt human again. . .even did a few lousy sketches. . .which the whole gang raved about. They said I looked like I'd just stepped out of a health club. . .shaved, spruced up. Knowing I could do it made me feel like a million. My folks called and asked me over for dinner with other people for the first time in years. They all treated me like a person. . .not like some piece of shit."

Helper: "Don't be discouraged that you've slipped back. Think about the tapes of those sessions. Listen to them. It happened once. You felt like somebody instead of a nobody. It will happen again. Keep up with the group. You've dropped in and out of it more than is good for you. You tell me they are the only people you trust or can make you believe in yourself, so it's important to keep in touch with them."

Loneliness and boredom are closely allied triggers in the addict's life. In the self-help addict groups I have conducted, they were often referred to as the bottom-line conscious reasons for turning to addictive practice—"to feel good". . . ."to relieve the monotony". . . ."to forget things and people that bother me". . . ."if I have to be home by myself, at least I can light up". . . ."shoot up". . . ."eat brownies". . . ."have a drink". . . ."jerk off". . . ."work till three a.m.". . . ."read the racing forms and bet on TV games." Otherwise, they say, "life is empty". . . ."one big colossal nothing". . . ."only lows, no highs". . . ."I'm dead inside."

Often they have confused, free-floating tension along with the loneliness and boredom. These triggers should be closely examined. Are they caused by inability to express emotions or to become involved with others? Does the addict use his practice as a solution to difficulty in facing problems and relating to people? He has to discover that loneliness and boredome both produce and result from the addictive behavior he uses to cope with a dysfunctional emotional and social life. His pseudocure only heightens his detachment and social isolation. At times he may use his loneliness in a self-pitying way and present himself as a pathetic loser to provoke guilt in people whose lives are more fulfilled than his. A helper must be alert to these maneuvers and not be trapped into feeling sorry for the addict and becoming a permissive monitor. If the addict's behavior is reinforced by such spurious support, he may use it to rationalize and justify his behavior.

The helper should confront any denial by the addict that there are alternatives to boredom and loneliness other than addictiveness. When a helper first tries this, he finds himself in a real power struggle. The addict constantly tries to defy the helper or enmesh him in controversy—an effort to affirm that addiction is his best alternative to boredom and loneliness. This becomes apparent when the helper suggests choices other than addictive agents and milieus. Because the addict always compares things to his addictive highs, it is difficult for him to imagine excitement or relief of his loneliness from other activities. Sometimes he even manipulates the helper into offering these suggestions, only to reduce them to absurdities or call them forms of control. "It's easy for you to go jogging or meet new people or get invited to parties. . .you don't have to face the world fat. . .it's an accomplishment for me to feel able to cross my legs. . .and going to the fridge is still better than staying in my room bored out of my skull."

To one such argument I replied, "Listen, you forget that when you went to Weight Watchers you did get out of yourself. You started to call that girl you met at the first meeting. You talked to her a lot about how you used to love to play the piano, told her that you had music in common. She's still studying music, even though she's fat and men don't call her. She doesn't seem to feel as sorry for herself or use her weight as an excuse to avoid everything else in life."

Addict: "You're right about one thing. I wasn't so lonely those nights. . .or so hungry. For once in years I got a little high on the phone with someone about my music. You know, I didn't tell you, I even got hot in the crotch talking to her. . . maybe I'll go from being a food freak to being one of those heavy breathers on the phone. You remember how you told me my mom always said she spent money just to fill her days and not live a dull life like my dad, working around the clock, and then how she stopped spending and turned into a health club freak. Well, I could get into sex more if I could see where it was under these layers of fat."

Helper: "You're making it seem impossible by using all this information negatively. The more you see how your mother used boredom and loneliness as an excuse, the sooner you'll understand yourself. When she replaced her addictive spending, she wasn't becoming a health freak; she used exercise and being with friends to fill some of the void. It was a replacement for your father, who wasn't around because he had to be on business trips. Your feeling sexy on the phone was a good sign. It doesn't have to become another excess. It can just be part of your feeling warm toward the girl."

These two triggers and many others are most powerfully counteracted by the addict voluntarily participating in a self-help group, with or without individual or group therapy. The therapist's most important function can be helping the addict to do so. The group becomes the core of his recovery. When I learned that groups did not exist for the sex addict, work addict, the anorexic, or the multiply addicted, I formed two groups for multiply and sexually addictive people. After four years as both a therapist and a peer workaholic member of these groups, I was convinced that they are absolutely necessary in any treatment program because of the change in my own addiction and new insights into patients I had previously seen only in individual therapy.

There is voluminous scientific literature confirming the value of self-help groups and group therapy. Many specialized forms of group therapy have been used recently to treat addictions—psychoanalytically oriented psychotherapy, psychodrama, family and adolescent and hospital peer groups, all male and all female groups, ethnic groups, audio and video playback groups, and others (see bibliography). I stress my conviction about the need for them because of the documentation of so much wasted time and money, the frustrations, discouragement, and heartaches for the addict and his helpers in dead-ended individual therapies. Many helpers have sworn, ''Never, never again will I work alone with an addict.'' Yet our own and the addict's ego and omnipotence lured us into more therapeutic failures.

No one helper will ever have enough time, energy, selflessness, insights, objectivity, dedication, patience, emotional flexibility, resilience in dealing with relapses, and constant availability that every addict needs. In the lives of most addicts who have received help over extended periods, there was more than one helper who vigorously, enthusiastically, but naively leaped on his or her charger to salvage, reform, or enlighten the addict, save him from deterioration, destruction, suicide, or some other kind of ruin. Few or none ever made it for long without calling in helpers, or departing worn, torn, and defeated. Those who remain do so out of their own neurotic, often masochistic or addictive-complementary needs. Some are closet fellow addicts not aware of their own deceptions.

A group in which at least some members are peer addicts or addictive complements offers these therapeutic aids:

1. Learning that change is possible by seeing it occur in peer addicts and by identifying with them.
2. Having more than one person to turn to and one place to go to during times of stress, isolation, crises, and inability to cope with addiction.
3. A source of encouragement, support, and appropriate responses to destructive attitudes and feelings of hopelessness, self-contempt, and self-devaluation.
4. The availability of hundreds of hours of dedicated helpers' time, energy, and other forms of involvement. Most groups offer this for low fees or free.
5. The addict learns about the depth, degree, and phase of his addiction, for he is in contact with people at all phases and degrees of addiction and recovery. He also comes to understand fellow addicts and their trial-and-error management of relapses.
6. The addict experiences some feelings he never felt before and exercises others he has spent his life suppressing. He sees others ventilate their emotions, giving him permission to express his own. He has an oasis of

emotional catharsis, a tolerant, confidential milieu of people who know what it is to have suffered. He feels what it is like not being condemned by others. He can confess to himself and others shame, guilt, fear, hostility, and other hidden, forbidden, socially unacceptable emotions.

This confessional element in group meetings is invaluable. Repressed and suppressed incidents have eroded the addict's self-esteem and removed him from other people, now, for the first time, they can be revealed. Old infections open up and drain instead of festering inside him; this reduces his susceptibility to addictive triggers. Unburdening himself of guilt and reaffirming his commitment to stopping addictive behavior is also central to the group's effectiveness. Even if the release from guilts is temporary and needs repetition, it is beneficial.

Every self-help group insists that one deal not only with one's addictive past but with the here and now. The addict's daily and hourly life is confessed to and closely examined. They explore the what, how much, where, when, with whom and, in some analytically oriented psychotherapy groups, the whys. Participating in this with other addicts makes it more difficult to use defense mechaniams. The addict's practices lay revealed to him at every turn by his fellow addicts. In some groups, fellow addicts can uncover denial and manipulations in an aggressive, forthright way that a professional therapist could never risk doing. Even anger and rebuke are possible, which the addict would not accept from nonaddicts; the addict's resistance to authoritarian, controlling nonaddicts are very great. Exchanges like this may occur:

Addict 1: "Don't tell me you went down to Greenwich Village just to get cheap paint supplies. You know that store is a block from the city's biggest meat rack (homosexual pickup area) and the place where you get amyl nitrate to take to the tubs—which are only four blocks away."

Addict 2: "The last few weeks you've really pissed me off with all your phony resolutions about no more sex binges with all that junk in you. Meanwhile, you've been laying a guilt trip on me about getting a bartender job as a cover for getting back into the bottle."

Addict 1: "Maybe you're both right. But I really couldn't take the doctor saying I'm deluding myself about wanting to give up endless impersonal orgasms because I still take the subways where I used to get blow jobs when I could just as well take buses to work. He has no faith in me. He doesn't know what it's like when I get my crotch fever. You guys all know what it's like."

At first the addict may discredit what he's learning because he cannot value a peer; still, didactic group activity can help him. Lectures and scientific information can also greatly help the addict who is ignorant of or has denied the facts of his addiction: "I went through this in such and such a fashion. You can get over it too, by doing so and so." The addict can best accept listening to a caring, recovered addict or to one who is a step ahead of him when he hears such advice as, "Weigh yourself every day, count calories and chart them. . .take each hour as a challenge to stay out of the bars. . .I used to go to the baths every time I was angry until I learned to express my anger right away, so just let your anger out. . .don't be such a Goody-Two-Shoes, you always look and sound weak after you've gone to the baths."

After attending self-help groups, many addicts say that they were triggered by the contact with other addicts. Even though the groups are motivated to lose their addiction, they may act as addictive complements; as they recount failures, relapses, subtle rationalizations, and the persistent need to practice their addictions, they can provoke an addictive response in the neophyte member. Furthermore, some addicts greatly fear contamination by the group's pathology. It is important to distinguish a genuine trigger from rationalizations to withdraw from help. The addict benefits most from a group that shows mutual care and giving:

Addict 1: "I can't take one more night of those fatties. It's food this and food that and all the goddam weigh-ins. They depress me with those self-pitying, sad-sack stories. I've got enough of my own. I get out of the meeting and head right for the first ice cream or candy shop I can find."

Addict 2: "There are two leaders in that group who go on and on about how great they are to have stayed clean for three years. They both think they're saving lost souls and sound like preachers. I've gotten that at home all my life from my rabbi father, who's still my biggest trigger. There's another guy who tells me he's been in and out of drug groups and rehabs for fifteen years. I think I'm going to call it quits."

Addict 3: "There's no doubt in my mind that Jane and Will care more for me than even my own parents ever have. They came over to my house at four in the morning and stayed for hours until I was conscious. I took all that stuff after the meeting because of a phone call. My sister screamed to me that I was disinherited. I'm dead broke, and I have liquor and gambling debts up to my eyeballs. That's what you guys call supertrigger time—no family, no money, and the wolves at my door. So why not just end it all, drug and debt myself into oblivion?"

In the group, the addict shows awareness of others and their needs for the first time. He says to himself, "There but for the grace of God go I." Giving to others becomes as important to him as taking, for he has quickly learned that he will receive from fellow addicts whatever he gives. He becomes more able to trust another person, even learns to depend on more than one for the support he may need. Great amounts of time and encouragement are available to him, compared to his emotionally impoverished existence before he entered the group.

Even within a group, the nonaddict helper always seems a risk to the addict; he has little or no reason for tolerating the addict's excessive, destructive taking and his depleting dependencies. In a mixed group (addicts and nonaddicts), if such a person is an addictive complement, or if he unconsciously wants to control the addict through guilt or by extracting more than he has given—or, conversely, if he has a neurotic need to tolerate these inequities—he will provoke the addiction. If the addict does not identify such pseudohelpers, others in the group will expose them.

As the addict begins to appreciate the pleasure of giving to fellow addicts, his self-esteem increases. He becomes willing to give up selfish addictive practices and life styles in order to gain those rewards. At first he must be shown how his addiction has made him totally self-oriented so that others receive little or nothing from him. Listening to addicts confess hundreds of selfish and dependent acts in the group is a powerful lesson about this. The addict becomes painfully aware that before he entered the group, addictive fantasies and acts had top priority in his life. He gave first and foremost to the addictive process! People, work, family, life crises, even danger to his physical being, came second or remained outside his consciousness because it had been invaded by his addictive self.

In the end stages of any addiction, but particularly in the multiply addicted, self-oriented and dependent behavior are as dramatic as the anarchy of tumorous tissue. Addictive thinking has driven out everything else. The biographies and auto-biographies of multiple addicts such as Montgomery Clift (an alcohol, drug, and sex addict) and Janis Joplin (alcohol, multiple drug, sex, and work addict) show such malignant effects. The addict's selfishness is one of the most destructive by-products of this stage. This makes it difficult or impossible for any friend, relative, lover, or professional helper who is not himself an addict in remission to tolerate the relationship. Ultimately the helper tries to intervene in the addict's excessive taking (narcissism and pathological dependency). For instance: ''Well, it's been two months since I asked all of you to make just one contribution to me, as no one is paying for my services. Remember, I asked you all to write out your alcoholic histories for my research, and it appears that no one has done that. I feel we should examine this.''

Addict 1: ''Well, you didn't ask often enough or make it clear when you needed it or why.''

Addict 2: ''I wrote some of it for me in my diary, and it was helpful, so I figured it's all you wanted it for and said forget it to myself.''

Addict 3: ''I did it on the phone one night with Addict 1, and he said he learned a lot. We compared notes and, like, we helped each other. It never occurred to me to think about you and your research. That's your responsibility! But it did make me feel good to listen to him and give him some of my time.''

Helper: ''What about the time I've given? You all forgot that I did spell it out, and I need these histories to complete my research.''

Addict 4: ''Aren't you getting enough out of us as guinea pigs, listening and using us every week for an hour and a half? Maybe it's you who's selfish, trying to do a guilt number on us. You're just like everyone else outside the group who wants to dump on us all the time.''

Addict 1: ''Not only that, but you and your machine answering service. . .I called it seven times yesterday, and I always get the same oily, 'This is Dr.—, at this moment I'm in session.' You know, that never happens when I call one of the group. I have all his numbers, and I called him at three in the morning. He picked up the phone and was with me all the way. We talked for a full hour. Would you ever do that? So what's all this 'feel sorry for me, I'm so cheated by you all' routine? It annoys me. Would you be there for me around the clock, giving me the answer?''

Helper: ''No. It isn't possible for me to offer that level of commitment to help you—ever, and you know that. But you all forget or choose not to remember that you did agree as part of our contract to bring in those histories. And you didn't. You do help each other in a very fair way, and that's the beginning of learning about giving and taking—an outgrowth of giving up what's most difficult of all, your drinking. I've gotten something out of our work, but not what I asked for.''

Group interactions provide many other things. The addict learns to socialize without his addictive agent. Some groups offer faith—spiritual beliefs that give him hope in powers beyond his control. Instead of himself or other people being in control of his addiction, he can release himself to this force. This has been unique to the AA groups, where I have found that those with religious backgrounds easily incorporate their religiosity into their response to the self-help group. They get into the program faster, show less resistance, attend more meetings, stay with it longer, and tend to proselitize other alcoholics more often than those without religious histories and activities. Their religious belief proved invaluable; morality and values are inevitably part of the recovery process in and out of the group. The use of emotionally charged words—liar, irresponsible, lazy—pushes the addict to scrutinize and alter many of his defective character traits. For instance:

''Attending these meetings makes my painfully aware of how destructive my drinking is to my wife and kids. I'm just a taker and a manipulator. . .and what's more, I do lie like the rest of them at AA. . .maybe about more than just my drinking. I see how my sober shit-kicking, smiling, good-guy routine is just a cover-up for a lot of unexpressed hate in me that only comes out when I'm tanked.''

In psychotherapy self-help groups, the addict expresses and examines distrust and interpersonal distortions, and he projects onto group members the roles of relatives he blames for his addiction. This corrective experience reduces alienation, self-contempt, and self-defeating ways of presenting himself to others. For instance:

''Look, my father could never be trusted. He always made promises he couldn't keep because he never had any money to keep them or the time. . .he was always in debt to the bookies. . .or at the trotters. He was and is a loser. Until this group experience, I never believed anyone would come through for me. . .thought I'd always be a loser, too. Now for the first time in my life am proud of what I do at work. All this happened here. I really feel I belong. It's like a family that's not all over the place. You feel some respect for each other, and that helps you face the next day feeling like somebody.''

Before the addict can experience any security in mastering his illness, he must find nonaddictive, pleasurable replacements for his addiction. If he does not consciously replace his addictive fantasies, impulses, and activities—in some cases, his entire life style—with a substitute acceptable to him and to society, he will feel a void in his life and remain vulnerable to relapses. Without relief from his addictive practices, he will experience various combinations of pain, apathy, anxiety, and depression; it must be made clear to him that at first he will devalue other activities as too dull, unacceptable, or not pleasurable enough. He has to try a variety of activities, peoples, places, and fantasies until he finds the right ones for himself.

The addict's unconscious is sly and slippery. He will try to use every pleasurable substitute but the viable ones, because he is attracted back to addictive people, practices, and environments. For some addicts, a diluted version of the past will be effective and not trigger a relapse; for most, especially those with long-standing addictions, the environmental triggers are so powerful that they will not be able to sustain even watered-down forms of their addictions. Most addicts are best off choosing people, activities, and places that are unrelated to their addictive past. This is difficult to get them to do:

Addict: ''My previous analyst played the stock market as much as I did. He was a closet gambler. He thought I should work as a race-horse trainer instead of betting on the side at the tracks because I love horses and the outdoors. I thought of running a backgammon club, but all my buddies are big betters at that game. Then the group suggested I invest in these run-down town houses and manage them. I thought, that's just another crazy gamble, they're filled with pimps and bookies. You know, my father taught me real estate. That's what I've done best, and I'd love to buy an old hotel and convert it into an apartment house for families. You know, I'm dropping a lot of friends who are into gambling, looking up old buddies who are married, and I feel great getting together with them. They're introducing me to different kinds of gals. . .not just the model, stewardess, lay-'em-and-leave-'em fast types.''

Helper: ''The group's been encouraging you in lots of ways. I heard that one of them also introduced you to someone so interesting that you didn't get out to the track that day. And you didn't rush home to get the basketball scores on TV and place bets with your old bookie.''

Addict: ''I still don't think I'll ever get off on the family scene after all these years of getting high on betting at some game. You know, I get high on the smells of those crisp, clear mornings at the track. It's like horses are in my blood.''

Helper: ''How about your other idea of a ranch or farm with horses?''

Addict: ''That's a great idea! I'll breed horses, then buy and sell the winners—my winners. And finally I'll be a winner.''

Helper: ''You seem to have to get back to gambling regardless of what you choose.''

Addict: ''It's hard to find other things that turn me on.''

Once the addict has found one or more nonaddictive forms of pleasure, he has to realize that he must be vigilant about using them to excess in order to deal with pain. He has a high potential for polarization in his thoughts, moods, acts, and values. He has to learn to distinguish between an activity or agent used recreationally, as an adaptive form of relaxation and release, and one that is easily abused and maladaptive.

He has to become convinced that when anxious, depressed, or in conflict and unable to cope, he has other ways of dealing with these problems than addiction. He invariably asks any and every helper, "What ways?"

Psychiatric and self-help literature are full of hundreds of techniques that therapists have experimented with in order to help the addict find satisfying, nonaddictive replacements for his addictive practice. They recommend physical exercise, yoga, transcendental meditation, relaxation, audio tapes, biofeedback, return to religious activity, dedication to a cause, philanthropic work, creative work, a new career, further education, and addict-free social groups that participate in pleasurable or work activities. The choices can grow from the addict's discovery of what has been underdeveloped, absent, repressed, or distorted in his emotional life.

If a person's addiction replaced or was used to deal with erotic feelings, he must begin to express and live them out. If anger, tenderness, or other emotions have been replaced by addictive practice, he must exercise them in his daily life. When he has done so, his addictive impulses become extinguished. He must observe whether expressing these emotions makes him feel and act less addictively in the following hours, days, and weeks. One addict who was making progress said to me:

"I guess being stone all the time did hide all sorts of things inside me. People thought I was a nice quiet guy, maybe a little spacey. Not now since I'm off of everything, I've begun to see that it pays to blow up at people when they take advantage of you, and I'm into balling chicks. I'd never been able to go all the way. It beats being zonked. I tell you, after I let my folks have it last week and met this girl who's great in the sack, I really was able to turn down the stuff my junkie pal wanted to sell me. All I need to do is let my temper out and get laid, maybe fall in love with the right chick, and I'll kick it once and for all. I've been a very tied-up guy."

The addict's almost reflex use of addictive behavior to solve any problem is a fact of life he must keep in mind every day. He must say to himself, "I have to face and solve this problem in any way except an addictive practice." If he finds that his addiction is on the increase, he must look for the reasons; he may not have realized that he was trying to solve a problem, feeling frustrated or angry, or had lost self-esteem. He has to ask himself, "What is really bothering me now?" Perhaps he wants a new career, more lovemaking, more money. Whatever it is, he must take a step toward doing it.

There are times when the addict cannot see the source of his addictive impulse. He must then avoid his lifelong trait of not being able to postpone gratification or tension release and of reaching impulsively for instant gratification. He now must learn to delay such behavior for as long as he can tolerate, using any device he can to reduce the feeling, thought, or fantasy that drives him toward an addictive act. Thus he interrupts the addictive cycle at any point he can. He can use or depend on others to help him in his delaying maneuver. People can fill the time, particularly if his contacts with them are pleasurable and rewarding. These contacts can soon become more rewarding than the addictive act or being with practicing addicts or in addictive milieus.

The technique of delay can be as simple as counting bites of foods or unwrapping a pack of cigarettes and writing down the number smoked that day and reasons for wanting to smoke at that moment. Or the addict may listen to a tape long enough for the fantasy or impulse to disappear. Any act should be used that restrains the addict to tolerate tension, anxiety, or dissatisfaction and increases his awareness of his addictive reflex.

It is the addict's responsibility to find through trial and error which delaying tactics work best for him and can be integrated into his life and the lives of those he loves and spends his days with. Something as simple as a slogan repeated to oneself can lead a person into an activity long enough for the addictive fever to pass. Mine is, "I love to be with my wife and kids. . .so I think I'll go to a movie with them or talk or play a game with them. . .instead of working today." I continue, "What's more, I'm getting old, and this work addiction will kill me before I've done the things and had the fun I want to have." I then find myself planning one of these activities and move on into some pleasure the replaces the compulsive high I know I can always get from work.

The one pitfall in turning exclusively to self-help peer groups is not making use of other resources. However, people struggling with long-standing malignant addictions may be able to stay addiction-free only in a peer subculture, such as the Synanon Community, or by daily attendance at AA meetings, becoming an AA worker, running a Weight Watchers unit, or working as a paraprofessional.

One must alert a less severely addicted person that he can become addicted to his therapy or to a therapeutic device, including the self-help group. Endless therapeutic talk and activity devitalize the addict and make him impossible to live with. I had an alcoholic patient who, after finally admitting that she was an alcoholic, went to AA meetings excessively, attended group therapy for alcoholics, joined a group doing megavitamin therapy for alcoholics, and attended my own multiple-addiction group. She was often on the phone with members of these groups who were going through crises. Finally, to be thorough, she had herself admitted to an alcohol detoxification center for thirty days of vigorous reprogramming. In therapy we often tried to analyze her excessive use of therapies. She finally gained insight into how they so drained her life that they began to trigger her into drinking. After her detoxification, she settled into more moderate treatment.

Any cure carried to excess can itself become a disease; the addict, with his tendency to excess, is especially vulnerable to this. Often therapy becomes a convenient avoidance of confrontations with the outside world, in which the addict has many insecurities. This very avoidance promotes a return to addictive practices. The addict must try his wings in new environments and with new people. If addictive people and places are ubiquitous, as they are for a smoker, the addict must strive to be with those who don't smoke, seek nonsmoking areas, get rid of ash trays, spend time with those who are or have been in Smoke Enders, etc. Immersion in nonaddictive places and people is a move in the right direction.

I worked with a sex addict who was vulnerable to entering subways and porno shops to be fellated. The first time in his addictive life when he had no impulse to do so was when he lived with his girlfriend and a farmer's family in Vermont. He was an artist, and the townspeople made a great fuss over him as the "town artist." He now thought of himself as an artist, not as a bisexual, homosexual, or sex addict. Even in an environment free of places that turned him on, he had to work at changing his fantasy life, which also spurred his addiction. But in Vermont he would have had to seek out a center of addictive activity—if, indeed, one existed—or turn to the use of porno, and he would do neither at the stage of awareness he had reached in therapy. When he returned to New York, under renewed pressures, he found himself back in subway urinals and porno peep-show booths, being fellated by strangers. He again began to think of himself as a sex addict and "the lowest kind of animal."

Once an addict has taken these first steps to control his addiction, he is faced with the test of remaining free of his addiction—"dry," "clean," "straight," "on the wagon," or whatever. Part of his mind and body have been possessed by his addiction, and it continually fights to repossess him. He will always live with at least the phantom of it. If it is sufficiently controlled, he will have to be vigilant only during times of great vulnerability. The frequency and degree of his relapses are directly proportional to the depth, intensity, duration, and kind of his addictive practices. Always they are greatest at times of crisis and when many triggers are at work. The addict must learn to identify the times when a relapse is predictable. Some addictions are more pernicious than others (i.e., chemical and food addictions). The addict with a history of periods of success in life, a strong sense of identity, and adequate self-esteem can tolerate more stress without his ego needing addictive repair. Those whose personalities and lives have been destroyed in many areas are most vulnerable to destructive relapses. Each relapse makes the mastery of the next slip more difficult, even seemingly impossible. *It is often more humane for the helper to prepare the chronic addict for a lifetime of anticipated slips.* The addict has to gain the insight to perceive a relapse as a temporary form of pseudoprotection, not necessarily the progressive problem it was in the earlier stages of the addictive process.

Usually in the last stages of any disease, the symptoms are more evident and debilitating. The smoking and eating and alcoholic addict pays with high incidences of cancer, emphysema, hypertension and liver and heart diseases. Especially for the alcoholic, many end-stage deteriorations set in. But research has shown that some addictions are self-extinguishing in the end stages. There are also instances of addiction being short-lived rather than chronic and progressive. And aging itself may somewhat distinguish addiction—or seem to. The addict's hangovers apparently disappear, his addiction seems less intense. The trigger mechanisms that spark and fuel addiction have decreased in number, frequency, and intensity. The addict has lived through the pressure-filled years of adolescence, with its erotic and gender crises and career preparations; early adulthood, with its many responsibilities; establishing love relationships, a family, independence; mid-life, and its passage to old age. Each phase might have kept the addiction alive. We have seen fewer addictions hanging on in the aged because less is expected or demanded of them.

However, this may be changing; recent research refutes the impression that addiction is less prevalent in the aged. The aged lead more complex, demanding lives; the Grey Panthers, a militant group of the aged, claim that more respect from the community has raised expectations of them. Since new pressures will be put on the aged by themselves and society, more aged addicts will surface. One addict said to me: "I'm seventy, but I couldn't retire even if I wanted to, because my clients still need me. I have to make myself available for them around the clock, and I do. I do all their tax work for their children, too. It's like there still aren't enough hours in the day. It's true I smoke too much and my breathing is bad, but you must know by now that without my work I might as well be dead. Sometimes I wonder what I'm working for. Maybe, as you said Doc, I'm addicted to money!"

Helper and addict have to assess the addict's capacity to stay abstinent—what he can realistically expect of himself without feeling added pain over minor periodic relapses. What is required for him to remain clean depends on his past performance and ego strength—not only his overall history but a detailed record of the daily and yearly predictable recurrences of addictive behavior and how intense they were.

An addict's previous responses to therapy give both helper and addict clues to his potential for change for avoiding relapses. Those who have responded to some valid form of therapy by being addiction-free for extended and increasing periods can be expected to control their addictions best and to experience few relapses. In my own work with many kinds of addictions in hundreds of addicts, I have experimented with a variety of techniques in dealing with relapses—taped conversations prepared by helpers, self-monitoring tapes, charts, combinations of positive and negative rein-forcements, rewards, and having them summon up visual imagery, internal monologues, and powerful one-liners that may help them.

For instance, one patient found a single line from a session that worked for him. He himself had picked it, which was important to him, for all other devices had failed: "Well, I guess I thought I tried every one of your little instant-cure numbers to keep myself from being stoned all the time. You know, I get stoned to get into my porno sex trip. I can't stand listening to those goddam tapes, making out silly charts, or beating up on my head about what a lowlife I am. They just don't work. I can't hack the time it takes. . .I'm too stoned to do them. . .but believe it or not, I hit one last week that's worked. My head's been clear for seven days. . .like a cloud has lifted. I kept saying over and over each time I grabbed a joint for a sex trip what I said to you in our last session—'I can get my cock and balls back. . .once I was on top of my class. . .top jock.' That line helped me realize I don't have to be a twenty-year-old down-the-drain pot and sex head. I can survive if I stay away from the stuff. Maybe I should put it on a tape.''

Sometimes the powerful line comes from someone else. A patient who was sent to see me at age sixteen by his family because of alcoholism returned twelve years later to report that he was no longer an alcoholic. He told me that when he had to be hospitalized by his physician for cirrhosis, a liver disease produced by excessive use of alcohol, he finally admitted the graveness of his illness. When I asked him how he managed to cease all drinking, he replied: ''The doctor placed his hand on my bedside and said in a compassionate and firm voice, 'The next time you return here for this illness, you will leave the hospital horizontally, not vertically.' From that day on I never had another drink. His words remain forever in my mind, and they've served me well ever since.'' The irony of his addictive saga was that he had returned with an acute depression, a history of repetitive venereal diseases, and inability to work caused by moving on to a sexual addiction—which we were able to arrest through treatment with the use of audio tapes.

It is relapses which most concern the addict and those who work with him. Self-help groups are still the most effective in handling relapses, and each has developed its own language to do so. Despite therapeutic zealousness, they are realistic about the varied forms and outcomes of relapses; they have observed a great many addicts in all phases of the process, and their successes and failures. Most are in acute, chronic, and malignant phases when they join groups. They must deal with relapses often, and the approach of AA and many other groups is that every addict must always cope with relapses as a fact of life. Similarly, in Weight Watchers groups, each member knows how many times someone lost weight and put it right back on again. The Smoke Ender learns to repeat the line, ''I just quit for the hundredth time.''

In treating any relapse, one has to develop a constructive attitude. The addict, facing the inevitable, must not be guilty or self-punitive. Becoming depressed will only hinder his ability to overcome the relapse. He should try to realize that there can be an end to the process, and he need not settle for a lifetime of only limited mastery of it. He must look back at the mechanisms that have provoked his worst relapses.

Some people's relapses are predictably seasonable or diurnal; there are rhythms in peoples' lives that no circumstances explain. The addict will find that over the years certain triggers always produced slips. When these triggers occur again, he must use the corrective techniques that worked best for him in the past. He may learn in his continuing examination of his addictive history that he could only partially arrest relapses despite his efforts, and that each new attempt to master a relapse brought greater comprehension and control of his addiction.

The least understood relapse is that which occurs suddenly after a long period of being addiction-free. The addict should first examine the people he has been involved with and his environment to learn whether he has been saturated with addictive stimuli. Second, he should scrutinize his life for unrecognized conflict and stress. Is his life in a state of transition or does he face changes not easily dealt with? Has there been a shift in his values or life style? Is he in love with or in daily contact with someone who is an addictive complement or closet addict? Repetitions of these relationships are the most disguised sources of relapse. Often in my work with alcoholics I have exposed and analyzed their unconscious gravitation to people with an addiction or an addictive history. They never seem to ask questions that might uncover this history. I get them to do so after they have slipped.

Acute or chronic physical or psychic fatigue can cause a person to slip back into an old addiction or move on to a new one. These are among the most common causes of relapse, and often the last to be recognized. Fatigue always lowers the addict's resistance, making him return to his early, primitive coping mechanisms—addictive agents, practices, milieus, or contacts. An addict and I once had this exchange:

Patient:	Nothing's different in my life this past year except my promotion. It's been great—I have the work, even if the hours are long, and the pay's terrific. We have money to burn these days. It's true, my wife keeps telling me I'm doing the job of three people. I look tired all the time, even fell asleep at the dinner table the other night, which really pissed her off.
Therapist:	You were really that tired?
Patient:	Not really. I guess I'm a little high on my job these days.
Therapist:	What did you say?
Patient:	No, don't tell me! That's an addiction too? But it's not really the same kind I used to get on booze. Working's a good kind of high isn't it?
Therapist:	Is it?
Patient:	Well, at least I'm not drinking, and we have all the money we need for everything. My wife used to bitch about our unpaid bills when I was a booze hound. I guess you just can't win can you?

Not infrequently the death of someone close, physical illness, being in a physically or emotionally weakened state, propels the former addict into a relapse. For example, an addict who had been alcohol-free for years discovered he had cancer. He had his first drink the day his physican told him. He then went on binges when he heard any new information about his cancer or even when the subject of cancer was discussed.

An addict may learn how to cope with his relapses without understanding how they are triggered by those who love him and live and work with him. Most people who live with addicts eventually lose patience with relapses and become hostile and distrustful. If healthy, they withdraw, stop caring, spend less time and attention and worst of all, give up hope that the addict will ever be clean. Helpers who are not aware of the nature of relapses increasingly devalue the addict with each slip. In turn, the addict reacts to those about him who aren't in touch with his subculture and plight as "they", enemies not to be trusted. He blames them for causing and perpetuating his relapses. He says *they* don't understand enough or "make me feel lower than low". . .tell me I'm full of promises I never keep. . .even though I did keep them one time. . .why don't "they" believe me?. . ."they" say it's gotten so bad that even if I wanted to tell the truth I wouldn't know how."

The addict must expect the worst from those who have lived with his relapses. The longer his addictive history, the more tolerance he has to develop for their negative response. His helpers, of course, must learn not to overreact and to deal with each relapse as if it were the last one. People with significant addictive histories must learn to say to themselves that there never is a last relapse, but that there are rewards and joy when they do stay clean. Sought-after punishment, self-punishment, self-denigration, blaming others, helpless and hopeless attitudes, all become self-fulfilling prophecies. It is far more helpful for an addict to have the attitude that he is striving to gain greater mastery, but that life is not predictable, and triggers can unexpectedly stimulate his addictive process. This is not a comforting or easy prospect, but it is a realistic one. Distinguishing manageable variables is the best he can hope to do.

Addicts who become highly conscious of what triggers and controls addiction can hope for some degree of control. They may find new mechanisms for coping with their pain that have no potentials for addiction. They will realize that any time they use pleasure in excess to do so, they revive the process. Moderation as an approach to life becomes the key to mellowing out the addictive process. The addict must learn to distinguish productive intensity from dysfunctional excess.

The wear and tear of an addictive life, we have said, can itself be a mellowing factor. Fatigue and loss of mental and physical functions may simulate recovery. Chronically addicted people who do not thus fade away pay their dues all at once in final phases of their addiction. They go out in a blaze of sudden destruction. The chronic smoking addicts develop cancer or emphysema; the obese have heart attacks; the workaholics develop suicidal depressions; some gamblers meet death by violence.

In my work on my own and others' addictions and in this book, I have only scratched the surface of man's fight against his potentially addictive nature. The vast literature, both scientific and popular, on the many forces involved (see bibliography) testifies to the complexity of addiction and the challenge it continues to pose. Too little has yet been said about what addictions have in common—that is, the process. I do know that as I have learned something about it, I have seen changes in my life, in those who have worked with me, and in their peer addicts. I have also discovered that dormant vulnerabilities can always be awakened to sabotage one's life. The ex-addict remains a potential addict; to be free is to never deny that the demon exists and can still be stirred. Mastery of it forever depends on *self-monitoring* and *awareness.*

PART IV
HELPFUL RESOURCES *

WHAT TO DO

In reading this book, you may think or suspect you have recognized yourself or someone close to you—someone vulnerable to or already enmeshed in the addictive process. Remember that we all worry about being or becoming addictive, but only those who meet the physical, psychological, and behavioral standards set forth in Part I are actually addicted. In case you have any doubts, I have included in this chapter some of the many major diagnostic, therapeutic, medical, research, community self-help, local, state, and national resources available. I have also suggested some appropriate private resources you can turn to when faced with the challenge of finding responsible, accredited institutions and individuals for help. Timing, sensitivity, and sound professional advice are crucial for diagnosis, treatment, and prevention of relapses. All this information is essential not only for the addict but for relatives, friends, lovers, peers, coworkers, addictive complements, and institutions in contact with the addict. What follows is a step-by-step approach for obtaining early and accurate assessment and diagnosis of anyone who is an addict or highly vulnerable to becoming one.

---

* Check phone numbers and addresses as they do change from year to year.

232

WHERE TO GO

I shall divide these resources into *General* (meant for any of the addictions) and *Specific* (for only one addiction); some fall in both categories. Rarely does one resource suffice. A multimodal approach is usually needed to treat addiction. In some cases, one resource does the majority of the work (e.g., Alcoholics Anonymous), but for maximum benefits, other people (Alanon), an ancillary professional (the family physician), or an institution (a detoxification and rehabilitation center) play a part somewhere along the way.

GENERAL DIAGNOSTIC RESOURCES

1. Your family physician or a psychiatrist, drug chemotherapist, psychologist, social worker, professional counselor, educational, religious, or industrial counselor, or a self-declared peer addict in a de-addiction facility.

2. General or specialized hospitals, in- or outpatient clinics, diagnostic centers, self-help groups, and therapeutic communities.

3. A family member, friend, coworker, or other informant who lives with the addictive person's behavior patterns every day. Such a person can often identify addictive behavior, helping a professional make an accurate diagnosis.

4. A physical exam, chemical tests (in certain addictions), and psychological tests (for example, the questionnaires administered by Alcoholics Anonymous and Gamblers Anonymous, and the smoker's self-testing kit) for early detection.

5. Self-help literature, audiovisual aids, instructional slides, films, television commercials, video, lectures, and other educational information that give clues to detection. These help remove the blind spots of those who continue to deny the obvious signs of their addictive processes, and help in identification of the vulnerable and addicted by those close to them.

After a diagnosis is made, an addict will continue to retreat, deny, or fight therapeutic follow-through. He may enter treatment by default, in order to salvage his health, economic survival, or personal relationships. He rarely does so otherwise, and certainly not in the early (pleasurable) or very late (fixated) phases. Therefore diagnosis continues to be therapy, and therapy is a constant reaffirmation of the diagnosis—except perhaps in food addiction, where the diagnosis is always self-evident.

GENERAL THERAPEUTIC RESOURCES

1. Psychiatrist, drug chemotherapist, psychologist, social worker, peer addict counselor, trained paraprofessional, and anyone who works in a de-addiction therapeutic center. These are the major therapeutic bridges by which an addict reaches the other therapeutic resources.
2. Self-help groups.
3. Psychiatric in- and outpatient facilities.
4. Therapeutic communities designed to treat addiction.
5. Detoxification and rehabilitation centers.
6. General hospitals with in- and outpatient facilities to treat addictions.
7. Industrial treatment programs.
8. Programs conducted by religious organizations.
9. Self-help literature, audiovisual and educational programs offered by family physicians and by community outreach programs for the addicted.

ALCOHOL

FOUR SPECIALIZED DIAGNOSTIC AND THERAPEUTIC FACILITIES

The following research, diagnostic, and therapeutic facilities which include acute withdrawal and detoxification centers should be used in conjunction with a primary care physician who can follow through the alcoholic's treatment using as many of the available facilities that are required and felt to be appropriate. Significant others (responsible relative—wife, husband, child, sibling, employer, etc.) should always be included. Treating an addiction always requires the total support of those close to the addict who can be a constructive as well as a destructive factor in any treatment program. Where specialized facilities are available, they have been described. For more detailed information on your local Alcoholics Anonymous Group or about the services offered by an Outpatient or Inpatient Alcoholic Service connected to your local or regional hospital, medical school or mental hygiene clinic, one need only look their phone number up in the Yellow Pages. They will tell you on the phone what is available for the addict in that facility. Should you not have any facilities in your immediate vicinity you can obtain such information as you need by calling your State's National Council on Alcoholism. Every State in the Union has such a Council.

Through your National Council on Alcoholism you can find out about the following services that are available to help the alcoholic and those who live with him.

Information and Referral

1.   Outpatient Treatment: Clinic-Private.

235

2.   Location and phone numbers of the Alcoholics Anonymous meeting places for your area.
3.   Detoxification services and Centers.
4.   Sobering-up stations.
5.   Rehabilitation Facilities.
6.   Residential facilities for the Alcoholic.
7.   Home-list resources for the aged.
8.   Adolescent services.
9.   Services to the significant others (wife-husband-child-sibling-relative).

Education and Training

1.   Educational literature, films, filmstrips, slides, audio-tapes, and lecture series on all aspects of alcoholism.
2.   Training of highly motivated and highly qualified laymen or ex-alcoholics and professionals (social workers, nurses, doctors, psychologists, psychiatrists, and educational/religious counsellors) to work with alcoholics or alcoholism within a community in a paraprofessional or professional status.

Industrial Programs

Advice and information as to how one can set up a Diagnostic and Treatment Unit in industry or other kinds of institutional organizations.

Should any of the above information be unavailable to you from a state, city or local information center you can contact the National Clearing House for Alcoholics Information, P. O. Box 2345, Rockville, Maryland 20852. Telephone number (301) 948-4450.

NATIONAL FACILITIES FOR ALCOHOLISM

Definition Facilities

Alcoholics Anonymous (AA) General Service Board
468 Park Avenue South
New York, New York 10016
(212) 686-1100

Center for Alcohol Studies
Rutgers, The State University of New Jersey
New Brunswick, New Jersey 08093
(201) 932-2190

Downstate Medical Center
Division of Alcoholism and Drug Dependence
450 Clarkson Avenue
Brooklyn, New York 11203
(212) 270-3131

Eagleville
Eagleville, Pennsylvania 19408
(215) 539-6000 Ext. 202

Haight-Ashbury Free Medical Clinic
558 Clayton Street
San Francisco, California
(415) 431-1714

National Council of Alcoholism (NCA)
2 Park Avenue, Suite 1720
New York, New York 10016
(212) 889-3160

Texas Research Institute for Mental Sciences
1300 Morsend
Houston, Texas 77025
(713) 522-8745

World Health Organization
Office of Mental Health
1211 Geneva 27, Switzerland

Facilities For the Diagnosis and Treatment of Acute Overdose

University of California at Irvine
Department of Psychiatry and Human Behavior
Irvine, California 92664
(714) 833-6413

Cornell University Medical College
Department of Psychiatry
411 E. 69th Street
New York, N. Y. 10021
(212) 472-5454

The Hartford Insurance Group
Hartford Plaza
Hartford, Connecticut 06115
(203) 547-5000

Harvard University
McLean Hospital
School of Medicine
Department of Psychiatry
Belmont, Massachusetts 02178
(617) 855-2201

Manhattan Bowery Project
8 East 3rd Street
New York, New York 10012
(212) 533-8400

National Institute on Alcohol Abuse and Alcoholism (NIAAA)
5600 Fishers Lane
Rockville, Maryland 20852
(301) 443-1056

Navaho Health Authority
Window Rock, Arizona 86515
(602) 871-4831

San Francisco General Hospital
San Francisco Detoxification Unit
Division of Clinical Pharmacology
1001 Petrero Avenue
San Francisco, California 94110
(415) 648-6016

Southern Illinois University
School of Medicine
Department of Medicine
Division of Emergency Medicine
Springfield, Illinois 62703
(217) 782-3318

Facilities For the Diagnosis and Treatment of Withdrawal States

Alaska Native Medical Center
Box 7-741

Anchorage, Alaska 99510
(907) 279-6661, Extension 252

Medical, detoxification, antabuse, and other medication; inpatient and outpatient treatment; occupational, recreational, aversion, individual, group, and family therapy.

Alcoholic Rehabilitation Unit
Tennessee Psychiatric Hospital and Institute
University of Tennessee—Medical Units
Memphis, Tennessee 38104
(901) 534-6806

Thirty bed inpatient unit and outpatient facilities. Also includes clinical facilities doing research in withdrawal from alcohol and the medication subsequently used in patient management. Works closely with Alcohol Research Center.

Alcohol Research Center
Tennessee Psychiatric Hospital and Institute
University of Tennessee—Medical Units
Memphis, Tennessee 38104
(901) 534-6806

Pure research unit in physiological complications of alcoholism and alcohol withdrawal. Currently investigating renal and cardiovascular complications with both human patients and animal subjects.

Alcoholism Services
Topeka State Hospital
2700 West Sixth Street
Topeka, Kansas 66606
(913) 296-4338

Type of Program: Facility provides inpatient treatment. Fixed fee.

Group counseling and therapy. Also, detoxification; family counseling; therapy; medication; social rehabilitation; in-service training to staff of this facility.

Beth Israel Medical Center
Morris Bernstein Institute
307 2nd Avenue
New York, New York 10003
(212) 677-2300

Inpatient detoxification (drugs and alcohol), methadone maintenance treatment program. Short term detoxification; inpatient treatment; individual, group, recreational, and family therapy. Therapy begins on intake in ward, continues on follow-up basis after discharge.

Department of Psychiatry
University of North Carolina, School of Medicine
Chapel Hill, North Carolina 27514
(919) 966-4285

Emergency and other medical; detoxification; individual, group, and family counseling; therapy; antabuse and other medication; aversion therapy; therapeutic community; sensitivity and/or awareness groups; occupational and recreational therapy; vocational and social rehabilitation; A-A services; and in-service training to staff of this facility.

Detoxification Medical Center
501 North Rampart Street
New Orleans, Louisiana 70130
(504) 524-4708

Detoxification, individual, group, family, recreational, and medical therapy. A.A. services; and in-service training to staff.

Downstate Medical Center
Addictive Disease Hospital
Division of Alcoholism
"K" Building, Box 9, Code #24
600 Albany Avenue
Brooklyn, New York 11203
(212) 630-4544

A large facility consisting of inpatient and outpatient clinical units, and research units specializing in problems of the withdrawal syndrome. Both clinical and physiological research is conducted with a current emphasis on sleep during intoxification and withdrawal.

Earl H. Mitchell, M. D.
2029 Q Street, N. W.
Washington, D. C. 20009
(202) 541-6675

Detoxification and individual, group, and family counseling. Also, therapy, antabuse medication, and A. A. services.

Fort Logan Mental Health Center—Alcoholism
3520 West Oxford Avenue
Denver, Colorado 80236
(303) 761-0220 Extension 246

Therapeutic community. Also, emergency and other medical, detoxification, individual, group, and family therapy; antabuse and other medication; sensitivity and/or awareness groups; occupational and recreational therapy; service training to staff of this facility, and community agencies and general public education.

Hope Rescue Mission
532 South Michigan Street
South Bend, Indiana 46601
(219) 288-4842 Extension 6

Emergency medical; detoxification; individual, group, and family counseling; antabuse and other medication; sensitivity and/or awareness groups; recreational therapy, and vocational rehabilitation.

Ivanhoe Sanitarium
2203 East Ivanhoe Place
Milwaukee, Wisconsin 53202
(404) 271-4030

Detoxification; individual, group, and family counseling, therapy; antabuse medication; vocational rehabilitation, and AA services.

La Hacienda Hospital and Rehabilitation Center
P. O. Box 1
Hunt, Indiana 78024
(512) 238-4222

Emergency and other medical; detoxification, individual, group, and family counseling; therapy; antabuse and other medication; aversion therapy; therapeutic community; sensitivity and/or awareness groups; occupational and recreational therapy; social rehabilitation; AA services; and in-service training to staff of this facility.

Lutheran General Hospital Alcoholism Rehabilitation Center
1775 Dempster Avenue
Park Ridge, Illinois 60068
(312) 696-2210

Therapeutic community. Also, emergency and other medical; detoxification; individual, group, and family counseling; therapy; recreational therapy; social rehabilitation; AA services; and in-service training to staff of this facility.

Manhattan Bowery Project
8 East 3rd Street
New York, New York
(212) 533-8400

Provides inpatient and outpatient treatment; diagnostic services; detoxification; halfway house; and aftercare for male residents of the Bowery.

Nebraska Psychiatric Institute
602 South 45th Street
Omaha, Nebraska 68105
Dependence Service
(402) 541-4684

Therapeutic community that provides emergency and other medical, detoxification, and individual and group and family counseling. Therapies include aversion,
occupational, and recreational therapy. Also provided are antabuse and other
medication; vocational and social rehabilitation; AA services; and in-service training
to the staff of this facility.

Provident Hospital
Detoxification Unit
2600 Liberty Heights Avenue
Baltimore, Maryland 21215
(301) 462-4700 Extension 2373

Emergency medical; detoxification; individual and group counseling; therapy;
antabuse and other medication; AA services; and in-service training to staff of this
facility.

Roosevelt Hospital Alcoholism Services
428 West 59th Street
New York, New York 10019
(212) 554-6725

This facility provides therapeutic, detoxification, aftercare, and information and
referral services on an inpatient, or outpatient basis, or in a therapeutic community
setting, depending on the phase of treatment. Group, family, and individual
counseling; occupational and vocational rehabilitation; and AA services are also
available to clients. Also in-service training to staff and community agencies. General
public education and professional education are included among the activities of this
center.

Salt Lake County Detoxification Center
Alcohol and Drug Problems Division
175 East 21st Street
Salt Lake City, Utah 84115
(801) 328-7045 and 328-7046

Detoxification. Also, individual and group counseling; therapy; aversion therapy;
AA services; general public education and referral.

San Francisco Detoxification Unit
San Francisco General Hospital

Ward 52
1001 Petrero Avenue
San Francisco, California 94110
(415) 648-6016

Detoxification. Also, emergency and other medical; individual, group, and family counseling; therapy; antabuse medication; social rehabilitation; AA services; and in-service training to staff of this facility.

St. Louis Detoxification Center
5400 Arsenal Street
St. Louis, Missouri 63139
(314) 644-5400 Extension 347 or 463

Detoxification. Also, emergency and other medical; individual counseling; therapy; antabuse medication; recreational therapy; vocational and social; rehabilitation; AA services; and in-service training to staff of this facility.

Veterans Administration Hospital
50 Irving Street, N. W.
Washington, D. C. 20422
(202) 483-6666

Medical. Also, emergency medical; detoxification; individual, group, and family counseling; therapy; antabuse and other medication; aversion therapy; occupational and recreational therapy; vocational and social rehabilitation; AA services; and in-service training to staffs of this facility.

Washington Center for Addictions
41 Morton Street
Boston, Massachusetts 02130
(617) 522-7151

Detoxification. Also medical; individual group, and family counseling; therapy; antabuse and other medication; sensitivity and/or awareness groups; occupational and recreational therapy; vocational and social rehabilitation; AA services; and in-service training to staffs of this facility.

West Center
Tucson General Hospital
1719 East Prince Road
Tucson, Arizona 85704
(602) 327-5431 Extension 347 or 348

Detoxification. Also, emergency medical; individual, group, and family counseling; therapy; antabuse and other medication recreational therapy; vocational rehabilitation; AA services; and in-service training to staff of this facility.

Woodland Park Hospital
Mental Health Unit
10300 Northeast Hancock Street
Portland, Oregon 97220
(503) 255-1313 Extension 345

Detoxification. Also, individual, group, and family counseling; therapy; antabuse and other medication; therapeutic community, sensitivity and/or awareness groups; occupational and recreational therapy; vocational and social rehabilitation; and in-service training to staff of this facility.

Facilities For Diagnosis and Treatment of Alcohol Abuse

Accept
New York Council on Alcoholism, Inc.
29 East 22nd Street
New York, New York 10028
212-674-8850

Inpatient and outpatient services, halfway house setting. Detoxification, family counseling, and therapy provided. Also antabuse medication; vocational and social rehabilitation; AA services; follow-up and outreach.

Alcohol Treatment and Training Center
309 Southwest 4th
Portland, Oregon 97204
503-229-5420

Group counseling, therapy. Also, medical; individual counseling; therapy; antabuse and other medication; sensitivity and/or awareness groups; vocational and social rehabilitation; and in-service training to staff of this facility.

Alcoholic Rehabilitation Unit
Tennessee Psychiatric Hospital and Institute
University of Tennessee—Medical Units
Memphis, Tennessee 38104
901-534-6671

Thirty bed inpatient unit and outpatient facilities providing clinical facilities. Doing research in withdrawal from alcohol and the medication subsequently used in patient management. Works closely with Alcohol Research Center.

Alcoholism Service
Long Beach General Hospital
2597 Redondo Avenue

Long Beach, California 90806
(213) 427-9951, 636-0784

Large treatment facility with satellite clinics in various other locations. Fifty bed detoxification unit; one hundred bed short term inpatient treatment unit; ambulatory detoxification unit; and other outpatient facilities. This facility maintains an interdisciplinary team approach with heavy reliance on group process under medical management. Training facilities for both professionals and paraprofessionals alike.

Alcoholism Services
Topeka State Hospital
2700 West Sixth Street
Topeka, Kansas 66606
913-296-4338

Group counseling; therapy; family counseling; therapy; medication; social rehabilitation; and in-service training to staff of this facility, to community agencies, and to general public education.

Alcoholism Treatment Unit
Rochester Methodist Hospital
Rochester, Minnesota 55901
507-282-4461, Extension 5371

Group counseling, therapy. Also, medical, individual, and family counseling; therapy; antabuse and other medication; recreational therapy; AA services; and in-service training to staff of this facility, and psychiatric evaluation.

Anchorage Social Development Center
Box 6540
Anchorage, Alaska 99502
907-272-8575, Extension 3

Therapeutic community; medical, individual, and group counseling, therapy; antabuse and other medication; aversion therapy; sensitivity and/or awareness groups; occupational and recreational therapy; vocational and social rehabilitation; AA services; and in-service training to staff of this facility and community agencies.

Appleton Treatment Center
McLean Hospital
115 Mill Street
Belmont, Massachusetts 02178
617-855-2782

Medical, individual, group, and family counseling; antabuse and other medication; therapeutic community; occupational and recreational therapy; vocational and social rehabilitation; AA services; in-service training to staff of this facility and community agencies; general public education and behavioral therapy; psychodrama; and detoxification.

Beech Hill Farm
Dublin, New Hampshire 03444
603-563-4271, 563-7601, 563-4781

Individual, group, and family counseling; therapy; medication; occupational and recreational therapy; social rehabilitation; AA services and in-service training to staff of this community.

Beverly Manor Hospital
Beverly Alcohol and Drug Problems
401 South Tustin Avenue
Orange, California 92666
714-633-9582

Group counseling, therapy. Also, emergency and other medical; individual and family counseling; therpy; therapeutic community; occupational and recreational therapy; vocational and social rehabilitation; AA services and in-service training to staff of this facility.

Charity Hospital of Louisiana at New Orleans
1532 Tulane Avenue, E 305
New Orleans, Louisiana 70140
504-524-3060, 524-3090

Emergency medical; individual, group, and family counseling; antabuse medication; aversion therapy; therapeutic community; sensitivity and/or awareness groups; occupational and recreational therapy; vocational and social rehabilitation; AA services; and in-service training to staff of this facility.

Chicago's Alcoholic Treatment Center
3026 South California Avenue
Chicago, Illinois 60608
312-254-3680

Therapeutic community. Also, emergency and other medical; individual, group, and family counseling; therapy; antabuse and other medication; recreational therapy; vocational and social rehabilitation; AA services; and in-service training to staff of this facility.

Chit Chat Farms
Box 277
Wernersville, Pennsylvania 19565

215-678-2332 (678-4541)

Emergency and other medical; individual, group, and family counseling; therapy; antabuse medication; therapeutic community; occupational and recreational therapy; vocational and social rehabilitation; AA services; and in-service training to staff of this facility.

Department of Psychiatry
University of North Carolina, School of Medicine
Chapel Hill, North Carolina 27514
919-966-4285

Emergency and other medical; individual, group, and family counseling; therapy; antabuse and other medication; aversion therapy; therapeutic community; sensitivity and/or awareness groups; occupational and recreational therapy; vocational and social rehabilitation; AA services and in-service training to staff of this facility.

Downstate Medical Center
Addictive Disease Hospital
Division of Alcoholism
"K" Building, Box 9 Code #24
600 Albany Avenue
Brooklyn, New York 11203
212-630-4544

A large facility consisting of inpatient and outpatient clinical units and research units specializing in problems of withdrawal syndrome. Both clinical and physiological research is conducted with a current emphasis on sleep during intoxication and withdrawal.

Eagleville
Eagleville, Pennsylvania 19408
215-539-6000 Extension 202

Fort Help
169 Eleventh Street
San Francisco, California 94103
415-864-4357

Individual counseling, therapy. Also, group and family counseling; therapy; and sensitivity and/or awareness groups.

Fort Logan Mental Health Center—Alcoholism
3520 West Oxford Avenue
Denver, Colorado 80236
303-761-0220, Extension 246

Therapeutic community. Also, emergency and other medical; individual, group, and family therapy; antabuse and other medication; sensitivity and/or awareness groups; occupational and recreational therapy; vocational and social rehabilitation; AA services; and in-service training to staff of this facility.

Halfway House
Box 26447
Tucson, Arizona 85713
602-622-9038

Type of Program: Facility provides halfway house and residential care. No fee.

Individual counseling and therapy. Also, group counseling; therapy; recreational therapy; vocational rehabilitation; and AA services.

Harrison Treatment and Rehabilitation Hospital
725 6th Avenue
Des Moines, Iowa 50309
515-288-7564, 8159 (or 274-4861, Ext. 185, 186, 233)

Services: Emergency and other medical; individual, group, and family counseling; therapy; antabuse and other medication; therapeutic community; sensitivity and/or awareness groups; vocational and social rehabilitation; AA services; and in-service training to staff of this facility.

Hazelden
Center City, Minnesota 55012
612-257-7184

Emergency and other medical; individual, group, and family counseling; therapy; antabuse and other medication; therapeutic community; occupational and recreational therapy; vocational and social rehabilitation; AA services; and in-service training to staff of this facility.

Inpatient Therapeutic Community
Work Therapy
Outpatient Facility
Halfway House

Treating drug addicts and alcoholics together primarily with group psychotherapy. An interdisciplinary team including usual professionals, paraprofessionals, and recovered patients. Two research projects examining the therapeutic community approach and the mixture of alcoholic and heroin addicts. A minimum of thirty days is recommended for career teacher to familiarize himself with the facility.

Malcolm Bliss Mental Health Center
Alcoholism Unit
1420 Grattan Street

St. Louis, Missouri 63104
314-241-7600, Extensions 433, 479, 240, 295

Emergency and other medical; individual, group, and family counseling; therapy; antabuse and other medication; aversion therapy; therapeutic community; sensitivity and/or awareness groups; occupational and recreational therapy; vocational and social rehabilitation; AA services; and in-service training to staff of this facility.

Manhattan Bowery Project
8 East 3rd Street
New York, New York 10003
212-533-8400

Provides inpatient and outpatient treatment; diagnostic services; detoxification; halfway house and aftercare for male residents of the Bowery.

Mesa Vista Hospital
7850 Vista Hill Avenue
San Diego, California 92123
714-278-4110

Medical, individual, and group counseling; therapy; antabuse and other medication; sensitivity and/or awareness groups; occupational therapy; social rehabilitation; AA services; and in-service training to staff of this facility.

Nebraska Psychiatric Institute
602 South 45th Street
Omaha, Nebraska 68105
Dependence Service
402-541-4684

Therapeutic community. Also, emergency and other medical; individual, group, and family counseling; therapy; antabuse and other medication; aversion therapy; sensitivity and/or awareness groups; occupational and recreational therapy; vocational and social rehabilitation; AA services; and in-service training to staff of this facility.

The University of Oklahoma
Department of Psychiatry and Behavioral Sciences
Health Sciences Center
Oklahoma Alcohol Research Center
Norman, Oklahoma 73069
405-524-0175

The Oklahoma Alcohol Research Center is in the Department of Psychiatry and Behavioral Sciences at the University of Oklahoma Health Sciences Center. An active research program with several investigators evaluating the influence of alcohol and other commonly abused drugs on sleep, information processing, and stage dependent learning (in animals). The center also is interested in the clinical aspects of alcoholism and has an active outpatient treatment program.

Palm Beach Institute
1014 North Olive Avenue
West Palm Beach, Florida 33401
305-833-7553

Medical, individual, group, and family counseling; therapy; antabuse medication; occupational and recreational therapy; vocational and social rehabilitation; AA services; and general public education.

Roosevelt Hospital Alcoholism Services
428 West 59th Street
New York, New York 10019
212-554-6725

This facility provides diagnostic, detoxification, aftercare, and information and referral services on an inpatient, or outpatient basis, or in a therapeutic community setting, depending on the phase of treatment. Group, family, and individual counseling; occupational and vocational rehabilitation; and AA services are also available. Also in-service training to staff and community agencies. General public education and professional education are included among the activities of this center.

Rush-Presbyterian-St. Luke's Medical Center
1753 West Congress Parkway
Chicago, Illinois 60612
312-942-5380

Emergency and other medical; individual, group, and family counseling; therapy; antabuse and other medication; therapeutic community; occupational and recreational therapy; social rehabilitation, and in-service training to staff of this facility.

Schick's Shadel Hospital, Inc.
12101 Ambaum Blvd., Southwest
Seattle, Washington 98146
206-244-8100

Aversion therapy, therapeutic community, and pentothal interviews. Also, emergency and other medical; individual, group, and family counseling; therapy; medication; and in-service training to staff of this facility.

Sheppard and Enoch Pratt Hospital
Box 6805, York Road

Towson, Maryland 21204
301-823-8200 Extension 552 or 553

Therapeutic community. Also, individual, group, and family counseling; therapy; antabuse and other medication; occupational and recreational therapy; vocational and social rehabilitation; AA services; and in-service training to staff of this facility.

Facilities of Non-Residential Self-Help Organizations

Send for the National Institute on Drug Abuse Services Research Report, *Non-Residential Self-Help Organizations and the Drug Abuse Problem: An Exploratory Conference,* Number (ADM) 78-752, July 1978, which can be obtained through the Services Research Branch, National Institute on Drug Abuse, 5600 Fishers Lane, Room 10-A-31, Rockville, Md. 20857. It provides a thorough description of the history, definition, ideology, structure, and functioning of the self-help organization with an up-to-date listing of seventeen non-residential self-help alcoholism and drug abuser organizations in eight states (California, Georgia, Indiana, Kentucky, New York, Ohio, Pennsylvania and Texas). If you wish to list your own self-help organization with the Service Research Branch, you may send your organization's name, address, and other particulars to the above address and they will list your non-residential self-help organization. They will make particulars available to those who inquire about the contact person, size of your group, and the type of services you offer to the addict or his family.

Psychological Factors Facilities

University of California at Irvine
Department of Psychiatry and Human Behavior
Irvine, California
(714) 833-5011

George Washington University Medical Center
901-23rd Street N.W.
Washington, D.C. 20037
(202) 331-2624

Harvard University
Department of Psychology
Cambridge, Massachusetts 02138
(617) 495-1000

Maryland Department of Health and Mental Hygiene
Division of Alcoholism Control

Baltimore, Maryland
(301) 383-2683

University of Maryland Medical School
Alcoholism and Drug Program
Baltimore, Maryland
(301) 528-6975

McLean Hospital
Department of Psychiatry
Harvard University
Belmont, Massachusetts
(617) 855-2201

University of Oklahoma
Department of Psychiatry and Behavioral Sciences
School of Medicine
Oklahoma City, Oklahoma
(405) 271-5555

University of Pittsburgh
Department of Pharmacology
School of Pharmacy
1106 Salk Hall
Pittsburgh, Pennsylvania 15261
(412) 624-3274

University of Pittsburgh
Departments of Special Education and Psychology
4616 Henry Street
Pittsburgh, Pennsylvania 15260
(412) 624-4141

Silver Hill Foundation
New Canaan, Connecticut 06880
(203) 966-3561

Prevention-Information Facilities

Adapt Corporation
201 Connecticut Avenue, N. W. Suite 611
Washington, D. C. 20008
(202) 244-5026

National Committee Against Mental Illness, Inc.
1101 17th Street N. W. Suite 812
Washington, D. C. 20036
(202) 296-4435

National Council of Alcoholism (NCA)
2 Park Avenue, Suite 1720
New York, New York 10016
(212) 889-3160

National Institute on Alcohol Abuse and Alcoholism (NIAAA)
5600 Fisher's Lane
Rockville, Maryland 20852
(301) 443-1056

New York Medical College
Department of Community & Preventive Medicine
Fifth Avenue & 106th Street
New York, N. Y. 10029
(212) TR 6-5500

University of Pittsburgh
Department of Special Education & Rehabilitation
Pittsburgh, Pennsylvania
(412) 624-4141

Associations and Conferences and Educational Resources Facilities

Alcohol and Drug Problem Association of North American (ADPA)
1130 Seventeenth Street, NW
Washington, D. C. 20036
(202) 452-0990

Alcoholism Anonymous (AA) General Service Board
468 Park Avenue South
New York, New York 10016
(212) 686-1100

American Medical Society on Alcoholism (AMSA)
2 Park Avenue, Suite 1720
New York, N. Y. 10016
(212) 889-3160

The Christopher D. Smithers Foundation, Inc.
41 East 57th Street
New York, New York 10022
(212) Plaza 2-4881

International Council on Alcoholism and Addictions (ICAA)
Cose Postale 140
1001 Lousanne
Switzerland
021-29-6485

National Clearinghouse of Alcohol Literature
   and Information (NCALI)
5600 Fishers Lane
Rockville, Maryland 20852
(301) 948-4450

National Coordination Council on Drug Education (NCCDE)
1512-18th Street N. W.
Washington, D. C. 20036
(202) 332-1512

National Council on Alcoholism (NCA)
2 Park Avenue, Suite 1720
New york, N. Y. 10016
(212) 889-3160

National Institute of Alcohol Abuse and Alcoholism (NIAAA)
5600 Fishers Lane
Rockville, Maryland 20852
(301) 443-1056

World Health Organization
Office of Mental Health
1211 Geneva 27, Switzerland

DRUGS

The initial diagnosis and early detection of drug addiction is not easy in most cases, and follow-through for treatment is more often than not studded with problems. A competent diagnostician (medical, paraprofessional, peer addict, or a relative who is aware of the addiction) is vital to establish the validity of the diagnosis and to confront the addict with the stage of his addiction. Each state has a *Drug Abuse Prevention Agency* that has up-to-date information about the exact location and services provided by all the drug abuse clinics in the state. A list of these agencies, drug abuse facilities, along with the Therapeutic Communities that exist throughout the country that are members of the Therapeutic Communities of America follow. A national office of the latter is located at 54 West 40th Street; Phone: (212) 354-6000.

The decision as to which of these facilities is most appropriate for an individual addict—in terms of what specific services are offered by each—is beyond the scope of this section. Every addict must receive treatment tailored to his individual history and needs. It is essential to coordinate the therapeutic plan of action decided upon by the diagnostician and agency with the primary care physician and the significant others who are involved in the addict's life and his care.

I have not listed the many clinics throughout the country that use methadone and other drug antagonists in conjunction with treatment. Use of such clinics should be based on the decision of a drug abuse specialist (e.g., a psychiatrist, internist or trained drug chemotherapist attached to such a facility) who feels that this course of therapeutic action should be taken in conjunction with the other therapeutic modalities. Because such facilities are often transient, you should check with your local hospital or physician, who will locate a methadone (or other drug antagonist) clinic for you that he knows to be dependable. If he cannot give you this information, call your state drug abuse prevention program, which can direct you to the nearest accredited facility.

State Drug Abuse Prevention and Program

ALABAMA

Division of Alcohol and Drug Abuse (205) 265-2301
135 Union Street
Montgomery Alabama 36130

ALASKA

Department of Health & Social Services (907) 586-6201
Office of Alcoholism & Drug Abuse (Seattle FTS
Pouch H-05F Operator
Juneau, Alaska 99811 8-399-0150)

ARIZONA

Drug Abuse Section (602) 255-1239
Bureau of Community Services
2500 East Van Buren Street
Phoenix, Arizona 85008

ARKANSAS

Arkansas Office of Alcohol & (501) 371-2604
 Drug Abuse Prevention
1515 West 7th Street
Little Rock, Arkansas 72202

CALIFORNIA

Department of Alcohol & Drug Abuse (916) 322-6690
825 15th Street
Sacramento, California 95814

COLORADO

Alcohol & Drug Abuse Division (303) 320-1167
Department of Health
4210 East 11th Avenue
Denver, Colorado 80220

CONNECTICUT

Connecticut Alcohol &   (203) 566-4145
  Drug Abuse Council
90 Washington Street
Hartford, Connecticut 06115

DELAWARE

Bureau of Substance Abuse   (302) 421-6101
Division of Mental Health
1901 North du Pont Highway
New Castle, Delaware 19720

DISTRICT OF COLUMBIA

Office of State Agency Affairs   (202) 724-5696
Department of Human Resources
1329 "E" Street, N.W.
Washington, D.C. 20004

FLORIDA

Drug Abuse Program, Mental   (904) 488-0900
  Health Program Office
1317 Winewood Boulevard
Tallahassee, Florida 32304

GEORGIA

Division of Mental Health &   (404) 894-4785
  Retardation, Georgia Department
  of Human Resources
618 Ponce de Leon Avenue, N.E.
Atlanta, Georgia 30308

HAWAII

State Substance Abuse Agency   (808) 548-7655
1270 Queen Emma Street   (San Francisco

Honolulu, Hawaii 96813

FTS Operator
8-556-0220)

IDAHO

Bureau of Substance Abuse
Statehouse
700 W. State Street
Boise, Idaho 83720

(208) 384-7706

ILLINOIS

Executive Director
Illinois Dangerous Drugs Commission
300 North State Street, Suite 1500
Chicago, Illinois 60610

(312) 822-9860

INDIANA

Assistant Commissioner
Division of Addiction Services
5 Indiana Square
Indianapolis, Indiana 46204

(317) 633-4477

MARYLAND

Drug Abuse Administration
201 West Preston Street
Baltimore, Maryland 21201

(301) 383-3959

MASSACHUSETTS

Division of Drug Rehabilitation
Department of Mental Health
160 N. Washington Street
Boston, Massachusetts 02114

(617) 727-8614

MICHIGAN

Office of Substance Abuse Services
3500 North Logan Street

(517) 373-8600

Lansing, Michigan 48909

MINNESOTA

Chemical Dependency-DPW   (612) 296-4610
Centennial Office Building
658 Cedar, 4th Floor
St. Paul, Minnesota 55155

MISSISSIPPI

Division of Alcohol &   (601) 354-7031
  Drug Abuse
619 Robert E. Lee Office Bldg.
Jackson, Mississippi 39201

MISSOURI

Division of Alcoholism and   (314) 751-4942
  Drug Abuse
2002 Missouri Boulevard
Jefferson City, Missouri 65101

MONTANA

Alcohol and Drug Division   (406) 449-2827
Department of Institutions
1539 11th Avenue
Helena, Montana 59601

NEBRASKA

Nebraska Commission on Drugs   (402) 471-2691
Post Office Box 94726
Lincoln, Nebraska 68509

NEVADA

Bureau of Alcohol & Drug Abuse   (702) 885-4790
505 East King Street
Carson City, Nevada 89710

NEW HAMPSHIRE

Office of Substance Abuse   (603) 271-2754
3 Capital Street, Room 405
Concord, New Hampshire 03301

NEW JERSEY

Alcohol, Narcotic, & Drug Abuse   (609) 292-5760
Department of Health
129 E. Hanover Street
Trenton, New Jersey 08608

NEW MEXICO

Substance Abuse Bureau   (505) 827-5271
Behavioral Health Services
Health & Environmental Department
Post Office Box 968
Santa Fe, New Mexico 87503

NEW YORK

New York State Division of   (518) 457-2061
   Substance Abuse Services
Executive Park South
Albany, New York 12203

NORTH CAROLINA

Alcohol and Drug Abuse   (919) 733-4555
325 North Salisbury Street
Raleigh, North Carolina 27611

NORTH DAKOTA

Division of Alcoholism & Drug Abuse   (701) 224-2767
Mental Health & Retardation
   Services
909 Basin Avenue
Bismarck, North Dakota 58505

OHIO

Ohio Bureau of Drug Abuse   (614) 466-9023
65 South Front Street, Room 211
Columbus, Ohio 43215

OKLAHOMA

Drug Abuse Services   (405) 521-2811
Post Office Box 53277
Oklahoma City, Oklahoma 73105

OREGON

Mental Health Division   (503) 378-2163
2575 Bittern Street, N.E.
Salem, Oregon 97310

PENNSYLVANIA

Governor's Council on Drug   (717) 787-9857
  and Alcohol Abuse
2101 North Front Street
Harrisburg, Pennsylvania 17120

RHODE ISLAND

Division of Substance Abuse   (401) 464-2091
Bldg. 303, General Hospital
R.I. Medical Center
Cranston, Rhode Island 02920

SOUTH CAROLINA

South Carolina Commission   (803) 758-2183
  on Alcohol and Drug Abuse
3700 Forest Drive
Columbia, South Carolina 29204

SOUTH DAKOTA

Division of Drugs and Substances   (605) 773-3123
    Control, Department of Health
Joe Foss Building
Pierre, South Dakota 57501

TENNESSEE

Alcohol & Drug Abuse Services   (615) 741-1921
501 Union Building
Nashville, Tennessee 37219

TEXAS

Drug Abuse Prevention Division   (512) 475-5566
Department of Community Affairs
210 Barton Springs Road
Austin, Texas 78704

UTAH

Division of Alcohol & Drugs   (801) 533-6532
150 W. North Temple
Room 350
Salt Lake City, Utah 84110

VERMONT

Alcohol & Drug Abuse Division   (802) 241-2170
Agency of Human Services
State Office Building
Montpelier, Vermont 05602

VIRGINIA

Virginia Department of Mental Health   (804) 786-5313
    and Mental Retardation
Post Office Box 1797
Richmond, Virginia 23214

WASHINGTON

Department of Social & Health Services   (206) 753-3073
OB-43E
Olympia, Washington 98504

WEST VIRGINIA

Director   (304) 348-3616
Alcohol and Drug Abuse Program
State Capitol
Charleston, West Virginia 25305

WISCONSIN

Director   (608) 266-2717
Bureau of Alcohol & Drug Abuse
1 West Wilson Street
Madison, Wisconsin 53702

WYOMING

Director   (307) 777-7115
Substance Abuse Program
Hathaway Building, Room 457
Cheyenne, Wyoming 82002

GUAM

Administrator, Guam Mental   (San Francisco
   Health & Substance Abuse   FTS Operator
   Agency   8-556-0220)
Post Office Box 20999   646-1255
Guam, Mariana Islands 96921

PACIFIC TRUST TERRITORIES

Chief   (San Francisco
Division of Mental Health   FTS Operator
Department of Health Services   8-556-0220
Office of the High Commissioner   9422 or 9355
Saipan, Marina Islands 96950

PUERTO RICO

Secretary
Department of Addiction Control Services
Post Office Box B-Y
Rio Piedras Station
Rio Piedras, Puerto Rico 00928

(809) 763-8957 or
(809) 763-7575
(DC FTS Op.
9-472-6620)

VIRGIN ISLANDS

Director, Division of Mental
Health, Alcoholism and Drug
Dependency
Post Office Box 520
Christiansted
St. Croix, Virgin Islands 00820

Dial Direct:
(809) 774-4888
or
(809) 249-7959

When writing or calling any of the above facilities, address your inquiry to the program director or to whatever individual is in charge of the required information. His title can be obtained by making a direct call to the facility. Should you wish to obtain information other than what can be supplied by your State Drug Abuse facility such as research monographs, educational programs, or any other data pertaining to diagnosis, treatment and prevention, you can call the National Institute on Drug Abuse (NIDA), telephone: (301) 443-4577. NIDA is part of the United States Department of Health, Education, and Welfare, the Public Health Service, and the Alcohol Drug Abuse and Mental Health Administration. They are all located at 5600 Fishers Lane, Rockville, Maryland 20857. You may address any one of the divisions.

Facilities For the Diagnosis and Treatment of Overdose

Center for Special Problems
2107 Van Ness Avenue
San Francisco, California 94109
415-558-4801

A specialized mental health center offering crisis intervention and outpatient assistance since November 1964. It is part of the Community Mental Health Service of the City and County of San Francisco.

Services provided; chemical detoxification; crisis intervention; individual therapy; methadone maintenance; drug free detoxification.

Corpus Christi Drug Abuse Council
425 South Broadway
Corpus Christi, Texas 78401
512-883-7483
512-884-2304 (Crisis Line)

Private, nonprofit drug prevention and rehabilitation organization. Services include crisis intervention; counseling; medical-surgical treatment.

Drug Abuse Treatment Unit
Veterans Administration Outpatient Clinic
17 Court Street
Boston, Massachusetts 02108
617-223-4571

Part of the Veterans Administration psychiatric service. Services offered are: crisis intervention; chemical detoxification; individual psychotherapy; methadone maintenance; medical-surgical treatment; drug free detoxification.

Drug Dependence Unit
Grady Memorial Hospital
80 Butler Street, S.E.
Atlanta, Georgia 30303
404-659-1212, Extensions 737, 880

Outpatient drug unit primarily for narcotic drug users, located in general hospital building. Services include crisis intervention; methadone maintenance; chemical detoxification; group counseling; medical-surgical treatment.

Haight-Ashbury Clinic
Drug Treatment Program
409 and 529 Clayton Street
San Francisco, California 94117
415-621-9758
415-621-2014

Component of Haight-Ashbury Free Clinic. Provides storefront, out-patient, and crisis assistance to drug abusers and their families.

Services include crisis intervention; group counseling; individual psychotherapy; chemical and drug free detoxification; medical-surgical treatment.

Illinois Drug Abuse Program
East Pavilion, Museum of Science and Industry
5700 South Lake Shore Drive
Chicago, Illinois 60617

312-955-9800, Extensions 40, 41, 42

Large organization providing comprehensive system of services for treatment and rehabilitation of drug abusers.

Services offered include crisis and legal intervention; medical-surgical treatment; methadone maintenance; counseling; drug free and chemical detoxification; cyclazocine therapy.

Institute for Clinical Toxicology
La Branch Street
Houston, Texas
713-524-4683

Los Angeles County Mental Health Department
1102 South Crenshaw
Los Angeles, California 90019
Drug Abuse Programs
213-937-2380

As a department of the Los Angeles county government, it has incorporated services for drug abusers into its ongoing mental health programs. The department works in conjunction with other county agencies in providing services to individual drug users, with emphasis on underlying psychiatric problems. Provides out-patient services in thirteen community centers. Fees are determined according to a sliding scale. Services offered include crisis intervention; drug free detoxification; and individual therapy.

Narcotics Treatment Administration
Drug Addiction Medical Service
D.C. General Hospital
1905 E Street, S.E.
Washington, D.C. 20003
202-626-5305 (inpatient)
202-626-5356 (outpatient)

Outpatient clinic plus inpatient treatment on hospital wards (501-1000). Services include chemical detoxification; medical-surgical treatment; methadone maintenance; counseling; individual psychotherapy.

Philadelphia General Hospital
Mills Building
Philadelphia, Pennsylvanias 19104
215-832-7496

Terros
1229 North First Street
Phoenix, Arizona 85004
602-252-6021

Free medical clinic and crisis center for drug abusers in two converted residences. Services offered: crisis intervention; medical-surgical treatment; referral; chemical detoxification.

Facilities for the Diagnosis and Treatment of Withdrawal States

Addiction Research and Treatment Corporation
927 Fulton Street
Brooklyn, New York 11238
212-636-1000, Extension 5

A private, nonprofit, research oriented drug abuse program encompassing many types of treatment; residential center, outpatient center, crisis center, daycare unit, and a converted Salvation Army Shelter.

Services include crisis and legal intervention; counseling; job placement; medical treatment; methadone maintenance; chemical detoxification.

Center for Special Problems
2107 Van Ness Avenue
San Francisco, Californias 94109
415-558-4801

A specialized mental heatlh center offering crisis intervention and outpatient assistance. Part of the Community Mental Health Service of the City and County of San Francisco.

Services offered include drug free detoxification; counseling; chemical detoxification; crisis intervention; meditation; individual therapy; methadone maintenance.

Columbia University
College of Physicians and Surgeons
630 West 168 Street
New York, New York 10032
212-568-4000, Extension 284

Haight-Ashbury Clinic
Drug Treatment Program
409 and 529 Clayton Street
San Francisco, California 94117
425-621-9758
415-621-2014

A component of the Haight-Ashbury Free Clinic, provides storefront, out-patient, and crisis assistance to drug abusers and their families.

Services include crisis intervention; counseling; individual psychotherapy; chemical and drug free detoxification; medical-surgical treatment.

Illinois Drug Abuse Program

East Pavilion, Museum of Science and Industry
5700 South Lake Shore Drive
Chicago, Illinois 60617
312-955-9800, Extensions 40, 41, 42

A large organization providing comprehensive system of services for treatment and rehabilitation of drug abusers.

Services include crisis and legal intervention; medical-surgical treatment; methadone maintenance; counseling; meditation; drug free and chemical detoxification; cyclazocine therapy.

Kings County Addictive Disease Hospital
600 Albany Avenue
Brooklyn, New York 11203
Drug Detoxification Unit
212-462-4000, Extensions 6548, 6115
212-270-3130

Inpatient detoxification primarily for narcotic addicts.

Services include chemical detoxification; crisis intervention; individual psychotherapy; legal intervention; medical-surgical treatment.

Los Angeles County Mental Health Department
1102 South Crenshaw
Los Angeles, California 90019
Drug Abuse Programs
213-937-2380

As a department of the Los Angeles county government, it has incorporated services for drug abusers into its ongoing mental health programs. The department works in conjunction with other county agencies in providing services to individual drug users, with emphasis on underlying psychiatric problems.

Services include crisis intervention; counseling; drug free detoxification; individual therapy.

Methadone Maintenance Program
Denver General Hospital, Ward 18
West 6th Avenue at Cherokee
Denver, Colorado 80204
303-893-6206

Outpatient methadone maintenance and ancillary services provided.

Services include methadone maintenance; crisis intervention; group counseling; individual therapy.

Methadone Maintenance Treatment Program
Beth Israel Medical Center
245 East 17th Street
New York, New York 10003
212-673-3000, Extensions 2951, 2952, 2953

Administers and is the primary resource for a large network of methadone maintenance clinics throughout the city. Three-phase maintenance program with outpatient and inpatient facilities. Many patients are stabilized on an ambulatory basis.

Services include methadone maintenance; medical-surgical treatment; group counseling; other group interaction; individual therapy; family counseling.

Narcotics Treatment Administration
Community Addiction Treatment Center
1400 Q Street, N.W.
Washington, D.C. 20009
202-629-5438

An outpatient center with services including chemical detoxification; group therapy and counseling; methadone maintenance.

University of Nevada
Anderson Health Science Building
Reno, Nevada 89507
702-784-4917

Rio Grande State Center for MH/MR
2115 North 28th Street
Harlingen, Texas 78550

The State Center, a psychiatric hospital, is central agency for three community mental health centers serving a ten-county area in South Texas. All use community centers located in each county they serve as outpatient facilities, and make hospital inpatient treatment available.

Services include chemical and drug free detoxification; methadone maintenance; family and group counseling; individual psychotherapy.

Facilities For the Diagnosis and Treatment of Abuse

Alcohol and Drug Dependence Division
Connecticut Department of Mental Health

51 Coventry Street
Hartford, Connecticut 06112
203-566-3554

Multicomponent, state-wide program of comprehensive services specifically for drug dependent persons. Services include chemical detoxification; medical-surgical treatment; methadone maintenance; group counseling; therapeutic community.

Alcohol and Drug Section
State of Oregon Mental Health Division
Henry Building, 6th Floor
309 S.W. Fourth Avenue
Portland, Oregon 97204
503-229-5089

Methadone maintenance and ancillary services provided on outpatient basis. Services include methadone maintenance; chemical detoxification; group interaction; occupational therapy.

Corpus Christi Drug Abuse Council
425 South Broadway
Corpus Christi, Texas 78401
512-883-7483
512-884-2304 (crisis line)

Private, nonprofit drug rehabilitation organization established January 1970. Offers crisis care and outpatient services in former residence. Services include group counseling; medical-surgical treatment; encounter and sensitivity groups; other group interaction; meditation; awareness; individual psychotherapy.

Daytop Village, Inc.
Administrative Headquarters
184 Fifth Avenue
New York, New York 10010
212-255-8850

A private, nonprofit comprehensive drug rehabilitation agency composed of residential and Community Outreach (daycare) programs with central administration and ten treatment facilities. Services include therapeutic community; encounter groups; education; family and group counseling; individual psychotherapy; drug free detoxification.

Diagnostic and Rehabilitation Center/Philadelphia
103-105 Arch Street

Philadelphia, Pennsylvania 19106
215-925-8844, Extension 214

Drug project within this multimodality addictive agency serves as the central diagnostic and evaluation center for a network of affiliated agencies. Services include chemical detoxification; group counseling; recreational therapy; therapeutic community; drug free detoxification.

Division of Drug Abuse
New Jersey College of Medicine and Dentistry
65 Bergen Street
Newark, New Jersey 07107
201-643-8800, Extension 711

Coordinating body for network of facilities which together provide comprehensive rehabilitation services for drug abusers. Services include chemical detoxification; crisis intervention; family counseling; group therapy; medical-surgical treatment; methadone maintenance; therapeutic community; drug free detoxification.

Drug Abuse Center
Johns Hopkins Hospital
1820 East Monument Street
Baltimore, Maryland 21205
301-955-5325
301-955-3501

Several specialized treatment units, together offering comprehensive services to narcotic addicts and other drug abusers, compose the drug abuse component of the hospital and multi-service health center. Therapeutic community (Project Exit) and detoxification, abstinence and methadone maintenance.

Drug Abuse Treatment Unit
Veterans Administration Outpatient Clinic
17 Court Street
Boston, Massachusetts 02108
617-223-4571

Part of the Veterans Administration psychiatric service. Outpatient services in hospital and community-based clinic. Services include crisis intervention; chemical detoxification; individual psychotherapy; methadone maintenance; educational and group counseling.

Drug Action of Wake County
P.O. Box 12021

Raleigh, North Carolina 27605
919-828-6292

Coordinates drug abuse outreach and education efforts in Raleigh and Wake County. Services include encounter and sensitivity groups; other group interaction; crisis intervention; chemical and drug free detoxification.

Drug Addiction Rehabilitation Enterprise, Inc. (DARE)
209-211 Littleton Avenue
P.O. Box 7117
Newark, New Jersey 07107
201-673-0636

Multi-service therapeutic community as well as central administrative offices for network of DARE outreach centers, residential care, and halfway house services in other cities of the state. Services include therapeutic community; drug free detoxification; encounter groups; group counseling; supervised work assignments; chemical detoxification.

Drug Dependence Unit
Grady Memorial Hospital
80 Butler Street, S.E.
Atlanta, Georgia 30303
404-659-1212, Extensions 737, 880

Outpatient drug unit primarily for narcotic drug users, located in general hospital building. Services include methadone maintenance; chemical detoxification; group counseling; medical-surgical treatment.

Drug Rehabilitation Center
Tulsa Psychiatric Center
1620 East 12th Street
Tulsa, Oklahoma 74120
918-582-2131

Branch of the Tulsa Psychiatric Center opened in November 1969. Services include encounter and sensitivity groups and group and individual therapy. Also chemical detoxification; educational and family counseling; meditation; therapeutic community.

Haight-Ashbury Clinic
Drug Treatment Program
409 and 529 Clayton Street
San Francisco, California 94117

415-621-9758
415-621-2014

Component of Haight-Ashbury Free Clinic, provides storefront, outpatient, and crisis assistance to large number of drug abusers and their families. Services include crisis intervention; group counseling; individual psychotherapy; encounter groups; chemical and drug free detoxification; medical-surgical treatment.

Herman Kiefer Hospital Drug Abuse Program
8809 John C. Lodge Fwy, Building 4
Detroit, Michigan 48202
313-224-3984, 3985

Hospital is central headquarters for outpatient methadone clinic system. Services include methadone maintenance; group therapy; chemical and drug free detoxification; therapeutic community.

Herrick-Berkeley Community Mental Health Center
2001 Dwight Way
Berkeley, California 94704
415-845-0130, Extension 487

Outpatient methadone program located in a hospital building. Services include methadone maintenance supplemented with encounter groups; family and group counseling; social services; vocational training.

Houston Teen Challenge
519 Sul Ross
Houston, Texas 77028
713-529-0696

Residential, crisis and halfway house care in converted residence. Emphasis on rehabilitation of addicts through religious involvement. Services include drug free detoxification; recreational therapy; religious counseling.

Illinois Drug Abuse Program
East Pavilion, Museum of Science and Industry
5700 South Lake Shore Drive
Chicago, Illinois 60617
312-955-9800, Extensions 40, 41, 42

Large organization providing comprehensive system of services for treatment and rehabilitation of drug abusers. Services include medical-surgical treatment; methadone maintenance; therapeutic community; encounter groups; group counseling; meditation; drug free and chemical detoxification; cyclazocine therapy.

Kings County Addictive Disease Hospital
600 Albany Avenue
Brooklyn, New York 11203
Benjamin Kissin, M.D., Director
212-270-3131
212-630-4548, 4549

General hospital and medical school, part of the State University of New York Downstate Medical Center and Kings County Hospital. Has eight specialized drug treatment components including a methadone maintenance treatment program; a polydrug clinic; a drug detoxification unit; and an adolescent day care program.

Los Angeles County Mental Health Department
1102 South Crenshaw
Los Angeles, California 90019
Drug Abuse Programs
213-937-2380

A department of the Los Angeles county government. Works in conjunction with other county agencies in providing services to individual drug users, among other categories of clients, with emphasis on underlying psychiatric problems. Provides outpatient services in 13 community centers. Services include crisis intervention; family and group counseling; drug free detoxification; and individual therapy.

Methadone Clinic
Colorado State Hospital
1600 West 24th Street
Pueblo, Colorado 81003
303-543-1170

Methadone maintenance program in outpatient clinic of Colorado State Hospital administration building. Services include methadone maintenance and chemical detoxification.

Methadone Maintenance Induction Center
259 Hyde Street
San Francisco, California 94102
415-558-2761

An outpatient methadone maintenance treatment program functioning as component of the Center for Special Problems. Services include methadone maintenance; crisis intervention; medical-surgical treatment.

Methadone Maintenance Program

Denver General Hospital, Ward 18
West 6th Avenue at Cherokee
Denver, Colorado 80204
303-893-6206

Outpatient methadone maintenance and ancillary services provided at the hospital. Services include methadone maintenance; crisis intervention; group counseling; and individual therapy.

Methadone Maintenance Treatment Program
Beth Israel Medical Center
245 East 17th Street
New York, New York 10003
212-673-3000, Extensions 2951, 2952, 2953

Administers and is the primary resource for a large network of methadone maintenance clinics throughout the city. Three-phase maintenance program with outpatient and inpatient facilities. Services include methadone maintenance; medical-surgical treatment; social services.

Narcotics Treatment Administration
122 C Street, N.W.
Washington, D.C. 20001
202-626-5305, 5356

Comprehensive agency servicing narcotic users through a number of specialized programs. NTA has a computerized information system containing intake data, treatment and progress notes, clients in all aspects of the program. Specific services provided by units include chemical detoxification; methadone maintenance; therapeutic community.

National Institute of Mental Health (NIMH)
  Clinical Research Center
Leestown Pike
Lexington, Kentucky 40507
Narcotic Addiction and Drug Abuse—NIMH
606-255-6812

A federal institution for rehabilitation of narcotic addicts, administered and funded by the National Institute of Mental Health, Division of Narcotic Addiction and Drug Abuse. Services include chemical detoxification; therapeutic community; individual psychotherapy; medical-surgical treatment.

Naturalism, Inc.

P.O. Box 3621
Hollywood, California 90028
213-466-7250

Nonprofit religious organization. Services include therapeutic community; encounter groups; group counseling; individual psychotherapy; meditation; religious counseling; drug free detoxification.

New York City Methadone Maintenance
Treatment Program
377 Broadway
New York, New York 10013
212-966-6308

Network of outpatient methadone maintenance centers under the auspices of the Health Services Administration of the City of New York. Services include methadone maintenance and medical-surgical treatment.

Odyssey House
309-311 East 6th Street
New York, New York 10003
212-614-9160

Central agency for complex of 18 drug abuse treatment programs. A psychiatrically oriented therapeutic community for people over the age of 25. Services include therapeutic community; group therapy; encounter groups; medical-surgical treatment; drug free detoxification.

The Open Door
162 West Street
Annapolis, Maryland 21401
301-268-4545

Outpatient, storefront operation working in conjunction with Anne Arundel County Health Department. Services include chemical and drug free detoxification; crisis intervention; group therapy; methadone maintenance.

Payne Whitney Clinic
New York Hospital Alcohol and Drug
  Abuse Treatment and Research Service
525 East 68 St.
New York, New York 10028
212-472-6455

This service offers inpatient detoxification, and a full outpatient department treatment program including group and individual treatment. They conduct a consultation and liaison service with the New York Hospital. They have affiliations with Alcoholics Anonymous and an Adolescent and Adult Methadone Treatment Clinic.

Puget Sound Social Programs, Inc.
Methadone Treatment Program
5212 15th Street, N.E.
Seattle, Washington 98105
206-522-0220

Medical social service organization provides aftercare treatment services for narcotic addicts. Services include methadone maintenance; drug free detoxification; family and group counseling; individual psychotherapy; medical-surgical treatment.

Rio Grand State Center for MH/MR
2115 North 28th Street
Harlingen, Texas 78550

The State Center, a psychiatric hospital, is central agency for three community mental health centers serving a ten-county area in South Texas, including Harlington, Kingsville and Laredo. Services include chemical and drug free detoxification; methadone maintenance; family and group counseling; individual psychotherapy. The Laredo Center offers a therapeutic community in addition to all of the above services.

Rubicon, Inc.
1208 West Franklin Street
Richmond, Virginia 23223
703-359-3257

Maintains four residential and outpatient centers in Richmond and surrounding area. Services include therapeutic community; chemical detoxification; encounter and sensitivity groups; medical-surgical treatment; group counseling; methadone support; drug free detoxification.

San Diego County Mental Health Services
P.O. Box 3067
San Diego, California 92103
714-291-7550

Agency administers residential and outpatient treatment, storefront and crisis centers at several locations. Services include chemical detoxification; methadone maintenance; therapeutic community; family and drug counseling; medical-surgical treatment; crisis intervention; drug free detoxification; individual psychotherapy.

Spectrum Programs, Inc.
900 S.E. First Avenue
Miami, Florida 33131
305-377-0716

Private, nonprofit organization which administers a complex of residential and community drug abuse treatment units in Dade and Broward Counties. Services offered include therapeutic community; drug free and chemical detoxification.

Terros
1229 North First Street
Phoenix, Arizona 85004
602-252-6021

Free medical clinic for drug abusers in two converted residences. Services include medical-surgical treatment and chemical detoxification.

Facilities of Non-residential Self-Help Organizations

The use of a *Drug Related Non-residential Self-Help Organization* facility is invaluable in the treatment program of any drug addicted patient particularly prior to and after he has been detoxified. The self-help organization plays a central role in his rehabilitation, helps him sustain a drug free life, and cope with his inevitable relapses. It can help him deal with his family and they with him, and often is the only means of getting him to confront his steadfast denials that block effective treatment of any kind.

The government has published an excellent report which not only describes the nature of self-help organizations in depth, but also has a comprehensive up-to-date listing of the locations and phone numbers of Drug Related Non-residential Self-Help Organizations which you can obtain free by requesting *The National Institute on Drug Abuse Services Research Report, Non-residential Self-Help Organizations and Drug Abuse Problem: An Exploratory Conference*, publication no. (ADM) 78-752, July 1978, from the Services Research Branch of the National Institute on Drug Abuse, 5600 Fishers Lane, Room 10-A-31, Rockville, Md. 20857. In this completely informative publication you will find listings for seventy-two organizations in California alone. Families Anonymous, Narcotics Anonymous, NarAnon, Narconon, Narcotics and Alcoholics Anonymous, Narcotics Education League, Parents United Project JUV II, Self-Help Center, Seventh Step Foundation, and Straight Ahead are among them.

Listings of drug related non residential self-help organizations for thirty five other States include some of those already mentioned and the following: Volunteers in Service to Substance Abuse (VISA), Parents Anonymous, Addicts Anonymous, Black Womens Program, Chemical Abuse Service Agency, Drug Abuse Services

Project, Metropolitan Institute on Black Chemical Abuse, On Top (Chemically Dependent Mothers), Acess, Americans Mobilized to End Narcotic Abuse (AMEN), Camelot, Project Create, Confront Inc., Women for Sobriety, Friends Anonymous, Pills Anonymous, Pilanon, Recover Inc., and Pot Smokers Anonymous.

To obtain detailed information about the exact services and function of any of these organizations you must call them up or visit them—or better still, find a member who has had an actual therapeutic experience in working with that organization. He or she will be the best informant as to its value. The telephone numbers on all the facilities described above, whether obtained through the government or other listings, may have changed since the publication of this book. They must be re-checked for accuracy in your local phone book, or by calling or writing to the Supportive Services and Evaluation, Services Research Branch of the Division of Resource Development, at the National Institute on Drug Abuse, 5600 Fishers Lane, Rockville, Md. 20857, (301) 443-4100.

The other major therapeutic modality is the *Residential Therapeutic Community*. To best understand the history, nature, functioning and current goals and services of *The Therapeutic Community*, I suggest that you write to the Alcohol, Drug Abuse and Mental Health Administration, 3600 Fishers Lane, Rockville, Maryland 20857, for their publication of The National Institute on Drug Abuse Services Research Report, *The Therapeutic Community: Proceedings of Therapeutic Communities of America Planning Conference, January 29-30, 1976*, edited by G. DeLeon and G. Beschner (DHEW Publication No. (ADM) 77-464, 1977). This conference was cosponsored by the National Institute on Drug Abuse and Therapeutic Communities of America.

Residential Therapeutic Communities: Members of Therapeutic Communities of America

ALASKA

Akeela House Inc.
135 N. Park St.
Anchorage, Alaska 99504
(907) 272-4476

ARIZONA

New Arizona Family, Inc.
1320 N. Second St.
Phoenix, Arizona 85004
(602) 252-3439

Tucson Awareness House, Inc.
P.O. Box 709
Tucson, Arizona 85702
(602) 622-2851

3 HO Drug Program
1050 N. Cherry Avenue
Tucson, Arizona 85719
(602) 327-1734

*Behavioral Health Agency of
   Central Arizona*
102 N. Florence Street
Casa Grande, Arizona 85222
(602) 836-1688

CALIFORNIA

*Tarzana Residential
   Treatment Program*
18646 Oxnard St.
Tarzana, CA 91356
(213) 996-1051

House of Metamorphosis
2970 Market St.
San Diego, CA 92102
(714) 236-9492

Brentwood Veterans Admin. Hosp.
RTC (116A24)
Wilshire & Sawtelle Blvd.
Los Angeles, CA 90073
(203) 478-3711

Impact Houses (Principles, Inc.)
1680 N. Fair Oaks Ave.
Pasadena, CA 91103
(213) 681-2575

My Family Inc.
3529 Vine St.
Riverside, CA 92507
(714) 682-4151

New Day Foundation, Inc.
2560 Pulgas Ave.
East Palo Alto, CA 94303
(415) 328-1065

Pacifica House
15519 Crenshaw Blvd.
Gardana, CA 90249
(213) 679-9031

Tuum EST Inc.
503 Ocean Front Walk
Venice, CA 90291
213-392-3070

Walden House Inc.
815 Buena Vista West
San Francisco, CA 94117
415-552-6440

The 3rd Floor
P.O. Box 12107
Fresno, CA 93776
(209) 237-6177

Sunflower House
125 Rigg Street
Santa Cruz, CA 95060
(408) 423-3890

Turning Point of Central Calif.
P.O. Box 3146
1845 So. Court

Visalia, CA 93277
(209) 732-8086

Straight Ahead, Inc.
34185 Coast Highway
Dana Point, CA 92629
(714) 831-0360

Crash, Inc.
P.O. Box 8057
San Diego, CA 92112
(714) 282-6877

Maac Project
(Substance Abuse Component)
827 "A" Avenue
National City, CA 92050
(714) 474-8227

Watsonville Drug Abuse Council, Inc.
278 Main Street
Watsonville, CA 95706
(408) 728-1791

CANADA

The Portage Program, Inc.
3418 Drummond St.
Montreal, Canada H3G 1Y1
(514) 282-0404

Spera Foundation, Inc.
2325 Center St.
Montreal Quebec, Canada H3K, 1J6
(514) 935-2515

X-Kalay Foundation (Manitoba), Inc.
P.O. Box 250
3514 Pembina Highway
St. Norbert, Manitoba R3V, 1L6
(204) 269-3430

COLORADO

New Horizons TC Colorado State Hosp.
1600 W. 24th Street

Pueblo, Colorado 81003
(303) 543-1170
Post House
715 Emery Street
Longmont, Colorado 80501
(303) 776-8118

CONNECTICUT

Connecticut Renaissance Inc.
21 Taylor Place
Westport, Conn. 06880
(203) 226-3353
Liberation House
119 Main St.
Stamford, Conn. 06901
(203) 325-4191
Vitam Center Inc.
57 West Rocks Rd.
Norwalk, Conn. 06851
(203) 846-2091

FLORIDA

Concept House, Inc.
162 N.E. 49th Street
Miami, Fla. 33137
(305) 751-6501
Disc Village
P.O. Box 6054
Tallahassee, Fla. 32301
(904) 878-1196
Here's Help, Inc.
14857 N.W. 7th Ave.
N. Miami, Fla. 33168
(305) 685-8201
Metamorphosis
732-734 N.E. 3rd Ave.
Gainesville, Fla. 32601
(904) 377-8787

Metatherapy Institute Inc.
27200 Old Dixie Highway
Miami, Fla. 33030
(305) 247-4515

Operation Par, Inc.
2400 Ninth St. So.
St. Petersburg, Fla. 33705
813-822-5242

The Village South Inc.
5810 Biscayne Blvd.
Miami, Fla. 33137
305-751-3856

Jacksonville Drug Abuse Program
515 W. 6th Street
Jacksonville, Fla. 32206
(904) 633-5150

Spectrum Programs
1 N.W. 67th Street
Miami, Fla. 33150
(305) 754-1683

HAWAII

Habilitat, Inc.
P.O. Box 801
Kaneohe, Hawaii 96744
(808) 235-6411/2/3/6617/8

Salvation Army/Alcohol Trtmnt Facility
3624 Waokanaka Street
Honolulu, Hawaii 96813
(808) 595-6371

ILLINOIS

Gateway Houses Fdn., Inc.
624 So. Michigan Ave.
Chicago, Ill. 60605
(312) 663-1130

Hill House Board Inc.
P.O. Box 287

Carbondale, Ill. 66605
(618) 549-7391

Stonehedge Programs
2621 N. Knoxville Ave.
Peoria, Ill. 61604
(309) 688-5627

Substance Abuse Services Inc.
1439 So. Michigan Ave.
Chicago, Ill. 60605
(312) 663-3610

Illinois Dangerous Drugs Rehab. Sys.
1439 So. Michigan Ave.
Chicago, Ill. 60605
(312) 663-0817

IOWA

Linwood T.C.
R.R. #2 School Road
Davenport, Iowa 52804
(319) 324-3529

MARYLAND

Second Genesis Inc.
4720 Montgomery Lane
Bethesda, MD 20024
(301) 424-8500

X-Cell Inc.
101 So. Wolfe St.
Baltimore, MD 21231
(301) 732-0600

MASSACHUSETTS

Concilio Human Svcs. Inc.
656 Massachusetts Ave.
Boston, Mass. 02118
(617) 267-2363

First, Inc.

167 Centre St.
Roxbury, Mass. 02119
(617) 427-1588/9

Spectrum House Inc.
P.O. Box 545
No. Grafton, Mass. 01536
(617) 839-4296

735, Inc.
81 Rowe St.
Melrose, Mass. 02176
(716) 662-8976

Project Concern
46 Perrin St.
Roxbury, Mass. 02119
(617) 445-1650

Third Nail Inc.
1179 Columbus Ave.
Boston, Mass. 02120
(617) 445-6142

Share Inc.
P.O. Box 1433
660 Middlesex St.
Lowell, Mass. 01853
(617) 459-2306

Women, Inc.
570 Warren St.
Dorchester, Mass. 02124
(617) 442-6166

MICHIGAN

Shar House Inc.
1842 W. Grand Blvd.
Detroit, Michigan 42808
(313) 894-8444

Alexandrine House Inc.
4139 Second Ave.
Detroit, Michigan 48201
(313) 833-7611

Project Rehab/Bullock House

200 Eastern SE
Grand Rapids, MI 49503
(616) 458-6131

MINNESOTA

Eden House
1025 Portland
Minneapolis, Minn. 55405
(612) 338-0723

Freedom House
3020 Lyndale Ave. So.
Minneapolis, Minn. 55408
(612) 827-3300

NEVADA

Fitzsimmons House, Inc.
201 N. 8th St.
Las Vegas, Nevada 89101
(702) 386-1929

NEW JERSEY

C.U.R.A. Inc.
75 Lincoln Park
Newark, NJ 07102
(201) 622-3570

N.A.R.C.O.
2006 Baltic Ave.
Atlantic City, NJ 08401
(609) 345-4035

Integrity Inc.
P.O. Box 1806
Newark, NJ 07101
(201) 623-0600

Damon House Inc.
105 Joyce Kilmer Avenue
New Brunswick, NJ 08901
(201) 828-3988

NEW YORK

Daytop Village
54 W. 40 Street
New York, NY 10018
(212) 354-6000

Educational Alliance, Inc.
371 E. 10 St.
New York, NY 10009
(212) 533-2470

Phoenix Houses Foundation, Inc.
164 W. 74 Street
New York, NY 10023
(212) 595-5810

Odyssey Houses Inc.
208-210 E. 18 St.
New York, NY 10003
(212) 741-9661

Project Return
444 Park Avenue So.
New York, NY 10016
(212) 683-6900

Samaritan Halfway Society
118-21 Queens Blvd.
Forest Hills, NY 11375
(212) 520-5207

Alba-Neck Halfway House
276 Albany Avenue
Amityville, NY 11701
(516) 842-6622

Su Casa Ctr.
Lower Eastside Service Center
46 E. Broadway
New York, NY 10002
(212) 431-4610

Veritas T.C. Inc.
203 W. 84 St.
New York, NY 10023
(212) 724-4141

Dynamite Youth Center Fdn., Inc.

1830 Coney Island Ave.
Brooklyn, NY 11230
(212) 376-7933

Areba
47 E. 51 Street
New York, NY 10022
(212) 593-0815/6/7

Greenwich House (Drug-Free Component)
27 Barrow St.
New York, NY 10014
(212) 242-4140

The Renaissance Project
481 Main St.
New Rochelle, NY 10801
(914) 576-3320

Hope House Inc.
261 N. Pearl St.
Albany, NY 12207
(518) 465-2441

OHIO

Cleveland Treatment Center
1127 Carnegie Ave.
Cleveland, Ohio 44115
(216) 861-4246

Encounter Programs Inc.
106 E. Whiteman Street
Yellow Springs, Ohio 45387
(513) 767-7309
(Alternatives to Trial &
   Incarceration Program)

Youth Drug Program
1833 No. Main St.
Dayton, Ohio 45405
(513) 278-4713

*The Family Tree Humanizing
   Comm. Inc.*
807 No. Superior

Toledo, Ohio 43684
(419) 248-4421

PENNSYLVANIA

Abraxas Foundation, Inc.
P.O. Box 59
Marionville, PA 16239
(814) 927-6615

C.A.R.E., Inc.
118 No. Main St.
Washington, PA 15301
(412) 288-2200

Eagleville Hospital &
  Rehabilitation Center
P.O. Box 45
Eagleville, PA 19408
(215) 539-6000

Gaudenzia, Inc.
39 East School House Lane
Philadelphia, PA 19144
(215) 849-7200

Genesis II, Inc.
1214 North Broad St.
Philadelphia, PA 19121
(215) 763-2650

Horizon House
1717 Point Breeze Ave.
Philadelphia, PA 19145
(215) 271-5353

House of the Crossroads
2012 Centre Ave.
Pittsburgh, PA 15219
(412) 281-5080

Mercer County Drug Council, Inc.
1055 No. Hermitage Rd.
Sharon, PA 16146
(412) 981-5155

Today, Inc.
P.O. Box 98

Newtown, PA 18940
(215) 968-4713

RHODE ISLAND

Marathon House, Inc.
170 Westminster St.
Providence, RI 02903
(401) 331-4250

TEXAS

Aliviane, Inc.
6040 Surety Drive
El Paso, Texas 79905
(915) 779-6669

WASHINGTON

Sea-Dur-Nar
P.O. Box 24344
Seattle, Washington 98124
(206) 767-0244
The Family House Inc.
200 W. Comstock
Seattle, Washington 98119
(206) 284-2010

WISCONSIN

The Wisconsin Family Inc.
2105 North Booth St.
Milwaukee, Wis. 53212
(414) 263-4481

WYOMING

State of Wyoming Drug Abuse Program
Hathaway Bldg.
Cheyenne, Wyoming 82002
(307) 777-7115

Polydrug Abuse Facilities

University of California—San Diego
University Hospital
Department of Psychiatry—Drug Abuse Programs
San Diego, California
215-387-5000

Center for Special Problems
2107 Van Ness Avenue
San Francisco, California 94109
415-558-4801

A specialized mental health center offering crisis intervention and outpatient assistance. Services include group counseling; other group interaction; chemical detoxification; individual therapy; methadone maintenance. Others available: drug free detoxification; family counseling; medical-surgical treatment.

Corpus Christi Drug Abuse Council
425 South Broadway
Corpus Christi, Texas 78401
512-883-7483

Private, nonprofit drug rehabilitation organization. Services offered include educational and group counseling; medical-surgical treatment; encounter and sensitivity groups; meditation; awareness and individual psychotherapy.

Drug Abuse Council
1828 L Street, N.W.
Washington, D.C. 20036
202-785-5200

Drug Addiction Rehabilitation Enterprise, Inc., (DARE)
209-211 Littleton Avenue
P. O. Box 7117
Newark, New Jersey 07107
201-673-0636

Multiservice therapeutic community as well as central administrative offices for network of DARE outreach centers, residential care, and halfway house services in other cities of the state.

Services include therapeutic community; drug free detoxification; encounter groups; group counseling; chemical detoxification; medical-surgical treatment; family counseling, occupational and recreational therapy; vocational training.

Illinois Drug Abuse Program
East Pavilion, Museum of Science and Industry
5700 South Lake Shore Drive
Chicago, Illinois 60617
312-955-9800, Extensions 40, 41, 42

Large organization providing comprehensive system of services for treatment and rehabilitation of drug abusers.

Services include medical-surgical treatment, methadone maintenance; therapeutic community; encounter groups; group counseling; meditation and self-awareness groups; vocational training.

Kings County Addictive Disease Hospital
600 Albany Avenue
Brooklyn, New York 11203
212-630-4507
212-630-4548

The Polydrug Clinic is an aspect of the General Hospital and medical school of the State University of New York and Kings County Hospital. Services provided include intense medical and psychiatric counseling services on an individual basis; vocational training; recreational therapy; group counseling.

Los Angeles County Mental Health Department
1102 South Crenshaw
Los Angeles, California 90019
213-937-2380

As a department of the Los Angeles county government, has incorporated services for drug abusers into its ongoing mental health programs. Works in conjunction with other county agencies in providing services to individual drug users with emphasis on underlying psychiatric problems.

Services include family and group counseling; drug free detoxification; individual therapy.

Naturalism, Inc.
P. O. Box 3621
Hollywood, California 90028
213-466-7250

Nonprofit religious organization; one of several programs in the United States and Canada. Services include therapeutic community; encounter groups; group counseling, individual psychotherapy; meditation; religious counseling.

San Francisco Polydrug Project

527 Irving Street
San Francisco, California 94122
415-621-9758, 2014

Stanford University
Institute for the Study of Human Problems
Psychopharmacology Project
Stanford, California 94305
415-497-2300

State University of New York at Buffalo
Department of Psychiatry
Buffalo, New York
716-831-9000

University of Kentucky
College of Medicine
Lexington, Kentucky 40506
606-258-9000

McLean Hospital
Department of Psychiatry
Harvard University
Belmont, Massachusetts 02178
617-855-2201

Methadone Maintenance Institute
8 South Michigan Avenue
Chicago, Illinois 60603
312-321-1230

Mid-Iowa Center for Drug Education and Research, Inc.
Iowa State University
Ames, Iowa 50010
515-294-4111

University of Missouri
School of Medicine
Narcotic Addiction Treatment Program
Department of Psychiatry
St. Louis, Missouri 63121
314-453-0111

Mount Sinai Hospital
Methadone Maintenance Treatment Program
5th Avenue and 100th Street
New York, New York 10029
212-876-2466

New York University Medical Center
566 1st Avenue
New York, New York 10016
212-679-3200

Tennessee Psychiatric Hospital and Institute
865 Poplar Avenue
Memphis, Tennessee 38104
901-534-6630

Prevention Facilities

Academy of Medicine of Cleveland
Drug Abuse Committee
10525 Carnegie Avenue
Cleveland, Ohio 44106
216-231-3500

Addiction Research and Treatment Corporation (ARTC)
437 Fulton Street
Brooklyn, New York 11238
212-636-1000, Extension 5

University of Arkansas
Medical Center
Room 3E24
Little Rock, Arkansas 72201
501-664-5000, Extension 385

Berkeley Free Clinic
2339 Durant Avenue
Berkeley, California 94704
415-548-2570

Community Organization for Drug Abuse Control (CODAC)
1807 North Central

Phoenix, Arizona 85004
602-252-7655

Colorado State Department of Health
Division of Alcoholism and Drug Dependence
4210 East 11th Avenue
Denver, Colorado 80220
303-388-6111

Hastings Regional Center
Ingleside, Nebraska 68953
402-463-2471

Illinois State Medical Society
Committee on Narcotics and Hazardous Substances
360 North Michigan Avenue
Chicago, Illinois 60601
312-782-1655

Odyssey House
309-311 East 6th Street
New York, New York 10003
212-674-9160

Regional Addiction Prevention, Inc.
1904 T Street, N.W.
Washington, D.C. 20009
202-462-7500

Association and Conferences on Drug Abuse Facilities

Addiction Research Foundation (ARF)
33 Russell Street
Toronto, Ontario
Ontario M 5S 2S1 Canada

Alcohol and Drug Problem Association of North America (ADPA)
1130 Seventeenth Street, N.W.
Washington, D.C. 20036
202-452-0990

Drug Abuse Council (DAC)

1828 L Street
Washington, D.C. 20036
202-785-5200

Drug Information Association (DIA)
c/o Mr. Robert Cuddihy
Managing Editor—Drug Information Bulletin
Sandoz
Route 10
Hanover, New Jersey 07936
201-386-1000

International Council on Alcoholism and Addictions (ICAA)
Cose Postale 140
1001 Lousanne
Switzerland
021-29-6485

National Association of State Drug Abuse Program Coordinators (NASDAPC)
1612 K Street, N.W.
Washington, D.C. 20006
202-659-7632

National Clearinghouse for Drug Abuse Information (NCDAI)
P.O. Box 1908
Rockville, Maryland 20850
301-443-6500

National Coordination Council on Drug Education (NCCDE)
1512 18th Street, N.W.
Washington, D.C. 20036
202-332-1512

National Institute on Drug Abuse (NIDA)
1400 Rockville Pike
Rockville, Maryland 20852
202-655-4000

World Health Organization
Office of Mental Health
1211 Geneva 27, Switzerland

FOOD

The diagnosis of a food addiction is the easiest to make. Except for secret boulimia, the symptoms—excessive weight gain or loss—are always evident.

A primary care physician should do a complete physical examination to rule out endocrine metabolic disorders or any other disease that could be causing changes in weight and eating patterns. Once all other bases for eating disorders are ruled out, the food addict can be referred to a psychiatrist or psychologist to determine the degree of emotional disorder present in the addict, and whether or not psychological treatment is necessary to supplement a weight control program.

Most weight reduction treatment programs do not include psychotherapy or group therapy because of the expense and unavailability of trained therapists. Because a psychological element always exists in case of food addiction, any insights obtained by the addict through therapy will improve the prognosis and decrease the chances of a relapse. There is a growing body of literature available that can help to shed light on the multidimensional psychological roots of eating disorders (see bibliography).

Many of the current treatment programs will take into account individual psychological factors along with the necessary behavioral modifications. Family, group (homogeneous for the specific disorder and mixed addictions) therapy, psychodrama, hypnotherapy, psychoanalytic psychotherapy, and even psychoanalysis have recently been used to treat food addiction. Each individual's treatment must take into account many factors that go beyond what is optimal, and as many of these variables as possible should be considered in deciding on the most effective program. The use of appetite suppressants (amphetamines, etc.) has gone out of vogue because of the addictive potentials of many of these drugs. Any program that includes them should be carefully monitored by the appropriate specialist (licensed medical nutritionist, psychiatrist or internist specializing in eating disorders).

The addict's visit to the dietician at the nutrition clinic at your local hospital can be beneficial in terms of establishing a livable diet that can be sustained. Because Weight Watchers has done the most extensive work in the field of behavioral weight control, their programs offer balanced diets and behavioral modification techniques that have proven to be effective over many years. I have listed this self-help group facility along with several other resources available to the food addict, where further diagnostic information and therapeutic activity is felt to be necessary.

SELF-HELP RESOURCES FOR EATING DISORDERS

Weight Watchers: established by Jean Neiditch in May, 1963, this organization is international in scope. It exists in fifty States, throughout Canada, and in twenty-six countries throughout the world. You may obtain information about their locations by looking them up in the yellow pages of your phone book under Reducing and Weight Control Services. Its programs are supervised and designed by medical, nutritional, and psychologically trained and licensed practitioners who have specialized in the physical and behavioral modification specialties. Weight Watchers has a Psychological Behavior Modification Director of Weight Control, a Director of Nutrition, and a Cardiologist attached to their standardized programs. Literature describing their programs, educational materials, diet books, and products, can be obtained through commercial sources or at their meeting places. These materials can be obtained by writing Weight Watchers International Inc., 800 Community Drive, Manhasset, N.Y. 11030, or by calling (516) 627-9200.

T.O.P.S. (Take Off Pounds Sensibly): This is the oldest and second largest self-help group. Its influence is most felt on the West coast of the United States. It exists in many states and can be located through the phone book.

Overeaters Anonymous, Diet Workshop, Diet Control Centers are among the other major weight reducing control services that can be located through your phone book's yellow pages. Should these resources not be available, you should check with your local hospital, teaching medical institution, or a private, medical nutritionist for the location of the nearest self-help group and individual treatment resource.

For all other information pertaining to eating disorder programs (and research, education, and nutrition), you can refer to your local Bureau of Nutrition through your city or state government. Also, write or call the U.S. Department of Agriculture's Department of Food and Nutrition, the Department of Health, Education, and Welfare's Community Nutritional Health Programs, and the National Institute of Health's Chronic Disease Division (which has a section on obesity). The Human Nutrition Institute, part of the United States Department of Agriculture, Washington, D.C. 20250, has weight control publications available at no cost. Other resources are The American Dietetic Association, located at 430 North Michigan Avenue, Chicago, Illinois 60611, phone (312) 822-0330, who can refer you to certified dieticians in each state that can provide materials and weight reduction programs. The Public Health Service Obesity Clinics of the Department of Health, Education, and Welfare can also offer help. The American Heart Association at 1320 Greenville Avenue, Dallas, Texas 75231, phone (214) 750-5300, has materials on how obesity can cause heart and other related diseases. This association exists in every state and can be located through your phone book's yellow pages.

Throughout America hundreds of non-residential and residential weight reduction programs and facilities have emerged. Some have become well-known because they are populated by the rich and famous and have effective programs. Others are less-known but equally effective. Beware of those that are fraudulent. It is important to check the credentials of all the personnal. A registered dietician (R.D.), physician (M.D.), both trained in eating disorder problems and other metabolic problems is a bare essential. A registered physical educator, knowledgeable of exercise physiology, is important also. The Green Mountain Weight Control Community For Young Women between eighteen and fifty-five in Poultney, Vermont 05764, phone (802) 287-9229 is exemplary of a residential weight reducing facility. Many hundreds more exist but have to pass the test. Each of these facilities operate with different programs and philosophies that must suit the food addicts specific needs. Have your physician nutritionist or therapist help you to determine the validity of the program.

The Association for Advancement of Behavior Therapy, which is a behavioral medicine special interest group with obesity as a subgroup interest, has a Directory of *Behavior Weight Control Programs* which has been compiled by Dennis R. Brightwell, M.D.. This directory describes the facilities and services offered for each of these weight control programs. Group therapy, workshops, behavioral self-control, assertiveness training, transactional analysis, physical fitness programming, medication, self-hypnosis, life-style modification, self-monitoring, stimulis control, chaining and response blocking, nutritional counseling, special diets, parental involvement, family therapy, token reinforcement, dietary education, ''self and food awareness'' educational techniques, contingency contracting, self-esteem change, relaxation techniques, social skills training and reinforcement, cognitive restructuring, aggressive, low profiled periodic follow-up programs are among the multi-modalities used by these weight control programs.

The following is the listings as of April 1979 (with a few added) that are residential centers but non-members of the AABT. If you write to Dennis R. Brightwell, M.D. (116A), Harry S. Truman Veterans Hospital, 800 Stadium Road, Columbia, Missouri 65201, you may obtain a detailed description of these programs. This list will no doubt grow and be updated each year. The value of having such a listing is the attempt on the part of the Association to bring professional credibility and interdisciplinary expertise which protects the public from fly-by-night fraudulent and exploitive programs.

Behavioral Medicine—Obesity Special Interest Subgroup

ARIZONA

Behavior Modification Clinic, Inc.
1130 E. Missouri Ave., Suite 520
Phoenix, Arizona 85014
(602) 264-5897

CALIFORNIA

Department of Psychology
California State University, Chico
Chico, California 95929
(916) 895-5178 or 895-5212

Gifford Mental Health Clinic
3427 Fourth Avenue
San Diego, California 92103

USC
734 West Adams Boulevard
Los Angeles, California 90007
(213) 741-2287

Habit Abatement Clinic
University of California
1490 Fifth Avenue
San Francisco, California 94143

The Lindner Clinic
12132 Garfield Avenue
Address Mail: P.O.B. 2097
South Gate, California 90280
(213) 634-2434

Department of Psychology
California State University
Los Angeles, California 90032
(213) 224-3841

Diet & Weight Control Clinic
P. O. Box 5203
Stanford, California
(415) 497-0322

CONNECTICUT

Connecticut State Department of Health
79 Elm Street
Hartford, Connecticut 06106

FLORIDA

Behavioral Medicine Institute, Inc.
10621 North Kendall Drive—Suite 121
Miami, Florida 33176
(303) 274-0901

Department of Psychology,
Florida State University
Tallahassee, Florida 32306
(904) 544-1454

IOWA

Student Counseling Service
Iowa State University
Ames, Iowa 50011
(515) 294-5056

Department of Family Practice
College of Medicine
The University of Iowa
Westlawn S-201
Iowa City, Iowa 52242
(319) 356-3518

ILLINOIS

Department of Psychology
Roosevelt University
430 South Michigan Avenue
Chicago, Illinois 60605
(312) 341-3757

INDIANA

Department of Psychological Services

Indiana Youth Center
P. O. Box 127
Plainfield, Indiana 46168

MISSOURI

Human Nutrition Laboratory
Lincoln University
Jefferson City, Missouri 65101
(314) 751-2310

Psychiatry Service (116A)
Harry S. Truman Memorial Veterans Hospital
800 Stadium Road
Columbia, Missouri 65201
(314) 443-2511, Ext. 6730

Behavior Therapy Clinic
Department of Psychology
Washington University
St. Louis, Missouri 63130
(314) 889-6527

MINNESOTA

Department of Psychology
University of Minnesota
Minneapolis, Minnesota 55455

MONTANA

Department of Psychology
University of Montana
Missoula, Montana 59812
(406) 243-4521

NEW JERSEY

Graduate School of Applied and Professional
    Psychology
Rutgers University
Box 819
Piscataway, New Jersey 08854
(201) 932-2004

NEW YORK

Department of Psychology
SUNY
Binghamton, New York 13901
(607) 798-2829

Department of Psychology
SUNY
1400 Washington Avenue
Albany, New York 12222

NORTH CAROLINA

Dietary Rehabilitation Clinic
Duke University Medical Center
Box 2914
Durham, North Carolina 27710
(919) 684-6331 (residential)

Structure House
707 Morehead Avenue
Durham, North Carolina 27707
(919) 688-7379

Department of Psychiatry
Duke Medical Center
Box 3837
Durham, North Carolina 27710

OHIO

Mt. Sinai Hospital Nutrition Service
University Circle
Cleveland, Ohio 44106
(216) 795-6000, Ext. 3201

OREGON

Mental Health Services
Sacred Heart Medical Center
1200 Alder Street
P. O. Box 10905
Eugene, Oregon 97401

PENNSYLVANIA

Obesity Research Group
Department of Psychiatry
University of Pennsylvania
205 Piersol Building
Philadelphia, Pennsylvania 19104
(215) 243-7316

Institute for Behavioral Education
Suite 105, Valley Forge Towers
King of Prussia, Pennsylvania 19406
(215) 783-0150

Clinical Psychology Center
University of Pittsburgh
Pittsburgh, Pennsylvania 15260
(412) 624-4971

Department of Psychology
Pennsylvania State University
University Park, Pennsylvania 16802
(841) 865-1711 or 7546

SOUTH CAROLINA

Department of Psychiatry and Behavioral Science
Weight Management Clinic
Medical University of South Carolina
171 Ashley Avenue
Charleston, South Carolina 29403
(803) 792-3051

Weight Control Center
Hilton Head Hospital
P. O. Box 1117
Hilton Head, South Carolina 29928
(non-member) (residential)

TENNESSEE

School of Nursing, Department of Psychology
Vanderbilt University
426 Godchaux Hall

Nashville, Tennessee 37240
(615) 322-3587

TEXAS

Diet Modification Clinic
6608 Fannin, Suite 1009
Houston, Texas 77030
(713) 790-2710

VERMONT

Green Mountain Weight Control
Community for Young Women (18-55)
Poultney, Vermont 05764
(802) 287-9229 (residential)

VIRGINIA

The Dominion Clinic
4501 North Witchduck Road
Virginia Beach, Virginia 23455
(804) 499-5473
Center Psychiatrists, Eating Disorder Unit
Crawford Parkway
Fort Lane
Portsmouth, Virginia 23704
(non-member)
(804) 397-7071

WASHINGTON

Department of Psychology
Western Washington University
Bellingham, Washington 98225
(206) 676-3579

WEST VIRGINIA

Department of Psychology

West Virginia University
Morgantown, West Virginia 26504
(303) 293-2511

WISCONSIN

Milwaukee Wellness Clinic, Inc.
204 East Capitol Drive
Milwaukee, Wisconsin 53212
(414) 961-1140

SMOKING

The diagnosis of a smoking addiction is one of the easiest to make, if one considers that the average one-pack-a-day cigarette smoker has found that the "modern cigarette is a highly efficient device for self-administering the drug nicotine. By inhaling, the smoker can get nicotine to his brain more rapidly than the heroin addict can get a "buzz" when he shoots heroin in his vein. It takes only seven seconds for nicotine in the lungs to reach the brain, compared with the fourteen seconds it takes for blood to flow from arm to brain. Further, the smoker gets a "shot" of nicotine after each inhaled puff. At ten puffs per cigarette, the pack-a-day smoker gets more than 70,000 nicotine shots to his brain in a year.* It is hardly surprising that cigarette smoking is so addictive. The two to four or more pack-a-day smoker need not go far to establish his diagnosis other than to admit to his over 70,000 shots of nicotine a year.

The National Institute of Drug Abuse has a variety of invaluable resources, research, education, diagnostic and therapeutic information for the addictive smoker. One can start out by subscribing to the *Smoking and Health Bulletin* which gives information every six weeks on the following relevant areas: behavioral and educational research and smoking cessation methods along with other health related subjects.

For a very brief but effective insight, the pamphlet *How to Choose a Stop Smoking Program*, written by Jerome L. Schwartz, Dr. P. H., and Alan Rice, M. P. H., can be obtained by writing to St. Helena Hospital and Health Center, Deer Park, California

* M. A. H. Russell, "Smoking Problems: An Overview," in *Research on Smoking Behavior,* edited by M. E. Jarvik, J. W. Cullen, E. R. Gritz, T. M. Vogt, and J. L. West. In National Institute on Drug Abuse Research Monograph 17: 1977, Department of Health, Education, and Welfare Publication No. (DM) 78-581 (1978).

94576, or by calling them at (707) 963-9455. Should you be interested in more complete, in-depth information, you can send for the *Review and Evaluation of Smoking Control Methods: The United States and Canada, 1969-1977*, by Jerome L. Schwartz, Dr. P. H. and Gail Rider (HEW Publication No. (CDC) 79-8369), which can be obtained from the U.S. Department of Health, Education and Welfare, Public Health Service, Center for Disease Control, Atlanta, Georgia 30333. You may also obtain the following extensive and comprehensive documents from the same address: *The Health Consequences of Smoking: A Reference Edition* HEW Publication No. (CDC) 78-8357, 1976; the second report to the Surgeon General, entitled *Smoking and Health*, which includes sections on "The Health Consequences of Smoking," "The Behavioral Aspects of Smoking," and "Education and Prevention," will be available in 1979-1980 through the U.S. Department of Health, Education, and Welfare, by writing to the National Clearing House for Smoking and Health (see address at end of this section).

SMOKING TREATMENT RESOURCES

There are currently many smoking cessation programs throughout the country. The largest is Smokenders, a profit organization with chapters in twenty states throughout the country and in Canada and Norway. Information can be obtained by looking up their local branches in your phone book or calling their toll-free number (800) 631-7676. The other long standing programs that exist are conducted by the American Cancer Society. They include the Schick program (method), the American Lung Association, the American Health Foundation in New York City, the Kaiser Foundation Health Plan in Oakland, California, and the Multiple Risk Factor Intervention Treatment project. They each have trigger films and other group methods that last from four to twelve weeks with follow-up maintenance sessions. Information concerning their specific forms of treatment and follow-up findings can be obtained in an excellent article by Jerome L. Schwartz, Ph.D., "Smoking Cures: Ways to Kick an Unhealthy Habit." It includes a listing of major smoking cessation programs throughout the world from 1963 to 1977. These programs include the following techniques: Self Care—devising a way of quitting by utilizing a guide tool (i.e., instructional manual, book, charting daily records, cassettes, self-monitoring audiotape, filter techniques, visual aids); Individual counseling; Educational; Group counseling; Medication; Hypnosis; Aversive conditioning; Self control; Mass Media, and Community. Each program's major method is briefly described, with a chart of cure rates used for the particular smoking cessation method—including follow-ups ranging from five months to four years. This publication can be obtained free from the government by writing for the NIDA Research Monograph 17, Research on Smoking Behavior, Department of Health, Education, and Welfare, publication number (ADM) 78-581, 1978, National Institute on Drug Abuse, Division of

Research, 5600 Fishers Lane, Rockville, Maryland 20857. You may also obtain free from the same department an excellent Self-Testing Kit and Teenage Self-Test. These kits have been used by several million persons. The kits help the smoker gain insight into attitudes, reasons, and emotions connected to smoking along with motivations to stop, explanations of the threats to health, and ways to discover factors that inhibit or help cessation.

Should you wish more detailed information refer to the following free publication by Jerome L. Schwartz, Ph.D. and Gail Rider, *Review and Evaluation of Smoking Control Methods: The United States and Canada, 1969-1977*, publication no. (CDC) 79-8369, U. S. Department of Health, Education, and Welfare, Public Health Service Center for Disease Control, Bureau of Health Education, Atlanta, Ga. 30333.

There are several helpful publications and an ongoing bulletin that will add to your knowledge of current research and treatment resources which can also be obtained free from the Technical Information Center Office on Smoking and Health, Park Building, Room 116, 5600 Fishers Lane, Rockville, Maryland 20857. You may also call (301) 443-1690 about any other of their invaluable publications; *The Health Consequences of Smoking, A Reference Edition*, publication no. (CDC) 78-8357; *Smoking and Health: An Annotated Bibliography of Public and Professional Education Materials*, publication no. (NIH) 78-1841; *Bibliography on Smoking and Health of the National Clearinghouse for Smoking and Health, Technical Information Center* (or call (404) 633-3311); *Summary and Implications of Review of Literature Related to Adolescent Smoking* by T. M. Williams, 1971; *Smokers Self-Testing Kit*, publication no. (CDC) 75-8716.

Facilities For Addiction Treatment and Research

American Cancer Society
Gipsy Trail
Carmel, New York 10512

American Health Foundation
1370 Avenue of Americas
New York, New York 10019

Department of Biological Psychiatric Institute
722 West 168th Street
New York, New York 10032

Department of Health Economics
School of Public Health, UCLA

Center for the Health Sciences
Los Angeles, California 90024

Department of Health Services
School of Public Health, UCLA
Center for the Health Sciences
Los Angeles, California 90024

Department of Pathology, UCLA
Center for the Health Sciences
Los Angeles, California 90024

Department of Psychiatry
Kaiser-Permanente Medical Center
1515 North Vermont Avenue
Los Angeles, California 90027

Department of Psychiatry and Biobehavioral Sciences
Associate Dean for Curricular and Student Affairs
UCLA School of Medicine
760 Westwood Plaza
Los Angeles, California 90024

Department of Psychiatry and Biobehavioral Sciences
UCLA School of Medicine, The Neuropsychiatric Institute
760 Westwood Plaza
Los Angeles, California 90024

Department of Psychiatry and Biobehavioral Sciences, UCLA
Psychology Department of the Veterans Administration Hospital Brentwood
Los Angeles, California 90073

Department of Psychology
University of Oregon
Eugene, Oregon 97403

Division of Cardiology, UCLA
Center for the Health Sciences
Los Angeles, California 90024

Division of Epidemiology
School of Public Health

University of Minnesota
1360 May Memorial Building
420 Delaware Street S. E.
Minneapolis, Minnesota 55455

Drug Dependence Treatment and Research Center
Philadelphia V. A. Hospital
University and Woodland Avenues
Philadelphia, Pennsylvania 19104

Health Care Research Office of Planning and Program Analysis
Department of Health, State of California
714 P Street
Sacramento, California 95814

Institute of Psychiatry
Maudsley Hospital
Addiction Research Unit
101 Denmanrk Hill
London, England

Psychopharmacology Unit
Veterans Administration Hospital Brentwood
Los Angeles, California 90073

Research Psychiatry Department, UCLA
Camarillo-Neuropsychiatric Institute Research Center
Box A
Camarillo, California 93010

School of Public Health, UCLA
Center for the Health Sciences
Los Angeles, California 90024

Social Science Office of Field Studies and Statistics
National Cancer Institute
National Institutes of Health
Bethesda, Maryland 20014

UCLA Cancer Center
Center for the Health Sciences
Los Angeles, California 90024

GAMBLING

The diagnoses of addictive gambling is usually made by the family, friends, employers, co-workers, and sometimes peer gamblers (with whom the gambler can always be located). Unpaid bills, debts, loss of jobs, credit, credibility, and the visible evidence of one or more forms of excessive gambling that interferes with familial, social, interpersonal, economic, and work life, makes the diagnoses far easier than many of the other addictions. Because gambling addiction results in the loss of money which is so central to one's survival and to those who depend upon the addictive gambler, the damage is often great and the by-products of the addicts life threatening. Depressions and false elations are common rollercoaster emotions sustained by the gambler and those who live with him. The deceit of his denials, false charm and exploitations often provoke retaliatory hostility that create dramatic episodes of destructiveness.

In their 1973-1976 reports, the National Commission on Compulsive Gambling estimated there were 1,100,000 gambling-addicted people in the United States. The National Council on Compulsive Gambling recently estimated that six million people were compulsive gamblers. Unfortunately, accurate statistics do not exist, although the number of gambling addicts is growing. Gambling is the most neglected of the addictions. Far too little diagnoses, research, treatment, and recognition of gambling as an illness has been done up to now. The American Psychiatric Association, for the first time, is listing it in their DSM3 under Pathological Gambling 312:1. A number of states are being presented with legislation which will recognize the needs for diagnostic, research, and treatment funds for the addicted gambler. The resources for help are growing as more pioneers in the field work toward extending help to the gambler and his family.

Facilities Available For the Addicted Gambler

Gamblers Anonymous organizations can be found listed in your telephone book. One hundred fifty such groups exist throughout the country—sixty in New York alone. This group was founded in 1957. They base their techniques on the twelve-step program of Alcoholics Anonymous. Organizations exist in Canada, Great Britain, Ireland, Scotland, Australia—thirteen foreign countries in all. They offer not only self-help treatment, but educational material as well, including their booklet, *Gamblers Anonymous* which includes "A Gambler's Twenty Question Test." You can send for starter kits if you wish to form your own Gamblers Anonymous (Gam-Anon) for spouses and significant others—at no cost. For information write Gamblers Anonymous, National Service Office, P.O. Box 17173, Los Angeles, Cal. 90017.

National Council on Compulsive Gambling is a central clearinghouse for organizational research or professional (psychiatric, psychological, social organizational contacts) liaison with the community, educational literature, and listings of Gamblers Anonymous Groups. A pioneer in this field is Monseigneur Joseph Dunn in the New York Chapter. His monthly publication, "The Christopher's News Notes" (12 East 48th Street, New York, New York 10017) contains information on signs, causes, life styles, and treatment programs for industry, insurance companies, etc. along with the latest research being conducted by ancillary professionals such as psychiatrists and psychologists. You may write to him in care of The National Council on Compulsive Gambling, 99 Park Avenue, New York, New York 10016. Telephone 212-686-6160.

CONCLUSION

If all else fails in your inquiry for help, turn to your yellow page listings for *Alcoholism Information and Treatment Centers* and *Drug Abuse Addiction Information and Treatment, Reducing and Weight Control Services* and *Smoke Information and Treatment Centers.* Make absolutely sure that these services are under the control of licensed and certified professionals recognized and referred to in your community by other professionals in these respective addictive fields.

Should none of these resources satisfy you and do not check out as legitimate, you may write to the National Clearing House for Drug Abuse Information, Parklawn Building, Room 10A56, 5600 Fishers Lane, Rockville, Maryland 20857. They have the capacity to review their data tapes of all current drug abuse programs and respond to individual requests for clinics/programs in single areas of the entire United States.

PART V
BIBLIOGRAPHICAL RESOURCES

For those interested in digging in to even greater depth to discover what is currently known about the *psychological* diagnoses, definition, causes, and treatment of the addictions, I have included a bibliography of works on addictions and self-help, and on therapeutic communities—the latter because of its increasingly potent role in the treatment of addications.

The literature on the addictions is voluminous. I have chosen a selective up-to-date bibliography for each addiction described in this book and for smoking and gambling. I have tailored the bibliography to the pragmatic needs of people interested in the psychological diagnosis, dynamics, and therapy of addiction. Because of this focus, I have excluded the vast literature on the genetic, constitutional, socioeconomic, cultural, chemical, epidemiologic, physiologic, biochemical, and genetic aspects of the addictions. These must be taken into account in order to understand and treat the addictive process, and reading about them is invaluable. The more comprehensive a picture you have of these elements, the better you will come to understand the incredible complexities of the addictive process. You will also become convinced of the absolute necessity for multimodal therapy. You will become aware of the enormity of past and current research done by an army of men and women who have continuously struggled to explore and treat addictions.

Except for a few source articles, this list covers the past fifteen years (1964-1979) and includes only each author's most relevant work. Many of these publications have comprehensive bibliographies. A list of all the significant recent contributions to our knowledge would require a book in itself. The scope of what has been written reflects the challenge of addiction to clinicians, researchers, and scholarly investigators. Even as I make this list, new contributors to the field work into the night or arise before dawn to add to our knowledge. Perhaps some, like myself, have approached the subject with addictive fervor only to perpetuate the tradition of excess on the subject of excess.

ALCOHOL

Ablon, A. "Abstinence Criteria: A Critique of Abstinence in the Treatment of Alcoholism." *Journal of Social Psychiatry* 14 (1968): 260-267.

———. "Al-Anon Family Group: Impetus for Change Through the Presentation of Alternatives." *American Journal of Psychotherapy* 28 (1974): 1-30.

———. *Alcohol and Health.* U. S. Department of Health, Education, and Welfare. December 1971.

———. "Family Structure and Behavior in Alcoholism." A review of the literature in *The Etiology and Biology of Alcoholism.* Edited by B. Lessen and N. Begleiter. Vol. 6 (1976).

Alcoholics Anonymous World Service, Inc. *This is Alcoholics Anonymous.* New York: Alcoholics Anonymous World Service, Inc., 1961.

Allman, L. R. "Group Drinking During Stress: Effects on Alcohol Intake and Group Process." *The International Journal of the Addictions* 8 (1973): 475-88.

Amark, C. A. "A Study in Alcoholism: Clinical, Social, Psychiatric and Genetic Investigations." *Acta Psychiatic Scandinavic Supplement* 70 (1951): 1-283.

American Medical Association. *Manual on Alcoholism.* Edited by R. J. Shearer. Chicago: American Medical Association, 1968.

Armor, D.; Polich, J. M.; and Stambul, H. B. *Alcoholism and Treatment.* Santa Monica, California: Rand Corporation, 1976.

Aronson, H., and Gilbert, A. "Preadolescent Sons of Male Alcoholics: An Experimental Study of Personality Patterning." *Archives of General Psychiatry* 8 (1963): 235-41.

Ashley, M. J.; LeRiche, W. H.; and Olin, J. S. "Social Class and Morbidity in Clinically Treated Alcoholics." *Drugs and Alcohol Dependence* 1(4) (1976): 263-76.

Bacon, M., and Jones, M. B. *Teenage Drinking.* New York: Thomas Y. Crowell Co., 1968.

Bacon, S. D. "The Process of Addiction to Alcohol: Social Aspects." *Quarterly Journal of Studies on Alcohol* 34 (1973): 1-27.

Baekland, F., and Lundwall, L. K. "Engaging the Alcoholic in Treatment and Keeping Him There." In *The Biology of Alcoholism: Treatment and Rehabilitation of the Chronic Alcoholic.* Vol. 5. Edited by B. Kissin and H. Begleiter. New York: Plenum Press, 1977.

Baekland, F.; Lundwall, L.; and Kissen, B. "Methods for the Treatment of Chronic Alcoholism." In *A Cultural Appraisal in Research Advances in Alcohol and Drug Problems.* Edited by Israel Y. John Wiley & Sons. New York: 1976.

Baekland, F.; Lundwall, L.; and Shanahan T. J. "Correlates of Patient Attrition in the Outpatient Treatment of Alcoholism." *Journal of Nervous and Mental Disease.* 157 (1973): 99-107.

Bailey, M. B. "Alcoholism and Marriage:

A Review of Research and Professional Literatures." *Quarterly Studies on Alcohol* 22 (1961): 81-97.

————. "Al-anon Family Groups as an Aid to Wives of Alcoholics." *Social Work* 10 (1965).

Bailey, M. B., and Stewart, J. "Normal Drinking by persons Reporting Previous Problem Drinking." *Quarterly Journal of Studies on Alcohol* 28 (1967): 305-15.

Baker, T. B.; Uden, H.; and Volger, R. E. "A Short Term Alcoholism Treatment Program Using Videotape and Self-Confrontation Techniques." Paper delivered at the 80th Convention of the American Psychology Association, Honolulu, 1972.

Barnes, G. E. "The Alcoholic Personality. A Reanalysis of The Literature." *Journal of Studies on Alcohol* 40, 7, (1979): 571-634.

Barr, H. L.; Rosen, A.; Ames, D. E.; and Ottenberg, D. K. "Two Years Followup Study of 724 Drug and Alcohol Addicts Treated Together in an Abstinence Community." Paper presented at 81st American Psychological Association Annual Convention, Montreal, Canada. 1973.

Barry, H., 3rd. "Sociocultural Aspects of Alcohol Addiction." *Residents Publications Association of Nervous and Mental Disease* 46 (1968): 455-71.

Bean M. "Alcoholics Anonymous." *Psychiatric Annals* 5 (1975): 3-4.

Bebbington, P. E. "The Efficacy of Alcoholics Anonymous: The Elusiveness of Hard Data." *British Journal of Psychiatry* 128 (1976): 572-580.

Beckman, L. J. "Women Alcoholics: A Review of Social and Psychological Studies." *Journal on Studies of Alcohol* 36(7) (1975): 797-824.

Bennett, R. M.; Boss, A. H.; and Carpenter, J. A. "Alcohol and Human Physical Aggression." *Quarterly Journal of Studies on Alcohol* 30 (1969): 870-76.

Bergin, A. E.; and Garfield, S. L., eds. *Handbook of Psychotherapy and Behavior Change*. New York: John Hiley & Sons, 1971.

Berman, K. K. "Multiple Conjoint Family Group in the Treatment of Alcoholism."

Journal of Medical Sociology, New Jersey 65 (1974): 6.

Bhakta, M. "Clinical Applications of Behavior Therapy in the Treatment of Alcohol." *The Journal of Alcoholism* 6 (1971): 75-83.

Blake, B. G. "The Application of Behavior Therapy to the Treatment of Alcoholism." *Behavior Research and Therapy* 5 (1967): 89-94.

————. "Issues in the Evaluation of Alcoholism Treatment." *Professional Psychology*. Special issue (1977): 593-608.

Blane, H. T. "Trends in the Prevention of Alcoholism." *Psychology Research Reports* 43 (1090) (1968): 24, 1-9.

Blane, H. T., and Barry H. "Birth Order and Alcoholism: A Review." *Quarterly Journal of Studies on Alcohol* 34 (1973): 837-52.

Blane, H. T., and Chafetz, M. E. "Dependency Conflict and Sex-role Identity in Drinking Delinquents." *Quarterly Journal of Studies on Alcohol* 32 (1971): 1025-39.

Blane, H. J.; Hill, M. J.; and Brown, E. "Self-esteem and Attitudes Toward Drinking in High School Students." *Quarterly Journal of Studies on Alcohol* 29 (1968): 350-54.

Blane, H. T., and Hill, M. J., eds. *Frontiers of Alcoholism*. New York: Science House, 1970.

Blane, H. T., and Meyers, W. R. "Social Class and Establishment of Treatment Relations by Alcoholics." *Journal of Clinical Psychology* 20 (1964): 287-90.

Blane, H. T.; Overton, Jr. W. F.; and Chafetz, M. E. "Social Factors in the Diagnosis of Alcoholism: Characteristics of the Patient." *Quarterly Journal of Studies on Alcohol* 24 (1963): 640-63.

Blum, E. M. "Psychoanalytic Views of Alcoholism: A Review." *Quarterly Journal of Studies on Alcohol* 27 (1966): 259-79.

Blum, E. M., and Blum, R. H. *Alcoholism: Modern Psychological Approaches to Treatment*. San Francisco: Jossey Bass, 1969.

Blum, H. T. *The Personality of the Alcoholic*. New York: Harper & Row, 1968.

Blum, I., and Levine, J. "Maturity, Depression and Life Events in Middle-aged Alcoholics.'' *Addictive Behaviors* 1(1) (1975): 37-45.

Bolmen, W. M. ''Abstinence Versus Permissiveness in the Psychotherapy of Alcoholism.'' *Archives of General Psychiatry* 12 (1965): 456-63.

Bowen, R. ''Alcoholism as Viewed Through Family Systems Theory and Family Psychotherapy.'' *Annals of the N.Y. Academy of Science* 233 (1974): 115.

Bromet, E., and Moos, R. H. ''Environmental Resources and the Post Treatment Functioning of Alcoholic Patients.'' *Journal of Health and Social Behavior* 18 (1977): 326-38.

Brun, K. ''Outcome of Different Types of Treatment of Alcoholics.'' *Quarterly Journal of Studies on Alcohol* 24 (1963): 280-88.

Bullock, S. C., and Mudd, E. H. ''The Inter-relatedness of Alcoholism and Marital Conflict Symposium: The Interaction of Alcoholic Husbands and Their Non-Alcoholic Wives During Counseling.'' *American Journal of Orthopsychiatry* 29 (1959): 519-27.

Burton, G., and Kaplan, H. M. ''Sexual Behavior and Adjustment of Married Alcoholics.'' *Quarterly Journal of Studies on Alcohol* 29 (1968): 603-9.

Burton, G.; Lupton, H. M.; and Mudd, E. H. ''Marriage Counseling With Alcoholics and Their Spouses.'' *British Journal of Addiction* 63 (1968): 151.

Burton, G. ''Group Counseling with Alcoholic Husbands and Their Wives.'' *Marriage and Family Living* 24 (1962): 56.

Cahalon, D. *Problem Drinkers.* San Francisco: Jossey-Bass, 1970.

Cahalon, D.; Cisen, I. H., and Crossly, H. M. *American Drinking Behavior and Attitudes.* Monograph No. 6, Rutgers Center of Alcohol Studies, New Brunswick, 1969.

Cahalon, D., and Room, R. *Problem Drinking Among American Men.* Report of Rutgers Center of Alcohol Studies, New Brunswick, N.J., 1974.

Cahn, S. *The Treatment of Alcoholics: An Evaluation Study.* New York: Oxford University Press, 1970.

Cain, A. C. *The Cured Alcoholic.* New York: John Day, 1964.

Cappell, H., and Herman, C. P. ''Alcohol and Tension Reduction: A Review.'' *Quarterly Journal of Studies on Alcohol* 33 (88 ref) (1972): 33-64.

Cappell, H., and LeBlanc, A. E. *Biological and Behavioral Approaches to Drug Dependence.* Report of Alcoholism and Drug Addiction Research Foundation, Ontario, Canada, 1975.

Cardoret, R. Y., and Winokowr, G. ''Depression in Alcoholism.'' *Annals of the N.Y. Academy of Science* 233 (1974): 34-9.

Caster, D. U. *Tailoring Treatment Modalities to Brain Functioning in Sobering Alcoholics.* Lecture presented to Psychotherapy Associates, Fourth Annual Winter Rx and Rehabilitation of Alcoholics Workshop, Colorado Springs, Colorado, 2 February 1978.

Caster, D. U., and Parsons, O. A. ''Locus of Control in Alcoholics and Treatment Outcome.'' *Journal of Studies of Alcohol* 38 (1977): 2087-95.

Caster, D. U., and Parsons, O. A. ''Relationship of Depression, Sociopathy and Locus of Control to Treatment Outcome in Alcoholics.'' *Journal of Consulting Clinical Psychology* 45 (1977): 751-56.

Catanzaro, R. J. *Alcoholism: The Total Treatment Approach.* Springfield: Thomas, 1968.

Cautela, J. R. ''The Treatment of Alcoholism by Covert Sensitization.'' *Psychotherapy: Theory, Research, and Practice* 7(2) (1970): 86-90.

Chafetz, M. E.; Hertzman, M.; and Berenson, D. ''Alcoholism: A Positive View.'' In *American Handbook of Psychiatry*, vol. 1. Edited by S. Ariete and E. B. Brody, New York: Basic Books.

———. ''Alcohol Excess.'' *Annals of the N.Y. Academy of Science* 133(3) (1966): 808-13.

———. ''Alcoholism.'' In *Comprehensive Textbook of Psychiatry.* Edited by A. M. Freedman and H. J. Kaplan. Baltimore: Williams and Wilkins, 1967.

———. ''Alcoholism Prevention and Reality.'' *Quarterly Journal of Studies on Alcohol* 28(2) (1967): 345-48.

————. "Clinical Syndromes of Liquor Drinkers." In *Alcohol and Alcoholism.* Edited by R. E. Popham. Toronto, Ontario: University of Toronto Press, 1970.

Chafetz, M. E. *Frontiers of Alcoholism.* Edited by H. T. Blane and M. J. Hill. New York: Science House, 1970.

————. "The Prevention of Alcoholism." *International Journal of Psychiatry* 9 (1970-71): 349-54.

————. *Proceedings of the 2nd Annual Alcoholism Conference of the National Institute on Alcoholism Abuse and Alcoholism.* Health, Education, and Welfare Publication, no. (NIH) 74-676, X, 247, 54:7836, 1973.

————. "Research in the Alcohol Clinic and Around-the Clock Psychiatric Service of Massachusetts General Hospital." 124(12) (1968): 1674-79.

Chandler, J.; Hensman, C.; and Edwards, G. "Determinants of what Happens to Alcoholics." *Quarterly Journal of Studies on Alcohol* 32 (1971): 349-63.

Clark, W. B., and Cahalan, D. "Changes in Problem Drinking Over a Four Year Span." *Addictive Behavior* 1 (1976): 251-59.

Cohen, M.; Liebson, J. A.; and Faillace, L. A. "Controlled Drinking in Chronic Alcoholics Over Extended Periods of Free Access." *Psychological Reports* 32 (1973): 1107-10.

Cohen, M. *The Modification of Drinking in Recent Advances in Studies of Alcoholism.* Edited by N. Mello and J. H. Mendelson. U. S. Government Printing Office, (1971): 745-66.

Cohen, M.; Liebson, J. A.; Faillace, L. A.; and Allen, R. P. "Moderate Drinking by Chronic Alcoholics: A Schedule-dependent Phenomenon." *Journal of Nervous and Mental Disease* 153 (1971): 434-44.

Cohen, M. and Speers, W. "Alcoholism: Controlled Drinking and Incentives for Abstinence." *Psychological Reports* 28 (1971): 575-80.

Cohen, S. "The Treatment of Alcoholism: Does It Work." *Drug Abuse and Alcoholism Newsletter.* Reprint #5680. 7:3 (1978): 1-4.

Cook, T. *Vagrant Alcoholics.* Routledge and Kegan Paul Ltd., 1975.

Cooperative Commission on the Study of Alcoholism. *Alcohol Problems: A Report to the Nation.* London: Oxford University Press, 1967.

Corder, B. F.; Corder, R. F.; and Laidlaw, N. Y. "An Intensive Treatment Program for Alcoholics and Their Wives." *Quarterly Journal of Studies on Alcohol 33* (1972): 1144.

Cork, M. *The Forgotten Children.* Report to the Alcohol and Drug Addiction Research Foundation, Toronto, 1969.

Corrigan, E. M. "Women and Problem Drinking: Notes on Beliefs and Facts." *Addictive Diseases* (2) (1974): 215-22.

Crawford, J. J.; Chalupsky, A. B.; and Hurly, M. M. *The Evaluation of Psychological Approaches to Alcoholism Treatment: a Methodological Review.* Final report AIR 96502-3/73-FR, Palo Alto, California: American Institute for Research, 1973.

Criteria Committee, National Council on Alcoholism. "Criteria For the Diagnosis of Alcoholism." *American Journal of Psychiatry* 120 (1972): 127-35.

Crowley, T. J.; Chesluk, D.; Pitts, S.; and Hart, R. "Drug and Alcohol Abuse Among Psychiatry Admissions." *Archive of General Psychiatry* 39(1) (1974): 1320.

Cudogen, R. "Marital Group Therapy in the Treatment of Alcoholism." *Quarterly Journal of Studies on Alcohol 34* (1973): 1187.

Curlee, J. "Attitudes That Facilitate or Hinder the Treatment of Alcoholism." *Psychotherapy: Theory, Research and Practice* 8 (1971): 68-70.

Curtis, J. "Family Treatment for Alcoholism: A Review." *Social Work* 23:2 (1978): 135-42.

Cutter, H. S., "Alcohol Drinking Patterns and Psychological Probability of Success." *Behavioral Science* 14 (1961): 19-27.

Cutter, H. S.; Key, J. C.; Rothstein, E.; and Jones, W. C. "Alcohol Power and Inhibition." *Quarterly Journal of Studies on Alcohol 34* (1973): 581-89.

Cutter, H. S.; Schwaabe, I. Jr.; and Nathan, P. E. "Effects of Alcohol on its Utility for Alcoholics and Non-Alcoholics." *Quarterly Journal of Studies on Alcohol 37* (1970): 369-78.

Cutting, J. "Specific Psychological Defects in Alcoholism." *British Journal of Psychiatry* 1:33 (1978): 119-22.

Davis, D. I.; Berenson, D.; Steinglass, P.; and Davis, S. "The Adaptive Consequence of Drinking." *Psychiatry* 37 (1974): 209.

DeLint, J. E. "Alcoholism, Birth Order and Parental Deprivation." *British Journal of Psychiatry* 130 (1964): 1062-65.

———. "Epidemological Aspects of Alcoholism." *International Journal of Mental Health* 5(1) (1976): 29-51.

Devernyi, P., and Wilson, M. "Barbiturate Abuse and Addiction and Their Relationship to Alcohol and Alcoholism." *Canadian Medical Association Journal* 104 (1971): 215-18.

Dohertz, J. "Controlled Drinking: Valid Approach or Deadly Snare?" *Alcohol and Health Resident World* Fall (1974): 2-8.

Donovan, D. M.; Radford, L. M.; Chaney, E. F., et al. "Perceived Locus of Control as a Function of Level of Depression Among Alcoholics and Non Alcoholics." *Journal of Clinical Psychology* 33 (1977): 582-84.

Dubourg, G. O. "Aftercare for Alcoholics —A Followup Study." *British Journal of Addiction* 64 (1969): 155-63.

Eagleston, J., and Mothersheed, A. *Alcoholism Program Monitorial System Procedures Manual,* vol. 1. Menlo Park, Cal.: Stamford Research Institute, 1975.

———. "Conjoint Family Therapy With Alcoholics." *British Journal of Addiction* 66 (1971): 251.

Easser, P. H. "Conjoint Family Therapy for Alcoholics." *British Journal of Addiction* 63 (1968): 177.

Edwards, P.; Harvey, C.; and Whitehead, P. C. "Wives of Alcoholics: A Critical Review and Analysis." *Quarterly Journal of Studies on Alcohol* 34 (1972): 112-32.

Einstein, R.; Hughes, I. E.; and Hindmerch, I. "Patterns of Use of Alcohol, Cannabis and Tobacco in a Student Population." *British Journal of Addiction* 70 (1975): 145-50.

Einstein, S.; Wolfson, E.; and Gecht, P. "What Matters in the Treatment Variable in Alcoholism." *International Journal of the Addictions* 5 (1970): 43-67.

Elkins, R. L. "Aversion Therapy for Alcoholism: Chemical, Electrical or Verbal Imagery." *International Journal of the Addictions* 8 (1973): 6.

Emrick, C. D. "A Review of Psychologically Oriented Treatment of Alcoholism: The Use and Interrelationship of Outcome Criteria and Drinking Behavior Following Treatment." *Quarterly Journal of Studies on Alcohol* 35 (1974): 523-48.

———. "A Review of Psychologically Oriented Treatment of Alcoholism: The Relative Effectiveness of Different Treatment Approaches and the Effectiveness of Treatment Versus No Treatment." *Journal of Studies on Alcohol* 36 (1975): 88-109.

Ends, E. J., and Page, W. A. "A Study of Three Types of Group Psychotherapy With Hospitalized Inebriates." *Quarterly Journal of Studies on Alcohol* 18 (1957): 263-77.

Engle, K. B. and Williams, T. K. "Effects of an Ounce of Vodka on Alcoholics' Desire for Alcohol." *Quarterly Journal of Studies on Alcohol* 33 (1973): 1099-1105.

Evenson, R. C.; Altman, H.; and Sle Hen, I. W. "Factors in the Description and Grouping of Alcoholics." *American Journal of Psychiatry* 130 (1973): 49-54.

Ewing, J. A. "Concurrent Group Psychotherapy of Alcoholic Patients and Their Wives." *International Journal of Group Psychotherapy* 11 (1961): 329.

———. "Some Recent Attempts to Inculcate Controlled Drinking in Patients Resistant to Alcoholics Anonymous." *Annals of the N.Y. Academy of Sciences* 233 (1974): 147-54.

Ewing, J. A., and Fox, R. E. "Family Therapy of Alcoholism, in *Current Psychiatric Therapies.* Edited by J. H. Masserman. New York: Green & Stratton. vol 8. 1968.

Faillance, L. A.; Flamer, R. N.; Imber, S. D.; and Ward, R. F. "Giving Alcohol to Alcoholics: An Evaluation." *Quarterly Journal of Studies on Alcohol* 33 (1972): 85-90.

Feemy, F. E.; Mindlin, D. F.; Minear, V. H.; and Short, E. T. "The Challenge of the Skid Row Alcoholic: A Social Psychologican and Psychiatric Comparison of the

Chronically Jailed Alcoholic and Cooperative Alcoholic Clinic Patients.'' *Quarterly Journal of Studies on Alcohol* 16 (1955): 465-77.

Feinstein, C., and Tameren, J. S. ''Induced Intoxication and Videotape Feedback in Alcoholism Treatment.'' *Quarterly Journal of Studies on Alcohol* 33 (1972): 408-16.

Fillmore, K. ''Drinking and Problem Drinking in Early Adulthood and Middle Age.'' *Quarterly Journal of Studies on Alcohol* 35 (1974): 819-40.

————. ''Relationships Between Specific Drinking Problems in Early Adulthood and Middle Age: An Exploratory 20 year Followup Study.'' *Journal of Studies on Alcohol* 36(7) (1975): 882-907.

Filstead, W. J.; Rossi, J. J.; and Keller, M., eds. ''Alcohol and Alcohol Problems.'' In *New Thinking and New Directions*. Cambridge, Mass.: Ballinger, 1976.

Fine, E.; Yudin, L.; and Holmes, J. *Behavior Disorders in Children With Parental Alcoholism*. Annual National Council on Alcoholism Conference, Milwaukee, Wis., 1975.

Finley, D. G. ''Alcoholism and Systems Theory: Building a Better Mousetrap.'' *Psychiatry* 41:3 (1978): 272-78.

————. ''Anxiety and the Alcoholic.'' *Social Work* 17 (1972): 29-33.

————. ''Effect of Role Network Pressures on Alcoholics Approach to Treatment.'' *Social Work* 11 (1966): 71.

Flaherty, J. A.; Spitzer, R. L.; and Gatski, R. ''The Psychodynamics of the 'Dry Drink'.'' *American Journal of Psychiatry* 112 (1955): 460-64.

Forrest, G. G. *Alcoholism as an Interpersonal Process* (text in press), 1978.

————. ''A Model for Training Addiction Counselors.'' Paper presented at the Rocky Mountain Counselor Education and Supervision Convention, Denver, Col., 3 October 1976.

————. *The Diagnoses and Treatment of Alcoholism*. Second Ed., Springfield: Thomas, 1978.

Fort, J. *Alcohol: Our Biggest Drug Problem. . .And Our Biggest Drug Industry*. New York: McGraw-Hill, 1973.

Fox, R. ''A Multidisciplinary Approach to the Treatment of Alcoholism.'' *Journal of Drug Issues* 2(2) (1972): 20.

————. *Alcoholism: Progress in Research and Treatment*. New York: Academic Press, 1973.

————. ''Treating the Alcoholic's Family.'' In *Alcoholism*. Edited by R. J. Cantanzaro, Springfield: Charles C. Thomas, 1968.

Fox, R., and Lyon, P. *Alcoholism—Its Scope, Cause, and Treatment*. New York: Academic Press, 1955.

Fox, R.; Graham, M. B.; and Gill, M. J. ''A Therapeutic Revolving Door.'' *Archives of General Psychiatry* 26(2) (1972): 181.

Fox, V. ''Alcoholism in Adolescence.'' *The Journal of School Health* 43 (1973): 32-35.

Franks, C. M. ''Conditioning and Conditional Aversion Therapies in Treatment of the Alcoholic.'' *International Journal of the Addictions* (1966): 161-98.

Freed, E. X. ''Alcoholism and Manic Depressive Disorders: Some Perspectives.'' *Quarterly Journal of Studies on Alcohol* 31 (1970): 62-89.

————. ''Drug Use by Alcoholics: A Review.'' *International Journal of Addictions* 8 (1973): 451-73.

Freedman, D. X. *Alcohol: A Model Explanation for Drug Dependence*. Second Edition. National Clearinghouse for Drug Abuse Information, 1972.

Galanter, M., ed. *Currents in Alcoholism*. Vol. 5, ''Biomedical Issues and Clinical Effects of Alcoholism.'' Vol. 6, ''Treatment Rehabilitation and Epidemiology.'' New York: Grune and Stratton, 1979.

Gallen, M.; Williams, B.; Cleveland, S. B.; O'Connell, W. E.; and Sando, P. A. ''A Short Term Followup of Two Contrasting Alcoholic Treatment Programs: A Preliminary Report.'' *Newsletter for Research in Mental Health and Behavioral Science* 15 (1973): 36-37.

Gallant, D. M.; Bishop, M. P.; Mouledoux, A.; Faulkner, M. A.; Brisolara, A.; and Swanson, W. A. ''The Revolving-door Alcoholic: An Impass in Treatment of the Chronic Alcoholic.'' *Archives of General Psychiatry* 28 (1973): 633-35.

———— Rich, A.; Bey, E.; and Terranova,

L. "Group Psychotherapy with Married Couples: A Successful Technique in New Orleans Alcoholism Clinic Patients." *Journal of Louisiana State Medical Society* 122 (1970): 41.

Gerard, D. L., and Saengen, G. *Out Patient Treatment of Alcoholism.* Toronto: Toronto University Press, 1966.

Gerard, D. L., and Wile, R. "The Abstinant Alcoholic." *Archives of General Psychiatry* 6 (1962): 83-95.

Gibson, S., and Becker, J. "Changes in Alcoholism, Self Reported Depression." *Quarterly Journal of Studies on Alcohol* 34 (1973): 829-36.

Gilbert, J. G., and Lombardi, D. M. "Personality Characteristics of Young Male Narcotic Addicts." *Journal of Consulting Psychology* 31 (1967): 536-38.

Gillies, M.; Laverty, S. G.; Smart, R. G.; and Aheeron, C. H. "Outcomes in Treated Alcoholics." *Journal of Alcoholism* 9 (1974): 125.

Gillis, L. J., and Keet, M. "Prognostic Factors in Treatment Results in Hospitalized Alcoholics." *Quarterly Journal of Studies on Alcohol* 30 (1969): 426-37.

Gitlow, S. E. "Alcoholism: A Disease." In *Alcoholism Progress in Research and Treatment.* Edited by P. B. Bourne and R. Fox. New York: Academic Press, 1973.

Glasscote, R. M.; Plaut, T. F.; and Hammersley, D. W., et al. *The Treatment of Alcoholism.* Joint Information Service of the National Institute of Mental Health and American Psychiatric Association, Washington, D.C., 1967.

Glasscote, R. M.; Sussex, J. N.; Jaffe, J. H.; Bull, J.; and Bull, L. *The Treatment of Drug Abuse: Programs, Problems, Proposals.* Joint Information Service of the National Institute of Mental Health and American Psychiatric Association, Washington, D.C., 1972.

———. *The Alcoholic and the Help He Needs.* London: Priory Press, 1970.

———. *Drugs, Society and Man: A Guide to Addiction and its Treatment.* New York: Halsted Press (Wiley), 1974.

———. "Psychotherapy of Drug Dependence: Some Theoretical Considerations." *British Journal of the Addictions* 65 (1970): 51-62.

———. "The Question of Moderate Drinking Despite Loss of Control." *British Journal of the Addictions* 62 (1967): 267-74.

Gleidman, L. H.; Nash, H. T.; and Webb, W. L. "Group Psychotherapy of Male Alcoholics and Their Wives." *Disease of the Nervous System* 17 September 1956, 90.

Gleidman, L. H. "Concurrent and Combined Group Rx of Chronic Alcoholics and Their Wives." *International Journal of Group Psychotherapy* 7 (1957): 414.

Gleidman, L. H.; Rosenthal, D.; Frants, D. C.; and Nash, H. T. "Group Therapy of Alcoholics With Concurrent Group Meetings With Their Wives." *Quarterly Journal of Studies on Alcohol* 17 (1956): 655.

Globetti, G. A. *A Survey of Teenage Drinking in Two Mississippi Communities.* (Preliminary Report no. 3). Social Science Research Center, Mississippi University, Miss. 1964.

Goldfried, M. B. "Prediction of Improvement in an Alcoholism Outpatient Clinic." *Quarterly Journal of Studies on Alcohol* 28 (1967): 76-104.

Goldman, M. S. "Drink or Not to Drink—Experimental Analysis of Group Drinking: Decision of Four Alcoholics." *American Journal of Psychiatry* 131 (1974): 1123-36.

Goodwin, D. W., "Familial Alcoholism: A Diagnostic Entity?" In *Critical Issues in Psychiatric Diagnoses.* Edited by R. L. Spitzer and D. F. Kileen. New York: Raven Press, 1978.

Goodwin, D. W.; David, D. H.; and Robins, L. N. "Drinking Amid Abundant Illicit Drugs: The Vietnam Case." *Archives of Psychiatry* 82 (1975): 230-33.

Goodwin, D. W., and Hill, S. "Chronic Effects of Alcohol and Other Psychoactive Drugs on Intellect, Learning and Memory." In *Alcohol, Drugs and Brain Damage.* Edited by R. J. Toronto. Ontario, Canada: Addiction Research Foundation Press, 1975.

Goodwin, D. W.; Schulsinger, F.; Hermansen, L., et al. "Alcohol Problems in Adoptees Raised Apart From Alcoholic Biological Parents." *Archives of General Psychiatry* 28 (1973): 238-43.

Goodwin, D. W.; Schulsinger, F.; Moller, N.; et al. "Drinking Problems in Adopted and Non-Adopted Sons of Alcoholics." *Archives of General Psychiatry* 31 (1974): 164-69.

Gorad, S. L. "Communicational Styles and Interaction of Alcoholics and Their Wives." *Family Process Bulletin* 10 (1971): 475-89.

Gossop, M. R., and Roy, A. "Hostility in Drug Dependent Individuals: Its Relation to Specific Drugs and Oral or Intravenous Use." *British Journal of Psychiatry* 128 (1976): 188-93.

Gottheil, E.; Alferman, A.; Skoloda, T.; and Murphy, B. "Alcoholics Patterns of Controlled Drinking." *American Journal of Psychiatry* 130 (1973): 418-22.

Gottheil, E.; Crawford, H. D.; and Cornelison, F. S. "The Alcoholics' Ability to Resist a Valuable Alcohol." *Disease of Nervous System* 34 (1974): 80-82.

Gottheil, E.; Corbert, L. O.; Grasberger, J. C.; and Cornelison, F. S. "Fixed Interval Drinking Decision: Research and Treatment Model." *Quarterly Journal of Studies on Alcohol* 33 (1972): 311-24.

―――. "Treating the Alcoholic in the Presence of Alcohol." *American Journal of Psychiatry* 128 (1971): 107-12.

Gottheil, E.; Murphy, B.; Skoloda, T.; and Corbert, L. O. "Fixed Interval Drinking Decisions: Drinking and Discomfort in 25 Alcoholics." *Quarterly Journal of Studies on Alcohol* 33 (1972): 325-40.

Griffith, R.; Bigelow; and Liebson, F. "Effect of Ethanol Self-administration on Choice Behavior Money Versus Socializing." *Pharmacology, Biology and Behavior* 3 (1975): 443-46.

―――. "Effect of Ethanol Self-administration in Alcoholics on Social Interactors in Alcoholics." *Psychopharmacologia* 38 (1974): 105-10.

―――. "Suppression of Ethanol Self-administration in Alcohols Lag Contingent Time-out from Social Interactions." *Behavior Research and Therapy* 12 (1974): 327-34.

Grittman, O. "The Psychodynamics of a Drug Addiction." *American Journal of Psychotherapy* 19 (1965): 653-65.

Gross, M. M. *Advances in Experimental Medicine and Biology―Alcohol Intoxication and Withdrawal: Experimental Studies II.* Vol. 59, New York: Plenum Press, 1975.

Gross, W. F., and Nerviano, V. J. "The Prediction of Dropouts from an Inpatient Alcoholism Program by Objective Personality Inventories." *Quarterly Journal of Studies on Alcohol* 34 (1973): 514-15.

Guzes, S. B.; Tuason, V. B.; Stewart, M. A.; and Picken, B. "The Drinking History: A Comparison of Reports by Subjects and Their Relatives." *Quarterly Journal of Studies on Alcohol* 24 (1963): 249-60.

Haberman, P. W. "Childhood Symptoms in Children of Alcoholics and Comparison Group Parents." *Journal of Marriage* 28 (1966): 152-54.

―――. "Some Characteristics of Alcoholics Differentiated by the Level of Deviance." *Journal of Marriage and Family* 27 (1965): 34-36.

Hamburg, S. "Behavior Therapy in Alcoholism: A Critical Review of Broad Spectrum Approaches." *Journal of Studies on Alcohol* 36 (1975): 69-87.

Hampton, P. J. "Representative Studies of Alcoholism and Personality." *Journal of Social Psychiatry* 34 (1957): 203-33.

―――. "Representative Studies of Alcoholism and Personality." *Journal Of Social Psychiatry* 35 (1952): 23-35.

Hanson, J. "College Students' Reason for Drinking: Twenty Year Trends." *College Student Journal* 9(3) (1975): 256-57.

Hartman, D. "A Study of Drug-taking Adolescents." *Psychoanalytic Study of The Child* 24 (1969): 384-98.

Hayman, M. "The Myth of Social Drinking." *American Journal of Psychiatry* 124 (1967): 585-92.

Hecht, M. "Children of Alcoholics are Children at Risk." *American Journal of Nursing* 3(10) (1973): 1764-67.

Hedberg, A. G. and Campbell, L. III. "A Comparison of Four Behavioral Treatments of Alcoholism." *Journal of Behavior Therapy and Experimental Psychiatry* 5 (1974): 251-56.

Hershon, H. I. "Alcohol Withdrawal Symptoms: Phenomenology and Implications." *British Journal of Addiction* 68(4)

(1973): 295-302.

Higgins, R. L., and Marlakt, G. A. "The Effects of Anxiety Arousal on Consumption of Alcohol by Alcoholics and Social Drinkers." *Journal of Counseling and Clinical Psychology* 41 (1973): 426-33.

Hill, M. J., and Blane, H. T. "Evaluation of Psychotherapy with Alcoholics: A Critical Review." In *Frontiers of Alcoholism*. New York: Science House, 1970.

————. "Evaluation of Psychotherapy with Alcoholics: A Critical Review." *Quarterly Journal of Studies on Alcohol* 28 (1967): 76-104.

Hill, M. J.; Haertzen, C. A.; and Davis, H. "An MMPI Factor Analutic Study of Alcoholics, Narcotic Addicts and Criminals." *Quarterly Journal of Studies on Alcohol* 33 (1962): 411-31.

Hindman, M. "Rational Emotive Therapy in Alcoholism Treatment." *Alcohol Health Research World* Spring (1976): 14-16.

Hoff, E. C. *Alcoholism: The Hidden Addiction*. New York: Seabury Press, 1974.

Hoff, E. L. "Group Therapy with Alcoholics." *Psychiatric Residency Report* 24 (1968): 61-70.

Hoffman, H., and Noem, A. "Social Background Variables, Referral Sources and Life Events of Male and Female Alcoholics." *Psychological Reports* 37(3) (1975): 1087-92.

Hoffman, H., and Jansen, D. G. "Relationships Among Discharge Variables and MMPI Scale Scores of Hospitalized Alcoholics." *Journal of Clinical Psychology* 29 (1973): 475-77.

Hore, B. D. "Life Events and Alcoholic Relapse." In *Alcohol Dependence and Smoking Behavior*. Edited by G. Edwards, M. A. H. Russel, D. Hawks, and M. McCaffertz. Farnborough, Hampshire, England: Sexon House, 1976.

————. "Craving for Alcohol." *British Journal of Addiction* 69 (1974): 137-40.

Hoy, R. M. "The Personality of Important Alcoholic Relation to Group Psychotherapy, as Measured by 16PF." *Quarterly Journal on Alcohol* 30 (1969): 401-07.

Hunt, G. M., and Azron, N. H. "A Community Reinforcement Approach to Alcoholism." *Behavioral Research and Therapy* 11 (1973): 91-104.

Hurwitz, J. F., and Lelos, D. A. "A Multilevel Interpersonal Profile of Employed Alcoholics." *Quarterly Journal of Studies on Alcohol* 29 (1968): 74-76.

Hyde, M. O. *Alcohol: Drink or Drug*. New York: McGraw-Hill, 1974.

Jackson, J. K. "Alcoholism and the Family." *Annals of the American Academy of Political and Social Science*, 1958.

————. "Alcoholism and the Family in Society." In *Culture and Drinking Patterns*. Edited by D. J. Pittman and C. R. Snyder. New York: Wiley, 1962.

————. "The Adjustment of the Family to the Crisis of Alcoholism." *Quarterly Journal of Studies on Alcohol* 15 (1954): 562.

Jackson, J. K.; James, J. E.; and Goldman. "Behavior Trends of Wives of Alcoholics." *Quarterly Journal of Studies on Alcohol* 32(2) (1971): 73-81.

Jackson, J. K., and Kogank, L. "The Search for Solutions, Help Seeking Patterns of Families of Active and Inactive Alcoholics." *Quarterly Journal of Studies on Alcohol* 24 (1963): 449-72.

Jacobson, G. R. *The Alcoholisms: Detection, Assessment, and Diagnosis.*, New York: Human Sciences Press, 1976.

Jellenick, E. M. "Phases of Alcohol Addiction." *Quarterly Journal of Studies on Alcohol* 13 (1952): 673-84.

————. *The Disease Concept of Alcoholism*. New Haven: Hullhouse Press, 1960.

————. "Phases in the Drinking History of Alcoholics: Analysis of a Survey Conducted by the Official Organ of Alcoholics Anonymous." *Quarterly Journal of Studies on Alcohol* 7 (1946): 1-88.

Jellenick, E. M.; Isbell, H.; Lindquist, G.; Tiebout, H. M.; Duchone, H.: Mardons, J.; and MacLeod, L. D. "The Craving for Alcohol, A Symposium by Members of the World Health Organization, Expert Committees on Mental Health and Alcohol." *Quarterly Journal of Studies on Alcohol* 16 (1955): 35-66.

Jellenick, E. M., and McFarland. R. A. "Analysis of Psychological Experiments on the Effects of Alcohol.'' *Quarterly Journal of Studies on Alcohol* J (1940): 272-371.

Jessor, R.; Carman, R. S.; and Grossman, P. H. ''Expectations of Need Satisfaction and Drinking Patterns of College Students.'' *Quarterly Journal of Studies on Alcohol* 29 (1968): 101-16.

Jessor, R.; Collins, M. I.; and Jessor, S. L. ''On Becoming a Drinker: Social-Psychological Aspects of Adolescent Transition.'' In *Nature and Nurture in Alcoholism.* Edited by F. E. Seixas. Annals of the N.Y. Academy of Science, 1972.

Jessor, R.; Graves, T. D.; Hansen, R. C.; and Jessor, S. L. *Society, Personality and Deviant Behavior—A Study of a Tri-ethnic Community.* New York: Holt, Rinehart, & Winston, 1968.

Jessor, R., and Jessor, S. L. ''Problem Drinking in Youth: Personality, Social and Behavioral Antecedents and Correlates.'' In *Research on Alcoholism: II Psychological and Social Factors in Drinking.* Washington, D.C.: U. S. Government Printing Office, (in press).

Johnson, V. E. *I'll Quit Tomorrow.* New York: Harper & Row, 1973.

Jones, H. *Alcoholic Addiction: A Psycho Social Approach to Abnormal Drinking.* London: Tavistock, 1953.

Jones, M. ''Personality Correlates and Antecedents of Drinking Patterns in Adult Males.'' *Journal of Consulting Clinical Psychology* 32 (1963): 2-12.

Kalant, H., and Sellers, E. M. ''Drug Therapy: Alcohol Intoxication and Withdrawal.'' *New England Journal of Medicine* 294(14) (April 1976): 757-62.

Kalant, H.; LeBlanc, A. E.; and Gibbins, R. J. ''Tolerance to, and Dependence on, Ethanol.'' In *Biological Basis of Alcoholism.* Edited by Y. Israel and J. Mardones. New York: Wiley-Interscience, 1971.

Kammeir, M. L. ''Adolescents from Families With and Without Alcoholic Problems.'' *Quarterly Journal of Studies on Alcohol* 32(2) (1971): 362-72.

Kaplan, E. H., and Weiden, H. ''Treatment and Conclusion.'' In *Drugs Take People—People Take Drugs.* New York: Lyle Stuart, 1974.

Keller, M., ed. ''Trends in Treatment of Alcoholism.'' In *Second Special Report to the U. S. Congress on Alcohol and Health, 1979.* Washington, D.C.: Department of Health, Education, and Welfare, 1979: 145-67.

———. ''Oddities of Alcoholics.'' *Quarterly Journal of Studies on Alcohol* 33(4) (1972): 1147-48.

———. ''On the Loss of Control Phenomena in Alcoholism.'' *British Journal of Addiction* 67 (1972): 153-66.

Kelly. ''Alcoholism and the Family.'' *Maryland State Medical Journal* 22(1) (1973): 25.

Kendall, R. E. ''Normal Drinking by Former Alcohol Addicts.'' *Quarterly Journal of Studies on Alcohol* 26 (1965): 247-57.

Kennedy, D. L. ''Behavior of Alcoholics and Spouses in Simulation Game Situation.'' *Journal of Nervous and Mental Disease* 162(1) (1967): 23-24.

Kessel, J. *The Road Back, A Report on Alcoholics Anonymous.* New York: Alfred A. Knopf, 1962.

Killers, P. G., and Well, C. L. ''Group Therapy of Alcoholics.'' *Current Psychiatric Therapy* 7 (1967): 174-78.

Kish, G. B., and Herman, H. T. ''The Fort Meade Alcoholism Treatment Program: A Followup Study.'' *Quarterly Journal of the Study of Alcohol* 32 (1971): 628-35.

Kissin, B., and Begleiter, H., eds. ''Clinical Pathology.'' In *Biology of Alcoholism.* Vol. 3., New York: Plenum Press, 1974.

———. eds. ''Treatment and Rehabilitation of the Chronic Alcoholic.'' In *Biology of Alcoholism.* Vol. 5., New York: Plenum Press, 1977.

———. Platz, A.; and Su, W. H. ''Social and Psychological Factors in the Treatment of Chronic Alcoholism.'' *Journal of Psychiatric Research* 8 (1970): 13-27.

Kissin, B.; Rosenblatt, S. M.; and Machover, S. M. ''Prognostic Factors in Alcoholism.'' *Psychiatric Resident Report* 24 (1968): 22-43.

———. ''Progressive Factors in Alcoholism.'' *Psychiatric Research Report* part I, 24 (1968): 22-43; part II, 24 (1968): 44-60.

Kleinknicht, R. A., and Goldstein, S. G. ''Neuropsychological Deficits Associated with Alcoholism." *Quarterly Journal of Studies on Alcohol* 33 (1972): 999-1019.

Knanert, A. P. *The Alcoholic Personality: Myth or Reality.* Lecture presented at Psychotherapy Association Third Winter Rx and Rehabilitation of the Alcoholic Workshop, Colorado Springs, Col., 31 January 1977.

Kogan, K. "Some Concomitants of Personal Difficulties in Wives of Alcoholics and Non-alcoholics." *Quarterly Journal of Studies on Alcohol* 26 (1965): 595-604.

Kogan, K., and Jackson, J. "Patterns of Atypical Perceptions of Self and Spouse in Wives of Alcoholics." *Quarterly Journal of Studies on Alcohol* 25 (1964): 55-57.

———. "Stress Personality and Emotional Disturbance in Wives of Alcoholics." *Quarterly Journal of Studies on Alcohol* 26 (1965): 486.

Koller, K. M., and Castinmast, H. "Family Background and Life Situation in Alcoholics." *Archives of General Psychiatry* 21 (1969): 603-10.

Krystal, H., and Moore, R. A. "Who is Qualified to Treat the Alcoholic? A Discussion." *Quarterly Journal of Studies on Alcohol* 24 (1963): 705-20.

Lazarus, H. A. "Toward the Understanding and Effective Treatment of Alcoholism." *South African Medical Journal* 39 (1965): 736-41.

Lenere, F. "Comment on Normal Drinking in Recovered Alcohol Adults." *Quarterly Journal of Studies on Alcohol* 24 (1963): 723-28.

Lester, D. "The Addictive Personality." *Psychology* 13:2 (1976): 53-57.

Levinson, T. *The Donwood Institute—A Five Year Followup Study.* Presented at 31st International Congress on Alcoholism and Drug Dependence, 1975.

Leventhal, H. "Fear for Your Health." *Psychology Today* 165 (1967): 54-58.

Leventhal, H. and Avis, N., "Pleasure, Addiction and Habit: Factors in Verbal Report or Factors in Smoking Behavior." *Journal of Abnormal Psychology* 85(5) (1976): 478-88.

Leventhal, H., and Niles, P. "A Field Experiment on Fear Arousal with Data on the Validity of Questionnaire Measures." *Journal of Personality and Social Psychology* 32(3) (1964): 459-79.

Leventhal, H.; Watts, J. C.; and Pagano, F. "Effects of Fear and Instructions on How to Cope with Danger." *Journal of Personality and Social Psychology* 6(3) (1967): 313-32.

Linsky, A. S. "Theories of Behavior and the Social Control of Alcoholism." *Social Psychiatry* 7 (1972): 47-52.

Lisman, S. A. "Alcoholic Blackout State Dependent Learning?" *Archives of General Psychiatry* 40(1) (1974): 46-53.

Lobell, H. "Craving for Alcohol." *Quarterly Journal of Studies on Alcohol* 16 (1955): 38-42.

Ludwing, A. M. "The First Drink-Psychological Aspects of Craving." *Archives of General Psychiatry* 30 (1979): 539-47.

———. "The Irresistable Rage and Unquenchable Thirst for Alcohol." Edited by M. E. Chaefitz. Proceedings of the 4th Annual Conference on Alcohol Abuse and Alcoholism Researching, Treatment, Prevention. Washington D.C.: Health, Education & Welfare, Publication #76 (1975): 284-322.

———. "On and Off the Wagon." *Quarterly Journal of Studies on Alcohol* 33 (1972): 91-96.

Ludwig, A. M.; Levens, J.; Stark, L. H.; and David L. S. *Alcoholism: A Clinical Study of Treatment Efficiency.* Springfield, Ill.: C. C. Thomas, 1970.

Ludwig, A. M., and Wikler, A. "Craving and Relapse to Drink." *Quarterly Journal of Studies on Alcohol* 35 (1974): 108-130.

Ludwig, A. M.; Wikler, A.; and Stark, L. H. "The First Drink: Psycho-Biological Aspects of Craving." *Archives of General Psychiatry* 30 (1974): 539-47.

MacAndrew, and Edgarton, R. B. *Drunken Comportment: A Social Explanation.* Chicago: Aldene Publishing Company, 1969.

MacDonald, D. E. "Group Psychotherapy With Wives of Alcoholics." *Quarterly Journal of Studies on Alcohol* 19 (1958): 125.

McCell and D.C. et al. *The Drinking Man.* The Free Press, 1972.

Machover, S., and Piszzop, F. S. "Clinical and Objective Studies of Personality Variables in Alcoholism." *Quarterly Journal of Studies on Alcohol* 20 (1959): 505-42.

Maddox, G. L., and McCall, B. C. *Drinking Among Teenagers.* Monograph of Rutgers Center of Alcoholic Studies, New Brunswick, N.J., 1964.

Madsen, W. *The American Alcoholic: The Nature-Nurture Controversies in Alcoholic Research and Therapy.* Springfield, Ill.: C. C. Thomas, 1974.

Mann, M. *New Primer on Alcoholism.* Second Edition. New York: Holt, Rinehart & Winston, 1968.

Marconi, J.; Fink, F.; and Maya, L. "Experimental Study on Alcoholics With an Inability to Stop." *British Journal of Psychiatry* 113 (1967): 543-45.

Marcovitz, E. "On the Nature of Addiction to Cigarettes." *Journal of the American Psychoanalytic Association* 17 (1969): 1074-96.

Margoles, M., and Siegel, S. "Psychotherapy with Alcoholic Offenders." *Quarterly Journal of Alcohol* 25 (1964): 85-99.

Marlatt, G. A.; Demming, B.; and Reid, J. B. "Loss of Control Drinking in Alcoholics: An Experimental Analogue." *Journal of Abnormal Psychology* 81 (1973): 233-41.

Mayer, J., and Black, R. *Child Care Issues in Families with Alcoholism.* National Council On Alcoholism Annual Forum, Washington, D.C., 1976.

Mayer, J., and Myerson, D. J. "Outpatient Treatment of Alcoholics, Effects of Status Stability and Nature of Treatment." *Quarterly Journal of Studies on Alcohol* 3 (1971): 620-27.

McClelland, D. C. "Cross Cultural Study of Folktale Comment on Drinking." *Sociometry* 29 (1966): 308-33.

McClelland, D. C.; Davis, W. N.; Kahn, R. and Warner, E. *The Drinking Man.* New York: Free Press, 1972.

McCord, S. "Etiological Factors in Alcoholism: Family and Personal Characteristics." *Quarterly Journal of Alcohol* 33 (1972): 1020-27.

McCord, W. and McCord, J. *Origins of Alcoholism.* Palo Alto, Cal.: Stanford University Press, 1960.

McCuen, E. R. *Social Variables of Geriatric Alcoholism.* Presented at National Council on Alcoholism Forum, Washington, D.C., May, 1976.

McGinnis, C. A. "The Effect of Group Therapy on the Ego Strength Scale Scores of Alcoholic Patients." *Journal of Clinical Psychology* 19 (1963): 346-347.

McGuire, M. T.; Stein, S.; and Mendelson, J. H. "Comparative Psychosocial Studies of Alcoholic and Non-alcoholic Subjects Undergoing Experimentally Induced Intoxication." *Psychosomatic Medicine* 28 (1966): 13-26.

McKay, J., R. "Juvenile Delinquency and Drinking Behavior." *Journal of Health and Social Behavior* 4 (Winter 1963): 276-82.

McNamee, H. B.; Mello, H. K.; and Mendelson, J. H. "Experimental Analysis of Drinking Patterns of Alcoholics: Concurrent Psychiatric Observations." *American Journal of Psychiatry* 124 (1968): 81-87.

McWilliams, J., and Brown, C. C. "Treatment Termination Variables, MMPI Scores and Frequencies of Relapse in Alcoholics." *Quarterly Journal of Studies on Alcohol* 38 (1977): 477-86.

Mello, N. K. "Behavioral Studies of Alcoholism." In *Biology of Alcoholism.* Edited by B. Kissin, H. Begleiter. Vol. 2, New York: Plenum Press, 1972.

Mello, N. K., and Mendelson, J. H. "Drinking Patterns During Work-Contingent and Non-Contingent Alcohol Acquisition." *Psychomatic Medicine* 34 (1972): 139-164.

———. "Experimentally Induced Intoxication in Alcoholics: A Comparison Between Programmed and Spontaneous Drinking." *Journal of Pharmacology* 173 (1970): 101-16.

———. "Operant Analysis of drinking Patterns of Chronic Alcoholics." *Nature* 206 (1965): 43-46.

———. "A Quantitative Analysis of Drinking Patterns in Alcoholics." *Archives of General Psychiatry* 25 (1971): 527-39.

Mellon, N. K.; McNamee, H. B.; and Mendelson, J. H. "Drinking Patterns of Chronic Alcoholics: Gambling and Motivations for Alcohol." *Psychiatric Research Report* 24 (1968): 83-118.

Mendelson, J. H. "Biologic Concommitants of Alcoholism." *New England Journal of Medicine* 283 (1970): (part 1), 24-32; (part 2), 71-81.

———. ed. "Experimentally Induced Chronic Intoxication and Withdrawal in Alcoholics." *Quarterly Journal of Studies on Alcohol*. Supplement no. 2, (1964).

Mendelson, J. H., and Mello, N. K. "Experimental Analysis of Drinking Behavior of Chronic Alcoholics." *Annals of the N.Y. Academy of Science* 133(3) (1966): 828-45.

Mendelson, J. H. and Mello, N. K. "Diagnosis" and Treatment of Alcoholism. New York: McGraw Hill, 1979.

Mendelson, J. H., and Steinglass, P. "Interactional Issues as Determinants of Alcoholism." *American Journal of Psychology* 128 (1971): 275-80.

Merry, J. "The Loss of Control Myth." *Lancet* I (1966): 1257-58.

Merrick, R., ed. *Life History Research in Psychopathology*. Vol. I. Minneapolis: University of Minnesota Press, 1970.

Miller, B. A.; Pokorny, A. D.; and Hanson, P. G. "A Study of Dropouts in an Inpatient Alcoholism Treatment Program." *Diseases of the Nervous System* 29 (1968): 91-99.

Miller, B. A.; Pokorny, A. D.; and Kanas, T. E. "Problems in Treating Homeless, Jobless Alcoholics." *Hospital and Community Psychiatry* 21 (1971): 98-99.

Miller, B. A.; Pokorny, A. D.; Valles, J.; and Cleveland, S. E. "Biased Sampling in Alcoholism Treatment Research." *Quarterly Journal of Studies on Alcohol* 31 (1970): 97-107.

Miller, D., and Jang, M. "Children of Alcoholics: A 20-Year Longitudinal Study." *Social Work Research and Abstracts* 13(4) (1977).

Miller, P. M. "The Use of Behavioral Contracting in the Treatment of Alcoholism: A Case Report." *Behavior Therapy* 3 (1972): 593-96.

Miller, P. M., and Barlow, D. H. "Behavioral Approaches to the Treatment of Alcoholics." *Journal of Nervous and Mental Disease* 157 (1973): 10-20.

Miller, P. M.; Hersen, M.; and Eisler, R. M. "Relative Effectiveness of Instructions, Agreements and Reinforcements in Behavioral Constructs with Alcoholics." *Journal of Abnormal Psychology* 83 (1974): 548-53.

Miller, P. M.; Hersen, M.; Eisler, R. M.; Epstein, L. H.; and Woolen, L. S. "Relationship of Alcohol Cues to Drinking Behavior of Alcoholics and Social Drinkers: An Analogue Study." *Psychological Record* 24 (1974): 61-66.

Miller, P. M.; Hersen, M.; Eisler, R. M.; and Hilsman, C. "Effects of Social Stress on Operant Drinking of Alcoholics and Social Drinkers." *Behavior Research and Therapy* 12 (1974): 67-72.

Miller, W. R. "Personal Communication." in Rohsenow, D. J. *Locus of Control and Treatment Outcome for Male Alcoholics.* Paper presented at Third Annual Conference of the University of Washington's Alcoholism and Drug Abuse Institute, Seattle, Washington, July, 1976.

Mills, K. C.; Sobell, M. B.; and Schaeffer, H. H. "Training Social Drinking as Alternative to Abstinence for Alcoholics." *Behavior Therapy* 2 (1971): 18-27.

Moore, R. A. "The Problem of Abstinence by the Patient as a requisite for the Psychotherapy of Alcoholism: The Need for Abstinence by the Alcoholic Patient During Treatment." *Quarterly Journal of Studies on Alcohol* 23 (1962): 105-11.

Nathan, P. E. "Alcoholism." In *Handbook of Behavior Modification and Behavior Therapy*. Edited by H. Leitenerger. Englewood Cliffs, N.J.: Prentice-Hall, 1976.

Nathan, P. E.; Goldman, M. S.; Lisman, S. A.; and Taylor, H. A. "Alcohol and Alcoholics: A Behavioral Approach." *Transactions of the N.Y. Academy of Sciences* 34 (1972): 602-27.

Nathan, P. E., and O'Brien, J. S. "An Experimental Analysis of the Behavior of Alcoholics and Non-alcoholics During Prolonged Experimental Drinking: A

Necessary Precursor of Behavior Therapy." *Behavior Therapy* 2 (1971): 455-76.

Nathan, P. E.; O'Brien, J. S.; and Norman, D. "Comparative Study of the Interpersonal and Affective Behavior of Alcoholics and Non-alcoholics During Prolonged Experimental drinking." In *Recent Advances in Studies of Alcoholism.* Edited by K. K. Mell and J. H. Mendelson. Washington, D.C.: U. S. Government Printing Office, 1971.

Nathan, P. E.; Titler, N. A.; Lowenstein, L. M.; Solomon, P.; and Rossi, A. M. "Behavioral Analysis of Chronic Alcoholism." *Archives of General Psychiatry* 22(1970): 419-30.

Nathan, P. E.; Wilson, G. T.; Steffen, J. J.; and Silverstein, S. J. "An Objective Look at Three Behavioral Treatment Approaches to Alcoholism." In *Biological and Behavioral Approaches to Drug Dependence.* Edited by H. D. Cappell and A. E. LeBlanc. Toronto, Canada: Addictions Research Foundation, 1976.

National Council on Alcoholism Criteria Committee. "Criteria for the Diagnoses of Alcoholism." *American Journal of Psychiatry* 129 (1972): 127-35.

Negrette, J. C.; MacPherson, S.; and Danely, T. E. "Comparative Study of Emotional and Social Problems of Active and Arrested Alcoholics." *Laval Medicine* 27 (1966): 162-67.

Nelson, P. C., and Hoffman, H. "Personalities of Alcoholics Who Leave and Seek Treatment." *Psychological Report* 30 (1972): 949-50.

Nir, Y., and Cutler, R. "The Unmotivated Patient Syndrome: Survey of Therapeutic Intervention." *American Journal of Psychiatry* 135:4 (1978): 442-47.

Nylander, I. "Children of Alcoholic Fathers." *Quarterly Journal of Studies on Alcohol* 24 (1963): 170-72.

O'Leary, M. R.; Rohsenow, D. J.; and Chang, E. F. "The Use of Multivariable Personality Strategies in Predicting Attrition From Alcoholism Treatment." *Journal of Clinical Psychiatry* April (1979): 190-93.

O'Leary, M. R.; Calsyn, D. A.; Chaney,

E. F.; et al. "Predicting Alcohol Treatment Program Drop-outs." *Diseases of the Nervous System* 38 (1977): 993-95.

O'Leary, M. R.; Rohsenow, D. J.; and Donovan, D. M. "Locus of Control and Patient Attrition From an Alcoholism Treatment Program." *Journal of Consulting Clinical Psychologists* 44 (1976): 686-87.

Omen, G. S., and Motolsky, A. G. "A Biochemical and Genetic Approach to Alcoholism." *Annals of the N.Y. Academy of Sciences* 197 (1972): 16-23.

Oxford, J. "A Comparison of Alcoholics Whose Drinking is Totally Uncontrolled and Those Whose Drinking is Mainly Controlled." *Behavior Research and Therapy* 11 (1973): 565-76; 13 (1975): 89-114.

———. "The Cohesiveness of Alcoholism-Complicated Marriage and its Influence on Treatment Outcome." *British Journal of Psychiatry* 128 (1972): 318-39.

———. "The Future of Alcoholism: A Commentary on the Rand Report." *Psychological Medicine* 8 (1978): 58.

———. "Notes on Ordering of Onset of Symptoms in Alcohol Dependence." *Psychological Medicine* 4 (1979): 281-88.

Oxford, J., and Edwards G. *Alcoholism: A Comparison of Treatment and Advice with a Study of the Influence of Marriage.* Monograph no. 26. Oxford University Press: Institute of Psychology, Moudsley, 1977.

Oxford, J.; Oppenheimer, E.; Egert, S.; and Hensman, C. "The Role of Excessive Drinking in Alcoholism-Complicated Marriage: A Study of Stability and Change Over a One Year Period." *International Journal of Addiction* B (1976).

Paolino, T. T., and McCrody, B. "Joint Admission As A Treatment Modality for Problem Drinkers: A Case Report." *American Journal of Psychiatry* 133 (1976): 22.

Paredes, A. "Denial Deception Maneuvers, and Consistency in the Behavior of Alcoholics." *Annals of the N.Y. Academy Sciences* 233 (1974): 23-33.

———. "Marital-Sexual Factors in Alcoholism." *Medical Aspects of Human Sexuality* 7 (1973): 98-114.

Paredes, A., and Cornelison, F. S. "Development of an Audiovisual Technique for the Rehabilitation of Alcoholics.'' *Quarterly Journal of Studies on Alcohol* 29 (1968): 84-92.

Paredes, A.; Gregory, D.; and Jones, B. M. ''Induced Drinking and Social Adjustment in Alcoholics: Development of a Therapeutic Model.'' *Quarterly Journal of Studies on Alcohol* 35 (1974): 1279-93.

Paredes, A.; Hood, W. R.; and Gregory, D. ''Microecology of Alcoholism: Implications for the Development of the Adolescent''. In *Current Issues in Adolescent Psychiatry*. Edited by J. C. Schoolar. New York: Brunner/Mazel, 1973.

Paredes, A.; Hood, W. R.; and Seymour, H. ''Sobriety as a Symptom of Alcohol Intoxication: A Clinical Commentary on Intoxication and Drunkeness.'' *British Journal of Addiction* 70 (1975): 233-43.

Paredes, A.; Hood, W. R.; Seymour, H.; and Gollob, M. ''Loss of Control in Alcoholism: An Investigation of the Hypothesis, with Experimental Findings.'' *Quarterly Journal of Studies on Alcohol* 34 (1973): 1146-61.

Paredes, A.; Ludwig, K. D.; Hassenfeld, I. N.; and Cornelison, F. S. ''A Clinical Study of Alcoholics Using Audiovisual Self-image Feedback.'' *Journal of Nervous and Mental Diseases* 148 (1969): 449-56.

―――. ''Filmed Representativs of Behavior and Responses to Self-observation in Alcoholics.'' In *Recent Advances in Studies of Alcoholism*. Edited by N. K. Mello and J. H. Mendelson. Washington, D.C.: Government Printing Office, 1971.

Park, P. ''Developmental Ordering of Experiences in Alcoholism.'' *Quarterly Journal of Studies on Alcohol* 34 (1973): 473-88.

Pattison, E. M. ''A Critique of Abstinence Critical in the Treatment of Alcoholism.'' *International Journal of Social Psychiatry* 14 (1968): 268-76.

―――. ''Non Abstinent Drinking Goals in the Treatment of Alcoholics.'' In *Research Advances in Alcohol and Drug Problems*. Edited by R. J. Gibbins and Y. Israel, et al. New York: John Wiley & Sons, 1976.

―――. ''Treatment of Alcoholic Families with Home Nurse Visits.'' *Family* 4 (1965): 77.

―――. *Trends in Treatment of Alcoholism*. Second Special Report to the Congress on Alcohol and Health, Washington, D.C., 1974, 145-67.

Pattison, E. M.; Courless, P.; Patti, R.; Mann, B.; and Muller, D. ''Diagnostic Therapeutic Intake Groups for Wives of Alcoholics.'' *Quarterly Journal of Studies on Alcohol* 26 (1965): 605-16.

Pattison, E. M.; DeFrancesco, C.; Wood, P.; and Frazier, H. *A Psychosocial Kinship Made for Family Therapy*. Presented at the American Psychiatric Association, May, 1975.

Pattison, E. M.; Headley, E. B.; Glaser, G. C.; and Gottschalk, L. A. *The Relation of Drinking Patterns to Overall Health in Successfully Treated Alcoholics*. Presented at the 21st Annual Meeting of American Psychiatric Association, May, 1965.

―――. ''Abstinence and Normal Drinking: An Assessment of Changes in Drinking Patterns in Alcoholics.'' *Quarterly Journal of Studies on Alcohol* 29 (1968): 610-33.

Pelz, D. C., and Shuman, S. H. *Drinking, Hostility and Alienation in Drinking of Young Men*. Presented at 3rd Annual Conference of National Institute on Alcoholism, Washington, D.C., June, 1973.

Pitts, F. N., and Winokur, G. ''Affective Disorder.'' In VII Alcoholism and Affective Disorder, *Journal of Psychiatric Research* 4 (1966): 37-50.

Pittman, D., and Gordon, C. W. *The Revolving Door*. New York: Free Press, 1958.

Pittman, D., and Tate, R. L. ''A Comparison of Two Treatment Programs for Alcoholics.'' *Quarterly Journal of Studies on Alcohol* 30 (1969): 388.

Plant, T. *Alcohol Problems: A Report to the Nation*. New York: Oxford University Press, 1967.

Pokorny, A. D., Miller, P. A.; and Cloveland, S. E. ''Responses to Treatment of Alcoholism: A Followup Study.'' *Quarterly Journal of Studies on Alcohol* 29 (1968): 364-68.

Pottinger, M., et al. ''The Frequency and Persistence of Depressive Symptoms in Alcohol Abuser.'' *Journal of Nervous and Mental Disease* 166:8 (1978): 562-620.

Premack, D., and Arglin, B. "On the Possibilities of Self-Control in Man and Animals." *Journal of Abnormal Psychology* 81 (1973): 137-51.

Quirk, D. A. "Former Alcoholics and Social Drinking." In *Journal of Abnormal Psychology* 81 (1973): 137-51.

Rae, J. B. "The Influence of Wives on the Treatment of Alcoholics: Followup Study at Two Years." *British Journal of Psychiatry* 120 (1972): 601-13.

Rae, J. B., and Dremery, J. "Interpersonal Patterns in Alcoholic Marriages." *British Journal of Psychiatry* 120 (1972): 615-21.

Rae, J. B., and Forbes, A. R. "Clinic and Psychometric Characteristics of Wives of Alcoholics." *British Journal of Psychiatry* 112 (1966): 197-200.

Ravensborg, M. R. "Mood Ratings in Early Termination From an Alcoholism Unit." *Psychology Report* 32 (1973): 1291-94.

Redlich, F. C., and Freedman, D. X. "Alcoholism." In *The Theory and Practice of Psychiatry*. New York: Basic Books, 1966.

Reinhart, R. E., and Bowen, W. T. "Social Drinking Followup Treatment for Alcoholism." *Bulletin of the Menninger Clinic* 32 (1968): 280-90.

Rimmer, J.; Reich, T.; and Winokur, G. "Alcoholism Versus Diagnosis and Clinical Variation Among Alcoholics." *Quarterly Journal of Studies on Alcohol* 33 (1972): 658-66.

Rimmer, J.; Pitts, F. N. Jr.; Reich, T.; and Winokur, G. "Alcoholism (II) Sex, Socioeconomic Status and Race in Two Hospitalized Samples." *Quarterly Journal of Studies on Alcohol* 32 (1971): 942-52.

Robinson, D. "The Alcohologists Addiction-Some Implication of Having Lost Control Over the Disease Concept of Alcoholism." *Quarterly Journal of Studies on Alcohol* 33 (1972): 1028-42.

———. *From Drinking to Alcoholism: A Sociological Commentary*. London: John Wiley and Sons, Ltd., 1976.

Rogers, D. A. "Psychological Interpretation of Alcoholism." *Annals of the N.Y. Academy of Sciences* 197 (1972): 222-25.

Room, R. "Normative Perspectives on Alcohol Use and Problems." *Journal of Drug Issues* 5(4) (1975): 358-68.

Rosebuck, J. B., and Kessler, R. G. *Etiology of Alcoholism*. Springfield, Ill.: Charles C. Thomas, 1972.

Rosma, W. G. "Children of Alcoholics—A Hidden Tragedy." *Maryland State Medical Journal* 21 (1) (1972): 34-36.

Ruff, C.; Ayers, J.; and Templer, D. I. "Alcoholics and Criminals' Similarity of Scores on the MacAndrew Alcoholism Scale." *Psychological Reports* 36(3) (1975): 921-22.

Sands, P. M., and Harson, P. G. "Psychotherapeutic Groups for Alcoholics and Relatives in an Outpatient Setting." *International Jouranl of Group Psychotherapy* 21 (1971): 23.

Schaefer, H. H. "Twelve-Month Follow-up of Behaviorally Trained Ex-Alcoholic Social Drinkers." *Behavior Therapy* 3 (1972): 286-89.

Schaefer, H. H.; Sobell, M. B.; and Mills, K. C. "Some Sobering Data on the Use of Self-Confrontation with Alcoholics." *Behavior Therapy* 2 (1971): 28-39.

Schaefer, H. H.; Sobell, M. B.; and Mills, K. C. "Baseline Drinking in Alcoholics and Social Drinkers: Levels of Drink and Sip Magnitudes." *Behavior Research and Therapy* 9 (1971): 23-27.

Schaefer, H. H.; Sobell, M. B.; and Sobell, L. C. "Twelve Months Follow-Up of Hospitalized Alcoholics Given Self-Confrontation Experiences by Videotape." *Behavior Therapy* 3 (1972): 283-85.

Schramm, C. J. *Alcoholism and Its Treatment in Industry*. Baltimore: Johns Hopkins University Press, 1977.

Schuckit, M. A., and Morrissen, E. R. "Alcoholism in Women: Some Clinical and Social Perspectives with an Emphasis on Possible Sub-types." In *Alcoholism Problems in Women and Children*. Edited by M. Greenblatt, and M. A. Schuckit. New York: Gome & Stratton, 1976.

Schuckit, M. D., and Winokur, G. "A Short Term Follow-Up of Women Alcoholics." *Diseases of the Nervous System* 33 (1972): 672-78.

Sclare, A. B. "Woman Alcoholic." *Journal of Alcoholism* 10 (1975): 134-37.

Seeley, J. R. "The WHO Definition of Alcoholism." *Quarterly Journal of Studies on Alcoholism* 20 (1959): 352-56.

Seiden, R. H. "The Use of Alcoholics Anonymous Members in Research on Alcoholism." *Quarterly Journal of Studies on Alcoholism* 21 (1960): 506-09.

Seixas, F. A. "New Priorities in Diagnosing and Treating Alcoholism." *Alcoholic Health and Research World* 54 (Summer Experimental Issue, 1973).

Seixas, F. A.; Cadoret, R.; and Eggleston, S. "The Person with Alcoholism." *Annals of the New York Academy of Science* 233, April 1974.

Seixas, F. A., and Eggleston, S., eds. "Alcoholism and the Central Nervous System." *Annals of the New York Academy of Science* 215 (1973): 1-389.

Seixas, F. A.; Omenn, G. S.; Burk, E. D.; and Eggleston, S., eds. "Nature and Nurture in Alcoholism." *Annals of the New York Academy of Science* 197 (1972): 1-229.

Selzer, M. L. "Alcoholism, Mental Illness and Stress in 96 Drinkers Causing Fatal Accidents." *Behavioral Science* 14 (1969): 1-10.

———. "The Personality of the Alcoholic as an Impediment to Psychotherapy." *Psychiatric Quarterly* 41 (1967): 38-45.

———. "The Michigan Alcoholism Screening Test: The Quest for a New Diagnostic Instrument." *American Journal of Psychiatry* 127 (1971): 1653-58.

Selzer, M. L.; Winocur, A.; and Wilson, T. D. "A Psychosocial Comparison of Drunken Drivers and Alcoholics." *Quarterly Journal of Studies on Alcoholism* 38 (1977): 1294-1312.

Shaw, J. A.; Donley, P.; Morgan, D. W.; and others. "Treatment of Depression in Alcoholics." *American Journal of Psychiatry* 132 (1975): 641-44.

Shea, J. E. "Psychoanalytic Therapy and Alcoholism." *Quarterly Journal of Studies on Alcoholism* 15 (1954): 595-605.

Singer, E.; Blane, H. T.; and Kasschua, R. "Alcoholism and Social Isolation." *Journal of Abnormal Social Psychology* 1 (1964-69): 681-85.

Skoloda, T. E.; Alterman, A. I.; Cornelisson,

F. S.; and Gottheil, E. "Treatment Outcome in a Drinking-Drivers Program." *Quarterly Journal of Studies on Alcohol* 36 (1975): 365-80.

Sloboda, S. "Children of Alcoholics: A Neglected Problem." *Hospital and Community Psychiatry* 25 (1974): 605-06.

Smart, R. B.; Schmidt, W.; and Moss, M. K. "Social Class as a Determinant of the Type and Duration of Therapy Received by Alcoholics." *International Journal of the Addictions* 4 (1969): 543-66.

Smith, C. J. "Alcoholics: Their Treatment and Their Wives." *British Journal of Psychiatry* 115 (1966): 1039.

Sobell, L. C., and Sobell, M. B. "Outpatient Alcoholics Give Valid Self Reports." *Journal of Nervous and Mental Disease* 161 (1975): 32-42.

Sobell, L. C., and Sammuels, F. H. "The Validity of Self-Reports of Prior Alcohol-Related Arrests by Alcoholics." *Quarterly Journal of Studies on Alcohol* 35 (1974): 276-80.

Sobell, L. C., and Sobell, M. B. "A Self-Feedback Technique to Monitor Drinking Behavior in Alcoholics." *Behavior Research and Therapy* 11 (1973): 237-38.

Sobell, M. B. "Alcoholics Treated by Individualized Behavior Therapy: One Year Treatment Oucome." *Behavior Research and Therapy* 11 (1973): 599-618.

———. "Individualized Behavior Therapy for Alcoholics." *Behavior Therapy* 4 (1973): 49-72.

———. "Individualized Behavior Therapy for Alcoholics: Rationale, Procedures, Preliminary Results, and Appendix." California Mental Health Research Monograph No. 13. Sacramento, Calif., 1972.

———. *Individualized Behavioral Treatment of Alcohol Problems.* New York: Plenum Press, 1977.

———. "The Need for Realism, Relevance, and Operational Assumptions in the Study of Substance Dependence." In *Biological and Behavioral Approaches to Drug Dependence.* Edited by H. D. Cappell and A. E. LeBlanc. Toronto Addiction Research Foundation, 1975.

———. "Second Year Treatment

Outcome of Alcoholics Treated by Individualized Behavior Therapy: Results.'' *Behavior Research and Therapy* 14 (1976): 195-215.

Sobell, M. B.; Schaeffer, H. H.; and Mills, M. K. ''Differences in Baseline Drinking Behaviors Between Alcoholics and Normal Drinkers.'' *Behavior Research and Therapy* 10 (1972): 257-68.

Sobell, M. B., and Sobell, J. J. ''Alcoholics Treated by Individualized Behavior Therapy: One Year Treatment Outcome.'' *Behavior Research and Therapy* 11 (1973): 237-38.

Stacey, B., and Davis, J. ''Drinking Behavior and Adolescence: An Evaluative Review.'' *British Journal of Addiction* 65 (1970): 203-12.

Steffen, J. J.; Nathan, P. E.; and Taylor, H. A. ''Tension-Reducing Effects of Alcohol: Further Evidence and Some Methodological Considerations.'' *Journal of Abnormal Psychology* 83 (1974): 542-47.

Stein, A., and Friedman, E. ''Group Therapy with Alcoholics.'' In *Groups and Drugs.* Edited by H. I. Kaplan and B. J. Sadock. New York: Dutton, 1972.

Steinbeck, A., and Blumenthal, M. ''Alcoholism Addiction and Body Build.'' *Acta Psychiatrica Scandinavica* 46 (1970): 224-31.

Steiner, C. M. ''The Alcoholic Game.'' *Quarterly Journal of Studies on Alcoholism* 30 (1969): 920-38.

————. *Games Alcoholics Play: Their Analysis and Self-Scripting.* New York: Grove Press, 1971.

Steinglass, P. ''Experimenting with Family Treatment Approaches to Alcoholism, 1950-1975: A Review.'' *Family Process* 15 (1976): 97-123.

Steinglass, P.; Donaldson, I.; and Berenson, D. ''Observations of Conjointly Hospitalized Alcoholic Couples During Sobriety and Intoxication: Implications for Theory and Therapy.'' *Family Process* 16 (1977): 1-16.

Steinglass, P.; Weiner, S.; and Mendelson, J. H. ''A Systems Approach to Alcoholism.'' *Archives of General Psychiatry* 24 (1971).

Sterne, M. W., and Pittman, D. J. ''The Concept of Motivation: A Source of Institutional and Professional Blockage in the Treatment of Alcoholism.'' *Quarterly Journal of Studies on Alcohol* 26 (1965): 41-57.

Straus, R. ''Alcohol and Society.'' *Psychiatric Annals of New York* 3 (1973): 8-107.

Straus, R. ''Problem Drinking in the Perspective of Social Change 1940-1973.'' In *Alcohol and Alcohol Problems.* Edited by W. Filstead, J. Rossi, and M. Leller. Cambridge, Mass.: Battinger, 1976.

Straus, R., and Bacon, S. *Drinking in College.* New Haven: Yale University Press, 1953.

Summers, T. ''Validity of Alcoholics' Self-Reported Drinking History.'' *Quarterly Journal of Studies on Alcohol* 31 (1970): 972-74.

Sutherland, E. H.; Schroeder, H. G.; and Tordella, O. L. ''Personality Traits and the Alcoholic: Critique of Existing Studies.'' *Quarterly Journal of Studies on Alcohol* 11 (1950): 547-56.

Swanson, D. W.; Weddige, R. L.; and Morse, R. M. ''Abuse of Prescription Drugs.'' *Mayo Clinic Proceedings* 48 (1973): 359-67.

Syme, L. ''Personality Characteristics of the Alcoholic.'' *Quarterly Journal of Studies on Alcoholism* 18 (1957): 288-301.

Szaz, T. S. ''Role of Counterphobic Mechanisms in Addiction.'' *Journal of the American Psychoanalytic Association* 6 (1958): 309-25.

Tamerin, J. S., et al. ''Alcohol and Memory: Amnesia and Short-Term Memory Function During Experimentally Induced Intoxication.'' *American Journal of Psychiatry* 127(12) (1971): 1659-64.

————. ''The Psychodynamics of Quitting Smoking in a Group.'' *American Journal of Psychoanalysis* 129(5) (1972): 589-95.

Tamerin, J. S., and Mendelson, J. H. ''The Psychodynamics of Chronic Inebriation: Observations of Chronic Alcoholics During the Process of Drinking in an Experimental Group Setting.'' *American Journal of Psychiatry* 125 (1969): 886-99.

Tamerin, J. S., and Neumann, C. P. ''The Alcoholic Stereotype: Clinical Reappraisal and Implications for Treatment.'' *Ameri-*

can *Journal of Psychoanalysis* 34(4) (1974): 315-23.

———. "Psychological Aspects of Treating Alcoholism." *Alcohol Health and Research World* Spring Exp. Issue (1974): 14-18.

Tamerin, J. S.; Toir, A.; and Harrington, B. "Sexual Differences in Alcoholics: A Comparison of Male and Female Alcoholics' Self and Spouse Perceptions." *American Journal of Drug and Alcohol Abuse* 3(3) (1976): 452-72.

Tamerin, J. S.; Tolot, A.; Holson, P.; and Neumann, C. P. "The Alcoholic's Perception of Self: A Retrospective Comparison of Mood Behavior During States of Sobriety and Intoxication." *Annals of the N.Y. Academy of Sciences* 233 (1974): 48-60.

Tamerin, J. S.; Weiner, S.; and Mendelson, J. H. "Alcoholics Expectancies and Recall of Experience During Intoxication." *American Journal of Psychiatry.*

Tartan, R. "Empirical Investigation of Psychological Deficits." In *Alcoholism: Interdisciplinary Approaches to an Enduring Problem.* Edited by R. Tartan, and A. A. Sugarman. Reading, Mass.: Addison-Wesley Publishing Co., 1976.

Toler, C. "The Personal Values of Alcoholics and Addicts." *Journal of Clinical Psychiatry* 31(3) (1975): 554-57.

———. "The Personal Values of Alcoholics and Addicts." *Newsletter for Research in Mental Health and Behavioral Science* 16(3) (1974): 17-20.

Toker, J. T.; Bunse, A. J.; Stefyre, R.; Napiur, D. A.; and Sodergren, J. A. "Emotional State and Behavioral Patterns in Alcoholics and Non-alcoholics." *Quarterly Journal of Studies on Alcohol* 34 (1973): 133-43.

Tomsovic, M. A. "A Followup Study of Discharged Alcoholics." *Hospital and Community Psychiatry* 21 (1970): 38-41.

Tracey, D. A.; Laden, R. B.; and Nathan, P. E. *An Experimental Analysis of the Behavior of Female Alcoholics.* Presented at the 8th Annual Meeting of the Association for Advancement of Behavior Therapy, Chicago, 1974.

Trice, H. M., and Roman P. M. "Sociopsychological Predictors of Affiliation with Alcoholics Anonymous: A Longitudinal Study of Treatment Success." *Social Psychiatry* 5 (1970): 51-59.

Trice, H. M.; Roman, P. M.; and Belasco, J. A. "Selection for Treatment; A Predictive Evaluation of an Alcoholism Treatment Regimen." *International Journal of Addictions* 4 (1969): 303-17.

Trice, H. M., and Wahl R. "A Rank Order Analysis of the Symptoms of Alcoholism." *Quarterly Journal of Studies on Alcohol* 19 (1958): 636-48.

Ullman, A. D. "The Psychological Mechanisms of Alcohol Addiction." *Quarterly Journal of Studies on Alcohol* 13 (1952): 602-08.

Uraa, C. W. "Alcoholism and the Treatment of Sexual Dysfunction." Lecture presented at the Fourth Annual Winter Workshop on the Treatment and Rehabilitation of the Alcoholic of the Psychotherapy Association, Colorado Springs, Colo. 3 February 1978.

Vaillant, G. "The Treatment of Alcoholics in Cambridge Alcoholic Clinic." Paper presented at a Symposium on Alcoholism, Boston University, Boston, Mass., 1974.

———. "Sociopathy as a Human Process." *Archives of General Psychiatry* 32 (1975): 178-83.

Vaillant, G. E., and Rasor, R. W. "The Role of Compulsory Supervision in the Treatment of Addiction." *Federal Probation* 30 (1966): 53-59.

Vanderpool, J. A. "Alcoholism and the Self-Concept." *Quarterly Journal of Studies on Alcoholism* 30 (1969): 59-77.

Van Dijk, W. K., and Van Dijk-Kofferman. "A Follow-Up Study of 211 Treated Male Alcoholic Addicts." *British Journal of Addiction* 68 (1973): 3-24.

Vogethin, W. L., and Lemere, F. "The Treatment of Alcohol Addiction: A Review of the Literature." *Quarterly Journal of Studies on Alcoholism* 2 (1942): 717-803.

Vogler, R. E.; Compton, J. V.; and Weissbach, J. A. "Integrated Behavior Change Techniques for Alcoholics." *Journal of Consulting and Clinical Psychology* 34 (1970): 302-07.

Wehmer, G.; Cooke, G.; and Gruber, J. "Evaluation of the Effects of Training Para-professionals in the Treatment of Alcoholism: A Pilot Study." *British Journal of Addiction* 69 (1974): 25-32.

Weingold, H. P.; Lachin, J. M.; Bell, A. H.; and others. "Depression as a Symptom of Alcoholism: Search for a Phenomenon." *Journal of Abnormal Psychology* 73 (1968): 195-97.

Weir, W. R. "Counseling Youth Whose Parents Are Alcoholic: A Means to an End as Well as an End in Itself." *Journal of Alcohol Education* 16 (1970): 13-19.

Wellman, M. "Management of the Late Withdrawal Symptoms of Alcohol." *Canadian Medical Association Journal* 71 (1954): 360-65.

Westfield, D. R. "Two Years Experience of Group Methods in the Treatment of Male Alcoholics in a Scottish Medical Hospital." *British Journal of Addiction* 67 (1972): 267.

Wilkinson, A. E.; Prado, W. M.; Williams, W. O.; and others. "Psychological Test Characteristics and Length of Stay in Alcoholism Treatment." *Quarterly Journal of Studies on Alcohol* 32 (1971): 60-65.

Willens, P. J. A.; Letemerdig, F. J. J.; and Arroyave, F. "A Categorization for Assessment of Prognosis and Outcome in the Treatment of Alcoholics." *British Journal of Psychiatry* 122 (1973): 649-54.

Winokur, G. "Family History Studies. VIII. Secondary Depression Is Alive and Well, and..." *Diseases of the Nervous System* 33 (1972): 94-99.

Winokur, G., and Clayton, P. J. "Family History Studies. IV. Comparison of Male and Female Alcoholics." *Quarterly Journal of Studies on Alcoholism* 29 (1968): 885-91.

Winokur, G.; Reich, T.; Rimmer, J.; and Pitts, F. N., Jr. "Alcoholism. III. Diagnosis and Familial Psychiatric Illness in 259 Alcoholic Probands." *Archives of General Psychiatry* 23 (1970): 104-111.

Winokur, G.; Rimmer, J.; and Reich, T. "Alcoholism. IV. Is There More Than One Type of Alcoholism?" *British Journal of Psychiatry* 118 (1971): 525-31.

World Health Organization Expert Committee on Drug Dependence. *Eighteenth Report.* Technical Report no. 437. Geneva: WHO, 1970.

Yalom, I. D., and others. "Alcoholics in Interactional Group Therapy: An Outcome Study." *Archives of General Psychiatry* 35 (1978): 415-25.

Zimberg; Wallace; and Blume, eds. "Practical Approaches to Alcoholism Psychotherapy." New York: Plenum Press, 1978.

POPULAR NOVELS ON ALCOHOLISM

Amis, Kingsley. *The Green Man.* New York: Harcourt, 1970.

Berryman, John. *Recovery.* New York: Farrar, Straus, 1973.

Bronte, Anne. *The Tenant of Wildfell Hall.* New York: Oxford, 1968.

Cookson, Catherine. *A Grand Man.* New York: Morrow, 1975.

Hemingway, Ernest. *Islands in the Stream.* New York: Scribner, 1970.

Hemingway, Ernest. *The Torrents of Spring.* New York: Scribner, 1972.

Jackson, Charles. *The Lost Weekend.* New York: Farrar, 1940.

Lowry, Malcolm. *Under the Volcano.* Philadelphia, Pa.: Lippincott, 1965.

O'Hara, John. *Appointment in Samarra.* New York: Harcourt, 1934.

Schulberg, Budd. *The Disenchanted.* New York: Random House, 1950.

Simenon, Georges. *November.* New York: Harcourt, 1970.

Styron, William. *Set This House on Fire.* New York: Random House, 1960.

Zola, Emile. *L'assommoir.* 1876.

DRUGS

Akers, R. I.; Burgess, R. T.; and Johnson, W. T. "Opiate Use, Addiction and Relapse." *Social Problems* 15 (1968): 459-69.

Aligulander, Christer. "Dependence on Sedative and Hypnotic Drugs: A Comparative Clinical and Social Study." *Acta Psychiatrica Scandinavica* 270 (1978): 270.

Alkesne, H.; Lieberman, L.; and Brill, L. "A Conceptual Model of the Life Cycle of Addiction." *International Journal of the Addictions* 2 (1968): 221-38.

Anderson, R. E. "Where's Dad? Parental Deprivation and Delinquency." *Archives of General Psychiatry* 18 (1968): 641-49.

Angrest, B., and Gershon, S. "Amphetamine Abuse in New York City 1966-1968." *Seminars in Psychiatry* 1 (1969): 195-207.

Arnold, L. E.; Strobl, D.; and Weisenberg, A. "Hyperkinetic Adult: Study of the Paradoxical Amphetamine Response." *Journal of the American Medical Association* 222 (1972): 693-94.

Arnon, D.; Kleinman, M. J.; and Kissin, B. "Psychological Differentiation in Heroin Addicts." *International Journal of the Addictions* 9 (1974): 151-59.

Aron, W. S. "Family Background and Personal Trauma Among Drug Addicts in the United States: Implications for Treatment." *British Journal of The Addictions* 79 (1975): 295-305.

"Aspects of Drug Dependency." *Annals of the New York Academy of Science* 233 (1974): 15-22.

Association for Research in Nervous and Mental Diseases. *The Addictive States 2 and 3.* New York, 1966.

Ausubel, D. P. *Drug Addiction: Psychological, Physiological and Sociological Aspects.* New York: Random House, 1958.

Baer, D., and Corrado, S. "Heroin Addict Relationships with Parents During Childhood and Early Adolescent Years." *Journal of Genetic Psychology* 12 (1974): 99-103.

Baldinger, R.; Goldsmith, B. M.; Capel, W. C.; and Stewart, G. T. "Pot Smokers, Junkies and Squares: A Comparative Study of Female Values." *International Journal of the Addictions* 7 (1972): 153-66.

Ball, J. C. "Marijuana Smoking and Onset of Heroin Use." *Baruch Journal of Criminology* 7 (1967): 408-13.

Barr, H. L. "In Summary Report of Technical Review on the Psychiatric Aspects of Opiate Dependence." Diagnostic and Therapeutic Research Issues, National Institute on Drug Abuse, Arlington, Va., 17 & 18 March 1977. Silver Spring, Md., Macro Systems, Inc., May 1977.

Battlegay, R.; Ludwig, D.; Muhlemann, R.; and Weidmann, M. "The Culture of Youth and Drug Abuse in Some European Countries." *International Journal of the Addictions* 11 (1976): 245-62.

Becker, H. S. "History, Culture and Subjective Experience: An Exploration of the Social Bases of Drug Induced Experiences." *Journal of Health and Social Behavior* 8 (1967): 163-76.

Bell, D. S., and Treshowar, M. B. "Amphetamine Addiction." *Journal of Nervous and Mental Disease* 133 (1961): 489-96.

Berman, Leon, E. A. "The Role of Amphetamine in a Case of Hysteria." *Journal of the American Psychoanalytic Association* 20 (1972): 325-40.

Bernhardson; Gunda; and Gunne, Lars M. "Forty-Six Cases of Psychosis in Cannabis Abusers." *International Journal of the Addictions* 7 (1972): 9-16.

Berzins, J. T.; Ross, W. F.; and Monroe, J. J. "A Multivariable Study of the Personality Characteristics of Hospitalized Narcotic Addicts on MMPI." *Journal of Clinical Psychology* 27 (1971): 174-81.

Black, F. W. "Personality Characteristics of Vietnam Veterans Identified as Heroin Abusers." *American Journal of Psychiatry* 132 (1975): 748-49.

Bloom, E. S. ed. *An Approach for Casual Drug Users.* National Institute on Drug Abuse, reprint no. 5644.

Bloomquist, E. R. *Marijuana.* Beverly Hills, Calif.: Glencoe Press, 1968.

Blum, Richard H. *Horatio Alger's Children: The Role of the Family in the Origin and Prevention of Drug Risk.* San Francisco: Jossey-Bass, 1973.

———. *Society and Drugs.* San Francisco: Jossey-Bass, 1969.

———. *Students and Drugs.* San Francisco: Jossey-Bass, 1969.

Boyd, P. "Heroin Addiction in Adolescents." *Journal of Psychosomatic Research* 14 (1970): 295-301.

Braen, W. R. "Drug Addiction." *Nature* 208 (1965): 825-87.

Brecher, E. M. *Licit and Illicit Drugs.* Mount Vernon, N.Y.: Consumers Union, 1972.

Brill, L. *The De-addiction Process: Studies in the De-addiction of Confirmed Heroin Addicts.* Springfield, Ill.: Charles C. Thomas, 1972.

———. *Rehabilitation in Drug Addiction.* U.S. Department of Health, Education, and Welfare Public Health Publication No. 1013. Washington, D.C.: U.S. Government Printing Office, 1964.

———. "Review of Innovative Programs and Techniques." In *Methadone: Experi-* *ences and Issues.* Edited by C. D. Chambers and L. Brill. New York: Behavioral Publications, 1973.

———. "The Treatment of Drug Abuse: Evolution of a Perspective." *American Journal of Psychiatry* 134 (1977): 157-60.

Brill, L., ed. *Major Modalities in the Treatment of Drug Abuse.* New York: Behavioral Publications, 1972.

Brill, L., and Lieberman, L. *Authority and Addiction.* Boston: Little, Brown, 1969.

Brill, N. Q., and Christie, R. L. "Marijuana Use and Social Adaptation." *Archives of General Psychiatry* 31 (1974): 713-19.

Brook, R.; Kaplan, J.; and Whitehead, P. C. "Personality Characteristics of Adolescent Amphetamine Users Measured by MMPI." *British Journal of Addiction* 69 (1974): 61-66.

Brook, R.; Szandorowoka, B.; and Whithead, P. C. "Psychosocial Dysfunctions as Precursors to Amphetamine Abuse Among Adolescents." *Addictive Diseases* 2 (1976): 465-78.

Brown, Claude. *Manchild in the Promised Land.* New York: Macmillan, 1965.

Brozovsky, M., and Winkler, E. G. "Glue Sniffing in Children and Adolescents." *New York State Journal of Medicine* 65 (1965): 1984-89.

Byler, R., ed. *Teach Us What We Want to Know.* New York: Mental Health Materials Center, 1969.

Byrd, O. E., ed. *Medical Readings on Drug Abuse.* Reading, Mass.: Addison-Wesley, 1970.

Calof, J. *A Study of Four Voluntary Treatment and Rehabilitation Programs for New York City Narcotic Addicts.* New York: Community Service Society of New York, 1967.

———. *Lifeline to Tomorrow: A Study of Voluntary Treatment Progrms for Narcotic Addicts.* New York: Community Service Society of New York, 1969.

Cappell, H. D., and Leblanc, A. E. *Biological and Behavioral Approaches to Drug Dependence.* Ontario: Alcoholism and Drug Addiction Research Foundation, 1975.

Carek, O. J.; Hendrickson, W. J.; and Holms, O. J. "Delinquency Addiction in

Parents." *Archives of General Psychiatriy* 4 (1961): 357-62.

Carlen, A. S., and Post, R. D. "Patterns of Drug Use Among Marijuana Smokers." *Journal of the American Medical Association* 213 (1971): 867-68.

Carmichael, J., and others. "Self Concept and Substance Abuse Treatment." *Comprehensive Psychiatry* 18 (1977): 357-62.

Casriel, D. *A Scream Away From Happiness.* New York: Grosset & Dunlap, 1972.

———. "The Acting Out Neurosis of Our Times." In *The Neurosis of Our Time: Acting Out.* Edited by D. S. Dilman and D. G. Goldman. Springfield, Ill.: Charles C. Thomas, 1973.

———. *So Fair a House: The Story of Synanon.* Englewood, N.J.: Prentice-Hall, 1963.

Casriel, D., and Amen, G. *Daytop: Three Addicts and Their Cure.* New York: Hill & Wang, 1971.

Casselman, B. W. "You Cannot Be a Drug Addict Without Really Trying." *Diseases of the Nervous System* 25 (1964): 161-63.

Cavior, M.; Kurtzberg, R.; and Lyston, D. "The Development and Validation of a Heroin Addiction Scale." *International Journal of the Addictions* 2 (1967): 128-38.

Chambers, C. D.; Moffett, A. D.; and Cuskey, W. R. "Five Patterns of Darvon Abuse." *International Journal of the Addictions* 6 (1971).

Chein, I.; Gerard, D.; Lee, R. S.; and Rosenfield, L. S. *The Road to H.* New York: Basic Books, 1964.

Chessik, R. D. "The 'Pharmacogenic Orgasm' in the Drug Addict." *Archives of General Psychiatry* 3 (1960): 545-56.

Clausen, J. A. "Social Patterns: Personality and Adolescent Drug Use." In *Explorations in Social Psychiatry.* Edited by A. H. Leighton, J. A. Clausen and R. Wilson. New York: Basic Books, 1957.

Cocchi, R., and Tornati, A. "Psychic Dependence? A Different Formulation of the Problem with a View to the Reorientation of Therapy for Chronic Drug Addiction." *Acta Psychiatrica Scandinavica* 56 (1977): 337-46.

Coghlen, A. J.; Gold, S. R.; Dohrenwend, E. F.; and Zimmerman, R. S. "A Psychobehavioral Residential Drug Abuse Program: A New Adventure in Adolescent Psychiatry." *International Journal of the Addictions* 8 (1973): 767-77.

Cohen, A. "Psychedelic Drugs and the Student: Educational Strategies." In *Drug Awareness.* Edited by R. Homan and A. Fox. New York: Avon, 1978.

———. "A Typology of Drug Addicts." Paper presented at the National Drug Abuse Conference, San Francisco, May 1977.

Cohen, C. P. "Marijuana Today." *Drug Abuse and Alcoholism Newsletter* 4 (1975).

———. "Prolonged Adverse Reactions to LSD." *Archives of General Psychiatry* 8 (1963): 475-80.

Cohen, C. P., and Ditman, K. S. "Complications Associated with Lysergic Acid Dietylamide" (LSD-25)." *Journal of the American Medical Association* 181 (1962): 161-62.

Cohen, C. P.; White, E. H.; and Scholaar, J. C. "Interpersonal Patterns of Personality for Drug Abusing Patients and Their Therapeutic Implications." *Archives of General Psychiatry* 24 (1971): 353-58.

Cohen, M., and Klein, D. M. "Post Hospital Adjustments of Psychiatrically Hospitalized Drug Users." *Archives of General Psychiatry* 31 (1974): 221-27.

Cohen, S. *The Beyond Within: The LSD Story.* New York: Atheneum, 1968.

———. *The Drug Dilemma.* New York: McGraw-Hill, 1969.

Coleman, S. B., and Davis, D. I. "Family Therapy and Drug Abuse: A National Survey." *Family Process* 17 (1978): 21-30.

Coles, A. *The Grass Pipe.* New York: Atlantic Monthly Press, 1969.

Coles, R.; Brenner, J. H.; and Meagher, D. *Drugs and Youth: Medical, Psychiatric and Legal Facts.* New York: Leveright, 1970.

Connell, ., and Dorn, N., eds. *Cannabis and Man: Psychological and Clinical Aspects and Patterns of Use.* Edinburgh, London and New York: Churchill Livingstone, 1975.

Copemann, D., and Shaw, P. L. "The Effect of Therapeutic Intervention on the Assessment Scores of Narcotic Addicts." *International Journal of the Addictions* 10 (1975): 921-26.

Corman, A. G.; Johnson, B.; Khantzian, E. J.; and Long, J. "Rehabilitation of Narcotic Addicts with Methadone and Public Health Approach vs. the Individual Perspective." *Contemporary Drug Problems* (Winter, 1973): 565-78.

Crowley, R. M. "Psychoanalytic Literature on Drug Addiction and Alcoholism." *Psychoanalytic Review* 26 (1939): 39-54.

Culver, C. M., and King, F. M. "Neuropsychological Assessment of Undergraduate Marijuana and LSD Users." *Archives of General Psychiatry* 31 (1974): 707-11.

Davis, D. M., and Klagsburn, M. "Substance Abuse and Family Interaction: A Review of the Literature and Recommendations for Future Research." Paper presented on Family Drug Abuse, Columbia, Md., 1977.

Davis, D. M.; Farnsworth, D. L.; Brotman, R.; Fredric, S.; Nahas, G.; and Greenwood, A. "Drug Abuse in America." *Psychiatric Annals* 3 (April 1973).

Davis, W. N. "The Treatment of Drug Addiction: Some Comparative Observations." *British Journal of Addiction* 65 (1970): 227-35.

De Bold, R. C., and Leaf, R. C. *LSD, Man and Society.* Middletown, Conn.: Wesleyan University Press, 1967.

De Forrest, J.; Roberts, P.; and Hays, J. "Drug Abuse: A Family Affair." *Journal of Drug Issues* (Spring 1974): 130-34.

De Leon, G.; Skodol, A.; and Rosenthal, M. S. "Phoenix House: Changes in Psychopathological Signs of Resident Drug Addicts." *Archives of General Psychiatry* 28 (1973): 131-35.

Densen-Gerber, J. A. *Child Abuse and Neglect as Related to Parental Drug Abuse and Other Antisocial Behavior.* New York: National Center of Child Abuse and Neglect, 1978.

———. *Drugs: For and Against.* New York: Hart Publishing Co., 1970.

———. "The Prevalence of Incestuous Experiences Among Male and Female Drug Abusers." Twenty-Eighth Annual Meeting of the American Academy of Forensic Sciences, Washington, D.C., 1976.

———. "Treatment Styles for Women." National Drug Abuse Conference, New York, 1976.

———. *Walk In My Shoes: An Odyssey into Womanlife.* New York: E. P. Dutton, 1976.

———. *We Mainline Dreams: The Odyssey House Story.* New York: Doubleday, 1973.

———. "Women and Stress." Conference of the Governor's Commission on the Status of Women, Louisiana, 1976.

Densen-Gerber, J. A., and Ament, M. "The Right to Be Well Born." Twenty-Seventh Annual Meeting of the American Academy of Forensic Sciences, 1975.

Densen-Gerber, J. A., and Benward, J. "Incest as a Causative Factor in Anti-Social Behavior: An Exploratory Study." Twenty-Seventh Annual Meeting of the American Academy of Forensic Sciences, 1975.

Densen-Gerber, J. A., and Drassner, D. "Odyssey House: A Structural Model for the Successful Employment and Re-Entry of the Ex-Drug Abuser." *Journal of Drug Issues,* Summer 1974.

Densen-Gerber, J. A., and Hutchinson, S. F. "Incest and Drug-Related Child Abuse: Systematic Neglect by the Legal and Medical Professions." Annual Meeting of the American Academy of Psychiatry and the Law, San Francisco, Calif., 1976.

Densen-Gerber, J. A.; Lyan, L.; and Griffin, W. "The Family Perspective: An Alternative Living Style." National Drug Abuse Conference, New York, N.Y., 1976.

Densen-Gerber, J. A.; Rohrs, C.; and Murphy, J. P. "The Therapeutic Community." *Proceedings of the International Drug Abuse Conference,* 1971.

Densen-Gerber, J. A., and Tissa Baden. *Drugs, Sex, Parents, and You.* New York: J. B. Lippincott, 1972.

Densen-Gerber, J. A., and Wahbeg, R. "Preliminary Report on Sociological Action in Child Abuse Deaths: Something Terrible Is Happening to American

Children.'' Drugs, Alcohol, and Women: A National Forum. Miami Beach, Fla., 1977.

de Rios, M. D., and Smith, D. E. ''Drug Use and Abuse in Cross Cultural Perspective.'' *Human Organization* 36 (1977): 14-21.

Dole, V. P. ''Research on Methadone Maintenance.'' In *Proceedings of the Second National Conference on Methadone Maintenance,* 1968.

Dole, V. P., and Nyswander, M. E. ''Methadone Maintenance and Its Implications for Theories of Narcotic Addiction.'' *Research Publication of the Association for Research in Journal of Nervous and Mental Diseases* 46 (1968): 359-66.

Dole, V. P., and Warner, A. ''Successful Treatment of 250 Criminal Addicts.'' *Journal of the American Medical Association* 206 (1968): 2710-11.

Droppa, D. C. ''Behavioral Treatment of Drug Addiction: A Review and Analysis.'' *International Journal of the Addictions* 8 (1973): 143-61.

Drug Abuse: Research in the Service of Mental Health. Report of the Research Task Force of NIMH. Julius Segal, Editor in Chief. Washington, D.C.: NIMH, 1976.

DuPont, R. L. ''Bridges between alcohol and drug problems.'' In *Proceedings of the ADPA 28th Annual Meeting Alcohol and Drug Problems Assocation of North America.* 25-29 September 1977; March 1978, 14-19.

————. ''Coming to grips with an urban heroin addiction epidemic.'' *The Journal of the American Medical Association,* (1973): 223(1), 46-48.

————. The drug abuse decade. *Journal of Drug Issues* 8(2), (1978): 173-87.

————. ''Equality for women in drug abuse.'' In *A National Forum Source Book.* Edited by M. Nellis. National Research and Communications Association, Inc., Washington, D.C., 1976, 7-13.

————. ''Getting it together for the long haul.'' *Drug Abuse: Modern Trends, Issues, and Perspectives—Proceedings of the Second National Drug Abuse Conference,* New Orleans, Louisiana, 1975, 1978, 13-29.

————. ''Heroin addiction treatment and crime reduction.'' *American Journal of Psychiatry* 128, (1972): 856-60.

————. ''How corrections can beat the high cost of heroin addiction.'' *Federal Probations,* 35(2) (1971): 43-50.

————. ''Just what can you tell your patients about marijuana?'' *Medical Times* 104(1) (1976): 120-31; also published in *Resident & Staff Physician,* 23(1) (1977): 103-10.

————. ''Marijuana: our next step.'' *Drug Abuse and Alcoholism Review* 1(1), (1978): 14-19; also, slightly modified version published in *Addictions* 5(4), (1977): 4-9; and *Focus on Alcohol and Drug Issues* 1(2), (1978): 7.

————. ''National strategies for drug abuse prevention: the United States experience.'' In *Proceedings of the 25th Iranian Medical Congress,* Ramsar, Iran (1977): 60-73.

————. ''New directions for the National Institute on Drug Abuse.'' In David E. Smith, et al eds., *A Multicultural View of Drug Abuse—Proceedings of the Fourth National Drug Abuse Conference,* San Francisco, California, 1977, Cambridge, Massachusetts: Schenkman Publishing Company, Inc., 1978, 11-22.

————. ''Overview of drug abuse.'' In *Proceedings of the First National Drug Abuse Conference,* Chicago, Illinois, 1974, 1975, 25-31.

————. ''Profile of a heroin-addiction epidemic.'' *New England Journal of Medicine* 285(6), (1971): 320-24.

————. ''The Treatment of Heroin Addicts: A Historical and Personal Review.'' *Career Directions* 3 (1973): 20.

————. ''Trying to treat all the heroin addicts in a community.'' *Proceedings of the Fourth National Conference on Methadone Treatment,* Washington, D.C., 1972, 77-80.

————. ''You alone can do it, but you cannot do it alone.'' In *Proceedings of the 2nd World Conference of Therapeutic Communities,* part I, 2(3,4) (1978): 34-40.

————. ''Urban crime and the rapid development of a large heroin addiction treatment program.'' *Proceedings of the Third National Conference on Methadone Treatment,* New York, New York, 1971, 115-20.

————. ''Veteran heroin addicts in Washington: a preliminary report.'' *Medical Annals of the District of Columbia* 40(8) (1971): 521-23.

DuPont, R. L., and Katon, R. N. ''Development of a heroin addiction treatment program: effect on urban crime.'' *The Journal of the American Medical Association* 216(8) (1971): 1320-24.

————. ''Physicians and the heroin addiction epidemic.'' *Modern Medicine* 39(13) (1971): 123-39.

Duvall, L. B., and Brill, L. ''Follow-Up Study of Narcotics Addicts Five Years After Hospitalization.'' *Public Health Reports* 78 (1963): 185-93.

Eben, D., ed. *The Drug Experience.* New York: Grove Press, 1961.

Ellinwood, E. H. ''Amphetamine Psychosis: I. Description of the Individuals and Process.'' *Journal of Nervous and Mental Disease* 144 (1967): 273-83.

————. ''Amphetamine Psychosis: A Multidimensional Process.'' *Seminars in Psychiatry* 1 (1969): 208-26.

Ellinwood, E. H.; Smith, W. E.; and Vaillant, G. E. ''Narcotic Addiction in Males and Females: A Comparison.'' *International Journal of the Addictions* 1 (1966): 33.

Essing, C. F. ''Addiction to Barbiturate and Nonbarbiturate Sedative Drugs.'' In *The Addictive States.* Association for Research in Nervous and Mental Disease. Baltimore: Williams & Wilkins, 1968.

————. ''Addiction to Nonbarbiturate Sedative and Tranquilizing Drugs.'' *Clinical Pharmacology and Therapeutics* 5 (1964): 334-43.

————. ''Drug Dependence of Barbiturate Type.'' *Drug Dependence* 5 (1970): 24-27.

————. ''Newer Sedative Drugs That Can Cause States of Intoxication and Dependence of Barbiturate Type.'' *Journal of the American Medical Association* 196 (1966): 714-17.

Evans, F., and Monet, C. ''Drug Use and Drug Dependence.'' In *Psychological Nursing.* Edited by F. Evans. New York: Macmillan, 1971.

Felix, F. H. ''An Appraisal of the Person-ality Types of the Addict.'' *American Journal of Psychology* 100 (1944): 462-67.

————. ''Some Comments on the Psychology of Drug Addiction.'' *Mental Hygiene* 23 (1939): 576-82.

Fenichel, D. *Drug Addiction in the Psychoanalytic Theory of Neurosis.* New York: W. W. Norton, 1945.

Fiddle, S. *Portraits from a Shooting Gallery.* New York: Harper & Row, 1967.

Forsythe, M. ''Youth and Drugs: Use and Abuse.'' *Ohio State Medical Journal* 65 (1969) 17-23.

Foxworth, J. M. ''Polydrug Abuse.'' *Psychiatric Forum* 7 (1978): 17-22.

Fram, D. H., and Hoffman, H. A. ''Treatment of Middle Class Heroin Abusers: Preliminary Observations.'' *Medical Annals of the District of Columbia* 41 (1972): 301-03.

Fram, D. H., and Hoffman, H. A. ''Family Therapy and the Treatment of Heroin Addiction.'' Unpublished.

Freedman, A. M., and Wilson, A. E. ''Childhood and Adolescent Addictive Behaviors.'' *Pediatrics* 134 (1964): 425-30.

Freedman, D. X. ''A Psychiatrist Looks at Psychedelics: Use and Abuse.'' In *Drug Abuse: A Course for Educators.* Edited by M. H. Weensing and D. W. Doerr. Indianapolis: Butler University, 1968.

————. ''On the Use and Abuse of LSD.'' *Archives of General Psychiatry* 18 (1968): 330-47.

Frosch, W. A. ''Psychoanalytic Evaluation of Addiction and Habituation.'' *Journal of the American Psychoanalytic Association* 18 (1970): 209-18.

Frosch, W. A.; Robbins, E. S.; and Stern, M. ''Untoward Reaction to LSD Resulting in Hospitalization.'' *New England Journal of Medicine* 273 (1965): 1235-39.

Gendreau, P., and Gendreau, L. P. ''The 'Addiction' Prone Personality: A Study of Canadian Heroin Addicts.'' *Canadian Journal of Behavioral Science* 2 (1970): 18-25.

Gerard, D. and Kormetsky, C. A. ''A Social and Psychiatric Study of Adolescent Opiate Addicts.'' *Psychiatric Quarterly* 28 (1954): 113-125.

Gilbert, J. G., and Lombardi, D. M. "Personality Characteristics of Young Male Narcotic Addicts." *Journal of Consulting Psychology* 31 (1967): 536-38.

Glasscote, R. M.; Sussex, J. N.; Jaffe, J. H.; Ball, J.; and Brill, L., eds. *The Treatment of Drug Abuse: Programs, Problems, Prospects.* Washington, D.C.: The Joint Information Service of the American Psychiatric Association and the National Association for Mental Health, 1972.

Glatt, M. M. "Psychotherapy of Drug Abuse: Some Theoretical Considerations." *British Journal of Addiction* 65 (1970): 51-62.

Glover, E. "On the Aetiology of Drug Addiction." *International Journal of Psychoanalysis* 13 (1932): 298-328.

Goldsmith, P. G. "Evaluation of Treatment Programs for Drug Abusers." Fifth International Institute of Prevention and Treatment of Drug Dependence, Copenhagen, 1974.

Goode, E. "Marijuana and the Politics of Reality." *Journal of Health and Social Behavior* 10 (1969): 83-94.

———. "Multiple Drug Use Among Marijuana Users." *Social Problems* 17 (1969): 48-64.

Gorsuch, R., and Butler, M. "Initial Drug Abuse: A Review of Predisposing Social and Psychological Factors." *Psychology Bulletin* 83 (1976): 120-37.

Gossop, M. "Drug Dependence: A Study of Relationships Between Rational, Cognitive, Social and Historical Factors and Treatment Variables." *Journal of Nervous and Mental Disease* 166 (1978): 44-50.

Granger, R., and Shugart, G. "The Heroin Addict's Pseudo-Assertive Behavior and Family Dynamics." *Social Casework* (December 1968): 643-49.

Greden, J. F.; Morgan, D. W.; and Frankel, S. "The Changing Drug Scene: 1970-1972." *American Journal of Psychiatry* 131 (1974): 77-81.

Greene, M. H.; Brown, B. S.; and DuPont, R. L. "Controlling the abuse of illicit methadone in Washington, D.C." *Archives of General Psychiatry,* 32 (1975): 221-26.

Greene, M. H.; Nightingale, S. L.; and DuPont, R. L. "Evolving patterns of drug abuse." *Annals of Internal Medicine* 83(3) (1975): 402-11.

Griffith, J. D. "Psychiatric Implications of Amphetamine Abuse." In *Amphetamine Abuse.* Edited by J. R. Russo. Springfield, Ill.: Charles C. Thomas, 1968.

Griffith, J. D. "Drug-seeking Behavior in Hospitalized Drug Addicts." Paper presented at the annual meeting of the American Psychiatric Association, Boston, Mass., 1968.

Grinspoon, L. *Marijuana Reconsidered.* Cambridge, Mass.: Harvard University Press, 1971.

Grinspoon, L., and Bakalar, J. B. *Cocaine: A Drug and Its Social Evolution.* New York: Basic Books, 1976.

Grinspoon, L., and Hedblom, P. *The Speed Culture: Amphetamine Use and Abuse in America.* Cambridge, Mass.: Harvard University Press, 1975.

Hafen, B. Q., ed. *Drug Abuse: Psychology, Sociology, Pharmacology.* Provo, Utah: Brigham Young University Press, 1973.

Halikas, J. A., and Rimmer, J. D. "Predictors of Multiple Drug Abuse." *Archives of General Psychiatry* 31 (1974): 414-18.

Hall, R. C. W., and others. "Concert Outpatient Drug Abuse." *Journal of Nervous and Mental Disease* 166 (1978): 343-48.

Harms, E. "Psychopathology of the Juvenile Drug Addict." In *Drugs and Youth: The Challenge of Today.* Edited by E. Harms. New York: Pergamon Press, 1973.

Hartin, H., and Mazur, M. "The Families of Drug Abusers: A Literature Review." *Family Process* 14 (1975): 411-31.

Hartman, D. "A Study of Drug-Taking Adolescents." *Psychoanalytic Study of the Child* 24 (1969): 384-98.

Hekimian, D. A., and Gershon, S. "Characteristics of Drug Abusers Admitted to Psychiatric Hospitals." *Journal of the American Medical Association* 205 (1968): 125-30.

Heller, M. E., and Mordkoff, A. M. "Personality Attributes of the Young Nonaddicted Drug Abuser." *International Journal of the Addictions* 7 (1972): 65-72.

Hendin, H. "Students on Amphetamines." *Journal of Nervous and Mental*

Disease 158 (1974): 255-67.

———. "Students on Heroin." *Journal of Nervous and Mental Disease* 158 (1974): 240-55.

Henriques, E.; Arseman, J.; Culter, H.; and Samaraweera, A. B. "Personality Characteristics and Drug of Choice." *International Journal of the Addictions* 7 (1972): 73-76.

Herman, R. "Application of Verbal Behavior Analysis to the Study of Psychological Defense Mechanisms: Speech Patterns Associated with Heroin Addiction." Unpublished manuscript. Abstract in L. Wurmser, *The Hidden Dimension: Psychodynamics in Compulsive Drug Use* (New York: Jason Aronson, 1978): 545 ff.

Hoffman, M. "Drug Addiction and Hypersexuality: Related Modes of Mastery Comprehension." *Psychiatry* 5 (1960): 262-70.

Hollister, L. *Clinical Use of Psychotherapeutic Drugs.* Springfield, Ill.: Charles C. Thomas, 1973.

———. "Marijuana in Man: Three Years Later." *Science* 172 (1971): 21-29.

Hughley, E. J. "Vocational and Social Adjustment of the Treated Juvenile Addicts." In *Drugs and Youth.* Edited by E. Harms. New York: Pergamon Press, 1973.

Jaffe, J. H. Verbal presentation given at Symposium on Drug Abuse Problems, Aspen, Colo., February 1975.

———. Verbal presentation given at National Academy of Sciences Meeting, McLean Hospital, Belmont, Mass., November 1975.

Jaffe, J. H.; Zaks, M. S.; and Washington, E. N. "Experience with the Use of Methadone in a Multimodality Program for Treatment of Narcotic Users." *International Journal of the Addictions* 4 (1969): 481-91.

Jessor, R., and Jessor, S. L. "Problem Drinking in Youth: Personality, Social, and Behavioral Antecedents and Correlates." Proceedings of the Second Annual Alcoholism Conference, Washington, D.C., NIAAA, 1972.

Jessor, R.; Jessor, S. L. and Finney, J. "A Social Psychology of Marijuana Use: Longitudinal Studies in High School and College Youth." *Journal of Personality and Social Psychology* 26 (1973): 1-15.

Judson, H. F. *Heroin Addiction in Britain.* New York: Harcourt Brace Jovanovich, 1973.

Kalant, O. J. *The Amphetamines: Toxicity and Addiction.* Second Edition. Toronto: University of Toronto Press, 1973.

Kaplan, E. H., and Weider, H. "Treatment and Conclusion." In *Drugs Don't Take People—People Take Drugs.* Secaucus, N.J.: Lyle Stuart, 1974.

Kaplan, H. S., and Meyerowitz, J. J. "Psychosocial Predictors of Postinstitutional Adjustment Among Male Drug Addicts." *Archives of General Psychiatry* 20 (1969): 278-89.

Kaplan, J. *Marijuana: The New Prohibition.* Cleveland: World, 1970.

Kaufman, E. "The Psychodynamics of Opiate Dependence: A New Look." *American Journal of Drug and Alcohol Abuse* 1 (1974): 349-70.

Keller, M. H. "Adverse Reaction to Marijuana." *American Journal of Psychiatry* 124 (1967): 128-31.

Khantzian, E. J. "A Preliminary Dynamic Formulation of the Psychopharmacologic Action of Methadone." In *Proceedings of the Fourth National Methadone Conference,* San Francisco, Calif., Jan. 1972.

———. "Opiate Addiction: A Critique of Theory and Some Implications for Treatment." *American Journal of Psychotherapy* 28 (1974): 59-70.

———. "Self Selection and Progression in Drug Dependence." *Psychiatry Digest* 36 (1975): 19-22.

———. "The Ego, the Self, and Opiate Addiction: Theoretical Considerations and Implications for Treatment." *Psychodynamic Aspects of Narcotics Addiction.* NIDA Technical Review, 1976.

———. "The Ego, the Self and Opiate Addiction: Theoretical and Treatment Considerations." *International Review of Psychoanalysis* 5 (1978): 189-98.

Khantzian, E. J.; Mack, J. E.; and Schatzberg, A. F. "Heroin Use as an Attempt to Cope: Clinical Observations." *American Journal of Psychiatry* 131 (1979): 160-64.

Kiev, Ari. *The Drug Epidemic.* New York:

Free Press, 1975.

Kohut, H. Preface to *Psychodynamics of Drug Dependence.* Edited by J. D. Blain and D. A. Julios. NIDA Research Monograph #12. Washington, D.C.: U.S. Government Printing Office, 1977.

Kolansky, H., and More, W. M. "Effects of Marijuana on Adolescents and Young Addicts." *Journal of the American Medical Association* 216 (1971): 128-31.

Kolansky, H., and Moore, W. T. "Toxic Effects of Chronic Marijuana Use." *Journal of the American Medical Association* 222 (1972): 34-51.

Kolb, L. "Clinical Contributions to Drug Addiction: The Struggle for Cure and the Conscious Reasons for Relapse." *Journal of Nervous and Mental Disease* 66 (1927): 22-43.

————. *Drug Addiction: A Medical Problem.* Springfield, Ill.: Charles C. Thomas, 1962.

————. "Types and Characteristics: Drug Addicts." *Mental Hygiene* 9 (1925): 300-13.

Kramer, J. C., and Littlefield, D. C. "Amphetamine Abusers: Patterns and Effects of High Doses Taken Intravenously." *Journal of the American Medical Association* 201 (1967): 305-09.

Kramer, R. A. "Adolescent Drug Abuse: A Problem or a Solution?" Reported at the Fifth International Institute on Prevention and Treatment of Drug Dependence, 1974.

Kreig, Margaret. *Black Market Medicine.* Englewood Cliffs, N.J.: Prentice-Hall, 1967.

Kron, Y. J., and Brown, E. M. *Mainline to Nowhere: The Making of a Heroin Addict.* New York: Pantheon, 1965.

Krystal, H. "A Review of *Drugs Don't Take People—People Take Drugs.*" *Psychoanalytic Quarterly* 43 (1974): 515-17.

————. "Tolerance." Paper presented at the annual meeting of the American Psychoanalytic Association, 1973.

————. "Withdrawal from Drugs." *Psychosomatics* 7 (1966): 199-302.

Krystal, H., and Raskin, H. A. *Drug Dependence: Aspects of Ego Function.* Detroit: Wayne State University Press, 1970.

Kurland, A. A. "The Narcotic Addict: Some Reflections on Treatment." *Maryland State Medical Journal* (March 1966): 37-39.

Kurland, A. A.; Wurmser, K. L.; and Kokowski, R. "Controls in the Treatment of the Narcotic Addict." *Journal of the American Psychiatric Association* 122 (1966): 739-42.

Landau, E. E. *The Underground Dictionary.* New York: Simon & Schuster, 1971.

Langerman, R. R. *Drugs from A to Z.* New York: McGraw-Hill, 1969.

Lehman, W. X. "A Unique Method of Therapy of the Adolescent Drug Abuser." Presented at the Fifth International Institute on Prevention and Treatment of Drug Dependence, Copenhagen, 1974.

Lemere, F. "The Danger of Amphetamine Dependency." *American Journal of Psychiatry* 123 (1966): 569-72.

Lester, D., and others. "The Addictive Personality." *Psychology* 13 (1976): 253-57.

Levine, D. G.; Leven, D. B.; Sloan, J. H.; and Chappel, J. M. "Personality Correlates of Success in Methadone Maintenance Programs." *American Journal of Psychiatry* 129 (1972): 456-60.

Lief, V. F. "Drug Abuse: Models of Treatment and Their Consequences." *International Pharmacopsychiatry* 7 (1972): 7-21.

Ling, W.; Holmes, E. D.; Post, G. R.; and Litaler, M. B. "A Systematic Psychiatric Study of the Heroin Addict." *National Conference on Methadone Treatment Proceedings* 1 (1973): 429-32.

Linn, L. S. "Psychopathology and Experience with Marijuana." *British Journal of Addiction* 67 (1972): 55-64.

Lloyd, R. A.; Katon, R. N.; and DuPont, R. L. "Evolution of a treatment approach for young heroin addicts." Comparison of three treatment modalities." *The International Journal of the Addictions* 9(2) (1974): 229-39.

Lombardi, D. N.; O'Brian, J.; and Isele, F. W. "Differential Responses of Addicts and Nonaddicts on the MMPI." *Journal of Protective Techniques* 32 (1968): 479-82.

Loomey, M. "The Dreams of Heroin

Addicts.'' *Social Work* 17 (1972): 23-28.

Louria, D. B. *The Drug Scene.* New York: McGraw-Hill, 1968.

Macleod, A. *Growing Up in America—A Background of Contemporary Drug Abuse.* Rockville, Md.: NIMH, 1973.

Malcolm X. *Autobiography of Malcolm X.* New York: McGraw Hill, 1970.

Maliom, A. I. *The Pursuit of Intoxication.* New York: Toronto Alcohol and Drug Addiction Research Foundation, 1971.

Marihuana-Hashish Epidemic and Its Impact on United States Security Hearings. Ninety-third Congress 9-21 May—13 June 1974. Superintendent of Documents, U.S. Government Printing Office, Washington, D.C. 20402.

The Marijuana Problem in the City of New York. Mayor LaGuardia's Committee on Marijuana. Published under the auspices of The Library of the New York Academy of Medicine. Metuchen, N.J.: Scarecrow Reprint Corporation, 1973.

McCracken, S. ''The Drugs of Habit and the Drugs of Belief.'' *Commentary* 51 (1971): 43-52.

McGlothlin, W. H., and West, L. J. ''The Marijuana Problem: An Overview.'' *American Journal of Psychiatry* 125 (1968): 370-78.

McLellan, A. T.; Luborsky, L.; O'Brien, C. P.; and Woody, G. E. ''Toward an Improved Diagnostic Evaluation of Substance Abuse Clients: Initial Findings with the Addiction Severity Index.'' In preparation.

Meerloo, J. A. M. ''Artificial Ecstasy.'' *Journal of Nervous and Mental Disease* 115 (1952): 246-66.

Mendhiratta; Sarabiji F. S.; and others. ''Some Psychological Correlates of Long Term Heavy Cannabis Users.'' *British Journal of Psychiatry* 132 (1978): 482-86.

Merry, J. ''Social Characteristics of Addiction to Heroin.'' *British Journal of Addiction* 67 (1972): 322-25.

Messinger, E., and Zitrin, A. ''A Statistical Study of Criminal Drug Addicts.'' *Crime and Delinquency* 11 (1965): 283-92.

Meyer, R. E., and Merin, S. M. *The Heroin Stimulus: Implications for a Theory of Addiction.* New York: Plenum, 1979.

Meyer, R. G. *Guide to Drug Rehabilitation.* Boston: Beacon Press, 1972.

Milkman, H., and Frosch, W. A. ''On the Preferential Abuse of Heroin and Amphetamine.'' *Journal of Nervous and Mental Disease* 156 (1973): 242-48.

Millman, R. B. ''Adolescent Drug Abuse.'' *Treatment Aspects of Drug Dependence.* Edited by A. Schecter. Cleveland: CRC Press, Inc. (1978): 99-108.

———. ''Drug Abuse in Adolescence—Current Issues.'' In *Developments in The Field of Drug Abuse.* Edited by E. Senay and V. Shorty. Proceedings of First National Drug Abuse Conference. National Association for the Prevention of Addiction to Narcotics, (1974): 18-24.

———. ''Drug and Alcohol Abuse.'' In *Handbook of Treatment of Mental Disorders in Childhood and Adolescence.* Edited by B. B. Wollman, J. Egan, and A. C. Ross. Englewood Cliffs, New Jersey: Prentice-Hall, Inc. (1978): 238-67.

———. ''Drug Abuse, Intoxication, and Addiction.'' In *Textbook of Medicine,* Edited by P. B. Beeson and W. McDermott, Fifteenth Edition. Philadelphia, Pa.: W. B. Saunders, 1979.

Millman, R. B., and E. T. Khuri. (Abstract) ''Treatment Approaches to the Youthful Drug Abuser.'' In *Developments in the Field of Drug Abuse.* Edited by E. Senay and V. Shorty. Proceedings of the First National Drug Abuse Conference. National Association for the Prevention of Addiction to Narcotics, Chicago, April, 1974.

———. (Panel Discussion) ''Trends and Issues in Adolescent Substance Abuse.'' In *Adolescent Health Care—A Multidisciplinary Approach.* Edited by J. E. Morgenthau. The Mount Sinai Hospital Adolescent Health Center, New York: (1976): 213-32.

Mintz, Morton. *By Prescription Only.* Boston: Houghton Mifflin, 1967.

Mirin, S. M.; Meyer, Roger E.; and McNarnel, Brian H. ''Psychopathology: Craving and Need During Heroin Acquisition: An Experimental Study.'' *International Journal of the Addictions* 11 (1976): 525-44.

Mojciechowsk, A. *Tuned Out.* New York: Harper & Row, 1967.

Monroe, J. J.; Ross, W. F.; and Berzins, J. I. "The Decline of the Addict as 'Psychopath': Implications for Community Care." *International Journal of the Addictions* 6 (1971): 601-08.

Moon, J. "Phenomenological Approach to Drug Dependence." *Australian Journal of Alcoholism and Drug Dependence* 1 (1974): 4-7.

Mott, J. "The Psychological Basis of Drug Dependence: The Intellectual and Personality Characteristics of Opiate Users." *British Journal of Addiction* 67 (1972): 89-99.

Myrin Institute for Adult Education Publications. 521 Park Avenue, New York, New York, 10021 (Small contribution required)

National Commission on Marijuana and Drug Abuse. *Drug Use in America: Problem in Perspective.* Second Report. Washington, D.C.: U.S. Government Printing Office, 1973.

National Institute for Drug Programs. *Bibliography on Drug Abuse: Prevention, Treatment, Research.* Washington, D.C.: Human Service Press, 1973.

National Institute on Drug Abuse Research. Superintendent of Documents, U.S. Government Printing Office, Washington, D.C. 20402.

    Vol. 1, *Findings of Drug Abuse Research.* GPO Stock #017-024-0467.

    Vol. 2, *Findings of Drug Abuse Research.* GPO Stock #017-024-0466-9.

    Vol. 5, *Young Men and Drugs: A Nationwide Survey.* Edited by John A. O'Donnell. GPO Stock #017-024-05511-8.

    Vol. 6, *Effects of Labeling the "Drug User": An Inquiry.* Edited by Jay R. Williams. GPO Stock #017-024-05512-6.

    Vol. 12, *Psychodynamics of Drug Dependence.* Edited by Jack D. Blaine and Demetrios A. Julius. GPO Stock #017-024-00842-4.

    Vol. 13, *Cocaine 1977.* Edited by Robert C. Peterson and Richard C. Stilman. GPO Stock #017-024-00642.

    Vol. 14, *Marihuana Research Findings 1976.* Edited by Robert C. Peterson. GPO Stock #017-024-00622-0

    Vol. 15, *Review of Inhalants: Euphoria to Dysfunction.* Edited by Charles Wm. Sharp and Mary Lee Brehm. In press.

    Vol. 16, *The Epidemiology of Heroin and Other Narcotics.* Edited by Joan Dunne Rittenhouse. In press.

New York City Board of Education Bureau for Health and Physical Education. *An Annotated Bibliography on Drugs.* 300 West 43rd Street, New York, N. Y. 10036.

"The Marijuana Decision." New York State Addiction Control Commission. Albany, N.Y., 1965.

Nowlis, H. H. *Drugs on the College Campus.* Garden City, N.Y.: Anchor Books, 1969.

Nyswander, M. *The Drug Addict as Parent.* New York and London: Grune & Stratton, 1971.

O'Brien, C. P.; Testa, T.; O'Brien, T; Brady, J. P.; and Wells, B. "Conditioned Narcotic Withdrawal in Humans." *Science* 19 (1977): 1000-1002.

O'Connor, G.; Wurmser, L.; Brown, T. C.; and Smith, J. "The Drug Addiction Business." *Drug Forum* 1 (1969): 3012.

O'Donnell, J. A. "A Follow-up of Narcotic Addicts: Mortality, Relapse and Abstinence." *American Journal of Orthopsychiatry* 34 (1964): 948-54.

―――. "Research Problems in Follow-up Studies of Addicts." In *Rehabilitating the Narcotic Addict.* Washington, D.C.: U.S. Government Printing Office, 1966.

O'Donnel, J. A., and Bull, C., eds. *Narcotic Addiction.* New York: Harper & Row, 1966.

Olson, Ray W. "MMPI Sex Differences in Narcotic Addicts." *Journal of General Psychology* 71 (1964): 257-66.

O'Malley, J. E.; Anderson, W. H.; and Lazore, A. "Failure of Outpatient Treatment of Drug Abuse: I. Heroin." *American Journal of Psychology* 128 (1972): 865-68.

O'Malley, J. E.; Anderson, W. H.; and Lazore, A. "Failure of Outpatient Treatment of Drug Abuse: II.

Amphetamines, Barbiturates and Hallucinogens.'' *American Journal of Psychology* 128 (1972): 1572-76.

Osnos, R.; and Leskowitt, D. A. "A Counselling Center for Drug Addicts." *Bulletin of Narcotics* 18 (1966): 4.

Ousler, W. *Marijuana: The Facts, the Truth.* New York: Paul S. Eriksson, 1968.

Partridge, M. "Drug Addiction: A Brief Review." *International Journal of the Addictions* 2 (1967): 207-20.

Pescor, M. J. "Follow-up Study of Treated Narcotic Drug Addicts." *Public Health Reports* 170 (Supplement, 1943).

Pittel, S. M. "Psychological Aspects of Heroin and Other Drug Dependence." *Journal of Psychedelic Drugs* 4 (1971): 44.

Pollard, J. C. "Some Comments on Non-narcotic Drug Abuse." Paper presented at the Nonnarcotic Drug Institute, Southern Illinois University, Edwardsville, Ill., June 1967.

"The Pot That Boils—Marijuana." *Science News,* 18 November 1967.

Powell, D. H. "A Pilot Study of Occasional Heroin Users." *Archives of General Psychiatry* 28 (1973): 586-94.

Preble, E., and Carey, J. J. "Taking Care of Business: The Heroin User's Life on the Street." *International Journal of the Addictions* 4 (1969): 1-24.

Proger, S. *The Medicated Society.* New York: Macmillan, 1968.

Proskauer, S., and Piolland, R. S. "Youth Who Use Drugs: Psychodynamic Diagnosis and Treatment Planning." *Journal of the American Academy of Child Psychiatry* 12 (1973): 32-47.

Quitken, F. M.; Rifkin, A.; Kaplan, J.; and Klein, D. F. "Phobic Anxiety Syndrome Complicated by Drug Dependence and Addiction." *Archives of General Psychiatry* 27 (1972): 159-62.

Radford, P.; Wiseberg, S.; and Yorke, C. "A Study of 'Mainline' Heroine Addiction: A Preliminary Report." *Psychoanalytic Study of the Child* 27 (1972): 156-80.

Rado, S. "Fighting Narcotic Bondage and Other Forms of Narcotic Disorders." *Comprehensive Psychiatry* 4 (1963): 160-67.

———. "Narcotic Bondage." *American Journal of Psychiatry* 114 (1957): 165.

———. "The Psychic Effects of Intoxicants: An Attempt to Evolve a Psychoanalytic Theory of Morbid Cravings." *International Journal of Psychoanalysis* 7 (1926): 396-413.

———. "The Psychoanalysis of Pharmacothymia (Drug Addiction)." *Psychoanalytic Quarterly* 2 (1933): 1-23.

Rafferty, M. *Drug Abuse.* Sacramento, Calif.: California State Department of Education, 1967.

Rasken, H. A.; Petty, T. A.; and Warren, M. A. "A Suggested Approach to the Problem of Narcotic Addiction." *American Journal of Psychiatry* 113 (1957): 1089-94.

Ray, O. S. *Drugs, Society, and Human Behavior.* St. Louis: C. V. Mosby, 1972.

Raynes, S. E., and others. "Factors Related to Imprisonment of Female Heroin Addicts." *International Journal of the Addictions* 9 (1974): 145-50.

Read, D. A. *Drugs and People.* Boston: Allyn and Bacon, 1969.

Renner, J. A., and Ruben, M. L. "Engaging Heroin Addicts in Treatment." *American Journal of Psychiatry* 130 (1973): 976-80.

Richards, Louise, G. "Patterns and Extent of Abuse." In *Drugs and Youth.* Edited by J. R. Wittenborn and others. Springfield, Ill.: Charles C. Thomas, 1970.

Robbins, P. R. "Depression and Drug Addiction." *Psychiatric Quarterly* 48 (1974): 374-86.

Robins, L. N.; Davis, D. H.; and Goodwin, D. W. "Drug Use by U.S. Army Enlisted Men in Vietnam: A Follow-up on Their Return Home." *American Journal of Epidemiology* 99 (1974): 235-45.

Robins, L. N., and Murphy, G. I. "Drug Use in Normal Population of Young Negro Men." *American Journal of Public Health* 67 (1967): 1580-96.

Rockwell, D. A., and Ostwald, P. "Amphetamine Use and Abuse in Psychiatric Patients." *Archives of General Psychiatry* 18 (1968): 612-16.

Romano, J., ed. "Drug Addiction." In *Yearbook of Psychiatry and Applied*

Mental Health. Edited by Francis J. Braceland and others. (1977) 339-46.

Room, R. "Social Psychology of Drug Dependence." In *The Epidemiology of Drug Dependence: Report of a Conference*. London and Copenhagen: World Health Organization, 1973.

Rosenfeld, H. A. "On Drug Addiction." In H. A. Rosenfeld, *Psychotic States*. London: Hogarth Press, 1965.

———. "The Psychopathology of Drug Addiction and Alcoholism: A Critical Survey of the Psychoanalytic Literature." In H. A. Rosenfeld, *Psychotic States*. International Universities Press, 1964.

Rosenthal, M. S., and Biase, D. U. "Phoenix House: Therapeutic Community for Drug Addicts." *Hospital and Community Psychiatry* 20 (1969): 26-30.

Rouse, B., and Ewing, J. A. "Marijuana and Other Drug Use by Women College Students: Associated Risk Taking and Coping Activities." *American Journal of Psychiatry* 130 (1973): 486-91.

Rubinow, D. R., and Canero, R. "The Bad Trip: An Epidemiological Survey of Youthful Hallucinogen Use." *Journal of Youth and Adolescence* 6 (1977): 1-10.

Rublonsky, J. *The Stoned Age: A History of Drugs in America*. New York: G. P. Putnam's Sons, 1974.

Russo, R. J. D., ed. *Amphetamine Abuse*. Springfield, Ill.: Charles C. Thomas, 1968.

St. Charles, Alwyn. *The Narcotic Menace*. Los Angeles: Borden Publishing Co., 1952.

Savitt, R. A. "Extramural Psychoanalytic Treatment of a Case of Narcotic Addiction." *Journal of the American Psychoanalytic Association* 2 (1954): 494-502.

———. "Psychoanalytic Studies on Addiction: Ego Structure in Narcotic Addiction." *Psychoanalytic Quarterly* 32 (1963): 43-57.

Schneider, R. J., and others. "Father-Distance and Drug Abuse in Young Men." *Journal of Nervous and Mental Disease* 165 (1977): 269-74.

Schur, E. M. *Narcotic Addiction in Britain and America*. Bloomington, Ind.: Indiana University Press, 1962.

Schwartzman, J. "Addict Abstinence and the Illusion of Alternatives." *Ethos* 5 (1977): 138-50.

———. "Systematic Aspects of Abstinence and Addiction." *British Journal of Medical Psychology* 50 (1977): 181-86.

———. "The Addict, Abstinence and the Family." *American Journal of Psychiatry* 13 (1975): 154-57.

Segal, B., and Merenda, P. "Locus of Control, Sensation-Seeking and Drug and Alcohol use in College Students." *Drug Forum*, 1975.

Seldin, N. E. "The Family of the Addict: A Review of the Literature." *International Journal of the Addictions* 7 (1972): 97-107.

Sells, H. F. *A Bibliography on Drug Dependence*. Fort Worth, Texas: Texas Christian University Press, 1967.

Senay, E. C.; Dorus, W. W.; and Meyer, E. P. *Psychopathology in Drug Abusers: Preliminary Report*. Department of Psychiatry, University of Chicago, Chicago, Ill., 1976.

Serger, A. "Mothering Practices and Heroin Addiction." *American Journal of Nursing* 74 (1974): 77-82.

Shafer, R. R. "Marijuana and Social Misunderstanding"; "Drug Use in America: Problem in Perspective." First and Second Annual Reports of the National Commission on Marijuana and Drug Abuse, R. P. Shafer, Chairman. Washington, D.C.: U.S. Government Printing Office, 1972-1973.

Sharoff, R. L. "Character Problems and Their Relationship to Drug Abuse." *American Journal of Psychoanalysis* 29 (1969): 186-93.

Shearn, C. R. "Survey of Reasons for Illicit Drug Use in a Population of Youthful Psychiatric In-Patients." *International Journal of the Addictions* 8 (1973): 623-33.

Shearn, C. R., and Fitzgibbons, D. J. "Patterns of Drug Use in a Population of Youthful Psychiatric Patients." *American Journal of Psychiatry* 128 (1972): 1381-87.

Sheppard, C.; Fracchia, J.; Recca, E.; and Meris, S. "Indications of Psychopathology in Male Narcotic Abusers, Their Effects and Relation to Treatment Effectiveness." *Journal of Psychology* 81 (1972): 351-60.

Sheppard, C.; Recca, E.; Fracchia, J.; and Merles, S. "Indications of Psychopathology in Applicants to a County Methadone Maintenance Program." *Psychological Reports* 33 (1973): 535-40.

Singer, J. L. "Daydreaming, Drug and Alcohol Use in College Students: A Factor Analytic Study." In *Addictive Behavior* vol. 1. New York: Pergamon Press, 1977.

Single, E.; Kandel, D.; and Faust, R. "Patterns of Multiple Drug Abuse in High School." *Journal of Health and Social Behavior* 15 (1974): 344-57.

Smart, R. G., and Jones, D. "Illicit LSD Users: Their Personality Characteristics and Psychopathology." *Journal of Abnormal Psychology* 75 (1970): 286-92.

Smith, G. M., and Fogg, C. P. "Psychological Predictors of Early Youth, Late Youth, and Nonuse of Marijuana Among Teenage Students." In *Longitudinal Research on Drug Use: Empirical Findings and Methodological Issues.* Edited by D. B. Kandel. Papers from a conference, San Juan, Puerto Rico, April 1976. Washington, D.C.: Hemisphere; and New York: Halsted (Wiley), 1978.

Smith, H. W., and Tullis, K. V. "Physician's Survey of Drug Abuse." *Southern Medicine* 61 (1973): 35-37.

Solas, S. A., and Weiland, F. W. "The Psychopathology of Narcotic-Dependent Individuals." Committee on Problems of Drug Dependence, National Research Council.

Solomon, D., ed. *LSD: The Consciousness Expanding Drug.* New York: G. P. Putnam's Sons, 1964.

Solomon, D., ed. *The Marijuana Papers.* New York: New American Library, 1966.

Stanton, D. M., and Todd, T. C. "Structural Family Therapy with Heroin Addicts: Some Outcome Data." Unpublished manuscript, 1976.

Stearns, J. *The Seekers.* New York: Doubleday, 1961.

Stefanis, C. L.; Aris, B.; Boulougouris, J.; Fink, M.; and Freedman, A. "Chronic Hashish use and Mental Disorder." *American Journal of Psychiatry* 133 (1976): 225-27.

Stein, L. "Chemistry of Reward and Punishment." In *Psychopharmacology: A Review of Progress.* Edited by D. E. Fron. U.S. Public Health Service Publication #1836. Washington, D.C.: U.S. Government Printing Office, 1968.

Surface, W. *The Poisoned Ivy.* New York: Coward-McCann, 1968.

Sutker, P. B. "Personality Differences and Sociopathy in Heroin Addicts and Nonaddict Prisoners." *Journal of Abnormal Psychology* 78 (1971): 247-51.

Sutker, P. B.; Allain, A. N.; and Cohen, G. H. "MMPI Indexes of Personality Change Following Short Term and Long Term Hospitalizations of Heroin Addicts." *Psychological Reports* 34 (1974): 495-500.

Sutker, P. B.; Cohen, G. H.; and Allan, A. N. "Prediction of Successful Response to Multimodality Treatment Among Heroin Addicts." *International Journal of the Addictions* 11 (1976): 861-79.

Szasz, T. S. "The Counterphobia Mechanism in Addiction." *Journal of the American Psychoanalytic Association* 6 (1958): 309-25.

———. "A Dialogue on Drugs." *Psychiatric Opinion* 14 (1977): 10-16.

Taylor, N. *Narcotics: Nature's Dangerous Gifts.* New York: Dell, 1966.

Taylor, S. D.; Wilbur, M.; and Osnos, R. "The Wives of Drug Addicts." *American Journal of Psychology* 123 (1966): 585-91.

Tec, Nechama. "Parent-Child Drug Abuse: Generation Continuity of Adolescent Deviancy?" *Adolescence* 9 (1974): 351-64.

Tennant, F. S. "Dependence Traits Among Parents of Drug Abusers." *Journal of Drug Education* 6 (1976): 83-88.

Tomin, B., and Glenn, A. "Psychotherapy with Drug Abusers in a Male Admitting Service." *Psychiatric Quarterly* 42 (1968): 144-55.

Torda, C. "Comments on the Character Structure and Psychodynamic Process of Heroin Addicts." *Perceptual and Motor Skills* 27 (1968): 143-46.

Tozman, S., and Delescio, E. "Portrait of a

Pusher: 'Mother.' " *Journal of Clinical Psychiatry* 39 (1978): 656-59.

Tylden, E. "A Case for Cannabis?" *British Medical Journal* 3 (1967): 556.

Uhr, L., and Miller, J. G. *Drugs and Behavior.* New York: John Wiley & Sons, 1966.

U.S. Department of Health, Education, and Welfare. *Rehabilitating the Narcotic Addict.* Washington, D.C.: U.S. Government Printing Office, 1966.

"The Up and Down Drugs—Amphetamines and Barbiturates." National Institute of Mental Health Service Publication #1830, Superintendent of Documents, Washington, D.C. 20402, March 1969.

"The Use and Misuse of Drugs." FDA's Life Protection Series, U.S. Department of Health, Education, and Welfare, Publication 46, U.S. Government Printing Office, October 1968.

Vaillant, G. E. "A 12-Year Follow-up of New York Narcotic Addicts. I. The Relation of Treatment to Outcome." *American Journal of Psychiatry* 122 (1966): 727-37.

———. "A 12-Year Follow-up of New York Narcotic Addicts. II. The Natural History of a Chronic Disease." *New England Journal of Medicine* 275 (1966): 1282-88.

———. "A 12-Year Follow-up of New York Narcotic Addicts. III. Some Social and Psychiatric Characteristics." *Archives of General Psychiatry* 15 (1966): 599-609.

———. "Sociopathy as a Human Process." *Archives of General Psychiatry* 32 (1975): 178-83.

Vaillant, G. E., and Rasor, R. W. "The Role of Compulsory Supervision in the Treatment of Addiction." *Federal Probation* 30 (1966?: 53-59.

Warren, L. "The Psychiatric Approach—Drug Addiction." *Journal of the Royal College of General Practitioners* 17 (Supplement, 1969): 2-8.

Weil, A. T.; Zinberg, N. E.; and Nelsen, J. M. "Chemical and Psychological Effects of Marijuana in Man." *Science* 162 (1968): 1234-42.

Wellman, B. "A Learning Theory

Approach to the Treatment of Substance Abuse." Paper presented at the Summer Institute of Drug Abuse, Colorado Springs, Colo. 1977.

Werder, H., and Kaplan, E. H. "Drug Use in Adolescents: Psychodynamic Meaning and Pharmacogenic Effect." *Psychoanalytic Study of the Child* 24 (1969): 399-431.

Wikler, A. A. "A Psychodynamic Study of a Patient During Experimental Self-Regulated Re-Addiction to Morphine." *Psychiatric Quarterly* 26 (1952): 270-93.

———. "Conditioning Factors in Opiate Addiction and Relapse." In *Narcotics.* Edited by D. M. Wilmer and C. G. Kassebaum. New York: McGraw Hill, 1965.

———. "Dynamics of Drug Dependence: Implications of a Conditioning Theory for Research and Treatment." In *Opiate Addiction: Origins and Treatment.* Edited by S. Fisher and A. M. Freeman. Washington, D.C.: Winston, 1974.

Wikler, A. A., and Rasor, R. W. "Psychiatric Aspects of Drug Addiction." *American Journal of Medicine* 14 (1953): 566-70.

Winick, C. "Maturing Out of Narcotics Addiction." *Bulletin of Narcotics* 14 (1962): 1-7.

Wishnie, H. "Opioid Addiction: A Masked Depression." In *Masked Depression.* Edited by S. Lessee. New York: J. Aronson, 1974.

Wishnie, H., and Cowan, R. "Schematic Techniques in Therapy with Addicts." *National Conference on Methadone Treatment Proceedings* 2 (1973): 1387-93.

Wittenborn, J. R.; Brill, L.; Smith, J. P.; and Wittenborn, S. A. *Drugs and Youth: Proceedings of the Rutgers Symposium on Drug Abuse.* Springfield, Ill.: Charles C. Thomas, 1969.

Woody, G. E., and Blaine, J. D. "Depression in Narcotics Addicts: Quite Possibly More Than a Chance Association." In *Handbook on Drug Abuse.* Edited by R. L. Dupont, A. Goldstein, J. O'Donnell, and B. Brown. Washington, D.C.: U.S. Government Printing Office. In press.

Woody, G. E.; O'Brien, C. P.; and Richards, H. "Depression and Anxiety in Heroin Addicts: A Placebo-Controlled

Study of Doxepen in Combination with Methadone." *American Journal of Psychiatry* 132 (1975): 447-50.

World Health Organization. *Youth and Drugs.* Report of a WHO Study Group. Technical Report No. 516. WHO: Geneva, 1973.

World Health Organization. *Twentieth Report of the Expert Committee on Drug Dependence.* Technical Report No. 550. WHO: Geneva, 1973.

World Health Organization Expert Committee on Drugs. "Drug Dependence: Its Significance and Characteristics." *Bulletin of the World Health Organization* 32 (1965): 721-33.

Wright, R. "The Psychology and Personality of Addicts." *Adolescence* 12 (1977): 359-401.

Wurmser, L. "Drug Addiction and Drug Abuse: A Synopsis." *Maryland State Medical Journal* 17 (1968): 68-80.

———. *The Hidden Dimension: Psychopathology of Compulsive Drug Use.* New York: Jason Aronson, 1978.

———. "Methadone and the Craving for Narcotics—Observations of Patients on Methadone Maintenance in Psychotherapy." *Proceedings of the Fourth National Methadone Conference,* 1972.

———. "Personality Disorders and Drug Dependence." In *Personality Disorder Diagnosis and Management.* Edited by John R. Leon. Baltimore: Williams & Wilkins, 1974.

———. "Principles of Prevention of Drug Abuse Presented to the U.S. Senate Committee on D.C. (Senator Tydings). In *Crime in the National Capital.* Washington, D.C.: U.S. Government Printing Office, 1970.

———. "Psychosocial Aspects of Drug Abuse. Part I. Etiological Considerations." *Maryland State Medical Journal* 22 (1973): 78-82.

———. "Psychosocial Aspects of Drug Abuse. Part 2. Treatment and the Role of the Family Physician." *Maryland State Medical Journal* 22 (1973): 99-101.

———. "Psychoanalytic Considerations of the Etiology of Compulsive Drug Use." *Journal of the American Psychoanalytic Association* 32 (1974): 820-43.

———. "Why People Take Drugs: Escape and Search." *Maryland State Medical Journal,* 1970, 62-64.

Wurmser, L.; Flowers, E.; and Weldon, S. "Methadone—Discipline and Revenge." *Proceedings of the Fifth National Methadone Conference,* 1973.

Wurmser, L.; Leven, L.; and Lewis, A. "Chronic Paranoid and Depressive Symptoms in Users of Marijuana and LSD as Observed in Psychotherapy." *Proceedings of the Thirty-First Annual Meeting of the Committee on Problems of Drug Dependence.* National Research Council, 1969.

Wurmser, L., and Spero, H. R. "Factors in Recognition and Management of Sociopathy and the Addictions." *Modern Treatment* 6 (1969): 704-19.

Yorke, C. "A Critical Review of Some Psychoanalytic Literature on Drug Addiction." *British Journal of Medical Psychology* 93 (1970): 141-55.

Zimmering, P.; Toolan, J.; Safrin, M. S.; and Works, S. P. "Drug Addiction in Relation to Problems of Adolescence." *American Journal of Psychiatry* 109 (1952): 272-78.

Zinberg, N. E. "Addiction and Ego Function." *Psychoanalytic Study of the Child* 30 (1975): 576-88.

———. *High States: A Beginning Study.* Washington, D.C.: The Drug Abuse Council, 1974.

Zuckerman, M.; Sola, S.; Masterson, J. W.; and Angelone, J. V. "MMPI Patterns in Drug Abusers Before the After Treatment in Therapeutic Communities." *Journal of Consulting and Clinical Psychology* 43 (1975): 286-96.

POPULAR NOVELS ON DRUG ADDICTION

Bagley, D. *The Spoilers.* New York: Doubleday, 1975.

Blum, R. *The Simultaneous Man.* Boston: Little, Brown, 1975.

Boulle, P. *The Virtues of Hell.* New York: Vanguard Press, 1974.

Caserta, Peggy. *Going Down with Janis* (Janis Joplin). New York: Dell, 1974.

Dickson, G. R. *The R Master.* New York: Lippincott, 1973.

Du Maurier, D. *The House on the Strand.* New York: Doubleday, 1969.

Hergescheimer, J. *Java Head.* New York: Knopf, 1946.

Herlihy, J. L. *The Season of the Witch.* New York: Simon & Schuster, 1975.

MacDonald, J. D. *Dress Her in Indigo.* New York: Lippincott, 1971.

MacLean, A. *The Way to Dusty Death.* New York: Doubleday, 1973.

Meyer, N. *The Seven-Per-Cent Solution.* New York: Dutton, 1974.

Motley, W. *Let No Man Write My Epitaph.* New York: Random House, 1958.

Pavese, C. *The Devil in the Hills.* New York: Farrar, Straus, 1968.

Robbe-Grillet, A. *La Maison de Rendez-Vous.* New York: Grove Press, 1975.

Silverberg, R. "How It Was When the Past Went Away." In *Three for Tomorrow-Nightwings.* New York: Walker & Co., 1975.

Stewart, R. *The Possession of Joel Delaney.* Boston: Little, Brown, 1970.

Tidgman, E. *Shaft.* New York: Macmillan, 1970.

Weslake, D. E. *The Busy Body.* New York: Random House, 1966.

Young, A. *Snakes.* New York: Holt, Rinehart and Winston, 1970.

FOOD

Abrahsom, E. E. "A Review of Behavioral Approaches to Weight Control." *Behavior Research Therapy* 11 (1973): 517-56.

Abram B. "Weight Watchers: A Total Approach to Weight Control." *Canada Home Economics Journal* 26 (1976): 4-10.

Allen, G. S. "A Practical Regimen for Weight Reduction in Family Practice. *The Journal of International Medical Research* 3 (1975): 40-44.

Ashwell, A. "Commerical Weight Loss Groups." *Recent Advances in Obesity Research*: 2. Edited by G. Bray. London: Newman Publishing Company. In press.

Ashwell, M., and Garrow, J. S. "A Survey of Three Slimming and Weight Control Organizations in the U.S." *Nutrition* 29 (1975): 347-56.

Atkinson, R. L.; Greenway, F. L.; Bray, G. A.; Dahms, W. T.; Molitch, M. E.; Hamilton K. and Rodin, J. "Treatment of Obesity: comparison of physician and non-physician therapists using placebo and anorectic drugs in a double-bline trial." *International Journal of Obesity* 1 (1977): 113-120.

Bauer, E. R. "Inhibition of Eating in the Obese: Cognition or Guilt?" *American Psychologist* 26 (1971): 739.

Bellack, A. S. "Behavioral Treatment for Obesity: Appraisal and Recommendations." *Progress in Behavior Modification,* vol. 4. Edited by M. Hersen; R. M. Eisler; and P. M. Miller. New York: Academic Press, 1976.

Bellack, A. S.; Schwartz, J.; and Rozensky, R. H. "The Contribution of External Control to Self-Control in a Weight Reduction Program." *Journal of Behavior Therapy and Experimentation Psychiatry* 5 (1972): 245-50.

Berman, E. M. "Factors Influencing Motivations in Dieting." *Journal of Nutritional Education* 7 (1975): 155-59.

Bernard, J. L. "Rapid Treatment of Gross Obesity by Operant Techniques." *Psychological Reports* 23 (1968): 663-66.

Booth, D. A. "Appetite and Satiety as Metabolic Expectancies." In *Food Intake and Chemical Senses.* Edited by Y. Katsuki; M. Sato; and S. F. Tagagi. Baltimore, Maryland: University Park Press, 1977.

———. "Approaches to Feeding Control." In *Appetite and Food Intake.* Edited by T. Silverston. Berlin: Abakon, 1976.

———. "First Steps Towards an Integrated Quantitative Approach to Human Feeding and Obesity with Some Implications for Research into Treatment." *Recent Advances in Obesity Research, II.* London: Newman, 1978.

———. "Satiety and Appetite are Conditioned Reactions." *Psychosomatic Medicine* 39 (1977): 76-81.

Booth, D. A.; Lee, M.; and McAleavy, C.

"Acquired Sensory Control of Satiation in Man." *British Journal of Psychology* 67 (1976): 137-47.

Booth, D. A. and Mather, P. "Prototype Model of Human Feeding. Growth and Obesity. In *Hunger Models: Computable Theory of Feeding Control*. Edited by E. A. Booth, London: Academic Press, 1978.

Boskind, Lodahl, Marlene, and Serlen. "The Gorging Purging Syndrome." *Psychology Today*, 10:10 (1977): 50-52, 82-85.

Bray, G. A. "Drug Therapy for The Obese Patient." In *The Obese Patient, Major Problems in Internal Medicine*. vol. 9, Philadelphia, Pa.: W. B. Saunders, 1976, 353-410.

Bray, G. A., ed. "Obesity in Perspective." *U.S. Government Printing Office*, Washington D.C., 1973, p. 498.

Brightwell, D. R. *Successful Followup of Obese Subjects Treated with Behavior Therapy*. Unpublished. 1975.

——. "Treating Obesity with Behavior Modification." *Postgraduate Medicine* 55 (1974): 52-58.

Brownell, K. D.; Heckerman, C. L.; Westlake, R. J.; et al. "The Effect of Couples Training and Partner Cooperativeness in the Behavioral Treatment of Obesity." Paper presented at the Annual Meeting of the Association for Advancement of Behavior Therapy, Atlanta, Ga., December 1977.

Brownell, K. D., and Stunkard, A. J. "Behavioral Treatment of Obesity in Children." *American Journal of Diseases of Children* 133 (1978): 403-12.

Bruch, H. "A Diet or A Psychiatrist? The Psychology of Obesity." *Medical Opinion* 2 (1973): 34-39.

——. "Conceptual Confusion in Eating Disorders." *Journal of Nervous and Mental Diseases* 133 (1961): 46.

——. "Depressive Factors in Adolescent Eating Disorders." In *Phenomenology and Treatment of Depression*. Edited by W. E. Founn, et al, 1977.

——. *Eating Disorders*. New York: Basic Books, 1973.

——. *The Golden Cage*. Cambridge, Mass.: Harvard University Press, 1978.

——. "Hunger and Instinct." *Journal of Nervous and Mental Diseases* 149 (1969): 91-114.

——. "Obesity and Anorexia Nervosa." *Psychosomatics* 19(4) (1978): 208-13.

——. "Transformation of Oral Impulses in Eating Disorders: A Conceptual Approach." *Psychiatric Quarterly* 35 (1961): 458-81.

Burdoin, R., and Mayer J. "Food Intakes of Obese and Non-obese Women." *Journal of American Dietetic Association* 29 (1953): 29-33.

Cautela, J. R. "Covert Sensitization." *Psychological Reports* 29 (1967): 459-68.

Cautela, J. R. "Treatment of Compulsive Behavior by Covert Sensitization." *Psychological Reports* 16 (1966): 33-41.

Chisholm, O. D. "Obesity in Adolescence." *Journal of Adolescence* 12 (1978): 177-194.

Collipp, P. J., ed. "Childhood Obesity." *Acton Massz Publishing Sciences Group, Inc.*, 1975.

Craighead, L.; O'Brien, R.; and Stunkard, A. "New Treatments for Obesity." Paper read at American Psychiatric Association meeting, Atlanta, Georgia, May 1978.

Davis, J. D.; Collins, B. J.; and Levine, M. W. "The Interaction Between Gustatory Stimulation and Gut Feedback in the Control of the Ingestion of Liquid Diets." In *Hunger Models: Computable Theory of Feeding Control*. Edited by D. A. Booth. London: Academic Press, 1978.

Decke, E. "Effects of Taste on the Eating Behavior of Obese and Normal Persons." In Schachter, S. *Emotion, Obesity, and Crime*. New York: Academic Press, 1971.

Dent, D. A.; Parsonage, S. R.; and Miller, D. S. "Comparison of Low Carbohydrate and Calorie Controlled Diets in Obese Subjects with a Sweeth Tooth." *General Practitioner*, 2 February 1973, 10-11.

DeRisi W. "Writing Behavioral Contracts to Control Problems." *Practical Psychology for Physicians* 2 (1975): 47-50.

DHSS/MRC. "Research on obesity." A report on the DHSS/MRC Group. London: HMSO, 1976.

Drabman, R. S.; Hammer, D.; and Jarvie,

G. J. "Eating Styles of Obese and Non-obese Black and White Children in a Natur-alistic Setting." *Addictive Behavior* 2 (1977): 83-86.

Duncan, G. C.; Jenson, W. K.; Frazer, R. L.; et al. "Correction and Control of Intractable Obesity." *Journal of the American Medical Association* 181 (1962): 309.

Dunkel, L. D., and Glaros, A. G. "Com-parison of Self-Instructional and Stimulus Control Treatments of Obesity." *Cognitive Therapy Research* 2 (1978): 75-78.

Elliott, C. H., and Denney, D. R. "Weight Control Through Covert Sensitization and False Feedback." *Journal of Consulting Clinical Psychology* 43 (1975): 842-50.

Erickson, M. A. "The Utilization of Patient Behavior in The Hypnotherapy of Obesity." *American Journal Clinical Hypnosis 3* (1960): 112-16.

Evans, R. I., and Hall, Y. "Social-Psychologic Perspective in Motivating Changes in Eating Behavior." *Journal of the American Dieticians Association* 72 (1978) 378.

Feinstein, A. R. "The Treatment of Obesity: An Analysis of Methods, Results, and Factors Which Influence Success." *Journal of Chronic Disease* 11 (1960): 349.

Fellows, H. H. "Study of Relatively Normal and Obese Individuals During and After Dietary Restriction." *American Journal of Medical Science* 181 (1931): 301-08.

Ferster, C. B.; Nurnberger, J. I.; and Levitt, E. B. "The Control of Eating." *Journal of Mathetics* 1 (1962): 87-109.

Foreyt, J. P., ed. *Behavioral Treatments of Obesity.* New York: Pergamon, 1977.

Foreyt, J. P., and Hagen, R. L. "Covert Sensitization: Conditioning or Suggestion?" *Journal of Abnormal Psychology 82* (1973) 17-23.

Foreyt, J. P., and Kennedy, W. A. "Treat-ment of Overweight by Aversion Therapy." *Behavior Research Therapy* 9 (1971): 29-34.

Fowler, R. S. "The Mouthful Diet." In *Be-havioral Programs for the Treatment of Obesity.* Edited by E. E. Abramson. New York: Springer, 1976.

Friedman, M. I., and Stricker, E. M. "The Physiological Psychology of Hunger: A Physiological Perspective." *Psychological Review* 83 (1976)L 409-37.

Garb, J. R., and Stunkard, A. J. "Effective-ness of Self-Help Group in Obesity Control." *Archives of Internal Medicine* 134 (1974): 716-20.

Glucksman, M. L. "Psychiatric Obser-vations on Obesity." *Advances of Psycho-somatic Medicine* 7 (1972): 194-216.

Glucksman, M. L., and Hirsch, J. "The Response of Obese Patients to Weight Reduction: A Clinical Evaluation of Behavior." *Psychosomatic Medicine* 30 (1968): 1-11.

Glucksman, M. L.; McCully, R. S.; Barron, B. A.; and Knittle, J. L. "The Response of Obese Patients to Weight Reduction: II. A Quantitative Evaluation of Behavior." *Psychosomatic Medicine* 30 (1968): 359-73.

Goldblatt, P. B.; Moore, M. E.; and Stunkard, A. J. "Social Factors in Obesity." *Journal of the American Medical Assodication* 192 (1965): 1039-44.

Goldman, D.; Jaffa, M.; and Schachter, S. "Yom Kippur, Air France, Dormitory Food, and Eating, behavior of obese and normal persons." *Journal of Personal and Social Psychology* 10 (1968): 117-23.

Hagen, R. L. *Group Therapy versus Biblio-therapy in Weight Reduction.* Thesis. University of Illinois, Champaign: 1969.

Hagen, R. L. "Theories of Obesity: Is there any hope for order?" *Obesity: Behavioral Approaches to Dietary Management.* Edited by B. J. Williams; S. Martin; and J. P. Foreyt. New York: Brunner-Mazel, 1976.

Hall, S. M., and Hall, R. G. "Outcome and Methodological Considerations in Behavioral Treatment of Obesity." *Behavior Therapy* 5 (1974): 352-64.

Harmatz, M. G., and Lapuc, P. "Behavior Modification of Overeating in a Psychiatric Population." *Journal of Consulting Clinical Psychology* 32 (1968): 583-87.

Harris, M. B. "Self-directed Program for Weight Control: A Pilot Study." *Journal* of Abnormal Psychology 74 (1969): 263-70.

Harris, M. B., and Hallbauer, E. S. "Self-directed Weight Control Through Eating and Exercise." Behavior Research Therapy 11 (1973): 523-29.

Hendry, L. B., and Billies, P. "Body Type, Body Esteem, School and Leisure: A Study of overweight, average and underweight adolescence." Journal Youth Adolescence 7:2 (1978): 181-96.

Herman, C. P., and Mack, D. "Restrained and Unrestrained Eating." Journal of Personality 43 (1975): 647-60.

Hibscher, J. A., and Herman, C. P. "Obesity, Dieting, and the Expression of 'Obese' Characteristics." Journal of Comparative Physiology and Psychology 91 (1977): 374-80.

Hirsch, J., and Knittle, J. L. "Cellularity of Obese and Non-Obese Human Adipose Tissue." Federal Procedure 29 (1970): 1516-21.

Hirsch, J. "Discussion (Disturbances in the Regulation of Food Intake)." Advances in Psychosomatic Medicine 7 (1972): 229-42.

Janda, L. H., and Rimm, D. C. "Covert Sensitization in the Treatment of Obesity." Journal of Abnormal Psychology 80 (1972): 37-42.

Jeffrey, D. B. "A Comparison of the Effects of External Control and Self-control on the Modification and Maintenance of Weight." Journal of Abnormal Psychology 83 (1974): 404-10.

Jeffery, R. W.; Wing, R. R.; and Stunkard, A. J. "Behavioral Treatment of Obesity: The State of the art 1976." Behavior Therapy. In press.

Johnson, M. L.; Burke, B. S.; and Mayer, J. "Relative Importance of Inactivity and Overeating in the Energy Balance of Obese High School Girls." American Journal of Clinical Nutrition 4 (1956): 37-44.

Jordan, H. S., and Levitz, L. S. "Behavior Modification in a Self-Help Group." Journal of the American Dietetic Assocation 62 (1973): 27-29.

Jordan, H. A., et al.: "Psychobiological Factors in Obesity." Psychosomatic Medicine: Its Clinical Applications. Edited by E. Witthower, and H. Warmes, 1977. 236-48.

Kalucy, R. S. "Obesity: An Attempt to Find a Common Ground Among Some of the Biological, Psychological, and Sociological Phenomena of the Obesity Overeating Syndromes." Modern Trends in Psychosomatic Medicine 3. Edited by Oskar Witell. (1976): 404-29.

Karpowitz, D. H., and Zein, F. R. "Personality and Behaviour Differences Among Obese and Non-obese Adolescents." In Recent Advances in Obesity Research. I. Edited by A. Howard. London: Newman, 1975.

Kaplan, H., and Kaplan, H. S. "The Psychosomatic Concept of Obesity." Journal of Nervous and Mental Disease 125 (1957): 181-201.

Kennedy, W. A., Foreyt, J. "Control of Eating Behavior in an Obese Patient by avoidance conditioning." Psychological Reports 22 (1968): 571-76.

Kolata, G. B. "Obesity, a Growing Problem." Science 198 (1977): 405.

Kopel, S., and Arkowitz, H. "The Role of Attribution and Self-Perception in Behavior Change: Implications for Behavior Therapy." Genetic Psychological Monograph 92 (1975): 175.

Le Magnen, J. "Sweet Preference and the Sensory Control of Caloric Intake." In Taste and Development: The Genesis of Sweet Preference. Edited by J. M. Weiffenbach. Washington, D.C.: U.S. Government Printing Office, 1977.

Leon, G. R. "Current Directions in the Treatment of Obesity., Psychological Bulletin 83 (1976): 557-78.

Levitz, L. "Behavior Therapy in Treating Obesity." Journal of the American Dietetic Association 62 (1973): 22-26.

Levitz, L. "The Susceptibility of Human Feeding to External Control." In Obesity in Perspective. Edited by G. A. Bray. Washington, D.C.: U.S. Government Printing Office, 1975.

Levitz, L., and Stunkard, A. J. "A Therapeutic Coalition for Obesity: Behavior Modification and Patient Self-Help." American Journal of Psychiatry 131 (1974): 423-47.

Maccuish, A. C.; Munro, J. F.; Duncun, L. J. P. "Follow-up Study of Refractory Obesity Treated by Fasting." *British Medical Journal* 1 (1968): 91-200.

Mahoney, B. K.; Rogers, T.; Straw, M. K.; et al. *Human Obesity: Assessment and Treatment.* Englewood Cliffs, New Jersey: Prentice-Hall. In press.

Mahoney, M. J. "The Obese Eating Style: Bites, Beliefs, and Behavior Modification." *Addictive Behavior* 1 (1975): 47-53.

———. "Self-Reward and Self-Monitoring Techniques for Weight Control." *Behavior Therapy* 5 (1974): 48-57.

Mahoney, M. J., and Mahoney, K. *Permanent Weight Control.* New York: W. W. Norton, 1976.

———. "Treatment of Obesity: A Clinical Exploration." In *Obesity: Behavioral Approaches to Dietary Management.* Edited by B. J. Williams; S. Martin; and J. P. Foreyt. New York: Brunner/Mazel (1976): 30-39.

Mahoney, M. J.; Moura, N. G.; Wade, T. C. "Relative Efficacy of Self-Reward, Self-Punishment, and Self-Monitoring Techniques for Weight Loss." *Journal of Consulting and Clinical Psychology* 40 (1973): 404-07.

Mahoney, M. J., and Thoresen, C. E. *Self-Control: Power to the Person.* Monterey, California: Brooks/Cole Publishing Co., 1974.

Manno, B., and Marston, A. R. "Weight Reduction As a Function of Negative covert reinforcement (sensitization) versus positive covert reinforcement." *Behavior Research Therapy* 10 (1972): 201-07.

Mayer, J. *Overweight: Causes, Cost and Control.* Englewood Cliffs, N.J.: Prentice-Hall, 1968.

Mehrabian, A. *Tactics of Social Influence.* Englewood Cliffs, N.J.: Prentice-Hall, 1970.

Meyer, J. E. "Psychopathology and Eating Disorders." In *Appetite and Food Intake.* Edited by T. Silverstone. Berlin: Abakon, 1976.

Meyer, V., and Crisp, A. H. "Aversion Therapy in Two Cases of Obesity." *Behavior Research Therapy* 2 (1964): 143-47.

Mikulas, W. L. "A Televised Self-Control Clinic." *Behavior Therapy* 17 (1976): 4.

Milgram, N. W.; Krames, L.; and Alloway, T. M., eds. *Food Aversion Learning.* New York: Plenum Press, 1977.

Miller, D. S., and Parsonage, S. "Resistance to Slimming. Adaptation or Illusion." *Lancet* 1 (1975): 733.

Monello, L. F. and Mayer, J. "Hunger and Satiety Sensations in Men, Women, Boys and Girls." *American Journal of Clinical Nutrition* 20 (1967): 253-61.

Morganstern, K. P. "Cigarette Smoke as a Noxious Stimulus in Self-Managed Aversion Therapy for Compulsive Eating: Technique and Case illustration." *Behavior Therapy* 5 (1974): 225-60.

Munro, J. F. "The Management of Obesity." In *Symposium on Anorexia Nervosa and Obesity.* Edited by R. F. Robertson and A. T. Proudfoot. Edinburgh: Royal College of Physicians (1973): 100-09.

Nisbett, R. E. "Determinants of Food Intake In Human Obesity." *Science* 159 (1968): 1254-55.

Nisbett, R. E., and Kanouse, D. "Obesity, Food Deprivation, and Supermarket Shopping Behavior." *Journal of Personal and Social Psychology* 12 (1969): 289-94.

Nisbett, R. E., and Storms, M. D. "Cognitive, Social, Physiological Determinants of Food Intake." In *Cognitive Modification of Emotional Behavior.* Edited by H. London and R. E. Nisbett. Chicago: Aldine, 1975.

Penick, S. B.; Filion, R.; Fox, S.; Stunkard, A. J. "Behavior Modification in the Treatment of Obesity." *Psychosomatic Medicine* 33 (1971): 49-55.

Penick, S. B., and Stunkard, A. J. "The Treatment of Obesity." *Advances in Psychosomatic Medicine* 7 (1972): 217-28.

Plotz, M. "Modern Management of Obesity—The Social Diet." *Journal of the American Medical Association* 170 (1959): 1513.

Pudel, J. E. "Psychological Observations on Experimental Feeding in the Obese." In *Recent Advances in Obesity Research –.* Edited by A. N. Howard. London: Newman (1975): 217-20.

Pudel, J. E., and Oetting, M. "Eating in the Laboratory: Behavioural Aspects of the Positive Energy Balance." *International Journal of Obesity* 1 (1977): 369-86.

Rand, C. S. W., and Stunkard, A. J. "Obesity and Psychoanalysis." *American Journal of the Academy of Psychoanalysis* 135 5 (1978): 547-51; (1977): 459-97.

Rascovsky, A.; DeRascovsky, M. W.; and Schlossberg, T. "Basic Psychic Structure of the Obese." *International Journal of Psychoanalysis* 31 (1950): 144-49.

Rodin, J. "Can Fat Be Beautiful? *Contemporary Psychology* 19 (1974): 630-31.

———. "Causes and Consequences of Time Perception Differences in Overweight and Normal-Weight People." *Journal of Personality and Social Psychology* 31 (1975): 898-910.

———. "Effects of Distraction on the Performance of Obese and Normal Subjects." *Journal of Comparative and Physiological Psychology* 8 (1973): 68-75.

———. "The Effects of Obesity and Set Point on Taste Responsiveness and Intake in Humans." *Journal of Comparative Physiology* 89 (1975): 1003-9.

———. "The Effects of Stimulus-Bound Behavior on Biological Self-Regulation: Feeding, Obesity, and External Control." In *Consciousness and Self-Regulation*, vol. 2. By G. Schwartz and D. Shapiro. New York: Plenum Press, 1978.

———. "Environmental Factors in Obesity." In *Psychiatric Clinics Symposium on Obesity.* Edited by A. J. Stunkard. Philadelphia: W. B. Saunders, 1978.

———. "External and Internal Controls." In *Recent Advances in Obesity Research II.* Edited by G. A. Bray. London: Newman, 1978.

———. "Human Obesity and External Behavior." In *Recent Advances in Obesity Research.* Edited by A. Howard. London: Newman Publishing Ltd., 1975.

———. "The Relationship Between External Responsiveness and the Development and Maintenanance of Obesity." In *Hunger, Basic Mechanisms and Clinical Implications.* Edited by I. D. Novin; W. Wyrwicka; and G. Bray. New York: Raven Press, 1976.

———. "Research and Eating Behavior and Obesity: Where Does It Fit In Personality and Social Psychology." *Personality and Social Psychology Bulletin* 3 (1977): 333-55.

———. "Responsiveness of the Obese to External Stimuli." In *Obesity in Perspective.* Edited by G. Bray; G. Cahill, Jr.; E. S. Horton; H. A. Jordon; F. R. McCrumb, Jr.; L. B. Salans; and E. A. H. Sims. Washington, D.C.: U.S. Government Printing Office, 1975.

———. The Role of Perception of Internal and External Signals on the Regulation of Feeding in Overweight and Nonobese Individuals." In *Appetite and Food Intake.* Edited by J. Silverstone. Berlin: Dahlem Konferenzen (1976): 265-83.

———. "The Role of Perception of Internal and External Signals on Regulation of Feeding in Overweight and Nonobese Individuals." In *Appetite and Food Intake.* Edited by T. Silverstone. Braunschweig: Pergamon Press/Vieweg, 1976.

Rodin, J.; Bray, G. A.; Atkinson, R. L.; Dahms, W. T.; Greenway, F. L.; Hamilton, K.; and Molitch, M. "Predictors of Successful Weight Loss in an Out-Patient Obesity Clinic." *International Journal of Obesity* 1 (1976): 12-16.

Rodin, J.; Moskowitz, H. R.; and Bray, G. A. "Relationship Between Obesity, Weight Loss, and Taste Responsiveness." *Physiology and Behavior* 17 (1976): 591-97.

Rodin, J. and Singer, J. L. "Eyeshift, Thought, and Obesity." *Journal of Personality* 44 (1976): 594-610.

Rodin, J., and Slochower, J. "Externality in the Nonobese: The Effects of Environmental Responsiveness on Weight." *Journal of Personality and Social Psychology* 33 (1976): 338-44; (1976): 557-65.

———. "Fat Chance for a Favor: Obese-Normal Differences in Compliance and Incidental Learning." *Journal of Personality and Social Psychology* 29 (1974): 557-65.

Rodin, J.; Slochower, J.; and Fleming, B. "The Effects of Degree of Obesity, Age of Onset, and Energy Deficit on External Responsiveness." *Journal of Comparative Physiology and Psychology* 91 (1977):

586-97.

Rosenthal, B. S. "The Role of a Significant Other in the Behavioral Treatment of Obesity." Paper presented to the American Psychological Association. Chicago, 1975.

Ross, L. D.; Pliner, P.; Nesbitt, P.; et al. "Patterns of Externality and Internality in Eating Behavior of Obese and Normal College Students." In *Emotion, Obesity, and Crime.* Edited by S. Schachter. New York: Academic Press, 1971.

Rozin, P. "Psychobiological and Cultural Determinants of Food Choice." In *Appetite and Food Intake.* Edited by T. Silverstone. Berlin: Abakon, 1976.

Sachs, L. B., and Ingram, G. L. "Covert Sensitization as a Treatment for Weight Control." *Psychological Reports* 30 (1972): 971-74.

Savitt, R. A. "Psychoanalytic Studies on Addiction, III: Food Addiction (Obesity)." Read at 1971 Spring Meeting, American Psychoanalytic Association. An unpublished manuscript.

Schachter, S. *Emotion, Obesity, and Crime.* New York: Academic Press, 1971.

———. "Obesity and Eating." *Science* 161 (1968): 751-56.

Schachter, S.; Goldman, R.; and Gordon, A. "Effects of Fear, Food Deprivation and Obesity on Eating." *Journal of Personal and Social Psychology* 10 (1968): 91-97.

Schachter, S., and Gross, L. "Manipulated Time and Eating Behavior." *Journal of Personal and Social Psychology* 10 (1968): 98-106.

Scoville, B. A. "Review of Amphetamine-like Drugs for the Food and Drug Administration: Clinical Data and Value Judgements." In *Obesity in Perspective.* Edited by G. A. Bray. Washington, D.C.: U.S. Government Printing Office (1976): 441-43.

Shipman, W. "Behavior Therapy With Obese Dieters." Annual report of the Institute for Psychosomatic and Psychiatric Research and Training. Chicago: Michael Reese Hospital and Medical Center 1970: 70-71.

Slochower, J. "Emotional Labeling and Overeating in Obese and Normal Weight Individuals." *Psychosomatic Medicine* 38 (1976): 131-39.

Stuart, R. B. *Act Thin: Stay Thin.* New York: W. W. Norton, 1978.

———. "Behavior Control of Overeating. *Behavior Research Therapy* 5 (1967): 357.

———. "Behavioral Control of Overeating: A Status Report." In *Obesity in Perspective.* Edited by G. A. Bray, et al. Fogarty International Center Series on Preventive Medicine. DHEW Publication No. (NIH) 75-708. Washington, D.C.: U.S. Government Printing Office, 1975.

———. *Trick or Treatment: How and When Psychotherapy Fails.* Champaign, Illinois: Research Press (1971): 183-94.

Stuart, R. B. and Davis, B. *Slim Chance in a Fat World: Behavioral Control of Obesity.* Champaign, Illinois: Research Press, 1972.

Stuart, R. B., and Guire, K. "Some Correlates in the Maintenance of Weight Loss Through Behavior Modification." *International Journal of Obesity.* In press.

Stuart, R. B., and Sachson, B. "Sex Differences in Obesity." In *Gender and Psychopathology.* Edited by Gomberg and E. Franks. New York: Brunnig Mazel. In press.

Stunkard, A. J. "From Explanation to Action in Psychosomatic Medicine: The Case of Obesity." *Psychosomatic Medicine* 37 (1975): 195-236.

———. "The Management of Obesity." *New York Journal of Medicine* 58 (1958): 69-87.

———. "New Therapies for the Eating Disorders." *Archives of General Psychiatry* 26 (1972): 391.

———. "Obesity and the Denial of Hunger." *Psychomatic Medicine* 21 (1959): 281-89.

———. "Obesity and the Social Environment: Current Status, Future Prospects." *Annals of the New York Academy of Science* 300 (1977): 298-320.

———. *The Pain of Obesity,* Palo Alto: Bull Press, 1976.

———. "Satiety is a Conditioned Reflex." *Psychosomatic Medicine* 37 (1975): 383-87.

Stunkard, A. J.; D'Aquili, E.; Fox, F.; et al. "Influence of Social Class on Obesity and Thinness in Children." *Journal of the American Medical Association* 221

(1972): 579-84.

Stunkard, A. J., and Fox, S. "The Relationship of Gastric Motility and Hunger: A Summary of the Evidence." *Psychosomatic Medicine* 33 (1971): 123-34.

Stunkard, A. J.; Fox, S.; and Levine, H. "The Management of Obesity: Patient Self-Help and Medical Treatment." *Archives of Internal Medicine* 125 (1970): 1067-72.

Stunkard, A. J., and Kaplan, D. "Eating in Public Places: A Review of Reports of the Direct Observation of Eating Behavior." *International Journal of Obesity* 1 (1977): 89-101.

Stunkard, A. J., and Koch, C. "The Interpretation of Gastric Motility: 1. Apparent Bias in the Reports of Hunger by Obese Persons." *Archives of General Psychiatry* 11 (1964): 74-82.

Stunkard, A. J., and Mahoney, M. J. "Behavioral Treatment of the Eating Disorders." In *Handbook of Behavior Modification and Behavior Therapy*. Edited by H. Leitenberg. Englewood Cliffs, New Jersey: Prentice-Hall (1976): 45-73.

Stunkard, A. J., and Levitx, L. S. "The Influence of Calorie Density and Availability on the Food Selections of Normal and Obese Subjects." University of Pennsylvania: Unpublished manuscript, 1973.

Stunkard, A. J., and Mazer, A. "Smorgasbord and Obesity." *Psychosomatic Medicine* 40(2) (1978): 173-75.

Stunkard, A. J., and McLaren-Hume M. "The Results of Treatment for Obesity." *Archives of Internal Medicine* 103 (1959): 79-85.

Stunkard, A. J., and Penick, S. B. "Behavior Modification in the Treatment of Obesity: The Problem of Maintaining Weight Loss." *Archives of General Psychiatry*. In Press.

Stunkard, A. J., and Reesh, A. J. "Dieting and Depression Reexamined: A Critical Review of Reports of Untoward Responses During Weight Reduction for Obesity." *Annals of Internal Medicine* 81 (1974): 526-33.

Sullivan, A. C. "An Overview of New Developments." In *Recent Advances in Obesity Research II*. Edited by G. A. Bray. London: Newman, 1978.

Swanson, D. W., and Dinello, F. A. "Follow-up of Patients Starved for Obesity." *Psychosomatic Medicine* 32 (1970): 209-14.

Thoreson, C. E., and Mahoney, M. J. *Behavioral Self-Control*. New York: Holt, Rinehart, and Winston, 1974.

Wagonfeld, S., and Wolowitz, H. "Obesity and The Self-Help Group: A Look at TOPS." *American Journal of Psychiatry* 125 (1968): 249-52.

Weil, W. B. "Current Controversies in Childhood Obesity." *Journal of Pediatrics* 91 (1977): 175.

Weiner, B. *Theories of Motivation from Mechanism to Cogniion*. Chicago: Rand McNally, 1972.

Williams, A. E., and Duncan, B. "A Commercial Weight-Reducing Organization: A critical analysis." *Medical Journal of Australia* 1 (1976): 781-85.

Williams, A. E., and Duncan, B. A. "Comparative Results of an Obesity Clinic and a Commercial Weight-Reducing Organization." *Medical Journal of Australia* 1 (1976): 800-02.

Wilson, G. T. "Behavioral Treatment of Obesity: Maintenance Strategies and Long-term efficacy." Unpublished manuscript. Rutgers University, 1978.

Winick, M. *Childhood Obesity*. New York: John Wiley and Sons, 1975.

Wollerscheim, J. P. "Effectiveness of Group Therapy Based Upon Learning Principles in The Treatment of Overweight Women." *Journal of Abnormal Psychology* 76 (1970): 462-74.

———. "Obesity and Behavioral Treatment Manuals." *American Psychological Association*. Reprint 5351 (1976): 48.

Wollerscheim, J. P., and Wooley, O. W. "Salivation to the Sight and Thought of food: A new measure of appetite." *Psychosomatic Medicine* 35 (1973): 136-41.

Wooley, O. W. "Long-Term Food Regulation in the Obese and Nonobese." *Psychosomatic Medicine* 33 (1971): 436-44.

Wooley, O. W., and Wooley, S. C. "The Experimental Psychology of Obesity. In *Obesity: Pathogenics and Managemnent*. Edited by T. Silverstone, and J. Fincham. Lancaster, Pennsylvania: Medical and

Technical Publication Co., Ltd., 1975.

Wooley, O. W.; Wooley, S. C.; and Woods, W. A. "Effect of Calories on Appetite for Palatable Food in Obese and Nonobese Humans. *Journal of Comparative Physiology and Psychology* 89 (1975): 619-25.

Wooley, S. "Physiologic verses Cognitive Factors in Short-Term Food Regulation in the Obese and Nonobese." *Psychosomatic Medicine* 34 (1972): 62.

Yates, B. T. "Improving the Cost Effectiveness of Obesity Programs: Three Basic Strategies for Reducing Cost Per Pound." *International Journal of Obesity.* In Press.

Young, C. M.; Scanlan, S. S.; Topping, C. M.; et al. "Frequency of Feeding, Weight Reduction, and Body Composition." *Journal of the American Dietetic Association* 59 (1971): 466-72.

Young, P. T. "Palatability: The Medonic Response to Foodstuffs." *Handbook of Physiology,* vol. 1, 1967, 353-66.

Yudkin, J., and Carey M. "The Treatment of Obesity by the 'High Fat' Diet. The Inevitability of Calories." *Lancet* 2 (1960): 939.

POPULAR BOOKS ON FOOD ADDICTION

Carey, P. *Fat Men In History*. New Zealand: Queensland University Press, 1976.

Greene, H., and Jones, C. *Diary Of A Food Addict*. New York: Grosset and Dunlop, 1974.

Lipsyte, R. *One Fat Summer*. New York: Bantam Books, 1977.

REFERENCES FOR ANOREXIA NERVOSA

Bachrach, A. J.; Erwin, W.; Mohr, J. P. "The Control of Eating Behavior in an Anorexic by Operant Conditioning Techniques." *Case Studies in Behavior Modification*. Edited by L. P. Ullmann, and L. Krasner. New York: Holt, Rinehart, and Winston (1965): 153-63.

Blinder, B. J.; Freeman, D. M. A.; Ringold, A.; et al. "Rapid Weight Restoration in Anorexia Nervosa." *Clinical Research* 15 (1967): 473.

Blinder, B. J., Stunkard, A. J. "Behavior Therapy and Anorexia Nervosa: Effectiveness of Activity as a Reinforcer of Weight Gain." *American Journal of Psychiatry* 126 (1970): 1093-98.

Blitzer, J. R.; Rollins; Nancy; and Blackwell, Amelia. "Children Who Starve Themselves: Anorexia Nervosa." *Psychosomatic Medicine* 23(5) (1961): 369-83.

Blundell, J. E. "Anorexic Drugs, Food Intake, and the Study of Obesity." *Nutrition* (London) 29 (1975): 5-18.

————. "Hunger and Satiety in the Control of Food Intake: Implications For The Treatment of Obesity." *Clinical Dietology* 4 (1977): 3-23.

Brady, John Paul, and Rieger, Wolfram. "Behavioral Treatment in Anorexia Nervosa." In *Applications of Behavior Modification*. Edited by Travis Thompson, and Willism S. Dockens, III. New York: Academic Press (1975): 45-63.

Bruch, Hilde. *Eating Disorders: Obesity, Anorexia and the Person Within*. New York: Basic Books (1973): 5.

————. *The Golden Cage: The Enigma of Anorexia Nervosa*. Cambridge, Mass: Harvard University Press, 1978.

————. "Perils of Behavior Modification in Treatment of Anorexia Nervosa." *Journal of the American Medical Association* 230(10) 9 December 1974: 1421.

Crisp, A. H. "Clinical and Therapeutic Aspects of Anorexia." *Journal of Psychosomatic Research* 9 (1965): 67-78.

————. "A Treatment Regime for Anorexia Nervosa." *British Journal of Psychiatry* 112 (1966): 505-12.

Crisp, A. H.; Kalucy, R. S.; Lacey, J. H.; and Harding, B. "The Long-Term Prognosis in Anorexia Nervosa: Some Factors Predictive of Outcome." In *Anorexia Nervosa*. Edited by Vigersky. New York: Raven Press, 1977.

Currey, H., et al. "Behavior Treatment of Obesity: Limitations and Results With the Chronically Obese." *Journal of The American Medical Association.* Reprint 5395 237:26 (1977): 2829-31.

Dally, P., and Sargant, W. "A New Treatment of Anorexia." *British Medical Journal* 1 (1960): 1770-73.
———. "Treatment and Outcome of Anorexia." *British Medical Journal* 2 (1966): 293-95.
Gifford, S.; Murawski, B. J.; and Pilot, M. L. "Anorexia Nervosa in One of Identical Twins." In *Anorexia and obesity.* Edited by Christopher V. Rowland, Jr. Boston: Little Brown (1970) 139-228.
Gladston, R. "Mind over Matter: Observations on Fifty Patients Hospitalized with Anorexia Nervosa." *Journal of the American Academy of Child Psychiatry* 13 (1974): 246-63.
Goetz, P. L.; Succop, R. A.; Reinhart, J. B.; and Miller, A. "Anorexia in Children: A Follow-Up Study." *American Journal of Orthopsychiatry* 47 (1977): 597-603.
Groen, J. J.; Feldman-Toledano, Z. "Educative Treatment of Patients and Parents in Anorexia Nervosa." *British Journal of Psychiatry* 112 (1966): 671-78.

Hallsten, E. A. Jr. "Adolescent Anorexia nervosa Treated by Desensitization." *Behavior Research Therapy* 3 (1965): 87-91.

Leitenberg, H.; Agras, W. S.; Thomson, L. E. "A Sequential Analysis of the Effect of Selective Positive Reinforcement in Modifying Anorexia Nervosa." *Behavior Research Therapy* 6 (1968): 211-18.
Lesser, L. I.; Ashenden, B. J.; Dubuskey, M.; and Eisenberg, L. "Anorexia Nervosa in Children." *American Journal of Orthopsychiatry* 30 (1960): 572-80.
Lucas, A. R.; Duncan, J. W.; and Piens, V. "The Treatment of Anorexia Nervosa." *American Journal of Psychiatry* 133 (1966): 1034-37.

Minuchin, Salvador; Montalvo, Braulio; Guerney, B. G., Jr.; Rosman, B. L.; and Schumer, F. *Families of the Slums: An Exploration of Their Structure and Treatment.* New York: Basic Books, 1967.

Pertshuk, M. J. "Behavior Therapy: Extended Follow-up." In *Anorexia Nervosa.* Edited by R. A. Vigersky. New York: Raven Press, 1977.

Rosman, Bernice; Minuchin, Salvador; and Liebman, Ronald. "Family Lunch Session: An Introduction to Family Therapy in Anorexia Nervosa." *American Journal of Orthopsychiatry.* 45(5) (October 1975): 846-53.
Rosman, Bernice; Minuchin, Salvador; Liebman, Ronald; and Baker, Lester. "Input and Outcome of Family Therapy in Anorexia Nervosa." In *Adolescent Psychiatry,* vol. 5. Edited by S. C. Feinstein, and P. L. Giovacchini. New York: Jason Aronson (1977): 319-22.
Russell, G. H. and Mezey, A. G. "An Analysis of Weight Gain in Patients with Anorexia Nervosa Treated with High Calorie Diets." *Clinical Science* 23 (1962): 449-61.

Schumacher, E. F. *Small is Beautiful.* New York: Harper & Row (1973): 14.
Selvini-Palazzoli, Mara *Self Starvation: From the Intrapsychic to the Transpersonal Approach to Anorexia Nervosa.* Translated by Arnold Pomerans. London: Chaucer; Human Context Book, 1974.
Shafii, Mohammed; Salguero, Carlos; and Finch, Stuart M. "Anorexia á Deux: Psychopathology and Treatment of Anorexia Nervosa in Latency Age Siblings." Paper presented at Annual Meeting of the American Academy of Child Psychiatry, New Orleans, October 1972.
Special Issue on Anorexia Nervosa. *Bul Mem Clinic* 41:5 (September 1977). Edited by Robert Vigorsky. New York: Raven Press, 1977.

Thomas, Helmut. *Anorexia Nervosa* New York: International University Press, 1967.
Tolstrup, K. "The Treatment of Anorexia Nervosa in Childhood and Adolescence." *Journal of Child Psychology and Psychiatry* 16 (1975): 75-78.

Warren, W. "A Study of Anorexia Nervosa in Young Girls." *Journal of Child Psychology and Psychiatry* 9 (1968): 27-40.

Williams, E. "Anorexia nervosa, a somatic disorder." *British Medical Jouranl* 2 (1958): 190-95.

Vigersky, ed. *Anorexia Nervosa* New York: Raven Press (1977): 277-382.

SEX

Auerbach, A. "Satyriasis and Nymphomania." *Medical Aspects of Human Sexuality* 2(9) (September 1968): 39-45.

Barry, A. "Sexual Arousal as an Anxiety Inhibitor." *Journal of Behavior Therapy and Experimental Psychiatry* 5(2) (September 1974): 151-52.

Bead, A. The Quarter is Our Turf. A Study of the Interface Between Gay and Straight Economy. Paper presented at the American Anthropological Association, (November 1974): 19-24.

Benedek, T. "Biology of the Depressive Constellation." *Journal of American Psychoanalytic Association* 4 (1956): 389-427.

Buber, I. "Heterosexuals Who Are Preoccupied with Homosexual Thoughts." *Medical Aspects of Human Sexuality* 94 (August 1975): 152-68.

Burke, T. "The New Homosexuality." *Esquire* 72(178) (1969): 304-18.

Cavan, S. "Interaction in Home Territories." *Berkeley Journal of Sociology* 8 (1968): 17-32.

Chapman, A. "The Rorschach Examination in a Case of Erotomaina." *Journal of Clinical Psychology* 9(2) (April 1953): 195-98.

Charham, R. "The Highly Sexed." *Forum* 41 (1974): 23-27.

Chesser, E. "The Nymphomaniac: Always Willing, Why?" *Sexology* 40(8) (1974): 10-14.

Conway, T. "Chickenhawks-The New Flesh Merchants." *Sexology* 403 (1975): 62-65.

Dahlberg, C. C. "Sexual Behavior in the Drug Culture." *Medical Aspects of Human Sexuality* 54 (1971): 64-71.

Dean, R. B. "Some Considerations on Promiscuity in Male Homosexuals." *Transcript* (1967): 13.

Ellis, A. *Nymphonia—A Study of the Oversexed Woman*. Edited by A. Ellis, and E. Sagrin. New York: Gilbert Press, 1964.

Flaxman, N. "Nymphomania—A Symptom." *Psychosis Medical Trial Technique Quarterly*, Part III (Winter 1973): 19, 30, 305-16.

Fenichel, O. *The Psychoanalytic Theory of Neurosis*. New York: W. W. Norton, (n.d.).

Latendresse, J. D. "Masturbation and its Relation to Addiction." *Review of Existential Psychology and Psychiatry* 8(1) (1968): 16-27.

Levilt, E. E. "Nymphomania." *Sexual Behavior* 3(3) (March 1973): 13-17.

Lewinson, R. "The Depraved Nymphomaniac Empress." *Sexology* 40(4) (November 1973): 21-25.

Machotka, P. "Incest as a Family Affair." *Family Process* 6(1) (1967): 98-116.

Mahler, M. S. *On Human Symbiosis and the Vicissitudes of Individuation*, vol 1. New York: International Universities Press, 1968.

McCray, J. L. "Nymphomania: A Case History." *Medical Aspects of Human Sexuality* 6(11) 152-210.

Marmor, J. "Crality in the Hysterical Personality." *Journal of American Psychoanalytic Association*, 1 (1953) 656-671.

———. "Sex for Nonsexual Reasons." *Medical Aspects of Human Sexuality.* June 1969.

Mathis, J. A. "Sexual Aspects of Heroin Addiction." *Medical Aspects of Human Sexuality* 4(9) (September 1970): 98-109.

Miller, I. "The Don Juan Character." *Medical Aspects of Human Sexuality* 3(4) (April 1969): 43-8.

Myrick, F. "The Homosexual Consumer: Some Consumption Patterns." Paper presented at Southern Markets Association, Dallas, Texas, 28-29 March 1974.

Podolsky, and Carlson. *Nymphomania.* New York: Eric Publishing Co. Inc., 1961.

Ponte, M. R. "Life in a Parking Lot: An Ethnograph of a Homosexual Drive in Deviations." Edited by Jerry Jacobs. Palo Alto, California: National Press Books (1974): 7-29.

Radin, S. S. "The Don Juan Sexual Behavior." *Medical Aspects of Human Sexuality* 11(5) (December 1972).

Rayben, J. B. "Homosexual Incest." *Journal of Nervous and Mental Disease* 148(2) (1969): 105-10.

Reiss, A. J. Jr. "The Social Integration of Queers and Peers." *Social Problems* 9(2) (Fall 1961): 102-20.

Sagarin, E. "Language of the Homosexual Subculture." *Medical Aspects of Human Sexuality* 4(4) (April 1971): 37-41.

———. "Sexual Acting Out in Psychotherapy." *American Journal of Psychoanalysis* 38(1) (1972): 3-8.

Saglier, M. T. "Homosexuality: Sexual Behavior of the Male Homosexual." *Archives of General Psychiatry* 21 (August 1969): 215-29.

Salzman, L. "The Highly Sexed Man." *Medical Aspects of Human Sexuality* 6(5) (May 1972): 36-49.

Savitt, R. A. "Psychoanalytic Studies on Addiction: II Hypersexuality (Love) Addiction." Paper read at Midwinter Meeting, American Psychoanalytic Association, 1968. Unpublished manuscript.

Schwarz, B. E. "The Man Who was Married Fifty-Five Times." *Journal of Nervous and Mental Diseases* 124(3) (September 1956): 287-51.

Gandy, P. "Comparison Study of Male Street Hustlers and Part Cruisers."

Ginsberg, K. "The 'Meat Rack'—A Study of the Male Homosexual Prostitute." *American Journal of Psychotherapy* 21(2) (n.d): 170-85.

Golden, J. S. "What is Sexual Promiscuity." *Medical Aspects of Human Sexuality.* (October 1968): 2, 10, 47-53.

Greenspan, B. "Some Reasons most Homosexual Relationships Don't Last." *Journal of Contemporary Psychotherapy* (Winter 1971): 4, 1, 34-36.

Hammer, M. "Hypersexuality in Reformatory Women." *Corrective Psychiatry and Journal of Social Therapy* 15(4) (Winter, 1969): 20-6.

Hatterer, L. J. "Changing Homosexuality in the Male." *Treatment for Men Troubled by Homosexuality.* New York: McGraw & Hill, 1970; New York: Delta, 1971.

Henn, F. A.; Herjanic, M.; Vanderpearl, R. H. "Forensic Psychiatry: Profiles of Two Types of Sex Offenders." *American Journal of Psychiatry* 2 133(b) (1976): 694-96.

Hollender, M. "Prostitution, the Body and Human Relatedness." *International Journal of Psychoanalysis* 42 (1961): 404-13.

"Homosexuality: Daisy-Chain" (audio record). one tape, 3 3/4 ips, sixty minutes surreptitious recording of a male homosexual's activity. Editorial comment by S.S. (Male L.3986). Chicago, 1958.

Humphreys, L. "New Styles in Homosexual Manliness.'' *Transaction* March 1971 38-46; April 1971 64-66.

———. ''The Tea Room Trade: Impersonal Sex in Public Places.'' AnnArbor, Michigan: Michigan University Microfilm, 1968.

———. ''They Meet in Bar-Rooms—A Preliminary Study of Participates in Homosexual Encounters.'' Paper presented at Washington University, St. Louis, Missouri, 5 May 1967.

———. ''What is Wrong with Public Sex.'' Paper presented at Meetings of American Sociology Association, San Francisco, Sept. 4, 1969.

Janus, S. S., and Bess, B. *A Sexual Profile of Men in Power.* New Jersey: Prentic Hall, 1977.

———. The Factors in the Successful Redemption of Prostitution. Paper read at the American Psychiatric Association Meetings, Detroit, Illinois, 1975.

———. Prostitution Option or Addiction. Paper read at the American Psychiatric Association Meetings, Toronto, Canada, 1977.

Kistner, R. W. ''Human 'She Wolves.' '' *International Journal of Sexology* 6(3) (February 1973): 168-71.

Klaf, K. S.; Bernhardt, J.; Haywood, B. J. *Nymphomania: A Psychiatric View.* New York: Lancer Books, 1963/1964.

Segal, M. H. ''Impulsive Sexuality: Some Clinical and Theoretical Observations.'' *International Journal of Psychoanalysis* 44 (1963): 407-18.

Shcerness, N. ''Nymphomania and Don Juanism.'' *Medical Triad Technique Quarterly* 15(1) (Summer 1972): 1-6.

Shulman, B. H. ''Uses and Abuses of Sex.'' *Medical Aspects of Human Sexuality* 2(48) (September 1968).

Siles, B. Jr. ''Sexual Activity as a Coping Mechanism.'' *Medical Aspects of Human Sexuality* 7(3) (March 1973): 40-61.

Sonenscheen, D. ''Aspects of Male Homosexual Promiscuity.'' Paper read at the Meeting of the South Western Psychological Association, Austin, Texas, 11-15 April 1969.

Staff, N. A. *A Diary of a Nymphomaniac.* New York: Lyle Stuart, 1961.

St. Louis, *The Oversexed Woman.* Dios Chemical Co., 1951.

Trorden, R. ''Homosexual Encounters in a Highway Rest Stop in Sexual Deviance and Sexual Deviants.'' Edited by E. Goode and R. Trorden. New York: Morrow (1974): 211-28.

Vassi, M. ''Steamy Sex.'' *Forum* 4(10) (July 1975): 38-42.

Willis, S. E. ''Hyperlibido.'' *Medical Aspects of Human Sexuality* 7(9) (September 1973): 72-85.

———. ''Sexual Behavior of Obese Married Women.'' Proceedings of the 79th Annual American Psychological Association, 1971.

———. ''Sexual Promiscuity as a Symptom of Personal and Cultural Anxiety.'' *Medical Aspects of Human Sexuality* 1(2) (October 1967): 16-23.

POPULAR BOOKS ON SEXUAL ADDICTION

Burgess, A. *A Tremor of Intent.* New York: W. W. Norton, 1966, 1975.

Donleavy, P. *A Singular Man.* New York: Delacorte, 1967.

Herlihy, J. L. *Midnight Cowbow.* New York: Simon & Schuster, 1965.

Jackson, C. *A Secondhand Life.* New York: Macmillan, 1975.

Mann, T. *The Kreutzer Sonata, The Devil, Death in Venice and other tales.* New York: Oxford Universities Press, 1957.

Mishima, Y. *The Temple of Dawn.* New York: Knopf, 1973.

———. *Thirst for Love.* New York: Knopf, 1969.

Moravia, A. *Agostino.* New York: Farrar, Straus, 1956, 1975.

Murdoch. *The Sacred and Profane Love Machine.* New York: Viking, 1974.

Nabokov, V. *Lolita.* New York: G. P. Putnam's Sons, 1958.

Roth, P. *Portnoy's Complaint.* New York: Random House, 1969.

Wakefield, D. *Going All the Way.* New York: Delacorte, 1970.

WORK

Bergler, E. "Work the Last Bastion engulf-ed in Neurosis." *Diseases of the Nervous System* 8 (1947): 317-19.

Hatterer, L. J. "Psychiatric Treatment of Creative Work Block." *Psychiatry Quarterly* 35 (1960): 634-47.

———. "Playing, Pleasures, and Placidity." In *Life Blueprint in Modern Man, Psychology and Sexuality of the Contemporary Male.* Edited by D. Goldman and D. S. Millman. Dubuque, Iowa: Kendall Hunt Publishing Co., 1979.

Holmes, D. A. "Contribution to a Psychoanalytic Theory of Work." In *The Psychoanalytic Study of the Child*, vol. 20. New York: International Universities Press Inc., 1968.

Horney, K. "Neurotic Disturbances in Work." *American Journal of Psychoanalysis* 10 (1950): 80-2.

Katz, J. "Balzor and Wolfe: A Study of Self Destructive Overproductivity." *Psychoanalysis, Journal of the National Psychological Association for Psychoanalysis* 3 (1957): 20.

Kets, de Vines, and Manfred, F. R. Defective Adaptation to Work: An Approach to Conceptualization." *Bulletin of the Menninger Clinic* 42 (1978): 35-50.

Kramer, Y. "Work Compulsion—A Psychoanalytic Study." *Psychoanalytic Quarterly* 46 (1977): 361-85.

Oberndorf, C. "Psychopathology of Work." *Bulletin of the Menninger Clinic* 15 (1951): 77-84.

Overbeck, T. J. "The Workaholic." *Psychology* 13:3 (1976): 36-42.

Reich, A. "Pathologic Forms of Self Esteem Regulation." In *The Psychoanalytic Study of the Child*, vol 15. New York: International University Press, Inc., 1960.

Robbins, B. "Neurotic Disturbances in Work." *American Journal of Psychiatry* 2 (1939): 333-42.

SMOKING

Bergler, E. "Psychology of Compulsive Smoking." *Psychiatric Quarterly* 20 (1946): 297-321.

Bernstein, D. A. "Modification of Smoking Behavior." *Psychological Bulletin* 71 (1969): 418-40.

Clausen, J. A. "Adolescent Antecedents of Cigarette Smoking: Data From the Oakland Study." *Social Sciences and Medicine* 1 (1968): 357-82.

Corti, E. *A History of Smoking.* New York: Harcourt Brace & Company, 1932.

DeLarue, N. C., and Moss, G. "The Toronto Smoking Withdrawal Centre: A Report Prepared for the Department of National Health and Welfare." A Smoking and Health Research Report, Ottawa, 1971.

Dengrove, E. "A Single-Treatment Method of Stop Smoking Using Ancillary Self-Hypnosis: Discussion." *International Journal of Clinical Experimental Hypnosis* 18 (1970): 251-56.

Eisinger, R. A. "Nicotine and Addiction to Cigarettes." *British Journal of Addiction* 66(2) (1971): 150-56.

Evans, R. I. "Smoking in Children: Developing a Social Psychology Strategy of Deterence." *Preventive Medicine* 5 (1976): 122-27.

Evans, R. I.; Rozelle, R. M.; Mittelmark, M. B.; Hansen, W. B.; Bane, A. L.; and Havis, J. "Deterring the Onset of Smoking in Children: Knowledge of Immediate Physiological Effects and Coping with Peer Pressure." *Journal of Applied Social Psychology.* In press.

———. "Deterring the Onset of Smoking in Children: Pressure, Media Pressure and Parent Modeling." *Journal of Applied Social Psychology* (1977).

Foss, R. "Personality, Social Influence and Cigarette Smoking." *Journal of Health and Social Behavior* 14 (1973): 279-86.

Francisco, J. W. "Modification of Smoking Behavior: A Comparison of Three Approaches." 33 (1973): 5511-12.

Freedman, A. M., and Laplan, H. I. *Comprehensive Textbook of Psychiatry.* Second edition. Baltimore: Williams and Williams Company, 1975.

Freedman, D. X., and Dyrud, J. E., eds. *American Handbook of Psychiatry: Treatment,* vol. 5. Second edition edited by Arieti, and E. B. Brody. New York: Basic Books, Inc. 1975.

Gaedeke, R., and Gehrmann, J. "Nicotine:

Drug Addiction Among Children and Adolescents with Particular Consideration of Habitual Sniffing." *Klinische Padiatrie* (German Language) 69 (1973): 10-16.

Goldfarb, T.; Gritz, E. R.; Jarvik, M. E.; and Stolerman, I. P. "Reactions to Cigarettes as a Function of Nicotine and Tar." *Clinical Pharmacology Therapy* 19(6) (1976): 767-72.

Goldfarb, T.; Jarvik, M. E.; and Glick, S. D. "Cigarette Nicotine Content as a Determinant of Human Smoking Behavior." *Psychomaracologia* (Berlin) 17 (1970): 89-93.

Gordon, T.; Kannel, W. B.; Dauber, T. R.; and McGee, D. "Changes Associated with Quitting Cigarette Smoking: The Framingham Study." *American Heart Journal* 90(3) (1975): 322-38.

Graham, S., and Gibson, R. W. "Cessation of Patterned Behavior: Withdrawal from Smoking." *Social Science and Medicine* 5 (1971): 319-37.

Gritz, E. R. "Smoking: The Prevention of Onset." Presented at the UCLA Research Conference on Smoking Behavior, 24 and 25 June 1977.

Hall, A., and Crasilneck, H. B. "Development of a Hypnotic Technique for Treating Chronic Cigarette Smoking." *International Journal of Clinical Experimental Hypnosis* 18 (1970): 283-89.

Hamburg, D., and Bodie, H. K., eds. *American Handbook of Psychiatry: In New Psychiatric Frontiers*, vol. 6. Second edition edited by S. Arieti, and E. B. Brody, 1975. New York: Basic Books, Inc., 1975.

Harris, E. *Tobacco: The Effects of Its Use As a Luxury on the Physical and Moral Nature of Men*. New York: W. Harrod, 1853.

Horn, D. "A Model for the Study of Personal Choice Health Behavior." *International Journal of Health Educaton* 19 (1976): 89-98.

Hunt, W. A., and Matarazzo, J. D. "Habit Mechanisms in Smoking." In *Learning Mechanisms in Smoking*. Edited by W. A. Hunt. Chicago, 1970.

Hunt, W. A., and Bespalec, D. A. "An Evaluation of Current Methods of Modifying Smoking Behavior." *Journal of Clinical Psychology* 30 (1974): 431-38.

Jacobs, M. A. "The Addictive Personality: Prediction of Success in a Smoking Withdrawal Program." *Psychosomatic Medicine* 34(1) (1972): 30-8.

Jarvik, M. E. *Smoking Behavior: Motives and Incentives*. Further observations on nicotine as the reinforcing agent in smoking—a special project of the Council for Tobacco Research, St. Maarten Island, French Netherlands Antilles, 12-15 January 1972. Washington, D.C.: Winston & Sons, 1973.

Jarvik, M. E.; Cullen, J. W.; Gritz, E. R.; Voight, T. M.; West, L. J. *Research on Smoking Behavior*. National Institute on Drug Abuse Research Monograph Series #GPO 017-024-00694-7, Washington, D.C.: Superintendent of Documents, U.S. Government Printing Office, 1977.

Jarvik, M. E.; Glick, S. D.; and Matanura, R. "Inhibition of Cigarette Smoking by Orally Administered Nicotine." *Clinical Pharmacology Therapy* 11 (1978): 574-76.

Johnson, L. M. "Tobacco Smoking and Nicotine." *Lancet* (1942): 742.

Johnstone, E., and Donoghue, J. R. "Hypnosis and Smoking: A Review of the Literature." *American Journal of Clinical Hypnosis* 13 (1971)L 265-72.

Kline, M. V. "The Use of Extended Group Hypnotherapy Sessions in Controlling Cigarette Habituation." *International Journal of Clinical Experimental Hypnosis* 18 (1970): 270-82.

Knapp, P.; Bliss, C. M.; and Wells, H. "Addictive Aspects in Heavy Cigarette Smoking." *American Journal of Psychiatry* 119 (1963): 966-72.

Kraft, T. "Desensitization and Reducation in Cigarette Consumption." *Journal of Psychology* 67(2) (1967): 323-29.

Kroger, W. S., and Fezler, W. D. "Excessive Smoking." In *Hypnosis and Behavior Modification: Imagery Conditioning*. Philadelphia, Pa.: J. B. Lippincott Co., 1976.

Kroger, W. L., and Libott, R. Y. *Thanks, Doctor, I've Stopped Smoking*. Springfield, Ill.: C. C. Thomas, 1967.

Lando, H. A. "Successful Treatment of Smokers with a Broad Spectrum Behavioral

Approach." *Journal of Consulting and Clinical Psychology* 45 (1977): 361-66.

Levanthal, H. A. "Pleasure Addiction and Habit Factors in Verbal Report or Factors in Smoking Behavior." *Journal of Abnormal Psychology* 85(5) (1976): 478-88.

Lichtenstein, E. *Current status and Further Directions for Behavior Modification of Smoking Behavior.* Report for the UCLA Research Conference on Smoking Behavior, 24 and 25 June 1977.

Lichtenstein, E., and Danaher, B. G. "Modification of Smoking Behavior: A Critical Analysis of Theory, Research, and Practice." In *Progress in Behavior Modification*, vol. 3. Edited by M. Herson, R. M. Eisler, and P. M. Miller. New York: Academic Press, 1976.

Lieberman Research Inc. *The Teenager Looks at Smoking.* Report for the American Cancer Society 1969.

McAlister, A. L. "Toward a Mass Communication of Behavioral Counseling: A Preliminary Experimental Study of a Televised Program to Assist in Smoking Cessation." Unpublished doctoral dissertation, Stanford University, 1976.

Metarazzo, J. d., and Matarazzo, R. G. "Smoking." *International Encyclopedia of Social Science* 14 (1968): 335-40.

Nuland, W. "A Single-treatment Method of Stop Smoking Using Ancillary Self-Hypnosis: Discussion." *International Journal of Clinical Experimental Hypnosis* 18 (1970): 257-60.

Nuland, W., and Field, P. B. "Smoking and Hypnosis: A Systematic Clinical Approach." *International Journal of Clinical Experimental Hypnosis* 18 (1970): 290-306.

Pederson, L. L.; Scrimgeour, W. G.; and Lefcoe, N. M. "Comparison of Hypnosis Plus Counseling, Counseling alone, and Hypnosis Alone in a Community Service Smoking Withdrawal Program." *Journal of Consulting Clinical Psychology* 31 (1975): 498-505.

Rustin, R. M. "Smoking Habits and Socio-biologic Factors." *Journal of Psychoanalytic Research* 22(2) (1978): 89-100.

Russell, M. A. H. "Cigarette Dependence Nature and Classification." *British Medical Journal* 5 (1971): 330-31.

Russell, M. A. H. "Cigarette Smoking, Natural History of a Dependence Disorder." *British Journal of Medical Psychology* 44 (1971): 1-16.

Russell, M. A. H. "Tobacco Smoking and Nicotine Dependence." In *Research Advances in Alcohol and Drug Problems*, vol. 3. Edited by R. J. Gibbons; H. Isreal; H. Kalent; R. E. Popham; W. Schmidt; and R. G. Smart, New York: Wiley (1976): 1-47.

Salber, E. J. *"Smoking Among Teenagers." Bulletin of the New York Academy of Medicine* 44 (1968): 1521.

Schwartz, J. L. "A Critical Review and Evaluation of Smoking Control Methods." *Public Health Report* 84 (1969): 483-506.

———. "Preliminary Report: Smoke Watchers Evaluation." Unpublished material. Berkeley, California: Institute for Health Research, 6 May 1973.

Schwartz, J. L., and Dubitzk, M. "Psycho-Social Factors Involved in Cigarette Smoking and Cessation." Berkely, California: Institute for Health Research, September 1968.

Schwartz, J. L., and Rider, G. "Smoking Cessation Methods in the United States and Canada: 1969-1974." In *Modifying the Risk for the Smoker*, vol. 2 of the Proceedings of the third World Conference on Smoking and Health. Edited by E. L. Wynder, D. Hoffman, and G. B. Gori. DHEW/Publication (NIH) 77-1413, 1977.

Schewchuk, L. A., and Wynden, E. L. "Guidelines on Smoking Cessation Clinics." *Preventive Medicine* 6 (1977): 130-33.

Spiegel, H. "A Single-treatment Method to Stop Smoking Using Ancillary Self-Hypnosis." *International Journal of Clinical Experimental Hypnosis* 18 (1970): 235-50.

———. "A Single-treatment Method to Stop Smoking Using Ancillary Self-Hypnosis: Final Remarks in Response to the Discussants." *International Journal of Clinical Experimental Hypnosis* 18 (1970): 268-69.

Srole, L, and Fischer, A. K. "The Social

Epidemiology of Smoking Behavior 1953 and 1970: The Midtown Manhattan Study.'' *Social Science and Medicine* 7 (1973): 341-58.

Tamerin, J. S. ''The Psychodynames of Quitting Smoking in a Group.'' *American Journal of Psychiatry* 129/5 (1972): 583-89.

Thomas, C. B. ''The Relationship of Smoking and Habits of Nervous Tension.'' In *Smoking Behavior: Motives and Incentives.* Edited by W. L. Dun and V. H. Winston & Sons, Washington, D.C., 1973.

Tomkins, S. S. ''Psychological Model for Smoking Behavior.'' *American Journal of Public Health and the Nation's Health* 56(12) (1966): 17-20.

U. S. Department of Health Education and Welfare, Public Service. ''Adult Use of Tobacco,'' NCSH, DHEW Publication no. (HSM) 73-8727, 1973.

———. ''Adult Use of Tobacco—1975,'' Center for Disease Control and National Cancer Institute, June 1976.

———. ''Teenage Smoking: National Patterns of Cigarette Smoking, Ages 12 Through 18, in 1972 and 1976.'' DHEW Publication no. (HSM) 73-8727, 1973.

Wright, M. E. ''A Single-treatment Method to Stop Smoking Using Ancillary Self-Hypnosis: Discussion.'' *International Journal of Clinical Experimental Hypnosis* 18 (1970): 261-67.

GAMBLING

Aubrey, W. E. "Altering the Gamblers Maladaptive Life Goals." *International Journal of the Addictions* 101 (1975): 29-33.

Beale, David, and Goldman, Clifford. Background paper of "Easy Money." Report of the Task Force on Legalized Gambling sponsored by the Fund for the City of New York and the Twentieth Century Fund. The Twentieth Fund/Kraus Reprint Company, Millwood, New York, 1975.

Bolden, D. W., and Boyd, W. H. "Gambling and the Gambler." *Archives of General Psychiatry* 18 (1968): 617-30.

Boyd, W. H., and Bolen, D. W. "The Compulsive Gambler and Spouse in Group Psychotherapy." *Journal of Group Psychotherapy* 20 (1970): 77-90.

Commission on the Review of the National Policy Toward Gambling: Final Report. *Gambling in America.* Washington, D.C., 15 October 1976.

Custer, R. L. "A Chart of Compulsive Gambling and Recovery."* National Council on Compulsive Gambling, 1978.

———. "An Overview of Compulsive Gambling." Unpublished paper. South Oaks Hospital, Amityville, L.I., N.Y., 1979.

———. "Characteristics of the Recovering Compulsive Gambler: A Survey of 150 Members of Gamblers Anonymous."* Unpublished paper. Fourth Annual Conference on Gambling, Reno, Nevada, December 1978.

———. "Compulsive Gambling (Pathological Gambling)."* Unpublished paper. Veterans Administration, August 1977.

———. "Description of Compulsive Gambling."* Unpublished paper. Third Annual Conference on Gambling, Las Vegas, Nevada, December 1976.

———. "The Gambling Scene—1977."* Unpublished paper. First International Conference of Gamblers Anonymous, Chicago, Illinois, 1977.

———. "Personality and Social Aspects of Compulsive Gambling."* Unpublished paper. American Psychological Association, Washington, D.C., September 1976.

———. "Twelve Principles in Treating the Compulsive Gambler."* Unpublished paper. Twelfth Annual Conclave of Gamblers Anonymous, Montreal, Canada, November 3, 1979.

Custer, R. L., et al. "Syllabus—Treatment of the Compulsive Gambler."* Unpublished paper. Presented at the Winter Session of the American Medical Association, December 1978.

Custer, R. L.; Glen, A.; and Burns, R. "Characteristics of Compulsive Gambling."*

Unpublished paper. Second Annual Conference on Gambling. Lake Tahoe, Nevada, June 1975.

Custer, R. L.; Glen, A.; and Burns, R. "In-Patient Treatment of Compulsive Gamblers."* Unpublished material. Second Annual Conference on Gambling, Lake Tahoe, nevada, June 1975.

* For further information concerning the unpublished papers write to Robert L. Custer, M.D.; Chief of Treatment Services, MH and BSS Veterans Administration Offices; Veterans Administration Department of Medicine and Surgery, Washington, D.C., 20420.

Ezell, John Samuel. *Fortune's Merry Wheel—The Lottery in America.* Cambridge, Mass.: Harvard University Press, 1960.

Fisher, A. "Blackjack Disease and Other Chromete Puzzles." Cutis 18(1) (1976): 21-22.

Gumblig, R. L. "An Interview: The Compulsive Gambler." *Today in Psychiatry*, reprint # 5337. 3:4 (1977): 1-3.

Hemsely, W. E. "Probability, Personality, Age and Risk-taking." *Journal of Psychology* 95:1 (1977): 131-38.

Lesieur, H. R. "The Compulsive Gambler's Spiral of Options and Involvement." *Psychiatry, Journal for the Study of Interpersonal Processes* 42 (1979): 79-87.

Livingston, J. *Compulsive Gambling: The Social Psychology of Action* Harvard Social Relations PhD. thesis, April 1963.

McAlister, A. L. "Behavioral Science Applied to Cardiovascular Health: Progress and Research Needs in the Modification of Risk Taking Habits in Adult Populations." *Health Education Monograph* 4(1) (1976): 45-74.

Moran, E. "Pathological Gambling." *British Journal of Psychiatry*. Special number (83 references) (9) (1975): 416-28.

University of Nevada, Las Vegas: Library. *A Gambling Bibliography.* Based on the Collection of Special Collections Librarian, Stephen Powell. Las Vegas, Nevada: University of Nevada, Las Vegas, 1972.

Pokorny, M. R. "Pathological Gambling." *British Journal of Psychiatry*. Special number (83 references) (9) (1975): 416-28.

Scarne, John. *Scarne's Complete Guide to Gambling.* New York: Simon and Schuster, 1961.

Svenson, O. "A Unifying Interpretation of Different Models for the Integration of Information When Evaluating Gamblers." *Scandinavian Journal of Psychology* 16:3 (1975): 187-92.

Roberts, G. C. "Sex and Achievement Motivation Efforts on Risk Taking." *Research Quarterly of the American Association of Health and Physical Education* 40:1 (1975): 56-70.

Weinstein, David, and Deitch, Lillian. *The Impact of Legalized Gambling: The Socioeconomic Consequences of Lotteries and Off-Track Betting.* New York: Praeger Publishing, 1974.

POPULAR BOOKS ON GAMBLING

Dostoevsky, F. *The Gambler; with Polena Suslova's Diary,* edited by Edward Wasiolek. Chicago: University of Chicago Press, 1972.

Edmonds, W. D. *The Wedding Journey.* Boston: Little, Brown, 1947.

Ferber, E. *Show Boat.* New York: Doubleday & Co., 1951 and 1975.

Fish, R. L. *The Wager.* New York: G. P. Putnam's Sons, 1974.

Fleming, L. *Casino Royale.* New York: Macmillan, 1966.

Franes, D. *Forfeit.* New York: Harper & Row, 1969.

Heyer, G. *Faro's Daughter*. New York: E. P. Dutton, 1967.

Higgens, G. V. *The Diggers Game*. New York, Knopf, 1973.

Keyes, F. P. *Steamboat Gothic*. New York: Messner, 1952.

Pharr, R. d. *The Book of Numbers*. New York: Doubleday, 1969.

Wilder, R. *An Affair of Honor*. New York: G. P. Putnam's Sons, 1969.

Papers available from the National Technical Information Service, U.S. Department of Commerce, Springfield, Va.:

Bell, Raymond, C. "Moral Views on Gambling Promulgated by Major American Religious Bodies." Accession no. PB 242817.

Duncan, Carol. "Gambling-Related Corruption." Accession no. PB 243818.

Fact Research, Inc. "Gambling in Perspective: A Review of the Written History of Gambling and an Assessment of its Effect on Modern American Society." Accession no. PB 243-820.

Joyce, Kathleen. "Social Aspects of Gambling." Accession no. PB 243821.

Rubenstein, Jonathan. "Gambling Enforcement and Police Corruption." Accession no. PB 243819.

CROSS/MULTIPLE ADDICTIONS

Adler, N. and Coleman, D. "Gambling and Alcoholism: Symptom Substitution and Functional Equivalents." *Quarterly Journal of Studies on Alcohol* 30 (3-a) (1969): 733-736.

Alkesne, H.; Lieberman, L.; Brill, L. "A Conceptual Model of the Life Cycle of Addiction." *International Journal of the Addictions* 2 (1978): 221-38.

Anant, S. S. "A Note on the Treatment of Alcoholics by Verbal Aversion Technique." *Canadian Psychologist* 8a (1) (1967): 819-22.

————. "Treatment of Alcoholics and Drug Addicts by Verbal Aversion Techniques." *International Journal of the Addictions* 33 (1968): 581-88.

Association for Research in Nervous and Mental Diseases. *The Addictive States.* Proceedings of the Association, 2 and 3 December 1966. New York, Baltimore: Williams and Wilkins, 1968.

Ayers, J.; Ruff, C. F.; and Templer, D. I. "Alcoholism, Cigarette Smoking, Coffee Drinking and Aversion." *Journal of Studies on Alcoholism* 37 (7) (1976): 983-85.

Barr, H. L., and Ottenberg, D. J. "The Cross-Use of Alcohol and Drugs by Addicts and Alcoholics. 1-Patterns of Previous Abuse of Alcohol in a Group of Hospitalized Drug Addicts." *Drug Forum* 4 (1). In press.

Barr, H. L.; Ottenberg, D. J.; and Cohen, A. "Drinking by Addicts." Presented at the North American Congress on Alcohol and Drug Problems, San Francisco, Cal., 12-18 December 1974.

Battlegay, R.; Muhlemann, R.; and Zehnder, R. "Comparative Investigations of the Abuse of Alcohol, Drugs and Nicotine for a Representative Group of 4,082 Men of Age." *Comprehensive Psychiatry* 16 (3) (2A) (1975): 247-54.

Belasco, J. A. "The Criterion Question Revisited." *British Journal of Addictions* (44) (1971): 39.

Birchard, C. "Alcohol and Other Drug Dependencies." *Canada S. Mental Health* 19 (5-6) (1967): 31-33.

Braucht, B. N. "A psychosocial Typology of Adolescent Alcohol and Drug Users." Third Annual Alcoholism Conference of NIAAA, Washington, D.C. 20-22 June 1973.

Brien, R. L.; Kleiman, J.; and Eisenman, R. "Personality and Drug Use: Heroin, Alcohol, Methadrin, Mixed Drug Dependency." *Corrective Psychiatry and Journal of Social Therapy* 18 (4) (1972): 22-23.

Brown, B. S.; Kozel, N. J.; Meyers, M. B.; and Dupont, R. L. "Use of Alcohol by Addict and Non Addict Populations." *American Journal of Psychiatry* 130 (1973): 599-601.

Chelton, L. G., and Whesnant, C. L. "The Comination of Alcohol and Drug Intoxication." *South Medical Journal* 59 (1966): 393.

Chessik, R. D.; Ollif, D. H.; and Price, H. G. "The Alcoholic Narcotic Addict." Quarterly Journal of Studies on Alcohol 22 (1961): 261-68.

Ciotola, P. V., and Peterson, J. F. "Personality Characteristics of Alcoholics and Drug Addicts in a Merged Treatment Program." *Journal of Studies on Alcohol* 39 (9) (1976): 1229-35.

Crowley, T. J.; Chesluk, D.; Dilts, S.; and Hart, R. "Drug and Alcohol Abuse Among Psychiatric Admissions." *Archives of General Psychiatry* 30 (1974): 13-20.

Denery, P., and Wilson, M. "Barbiturate Abuse and Addiction and Their Relationship to Alcohol and Alcoholism." *Canadian Medical Association* 104 (1971): 215-18.

———. "Abuse of Barbiturates in an Alcoholic Population." *Canadian Medical Association* 104 (1971): 219-21.

Dreher, K. F., and Fraser, J. G. "Smoking Habits of Alcoholic Out Patients." *International Journal of Addictions* 33 (1968): 65-80.

Driscoll, G. Z. "Comparative Study of Drug Dependent and Alcoholic Men." Presented at the Twenty-Second Annual Meeting of the Alcohol and Drug Problems Association, Hartford, Conn. September 1971.

Eagleville Hospital and Rehabilitation Center. "Is the Alcoholic or Addict Mentally Ill?" In *Proceedings of the Seventh Annual Eagleville Conference,* Eagleville, Pa., June 1974.

Edwards, G.; Russell, M. A.; Hawks, D.; and MacCafferty, M. M., eds. *Alcohol Dependence and Smoking Behavior.* New York: Farnborough, 1976.

Einstein, R.; Hughes, I. E.; and Hindmark, I. "Patterns of Use of Alcohol, Cannabis, and Tobacco in a Student Population." *British Journal of Addiction* 70 (2) (1975): 145-50.

Eisenthal, S., and Udin, H. "Psychological Factors Associated with Drug and Alcohol Usage among Neighborhood Youth Corps Enrollees." *Developmental Psychology* 7 (2) (1972): 119-23.

Ferneau, E. W. "Drug Abuser and the Alcoholic: Some Similarities." *Addictions* 20 (1) (1973): 52-61.

Fischer, H. K. "Some Aspects of Psychotherapy in Patients with Addictive Personality Traits." *Psychosomatics* 14 (1) (1973): 27-32.

Fox, R. "Alcoholism and Reliance upon Drugs as Depressive Equivalents." *American Journal of Psychotherapy* 67 (21) (3): 585-96.

Freed, E. X. "Drug Abuse by Alcoholics: A Review." *International Journal of the Addictions* 8 (3) (1973): 451-73.

Freudenberger, H. L. "The Gay Addict in a Drug and Alcohol Abuse Therapeutic Community." *Homosexual Counseling Journal* 3 (1) (1976): 34-45.

Gale, E. N., and Gale, D. S. "Level of Activation and Choice of Drug." In *Proceedings of the 30th International Congress on Alcoholism and Drug Dependence* (Amsterdam, Netherlands). Lausanne, Switzerland: International Council on Alcohol and Addictions, 1972.

Gary, A. L., and Hammond, R. "Self-disclosures of Alcoholics and Drug Addicts." *Psychotherapy Theory, Research, and Practice* 7 (3) (1970): 142-43.

Gibbons, R. L. *Research Advances in Alcohol and Drug Problems,* vol. 1. New York: John Wiley and Sons, 1979.

Gibbons, R. J., and Israel, Y. eds. *Research Advances in Alcohol and Drug Problems,* vol. 2. New York: John Wiley and Sons, 1975.

Glatt, M. "Who Is Vulnerable?" *Mental Health* 28 (3) (1966): 26-28.

Gnepp, E. H. "A Causal Theory of Alcoholism and Drug Addiction." *Psychology* 13 (2) (1976): 3-23.

Goodwin, D. W.; Davis, D. H.; and Robins, L. N. "Drinking amid Abundant Illicit Drugs: The Vietnam Case." *Archives of General Psychiatry* 32 (1975): 230-33.

Gordon, W. W. "The Treatment of Alcohol and Tobacco Addiction by Differential Conditioning. New Manual and Medical Methods." *American Journal of*

Psychotherapy 25 (3) (1971): 394-417.

Greenwald, S.; Carter, D.; and Stein, E. "Differences between Background Attitude Functioning and Mood of Drug Addicts, Alcoholics, and Orthopedic Patients." *International Journal of the Addictions* 8 (5) (1973): 865-74.

Griffiths, R. R., et al. "Relationships between Anorectic and Reinforcing properties of Appetite Suppressant Drugs: Implications for Assessment of Abusive Liability." *Biological Psychiatry* 13 (2) (1978): 283-90.

Haberman, P. W., and Baden, M. M. "Drinking, Drugs, and Death." *International Journal of the Addictions* 2 (1967): 115-28.

Haertzen, C. A., and Hooks, N. T. "Dictionary of Drug Associations to Heroin, Benzedrine, Alcohol, Barbiturates, and Marijuana." *Journal of Clinical Psychology* 29 (2) (1973): 115-64.

Haertzen, C. A., and Panton, J. "Development of a Psychophobic Scale for the Addiction Research Center Inventory (ARCI)." *International Journal of the Addictions* 2 (1967): 115-28.

Heilman, R. O. "Dynamics of Drug Dependency." *Minnesota Medicine* 56 (1973): 179-82.

Hemmink, E. "Tobacco, Alcohol, Medicines and Illegal Drug Taking." *Adolescence* 9 (35) (1974): 421-29.

Hunt, W. A.; Barnett, L. W.; and Branch, L. G. "Relapse Rates in Addiction Programs." *Journal of Clinical Psychology* 27 (4) (1971): 455-56.

Hunt, W. G. "Smoking and Alcoholism: A Brief Report." *American Journal of Psychiatry* 128 (11) (1972): 1455-56.

Huntington, A. R. "Management Looks at Alcohol and Drug Dependency." In "Drugs and Alcohol: Their Effect on Industry." Unpublished seminar. Vancouver: Workmen's Compensation Board of British Columbia, Canada, 1972.

Jackson, G. W., and Richman, A. "Alcohol Use among Narcotic Addicts." In *Proceedings of the 30th International Congress on Alcoholism and Drug Dependence* (Amsterdam, Netherland). Lausanne,

Switzerland: International Council on Alcohol and Addictions, 1972.

Jacobs, M. A. "The Addictive Personality: Prediction of Success in a Smoking Withdrawl Program." *Psychosomatic Medicine* 34 (1) (1972): 30-38.

Kopell, B. S.; Tinklenberg, J. R.; and Hollister, L. E. "Contingent Negative Variation Amplitudes: Marihuana and Alcohol." *Archives of General Psychiatry* 27 (1972): 809-11.

Kupperman, A., and Fine, E. "Combined Use of Alcohol and Amphetamines." *American Journal of Psychiatry* 131 (11) (1974): 1277-80.

Latendresse, J. D. "Masturbation and Its Relation to Addiction." *Review of Existential Psychology and Psychiatry* 8 (1) (1968): 54-64.

Lipp, M., et al. "Medical Student Use of Marijuana, Alcohol, and Cigarettes: A Study of Four Schools." *International Journal of Addictions* 7 (1) (1972): 141-52.

Lorefice, L.; Steer, R. A.; Fine, E. W.; Schut, J. R. "Personality Traits and Moods of Alcoholics and Heroin Addicts." *Journal of Studies on Alcoholism* 30 (5) (1976): 687-89.

MacDonough, T. S. "Evaluation of the Effectiveness of Intensive Confrontation in Changing the Behavior of Alcohol and Drug Abusers." *Behavior Therapy* 7 (3) (1976): 409.

————. "The Relative Effectiveness of a Medical Hospitalization Program vs. a Feedback-Behavior Modification Program in Treating Alcohol and Drug Abusers." *International Journal of the Addictions* 11 (2) (1976): 269-82.

————. "The Validity of Self-Recording Reports Made by Drug and Alcohol Abusers in a Residential Setting." *International Journal of the Addictions* 11 (3) (1976): 447-66.

McLachland, F. "An MMPI Discriminant Function to Distinguish Alcoholics from Narcotics Addicts: Effects of Age, Sex, and Psychopathology." *Journal of Clinical Psychology* 31 (1) (1975): 163-65.

Madden, J. S.; Walker, R.; and Kenyon, W. H. *Alcoholism and Drug Dependence*. New

York: Plenum Press, 1977.

Manheimer, D. I.; Mellinger, G. D.; and Somers, R. H. "Use of Mood-Changing Drugs among American Adults." In *Proceedings of the 30th International Congress on Alcoholism and Drug Dependence* (Amsterdam, Netherlands). Lausanne, Switzerland: International Council on Alcohol and Addictions, 1972.

Manry, W. E. "Alcoholism, Obesity, Nicotine, Etc." *Journal of the Florida Medical Association* 61 (7) (1974): 57.

Milman, R. B. "Drug and Alcohol Abuse." In *Handbook of Treatment of Mental Disorders in Childhood and Adolexcence.* Edited by B. B. Waltman, et al. Englewood Cliffs, New Jersey: Prentic Hall, 1978.

Milner, G. "Drug Abuse, Alcohol and Marihuana Problems: Errors, Costs, and Concepts." *Medical Journal of Australia* 2 (1973): 285-90.

Monroe, J. J.; English, G. E.; and Haertzen, C. A. "The Language of Addiction Scales: Validity Generalization of Effects of Labeling as Drug Addict or Alcoholic." *Quarterly Journal of Studies on Alcohol* 32 (4) (1971): 1049-54.

Orcutt, J. D. "Social Determinants of Alcohol and Marijuana Effects: A Systematic Theory." *International Journal of the Addictions* 10 (6) (1975): 1021-33.

Ottenberg, D. J. "Addiction as Metaphor." *Alcohol, Health and Research World* (Fall 1974) Expimental Issue: 18-20.

Ottenberg, D. J., and Rosen, A. "Combined Treatment of Alcoholics and Drug Addicts." Presented at North American Congress on Alcohol and Drug Problems, San Francisco, Calif., 12-18 December 1974.

———. "Merging the Treatment of Drug Addicts into an Existing Program for Alcoholics." *Quarterly Journal of Studies on Alcohol* 32 (1) (1971): 94-103.

Overall, J. E. "MMPI Personality Patterns of Alcoholics and Narcotic Addicts." *Quarterly Journal of Studies on Alcohol* 34 (1973): 104-111.

Platt, J. J. "Addiction Proneness and Personality in Heroin Addicts." *Journal of*

Abnormal Psychology 84 (3) (1975): 303-6.

Prendergast, T. J.; Preble, M. R.; and Tennant, F. S. "Drug Use and Its Relation to Alcohol and Cigarette Consumption in the Military Community of West Germany (Drugs, Alcohol, Cigarettes in a Military Setting)." *International Journal of the Addictions* 8 (5) (1973): 741-54.

Purdue Opinion Panel. "Report of Poll 86, Current Views of High School Students towards the Use of Tobacco, Alcohol, and Drugs." Narcotics Measurement and Research Center, Purdue University, Lafayette, Indiana, 1969.

Rathbone, J. L. *Tobacco, Alcohol, and Narcotics.* New York: Oxford Book Co., 1952.

Raynes, A. E.; Levine, G. L.; and Patch, V. D. "Epidemiology and Treatment of Polydrug Abuse." Presented at North American Congress on Alcohol and Drug Problems, San Francisco, Cal., 12-18 December 1974.

Robbins, P. R., and Nugent, J. F. "Perceived Consequences of Addiction: A Comparison between Alcoholics and Heroin Addict Patients." *Journal of Clinical Psychology* 32(2) (1975): 367-69.

Robbins, P. R.; Tanck, R. H.; and Meyerberg, H. A. "Psychological Factors in Smoking, Drinking, and Drug Experimentation." *Journal of Clinical Psychology* 27 (4) (1971): 450-52.

Rosen, A.; Ottenberg, D. J.; Barr, H. L. "Patterns of Previous Abuse of Alcohol in a Group of Hospitalized Drug Addicts." *Drug Forum* 75 (4) (3): 261-272.

Sand, W. T. "Psychosocial Factors and the Types of Sociopathy." *Dissertation Abstracts* 66 (27) (4-A): 1112-13.

Savitt, R. A. "Extramural Psychoanalytic Treatment of a Case of Narcotic Addiction." *Journal of the American Psychoanalytic Association* 2 (1954): 494-52.

———. "Psychoanalytic Studies of Addiction: The Method of Dealing with Narcotic Addiction." *Revista de Psicoanalisis* 23 (3) (1966): 334-44.

———. "Psychoanalytic Studies on Addiction: Ego Structure in Narcotic Addiction." *Psychoanalytic Quarterly* 32 (1963): 43-57.

————. "Psychoanalytic Studies on Addiction, II: Hypersexuality (Love Addiction). Paper read at Midwinter meeting of the American Psychoanalytic Association. Unpublished. 1965.

————. "Psychoanalytic Studies on Addiction, III: Food Addiction (Obesity). Paper read at Spring meeting of the American Psychoanalytic Association. Unpublished. 1971.

————. "The Psychopathology of the Addiction Process." *Journal of Hillside Hospital* 17 (1968): 277-86.

————. "Transference, Somatization, and Symbiotic Need." *Journal of the American Psychoanalytic Association* 17 (1969): 1030-54.

Schonfeld, W. A. "Socioeconomic Affluence as a Factor." *New York State Journal of Medicine* 67 (14) (1967): 1981-90.

Schonfield, J. "Differences in Smoking, Drinking, and Social Behavior by Race and Delinquency Status in Adolescent Males." *Adolescence* 1 (4) (1966): 367-80.

Seevers, M. H. "Discussion of a Paper." In *The Addictive States.* Edited by A. Wikler. Baltimore: The Williams and Wilkens Company (1968): 244.

Seevers, M. H. "Medical Perspectives on Habituation and Addiction." *Journal of the American Medical Association* 181 (1962): 92-8.

Singh, R. N., and Hadely, L. E. "Alcohol Consumption and the Student's Use of Hallucinogenic Drugs." *West Virginia Medical Journal* 69 (4) (1973): 88-90.

Straus, R. "Public Attitudes Regarding Problem Drinking and Problem EAting." *Annals of the New York Academy of Sciences* 133 (3) (1966): 792-802.

Sutker, P. B. "Personality Differences and Sociopathy in Heroin Addicts and Non-Addict Prisoners." *Journal of Abnormal Psychology* 78 (3) (1971): 247-51.

Tamerin, J. S., and Neuman, C. P. "Prognostic Factors in the Evaluation of Addicted Individuals." *International Pharmacopsych.* 6 (2) (1971): 69-76.

Thomasina, M. "Adolescent Drug and Alcohol Survey." *Journal of Perth Amboy General Hospital* 3 (4) (1974): 36-37.

Toler, C. "The Personal Values of Alcoholics and Addicts." *Journal of Clinical Psychology* 31 (3) (1975): 554-57.

————. "The Personal Values of Alcoholics and Addicts." *Newsletter for Research in Mental Health and Behavioral Sciences* 16 (3) (1979): 17-20.

Valliant, G. E. "Alcoholism and Drug Dependence." In *The Harvard Guide to Modern Psychology.* Edited by A. M. Nicholi, Jr. (1978): 567.

Wikler, A. "The Search for the Psyche in Drug Dependence." *Journal of Nervous Mental Disease* 165 (1) (1977): 29-40.

William, H. "Heroin vs. Alcohol Addiction: Quantifiable Psychosocial Similarities and Differences." *Journal of Psychosomatic Research* 18 (5) (1974): 327-35.

Wilson, S., and Lennard, D. "The Extraverting Effect of Treatment in a Therapeutic Community for Drug Users." *British Journal of Psychiatry* 132 (1978): 296-99.

Wishnie, H. *The Compulsive Personality: Understanding People with Destructive Character Disorders.* New York: Plenum Press, 1977.

Zinberg, N. E., and Robertson, J. A. *Drugs and the Public.* New York: Simon and Schuster, 1972.

Zucker, R. A. "Sex-Role Identity Patterns and Drinking Behavior of Adolescents." *Quarterly Journal of Studies on Alcohol* 43:6882 (29) (4-A) (1968): 868-84.

Zucker, R. A., and Van Horn, H. "Sibling Social Structure and Oral Behavior: Drinking and Smoking in Adolescence." *Quarterly Journal of Studies on Alcohol* 51:912 (33) (1-A) (1972): 193-97.

Zuckerman, M. "Dimensions of Sensation-Seeking." *Journal of Consulting and Clinical Psychology* 36 (1971): 45-52.

————. "Drug Usage As One Manifestation of a Sensation-Seeking Trait." In *Drug Abuse: Current Concepts and Research.* Edited by J. Keup. Springfield, Illinois: C. C. Thomas, 1972.

POPULAR BOOKS ON CROSS/MULTIPLE ADDICTIONS

Brown, C. *Manchild in a Promised Land.* New York: New American Library, 1976.

Halley, A. *The Autobiography of Malcolm X.* New York: Ballantine, 1976.

LaGuardia, R. *Monty* (A Biography of Montgomery Clift). New York: Avon Books, 1977.

Peele, S. *Love and Addiction.* New York: New American Library, 1976.

SELF-HELP GROUPS AND
THERAPEUTIC COMMUNITIES

Abrahams, Ruby B. "Mutual Helping: Styles of Caregiving in a Mutual Aid Program." In *Support Systems and Mutual Help: Multi-Disciplinary Explorations.* Edited by Gerald Caplan and Marie Killilea. New York: Grune & Stratton, 1976.

Adler, H. M., and Hammett, V. B. O. "Crisis, Conversion, and Cult Formation." *American Journal of Psychiatry* 13 (August 1973).

Alcoholics Anonymous: The Story of How Many Thousands of Men and Women Have Recovered from Alcoholism. New York: Alcoholics Anonymous World Services, 1955.

Anthony, E. J. "Age and Syndrome in Group Psychotherapy." *Journal of Long Island Consultation Center* 1:3 (1960).

Bacon, S. D. "A Sociologist Looks at Alcoholics Anonymous." *Minnesota Welfare* 10 (1957): 35-44.

Bailey, M. B. "Al-Anon Family Groups as an Aid to Wives of Alcoholics." *Social Work* (January 1965): 68-74.

Bales, R. F. "The Therapeutic Role of Alcoholics Anonymous as Seen by a Sociologist." *Quarterly Journal of Studies on Alcohol* 5 (1944): 267-78.

———. "The Therapeutic Role of Alcoholics Anonymous as Seen by a Sociologist." In *Society, Culture, and Drinking Patterns.* Edited by D. J. Pittman and C. R. Snyder. New York: Wiley, 1962.

———. "Social Therapy for a Social Disorder—Compulsive Drinking." *Journal of Social Issues* 1 (1945): 14-22.

Barish, Herbert. "Self-Help Groups." *Encyclopedia of Social Work* 2 (1971): 1164.

Bassin, Alexander. "Daytop Village." *Psychology Today* (December 1968): 48.

Blum, E. M., and Blum, R. Alcoholism: *Modern Psychological Approaches to Treatment.* San Francisco: Jossey-Bass, 1967.

Blumbalo, J. A., and Young, D. E. "The Self-Help Phenomenon." *American Journal of Nursing* 158 (1973): 8-9.

C. B. "The Growth and Effectiveness of Alcoholics Anonymous in a Southwestern City, 1948-1962." *Quarterly Journal of Studies on Alcohol* 26 (1965): 279-84.

Caplan, Gerald. *Support Systems and Community Mental Health.* New York: Behavioral Publications, 1974.

Carner, Charles. "Now: Clubs for Mutual Mental Health." *Today's Health* (March 1968): 41.

Cherkes, Marshall S. "Synanon Foundation—A Radical Approach to the Problem of Addiction." *American Journal of Psychi-*

atry 121 (1965): 1066.

Cohen, F. "Personality Change Among Members of A. A." *Mental Hygiene* 46 (1962): 427-37.

Collier, Peter. "The Houses of Synanon." *Ramparts* (October 1967): 93-100.

Davis, C. N. "Alcoholics Anonymous." *Archives of Neurological Psychiatry* 57 (1947): 516-18.

DeLeon, G. *Phoenix House: Studies in a Therapeutic Community (1968-1973).* New York: MSS Information, 1974.

Dumont, Matthew P. "Self-Help Treatment Programs." *American Journal of Psychiatry* 131 (1974): 631-35.

Eckhardt, W. "Alcoholic Values and Alcoholics Anonymous." Presented at the 1965 Meeting of the Southwest Psychology Association.

Edwards, G., et al. "Who Goes to Alcoholics Anonymous?" *Lancet* 13 August 1966: 382-84.

Emrik, C. D.; Lassen, C. L.; and Edwards, M. T. "Nonprofessional Peers as Therapeutic Agents." In *Effective Psychotherapy.* Edited by A. S. Gurman and A. M. Razin. Oxford: Pergamon Press, 1977.

Enright, John B. "Synanon: A Challenge to Middle-Class Views of Mental Health." In *Community Psychology and Mental Health: Perspectives and Challenges.* Edited by Daniel Adelson and Betty L. Kalis. Scranton, Pa.: Chandler Publishing Company, 1970.

Gartner, Alan. "Self-Help and Mental Health: The Anonymous Groups." *Reflections* 14 (1979): 25-56.

Glatzer, H. T. "The Relative Effectiveness of Clinically Homogeneous and Heterogeneous Psychotherapy Groups." *International Journal of Group Psychotherapy* 3 (1956): 258.

Glazer, F. B. "Gaudenzia, Incorporated: Historical and Theoretical Background of a Self Help Addiction Treatment Program." *International Journal of the Addictions* 6 (1971): 615-26.

Goffman, Erving. *Stigma: Notes on the Management of Spoiled Identities.* Englewood, N.J.: Prentice-Hall, 1963.

Grosz, Hanus J. *Recovery, Inc., Survey.* Chicago: Recovery, Inc., 1973.

Gurman, A. S., and Raisin, A. M., eds. *Effective Psychotherapy: A Handbook of Research.* Oxford: Pergamon Press, 1977. Emerick, Chad D., Lasson, Carol L., and Edwards, Miles T. Chapter 7, "Non-Professional Peers as Therapeutic Agents." (246 references).

Gussow, Zachary, and Tracy, George S. "Interim Status Report: Voluntary Self-Help Organizations—A Study in Human Support Systems." September 1973.

————. "The Role of Self-Help Clubs in Adaptation to Chronic Illness and Disability," n.d.

Hartrup, W. W. "Peer Interaction and Social Organization." In *Carmichael's Manual of Child Psychology* vol. 2 (3d ed.) Edited by P. H. Mussen. New York: Wiley, 1970.

————. "Peer Self-Help Psychotherapy Groups: Psychotherapy Without Psychotherapists." In *The Sociology of Psychotherapy.* Edited by Roman P. Trice, New York: Jason Aronson, 1973.

Hurvitz, Nathan. "Peer Self-Help Psychotherapy Groups and Their Implications for Psychotherapy." *Psychotherapy: Theory, Research and Practice* 7 (Spring 1970).

"Jack, M." In *Explorations in Self-Help and Mutual Aid.* Edited by Leonard D. Borman. Proceedings of the Self-Help Workshop held 9-12 June, in Chicago, under the auspices of the W. Clement and Jessie V. Stone Foundation. Evanston, Ill.: Center for Urban Affairs, Northwestern University, 1975.

Kaplan, S. R., and Ahmed, B. M. "Group Strategies for Disadvantaged Populations: The Role of the Public Mental Health Setting." In *Group Counseling and Group Psychotherapy with Rehabilitation Clients.* Edited by M. Seligman. Springfield, Ill.: Charles C. Thomas, 1977.

Kaplan, S. R.; Boyajian, L. Z.; and Meltzer, B. "The Role of the Nonprofessional Worker." In *The Practice of Community Mental Health.* Edited by H. Grunebaum. Boston: Little, Brown, 1970.

Kaplan, S.R., and Razin, A. M. "The Psychological Substrate of Self-Help Groups." *Journal of Operational Psychiatry*, vol. 2 (1978): 58-66.

Katz, A. H. "Application of Self Help Concepts in Current Social Welfare." *Social Work* 10 (1965): 67-74.

———. "Self Help in Rehabilitation: Some Theoretical Aspects." *Rehabilitation Literature* 28 (1967): 10-11.

———. "Self Help Groups." *Social Work* 17 (1972): 120-21.

———. "Self Help Organizations and Volunteer Participation in Social Welfare." *Social Work* 15 (1970): 51-60.

Katz, A. H., and Bender, E. I., eds. *The Strength in Us: Self-Help Groups in the Modern World.* New York: New Viewpoints, 1976.

Killilea, Marie. "Mutual Help Organizations: Interpretations in the Literature." In *Support Systems and Mutual Help: Multi-Disciplinary Explorations.* Edited by Gerald Caplan and Marie Killilea. New York: Grune & Stratton, 1976.

Kohut, H. *Analysis of the Self.* New York: International Universities Press, 1971.

Leach, B., et al. "Dimensions of Alcoholics Anonymous." *International Journal of the Addictions* 4 (1969): 507-41.

Lee, Donald T. "Therapeutic Type: Recovery Inc." In *The Strength in Us: Self-Help Groups in the Modern World.* Edited by A. H. Katz and E. I. Bender. New York: New Viewpoints, 1976.

Lindt, H. "The 'Rescue Fantasy' in Group Therapy of Alcoholics." *Journal of Group Psychotherapy* 9 (1959): 43-52.

Loftland, J. F., and Lejeune, R. A. "Initial Interaction of Newcomers in Alcoholics Anonymous: A Field Experiment in Class Symbols and Socialization." *Social Problems* 8 (1960): 102-11.

Lolli, G. "Alcoholism as a Disorder of the Love Disposition." *Quarterly Journal of Studies on Alcohol* 17 (1956): 96-107.

Maxwell, M. A. "Alcoholics Anonymous: An Interpretation." In *Society, Culture, and Drinking Patterns.* Edited by D. J. Dittman and C. P. Snyder. New York: John Wiley & Sons, 1962.

Narcotics Anonymous. Sun Valley, Calif.: NA World Service Organization, 1976.

Neurotics Anonymous: An Introductio. Washington, D.C.: Neurotics Anonymous International Liaison, 1966.

Norris, J. "Alcoholics Anonymous." In *World Dialogue on Alcohol and Drug Dependency.* Edited by E. D. Whitney. Boston: Beacon Press, 1970.

Parents Anonymous. *I Am A Parents Anonymous Parent.* Redondo Beach, Calif.: Parents Anonymous, Inc., 1974.

Patterson, G. R., and Anderson, D. "Peers as Social Inforcers." *Child Development* 35 (1964): 951-60.

Phillips, Julianne. *Alcoholics Anonymous: An Annotated Bibliography, 1935-1972.* Cincinnati, Ohio: Central Ohio Publishing Company, 1973.

Reissman, F. "The Helper Therapy Principles." *Social Work* 10 (April 1968).

Ripley, H. S., and Jackson, J. K. "Therapeutic Factors in Alcoholics Anonymous." *American Journal of Psychiatry* 116 (1959): 44-50.

Ritchie, Oscar W. "A Sociohistorical Analysis of Alcoholics Anonymous." *Quarterly Journal of Studies on Alcohol* 9 (1948): 119.

Rubington, E. *Alcohol Problems and Social Control.* Columbus, Ohio: Charles E. Merrill Publishing Company, 1973.

Sagarin, E. *Odd Man In: Societies of Deviants in America.* Chicago: Quadrangle Books, 1969.

Scodel, Alvin. "Inspirational Group Therapy: A Study of Gamblers Anonymous." *American Journal of Psychotherapy* 18 (1964): 117.

Silverman, Phyllis Rolfe. "The Widow as a Caregiver in a Program of Preventive Intervention with Other Widows." *Mental Hygiene* 54 (1970): 545-46.

Speigel, D. "Going Public and Self Help." Paper presented in a seminar on Support Systems at the Laboratory for Community Psychiatry, Boston, Mass., Spring, 1974.

Stabler, Brian; Gibson, Frank W., Jr.; and Cutting, D. Scott. "Parents as Therapists: An Innovative Community-Based Model." *Professional Psychology* 4 (1973):

397-402.

Stunkard, A.; Levine, H.; and Fox, S. "The Management of Obesity: Patient Self-Help and Medical Treatment." *Archives of Internal Medicine* 125 (1970): 1067-72.

Thomsen, Robert. *Bill W.* New York: Harper & Row, 1975.

Tiebout, H. M. "The Act of Surrender in the Therapeutic Process with Special Reference to Alcoholism." *Quarterly Journal of Studies on Alcohol* 10 (1949): 48-58.

———. "The Affiliation Motive and Readiness to Join Alcoholics Anonymous." *Quarterly Journal of Studies on Alcohol* 20 (1959): 313-20.

———. "Alcoholics Anonymous, an Experiment of Nature." *Quarterly Journal of Studies on Alcohol* 22 (1961): 52-68.

———. "Delabeling, Relabeling and Alcoholics Anonymous." *Social Problems* 17 (Spring 1970).

———. "Psychological Factors Operating in Alcoholics Anonymous." In *Current Therapies of Personality Disorders.* Edited by B. Glueck. New York: Grune & Stratton, 1946.

———. "Therapeutic Mechanisms of Alcoholics Anonymous." *American Journal of Psychiatry* 100 (1944): 468-73.

———. "Some Aspects of the Problem of Alcoholism." *New York State Journal of Medicine* 50 (1950): 1706.

Trice, H. M. "A Study of the Process of Affiliation with Alcoholics Anonymous." *Quarterly Journal of Studies on Alcohol* 18 (1957): 39.

Trice, H. M., and Roman, P. M. "Sociopsychological Predicators of Affiliation with A.A.: A Longitudinal Study of Treatment Success." *Social Psychology* 5 (1970): 51-59.

Twelve Steps and Twelve Traditions. New York: Alcoholics Anonymous World Services, Inc., The A.A. Grapevine, Inc., 1952.

Van Stone, William, and Gilbert, Robert. "Peer Confrontation Groups: What, Why, Whither." *American Journal of Psychiatry* 129 (1972): 583.

Vattano, Anthony J. "Power to the People: Self-Help Groups." *Social Work* 17 (1972): 10.

W., Bill. *Alcoholics Anonymous Comes of Age.* New York: Harper & Brothers, 1957.

W. W. co-founder: "The Society of Alcoholics Anonymous." *American Journal of Psychiatry* 106 (1949): 370-75.

Wahler, R. G. "Oppositional Children: A Quest for Parental Reinforcement Control." *Journal of Applied Behavior Analysis* 2 (1969): 159-70.

Wechsler, Henry. "The Ex-patient Organization: A Survey." *Journal of Social Issues* 16 (1960): 50.

Yablonsky, L., and Dederick, C. E. "Synanon: An Analysis of Some Dimensions of the Social Structure of an Antiaddiction Society." In *Narcotics.* Edited by D. M. Wilner and G. G. Kassenbaum. New York: McGraw-Hill, 1965.

Yablonsky, L. *Synanon: The Tunnel Back.* Baltimore: Penguin Books, 1965.

Young People and A.A. New York: Alcoholics Anonymous World Services, Inc., 1969.